Modern econometrics

Modern econometrics

An introduction

R.L. Thomas

Department of Economics,
Manchester Metropolitan University

Addison-Wesley

Harlow, England • Reading, Massachusetts
Menlo Park, California • New York
Don Mills, Ontario • Amsterdam • Bonn
Sydney • Singapore • Tokyo • Madrid • San Juan
Milan • Mexico City • Seoul • Taipei

Addison Wesley Longman Limited
Edinburgh Gate, Harlow,
Essex, CM20 2JE, England

and Associated Companies throughout the World.

Visit Addison Wesley Longman on the World Wide Web at:
http://www.awl-he.com

Cover designed by Op den Brouw, Design & Illustration, Reading, UK
and printed by The Riverside Printing Co. Ltd., Reading, UK
Text design by Sally Grover Castle
Illustrations by Chartwell Illustrators, Croydon, UK
Typeset by Techset Composition, Salisbury, UK
Printed and bound by T J Press, Padstow, UK

First printed 1996, Reprinted 1998

ISBN 0–201–87694–9

Printed in China
NPCC/03

British Library Cataloguing-in-Publication Data

A catalogue record for this book is available from the British Library

Library of Congress Cataloging-in-Publication Data is available

preface

Econometrics has experienced remarkable changes in the past 15 years, particularly in the area of time series analysis. The development of cointegration techniques has, for the first time, enabled econometricians to make a serious attempt at dealing with the problems of spurious regressions and non-stationary time series. Parallel with this development has come the increased acceptance of the so-called general-to-specific methodology, combined with the use of error correction models.

Unfortunately, the above changes have generally not been properly reflected in introductory undergraduate textbooks. If such topics appear at all in such texts, they tend to be tagged on at the end, after previous material that is becoming increasingly dated. In this book I have tried to provide a text that not only includes substantial material on the more recent topics but, where necessary, integrates these new ideas with more traditional material. Thus, while the techniques developed in recent decades are mainly covered in the last third of this text, the earlier chapters frequently look ahead to these innovations.

While the text is an undergraduate one, it may also prove useful to postgraduates whose training in econometrics has been less full than is desirable. Also, such is the variation in the mathematical calibre of undergraduates across the universities of today, it would be unwise to categorize this book as being unequivocally for 'second year' or for 'third year'. For many universities where the mathematical background of students is more limited, it should clearly serve as a third-year text. The material of the early chapters might then constitute (probably necessary) revision. In a minority of universities, however, the book may find use in both second and third years. It could serve as the main text in the second year, with some of the later material being omitted at this stage. In the third year it might then, however, need to be supplemented by, for example, Charemza and Deadman's excellent, if somewhat specialized, 1992 text on new directions in econometrics.

I would like to thank John Pu for his invaluable assistance with the simulation studies contained in the text. I am also indebted to three anonymous Addison-Wesley readers for comments on an earlier draft. Needless to say, any mistakes that remain in the text are my own.

R L Thomas, July 1996

contents

contents

4   Two-variable regression analysis   75

5   Estimators and methods of estimation   106

6   The classical two-variable regression model   135

Appendix I   Introduction to matrix algebra   479

Appendix II Answers to numerical exercises   501

Appendix III The data sets and the floppy disk   511

Appendix IV Statistical tables   520

Bibliography   527

Index   531

*An asterisk indicates a section containing material of greater conceptual or mathematical complexity. See Introduction, page 7, for more details.

1 Introduction

1.1 What is econometrics?

Econometrics has been defined as 'the application of mathematical statistics to economic data to lend empirical support to the models constructed by mathematical economics and to obtain numerical estimates' (Samuelson et al., 1954, pp. 141–6). More succinctly, the basic task of econometrics 'is to put *empirical* flesh and blood on theoretical structures' (Johnston, 1984, p. 5).

Economic theory deduces or predicts various relationships between variables. Examples spring easily to mind – a demand curve, a production function, a consumption function. An econometrician is concerned

(a) to measure such relationships, and to estimate the parameters they involve;

(b) to test the theoretical ideas represented by such relationships;

(c) to use such relationships for quantitative predictions or forecasts.

Econometrics involves the coming together of mathematical economics, economic statistics and statistical inference. Mathematical economics expresses the theories and ideas of economics in mathematical form. However, these mathematical forms are qualitative rather than quantitative – that is, they do not involve numbers. Economic statistics involves the collection and processing of economic data and their expression in readily understandable form. Econometrics

1

takes the equations of mathematical economics and by confronting them with economic data seeks to use the techniques of statistical inference to give these equations quantitative form.

An example should make the above clearer. Monetary theory suggests that the aggregate demand for money in an economy may depend on a 'scale' variable such as national income or national wealth and an interest rate variable representing the opportunity cost of holding money. That is,

$$M = f(Y, r) \tag{1.1}$$

where M, the demand for money, and Y, the scale variable, are defined in real terms and r is the interest rate variable.

Notice that theory specifies a relationship between the real values M and Y that is independent of the general price level. Theory also suggests that a rise in the scale variable should result in a rise in the demand for money, whereas a rise in the rate of interest leads to a fall in M.

Theory, however, leaves us with a whole series of unanswered questions. First, it does not tell us how we should define our variables. Should we adopt a 'narrow' definition of money or a 'broad' one? Which scale variable should we use, and which of the many interest rates in an economy best represents the opportunity cost of holding money?

Secondly, theory tells us nothing about the precise functional form of Equation (1.1). It is unlikely to be of the simple linear form

$$M = \alpha + \beta Y + \gamma r, \quad \beta > 0, \quad \gamma < 0 \tag{1.2}$$

It could be of the convenient constant-elasticity form[1]

$$M = AY^{\beta} r^{\gamma}, \quad \beta > 0, \quad \gamma < 0 \tag{1.3}$$

but many other nonlinear functional forms are equally consistent with the information that theory provides us with.

Thirdly, theory provides us with only qualitative information on how Y and r influence the demand for money. For example, suppose there is a rise of 5% in the scale variable Y. Theory suggests that this will result in a rise in the demand for money, but it does not tell us by how much. That is, it provides no quantitative information. However, quantitative information on, for example, the elasticities β and γ in (1.3) is of the greatest importance in deciding government policy.

Fourthly, theory generally refers to what economists call the long run. That is, it tells us about equilibrium positions. For example, in equilibrium, the demand for and the supply of money can be regarded as equal. Thus, under such conditions, we would be justified in using data series on the supply of money to represent the demand for money. However, the money market is seldom if ever in equilibrium. When it is in disequilibrium, are we justified in using observed supply of money data to represent the demand for money in equations such as (1.1), (1.2) and (1.3)? More generally, economic theory often has very little to say about how an economy or market moves from one equilibrium to another. That is, theory rarely describes the adjustment process. Unfortunately, economic data usually refers to this adjustment process rather than to successive equilibrium positions.

To a greater or lesser extent, econometrics seeks to provide the answers to the above questions that economic theory leaves unanswered. In particular, it seeks to find numerical estimates of the parameters in equations such as (1.2) and (1.3). It also aims to test some of the predictions of theory. For example, we saw above that monetary theory implies that demand-for-money functions such as (1.1) are independent of the general price level. The econometrician's approach to testing this theoretical prediction would be to generalize equations such as (1.2) or (1.3) to allow for possible price effects. For example, (1.2) might be changed to

$$M = \alpha + \beta Y + \gamma r + \delta P \tag{1.4}$$

where P is the general price level. If $\delta = 0$ then the price level has no effect on the demand for money. The statistical techniques used to estimate the parameters β and γ can also be used to obtain an estimate of δ. If this turns out to be significantly different from zero then the prediction of theory is contradicted.

Up until now, the way we have written equations suggests that economic relationships are exact or deterministic. However, this is virtually never the case, since the behaviour of human economic agents is never totally predictable. Econometricians allow for this by adding a 'random' **disturbance** to equations such as (1.2). That is, we rewrite (1.2) as

$$M = \alpha + \beta Y + \gamma r + \epsilon \tag{1.5}$$

where ϵ is the disturbance term, which might be positive or negative. The inclusion of ϵ in Equation (1.5) means that the same given levels of Y and r will not always result in the same exact value for the demand for money, M. There will be some entirely random variation depending on the size and sign of the disturbance.[2]

The existence of the disturbance in (1.5) means that it is impossible to measure parameters such as α, β and γ exactly. That is why we talked above of using the techniques of statistical inference to provide *estimates* of parameters. Such estimates can never be exact.

1.2   The plan of this text

As we have seen, econometrics combines economic theory with mathematics and statistical inference. It is assumed that the reader has a knowledge of economic theory up to second-year university level. As far as mathematics is concerned, a knowledge of basic algebra and basic differential calculus is assumed. Some of the following chapters make use of matrix algebra, although this is kept to a minimum. Readers unfamiliar with matrices are advised to spend some time reading Appendix I at the end of the text. All the matrix algebra needed to follow this text is contained within this appendix.

A good (even if at times intuitive) understanding of various concepts in probability and statistical inference is necessary for any worthwhile study of econometrics. Chapters 2 and 3 attempt to provide this. In Chapter 4 on two-variable regression analysis we consider, in a descriptive manner, relationships between two variables, introducing the so-called least squares method of estimating parameters.

Many readers may already have some familiarity with two-variable regression and least squares. Essentially, this involves fitting a straight line to a scatter of points. For example, suppose we were concerned with the relationship between household income, Y, and household expenditure on consumer goods, C. We might hypothesize a linear **consumption function** of the kind

$$C = \alpha + \beta Y + \epsilon \qquad (1.6)$$

where α and β are parameters we wish to estimate. For example, β is the marginal propensity to consume. ϵ is a disturbance similar to that in Equation (1.5).

Suppose now that we have data on the income and consumption of 10 households. This data can be represented by 10 points in a scatter diagram such as that of Figure 1.1. The coordinates of each point refer to the income and consumption of a particular household. Two-variable regression analysis fits, by some means or other, a straight line to such a scatter of points as indicated. The intercept and slope of this line then provide the required estimates of α and β respectively. The best known method of fitting such a line is that of least squares, where the line is chosen so as to minimize the sum of the squares of the vertical distances of the points from the line.[3] Much of econometrics consists of generalizations of the procedure just described.

Clearly, we would like our estimates of parameters such as α and β in Equation (1.6) to be as 'good' as possible. Chapter 5 is concerned with estimators in general. We consider the properties our estimators need to have if we are to be happy with them, and we consider various different methods of estimation. In Chapter 6 we put

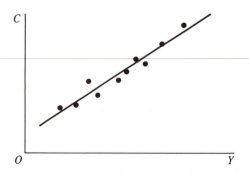

Figure 1.1 A typical scatter diagram.

together what we have learnt about inference, estimation and two-variable regression. That is, we examine what is known as the classical two-variable regression model.

It is in Chapter 7 that we begin to study what might be termed econometrics proper. Economic relationships typically involve more than the two variables of Equation (1.6). For example, our demand-for-money equations (1.1), (1.2) and (1.3) involve three variables. The two-variable regression of Chapters 4 and 6 is therefore not suitable for the analysis of such relationships.

Suppose we were faced with the problem of estimating the parameters of a relationship such as (1.2). Note that, in this case, the scale variable parameter β measures the effect on the demand for money of a unit rise in the scale variable Y under the *ceteris paribus* assumption that the interest rate r is held constant.[4] Ideally, to estimate β, we would like to set up some kind of laboratory experiment in which we hold the interest rate r constant but vary the scale variable Y. We would then be faced with a relationship

$$M = (\alpha + \gamma r) + \beta Y$$

where $(\alpha + \gamma r)$ is a constant. We are now back in the world of two-variable relationships, and could observe the effect on M of *ceteris paribus* unit changes in Y. By plotting a scatter diagram of M against Y, we could then obtain some estimate of the parameter β. However, to obtain an estimate of the interest rate parameter γ, a separate experiment, in which we hold the scale variable Y constant but vary the rate of interest, would be necessary.

The above approach might be feasible in the physical sciences. Unfortunately, laboratory experiments are rarely, if ever, possible in economics. We have to make do with non-experimental data in which, typically, all variables of interest vary simultaneously. In Chapter 7 we introduce the classical multiple regression model. This is an extension of the two-variable model of earlier chapters in which the least squares method is generalized to allow for three or more variables. Multiple regression is the econometrician's substitute for the laboratory experiment of the physical scientist. Virtually all econometric analysis involves multiple regression of some form or other. Chapter 7 therefore deals with the so-called classical multiple regression model and the assumptions that underpin it.

Unfortunately, the assumptions of the classical multiple regression model are rather restrictive. It turns out that some or all of these assumptions very often turn out to be invalid when applied to typical economic data. Chapters 8 and 10 therefore consider the consequences for the classical model of breakdowns in these assumptions. Some alternative procedures are also suggested. Meanwhile, in Chapter 9 some extensions to the classical model that are particularly relevant for economic data are developed.

In Chapter 11 we make a first attempt at tackling the problem, mentioned above, of modelling the behaviour of economic agents as they adjust to positions of disequilibrium. As noted earlier, most economic theory refers to equilibrium positions – that is, it is static in nature. However, economic data almost invariably relate to agents or markets that are in disequilibrium. Dynamic models therefore have to be formed and estimated if we are to handle such data. Some simple dynamic models are introduced in this chapter.

Much of the material found in this text up until Chapter 11 could have been found in any introductory econometrics text 10 or 15 years ago. It remains the basic 'bread and butter' of econometrics. However, during the past decade or so, the approach of applied econometricians, particularly when faced with time series data, has undergone a significant change. It is this changed approach and the new techniques associated with it that are the subjects of Chapters 12–15 of this text.

The changed approach became necessary when econometricians at last faced up to what is usually termed the 'spurious regression problem'. This was not a new problem, but was one to which applied workers had been content to turn a very blind eye until recently. We shall obviously discuss this problem in detail in the main body of the text. For now, it is sufficient to note that the non-experimental nature of economic data makes it very easy to uncover relationships between variables that are apparently strong but in actual fact are **spurious** or 'sham' relationships. This is particularly the case when data on variables trend consistently upwards over time. Such variables are certain to be highly correlated, even in the absence of any causal relationships between them.

Hand in hand with attempts to deal with the spurious regression problem, there has also been a new approach to the problem of discriminating between competing theories or models. Traditional econometrics was seriously lacking in this respect. Yet economists have been justly famous for providing alternative theories to fit the same set of facts! In Chapter 12 we therefore consider the problem of how to select the best model, and we describe the so-called 'general-to-specific' approach. In Chapter 13 we combine the approach of Chapter 12 with a dynamic type of model that has been extensively used during the past two decades. This is the 'error correction model'. It turns out that this model is particularly appropriate for handling data in which variables are trending strongly upwards. Recall from the last paragraph that it is with data of this nature that so-called spurious regression problems are most likely to arise.

In Chapters 14 and 15 we introduce procedures that have been developed specifically to deal with the problem of spurious regressions. These chapters are inevitably more technical in nature, but an intuitive approach is adopted, with the degree of mathematical difficulty kept to a minimum. The final chapter is devoted to selected further topics. Some knowledge of these topics, particularly vector autoregressions and limited dependent variables, is essential to any modern applied econometrician.

In a number of chapters the reader will find what are referred to as Monte Carlo or simulation studies. As will be seen, such studies are the nearest approach that econometricians can make to the laboratory experiments of the physical sciences. They have been included for two reasons. First, simulation studies are a useful way of reinforcing or checking theoretical results. They can help provide an intuitive understanding of the meaning of such results. Secondly, many of the techniques used in recent years to tackle the spurious regression problems mentioned above rely on the results of simulation studies. A proper appreciation of this area is therefore not possible without some understanding of how simulation studies proceed.

In many of the later chapters the reader will encounter sections marked with an asterisk. These 'starred' sections contain material that is of a greater conceptual and/or mathematical complexity than the rest of the text. While it would sometimes be unwise to leave these sections out entirely, a general, even vague, understanding of what they contain should be enough to enable the reader to follow everything in the main body of the text.

1.3 Exercises

Numerical exercises are included in all chapters, and are an essential part of the text. While the exercises in the early chapters can be tackled with a simple hand calculator, the computer exercises that appear from Chapter 7 onwards will require the use of regression software. Computer work is an inescapable part of the training of any applied econometrician, and readers are expected to attempt all the computer exercises. The data for these exercises can be found both in Appendix IV at the end of this text and in ASCII text files on the floppy disk enclosed with the text. The exercises themselves, however, are not tied to the use of any particular multiple regression program. There are a number of standard packages that are available, and virtually all would be suitable for use with this text. Examples are MICROFIT, PCGIVE, RATS and SHAZAM.

The computer exercises all involve the estimation of multiple regression equations of some kind. In many exercises some of the estimated equations will actually appear in the text. However, the reader should not take these on trust, but should replicate them using the data supplied.

Appendix 1A

Notes to Chapter 1

1. In Equation (1.3) β and γ are the income and interest elasticities of demand for money respectively. For example, since $\partial M / \partial Y = \beta A Y^{\beta-1} r^{\gamma}$, the income elasticity is $(\partial M / \partial Y)(Y / M) = \beta$.

2. The disturbance may also reflect other influences. For example, it might reflect the effect of whatever other minor factors, other than Y and r, influence the demand for money. Also, it can be regarded as reflecting the fact that errors of measurement are frequently made when we deal with economic variables.

3. The presence of the disturbance in Equation (1.6) ensures that the points in the scatter do not lie exactly on a straight line. In the absence of the disturbance ϵ, (1.6) would describe an exact linear relationship.

4. If a disturbance akin to that in Equation (1.6) were included in (1.2) then the *ceteris paribus* assumption would also apply to this disturbance.

2 Probability distributions

Some basic knowledge of probability and statistical inference is a prerequisite for any study of econometrics. This and the following chapter attempt to provide such knowledge. In this chapter we assume that the reader has some previous knowledge of probability and probability distributions. However, we revise and stress certain concepts that will be particularly useful later in the text.

2.1 Stochastic variables and probability distributions

Consider a simple experiment involving a six-sided die. A 'trial' of this experiment involves rolling the die twice. There are 36 possible outcomes to such a trial, and these are listed in Table 2.1. Provided we have a 'fair' die, all the 36 outcomes will be equally likely, so each will have a probability $1/36$ of occurring on any one particular trial of the experiment.

We now define a variable X, equal to the sum of the spots observed on both rolls of the die for any single trial of the experiment. X will obviously vary from trial to trial, and its possible values are shown to the right of the various outcomes in Table 2.1. These X values range from 2 (a double 1) to 12 (a double 6).

X is an example of a random or stochastic variable. A **stochastic variable** is simply a variable whose values are determined by some chance mechanism. In the

Table 2.1 Sample space

(1, 1) 2	(2, 1) 3	(3, 1) 4	(4, 1) 5	(5, 1) 6	(6, 1) 7
(1, 2) 3	(2, 2) 4	(3, 2) 5	(4, 2) 6	(5, 2) 7	(6, 2) 8
(1, 3) 4	(2, 3) 5	(3, 3) 6	(4, 3) 7	(5, 3) 8	(6, 3) 9
(1, 4) 5	(2, 4) 6	(3, 4) 7	(4, 4) 8	(5, 4) 9	(6, 4) 10
(1, 5) 6	(2, 5) 7	(3, 5) 8	(4, 5) 9	(5, 5) 10	(6, 5) 11
(1, 6) 7	(2, 6) 8	(3, 6) 9	(4, 6) 10	(5, 6) 11	(6, 6) 12

present case the chance mechanism is of course the six-sided die. The variable X is also a **discrete variable**. That is, it can take only certain values within its range of 2–12. For example X cannot take the value 3.77 or 8.5.

We now derive the **probability distribution** for X. This probability distribution simply involves a listing of all values that X can take, together with the probabilities associated with each and every such X value. For example, to obtain the probability that $X = 4$ on any trial, we observe that 3 of the 36 outcomes in Table 2.1 yield this value for X, namely the outcomes (1, 3), (2, 2) and (3, 1). Since each such outcome has a probability of 1/36 of occurring, the probability that $X = 4$ must therefore equal 3/36. That is $\Pr(X = 4) = 3/36$.

The probabilities of X equalling any of its possible values from 2 to 12 can be calculated in a similar manner. The full range of probabilities is shown in Table 2.2, where we have introduced the notation $p(X)$ for the probability of obtaining X spots on any trial of the experiment. Thus, for example, $p(7) = \Pr(X = 7)$ etc. Table 2.2 shows the full probability distribution for X. Note that, since we cover all possible values for X, the sum of all the probabilities in a probability distribution will always be unity. That is, $\sum p(X) = 1$.

Table 2.2 Probability distribution

x	2	3	4	5	6	7	8	9	10	11	12
$p(x)$	1/36	2/36	3/36	4/36	5/36	6/36	5/36	4/36	3/36	2/36	1/36

Exercise 2.1

A coin is tossed 4 times. List the elements of the sample space corresponding to this experiment. If X is the number of 'heads' obtained on a trial of this experiment, find the probability distribution for X.

Exercise 2.2

A pot contains 2 red balls and 5 white balls. Three balls are withdrawn from the pot, *none being replaced before the next is drawn*. Find the probability distribution for the number of red balls drawn. [*Hint*: in this case the outcomes of the sample space are *not* all equally likely.]

Mathematical expectations

Consider n trials of the above die rolling experiment, where n is some very large number. Suppose we wish to know the mean or average value taken by the variable X. That is, we require the average number of spots obtained per trial. Clearly, it will not be good enough to compute a straightforward mean of all the possible X values, since some X values will occur more frequently than others. What we must do is take a weighted mean of the X values, with weights equal to the proportion of times each X value occurs. That is, we must use the probabilities in Table 2.2 as the weights, so that

$$\text{average value of } X = 2p(2) + 3p(3) + 4p(4) + \cdots + 12p(12)$$
$$= \sum Xp(X)$$

where the summation is over all values of X. If we work out this quantity for Table 2.2, we obtain

$$\sum Xp(X) = \tfrac{2}{36} + \tfrac{6}{36} + \tfrac{12}{36} + \tfrac{20}{36} + \tfrac{30}{36} + \tfrac{42}{36} + \tfrac{40}{36} + \tfrac{36}{36} + \tfrac{30}{36} + \tfrac{22}{36} + \tfrac{12}{36} = 7$$

Thus the average number of spots per trial equals 7.

The quantity $\sum Xp(X)$ is known as the **mean of the probability distribution** for X and is given the symbol μ. It is also referred to as the **expected value** or the **mathematical expectation** of X, written E(X). That is,

$$\mu = \text{E}(X) = \sum Xp(X) \tag{2.1}$$

The symbol E in (2.1) is known as the **expectations operator**.

Suppose now that every time we perform a trial of our experiment we not only count the number of spots obtained, X, but also square this number, thus obtaining X^2. What would be the average value of X^2 obtained over n trials if n were very large? Using the terminology introduced above, we require the expected value or mathematical expectation of X^2, that is, E(X^2).

Possible values of X^2 are $4, 9, 16, 25, \ldots, 144$. To find E($X^2$), we simply take a weighted mean of the possible values for X^2, using the probabilities in Table 2.2 as weights once again. That is,

$$\text{E}(X^2) = \sum X^2 p(X) \tag{2.2}$$

Computing (2.2) for the probability distribution in Table 2.2 gives

$$\text{E}(X^2) = \tfrac{4}{36} + \tfrac{18}{36} + \tfrac{48}{36} + \tfrac{100}{36} + \tfrac{180}{36} + \tfrac{294}{36} + \tfrac{320}{36} + \tfrac{324}{36} + \tfrac{300}{36} + \tfrac{242}{36} + \tfrac{144}{36} = 54.83$$

Thus the average value for X^2 that we would obtain over many trials is 54.83.

Notice that it is *not* the case that $E(X^2) = [E(X)]^2$. Obviously $[E(X)]^2 = [7]^2 = 49$. In general,

$$E(X^2) \neq [E(X)]^2 \tag{2.3}$$

This inequality illustrates the fact that we should take care when manipulating expected values. What might appear to follow from the normal rules of arithmetic does not necessarily follow. We shall give attention later in this chapter to what can and cannot be done with the expectations operator.

The technique used above for finding expected values can be applied to any function of a variable X. For example,

$$E(X^3) = \sum X^3 p(X), \qquad E[(X+4)^5] = \sum (X+4)^5 p(X),$$

$$E(1/X) = \sum (1/X) p(X)$$

In general, it will be the case that if $f(X)$ is any function of a stochastic variable X then

$$E[f(X)] = \sum f(X) p(X) \tag{2.4}$$

where the summation is always over all possible values of X.

Variance of a probability distribution

An important mathematical expectation is

$$E[(X - \mu)^2] = \sum (X - \mu)^2 p(X) \tag{2.5}$$

where $\mu = \sum X p(X)$ is the mean of the probability distribution. The quantity in Equation (2.5) is referred to as the **variance of the probability distribution**, written Var(X), and is normally given the symbol σ^2. For example, in our die rolling example $\mu = 7$ and $\sigma^2 = E(X-7)^2$. The variance is therefore a measure of the average distance between X on a trial and the mean value of X, which is 7. The variance is a measure of the extent to which all the values of X we would obtain from many trials spread themselves out about their central value of 7. Since the extent of this spread or dispersion depends on the probabilities in Table 2.2, the variance is a measure of the spread or dispersion of probabilities in a probability distribution.

One method of computing a variance from a probability distribution is to use the expectation in the definition (2.5). However, it is more easily computed if we note that

$$\begin{aligned}
\sigma^2 = \sum (X - \mu)^2 p(X) &= \sum X^2 p(X) + \mu^2 \sum p(X) - 2\mu \sum X p(X) \\
&= \sum X^2 p(X) + \mu^2 - 2\mu^2 \\
&= E(X^2) - \mu^2
\end{aligned} \tag{2.6}$$

We already have $\mu = 7$ and $E(X^2) = 54.83$ for our die rolling example, so the variance of the probability distribution in Table 2.2 is, using (2.6),

$$\text{Var}(X) = 54.83 - (7)^2 = 5.83$$

Although we may know that the variance is a measure of the spread or dispersion of a probability distribution and that higher values for σ^2 imply larger spreads, it is not easy to attach any particular meaning to a single value such as $\sigma^2 = 5.83$. To help in this respect, we define the **standard deviation** σ of a probability distribution as the positive square root of the variance. In the present case, therefore, $\sigma = \sqrt{5.83} = 2.41$.

It is possible to give a very rough and ready meaning to this value of 2.42. We can say that, very roughly, over many trials of the die rolling experiment, our variable X on average will be a distance of 2.41 away from its mean value of 7. This is not a precise interpretation of the standard deviation, but it is a useful guide to interpreting absolute values for σ.

Exercise 2.3

Find the mean and variance of the probability distribution obtained in Exercise 2.1. Also find $E(X^3)$ and $E[1/(1 + X)]$.

Pictorial representation of probability distributions

It is sometimes useful to present a pictorial representation of a probability distribution such as that in Table 2.2. This can be done by means of a probability histogram. For the distribution in Table 2.2, such a histogram is shown in Figure 2.1(a).

While possible values for X are shown on the horizontal axis in a probability histogram, the vertical axis measures something a little more complex than simply probability. We stress that it is the areas rather than the heights of the blocks in Figure 2.1(a) that must represent probabilities. To make this clear, suppose for the moment that we were unaware of the individual probabilities $p(2)$ and $p(3)$ in Table 2.2, but knew only that the probability of getting a value for X equal to *either* 2 *or* 3 was equal to 3/36. If we tried to represent this in a histogram in which heights rather than areas represented probabilities, we would obtain Figure 2.1(b). This clearly gives a false impression of the true probability of obtaining $X = 2$ or 3. However, if we let areas represent probabilities, we obtain the histogram in Figure 2.1(c). Since the width of the $X = 2$ or 3 block is twice that of all other blocks, we have given it a height equal to just half of the probability 3/36. The histogram in Figure 2.1(c) is clearly a better representation of the true situation, since the area of its $X = 2$ or 3 block is exactly equal to the sum of the true $X = 2$ and $X = 3$ blocks in Figure 2.1(a).

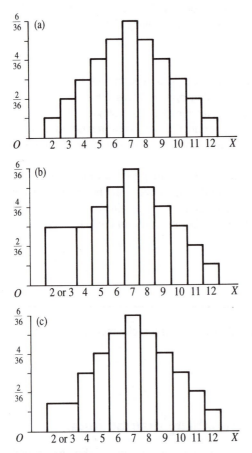

Figure 2.1 (a) Probability histogram for X. (b) Faulty representation. (c) Correct representation.

Areas not heights, then, must represent probabilities in any pictorial representation. What is therefore represented on the vertical axis in the figures is the probability per unit distance along the X axis. This is referred to as the **probability density**. For example, in Figure 2.1(c) the block for $X = 2$ or 3 has a width of 2 and a probability density (height) of $1.5(1/36)$. Its area is therefore $3/36$, representing the probability of getting $X = 2$ or 3. The block for $X = 4$, however, has a width of only 1 unit and a probability density of $3/36$, so that its area equals $3/36$, representing the probability of getting $X = 4$. The concept of probability density will be of considerable importance in the next section.

Exercise 2.4

Given the following probability histogram, find the probability that (a) $X = 4$, (b) X equals either 4 or 5 or 6, and (c) X equals 7 or 8 or 9 or 10.

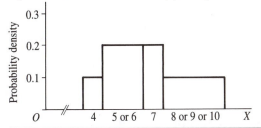

It is important in this chapter that readers obtain a thorough grasp of what can and what cannot be done with the expectations operator E. We shall therefore present, at various stages, a series of theorems outlining the properties of this operator. The first of such theorems is presented here.

THEOREM 2.1

If X is a random variable then, if a and b are constants,
$$E(a + bX) = a + bE(X)$$
and
$$\mathrm{Var}\,(a + bX) = b^2\,\mathrm{Var}\,(X)$$

Proof

$$\begin{aligned}
E(a + bX) &= \sum(a + bX)p(X) \quad \text{(using the definition of expected value)} \\
&= \sum ap(X) + \sum bXp(X) \\
&= a\sum p(X) + b\sum Xp(X) \quad \text{(since } a \text{ and } b \text{ are constants)} \\
&= a + bE(X)
\end{aligned}$$

Also,
$$\mathrm{Var}\,(a + bX) = E\{[a + bX - E(a + bX)]^2\}$$

(using the definition of variance)

But
$$E(a + bX) = a + bE(X) = a + b\mu, \quad \text{where } \mu = E(X)$$
Hence
$$\begin{aligned}
\mathrm{Var}\,(a + bX) &= E[(a + bX - a - b\mu)^2] \\
&= E\{[b(X - \mu)]^2\} = E[b^2(X - \mu)^2] \\
&= b^2 E[(X - \mu)^2] = b^2\,\mathrm{Var}\,(X)
\end{aligned}$$

Notice in particular that while, for example, $E(6X) = 6E(X)$, it is not the case that $Var(6X) = 6 Var(X)$. Rather, $Var(6X) = 36 Var(X)$. However, since the standard deviation is the square root of the variance, the standard deviation of $6X$ does equal 6 times the standard deviation of X.

Exercise 2.5

Suppose $E(X) = 3$ and $Var(X) = 7$. If $Y = 5X - 4$, find $E(Y)$ and $Var(Y)$.

Some well-known discrete probability distributions

The binomial distribution

Consider an experiment with just two possible outcomes, which we shall refer to as 'success' and 'failure'. Suppose that all trials of this experiment can be regarded as independent of each other. That is, the outcome of any one trial does not influence and is not influenced by the outcome of any other trial. The probability of 'success' on any one trial of the experiment can therefore be regarded as a constant, which we denote by π. An obvious example would be the experiment of tossing a coin. If we regard tossing a 'head' as success then $\pi = 0.5$. Another example might concern a trade union 80% of whose membership favour industrial action, the rest opposing action. Each member of the union would represent an independent 'trial', and if being in favour of action is regarded as 'success' then $\pi = 0.8$.

Consider n trials of such a 'binomial' experiment. Let X be the number of successes obtained in these n trials. Thus X can take any of the values $1, 2, 3, \ldots, n$. It can be shown that the probability distribution for X can be obtained by using the expression

$$p(X) = \frac{n!}{(n-X)!X!} \pi^X (1 - \pi)^{n-X} \tag{2.7}$$

Equation (2.7) defines the **binomial distribution**, which can be shown to have mean $E(X) = n\pi$ and variance $Var(X) = n\pi(1 - \pi)$.

For example, in the above trade union example with $\pi = 0.8$, if we interviewed 8 members then, using (2.7), the probability of finding $X = 6$ of them in favour of industrial action is

$$p(6) = \frac{8!}{(8-6)!6!} (0.8)^6 (0.2)^{8-6} = 0.294$$

Exercise 2.6

The probability that a 60-year-old male will be alive in 20 years time is 0.2. Given a sample of 5 such males, let X be the number in the sample who will be alive in 20 years time. Use (2.7) to obtain the probability distribution for X. Sketch a probability histogram of the distribution.

The Poisson distribution

Consider again a binomial experiment. Suppose that the number of trials of the experiment, n, is very large and that the constant probability of success, π, is very small. In such a situation it can be shown that (2.7) may be approximated very well by

$$p(X) = \left(\frac{n\pi^X}{X!}\right)e^{-n\pi} \tag{2.8}$$

where $n\pi$ again equals the mean number of successes in n trials.

Equation (2.8) is particularly useful when n and π are unknown but their product $n\pi$ is known. In this case Equation (2.8) becomes

$$p(X) = \frac{\lambda^X}{X!}e^{-\lambda}, \qquad \lambda = n\pi \tag{2.9}$$

where X is again the number of successes obtained and λ the mean number of successes. Equation (2.9) defines the **Poisson distribution**.

As an example of the use of the Poisson distribution, consider a bank that receives *on average* 3 'dud' cheques per working day. Suppose we require the probability of obtaining exactly 5 dud cheques on a single day.

Let X be the number of dud cheques received in a day. We split the working day up into very many 'moments' or 'split seconds'. Each such split second can be regarded as the trial of an experiment that is a success if a dud cheque arrives at that moment but a failure otherwise. Since the length of a split second is unspecified, we do not know the number of trials, n, that occur in a day, but we do know that n is very large.

The probability π of a dud cheque arriving during any given split second is very small but unknown. It may be assumed, however, that π is the same for all split seconds in the day. That is, the likelihood of a dud cheque arriving is the same at 10 a.m. as it is at 3 p.m.

Although n and π are both unknown in this situation, we do know that $\lambda = n\pi$. $\lambda = 3$ because we know that the mean number of dud cheques per day is 3. Since n is large and π is small, we may therefore use (2.9) to find the probability of 5 cheques arriving in a day. Equation (2.9) in fact yields

$$p(5) = \frac{3^5}{5!}e^{-3} = 0.101$$

Exercise 2.7

Deaths from malaria in a tropical city occur at a rate of 8 per week. Use (2.9) to find (a) the probability of 5 deaths occurring in a week and (b) the probability of at least one death occurring in a week. What assumption have you made in deriving your answers?

The geometric distribution

Consider again a binomial experiment with independent trials for which the fixed probability of success is π. Suppose that X is the number of trials performed *before* the first failure is obtained. That is, if the first failure is obtained on the 5th trial, for example, then $X = 4$. It can easily be shown that the probability distribution for X can be obtained by using the expression

$$p(X) = (1 - \pi)\pi^X \tag{2.10}$$

Equation (2.10) defines the **geometric distribution**, which can be shown to have a mean $E(X) = \pi/(1 - \pi)$ and variance $\text{Var}(X) = \pi/(1 - \pi)^2$. Thus, if a coin is repeatedly tossed, the probability of getting the first head on the 3rd toss is

$$p(2) = (0.5)^2(0.5) = 0.125$$

2.2 Continuous stochastic variables

In this section we shall take as our variable X the height of a female university student in the UK. Since any individual student's height can in principle take any value within the full range of such heights (e.g. a student could be 64.3742 inches tall), X is a **continuous variable**, in contrast to the discrete variables of the last section.

Suppose we carry out an exhaustive survey and actually measure the heights of the many thousand female UK students, initially measuring such heights to the nearest inch. We could then calculate the proportion or relative frequency of students having various heights. For example, the relative frequency of students having a height of 63 inches (this would in fact include all heights within the range $62.5 \leqslant X < 63.5$ inches, assuming we round 62.5 and 63.5 upwards) might be 0.094 or 9.4%. Since we are dealing with a very large number of students, we can interpret this relative frequency as a probability. Thus we can say that if we select a student at random from this population of students, and measure her height to the nearest inch, then the probability of obtaining $X = 63$ is 0.094. In this context X becomes a stochastic variable, and we can build up its probability distribution from the various relative frequencies calculated from our survey. A probability histogram for this distribution will look something like that in Figure 2.2.

Notice that in Figure 2.2 it is probability density that, as usual, is measured on the vertical axis. Thus, since the $X = 63$ block, for example, is 1 inch wide, the probability density for this block is 0.094, making its area equal to the required probability of 0.094. Again, it is the area not the height of the block that represents the probability.

Now suppose that in our survey of all students, instead of measuring heights to the nearest inch, we measured them to the nearest half-inch. That is, we classify students as having heights of 61.5 inches or 62 inches or 62.5 inches etc. We could

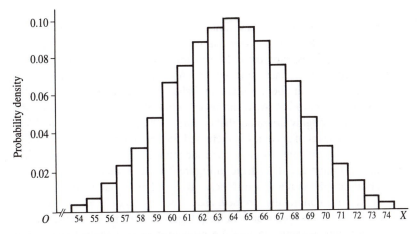

Figure 2.2 Histogram of heights measured to nearest inch.

again compute relative frequencies for various heights and again interpret such relative frequencies as probabilities. For example, we might find that the relative frequency and hence probability of heights of $X = 63$ inches (i.e. all heights now in the range $62.75 \leqslant X < 63.25$) was 0.046. Arranging such values in a probability histogram, we should obtain something like Figure 2.3.

Since we have used the same scale on the horizontal axis in Figure 2.3 as in Figure 2.2, the blocks in Figure 2.3 are only half as wide as those in Figure 2.2. The probability density associated with the $X = 63$ block is 0.092, giving an area for this block equal to the required probability, 0.046. As always, it is the areas not the heights of blocks that represent probabilities. Because of this, the heights of the blocks in Figure 2.3 are similar to those in Figure 2.2.

Clearly, we could increase the accuracy of our height measurement further. For example, if we measured all heights to the nearest tenth of an inch, we should

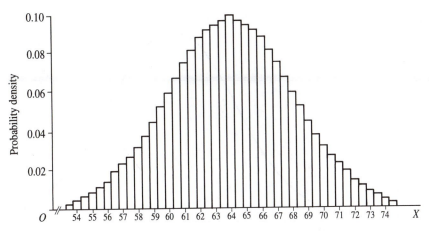

Figure 2.3 Histogram of heights measured to nearest half-inch.

eventually obtain a probability histogram similar in general height and shape to that in Figure 2.3 but with blocks only one-tenth as wide and with a rather less 'jagged' outline. Nor need the process stop there. In principle, heights could be measured to the nearest hundredth of an inch, and so on. As we increase the accuracy of measurement, the blocks in the resultant probability histograms will obviously become narrower and narrower. Also, however, while the general outline of the histogram will remain roughly the same, that outline is likely to become less and less jagged. In fact, as the level of accuracy is increased further and further, the outline of the histogram, almost certainly, will approach the smooth bell-shaped symmetrical curve illustrated in Figure 2.4. The shape in Figure 2.4 can in fact be thought of as being made up of an infinite number of blocks, all of infinitesimal width.

Since, as we have continually stressed, areas not heights of blocks are used to represent probability, to find probabilities from Figure 2.4 we must calculate areas beneath the curve. For example, to find the probability that a student selected at random will have a height between 61 and 64 inches, we need to find the area beneath the curve between these two values. If the equation representing the curve can be found, this is most easily done by integrating this function between the limits 61 and 64. Fortunately, statisticians have known the function representing such curves for many years. It is[1]

$$p(X) = (2\pi\sigma^2)^{-0.5} \exp\left[-(x - \mu)^2/2\sigma^2\right] \tag{2.11}$$

where $\mu = \mathrm{E}(X)$ is the mean of the probability distribution and σ^2 is its variance. The probability distribution described by (2.11) is known as the **normal distribution**. Many variables in nature, for example weights, waist measurements and the heights of oak trees, turn out to be normally distributed. The distribution is also important, as we shall see in the next chapter, in statistical theory.

Since $p(X)$ tells us the probability density for various values of X, functions such as (2.11), that is, probability distributions for continuous variables, are referred to as **probability density functions**.

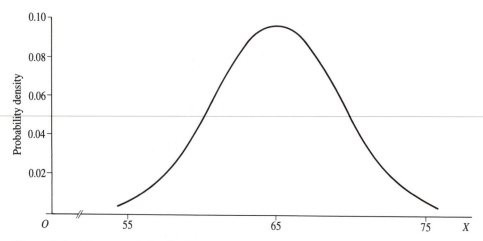

Figure 2.4 The normal distribution.

Not all continuous variables have normal distributions of course. However, in general, if a continuous variable X has a probability density function $f(X)$ then it can be shown that its mean is given by

$$E(X) = \int_{-\infty}^{+\infty} Xf(X)\,dX \qquad (2.12)$$

and its variance by

$$\mathrm{Var}\,(X) = \int_{-\infty}^{+\infty} [X - E(X)]^2 f(X)\,dX \qquad (2.13)$$

The expressions (2.12) and (2.13) should be compared with (2.1) and (2.5) for discrete variables. Because (2.12) and (2.13) are often harder to work out than (2.1) and (2.5), we shall not make use of them in this text. However, if they are applied to the normal probability density function (2.11), it can be shown that we do in fact obtain $E(X) = \mu$ for the mean and $\mathrm{Var}\,(X) = \sigma^2$ for the variance of this distribution.

A variable with the probability density function (2.11) is normally distributed with mean μ and variance σ^2. A statistician's shorthand for this is to write

$$X \text{ is } N(\mu, \sigma^2)$$

Thus, for example, if X is N(4, 25) then it is normally distributed with mean 4 and variance 25.

As we observed above, areas under the normal curve in Figure 2.4 represent probabilities, and these can be calculated by integrating (2.11) between definite limits. However, the integration process is complicated, and its continuous use is tedious. For this reason, tables have been prepared giving areas under one particular normal distribution – the **standard normal distribution**.

The standard normal distribution is the normal distribution that has zero mean and unit variance. That is, it is the N(0, 1) distribution. Setting $\mu = 0$ and $\sigma^2 = 1$ in (2.11), we see that the probability density function for the standard normal distribution is

$$p(X) = (2\pi)^{-0.5} \exp\left[-x^2/2\right]$$

The standard normal distribution is illustrated in Figure 2.5. It is centred about $X = 0$ and, like all normal curves, has a smooth bell-shaped symmetrical shape.

A table of areas under the standard normal curve and a brief description of how to use it are presented in Appendix IV at the end of this text. We assume that readers are familiar with this procedure, but will revise the process by which the table may be used to find areas under *any* normal curve, whatever its mean and variance.

First, we demonstrate that any normally distributed variable can be very easily transformed into a standard normal or N(0, 1) variable. Referring back to our population of female students, suppose that heights of such students are normally distributed with a mean of 64.3 inches and a variance of 9.8, that is, a standard deviation of 3.13 inches. Thus

$$X \text{ is } N(64.3, 9.8)$$

Subtracting the mean, 64.3, from all values of X, we obtain a new variable Y, where

$$Y = X - 64.3 \text{ is } N(0, 9.8) \qquad (2.14)$$

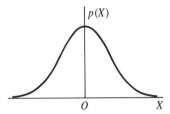

Figure 2.5 The standard normal distribution.

To obtain (2.14), we have used the first part of Theorem 2.1 and the fact that subtracting a constant from a variable does not change the shape of its probability density function.

If we divide Y by its standard deviation, 3.13, we obtain a further variable Z, where

$$Z = \frac{X - 64.3}{3.13} \quad \text{is} \ N(0, 1) \tag{2.15}$$

That is, Z is a standard normal variable. To obtain (2.15), we have used the second part of Theorem 2.1 on variances and the fact that dividing a variable by a constant does not change the shape of that variable's probability density function.

Notice that to turn the variable X into a $N(0, 1)$ variable, we had to first subtract its mean, 64.3, and then divide by its standard deviation, 3.13. *It should be clear that, in general, if X is normally distributed with mean μ and variance σ^2 then X can always be converted into a standard normal Z variable by subtracting the mean μ from X and then dividing by the standard deviation σ. That is,*

$$Z = \frac{X - \mu}{\sigma} \quad \text{is} \ N(0, 1) \tag{2.16}$$

Suppose we require the probability that a female student, selected at random, has a height in excess of 69 inches. This is a 'question about X', and the trick is to turn it into a 'question about Z', which we can answer using our standard normal tables.

We require

$$\Pr(X > 69) = \Pr\left(\frac{X - 64.3}{3.13} > \frac{69 - 64.3}{3.13}\right)$$

$$= \Pr(Z > 1.50) \quad \text{(using (2.15))}$$

$$= 0.5 - \text{area} \ A = 0.5 - 0.4332 = 0.0668 \tag{2.17}$$

We have used Figure 2.6 and the standard normal table for the last line in (2.17).

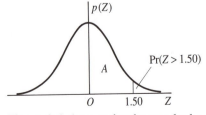

Figure 2.6 Area under the standard normal curve.

Thus the required probability is 0.0668, or we can say that 6.68% of all female UK students have a height in excess of 69 inches.

Exercise 2.8

The weekly food expenditure £ of single adult females is N(48, 5). Find the proportion of such females (a) with an expenditure greater than 52, (b) with an expenditure between 46.5 and 51.5, and (c) with an expenditure equal to 46.

Exercise 2.9

Student marks in an examination are normally distributed, with a mean of 54 and a standard deviation of 12. It is decided to give 10% of students a grade A. What mark must a student obtain to achieve a grade A?

Perhaps we should stress at this point that continuous variables are not necessarily normally distributed. We shall encounter other probability density functions in the next chapter. These distributions do not, however, occur naturally and are in fact constructed out of standard normal variables. A probability density function that does occur naturally, though, is the so-called 'negative exponential distribution'.

Suppose a machine tends to break down. The number of breakdowns per hour is a discrete random variable. Suppose this variable has the Poisson probability distribution defined by Equation (2.9). It can then be shown that the time in hours between successive breakdowns, X (a continuous variable), has a probability density function given by

$$p(X) = \theta e^{-\theta X} \tag{2.18}$$

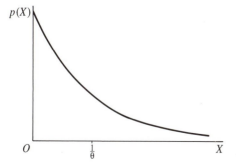

Figure 2.7 The negative exponential distribution.

Equation (2.18) defines the **negative exponential distribution**. It has a mean of $1/\theta$ with variance $1/\theta^2$, and is illustrated in Figure 2.7. As with all probability density functions, areas under this curve represent probabilities.

2.3   Joint, marginal and conditional probability distributions

Consider an experiment where a coin is tossed 4 times. The sample space for this experiment consists of 16 possible outcomes, and is shown in Table 2.3, where H stands for 'heads' and T for 'tails'. Provided the coin is a fair one, each outcome has a probability $1/16$ of occurring on any given trial of the experiment. We now define two discrete random variables as follows:

$X =$ number of heads obtained on the first 3 tosses of the coin

$Y =$ number of heads obtained on all 4 tosses of the coin

The values of X and Y for all possible outcomes are shown in Table 2.3, and constitute the sample space for this experiment.

Now consider Table 2.4. The values shown in the main body of this table are **joint probabilities** concerning X and Y. For example, the value $3/16$ in the $X = 2$ row and the $Y = 3$ column represents the joint probability of getting both $X = 2$ *and $Y = 3$* on the same trial of the experiment. Referring back to the sample space in Table 2.3, we see that 3 of the 16 outcomes result in this combination of X and Y – hence the joint probability of $3/16$. Similarly, the combination $X = 0$ and $Y = 1$ appears only once in the sample space, (TTTH), and hence has a joint probability of $1/16$. Many of the joint probabilities are zero, since a number of combinations for X and Y are impossible. For example, if there are no heads on the first 3 tosses of the coin, it is impossible to get 2, 3 or 4 heads from all 4 tosses.

The array of joint probabilities in the main body of Table 2.4 make up what is called the **joint probability distribution** for X and Y. Such a joint probability

Table 2.3   Sample space

	X	Y		X	Y		X	Y		X	Y
(HHHH)	3	4	(HHHT)	3	3	(TTHH)	1	2	(THTT)	1	1
(THHH)	2	3	(HHTT)	2	2	(THTH)	1	2	(TTHT)	1	1
(HTHH)	2	3	(HTHT)	2	2	(THHT)	2	2	(TTTH)	0	1
(HHTH)	2	3	(HTTH)	1	2	(HTTT)	1	1	(TTTT)	0	0

Table 2.4   Joint and marginal probability distributions

X \ Y	0	1	2	3	4	$f(X)$
0	1/16	1/16	0	0	0	1/8
1	0	3/16	3/16	0	0	3/8
2	0	0	3/16	3/16	0	3/8
3	0	0	0	1/16	1/16	1/8
$g(Y)$	1/16	1/4	3/8	1/4	1/16	

distribution therefore consists of a listing of all possible combinations of X and Y, together with the joint probabilities associated with each such combination. It is most conveniently presented as a two-dimensional array as in Table 2.4.

We shall denote our joint probability distribution by $p(X, Y)$. Thus our notation will be, for example, to write $p(3, 4)$ for $\Pr(X = 3$ and $Y = 4)$. Thus $p(3, 4) = 1/16$ and $p(2, 2) = 3/16$ etc. Note that the sum of all the probabilities in a joint distribution will always be unity, since we cover all possible combinations of X and Y.

Let us now concentrate on the X variable, ignoring for the moment the value taken by Y. That is, we consider only the first 3 tosses of the coin. The probability that X takes a certain value, regardless of the value of Y, is known as a **marginal probability**, and the distribution of such probabilities as the **marginal probability distribution** for X. These marginal probabilities are shown in the far-right column of Table 2.4, with the relevant X-values in the far-left column. For example, the value $3/8$ is the simple marginal probability of obtaining $X = 1$. This value can be obtained by referring back to the sample space in Table 2.3. Ignoring the Y-values, we see that 6 of the 16 outcomes possible on each trial of the experiment result in just 1 head on the first 3 tosses. Hence the marginal probability of $3/8$. Similarly, the marginal probability that $X = 3$ is $1/8$, because 2 of the 16 outcomes imply 3 heads in the first 3 tosses.

We denote the marginal probability distribution for X by $f(X)$. Thus by $f(1)$ we mean $\Pr(X = 1)$, which is $3/8$. Similarly $f(3) = 1/8$ etc. For this reason, the column of marginal probabilities for X is headed $f(X)$.

We can also, of course, obtain a marginal probability distribution for Y. The marginal probabilities for Y are shown in the bottom row of Table 2.4, with the relevant values of Y in the top row. The marginal probabilities have again been obtained by referring back to the sample space in Table 2.3. For example, this time ignoring the X-values, 4 of the 16 outcomes yield a value of $Y = 1$. Thus $\Pr(Y = 1) = 1/4$, and this value appears under $Y = 1$ in the bottom row of Table 2.4.

We denote the marginal probability distribution for Y by $g(Y)$. Thus, for example, $g(1) = \Pr(Y = 1)$, which we know is $1/4$. Similarly $g(2) = 3/8$ etc. The row of marginal probabilities for Y is therefore marked as $g(Y)$ in Table 2.4.

Notice from Table 2.4 that the joint and marginal probabilities are closely related. For example, each row of joint probabilities sums to the marginal probability on the right-hand side. A little thought will indicate why this must always be so. For example, to find the marginal probability that $X = 2$, we need to list all the separate ways in which it is possible to obtain $X = 2$ (there are in fact only two such ways: $X = 2$, $Y = 2$ and $X = 2$, $Y = 3$). These possibilities are mutually exclusive, so their probabilities have to be added together to obtain the required marginal probability. But that is exactly what we do if we add the joint probabilities in the $X = 2$ row.

For the same reason, each column of joint probabilities will always sum to the marginal probability at its foot. For example, $g(3)$ in Table 2.4 is the sum of the joint probabilities in the column above it.

This relationship between marginal and joint probabilities means that once we have the joint probability distribution for any two variables X and Y, we can obtain the marginal distributions by simply summing rows and columns. For example, we do not have to refer back to the sample space, as we did originally, to find the marginal probabilities in Table 2.4.

It is possible to find the mean and variance of a marginal distribution in the manner of Section 2.1. For example, taking the marginal distribution for Y in Table 2.4, its mean and variance are given by

$$E(Y) = \sum Yg(Y) = 2 \quad \text{and} \quad \text{Var}(Y) = E(Y^2) - [E(Y)]^2 = 5 - (2)^2 = 1$$

Exercise 2.10

A four-sided die has the numbers 1, 2, 3 and 4 on its sides. It is tossed twice. (a) Set up the sample space for this experiment. (b) If X is the higher of the two numbers obtained and Y is the lower, find the joint probability distribution for X and Y, and the marginal probability distributions for X and Y. (c) Find the mean and variance of the marginal distribution for X. [*Note*: if, for example, a double 3 is tossed then $X = 3$ and $Y = 3$ etc.]

Conditional probability distributions

Let us concentrate for the moment on those trials of the above experiment where we obtain $X = 2$, that is, obtain 2 heads on the first 3 tosses of the coin. Suppose we wish to know the proportion of such trials that end up with $Y = 3$, that is, 3 heads on all 4 tosses. What we in fact seek is the **conditional probability** of obtaining $Y = 3$ given that $X = 2$. We can find this by simply using the definition of a conditional probability:

$$\Pr(Y = 3 \mid X = 2) = \frac{\Pr(X = 2, Y = 3)}{\Pr(X = 2)} = \frac{p(2, 3)}{f(2)} = \frac{3/16}{3/8} = 0.5$$

Notice that to obtain this conditional probability, we take a joint probability from the main body of Table 2.4 and divide it by a marginal probability for X. The value of 0.5 that we obtain simply means that, out of all trials of the experiment that have 2 heads on the first 3 tosses, one-half end with 3 heads on all 4 tosses.

Similarly, we can find the conditional probabilities of obtaining $Y = 0, 1, 2$ or 4, given that $X = 2$:

$$\Pr\,(Y = 0 \mid X = 2) = \frac{p(2, 0)}{f(2)} = \frac{0}{3/8} = 0$$

$$\Pr\,(Y = 1 \mid X = 2) = \frac{p(2, 1)}{f(2)} = \frac{0}{3/8} = 0$$

$$\Pr\,(Y = 2 \mid X = 2) = \frac{p(2, 2)}{f(2)} = \frac{3/16}{3/8} = 0.5$$

$$\Pr\,(Y = 4 \mid X = 2) = \frac{p(2, 4)}{f(2)} = \frac{0}{3/8} = 0$$

In each case the conditional probability is again obtained by dividing a joint probability from the main body of Table 2.4 by the same marginal probability that $X = 2$.

The above conditional probabilities are arrayed in Table 2.5. They make up the **conditional probability distribution** for Y given that $X = 2$. Notice that some of the conditional probabilities are zero. This is because if, for example, we obtain $X = 2$ heads on the first 3 tosses then there is no way in which we can obtain $Y = 0, 1$ or 4 heads on all 4 tosses.

We denote conditional probabilities for Y given some value for X by $g(Y \mid X)$. Thus $g(3 \mid 2)$ denotes the conditional probability of obtaining $Y = 3$ given $X = 2$. Similarly $g(4 \mid 3)$ is the conditional probability of obtaining $Y = 4$ given $X = 3$. A conditional probability distribution for Y is therefore written as

$$g(Y \mid X) \quad \text{for all } Y \tag{2.19}$$

Thus the conditional distribution in Table 2.5 is labelled $g(Y \mid 2)$.

Table 2.5   Conditional distribution for Y given $X=2$

Y	0	1	2	3	4
$g(Y \mid 2)$	0	0	0.5	0.5	0

Once a table of joint and marginal probabilities has been drawn up, conditional probability distributions can be swiftly obtained. For example, in Table 2.5 we have obtained the conditional probabilities by dividing joint probabilities by the marginal probability $f(2)$, because the distribution was conditional on $X = 2$. The required joint probabilities are simply those in the row to the left of $f(2)$ in Table 2.4. Dividing them by $f(2)$ immediately gives the conditional probabilities in Table 2.5.

Obviously we can also have conditional probability distributions for X given Y. For example, consider the conditional distribution for X given $Y = 3$. This is presented in Table 2.6. To obtain these conditional probabilities, we concentrate simply on trials of the experiment that result in $Y = 3$. The marginal probability of $Y = 3$ is $g(3)$. The required joint probabilities are those in the column above $g(3)$ in Table 2.4. Dividing them in turn by $g(3) = 1/4$ yields the conditional probability distribution in Table 2.6. For example, the conditional probability of obtaining $X = 2$ given $Y = 3$ is 0.75. That is, out of all trials that result in $Y = 3$ heads altogether, three-quarters will have shown $X = 2$ heads on the first 3 tosses.

Extending our notation slightly, we denote conditional probabilities for X given Y by $f(X | Y)$. Thus $f(1 | 2) = \Pr(X = 1 | Y = 2)$ etc. A conditional distribution for X given Y is therefore written as

$$f(X | Y) \quad \text{for all } X \tag{2.20}$$

Thus the conditional distribution in Table 2.6 is labelled $f(X | 3)$.

Table 2.6   Conditional distribution for X given $Y = 3$

X	0	1	2	3
$f(X \mid 3)$	0	0	0.75	0.25

Conditional means and variances

It was a simple matter to find the mean and variance of, for example, Y from Table 2.4. We simply applied the techniques of Section 2.1 to the marginal distribution for Y, $g(Y)$. Thus $E(Y) = \sum Yg(Y)$, and $\text{Var}(Y) = E(Y^2) - [E(Y)]^2$. Similarly, the mean and variance of X can be obtained from $f(X)$. In this context, however, such quantities are known as **unconditional means and variances**. It is also possible to find means and variances for conditional distributions.

Consider Table 2.5, where we have the conditional distribution for Y given that $X = 2$, that is, $g(Y | 2)$. The mean of this distribution is known as the **conditional mean** of Y given $X = 2$, and is found by applying the techniques of Section 2.1 to the conditional distribution in Table 2.5. Thus

$$\text{conditional mean} = E(Y | 2) = \sum Yg(Y | 2) = 2(1/2) + 3(1/2) = 2.5$$

The value of 2.5 found for this conditional mean simply implies that if we consider just those trials of our coin experiment that resulted in $X = 2$ then the mean value of Y will be 2.5.

Similarly, the variance of the distribution in Table 2.5 is known as the **conditional variance** of Y given $X = 2$, and this can also be found using the techniques of Section 2.1. Thus

$$E(Y^2 \,|\, X = 2) = \sum Y^2 g(Y \,|\, 2) = (2)^2(1/2) + (3)^2(1/2) = 6.5$$
$$\text{Var}\,(Y \,|\, 2) = E(Y^2 \,|\, X = 2) - [E(Y \,|\, 2)]^2 = 6.5 - (2.5)^2 = 0.25$$

The means and variances of any conditional distribution, for example that in Table 2.6, can be found in the same manner.

Exercise 2.11

For the variables in Exercise 2.10, find (a) the conditional probability distribution for Y given that $X = 4$, and (b) the conditional distribution for X given that $Y = 2$. (c) Find the conditional mean and variance for the first of these distributions and interpret the values obtained.

2.4 Mathematical expectations of functions of more than one variable

Consider again the coin tossing experiment of the previous section. Suppose, on each trial of the experiment, that after finding X and Y we compute their product XY. How can we find $E(XY)$, that is, the average value of XY obtained over very many trials? Just as we found $E(X)$ by taking $\sum Xf(x)$ and $E(Y)$ by taking $\sum Yg(Y)$, it can be shown that we can obtain $E(XY)$ by taking the double summation

$$E(XY) = \sum_X \sum_Y XYp(X, Y) \tag{2.21}$$

where $p(X, Y)$ is the joint probability distribution for X and Y. The double summation in (2.21) means that for every possible combination of X and Y, we multiply XY by the joint probability of that X and Y combination and then sum. The joint probabilities are given in Table 2.4, and the product XY is given in Table 2.7(a) for all possible combinations. Thus, to form $E(XY)$, the numbers in Table 2.4 are multiplied into the corresponding numbers in Table 2.7(a) and then summed. This

Table 2.7(a) Values of XY

X \ Y	0	1	2	3	4
0	0	0	0	0	0
1	0	1	2	3	4
2	0	2	4	6	8
3	0	3	6	9	12

Table 2.7(b) Values of X^3Y^2

X \ Y	0	1	2	3	4
0	0	0	0	0	0
1	0	1	4	9	16
2	0	8	32	72	128
3	0	27	108	243	432

gives (many of the $XYp(X, Y)$ terms are zero)

$$E(XY) = 3/16 + 6/16 + 12/16 + 18/16 + 9/16 + 12/16 = 3.75$$

Thus, over many trials, the average value obtained for the product of X and Y is 3.75. Notice that, although the average value of X over many trials is $E(X) = 1.5$ and the average value of Y is $E(Y) = 2$, it is *not* the case that $E(XY) = 1.5 \times 2 = 3$. In general,

$$E(XY) \neq E(X)E(Y) \tag{2.22}$$

As we saw in Section 2.1, one has to be careful when manipulating the expectations operator!

Suppose, for some (obscure) reason, we had wished to find not $E(XY)$ but $E(X^3Y^2)$, the average value of X^3Y^2 over very many trials. To find this, we compute the double summation

$$E(X^3Y^2) = \sum_X \sum_Y X^3Y^2 p(X, Y) \tag{2.23}$$

That is, for each combination of X and Y, we form X^3Y^2, multiply it into the corresponding joint probability $p(X, Y)$, and sum. The values of X^3Y^2 are shown in Table 2.7(b). For example, when $X = 2$ and $Y = 3$, the value of $X^3Y^2 = 72$. The double summation in (2.23) yields

$$E(X^3Y^2) = 3/16 + 12/16 + 96/16 + 216/16 + 243/16 + 432/16 = 62.625$$

The reader should verify that it is *not* the case that $E(X^3Y^2) = E(X^3)E(Y^2)$.

In a similar manner, we can find the expected value of any function of X and Y, $h(X, Y)$, by taking the double summation

$$E[h(X, Y)] = \sum_X \sum_Y h(X, Y)p(X, Y) \tag{2.24}$$

We note, at this point, a further useful property of the expectations operator.

THEOREM 2.2

If X and Y are two random variables then, if a and b are constants,

$$E(aX + bY) = aE(X) + bE(Y)$$

★ Proof

$$E(aX + bY) = \sum_X \sum_Y (aX + bY)p(X, Y)$$

$$= \sum_X \sum_Y aXp(X, Y) + \sum_X \sum_Y bYp(X, Y)$$

$$= a\sum_X X\sum_Y p(X, Y) + b\sum_Y Y\sum_X p(X, Y)$$

$$= a\sum_X Xf(X) + b\sum_Y Yg(Y)$$

$$= aE(X) + bE(Y)$$

where in the fourth line we have used the relationship between joint and marginal probabilities.

Readers unused to handling summation operations may be a little baffled by the proof of Theorem 2.2, but the main point to understand is that it *is* the case that, for example, $E(5X + 3Y) = 5E(X) + 3E(Y)$ and $E(2X - 4Y) = 2E(X) - 4E(Y)$. Hence, although, as we have seen, $E(XY)$ does not normally equal $E(X)E(Y)$, if we set a and b equal to 1 in Theorem 2.2, we obtain $E(X + Y) = E(X) + E(Y)$. The reader should verify that this is indeed the case for our coin tossing example above.

Theorem 2.2 can in fact be extended to more than two random variables. For example,

$$E(aX + bY + cZ + dW) = aE(X) + bE(Y) + cE(Z) + dE(W)$$

Covariances and correlations

The **covariance** between any two random variables X and Y is defined as

$$\text{Cov}(X, Y) = E[X - E(X)][Y - E(Y)] \tag{2.25}$$

It is a measure of the strength and direction of any linear relationship between X and Y. For example, in our coin tossing example with $E(X) = 1.5$ and $E(Y) = 2$, we are calculating in (2.25) the average value of $(X - 1.5)(Y - 2)$ over many trials of the experiment. Suppose there is an inverse linear association or relationship between X and Y (i.e. with X rising as Y falls). This implies that, over many trials, positive values of $(X - 1.5)$ will tend to coincide with negative values of $(Y - 2)$, whereas negative values of $(X - 1.5)$ will tend to coincide with positive values of $(Y - 2)$.

Thus the product $(X - 1.5)(Y - 2)$ will tend to be negative, so that its average value over many trials, $E[(X - 1.5)(Y - 2)]$, will clearly be negative. Moreover, the stronger the inverse linear association or relationship between X and Y, the more negative the covariance will become.

If, on the other hand, there is a direct linear association between X and Y (i.e. with X rising as Y rises) then the product $[X - E(X)][Y - E(Y)]$ will tend to be positive. Thus its expected value, the covariance, will be positive. Again, the stronger the direct linear relationship between X and Y, the more positive will the covariance become.

One way of evaluating the covariance (2.25) is to use the double summation $\sum_X \sum_Y [X - E(X)][Y - E(Y)]p(X, Y)$. However, there is a simpler way than this, since

$$
\begin{aligned}
\text{Cov} (X, Y) &= E[X - E(X)][Y - E(Y)] \\
&= E[XY - XE(Y) - YE(X) + E(X)E(Y)] \\
&= E(XY) - E(Y)E(X) - E(X)E(Y) + E(X)E(Y) \quad\quad (2.26)
\end{aligned}
$$

In (2.26) we have used the fact that $E(X)$ and $E(Y)$ are constants and hence, by Theorem 2.1, can be taken outside the expectations operator. It follows that

$$
\text{Cov} (X, Y) = E(XY) - E(X)E(Y) \quad\quad (2.27)
$$

The expression (2.27) is normally easier to evaluate than the equivalent double summation. For example, in our coin tossing example we know that $E(XY) = 3.75$ and that $E(X) = 1.5$ and $E(Y) = 2$. Thus in this case we have

$$
\text{Cov} (X, Y) = 3.75 - 1.5(2) = 0.75
$$

The positive value of 0.75 for the covariance implies a direct positive linear association between X and Y in this example. This is what we would expect, since, obviously, the more heads we obtain on the first 3 tosses of the coin, the more heads we shall obtain from all 4 tosses.

The problem with the covariance, as a measure of the strength of the association between X and Y, is that we have no absolute standard against which to judge it. A higher covariance implies a stronger linear association, but does the above value of 0.75 mean a strong association or a weak one? To resolve this problem, statisticians therefore work out the so-called correlation between X and Y.

The **correlation** between X and Y, denoted by ρ, is defined as

$$
\rho = \frac{\text{Cov} (X, Y)}{\sqrt{\text{Var} (X)} \sqrt{\text{Var} (Y)}} = \frac{E[X - E(X)][Y - E(Y)]}{\sqrt{E[X - E(X)]^2} \sqrt{E[Y - E(Y)]^2}} \quad\quad (2.28)
$$

The correlation has the advantage that its value always lies in the range -1 to $+1$. It takes the value zero whenever the covariance is zero, that is, when there is no linear association between X and Y. If there is an exact positive or direct linear association between X and Y then it takes a value equal to $+1$, but if there is an exact negative or inverse linear association then it takes a value of -1.

To see this, suppose an exact linear relationship $Y = \alpha + \beta X$ does exist. Hence, by Theorem 2.1, $E(Y) = \alpha + \beta E(X)$. Substituting for Y and $E(Y)$ in the numerator of (2.28) yields

$$E[X - E(X)][\alpha + \beta X - \alpha - \beta E(X)] = \beta E[X - E(X)]^2$$

Similarly, substituting into the denominator of (2.28) yields

$$\sqrt{E[X - E(X)]^2}\sqrt{E[\alpha + \beta X - \alpha - \beta E(X)]^2} = \sqrt{\beta^2\{E[X - E(X)]^2\}^2}$$
$$= + \beta E[X - E(X)]^2$$

where we always take the *positive* value of the square root. Thus if $\beta > 0$, so that the linear relationship is positive, then by dividing numerator by denominator in (2.28) we obtain a value $\rho = +1$. However, if $\beta < 0$, so that the linear relationship is an inverse one, we obtain $\rho = -1$.

We now compute the correlation ρ for X and Y in our coin tossing example. We already know the covariance in the numerator of (2.28). We computed this as 0.75 above. For the two variances in the denominator of (2.28), we have

$$E[X - E(X)]^2 = E(X^2) - [E(X)]^2 = 3 - (1.5)^2 = 0.75 \qquad (2.29)$$

and

$$E[Y - E(Y)]^2 = E(Y^2) - [E(Y)]^2 = 5 - (2)^2 = 1 \qquad (2.30)$$

To obtain $E(X^2)$ and $E(Y^2)$ in (2.29) and (2.30), we have used $\sum X^2 f(X)$ and $\sum Y^2 g(Y)$ respectively. We can now use (2.28) to find the correlation. This gives

$$\rho = \frac{0.75}{\sqrt{0.75}\sqrt{1}} = 0.87$$

Since 0.87 is much closer to unity than to zero, we can now say that there is a strong positive linear association between X and Y. This is as expected, given the nature of X and Y.

Exercise 2.12

For the variables in Exercise 2.10, (a) find the covariance between X and Y, and (b) find the variance of X, the variance of Y and hence the correlation between X and Y.

Exercise 2.13

A box contains 9 balls, 2 of which are white and 7 red. Three balls are drawn from the box – *none being replaced before the next is drawn*. Let X be the number of white balls drawn and Y the number of red balls drawn. Find the joint probability distribution for X and Y. Hence show that the correlation between X and Y is -1, and explain why this should be so.

We now introduce two further theorems concerning expectations and variances.

THEOREM 2.3

If two random variables X and Y are uncorrelated then $E(XY) = E(X)E(Y)$.

Proof

Recall that Cov $(X, Y) = E(XY) - E(X)E(Y)$. But if X and Y are uncorrelated then Cov $(X, Y) = 0$. Hence

$$E(XY) - E(X)E(Y) = 0, \quad \text{so that} \quad E(XY) = E(X)E(Y)$$

As we saw earlier in the chapter, it is not generally the case that $E(XY) = E(X)E(Y)$. Theorem 2.3 simply states that this equality will hold only when the two variables concerned are uncorrelated. The theorem can be expanded to cover more than two random variables. For example, $E(XYZ) = E(X)E(Y)E(Z)$ only when X, Y and Z are all uncorrelated with one another.

THEOREM 2.4

If X and Y are two random variables then, if a and b are constants,

$$\text{Var}(aX + bY) = a^2 \text{ Var}(X) + b^2 \text{ Var}(Y) + 2ab \text{ Cov}(X, Y)$$

Proof

$$\text{Var}(aX + bY) = E[aX + bY - E(aX + bY)]^2$$
$$\text{(using the definition of a variance)}$$
$$= E[aX - aE(X) + bY - bE(Y)]^2$$
$$\text{(using Theorem 2.2)}$$
$$= E\{a^2[X - E(X)]^2 + b^2[Y - E(Y)]^2 + 2ab[X - E(X)][Y - E(Y)]\}$$
$$= a^2 E[X - E(X)]^2 + b^2 E[Y - E(Y)]^2 + 2ab E[X - E(X)][Y - E(Y)]$$
$$= a^2 \text{ Var}(X) + b^2 \text{ Var}(Y) + 2ab \text{ Cov}(X, Y)$$

Note that if X and Y are uncorrelated, in which case Cov $(X, Y) = 0$, then Theorem 2.4 reduces to

$$\text{Var}(aX + bY) = a^2 \text{ Var}(X) + b^2 \text{ Var}(Y) \tag{2.31}$$

However, if X and Y are correlated then a covariance term enters into (2.31).

There are a number of useful special cases of Theorem 2.4. For example, if $a = 1$ and $b = 1$ then we have

$$\text{Var}\,(X + Y) = \text{Var}\,(X) + \text{Var}\,(Y) + 2\,\text{Cov}\,(X, Y) \qquad (2.32)$$

whereas setting $a = 1$ and $b = -1$ yields

$$\text{Var}\,(X - Y) = \text{Var}\,(X) + \text{Var}\,(Y) - 2\,\text{Cov}\,(X, Y) \qquad (2.33)$$

If X and Y are uncorrelated then the covariance terms drop out of (2.32) and (2.33), and we obtain

$$\text{Var}\,(X + Y) = \text{Var}\,(X - Y) = \text{Var}\,(X) + \text{Var}\,(Y) \qquad (2.34)$$

Exercise 2.14

X, Y and Z are random variables with

$$E(X) = 3, \qquad E(Y) = -4, \qquad E(Z) = 11$$
$$\text{Var}\,(X) = 12, \qquad \text{Var}\,(Y) = 8, \qquad \text{Var}\,(Z) = 34$$

Y and Z are uncorrelated, but $\text{Cov}\,(X, Y) = 8$. If $U = 4Y + Z$, $V = X + Y$ and $W = 4X - 3Y$ are three further random variables, find $E(U)$ and $\text{Var}\,(U)$, $E(V)$ and $\text{Var}\,(V)$, and $E(W)$ and $\text{Var}\,(W)$.

Exercise 2.15

Two random variables X and Y have the following means, variances and covariance:

$$E(X) = 5, \quad \text{Var}\,(X) = 10, \quad E(Y) = 2, \quad \text{Var}\,(Y) = 20, \quad \text{Cov}\,(X, Y) = 5$$

If $A = 2X + Y$ and $B = X - 2Y$, find the means and variances of A and B. Show that $E(AB) = 2E(X^2) - 2E(Y^2) - 3E(XY)$. Hence find the covariance between A and B.

Sample covariances and correlations

It is likely that the reader will have come across the term 'correlation' before. However, the definition of correlation given by (2.28) may well be unfamiliar. This is because correlations are most often worked out for *samples*.

Consider the experiment introduced at the beginning of Section 2.3, where a coin was tossed 4 times and 2 random variables X and Y defined. Suppose we consider $n = 10$ trials of this experiment. For each trial, we shall have a value for X and a value for Y. We shall therefore have 10 pairs of such values, which we can regard as a sample, of size $n = 10$, drawn randomly from a *population* of such pairs of

Table 2.8 Sample values for X and Y

X	Y	$X - \bar{X}$	$(X - \bar{X})^2$	$Y - \bar{Y}$	$(Y - \bar{Y})^2$	$(X - \bar{X})(Y - \bar{Y})$
2	3	0.3	0.09	0.8	0.64	0.24
1	2	−0.7	0.49	−0.2	0.04	0.14
2	2	0.3	0.09	−0.2	0.04	−0.06
0	0	−1.7	2.89	−2.2	4.84	3.74
2	2	0.3	0.09	−0.2	0.04	−0.06
3	4	1.3	1.69	1.8	3.24	2.34
1	1	−0.7	0.49	−1.2	1.44	0.84
1	2	−0.7	0.49	−0.2	0.04	0.14
2	3	0.3	0.09	0.8	0.64	0.24
3	3	1.3	1.69	0.8	0.64	1.04
17	22		8.10		11.60	8.84

values, the population being characterized by the joint probability distribution of Table 2.4. A typical such sample is shown in the first two columns of Table 2.8.

For all the measures – means, variances, covariance and correlation – worked out earlier for the population (i.e. from the joint and marginal probability distributions in Table 2.4), there are corresponding measures that can be worked out for the sample. First, corresponding to the means $E(X)$ and $E(Y)$ of the marginal distributions in Table 2.4, we can define a sample mean $\bar{X}$ equal to the average of all the X values in the sample, and a sample mean $\bar{Y}$ equal to the average of the Y values. That is,

$$\bar{X} = \sum X/n, \quad \bar{Y} = \sum Y/n \tag{2.35}$$

For the sample in Table 2.8, for example, we have $\bar{X} = 1.7$ and $\bar{Y} = 2.2$.

Next, corresponding to the population variances $E[X - E(X)]^2$ and $E[Y - E(Y)]^2$, we define a variance of the sample X values, s_X^2, and a variance of the sample Y values, s_Y^2. Just as the population variances measure the dispersions or 'spreads' of X and Y, the **sample variances** measure the dispersions in the sample X values and sample Y values:

$$s_X^2 = \sum (X - \bar{X})^2/n, \quad s_Y^2 = \sum (Y - \bar{Y})^2/n \tag{2.36}$$

Notice that, for example, both population and sample variances of X can be expressed in words as 'the average value of X-minus-its-mean all squared'. However, whereas when calculating the population variance we take the average over an infinite number of trials of the experiment, when calculating the sample variance we take the average over the n trials that form our sample.[2] A similar relationship obviously holds between the population and sample variances of Y.

For the sample in Table 2.8, values of $(X - \bar{X})^2$ and $(Y - \bar{Y})^2$ are shown in the fourth and sixth columns, with their sums at the foot. For our sample, we therefore have, using (2.36), the variance of X, $s_X^2 = 0.81$ and the variance of Y, $s_Y^2 = 1.16$.

The population covariance, defined by (2.25), can be expressed in words as 'the average value of $[X - E(X)][Y - E(Y)]$ over an infinite number of trials of the experiment'. To obtain a similar measure for the n pairs of values in a sample, we calculate

$$s_{XY} = \sum(X - \bar{X})(Y - \bar{Y})/n \tag{2.37}$$

where the summation is over all pairs of values of X and Y.

s_{XY} defines the **sample covariance**. Like the population covariance, the sample covariance is a measure of the strength of any linear association between X and Y, but this time referring to the X and Y values in a sample. For the sample in Table 2.8, values of $(X - \bar{X})(Y - \bar{Y})$ are shown in the seventh column, again with their sum at the foot. Using (2.37), the sample covariance is therefore $s_{XY} = 0.884$, the positive value reflecting the direct rather than inverse association between X and Y in the sample.

Finally, corresponding to the population correlation, defined by (2.28), we have a **sample correlation**. To compute the sample correlation, the population covariance and variances in the expression (2.28) are simply replaced by the sample covariance (2.37) and the sample variances (2.36). That is,

$$R = \frac{s_{XY}}{s_X s_Y} = \frac{\sum(X - \bar{X})(Y - \bar{Y})}{\sqrt{\sum(X - \bar{X})^2}\sqrt{\sum(Y - \bar{Y})^2}} \tag{2.38}$$

where R is the sample correlation.

For the sample in Table 2.8, the sample correlation is

$$R = \frac{0.884}{\sqrt{0.81}\sqrt{1.16}} = 0.91$$

Like the population correlation, the sample correlation must lie between -1 and $+1$, positive values indicating a direct linear association and negative values an inverse one. The value of $R = 0.91$ reflects the strong positive linear relationship between X and Y in our sample.

Notice that the values for the sample means, variances and correlation differ from the corresponding population values calculated earlier. This is not surprising, since the sample values refer only to $n = 10$ trials. If we carried out a further 10 trials, thus generating another sample, it should be fairly obvious that we would, almost certainly, obtain different values for the sample means, variances and correlation. These would, very likely, again be different from the population values. In fact, sample values can be regarded as *estimators* of the corresponding population measures. However, we shall discuss estimators at much greater length in Chapter 5. We shall also look again at the sample correlation when we discuss two-variable regression analysis in Chapter 4.

2.5 Independence versus non-correlation

We have seen that the correlation between two random variables is a measure of the strength of the *linear* association between them. A zero correlation coefficient therefore implies the absence of any such linear association. However, it does not rule out the presence of more complicated nonlinear associations between X and Y. Such relationships could be strong and almost exact, or they could be weak and tenuous. If all types of associations between X and Y, both linear and nonlinear, are to be ruled out then X and Y have to be *independent* variables.

Two events A and B are **independent** if $\Pr(A, B) = \Pr(A) \Pr(B)$. That is, the joint probability of both events occurring must equal the product of the marginal probabilities of the two individual events. In the context of our coin tossing example of Section 2.3, suppose that A is the event $X = 2$, that is, obtaining 2 heads on the first 2 tosses of the coin, and that B is the event $Y = 3$, that is, obtaining 3 heads in all. For these two events to be independent, it would be necessary, using the notation of Section 2.3, that $p(2, 3) = f(2)g(3)$. That is, the joint probability of the two events must equal the product of the marginal probabilities. From Table 2.4, it can be seen that this is obviously not the case. This reflects the fact that X and Y are not independent in our example.

For two random *variables* to be independent, it is necessary that joint probabilities should be equal to the product of the relevant marginal probabilities *for all possible combinations of X and Y*. That is, we require

$$p(X, Y) = f(X)g(Y) \quad \text{for all values of } X \text{ and } Y \tag{2.39}$$

In Table 2.9 we have a joint probability distribution in which it can easily be seen that (2.39) holds for all the joint probabilities. Hence in this case X and Y are independent random variables. We stress that (2.39) must hold *in all cases* if X and Y are to be independent.

Since independence rules out all possible types of association between X and Y, whereas non-correlation implies only the absence of any linear association, independence is clearly a stronger condition than non-correlation. Independence implies non-

Table 2.9 Joint distribution for independent variables

Y \ X	2	4	6	8	10	g(Y)
20	0.08	0.08	0.12	0.08	0.04	0.4
30	0.04	0.04	0.06	0.04	0.02	0.2
40	0.08	0.08	0.12	0.08	0.04	0.4
f(X)	0.2	0.2	0.3	0.2	0.1	

Table 2.10 Conditional distribution for X given $Y=20$

X	2	4	6	8	10
$f(X\,|\,20)$	0.2	0.2	0.3	0.2	0.1

correlation, but non-correlation does not necessarily mean independence. Thus the equality $E(XY) = E(X)E(Y)$, which we have seen implies zero correlation, does *not* necessarily imply independence. We also require the condition (2.39) for independence.

A consequence of independence between two variables is that *the conditional probability distributions for the variables are identical to the marginal probability distributions*. For example, in Table 2.9 the marginal probability that $X = 6$ regardless of the value of Y is $f(6) = 0.3$. But since X and Y are independent, the value taken by X is completely uninfluenced by that taken by Y anyway. Thus the probability that $X = 6$ given that $Y = 20$ must also be 0.3. That is, $f(6\,|\,20) = 0.3$. In fact, if we find the conditional distribution for X given that $Y = 20$ in the usual way, we obtain the distribution in Table 2.10, which is the same as the marginal distribution for X in Table 2.9.

It is easily verified that the conditional distributions for X given any value of Y are all identical to the marginal distribution for X. That is,

$$f(X\,|\,Y) = f(X) \quad \text{if } X \text{ and } Y \text{ are independent} \tag{2.40}$$

Similarly, the conditional distributions for Y are identical to the marginal distribution for Y in Table 2.9. That is,

$$g(Y\,|\,X) = g(Y) \quad \text{if } X \text{ and } Y \text{ are independent} \tag{2.41}$$

Exercise 2.16

Compute $E(X)$, $E(Y)$ and $E(XY)$ for the following joint distribution:

Y \ X	0	1	2	3
1	0.125	0	0	0.125
2	0	0.25	0.25	0
3	0	0.125	0.125	0

Do your results mean that X and Y are independent?

Exercise 2.17

Two variables X and Y are independent and have the following marginal distributions:

X	1	2	3	4	5
$f(X)$	0.1	0.2	0.3	0.2	0.2

Y	3	6	9
$g(Y)$	0.3	0.4	0.3

Write down the joint probability distribution for X and Y. Verify that $E(XY) = E(X)E(Y)$ in this case. Also verify that the conditional distribution for X given $Y = 6$ is identical to the above marginal distribution for X.

The concepts of non-correlation and independence apply equally well to continuous variables as to the discrete variables in the above examples. However, when the continuous variables under consideration are normally distributed, it turns out that the distinction between non-correlation and independence disappears. In fact, it can be shown that *if two **normally** distributed variables X and Y are uncorrelated then they must also be independent variables*. We shall have cause to recall this fact in later chapters.

We close this chapter with one final theorem, quoted without proof, concerning normally distributed variables that happen to be independent.

THEOREM 2.5

If $Z_1, Z_2, Z_3, \ldots, Z_n$ are all independent and normally distributed variables then any linear function of these variables will also be normally distributed.

As we shall see later, this is an extremely useful property. It implies for example that if W, X and Y are all independent and normally distributed then a linear function such as $Z = 3 - 2W + 6X - 4Y$ can also be treated as a normally distributed variable.

Appendix 2A

Notes to Chapter 2

1. In this text we sometimes denote the exponential function e^x by $\exp(x)$.

2. For reasons to be made clear in the next chapter, it is often the case that a sample variance is computed by dividing by $n-1$ rather than n. That is, $s_X^2 = \sum(X - \bar{X})^2/(n-1)$. However, s_X^2 remains a measure of the dispersion in sample X values, and for large n the change in definition makes little difference.

Further reading

For a more detailed discussion of discrete and continuous probability distributions than we have room for here, see Greene (1993), Chapter 3 and Judge et al. (1988), Chapter 2.

3 Statistical inference

In this chapter we begin by considering certain basic ideas concerning statistical inference. We then discuss the formation of confidence intervals and the testing of hypotheses. Finally, we define and consider certain probability density functions that arise frequently in problems of inference.

3.1 Some basic concepts of statistical inference

Whenever we wish to observe or investigate a phenomenon or variable, there are two basic types of data source that we might use. First, we might have access to the **population**. By this, we mean that we have access to all possible observations, past, present and future, on the variable of interest. For example, if our variable were the earnings in the first week of March 1995 of an adult male worker in the steel industry of Arcadia, and we had access to a complete survey of such earnings, then we would be dealing with the population of observations on this variable.

Very often, unfortunately, we do not have access to the population. For example, a complete survey of earnings in the Arcadian steel industry might not exist. Under such circumstances we have to make do with a **sample** of observations on our variable. That is, for example, data on the weekly earnings of 100 steelworkers whom we have actually interviewed.

The sample is the second type of data source with which we can find ourselves dealing. Typically, statisticians have available samples of data only. On the basis of their sample, they have to deduce or infer facts about the population from which the sample is drawn. This process is known as **statistical inference**.

As a typical problem in statistical inference, suppose that, in the first week in March 1994, earnings in the Arcadian steel industry had been fully surveyed so that we knew that average weekly earnings had been $540. It is now the first week in March 1995, and we wish to determine whether average weekly earnings have risen since a year ago. We do not have access to a survey for this March, and have time to interview only 100 workers. This sample of 100 workers proves to have mean weekly earnings of $565. Can we *infer*, on the basis of this sample evidence, that mean weekly earnings have risen for the industry as a whole?

Clearly, had the sample mean earnings been $700, we could have claimed very confidently that industry earnings had risen. If the sample mean had only been $543, we would suspect very strongly that they had not. But we have obtained a sample mean of $565. What can we infer from this? The problem of inference becomes one of deciding by how much the *sample* mean has to exceed last year's industry or *population* mean before we can claim a general increase in earnings.

A major problem in all problems of statistical inference is what is termed **sampling variability**. By this, we mean that different samples will yield different outcomes. For example, if in March 1995 we took a second sample of 100 steelworkers, it would almost certainly have a mean earnings different from that of the first sample we took. Similarly, a third sample would yield yet another value for its mean earnings. Clearly, there is a danger that the answer we come to regarding industry earnings will depend very much on what actual sample we take.

Luckily, provided we take our sample in a particular way, sampling variability follows a systematic pattern about which much is known. In fact, if we are to be able to handle the problem of sampling variability, then it is necessary that samples be *random* samples.

A sample of size n is said to be **random** *if every combination of n items or members in the population has an equal chance of becoming the sample that is actually drawn.*

Drawing a random sample is by no means a trivial matter. For example, drawing a random sample of 100 workers from the Arcadian steel industry would involve, first, acquiring a complete list of workers in the industry. Having next allocated a number to every worker on the list, we would then have to invoke some purely chance mechanism to select 100 numbers from this list. We shall, however, sidestep these problems and assume, somewhat heroically, that all the samples we deal with or discuss in this text have been randomly drawn.

The sampling distribution of the mean

Let X be the weekly earnings of an Arcadian steelworker in March 1995 and suppose, at this time, that our population of steelworkers has a mean weekly earnings of μ with a variance of σ^2. That is, $E(X) = \mu$ and Var $(X) = \sigma^2$. The variance of X is simply a measure of the extent to which the earnings of individual workers are dispersed or 'spread' out about their mean of μ. μ and σ^2 are known as **population parameters**. They are *fixed* but typically *unknown* quantities.

Notice that we have labelled the population mean and variance with the same symbols as we used for the mean and variance of a probability distribution in the last chapter. This is because, with such a large population, we can interpret as a probability the relative frequency with which a particular level of earnings occurs. Indeed, the population can be regarded as analogous to a probability distribution for the variable X.

Suppose a random sample of n workers is drawn from the population. We denote the mean earnings of workers in this sample by $\bar{X}$. That is,

$$\bar{X} = \frac{\sum X_i}{n} \tag{3.1}$$

where X_i is the earnings of the ith worker in the sample and the summation is over all i.

A single sample drawn from the population might yield a sample mean of, for example, $\bar{X} = \$560$. However, as noted above, different samples yield different outcomes, so that a second sample might yield $\bar{X} = \$558$, a third $\bar{X} = \$564$, a fourth $\bar{X} = \$567$, etc. Imagine a situation where very many, maybe thousands of samples, all the same size n, were taken from this single population. It would now be possible to build up a distribution of relative frequencies for $\bar{X}$, the mean of a random sample size n. For example, a mean of $\bar{X} = 564$ might occur with a relative frequency of 0.18. Since very many samples have been taken, such relative frequencies could be interpreted as probabilities, so that we could claim, for example, that $Pr(\bar{X} = 564) = 0.18$. In this way, it is possible to build up a probability distribution for $\bar{X}$. It might, for example, look something like that illustrated in Figure 3.1.

The probability distribution for $\bar{X}$ just described is known as the **sampling distribution of the mean** of a random sample size n. Sampling distributions of this kind are of crucial importance in statistical inference, and we shall have much to say about them in this chapter.

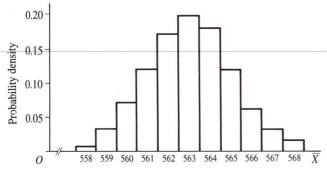

Figure 3.1 Sampling distribution for the mean.

In practice, of course, sampling distributions are rarely built up empirically in the above manner. Normally we have evidence from a single sample, and it is not practicable to take 'very many' samples. Fortunately, however, much can be stated about the sampling distribution of the mean without the necessity of taking more than a single sample. First, we can use the knowledge of expected values and variances, obtained in the last chapter, to derive expressions for the mean and variance of the sampling distribution.

THEOREM 3.1

If random samples size n are taken from an infinitely sized population with mean μ and variance σ^2 then the sampling distribution of the sample mean $\bar{X}$ will have

$$\text{mean } E(\bar{X}) = \mu \quad \text{and} \quad \text{variance } \sigma^2_{\bar{X}} = \text{Var}(\bar{X}) = \sigma^2/n$$

Proof

The sample mean $\bar{X}$ can be written as

$$\bar{X} = \frac{\sum X_i}{n} = \frac{1}{n}X_1 + \frac{1}{n}X_2 + \frac{1}{n}X_3 + \cdots + \frac{1}{n}X_n \tag{3.2}$$

Since $X_1, X_2, X_3, \ldots, X_n$ will vary from sample to sample, they can be regarded as variables in their own right, each with mean μ and variance σ^2. Moreover, if the sample is random, we can treat them as independent and hence uncorrelated variables.

Using Equation (3.2) and Theorem 2.2 from the last chapter, we have, first,

$$E(\bar{X}) = \frac{1}{n}E(X_1) + \frac{1}{n}E(X_2) + \frac{1}{n}E(X_3) + \cdots + \frac{1}{n}E(X_n)$$

$$= \frac{1}{n}\mu + \frac{1}{n}\mu + \frac{1}{n}\mu + \cdots + \frac{1}{n}\mu$$

$$= \frac{1}{n}n\mu = \mu$$

Secondly, using (3.2) and Theorem 2.4 from the last chapter, we have, since the X_i are uncorrelated so that all covariances are zero,

$$\sigma^2_{\bar{X}} = \text{Var}(X) = \frac{1}{n^2}\text{Var}(X_1) + \frac{1}{n^2}\text{Var}(X_2) + \frac{1}{n^2}\text{Var}(X_3) + \cdots + \frac{1}{n^2}\text{Var}(X_n)$$

$$= \frac{1}{n^2}\sigma^2 + \frac{1}{n^2}\sigma^2 + \frac{1}{n^2}\sigma^2 + \cdots + \frac{1}{n^2}\sigma^2$$

$$= \frac{1}{n^2}(n\sigma^2) = \frac{\sigma^2}{n}$$

Theorem 3.1 is, in fact, saying three things about the sampling distribution for $\bar{X}$ obtained when we take 'very many' samples, all of size n, from our population. First, the theorem states that, if we calculate $E(\bar{X})$, the average of the $\bar{X}$s obtained from our many samples, we will find that this equals μ, the mean of the Xs in the population. The theorem also states that the variability (as measured by $\sigma_{\bar{X}}^2 = \sigma^2/n$) in the $\bar{X}$s we obtain from the many samples taken will depend on two factors: first, the constant size n of the samples taken and, secondly, the variability (as measured by σ^2) of the Xs in the original population. The greater the sample size n, the smaller the variability of the $\bar{X}$s, σ^2/n, obtained. The greater the variability σ^2 in the original population, the greater the variability in the $\bar{X}$s, σ^2/n, obtained from the many samples.

Recall from the last chapter that many real world variables tend to be normally distributed. If it should be the case that the population referred to in the above theorem is normally distributed, that is X is $N(\mu, \sigma^2)$, then we can make a further useful statement about the sampling distribution for $\bar{X}$. As Equation (3.2) makes clear, $\bar{X}$ is a linear function of the X_i. Hence if all the X_i are normally distributed then, by Theorem 2.5 of the last chapter, $\bar{X}$ itself must be normally distributed. That is,

$$\text{if } X \text{ is } N(\mu, \sigma^2) \quad \text{then} \quad \bar{X} \text{ is } N(\mu, \sigma^2/n) \tag{3.3}$$

As noted earlier, population parameters such as μ and σ^2 are generally unknown and we have to make inferences about them, using sample information. However, as an aid to the proper understanding of the above theorem, consider the following example in which the population parameters are known.

WORKED EXAMPLE

The population of Arcadian steelworkers has mean weekly earnings of $560, with a standard deviation of $12. The weekly earnings of workers may be assumed to be normally distributed. If a random sample of 100 workers is drawn from this population, what is the probability that the mean weekly earnings of workers in the sample will exceed $562?

Letting X represent the earnings of a single worker, we require $\Pr(\bar{X} > 562)$ given that X is $N(560, 144)$.

Using Theorem 3.1, $E(\bar{X}) = \mu = 560$ and $\text{Var}(\bar{X}) = \sigma^2/n = 1.44$. Hence, since the population is normally distributed, we have, using (3.3),

$$\bar{X} \text{ is } N(560, 1.44)$$

We can transform $\bar{X}$ into a standard normal distribution by, as in the last chapter, subtracting the mean and dividing by the standard deviation. Thus

$$Z = \frac{\bar{X} - 560}{1.2} \text{ has a } N(0, 1) \text{ distribution}$$

Thus, converting the question about $\bar{X}$ into a question about Z,

$$\Pr(\bar{X} > 562) = \Pr\left(\frac{\bar{X} - 560}{1.2} > \frac{562 - 560}{1.2}\right) = \Pr(Z > 1.67) = 0.0475$$

The final probability is worked out, in the usual way, using the standard normal table in Appendix IV. There is therefore a rather small probability of obtaining a sample mean in excess of $562.

Our ability to tackle the above example depended not merely on Theorem 3.1 but also on our assumption that the population was normally distributed. Without this assumption, would it still have been reasonable to make use of standard normal tables? The answer to that question is provided by the following famous theorem.

THEOREM 3.2 (The Central Limit Theorem)

If large samples are randomly selected from a population with mean μ and variance σ^2 then the sampling distribution of the mean will be approximately normally distributed with mean $E(\bar{X}) = \mu$ and variance $\sigma_{\bar{X}}^2 = \sigma^2/n$, regardless of the shape of the distribution of the parent population.

A proof of the above theorem is unfortunately beyond our scope. However, the theorem states that, provided the samples we take are sufficiently large, then, even if the population is non-normally distributed (for example, its distribution might take any of the shapes illustrated in Figure 3.2), the sampling distribution of the mean can still be approximated by a normal distribution. In fact, *the larger the samples taken, the closer is the approximation*. Notice that there is no clear distinction between what is a 'large' and what is a 'small' sample. In practice, if the sample size is 30 or larger, we can feel safe in assuming the sampling distribution has a shape close to the normal form.

Referring back to the above worked example, it should be clear that, in obtaining the answer that Pr $(\bar{X} > 562) = 0.0475$, we did not in fact need to make the assumption that the population of weekly earnings was normally distributed. Since the sample size is as large as 100, we can safely appeal to the Central Limit Theorem, and claim that our answer is valid, regardless of the shape of the parent population. However, it would have been a different matter had the sample size been only 10.

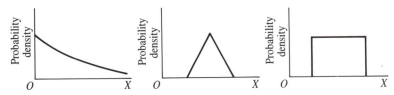

Figure 3.2 Alternative possible population distributions.

Exercise 3.1

The monthly food expenditures of single adult males in a large city have a mean of $480, with a standard deviation of 115. If a random sample, size 60, is drawn from this population, what is the probability that mean expenditures in the sample will (a) lie between $460 and $510; (b) exceed $500?

Exercise 3.2

It is claimed that the weights of 8-year-old girls in a county have a mean of 20 kg with a variance of 25. If this claim is true and a sample, size 40, is to be drawn from this population, what is the probability that the sample mean weight will prove to be less than 18.5 kg.

　　If the sample is taken and in fact does have a mean of less than 18.5 kg, would this make you doubt the original claim that weights had a population mean of 20 kg? What would you feel about the claim if the sample turned out to have a mean of less than 18 kg?

Exercise 3.3

Parcels have a mean weight of 300 kg, with a standard deviation of 50. A random sample of 25 parcels is loaded on to an elevator. Find the probability that the combined weight of the parcels will exceed a specified safety limit for the elevator of 8200 kg.

　　In the above numerical examples the population parameters, μ and σ^2, were assumed known and we used the Central Limit Theorem to calculate probabilities about a sample. In practice, the normal situation is that the population parameters are unknown and we have to use known sample information to make inferences about them. Statistical inference can be divided into two broad areas – estimation and hypothesis testing – and we discuss each in turn.

3.2 Estimation of a population mean

If a population parameter is unknown there are two ways in which it may be *estimated*. First, we may estimate the parameter by a single number or *point estimate*, or, secondly, we may specify a range within which we are confident the true parameter lies.

Point estimates

These are single-number estimates. For example, we might estimate the mean weekly earnings of a population of steelworkers by $480 or by $520. In fact the obvious way to estimate an unknown population mean μ is to use the known sample mean $\bar{X}$. There is an advantage in using the **estimator** $\bar{X}$. From Theorem 3.1, we know that $E(\bar{X}) = \mu$. That is, we know that *if* we took 'very many' samples from the population then we would obtain a sampling distribution akin to that in Figure 3.3(a), and 'on average' we would obtain a value equal to the true but unknown μ. Although in practice we only take one sample, it is comforting to know that there is no systematic error or **bias** in our estimation procedure. Because $E(\bar{X}) = \mu$, $\bar{X}$ is said to be an **unbiased point estimator** of μ.

There will also be occasions when we wish to estimate a population variance σ^2. The obvious point estimate of σ^2 is the sample variance given by

$$v^2 = \frac{\sum(X_i - \bar{X})^2}{n} \tag{3.4}$$

For example, given data on the weekly earnings of a random sample of n steelworkers, we simply use the normal expression for the variance of a set of n numbers. The problem with (3.4) is that, like $\bar{X}$, it will take different values in different samples, and unfortunately it can be shown that

$$E(v^2) = \left(\frac{n-1}{n}\right)\sigma^2 \neq \sigma^2 \tag{3.5}$$

That is, the sampling distribution for v^2 looks something like that in Figure 3.3(b). Hence, if 'very many' samples were taken then 'on average' v^2 would give us a value rather less than the true σ^2. Thus in this case there is a systematic tendency towards error, and v^2 is said to be a **biased point estimator** of σ^2.

To overcome this problem of bias, a population variance σ^2 is normally estimated by

$$s^2 = \frac{\sum(X_i - \bar{X})^2}{n-1} \tag{3.6}$$

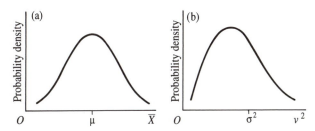

Figure 3.3 (a) Unbiased point estimator of μ. (b) Biased point estimator of σ^2.

This is because $s^2 = [n/(n-1)]v^2$, so that

$$E(s^2) = E\left(\frac{n}{n-1}v^2\right) = \left(\frac{n}{n-1}\right)\left(\frac{n-1}{n}\right)\sigma^2 = \sigma^2 \quad \text{(using (3.5))}$$

Thus s^2 is an unbiased point estimate of σ^2.

We shall have considerably more to say about point estimates and their properties in Chapter 5.

Confidence intervals

It will sometimes be the case that a single number or point estimate of a parameter will not suffice. We may want to specify in some way the level of confidence we have in our estimate. One way of doing this is to try and find a 'range' of values within which we are '95% confident' that a parameter lies. We tackle this problem, taking the population mean μ as our example, in the following way.

Suppose we wish to find a range of values between $\bar{X} + E$ and $\bar{X} - E$, such that, before we take our sample, there is a 0.95 probability that the range eventually obtained will include the unknown parameter μ.

Since $\bar{X}$, the sample mean, is an unbiased estimator of μ, it makes sense to place it at the centre of the range we seek. E is simply an expression or formula that we have to find.

If our sample is large then we know by the central limit theorem that $\bar{X}$ is $N(\mu, \sigma^2/n)$. Hence we can say that

$$Z = \frac{\bar{X} - \mu}{\sigma/\sqrt{n}} \quad \text{has a N(0, 1) distribution} \tag{3.7}$$

Use of the standard normal tables in Appendix IV and of Figure 3.4(a) indicates that

$$\Pr(-1.96 < Z < 1.96) = 0.95 \tag{3.8}$$

Using (3.7) to substitute for Z in (3.8) gives

$$\Pr\left(-1.96 < \frac{\bar{X} - \mu}{\sigma/\sqrt{n}} < 1.96\right) = 0.95 \tag{3.9}$$

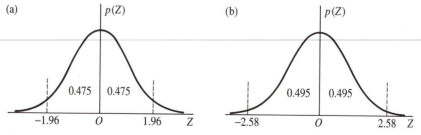

Figure 3.4 (a) Area between $Z = +1.96$ and $Z = -1.96$. (b) Area between $Z = +2.58$ and $Z = -2.58$.

Manipulation of the quantities inside the probability parentheses soon gives

$$\Pr\left(\bar{X} + 1.96\frac{\sigma}{\sqrt{n}} > \mu > \bar{X} - 1.96\frac{\sigma}{\sqrt{n}}\right) = 0.95 \tag{3.10}$$

Examination of (3.10) indicates that we have found what we were looking for: a range that has a 0.95 probability of containing the unknown μ. The expression E we sought is in fact $1.96\sigma/\sqrt{n}$.

The range we have obtained is normally referred to as a **95% confidence interval** for μ. The only problem with this range is that $E = 1.96\sigma/\sqrt{n}$ depends on σ, which, like μ, is unknown. In practice, when computing a confidence interval, σ has to be replaced by s, the sample standard deviation, worked out using (3.6) to ensure an unbiased estimate. The 95% large-sample confidence interval for μ is therefore written as $\bar{X} \pm E$, or

$$\bar{X} \pm 1.96\frac{s}{\sqrt{n}} \tag{3.11}$$

It is of course possible that we may wish to be more than '95% confident' that our interval will contain μ. However to raise the confidence level simply involves reading a different number from the standard normal tables. For example, Figure 3.4(b) indicates that to form a 99% confidence interval we replace the above 1.96 by 2.58 and obtain

$$\bar{X} \pm 2.58\frac{s}{\sqrt{n}} \tag{3.12}$$

Once the basic expressions are derived, confidence intervals are very easy to compute. For example if, in our steelworker example, a sample size $n = 80$ should yield mean earnings $\bar{X} = 574$ with $s = 94$ then substituting in (3.11) yields a 95% confidence interval of

$$574 \pm 1.96\frac{94}{\sqrt{80}} = 574 \pm 20.6$$

The required interval is therefore from 553.4 to 594.6.

Although confidence intervals are easy to compute, they are more slippery to interpret than one might imagine. It has to be remembered that the population mean μ, although unknown, is a fixed constant. It must therefore either lie within the range 553.4–594.6 that we have computed or lie outside it. If it lies within then there is a probability of unity that it does so. If it lies outside then the probability that it lies within must be zero. Therefore we cannot say that there is a 0.95 probability that it lies within the range 553.4–594.6! So, what do our computations mean?

The key to this question is to remember that different samples will yield different means $\bar{X}$ and different standard deviations s. Hence different samples will yield, on substitution into (3.11), *different confidence intervals*. If 'very many' samples were taken, 95% of these intervals would contain the unknown μ but 5% would not. *The intervals vary from sample to sample, but μ is fixed.* Because of this, what we can say is that, before we take our sample, there is a 0.95 probability that the interval we eventually compute will contain μ. Unfortunately, once we have taken the sample and computed the interval, we cannot, strictly speaking, still say this! Thus the interpretation of actual confidence intervals is not straightforward.

As we shall see, we often compute confidence intervals for population parameters other than a population mean μ. However, the process is always similar to that above. The standard deviation of the sampling distribution of an estimator is known as the **standard error of the estimate**. For example, the standard error of the estimate $\bar{X}$ is simply $s_{\bar{X}} = s/\sqrt{n}$, that is, the standard deviation of its sampling distribution. Given an unbiased point estimate and providing its sampling distribution is symmetric, confidence intervals in fact always take the form

$$\text{point estimate} \pm (\text{critical value})(\text{standard error of estimate}) \qquad (3.13)$$

The 'critical value' in (3.13) is taken from some table of distribution values such as the standard normal table. For example, in (3.11) and (3.12), the point estimate is $\bar{X}$, the critical value comes from the standard normal table in Appendix IV, and the standard error is $s/\sqrt{n}$.

Exercise 3.4

A random sample of 8 automobiles (all the same model) are found to perform with the following mileages per gallon:

37.1	35.6	37.7	36.2	36.1	36.5	37.6	35.2

Obtain unbiased estimates of (a) the population mean, (b) the population variance.

Exercise 3.5

In a random sample of 40 law firms, legal charges per hour are found to have a mean of $25 with a standard deviation $s = \$3.7$. Obtain a 95% confidence interval for the average legal charge per hour in the law profession as a whole.

Exercise 3.6

38 randomly selected three room apartments have a mean monthly rent of $135, with a standard deviation $s = \$22$. Find a 99% confidence interval for the true mean rent of such apartments. If you wished to estimate the true mean rent to within $2.00 with 99% confidence, how large a sample should you take?

3.3   Testing hypotheses about a population mean

There will be occasions when, instead of simply wishing to estimate a population parameter, we may have an interest in whether or not such a parameter takes a specific value. At the beginning of this chapter, as an example of a typical problem in inference, we considered a situation where the mean earnings of Arcadian steel-workers in the first week in March 1994 was known to be $540. A year later, in the first week in March 1995, we were faced with the problem of how, given just a sample of 100 workers, we could decide whether or not there had been an increase in population mean earnings during the past year. We are now in a position to tackle this problem.

We begin by formulating two hypotheses. First, we formulate a so-called **null hypothesis** that population mean earnings have not risen during the past year. That is, μ still equals $540. A null hypothesis is usually given the designation H_0. Thus we have

$$\text{null hypothesis } H_0 : \quad \mu = 540 \quad \text{(no change in earnings)} \tag{3.14}$$

Note that the μ referred to in (3.14) is the 1995 population mean.

Next we formulate an **alternative hypothesis**, designated H_A, which covers all reasonable alternatives to the null H_0. Since the 1990s are inflationary times, we shall rule out, for the moment, the possibility that earnings have fallen since 1994, and adopt as the alternative the hypothesis that they have risen:

$$\text{alternative hypothesis } H_A : \quad \mu > 540 \quad \text{(rise in earnings)} \tag{3.15}$$

Our problem thus becomes that of choosing between H_0 and H_A, that is, between null and alternative hypotheses. We must do this on the basis of information from a sample size $n = 100$.

Once the sample has been taken, we will know the value of the sample mean $\bar{X}$. Clearly it will make sense to *reject* the null hypothesis H_0, that earnings have not risen, if $\bar{X}$ turns out to be 'much larger' than last year's population value of $540. The important question, of course, is how much larger $\bar{X}$ needs to be before we reject H_0 and *accept* the alternative H_A, that population earnings have risen.

The crucial tool we have for tackling this question is the Central Limit Theorem. Since our sample is a relatively large one, we know that the sampling distribution for $\bar{X}$ is $N(\mu, \sigma^2/n)$. Thus Equation (3.7) must hold.

Suppose for a moment that the null hypothesis H_0 is *true* and earnings have not risen. Given the null hypothesis, that is, under H_0, $\mu = 540$, so that, substituting into (3.7), we have

$$\text{TS} = \frac{\bar{X} - 540}{\sigma/\sqrt{n}} \quad \text{has a N(0, 1) distribution} \tag{3.16}$$

The quantity $(\bar{X} - 540)/(\sigma/\sqrt{n})$ is known as a **test statistic** (TS). We shall encounter many such test statistics in this text. The crucial point about this test statistic is that it *only has a* N(0, 1) *distribution when the null hypothesis* H_0 *is true*. If H_0 is not true but *false* then (3.16) will not hold, since μ will now take some value other than 540.

As can be seen from Figure 3.5, the standard normal or N(0, 1) distribution is centred about zero. Recall that areas under this curve represent probabilities. It follows that if the null hypothesis is true, that is, under H_0, there is a large probability that TS will take a value around zero. If it should take a value very different from zero then we will be inclined to doubt whether H_0 is true. For, if H_0 is false, there is no reason why TS should not take a value far from zero. The test statistic therefore provides a means of 'testing' whether H_0 is true.

Notice that TS is based on the difference between $\bar{X}$ and the value $540 that appears in H_0. The greater the extent by which the sample mean $\bar{X}$ exceeds $540, the larger (more positive) the test statistic will be. As argued previously, commonsense indicates that we should reject H_0 if $\bar{X}$ is sufficiently greater than $540. Thus the more *positive* is TS, the test statistic, the more we will be inclined to reject H_0 in favour of H_A and say that we believe population earnings have risen.

Suppose our sample of 100 workers is taken and TS $= (\bar{X} - 540)/(\sigma/\sqrt{n})$ computed (if necessary, using the sample standard deviation s as an estimate of σ). Suppose, further, that TS > 1.64. The number 1.64 has not been arbitrarily chosen. As can be seen from Figure 3.5, the area under the standard normal curve to the right of 1.64 happens to be exactly equal to 0.05.

The number 1.64 is clearly positive, but is TS > 1.64 sufficiently positive to make us doubt the null hypothesis H_0 that earnings have not risen? In fact if TS > 1.64, we must take up one of two possible positions.

First, we could still maintain that H_0 is true. However, if we adopt this position, we have to claim that something rather unusual has occurred. If H_0 is true then (3.16) is valid, and the curves in Figure 3.5 represent the distribution of the test statistic. If this is the case then the probability of getting a value for TS in excess of 1.64 is only 0.05, that is, only 1 in 20. Most people would regard the occurrence of an event that has only a 1 in 20 chance of happening as rather strange.

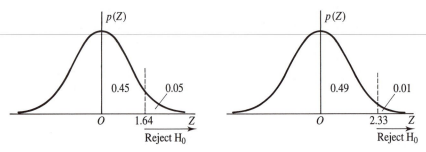

Figure 3.5 Rejection of H_0 at 0.05 and 0.01 levels of significance.

Alternatively, of course, if TS > 1.64, we could reject H_0 and maintain instead that H_A is true and that earnings have risen since 1994. If the alternative hypothesis is true then, under H_A, there is no reason why Figure 3.5 should represent the distribution of the test statistic. TS might be distributed around 1.5 or 2, in which case there would be nothing unusual in obtaining TS > 1.64. However, if we reject H_0 in favour of H_A, we must remember that there always remains that small probability of up to 0.05 that H_0 is in fact true. That is, if we reject H_0 and maintain that earnings have risen, there is a probability, maybe as great as 0.05, that we are wrong to do so.

When a statistician obtains a value for the test statistic in excess of 1.64, s(he) normally states that s(he) 'rejects the null hypothesis at the 0.05 **level of significance**'. This is simply statistical jargon for rejecting H_0 but admitting there is a 0.05 probability that it is wrong to do so. Thus the level of significance represents the probability of error when rejecting H_0. The probability of this kind of error is normally given the symbol α. That is,

level of significance $\alpha =$ Pr (reject $H_0 \mid H_0$ is true)

As we shall see, the level of significance is not the only type of error that can be made in hypothesis testing.

To make the above absolutely clear, let us consider in a slightly different manner what is implied when we 'reject H_0' if TS > 1.64. From (3.16), if TS > 1.64 then

$$\bar{X} > 540 + 1.64\sigma/\sqrt{n} \tag{3.17}$$

Thus we are rejecting H_0 if $\bar{X}$ exceeds some critical number given by the right-hand side of (3.17). Given an estimate of σ, this number could be computed.[1] But if H_0 is true then $\bar{X}$ is $N(540, \sigma^2/n)$, and the probability of (3.17) occurring can be easily computed as

$$\text{Pr } (\bar{X} > 540 + 1.64\sigma/\sqrt{n}) = \text{Pr } (Z > 1.64) = 0.05$$

Thus if H_0 is true there is only a 0.05 probability of obtaining a value for $\bar{X}$ that exceeds the critical value in (3.17). Hence, if we do obtain such a value, we consider this such an unlikely occurrence that we 'reject H_0 at the 0.05 level of significance'.

There is nothing particularly special about the number 1.64 or a level of significance of 0.05. Alternatively, we could decide to reject H_0 and maintain that earnings have risen if TS > 2.33. The point about the number 2.33 is that the area to the right of it under the standard normal curve in Figure 3.5 is 0.01. Following the same argument as above, given TS > 2.33, we can either accept H_0 as true, but now claim that an event with a probability as low as 0.01 has occurred, or we can reject H_0. However, if we reject H_0, we must remember that there is still a probability of error, albeit now as low as 0.01. In statisticians' jargon, if TS > 2.33, we 'reject H_0 at the 0.01 level of significance'.

Notice that the smaller the level of significance at which we can reject H_0, the stronger is the rejection. For example, a rejection of H_0 at the 0.01 level of significance is a stronger rejection than one at only the 0.05 level, because the chance of error is smaller. Notice also that it is impossible to reduce the level of significance to zero, since the tails of the standard normal curve only approach the Z-

axis in Figure 3.5 asymptotically (that is, they never quite get there!). The level of significance can be made extremely small if necessary, but, as we shall see, this leads to a different problem.

Introducing some numbers into the hypothesis testing process, suppose our sample of 100 workers turns out to have mean earnings $\bar{X} = \$564$, with a sample standard deviation of $s = 75$. Substituting into the test statistic (3.16), using s instead of the unknown σ, gives

$$\text{TS} = \frac{564 - 540}{75/\sqrt{100}} = 3.2$$

Thus the test statistic exceeds not only 1.64 but also 2.33. We can therefore reject the null hypothesis (that earnings are unchanged since last year) at both the 0.05 and, more strongly, the 0.01 levels of significance.

Two-tail tests

In the above example we ruled out the possibility that earnings might have fallen since 1994. Suppose, however, we had felt unable to rule out this possibility and had simply wished to test whether mean earnings had changed. We can proceed with the same null hypothesis as previously. However, the alternative hypothesis covering all other reasonable possibilities must now simply be that mean earnings have changed from last year's value of $540. That is, we now have

null hypothesis H_0 : $\quad \mu = 540 \quad$ (no change in earnings)

alternative hypothesis H_A : $\quad \mu \neq 540 \quad$ (change in earnings)

Once we have taken our sample, it now makes sense to reject H_0, that population mean earnings still equal $540, *either* if the sample mean $\bar{X}$ is very much greater than $540 *or* if $\bar{X}$ is very much smaller than $540. Remember that, in the previous case, we only rejected H_0 when $\bar{X}$ was very much greater than $540. This was justified because in the previous case we had ruled out the possibility that population earnings might have fallen.

Interpreting our revised criterion for rejection of H_0 in terms of the test statistic (3.16), we now see that we should reject H_0 and claim earnings have changed *either* if TS is very much greater than zero (very positive) *or* if TS is very much less than zero (very negative). How positive or how negative the test statistic must be is decided again by reference to standard normal tables. For example, examination of Figure 3.6 indicates that if we adopt a 0.05 level of significance then we should reject H_0 and claim earnings have *changed* either if the test statistic is more negative than -1.96 or if it is more positive than $+1.96$. Notice that the 0.05 probability of error is now distributed equally between the two tails of the standard normal distribution. For this reason, this kind of test is known as a **two-tail test**, whereas that described by Figure 3.5 is, for obvious reasons, referred to as a **one-tail test**.

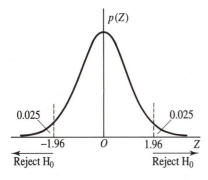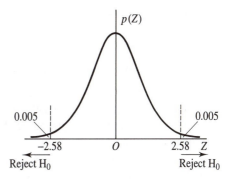

Figure 3.6 Two-tail rejection regions.

We can re-express our **decision** or **test criterion** for the two-tail test in terms of the absolute value of the test statistic by writing

'reject H_0 at the 0.05 level of significance if $|TS| > 1.96$'

Similarly, inspection of Figure 3.6 indicates that we

'reject H_0 at the 0.01 level of significance if $|TS| > 2.58$'

In this second case the 0.01 probability of error is equally distributed between the two tails of the standard normal distribution.

Exercise 3.7

The mean lifetime of a random sample of 80 light bulbs produced by a factory is found to be 1460 hours, with a standard deviation $s = 110$ hours. If μ is the mean lifetime of all the light bulbs produced by the factory, test the hypothesis $\mu = 1500$ against an alternative hypothesis that $\mu \neq 1500$, using level of significance (a) 0.05; (b) 0.01.

Exercise 3.8

The breaking strength of a manufacturer's cables has a mean of 905 kg, with variance 2500 kg^2. It is claimed that breaking strength can be increased by a new manufacturing technique. To test this claim, a sample of 40 cables, manufactured using the new technique, is tested and found to have a mean breaking strength of 930 kg. Test the claim at the 0.05 level of significance. Justify your choice of alternative hypothesis.

Types of error

Implicit in the above example and analysis is a **decision** or **test criterion** of the kind

$$\text{reject } H_0 \text{ if } |TS| > k \text{ but accept } H_0 \text{ if } |TS| < k \tag{3.18}$$

The value of k is taken from standard normal tables, and will depend on the level of significance adopted and on whether the test is one-tail or two-tail. Rejection of H_0 automatically implies acceptance of the alternative H_A, while acceptance of H_0 implies rejection of H_A.

Given a decision criterion of the form (3.18), there are two types of error we could make when carrying out a test. Since either H_0 is true (in which case H_A is false), or H_0 is false (in which case H_A is true), and since we either reject or accept H_0, these types of error are as illustrated in Table 3.1.

Clearly, if we accept H_0 when it is true or reject H_0 when it is false then we are not making an error. If we reject H_0 when it is true, we are making what statisticians call a **type I error**. As we saw earlier, the probability of making this type of error is in fact the level of significance of the test. On the other hand, if we accept H_0 when it is false, we are making what is referred to as a **type II error**.

Nobody likes making errors of any kind, and at the very least we might want to keep the probabilities of type I and type II errors as small as possible. Ideally, we would like to be able to choose some value of k in the test criterion (3.18) that makes both Pr (type I error) and Pr (type II error) very small indeed. Unfortunately, this is very rarely possible, for the following reasons.

First, it turns out that if we vary k in the criterion (3.18), *the smaller we make* Pr (type I error) *the larger becomes* Pr (type II error), *and vice versa*. It is not normally possible to make both probabilities very small at the same time. To understand this, let us revert to our steelworker example, where we had the null and alternative hypotheses

$$H_0 : \quad \mu = 540, \quad H_A : \quad \mu \neq 540$$

The decision criterion (3.18) implies that we reject H_0 if

$$TS = \frac{\bar{X} - 540}{\sigma / \sqrt{n}} \text{ is either } > k \text{ or } < -k$$

Table 3.1 Types of error

	H_0 is true	H_0 is false
Reject H_0	Type I error	
Accept H_0		Type II error

We can rewrite this as

$$\text{reject } H_0 \text{ if } \bar{X} > 540 + \frac{k\sigma}{\sqrt{n}} \quad \text{or} \quad \text{if } \bar{X} < 540 - \frac{k\sigma}{\sqrt{n}} \tag{3.19}$$

The value of k, as usual, depends on the level of significance chosen.

We know that, under H_0, $\mu = 540$, so that the sample mean $\bar{X}$ is $N(540, \sigma^2/n)$. This distribution is shown as the left-hand curve in Figure 3.7, centred around $\bar{X} = 540$. The points R' and R in Figure 3.7 are at $540 - k\sigma/\sqrt{n}$ and $540 + k\sigma/\sqrt{n}$ respectively on the $\bar{X}$ axis. Our decision criterion (3.19) is such that, if the sample mean $\bar{X}$ takes a value to the left of R' or to the right of R, we reject H_0. The probability of a type I error, that is rejecting H_0 when it is true and the left-hand curve represents the distribution of $\bar{X}$, is equal to the sum of the areas under the curve to the left of R' and to the right of R. It is therefore equal to twice the lined area to the right of R.

Suppose now that it is H_A that is true and not H_0. H_A just implies $\mu \neq 540$, but let us take the particular case where $\mu = 560$. If $\mu = 560$ then the sample mean $\bar{X}$ is $N(560, \sigma^2/n)$. This distribution is shown as the right-hand curve in Figure 3.7. Since it has the same variance as the first curve but a larger mean, its shape is identical to the first curve but is shifted rightwards along the $\bar{X}$ axis.

Under our decision criterion we *accept* H_0 if $\bar{X}$ takes a value between R' and R. However, if H_A rather than H_0 is true then the distribution of $\bar{X}$ is the right-hand curve. Hence if H_A is true, the probability of incorrectly accepting H_0 is given by the dotted area under the right-hand curve to the left of R. This dotted area therefore represents the probability of a type II error, that is, the probability of accepting H_0 when H_0 is false.

It is now possible to see why reducing Pr (type I error) increases Pr (type II error), and vice versa. If we vary k in our test criterion (3.19) (that is, change the level of significance), this causes the points R' and, more importantly, R in Figure 3.7 to move. If k is increased and R moved to the right then the shaded area under the left-hand curve is reduced and this implies a *reduction* in Pr (type I error). But a movement to the right by R increases the dotted area under the right-hand curve and hence *increases* Pr (type II error). Similarly, if R is moved to the left, this reduces Pr (type II error) but simultaneously increases Pr (type I error). We find ourselves caught in a cleft stick.

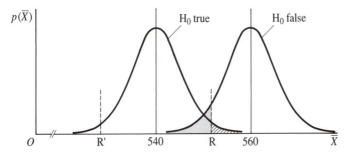

Figure 3.7 Type I and type II errors.

There is a second problem with test criteria of the form (3.18) and (3.19). In Figure 3.7 we have assumed that when H_A rather than H_0 is true, $\mu = 560$. But H_A simply states that $\mu \neq 540$. Suppose, instead, H_A is true but $\mu = 550$. The right-hand curve in Figure 3.7 would now lie much closer to the left-hand curve. Consequently, with R in a given position, that is, for given Pr (type I error), there will be a larger Pr (type II error).

In general, for a given Pr (type I error), it should be clear that Pr (type II error) will depend on the position of the second curve and hence on the value taken by μ when H_0 is false. But, with hypotheses of the above kind, if H_0 is false, we will not know the value of μ. H_A does not specify this – it merely states that $\mu \neq 540$. Thus, in general, *we cannot know the probability of a type II error.*

There are, then, two related problems with test criteria of the form (3.18) and (3.19). First, we cannot know the probability of a type II error. Secondly, the smaller we make the probability of a type I error, the larger becomes the probability of a type II error (whatever this happens to be).

It is possible in principle to get round the second of these problems by increasing the sample size. In general, this will reduce Pr (type II error) for a given Pr (type I error). In terms of Figure 3.7, increasing the sample size leads to a smaller spread in both the distributions shown.[2] However economic data series are often limited and this option will not often be open to us.

Exercise 3.9

When testing a null hypothesis H_0: $\mu = 60$ against an alternative H_A: $\mu > 60$, the test statistic

$$TS = \frac{\bar{X} - 60}{\sigma/\sqrt{n}}$$

is used. The following test criterion is adopted:

reject H_0 if $TS > 2.1$ but accept H_0 if $TS < 2.1$

If the test statistic has a standard normal distribution under H_0, calculate the probability of a type I error. Given $n = 100$ and $\sigma = 12$, calculate the probability of a type II error when (a) $\mu = 75$; (b) $\mu = 62$; (c) $\mu = 60.5$.

Because of the above difficulties concerning type II errors, statisticians often use test criteria slightly different from (3.18). The type of criteria we shall adopt in this text have the form

reject H_0 if $|TS| > k$ but reserve judgement if $|TS| < k$ \hfill (3.20)

where k again depends on the level of significance adopted.

Notice that, with test criterion (3.20), we *never accept the null hypothesis* H_0. We either reject it (and accept H_A) or we simply reserve judgement on whether H_0 is true or false. Because we never actually accept H_0, we cannot now make a type II error, since this involves accepting H_0 when it is false. The reason we never accept H_0 is because we do not know Pr (type II error) but suspect that it could be large.

Since we cannot now make a type II error, this leaves us free to concentrate on type I errors and make their probability (the level of significance) as small as is appropriate. In practice, significance levels of 0.05 and 0.01 are usually adopted. However, if the real-world consequences of a type I error were serious or costly, an even lower significance level might be adopted.

The power of a test

If we adopt a decision criterion of the form (3.20), clearly we must hope that, if a null hypothesis H_0 is false then we will reject it in favour of the alternative H_A. However, further examination of Figure 3.7 indicates that this may not happen. If H_0 is false and the true distribution of the sample mean $\bar{X}$ is the right-hand curve, there is still a probability that we may obtain an $\bar{X}$ to the left of the point R and end up not rejecting H_0, as we should, but reserving judgement. The probability in this situation of rejecting H_0 when it is false is given by the area to the right of the point R under the right-hand curve. This probability is clearly less than unity.

The probability of rejecting the null hypothesis H_0 when we should, because it is false, is known as the **power of the test**. It measures the probability of detecting a false null hypothesis.

Obviously, we would like the power of a test to be high, and, if possible, close to unity. However, further study of Figure 3.7 reveals that, given the point R, the closer the right-hand distribution curve is to the left-hand distribution curve, the smaller is the power of the test.

In Figure 3.7, H_0 is $\mu = 540$. If H_0 is false and μ is much greater than 540 then the distribution curves will be far apart, so that the power of the test is high. That is, the probability of detecting the false H_0 is large. If, however, H_0 is false but μ is very close to 540 (as, for example, in Figure 3.8, where $\mu = 542$), the curves will be close together and the power of the test to detect the false H_0 will be small. In Figure 3.8 the probability of detecting the false H_0 is given by the rather small shaded area, which is considerably less than unity.

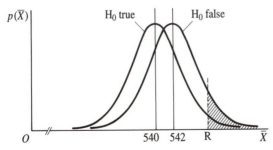

Figure 3.8 The power of a test.

This is fairly reassuring. For example, in our steelworker case, where H_0 actually was $\mu = 540$, suppose earnings had risen very slightly from last year, so that μ was now 542. As we have seen, our test criterion (3.20) will have low power for this value of μ. But, because this change in earnings is so small, the fact that our test does not pick it up may not matter. If, however, earnings had risen to a figure as large as, for example, 580 then, for this value of μ, the power of the test will be much higher. Thus our test is much more likely to pick up this much larger rise in earnings.

The power of a test clearly depends on the true value taken by μ. This determines the position of the right-hand curve in Figures 3.7 and 3.8. The relationship between the power of a test and a parameter such as μ is known as a **power function**. We do not have the space to investigate the nature of power functions. However, it should be clear that, ideally, given a choice of tests, we would prefer that test which has the higher power over a wide range of possible values for μ.

Summary of testing procedure

We may summarize the testing procedure described above as follows.

(1) Formulate appropriate null and alternative hypotheses. The null hypothesis will normally contain an equality sign and be of the type

$$H_0: \quad \mu = \mu_0$$

where μ_0 is some constant. The alternative hypothesis will depend on whether a one-tail or two-tail test is required.

(2) Decide on the appropriate test statistic. This will take the form $(\bar{X} - \mu_0)/(s/\sqrt{n})$, where μ_0 is the constant appearing in the null hypothesis.

(3) Select the level of significance or Pr (type I error). This will depend on the seriousness of the consequences of a type I error, but is usually set at 0.05 or 0.01.

(4) Formulate an appropriate test criterion of the kind (3.20). The precise form of the criterion will depend on the level of significance decided on in (3) and on whether you have decided on a one-tail or two-tail test.

(5) Take the sample or examine the sample information, calculating $\bar{X}$ and s.

(6) Compute the test statistic derived in (2) using the sample information.

(7) Apply the test criterion formulated in (4).

It is important to get into the habit of tackling hypothesis testing in the above sequential manner. Adopting a systematic approach at the outset will help later when we encounter more complicated hypothesis testing situations.

Exercise 3.10

A random sample of 200 adult males is found to be on average 8 kg overweight, with standard deviation $s = 2.4$ kg. Does this evidence support a claim that the adult male population as a whole is on average overweight by 6.5 kg?

Exercise 3.11

It is claimed that the average weekly food expenditure of families with 2 children is £95. A random sample of 100 such families is taken to test this claim. The families in the sample have a mean expenditure of £92.80, with a standard deviation of £10.30. Test at the 0.05 and 0.01 levels of significance whether this evidence contradicts the claim. If you reach different conclusions at different levels of significance, how would you explain this to a non-statistician?

3.4   Some other important test statistics and their distributions

In the last two sections we introduced the ideas of statistical inference almost entirely in the context of a population mean. However, there are frequently occasions when we may wish to make inferences about other population parameters – an obvious example is the population variance σ^2. In addition, as we shall see, statistical inference has an important role in regression analysis. In the last two sections, we also restricted our analysis to large samples. Unfortunately, in economics we frequently have to deal with samples smaller than that assumed so far.

Before we are equipped to deal with the above problems, we have to familiarize ourselves with a number of additional probability distributions/density functions. All these density functions, however, involve the concept of 'degrees of freedom', to which we first turn.

Degrees of freedom

Consider n continuous random variables, $X_1, X_2, X_3, \ldots, X_n$, and the sum of squares $\sum_{i=1}^{n} X_i^2$. **Degrees of freedom** is a concept associated with such sums of squares.

For example, suppose $n = 5$ and there happen to be 2 linear restrictions placed on the X variables. These might be $X_1 + X_2 + X_3 = 0$ and $2X_4 + 3X_5 = 8$. If we select values for three of the X variables then, given the restrictions, the values of the remaining two X variables are also determined. For example, if we select $X_1 = 2$, $X_2 = -3$ and $X_4 = 1$ then, by the first restriction, X_3 must take the value 1, and, by the second restriction, X_5 must take the value 2. In selecting values for the Xs, we are said to have only three degrees of freedom, since only three such values can be selected independently of the others. The associated sum of squares is then also said to have three degrees of freedom.

In general, if we have n variables, and r restrictions are placed on them, then we will have $n - r$ degrees of freedom. The sum of squares $\sum_i X_i^2$ is then also said to have $n - r$ degrees of freedom.

As an example, suppose we have a population of X values from which we take a sample size n, consisting of the values $X_1, X_2, X_3, \ldots, X_n$. Suppose we now compute the sum of squares $\sum_{i=1}^{n}(X_1 - \bar{X})^2$, where $\bar{X}$ is the sample mean. Since[3] $\sum_i(X_i - \bar{X}) = 0$, there is a single restriction placed on the n variables $X_i - \bar{X}$. Thus the sum of squares $\sum_i(X_i - \bar{X})^2$ is said to have $n - 1$ degrees of freedom.

Suppose, however, that the population mean μ is known and, instead of computing $\sum_i(X_i - \bar{X})^2$, we compute the sum of squares $\sum_i(X_i - \mu)^2$. Since there is no reason why $\sum_i(X_i - \mu)$ should equal zero, no restrictions are placed on the n variables $X_i - \mu$, so the sum of squares $\sum_i(X_i - \mu)^2$ has the 'full' n degrees of freedom.

Notice that replacing a population parameter μ by its sample estimate $\bar{X}$ in the above sums of squares leads to the 'loss' of one degree of freedom. This result is in fact quite general. Whenever we have to replace a population parameter by its sample estimate to compute a sum of squares, we shall find that this involves the placing of a restriction on the variables being squared and summed. This leads to a reduction of one in the degrees of freedom associated with the sum of squares. In the above case, for example, replacing μ by $\bar{X}$ involved the imposition of the restriction $\sum_i(X_i - \bar{X}) = 0$ on the variables to be squared and summed.

Given the above, we can say that *the number of degrees of freedom (d.f.) associated with a sum of squares is given by the number of observations used to compute the sum of squares minus the number of parameters that have to be replaced by their sample estimates.* As we have seen, the number of parameters replaced always turns out to equal the number of restrictions placed on the variables used to form the sum of squares.

The χ^2 distribution

If $Z_1, Z_2, Z_3, \ldots, Z_n$ are all independently distributed standard normal or $N(0, 1)$ variables then the sum of squares $\sum_{i=1}^{n} Z_i^2$ is said to have a χ^2 **distribution with** n **degrees of freedom**. The degrees of freedom associated with the distribution are those of the underlying sum of squares. Since the Z variables are independent, this sum of squares has the full n degrees of freedom. A χ^2 variable with n degrees of freedom is written χ_n^2.

The shapes of selected χ^2 distributions for various numbers of degrees of freedom are shown in Figure 3.9. It can be shown that the total area between each of these curves and the horizontal axis equals unity. We are therefore justified in

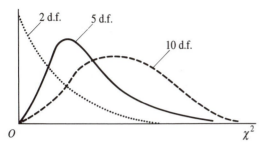

Figure 3.9 χ^2 distributions with 2, 5 and 10 degrees of freedom.

referring to them as distributions or probability density functions. Areas under the curve can be interpreted as probabilities and probability densities are measured on the vertical axis. Since sums of squares can never be negative, the distributions lie entirely in the positive quadrant. The distributions are non-symmetrical and have long right-hand tails. This is a result of the shape of the underlying standard normal distributions.

Given the above definition, the mean of the χ_n^2 distribution can easily be derived. For all i,

$$\text{Var}(Z_i) = \text{E}(Z_i^2) - [\text{E}(Z_i)]^2 \quad \text{(by definition)}$$

$$= \text{E}(Z_i^2) \qquad\qquad \text{(since each } Z_i \text{ has a mean of zero)}$$

But the Z_i are all $N(0, 1)$, and therefore all have a variance of unity. Thus we have that $\text{E}(Z_i^2) = 1$ for all i.

The mean of the χ_n^2 distribution is therefore given by

$$\text{E}(\chi_n^2) = \text{E}\left(\sum_i Z_i^2\right) = \sum_i \text{E}(Z_i^2) = \sum_i (1) = n$$

Thus the mean of the χ_n^2 distribution equals its degrees of freedom. Because of this, the smaller the number of degrees of freedom associated with the distribution, the closer its peak lies to the vertical axis in Figure 3.9.

A use of the χ^2 distribution

A well-known use of the χ^2 distribution is in the making of inferences about a population variance σ^2. Suppose we have a sample of n observations, $X_1, X_2, X_3, \ldots, X_n$, from a $N(\mu, \sigma^2)$ distribution. It follows that

$$\frac{X_i - \mu}{\sigma} \quad \text{has a } N(0, 1) \text{ distribution for all } i \tag{3.21}$$

Consider the sample variance s^2 given by (3.6) and also

$$\frac{s^2(n-1)}{\sigma^2} = \frac{\sum_i (X_i - \bar{X})^2}{\sigma^2} \tag{3.22}$$

It follows from (3.21) that

$$\sum_i \left(\frac{X_i - \mu}{\sigma}\right)^2 \text{ has a } \chi^2 \text{ distribution with } n \text{ d.f.} \qquad (3.23)$$

since it is the sum of squares of n standard normal variables that will be independently distributed if the sample of X values is random.

Hence, using (3.22),

$$\frac{s^2(n-1)}{\sigma^2} \text{ has a } \chi^2 \text{ distribution with } n-1 \text{ d.f.} \qquad (3.24)$$

We now have $n - 1$ degrees of freedom, because in moving from the sum of squares in (3.23) to that in (3.22) and (3.24), we have replaced the parameter μ by its sample estimate $\bar{X}$.

What (3.24) implies is that if we take many samples of size n from the $N(\mu, \sigma^2)$ population then we will obtain a sampling distribution of values for s^2. Different samples, just as they will yield different values for $\bar{X}$, will yield different values for s^2. If, however, for each sample we compute $s^2(n - 1)/\sigma^2$ then the sampling distribution for this statistic will be the χ^2 distribution with $n - 1$ degrees of freedom.

WORKED EXAMPLE

In the past, the time taken to complete a certain section of a production process has had a standard deviation of 35 seconds. Such variability in times, however, causes disruption to the production process, and it is believed that a new method of operating might reduce this standard deviation.

In an experiment, 20 timings using the new method of operating prove to have a standard deviation $s = 28$ seconds. On the basis of this evidence, determine whether the new method represents an improvement.

Let us begin by formulating null and alternative hypotheses. The null hypothesis is that the new method is no better than the old. That is, the variance, if the new method were permanently adopted, would still be $(35)^2 = 1225$. Thus

$$H_0 : \quad \sigma^2 = 1225$$

The alternative hypothesis is that the variance, using the new method, is less than the 1225 of the original method. That is,

$$H_A : \quad \sigma^2 < 1225$$

We use (3.24) to derive a test statistic. Under H_0,

$$TS = \frac{s^2(n-1)}{1225} \text{ has a } \chi^2 \text{ distribution with } n-1 \text{ d.f.} \qquad (3.25)$$

Since χ^2_{n-1} has a mean of $n - 1$, this means that, under H_0, we expect this test statistic to take a value close to $n - 1$. We obviously reject H_0 in favour of H_A, and say that the new method is an improvement, if the sample variance s^2 is sufficiently less than the 1225 in H_0. This means that TS must be sufficiently *less* than $n - 1$ if we are to reject H_0.

To decide what we mean by 'sufficiently less than $n - 1$', we refer to Figure 3.10 and a table of critical χ^2 values. Such a table, with a description of its use, is provided in Appendix IV. Examination of Figure 3.10 indicates that, at the 0.05 level of significance, we should

reject H_0 if TS $< \chi^2_{0.95}$ but reserve judgement if TS $> \chi^2_{0.95}$

This is our test criterion, with the precise value of $\chi^2_{0.95}$ depending on the degrees of freedom and hence the sample size. In fact, with $n - 1 = 19$ d.f., the χ^2 table indicates that $\chi^2_{0.95} = 10.12$.

The sample consists of the $n = 20$ actual timings using the new method of operation. This had a variance $s^2 = (28)^2 = 784$. The value of the test statistic (3.25) is therefore

$$\text{TS} = \frac{784 \times 19}{1225} = 12.16$$

Applying our test criterion, we therefore see that we must reserve judgement on H_0 at the 0.05 level of significance. Thus we find that the evidence is insufficient to say that the new method of operation represents an improvement.

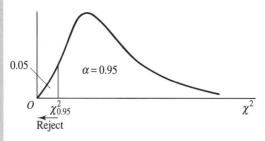

Figure 3.10 Testing an hypothesis about a population variance.

Exercise 3.12

A company plans to purchase light bulbs for one of its factories. It is necessary to have bulbs that possess not only a long life but also a high degree of uniformity. On the basis of past experience, it is decided that the variance of the lifetime of light bulbs purchased should not exceed 300 hours^2. A test of 25 bulbs of a certain make proves to have a variance of 340 hours^2. Test at the 0.05 level of significance whether this make of light bulb fails to meet the required specification.

An important property of χ^2 distributions

The χ^2 distribution is formed by taking the sum of squares, $\sum_i Z_i^2$, of n standard normal variables. If these variables are all independent of one another then the distribution obtained has n degrees of freedom. If, however, only r of the standard normal variables are independent, with the remainder depending on these r, then the sum of squares, $\sum_i Z_i^2$, will have only r degrees of freedom. Thus the χ^2 distribution formed will also have only r degrees of freedom. We have implicitly used this fact in the previous worked example. However, it follows from this that χ^2 variables have the following important property.

THEOREM 3.3

If χ_u^2 and χ_v^2 are two independent χ^2 distributions with u and v d.f. respectively then $\chi_u^2 + \chi_v^2$ will have a χ^2 distribution with $u + v$ d.f.

Thus the sum of two independent χ^2 distributions is also a χ^2 distribution and the degrees of freedom associated with this new distribution equals the sum of the degrees of freedom associated with the original distributions.

Theorem 3.3 is in fact fairly obvious. Clearly, the sum of two sums of squares must itself be a sum of squares. Also the number of restrictions on the variables in the new sum of squares must equal the sum of the two sets of restrictions on the original sums of squares. This relatively obvious property has, as we shall see in later chapters, a number of very important uses in regression analysis.

The Student's t distribution

If $Z_0, Z_1, Z_2, Z_3, \ldots, Z_n$ are all independently distributed standard normal variables then the quantity

$$t = \frac{Z_0}{\sqrt{\sum_{i=1}^{n} Z_i^2 / n}} \tag{3.26}$$

is said to have a **Student's t distribution with n degrees of freedom**.

It can be seen that inside the square root of the denominator of (3.26) we have $(1/n)\sum_{i=1}^{n} Z_i^2$, which is a χ_n^2 variable divided by its degrees of freedom. An alternative definition of t is therefore that *it is the ratio of a standard normal variable to the square root of an independent χ^2 variable that has been divided by its degrees of freedom*. Note that the Student's t distribution obtains its degrees of freedom from the χ^2 distribution that appears in its denominator.

The shape of the Student's t distribution is illustrated in Figure 3.11. It can be shown that the total area between the curve and the horizontal axis is equal to unity, so that, like χ^2, we are justified in referring to it as a distribution or probability density

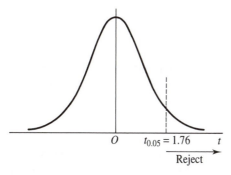

Figure 3.11 The Student's t distribution.

function. That is, areas under the curve can be regarded as probabilities, with probability densities measured on the vertical axis. The shape is very similar to that of the standard normal distribution, being symmetrical about zero, but with a slightly larger probability of getting values in the two tails.

The precise shape of the Student's t distribution depends on n, its degrees of freedom. *It can be shown that as $n \to \infty$, the shape tends to that of the standard normal distribution.* In fact, for $n > 50$, differences between the two distributions can be ignored for all practical purposes.

A use of the Student's t distribution

In the last section we considered large-sample tests concerning population means. Since the samples involved were 'large', we could invoke the central limit theorem to derive an appropriate test statistic.

Even if samples are small, recall that, provided the population is normally distributed, the sampling distribution of the mean $\bar{X}$ is still $N(\mu, \sigma^2/n)$. Thus it is still the case that $(\bar{X} - \mu)/(\sigma/\sqrt{n})$ has a standard normal distribution. Thus if σ were known, we could still form a test statistic that was standard normal under a null hypothesis that μ equals some given value μ_0.

The population standard deviation σ is, however, usually unknown, and has to be replaced by the sample standard deviation s. Unfortunately, in small samples, there is no reason why $(\bar{X} - \mu)/(s/\sqrt{n})$ should be a standard normal variable. However, we shall now show that, provided the population is normally distributed,

$$\frac{\bar{X} - \mu}{s/\sqrt{n}} \text{ has a Student's } t \text{ distribution with } n - 1 \text{ d.f.} \tag{3.27}$$

For samples drawn from a normal population, it is the case that

$$\frac{\bar{X} - \mu}{\sigma/\sqrt{n}} \text{ has a standard normal distribution} \tag{3.28}$$

and also, reproducing (3.24), that

$$\frac{s^2(n-1)}{\sigma^2} \text{ has a } \chi^2 \text{ distribution with } n-1 \text{ d.f.} \tag{3.29}$$

Recalling the alternative definition of a t variable below (3.26), let us take the ratio of (3.28) to the square root of (3.29) divided by its degrees of freedom:

$$\frac{(\bar{X}-\mu)/(\sigma/\sqrt{n})}{\sqrt{s^2/\sigma^2}} = \frac{(\bar{X}-\mu)}{(\sigma/\sqrt{n})(s/\sigma)} = \frac{\bar{X}-\mu}{s/\sqrt{n}} \tag{3.30}$$

Hence $(\bar{X}-\mu)/(s/\sqrt{n})$ will have a Student's t distribution, and, moreover, the degrees of freedom associated with this distribution will be those of the χ^2 distribution in the denominator of (3.30), that is, $n-1$. Thus (3.27) has been shown to be true.

WORKED EXAMPLE

Referring back to our population of steelworkers introduced earlier in this chapter, suppose we again wish to test the null hypothesis H_0: $\mu = 540$ against the alternative H_A: $\mu > 540$. On this occasion, however, suppose we have available a small sample size, $n = 15$, for which $\bar{X} = \$556$ and $s = \$68$.

Provided the *population* of steelworker earnings is normally distributed, we can derive a test statistic by noting that, under H_0,

$$\text{TS} = \frac{\bar{X}-540}{s/\sqrt{n}} \text{ has a Student's } t \text{ distribution with } n-1 \text{ d.f.}$$

With a one-tail test, we again reject H_0 if the test statistic is sufficiently greater than zero. Now, however, we have to determine what is 'sufficiently greater' by reference to Figure 3.11 and a table of critical values for the t distribution. Such a table, with directions to its use, is provided in Appendix IV. Using a 0.05 level of significance, we see that, with $n-1 = 14$ d.f., our test criterion in this case is

reject H_0 if TS > $t_{0.05} = 1.76$, but reserve judgement if TS < 1.76

For our sample, the test statistic takes a value of TS = 0.91. Thus, applying the above test criterion, we have to reserve judgement on the hypothesis. That is, there is insufficient evidence in this sample for us to claim that earnings now exceed \$540.

Exercise 3.13

A large firm claims that the average hours worked by its employees does not exceed 40 hours. A random sample of ten workers are found to work the following hours in a given week:

43	39	44	40	42	38	45	39	46	44

Test whether the firm's claim is correct.

Exercise 3.14

A machine is designed to produce washers with an average thickness of 0.5 cm, with a standard deviation of not more than 0.01 cm. The thickness of washers is normally distributed. To determine whether the machine is in proper working order, a random sample of 11 washers was examined and found to have the following thicknesses:

0.48	0.51	0.49	0.50	0.48	0.48	0.49	0.48	0.50	0.47	0.51

Carry out whatever statistical tests you think are appropriate to decide whether the machine is working properly.

Small-sample confidence intervals for a population mean

In Section 3.2 we derived large-sample confidence intervals for a population mean μ. If the sample is small, however, we can no longer make use of the central limit theorem and the standard normal distribution. But, provided the population is normally distributed, we can make use of (3.27) and use the Student's t distribution instead.

Recalling the general expression for a confidence interval, (3.13), it follows that, for small samples, a 95% confidence interval for a population mean μ is given by

$$\bar{X} \pm t_{0.025} \frac{s}{\sqrt{n}} \tag{3.31}$$

The critical value $t_{0.025}$ will depend on the degrees of freedom involved; it is taken from the t table in Appendix IV, and replaces the 1.96, taken from standard normal tables for the large-sample case.

Reverting again to our steelworker earnings example, suppose we had a sample size 20 with $\bar{X} = \$566$ and $s = \$72$. Then, since we have $n - 1 = 19$ degrees of freedom, $t_{0.025} = 2.093$, so that a 95% confidence interval for population mean earnings would be

$$566 \pm 2.093 \frac{s}{\sqrt{n}} = 566 \pm 33.70$$

In general, a $100(1 - \alpha)\%$ confidence interval for μ will be given by

$$\bar{X} \pm t_{\alpha/2} \frac{s}{\sqrt{n}} \tag{3.32}$$

Exercise 3.15

For the firm in Exercise 3.13, obtain a 99% confidence interval for the mean weekly hours worked by its employees.

The F distribution

There is one further distribution that we will make considerable use of in later chapters. Suppose χ^2_u and χ^2_v are two independently distributed χ^2 variables with u and v degrees of freedom respectively. The ratio

$$F = \frac{\chi^2_u / u}{\chi^2_v / v}$$

is then said to have an F **distribution with** $[u, v]$ **degrees of freedom**. Thus an F variable is *the ratio of two independent χ^2 variables each divided by their respective degrees of freedom.*

The shape of an F distribution is shown in Figure 3.12. It is similar to the shape of the χ^2 distribution with a long right-hand tail. The total area beneath the curve can be shown to equal unity, so again we are justified in referring to it as a probability density function. The precise shape of the F distribution depends on u and v, the degrees of freedom associated with the underlying χ^2 distributions. Critical values for the distribution are normally presented in two tables, one for the 0.05 level and another for the 0.01 level of significance. Such tables, with instructions as to use, are again contained in Appendix IV.

A use of the F distribution

The F distribution may be used to test a null hypothesis that two normally distributed populations have the same variance. This is usually tested against an alternative hypothesis that one of the variances is greater than the other. That is, if σ_1^2 and σ_2^2 are

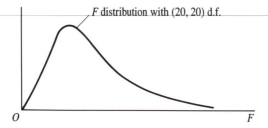

Figure 3.12 The F distribution with (20, 20) degrees of freedom.

the two variances, we have

$$H_0: \quad \sigma_1^2 = \sigma_2^2$$
$$H_A: \quad \sigma_1^2 > \sigma_2^2$$

where the population we suspect has the *larger* variance has been labelled 'population 1'.

Suppose random samples, of sizes n_1 and n_2 respectively, are drawn from the two populations and their variances s_1^2 and s_2^2 computed. Consider the ratio s_1^2/s_2^2. It makes sense to reject H_0 in favour of H_A and say that σ_1^2 exceeds σ_2^2 if this ratio is sufficiently large. As usual, we need to decide how large.

Under H_0 the two population variances are the same, so that

$$\frac{s_1^2}{s_2^2} = \frac{s_1^2/\sigma_1^2}{s_2^2/\sigma_2^2} = \frac{s_1^2(n_1 - 1)/\sigma_1^2(n_1 - 1)}{s_2^2(n_2 - 1)/\sigma_2^2(n_2 - 1)} \tag{3.33}$$

Using (3.24), we see that the numerator of the last expression in (3.33) is a χ^2 variable with $n_1 - 1$ degrees of freedom, divided by those degrees of freedom. Similarly, the denominator is a χ^2 variable with n_2 degrees of freedom, divided by those degrees of freedom. Hence, from the definition of an F variable, we can say that, under H_0,

$$\text{TS} = s_1^2/s_2^2 \text{ has an } F \text{ distribution with } [n_1 - 1, n_2 - 1] \text{ d.f.}$$

We may therefore use F tables to determine whether the test statistic is sufficiently large for us to reject H_0 and say that the first population has the larger variance.

Suppose, for example, that the first sample was of size $n_1 = 11$, with $s_1^2 = 248$, while the second sample was of size $n_2 = 20$, with $s_2^2 = 164$. Using the F table for the 0.05 level of significance, and with $[10, 19]$ degrees of freedom, the critical value for F is $F_{0.05} = 2.38$. The required test criterion is therefore

reject H_0 if TS > 2.38, but reserve judgement if TS < 2.38

For the two given samples, $\text{TS} = s_1^2/s_2^2 = 1.51$. Applying the test criterion, we see that we must reserve judgement at the 0.05 level of significance. Thus there is insufficient evidence to say that the variance of the first population exceeds that of the second.

Exercise 3.16

Two methods are being considered for performing a certain task. In a time and motion study, the times taken by 10 workers performing the task by the first method had a standard deviation of $s_1 = 20$ minutes, while the time taken by 15 workers performing the task by the second method had a standard deviation of $s_2 = 50$ minutes. Test whether there is more variability in the time taken to perform the task when the second method is used. If the first method is eventually adopted, test the hypothesis that the variance of times taken would be less than 625 minutes^2.

Appendix 3A

Notes to Chapter 3

1. For example, with a sample size $n = 100$ and an estimate of σ given by a sample standard deviation of $s = 75$, (3.17) becomes $\bar{X} > 552.3$. Thus, if $\bar{X}$ exceeds 552.3, we say that this is sufficiently greater than 540 for us to reject H_0: $\mu = 540$.
2. Recall that the variance of $\bar{X}$, and hence of both the distributions in Figure 3.7, is σ^2/n. Thus an increase in n will reduce this variance.
3. Since we are summing over all n variables,

$$\sum_i (X_i - \bar{X}) = \sum_i X_i - n\bar{X} = \sum_i X_i - \sum_i X_i = 0$$

Further reading

Good introductory material on statistical inference can be found in Griffiths et al. (1993), Chapters 3 and 4. See also Judge et al. (1988), Chapter 3. Greene (1993), Chapter 4, provides more advanced material.

4 Two-variable regression analysis

We begin this chapter by considering the data set contained in Table 4.1. This refers to a random sample of 25 four-person (two adults) households taken from the population of Transvenia, a modern industrial country. It contains information in hundreds of dollars on their annual disposable income and their annual total expenditure on non-durable goods and services. Since the data all refer to the year 1995, it may be assumed that all the households face the same array of prices for the goods and services that they purchase.

The expenditure data in the table excludes spending on durable goods, and hence is a reasonable approximation to the economist's definition of 'consumption'. Moreover, since all Transvenian households face the same prices, we need not concern ourselves with differences between real and nominal consumption or between real and nominal income.

We shall now investigate the relationship between the consumption and disposable income of Transvenian households of the above type. When we consider the nature and form of a relationship between any two or more variables, the analysis is referred to as **regression analysis**. In this chapter we consider two-variable regression analysis, leaving the problem of relationships between more than two variables until later chapters. The reader may well object that other factors may enter into the relationship between income and consumption, but for the moment we abstract from such influences.[1]

Table 4.1   Household income X and consumption Y

Household	Y	X
1	52.30	36.40
2	78.44	46.80
3	88.76	57.20
4	54.08	67.60
5	111.44	74.30
6	105.20	86.50
7	45.73	91.30
8	122.35	102.80
9	142.24	114.50
10	86.22	120.90
11	174.50	135.00
12	185.20	144.00
13	111.80	156.00
14	214.60	173.70
15	144.60	182.00
16	174.36	199.20
17	215.40	208.00
18	286.24	217.80
19	188.56	223.20
20	237.20	234.00
21	181.80	251.00
22	373.00	260.00
23	191.60	289.50
24	247.12	296.40
25	269.60	312.00

In regression analysis an important issue is the 'direction of causation' between variables. It should be clear that, in the present case, the direction of causation runs from disposable income to consumption and not vice versa. That is, income 'explains' consumption. Alternatively, consumption 'depends' on income. We shall therefore refer to consumption as the **dependent variable**, giving it the symbol Y, and refer to disposable income as the **explanatory variable**, giving it the symbol X. Although it is customary in economics to give the symbol Y to income, in statistics it is normal to give this symbol to the dependent variable, and we shall follow this practice, despite any slight initial confusion this may cause.

A scatter diagram of consumption against disposable income is plotted in Figure 4.1. Note that, as is customary, the dependent variable Y is measured on the vertical axis and the explanatory variable X on the horizontal axis. Casual observation of the scatter suggests that the relationship between income and consumption is 'positive' in that consumption rises as income rises. Also, the relationship may well be linear in the sense that a straight line looks likely to 'fit' the scatter of points in Figure 4.1 as well as any curve.

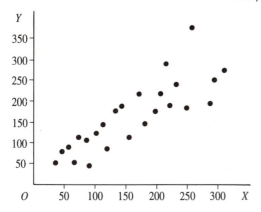

Figure 4.1 Scatter diagram of income X and consumption Y.

4.1 The population and sample regression lines

Before we can further analyse the relationship we have apparently discovered, we need to develop a formal model that might describe such a relationship. Our sample of 25 four-person households is drawn from a population of thousands, possibly millions, of such Transvenian households. Let us assume that the consumption Y and income X of these households are linked by the relationship

$$E(Y) = \alpha + \beta X \tag{4.1}$$

where $E(Y)$ represents the expected consumption of a household with given income X, and α and β are unknown population parameters. $E(Y)$ in (4.1) could be interpreted as the 'average consumption' of 'very many' households all with the same given income X. Equation (4.1) is known as the **population regression equation**. Notice that it expresses expected consumption as a *linear* function of household income. As we shall see, such relationships need not necessarily be linear, but, for simplicity, we make this assumption for now. The graph of (4.1) is shown as the broken line in Figure 4.2, and is known as the **population regression line**. The parameters α and β are the intercept and slope respectively of this line.

The actual consumption Y of a household will not always equal its expected value $E(Y)$. Actual consumption of a household may be 'disturbed' from its expected value by any one of innumerable factors, and we shall therefore write actual consumption as

$$Y = E(Y) + \epsilon \tag{4.2}$$

or

$$Y = \alpha + \beta X + \epsilon \tag{4.3}$$

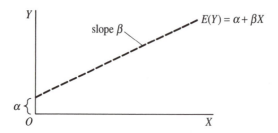

Figure 4.2 The population regression line.

where ϵ is a **disturbance**, which may be positive or negative. The disturbance term represents two sets of factors. First, it represents the effect on household consumption of all variables other than income. For the moment, we are implicitly assuming that such effects are small. Otherwise we might want to redesign our basic model (4.1). Secondly, even if income X were the only identifiable variable influencing consumption Y, we would not expect a household with a given income always to have the same level of consumption year after year. ϵ therefore is also included to allow for the basic *random* unpredictability of human behaviour.

Up to this point, we have used the symbol Y simply as a shorthand for the variable it is intended to represent, namely consumption. Similarly, X has been our shorthand for income. We now extend this notation. Writing n for the size of the sample ($n = 25$ in the present case), we number the households from 1 to n. We shall write Y_i for the consumption of the ith household and X_i for the income of the ith household. Thus Y_{10} is the consumption of household 10, and is simply the number 86.22, taken from Table 4.1. Similarly, X_{14} is the income of household 14, and is simply the number 173.70 taken from Table 4.1. Summarizing, the symbols Y and X without subscripts are simply shorthand for the variables they represent. However, when X and Y appear with subscripts (e.g. as Y_{18} or X_{12}), they are to be interpreted as actual numbers referring to specific households. We shall use this type of notation throughout this book.

The fact that we are assuming Equations (4.1) and (4.3) hold for all households in our sample can be expressed symbolically in our extended notation as

$$E(Y_i) = \alpha + \beta X_i \quad \text{for } i = 1, 2, 3, \ldots, n \tag{4.4}$$

and

$$Y_i = \alpha + \beta X_i + \epsilon_i \quad \text{for } i = 1, 2, 3, \ldots, n \tag{4.5}$$

where ϵ_i in (4.5) is the (unobserved) value of the disturbance ϵ for the ith household. For example, ϵ_7 is the disturbance associated with the seventh household.

We stress at this point that the population regression equation (4.1) is unknown to any investigator, and remains unknown. The investigator has to estimate it, using the data in the sample on consumption and disposable income. To do this (s)he has, by some method or another, to fit a straight line to the scatter of points in Figure 4.1. This line can then be regarded as an 'estimate' of that in Figure 4.2. We shall have a considerable amount to say about how such a line should be fitted to a scatter in the rest of this book, but, for the moment, let us assume that the investigator, by some unspecified method, has fitted a line that we write as

$$\hat{Y} = \hat{\alpha} + \hat{\beta}X \tag{4.6}$$

Equation (4.6) is referred to as the **sample regression equation**, and represents a straight line with intercept $\hat{\alpha}$ and slope $\hat{\beta}$. $\hat{\alpha}$ and $\hat{\beta}$ are in fact estimates of the population parameters α and β that appear in the population regression equation (4.1). $\hat{Y}$ in (4.6) is known as the **predicted value of** Y. It is given this name because, once a sample regression equation line has been obtained (i.e. once we have estimates $\hat{\alpha}$ and $\hat{\beta}$), it is possible to obtain a predicted consumption level $\hat{Y}$ for any household in our sample by substituting the income value X for that household into (4.6). For example, household 14 has income $X_{14} = 173.70$. Therefore it has a predicted consumption level of $\hat{Y}_{14} = \hat{\alpha} + 173.70\hat{\beta}$.

It should be clear that, given estimated values $\hat{\alpha}$ and $\hat{\beta}$, we can use the sample regression equation to obtain a predicted consumption level for every household in the sample, simply by substituting in the relevant values of household income. That is, we have

$$\hat{Y}_i = \hat{\alpha} + \hat{\beta}X_i \quad \text{for } i = 1, 2, 3, \ldots, n \tag{4.7}$$

The predicted values of consumption, given by (4.7), are unlikely to coincide with the actual consumption values in Table 4.1. Indeed, if they did, all the points in the scatter diagram in Figure 4.1 would lie exactly on the fitted sample regression line, a highly unlikely occurrence. The difference between an actual consumption value (a Y_i) and a predicted consumption value (a $\hat{Y}_i$) is known as a **residual**, and we write it as e_i. That is,

$$Y_i = \hat{Y}_i + e_i \quad \text{for } i = 1, 2, 3, \ldots, n \tag{4.8}$$

Thus, for example, e_{10} is the residual associated with the 10th household and is simply the difference between actual consumption Y_{10} and predicted consumption $\hat{Y}_{10}$ for that household. Clearly, as (4.8) implies, there will be a residual for every household in the sample.

It is important that the reader should grasp clearly the distinction between the disturbances, introduced earlier, and the residuals. Consideration of Figure 4.3 should help. In Figure 4.3 the broken line again represents the unknown population regression equation (4.1). This is and remains *unknown to the investigator*. The point marked with a cross represents the actual values for consumption and income for the 14th household in Table 4.1. It is therefore just one of the points from the scatter diagram in Figure 4.1.

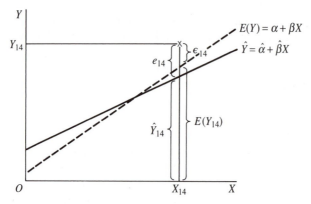

Figure 4.3 Disturbances and residuals.

Examination of Equations (4.4) and (4.5), which together imply

$$Y_i = E(Y_i) + \epsilon_i \quad \text{for } i = 1, 2, 3, \dots, n \tag{4.9}$$

should make it clear that the disturbance associated with the 14th household, ϵ_{14}, is in fact the vertical distance between the cross in Figure 4.3 and the population regression line. That is, $\epsilon_{14} = Y_{14} - E(Y_{14})$. Although an investigator knows where the cross is, since (s)he does not know the underlying population regression line, the distance ϵ_{14} (i.e. the disturbance) is and must remain unknown.

For every household in our sample, there is a point in the associated scatter diagram, and hence a disturbance represented by the vertical distance between point and population regression line. If a point happens to lie below the population regression line, this simply means the disturbance is negative. We stress, however, that all disturbances are and remain unknown.

The unbroken line in Figure 4.3 represents the sample regression equation (4.6), 'fitted' to the scatter of points in Figure 4.1 by some still unspecified method. From (4.8), it can be deduced that e_{14}, the residual associated with household 14, is in fact the vertical distance between the cross and the sample regression line. Similarly, the residual for any household in the sample can be represented by the vertical distance between the relevant point in the scatter and the sample regression line. Points below the line represent households with negative residuals. Notice that since, like the points in the scatter, the sample regression line is known (it has been fitted by the investigator), *residuals, unlike disturbances, are known quantities.* As we shall see in later chapters, the known residuals often have to be treated as estimates of the unknown disturbances.

We have deliberately said nothing so far about how the sample regression line is obtained. However, it should be clear that, whatever method is adopted for fitting a line to a scatter of points, a set of residuals (e_i, $i = 1, 2, \dots, n$) will result.

4.2   The ordinary least squares estimation method

When we fit a sample regression line to a scatter of points, it obviously makes sense to select a line (that is, choose values for $\hat{\alpha}$ and $\hat{\beta}$) such that the residuals given by (4.8) that result are in some sense small. This will ensure that the predicted consumption levels yielded by our sample regression equation will be fairly close to the actual consumption levels of the households in the sample. The most popular and best known way of ensuring this is to choose $\hat{\alpha}$ and $\hat{\beta}$ so as to minimize the sum of the squares of the residuals. That is we choose the sample regression equation that minimizes $\sum_i e_i^2$. This method of estimating the parameters α and β is known as the method of **ordinary least squares** (OLS). Its popularity stems from the fact that, *provided a whole series of further assumptions are valid*, the OLS method can be shown to provide 'good' estimators of α and β. We shall define what we mean by 'good' in Chapter 5, and will be examining the required further assumptions in Chapter 6. For the moment, though, we merely note that many of these assumptions are highly unlikely to hold when we are dealing with economic-type data. For this reason, the OLS estimating method is rather more popular than it deserves to be. For now, however, we shall simply concentrate on the technical question of actually deriving the OLS estimators.

Using the symbol S for the sum of the squared residuals, we have, using Equation (4.8) and then (4.7),

$$S = \sum e_i^2 = \sum (Y_i - \hat{Y}_i)^2 = \sum (Y_i - \hat{\alpha} - \hat{\beta} X_i)^2 \tag{4.10}$$

where summations are from $i = 1$ to $i = n$, that is over all households. The OLS estimation method chooses $\hat{\alpha}$ and $\hat{\beta}$ in (4.10) so as to minimize S.

To minimize (4.10), we partially differentiate with respect to $\hat{\alpha}$ and $\hat{\beta}$, setting the resultant derivatives to zero. This gives[2]

$$\frac{\partial S}{\partial \hat{\alpha}} = -2 \sum (Y_i - \hat{\alpha} - \hat{\beta} X_i) = 0 \tag{4.11}$$

and

$$\frac{\partial S}{\partial \hat{\beta}} = -2 \sum X_i (Y_i - \hat{\alpha} - \hat{\beta} X_i) = 0 \tag{4.12}$$

(Recall that all the X_i and Y_i in (4.10) refer to observations in our sample, and hence are constants as far as the differentiation is concerned.)

Note, at this point, that the term in parentheses in Equations (4.11) and (4.12) is in fact the residual, $e_i = Y_i - \hat{\alpha} - \hat{\beta} X_i$. Hence it is possible to rewrite (4.11) and (4.12) as $-2 \sum e_i = 0$ and $-2 \sum X_i e_i = 0$. It follows that

$$\sum e_i = 0 \quad \text{and} \quad \sum X_i e_i = 0 \tag{4.13}$$

The residuals in OLS regression must therefore always obey the relationships (4.13).

We shall have reason to refer to these properties of OLS residuals on a number of future occasions.

Noting that, since all summations are from $i = 1$ to $i = n$, $\sum \hat{\alpha} = n\hat{\alpha}$, we can rearrange Equations (4.11) and (4.12) as

$$\sum Y_i = n\hat{\alpha} + \hat{\beta} \sum X_i \tag{4.14}$$

and

$$\sum X_i Y_i = \hat{\alpha} \sum X_i + \hat{\beta} \sum X_i^2 \tag{4.15}$$

Equations (4.14) and (4.15) are often referred to as the **normal equations** of the two-variable regression model. Since quantities such as $\sum X_i$ and $\sum X_i Y_i$ can be calculated from the sample data set, and n is the sample size, the only unknowns in (4.14) and (4.15) are $\hat{\alpha}$ and $\hat{\beta}$. The normal equations may therefore be solved to yield expressions for $\hat{\alpha}$ and $\hat{\beta}$, the ordinary least squares estimators.

To obtain such expressions, first, we divide (4.14) throughout by n and rearrange to obtain

$$\hat{\alpha} = \bar{Y} - \hat{\beta}\bar{X} \tag{4.16}$$

where $\bar{Y} = \sum Y_i / n$ and $\bar{X} = \sum X_i / n$. That is, $\bar{Y}$ and $\bar{X}$ are means of the sample values for Y and X respectively.

Substituting for $\hat{\alpha}$ in (4.15) gives

$$\sum X_i Y_i = \bar{Y} \sum X_i - \hat{\beta}\bar{X} \sum X_i + \hat{\beta} \sum X_i^2$$

or

$$\sum X_i Y_i = \frac{1}{n} \sum X_i \sum Y_i + \hat{\beta} \left[\sum X_i^2 - \frac{1}{n} \left(\sum X_i \right)^2 \right]$$

Thus

$$\hat{\beta} = \frac{\sum X_i Y_i - (1/n) \sum X_i \sum Y_i}{\sum X_i^2 - (1/n)(\sum X_i)^2} \tag{4.17}$$

Given $\hat{\beta}$, we can now use (4.16) to obtain $\hat{\alpha}$.

Noting that

$$\sum (X_i - \bar{X})^2 = \sum X_i^2 - \frac{1}{n} \left(\sum X_i \right)^2$$

and

$$\sum (X_i - \bar{X})(Y_i - \bar{Y}) = \sum X_i Y_i - \frac{1}{n} \sum X_i \sum Y_i$$

we can rewrite the OLS estimator $\hat{\beta}$ in a simpler and more convenient way as

$$\hat{\beta} = \frac{\sum x_i y_i}{\sum x_i^2} \tag{4.18}$$

where $x_i = X_i - \bar{X}$ and $y_i = Y_i - \bar{Y}$. That is, x_i is the **deviation** of X_i from its mean value $\bar{X}$, and, similarly, y_i is the deviation of Y_i from $\bar{Y}$.

Table 4.2   Basic calculations for two-variable regression

Y	X	Y^2	X^2	XY
52.30	36.40	2 735.3	1 325.0	1 903.7
78.44	46.80	6 152.8	2 190.2	3 671.0
88.76	57.20	7 878.3	3 271.8	5 077.1
54.08	67.60	2 924.6	4 569.8	3 655.8
111.44	74.30	12 418.9	5 520.5	8 280.0
105.20	86.50	11 067.0	7 482.3	9 099.8
45.73	91.30	2 091.2	8 335.7	4 175.1
122.35	102.80	14 969.5	10 567.8	12 577.6
142.24	114.50	20 232.2	13 110.3	16 286.5
86.22	120.90	7 433.9	14 616.8	10 424.0
174.50	135.00	30 450.3	18 225.0	23 557.5
185.20	144.00	34 299.0	20 736.0	26 668.8
111.80	156.00	12 499.2	24 336.0	17 440.8
214.60	173.70	46 053.2	30 171.7	37 276.0
144.60	182.00	20 909.2	33 124.0	26 317.2
174.36	199.20	30 401.4	39 680.6	37 732.5
215.40	208.00	46 397.2	43 264.0	44 803.2
286.24	217.80	81 933.3	47 436.8	62 343.1
188.56	223.20	35 554.9	49 818.2	42 086.6
237.20	234.00	56 263.8	54 756.0	55 504.8
181.80	251.00	33 051.2	63 001.0	45 631.8
373.00	260.00	139 129.0	67 600.0	96 980.0
191.60	289.50	36 710.6	83 810.3	55 468.2
247.12	296.40	61 068.3	87 853.0	73 246.4
269.60	312.00	72 684.2	97 344.0	84 115.2
4082.34	4080.10	825 308.5	832 146.8	801 322.7

Equations (4.16) and (4.18) are the most convenient expressions for the **ordinary least squares estimators** of the parameters α and β in the population regression equation (4.1). We can now compute these estimators for our present example, using the data on consumption Y and disposable income X in Table 4.1. Some basic calculations are given in Table 4.2. The sums of the columns in Table 4.2 give us respectively $\sum Y_i$, $\sum X_i$, $\sum Y_i^2$, $\sum X_i^2$ and $\sum X_i Y_i$, although we do not as yet need $\sum Y_i^2$. We can now calculate the sample means of consumption and income as

$$\bar{Y} = \frac{\sum Y_i}{n} = 163.29 \quad \text{and} \quad \bar{X} = \frac{\sum X_i}{n} = 163.20 \tag{4.19}$$

Next we can calculate what may be called the **three basic building blocks** of two-variable regression. That is,

$$\sum x_i^2 = \sum X_i^2 - \frac{1}{n}\left(\sum X_i\right)^2$$

$$= 832\ 146.8 - \frac{1}{25}(4080.1)^2 = 166\ 258.2 \tag{4.20}$$

$$\sum x_i y_i = \sum X_i Y_i - \frac{1}{n}\left(\sum X_i\right)\left(\sum Y_i\right)$$

$$= 801\ 322.7 - \frac{1}{25}(4080.1)(4082.34) = 135\ 068.5 \tag{4.21}$$

$$\sum y_i^2 = \sum Y_i^2 - \frac{1}{n}\left(\sum Y_i\right)^2$$

$$= 825\ 308.5 - \frac{1}{25}(4082.34)^2 = 158\ 688.5 \tag{4.22}$$

We shall find that the quantities $\sum x_i^2$, $\sum x_i y_i$ and $\sum y_i^2$ crop up repeatedly in computations concerning two-variable regression. Although we do not need (4.22) just yet, we can use (4.20) and (4.21) immediately to find $\hat{\beta}$, the OLS estimator of the slope parameter β. That is, using (4.18),

$$\hat{\beta} = \frac{\sum x_i y_i}{\sum x_i^2} = \frac{135\ 068.5}{166\ 258.2} = 0.812 \tag{4.23}$$

Given $\hat{\beta}$, we can now use (4.16), together with (4.19), to find $\hat{\alpha}$, the OLS estimator of the intercept parameter α. That is,

$$\hat{\alpha} = \bar{Y} - \hat{\beta}\bar{X} = 163.29 - (0.812)(163.2) = 30.71 \tag{4.24}$$

We have now obtained our sample regression equation (4.6), using the OLS estimation method:

$$\hat{Y} = 30.71 + 0.812X \tag{4.25}$$

In Figure 4.4 the sample regression equation (4.25) is plotted on the original scatter diagram from Figure 4.1. Note that it passes fairly near to all the points in the scatter.

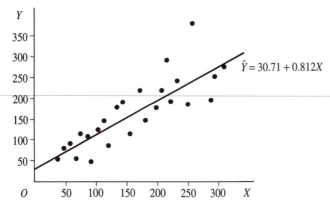

Figure 4.4 The sample regression line.

We can now use our estimated equation to work out predicted consumption levels for each household in our sample. Considering for example household 18, we have from Table 4.1 that actual consumption, $Y_{18} = 286.24$. Since the income of household 18 is $X_{18} = 217.8$, we can use (4.25) to find the predicted consumption for household 18. That is,

$$\hat{Y}_{18} = 30.71 + 0.812(X_{18}) = 207.55$$

Recalling that a residual is the difference between actual and predicted consumption we have, using (4.8), that the residual for household 18 is

$$e_{18} = Y_{18} - \hat{Y}_{18} = 78.69$$

Recall that e_{18} is simply the vertical distance between the point in our scatter corresponding to household 18 and the sample regression line. In a similar manner, we can calculate predicted values and hence residuals for all households in the sample.

Our sample regression equation can also be used to predict consumption levels for households other than those in our particular sample. For example, suppose we wish to predict the consumption level of a four-person household (let us call it household 26) that has an income of $X_{26} = 247.3$. Predicted consumption is simply

$$\hat{Y}_{26} = 30.71 + 0.812X_{26} = 231.5$$

Clearly, we can use Equation (4.25) for prediction purposes, but how are the OLS estimates $\hat{\alpha} = 30.71$ and $\hat{\beta} = 0.812$ of the parameters in the population equation (4.1) to be interpreted? First, $\hat{\beta}$, the estimate of the slope parameter β, is our estimate of the extent to which mean or expected consumption of a household increases when it experiences an increase of one unit in its disposable income. It is therefore an estimate of the **marginal propensity to consume** of four-person (two adults) Transvenian households.

$\hat{\alpha}$, the estimate of the intercept α in the population regression equation (4.1), is really an estimate of the expected consumption of a household with zero income. Since in modern industrial economies no four-person households have zero income, it is doubtful whether the α estimate has any realistic interpretation on this occasion. However, it could be interpreted as a subsistence level of consumption, which Transvenian households on zero income are able to maintain by a process of dissaving.

Exercise 4.1

The following data refers to the demand for apples Y, in kg, and the price of apples X, in pence per kg, on 10 different market stalls:

Y	99	91	70	79	60	55	70	101	81	67
X	22	24	23	26	27	24	25	23	22	26

(a) Verify that $\sum Y^2 = 61\ 999$, $\sum X^2 = 5884$ and $\sum XY = 18\ 563$.
(b) Find $\sum y^2$, $\sum x^2$ and $\sum xy$.
(c) Assuming $Y = \alpha + \beta X + \epsilon$, obtain the OLS estimators of α and β.
(d) On a scatter diagram of the data, draw in your OLS sample regression line.
(e) Estimate the elasticity of demand for apples at the point of sample means (i.e. when $Y = \bar{Y}$ and $X = \bar{X}$).

Exercise 4.2

The following refer to the demand for money M ($billions) and the rate of interest R (%) in 8 different economies:

M	36	50	46	30	20	35	37	61
R	6.3	4.6	5.1	7.3	8.9	5.3	6.7	3.5

$$\sum m^2 = 1124, \qquad \sum r^2 = 20.3, \qquad \sum mr = -142$$

(lower-case letters denote deviations of variables from their means, i.e. $m = M - \bar{M}$ etc.).
(a) Assuming a relationship $M = \alpha + \beta R + \epsilon$, obtain the OLS estimators of α and β.
(b) If in a 9th economy the rate of interest is $R = 8.1$, predict the demand for money in this economy.

Exercise 4.3

The following data refers to the outputs Q of 6 firms and their *average* costs per unit of output, A:

Q	18	25	52	9	39	31
A	294	247	153	600	173	218

$$\sum q^2 = 1170, \qquad \sum a^2 = 135\ 103, \qquad \sum aq = -10\ 537$$

(lower-case letters denote deviations from means).
Use the data to estimate a regression equation of the form $\hat{A} = \hat{\alpha} + \hat{\beta} Q$, and sketch this equation on a scatter diagram.

4.3 Measuring closeness of fit

We have noted that the sample regression equation (4.25) fits the scatter in Figure 4.4 fairly closely. 'Fairly closely' is, however, a vague expression, and it is often convenient to have a precise **summary statistic** (that is, a single number) by which we can assess and compare the closeness of fit of different scatters and different sample regression lines.

To derive such a summary statistic, we consider the following question: *What proportion of the variation in consumption among our 25 households can we attribute to the variation in their incomes?* Clearly, if we can explain a large proportion of consumption variations then this must reflect a closely fitting sample regression line.

To answer the question posed, consider Figure 4.5, on which is drawn a horizontal line corresponding to mean sample consumption $\bar{Y} = 163.29$. The single point from the scatter shown in Figure 4.5 refers to household 18, for which, as we have seen, $Y_{18} = 286.24$ and $\hat{Y}_{18} = 207.55$, but what follows applies equally well to any point in the scatter. We shall measure variations in consumption levels about their mean value $\bar{Y}$, so, for the point shown, the *total* variation of consumption from its mean is $Y_{18} - \bar{Y} = 122.95$. However, for this household, the variation in Y *that can be attributed to the influence of income, X* (i.e. is due to the regression line) is given by the vertical distance $\hat{Y}_{18} - \bar{Y} = 44.26$. That part of the total variation in consumption about $\bar{Y}$ that cannot be attributed to income can now be seen to be equal to the residual $e_{18} = 78.69$ associated with the 18th household. For this reason, we refer to it as the **residual variation** in Y. From Figure 4.5, we see that

total variation = variation due to X + residual variation

$$Y_{18} - \bar{Y} = \qquad \hat{Y}_{18} - \bar{Y} \qquad + \qquad e_{18}$$

Proceeding in this way, it is clear that, for each point in the scatter, we can divide the total variation in Y into that which can be attributed to X and a remaining

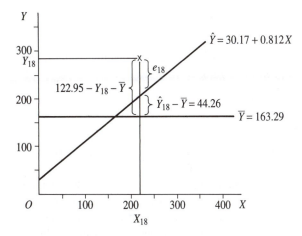

Figure 4.5 Decomposition of the variation in Y.

residual variation. That is,

$$Y_i - \bar{Y} = \hat{Y}_i - \bar{Y} + e_i \quad \text{for } i = 1, 2, 3, \ldots, n \tag{4.26}$$

What we now require is an overall measure of the above division that covers all households. For all households in our sample, that is, for all points in the scatter, an obvious overall measure of the **total variation** in Y about its mean is $\sum(Y_i - \bar{Y})^2$. (If we divided this measure by the sample size n, it would simply be the sample variance.) The measure is often also referred to as the **total sum of squares** (SST).

Over all points in the scatter, a similar measure of the variation in Y about its mean that can be attributed to the X variable is $\sum(\hat{Y}_i - \bar{Y})^2$. That is, we take the sum of squares of the explained variations, obtained above, for each point in the scatter. This quantity is normally referred to as the **explained sum of squares** (SSE) or the **explained variation** in Y. Finally, the obvious measure of the remaining or **residual variation** in Y about its mean is $\sum e_i^2$, the **residual sum of squares** (SSR).

We now present an important result. We shall show presently that, *provided our method of estimation is ordinary least squares*, it follows from (4.26) that

$$\sum(Y_i - \bar{Y})^2 = \sum(\hat{Y}_i - \bar{Y})^2 + \sum e_i^2 \tag{4.27}$$

That is, over all points in a scatter (i.e. over all sample observations), *provided we define our measures as above*,

total variation in Y = variation due to X + residual variation

or

total sum of squares (SST) = explained sum of squares (SSE)
+ residual sum of squares (SSR)

Note that (4.27) does not follow automatically from (4.26). If we square each side of (4.26) and sum over all observations, we obtain

$$\sum(Y_i - \bar{Y})^2 = \sum(\hat{Y}_i - \bar{Y})^2 + \sum e_i^2 + 2\sum e_i(\hat{Y}_i - \bar{Y}) \tag{4.28}$$

If (4.28) is to reduce to (4.27) as required then it is necessary that the last term on the right-hand side of (4.28) be shown to be zero. Now,

$$\sum e_i(\hat{Y}_i - \bar{Y}) = \sum e_i(\hat{\alpha} + \hat{\beta}X_i - \bar{Y})$$
$$= \hat{\alpha}\sum e_i + \hat{\beta}\sum X_i e_i - \bar{Y}\sum e_i = 0$$

using the properties (4.13) of OLS residuals. Hence the last term on the right-hand side of (4.28) is indeed zero, so (4.28) does in fact reduce to (4.27).

Note that we have been able to demonstrate the exact split of the total variation in Y given by (4.27) only by invoking the properties of *ordinary least squares residuals*. It follows that (4.27) holds *if the method of estimation is ordinary least squares*, but does not necessarily hold for other methods of estimation. This may appear strange, since commonsense suggests that the total variation in Y must always be the sum of the variation that can be explained and that which cannot be explained. However, we have defined particular measures of total variation, explained variation and residual variation, and these are not the only possible measures. The point is that, *for the measures we have selected*, the commonsense division of total variation into explained and unexplained components will be valid if the method of estimation is ordinary least squares. We shall encounter a number of alternative methods of estimating population regression equations later in this book, and it is always worth remembering that the relationship (4.27) will not necessarily hold for them.

We are now in a position to answer the question posed at the beginning of this section. We define the **coefficient of determination** R^2, as the proportion of the sample variation in Y that can be attributed to the sample variation in X. Thus, given the relationship (4.27), and using the above terminology,

$$R^2 = \frac{\text{variation attributed to } X}{\text{total variation in } Y} = \frac{\text{SSE}}{\text{SST}} \tag{4.29}$$

To evaluate R^2, we require convenient expressions for both numerator and denominator in (4.29). We know that $\text{SST} = \sum y_i^2$, while

$$\begin{aligned} \text{SSE} &= \sum (\hat{Y}_i - \bar{Y})^2 = \sum (\hat{\alpha} + \hat{\beta} X_i - \bar{Y})^2 \\ &= \sum (\hat{\beta} X_i - \hat{\beta} \bar{X})^2 \quad \text{(using (4.16))} \\ &= \sum \hat{\beta}^2 (X_i - \bar{X})^2 = \hat{\beta}^2 \sum x_i^2 \end{aligned} \tag{4.30}$$

Hence, substituting for SSE and SST in (4.29), we obtain

$$R^2 = \frac{\hat{\beta}^2 \sum x_i^2}{\sum y_i^2} \tag{4.31}$$

Although (4.31) is the most convenient expression for the coefficient of determination in two-variable regression, since $\text{SST} = \text{SSE} + \text{SSR}$, we can also rewrite (4.29) as

$$R^2 = \frac{\text{SSE}}{\text{SST}} = \frac{\text{SST} - \text{SSR}}{\text{SST}} = 1 - \frac{\text{SSR}}{\text{SST}} = 1 - \frac{\sum e_i^2}{\sum y_i^2} \tag{4.32}$$

Equation (4.31) is the most convenient expression for computing R^2 because, for our sample of 25 households, we already have figures for $\hat{\beta} = 0.812$, $\sum y_i^2 = 158\ 688.5$ and $\sum x_i^2 = 166\ 258.2$. Making use of these values gives the value $R^2 = 0.691$. Thus we can say that 69.1% of the variation in consumption among our 25 households can be attributed to variations in their incomes.

Notice that, since R^2 is a proportion, its value must always lie between zero and one. Thus we can assess how closely an OLS regression line fits a scatter of points by computing a value for the coefficient of determination. The closer the coefficient is to one, the better the line will fit the points. Finally, remember that, since we have fitted a *straight line* to our scatter, R^2 measures the proportion of the total variation in Y that can be attributed to a *linear* relationship between X and Y. As we shall see later, it is sometimes possible to obtain closer fits to a scatter of points by employing nonlinear relationships.

The correlation coefficient

The coefficient of determination R^2 is closely related to another measure of the strength of the relationship between X and Y that we have encountered before. Its square root R can in fact be shown to be identical to the sample *correlation* described in Section 2.4.

Before demonstrating this relationship, we work out the sample correlation between X and Y for the data on our 25 households in Table 4.1. In the notation of this chapter, the sample correlation, or **correlation coefficient** as it is often called, given by the definition (2.38), becomes

$$R = \frac{\sum x_i y_i}{\sqrt{\sum x_i^2}\sqrt{\sum y_i^2}} \tag{4.33}$$

Thus, the correlation between X and Y can be computed easily, using the basic building bricks (4.20)–(4.22). Substituting these values into (4.33) gives

$$R = \frac{135\,068.5}{\sqrt{166\,258.2}\sqrt{158\,688.5}} = +0.832$$

Notice that the coefficient of correlation R is indeed the square root of the coefficient of determination obtained above as 0.691. In addition, the positive sign of R in this case indicates that the linear relationship between X and Y is a positive one.

We now demonstrate that it is always the case that the square of the coefficient of correlation is the coefficient of determination. Squaring the expression for R in (4.33) gives

$$\frac{(\sum x_i y_i)^2}{\sum x_i^2 \sum y_i^2} = \frac{(\sum x_i y_i)^2 / \sum x_i^2}{\sum y_i^2}$$

$$= \frac{(\sum x_i y_i / \sum x_i^2)^2 (\sum x_i^2)}{\sum y_i^2} = \frac{\hat{\beta}^2 \sum x_i^2}{\sum y_i^2}$$

which is the expression for R^2 given in (4.31).

Since the coefficient of determination, R^2, varies between 0 and 1, it follows that the correlation coefficient R must vary between $+1$ and -1. For example, in Figure 4.6(a) all the points in the scatter lie on an upward-sloping straight line. In such an unlikely case it is clear that all the variation in Y can be attributed to X, so that $R^2 = 1$. The correlation coefficient in this case will be $R = +1$, indicating a perfect positive linear relationship between X and Y. In Figure 4.6(b), however, the points all lie on a downward-sloping straight line, so that, although again we have $R^2 = 1$, on this occasion $R = -1$, indicating an exact negative or inverse linear relationship between X and Y. Finally, in Figure 4.6(c) the points in the scatter are

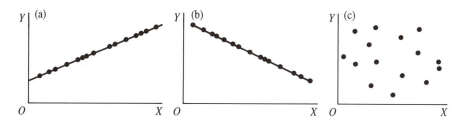

Figure 4.6 (a) A correlation of $+1$. (b) A correlation of -1. (c) A correlation of zero.

exactly evenly spread out, and clearly none of the variation in Y can be attributed to X, so that $R^2 = 0$. In this case the correlation coefficient R is also zero, indicating no detectable linear association between the two variables.

We now consider the uses that are made of the coefficients of correlation and determination. A statistician uses the correlation coefficient simply as a measure of the strength of the linear association or relationship between two variables. Nothing is inferred about the direction of causation between the variables. For example, a statistician would interpret the above correlation of $+0.832$ between the income and consumption of our 25 households as a strong positive or direct linear association. But (s)he would not necessarily infer that there was any causal link between the two variables. In particular, (s)he would not infer, from the correlation coefficient alone, that it was income that affected consumption and not vice versa. Correlation is simply a measure of the extent to which variables 'move together', and has nothing to say about causation.

Strictly speaking, since the coefficient of determination, R^2, is merely the square of the correlation coefficient, it too is simply a measure of the strength of the association between variables. However, the coefficient of determination is usually used in the context of regression analysis, in which, as we have seen, some assumption about the direction of causation between variables is made at the outset. Hence R^2 is usually interpreted by econometricians as above, that is, as measuring the proportion of the variation in the dependent Y variable that can be attributed to variations in X.

Exercise 4.4

Calculate the coefficient of determination using (4.31) and the correlation coefficient using (4.33) for the data in Exercise 4.1. Verify that, for this data, the coefficient of determination is the square of the correlation coefficient.

Exercise 4.5

Calculate the coefficient of determination, R^2, for the data in Exercise 4.3, and interpret its value.

Time series data

The data in Table 4.3 again refer to the consumption expenditure and disposable income of households. In this case, however, the data is **aggregate time series data** for the 20 years from 1971 to 1990. That is, each observation (i.e. each pair of numbers) refers to the average consumption per capita, Y, and average disposable income per capita, X, in hundreds of dollars at constant 1980 prices, for all households in the Transvenian economy during a particular year.[3] This data set is to be contrasted with that in Table 4.1, where all observations referred to a single household in the same year, but there were different observations for each household. The data set in Table 4.1 is an example of what is referred to as **cross-sectional data**.

Time series and cross-sectional data are the two types of data typically available to the econometrician. Time series data need not necessarily be aggregate as in Table 4.3, but its basic characteristic is that observations refer to consecutive time intervals. For example, data on a consumer price index for all quarters, from the first quarter of 1956 to the third quarter of 1993, make up a time series covering 151 consecutive quarters. Observations in a cross-section, however, all refer to the same

Table 4.3 Time series data on income X and consumption Y

Year	Y	X
1971	48.34	52.02
1972	48.54	52.41
1973	47.44	51.55
1974	54.58	58.88
1975	55.00	59.66
1976	63.49	68.42
1977	59.22	64.27
1978	57.77	63.01
1979	60.22	65.61
1980	55.40	61.05
1981	57.17	63.36
1982	60.84	67.42
1983	60.73	67.86
1984	76.04	83.39
1985	76.42	84.26
1986	69.34	77.41
1987	61.75	70.08
1988	68.78	77.44
1989	67.07	75.79
1990	72.94	81.89

time period but to different economic units. For example, data on the value of sales at 200 drug stores in Boston during 1993 would constitute a cross-sectional data set.

We can apply regression analysis to the time series data in Table 4.3 just as we did to the cross-sectional data in Table 4.1. However, the population regression line (4.1) must now be regarded as defining a linear relationship between average or aggregate disposable income and consumption. We again assume that any influence on consumption, other than that of income, can be captured by a disturbance ϵ, as in Equations (4.2) and (4.3).

A scatter diagram of the observations in Table 4.3 is shown in Figure 4.7. We now fit a line to this scatter, using the method of ordinary least squares outlined in Section 4.2. For the present data set, to 5 significant figures,

$$\sum X_i = 1345.8, \quad \sum Y_i = 1221.1$$
$$\sum X_i^2 = 92\,520, \quad \sum Y_i^2 = 75\,969, \quad \sum X_i Y_i = 83\,826$$

Our basic building blocks, (4.20), (4.21) and (4.22), are in this case

$$\sum x_i^2 = 1961.1, \quad \sum y_i^2 = 1414.7, \quad \sum x_i y_i = 1658.2 \tag{4.34}$$

Hence the OLS estimate of the slope β of the population regression line is, using (4.18), $\hat{\beta} = 0.846$.

Since the sample size $n = 20$, we have $\bar{X} = 67.3$ and $\bar{Y} = 61.1$, so that the OLS estimate of the intercept parameter α is, using (4.16), $\hat{\alpha} = 4.16$. We therefore obtain an OLS sample regression equation

$$\hat{Y} = 4.16 + 0.846X \tag{4.35}$$

The sample regression equation (4.35) is plotted on the scatter diagram in Figure 4.7. As can be seen, the line fits the points very closely, and we can again obtain a quantitative assessment of this closeness of fit by computing the coefficient of determination. Using the expression (4.31) and the calculations in (4.34) and

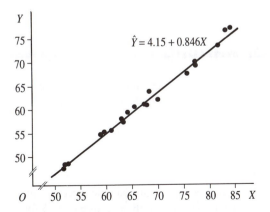

Figure 4.7 Time series scatter and sample regression line.

(4.35) gives a value for R^2 equal to 0.992. Hence, we can say that 99.2% of the variation in aggregate consumption can be attributed to variations in aggregate disposable income. Interpretation of the OLS line (4.35) is analogous to the interpretation of the line in Section 4.2. $\hat{\beta}=0.846$ is our estimate of the effect on aggregate consumption per capita of a one-unit rise in aggregate disposable income per capita. That is, it is an estimate of the aggregate marginal propensity to consume. The estimate, $\hat{\alpha}=4.16$, is our estimate of what aggregate consumption would be if aggregate income per capita were zero. It could again be given an interpretation in terms of subsistence consumption expenditure.

Clearly, the OLS line (4.35) could again be used for predictive purposes. For example, if the above line had been estimated in 1992 and, at that time, it was forecast that in 1995 aggregate disposable income per capita would be $X_{95}=92.43$, then we could predict aggregate consumption per capita in 1995 as

$$\hat{Y}_{95} = 4.16 + 0.846(92.43) = 82.36$$

Exercise 4.6

The following data refers to transaction demand for cash balances M ($billions) and national income Y ($billions) for an economy over 11 consecutive years:

M	21.3	24.2	26.4	27.1	28.5	29.2	30.1	33.2	34.7	37.2	39.0
Y	80.6	95.1	103.4	110.3	114.3	117.3	120.8	134.4	139.2	150.3	156.2

$$\sum m^2 = 298.9, \quad \sum y^2 = 5386.7, \quad \sum my = 1265.9$$

(lower-case letters denote deviations from means).

Assuming a relationship of the form $M = \alpha + \beta Y + \epsilon$, obtain the OLS estimators of α and β. Find and interpret the coefficient of determination for this data.

4.4 Some words of warning

There are two reasons to be very cautious when calculating standard regression statistics such as the OLS estimators $\hat{\alpha}$ and $\hat{\beta}$, and the coefficients of determination and correlation.

Sampling variability

First, any set of regression statistics are specific to the sample used in their calculation. For example, in Section 4.2 we used a cross-sectional sample of 25 four-person households to calculate the OLS estimators of the intercept and slope of the population regression line (4.1). However, if we selected a second sample of 25 four-person households from the same population then almost certainly these households would have different incomes and expenditures from those in the first sample. Thus the X_i and Y_i used to compute $\hat{\alpha}$ and $\hat{\beta}$ would be different, so that our second sample would lead to different values for the OLS estimators. Similarly, a third sample would lead to yet different estimates again. The OLS estimators are subject to **sampling variability**.

It should be clear that if we visualize a situation where many samples of four-person households, all size 25, are taken from the given population then **sampling distributions** for the OLS estimators will arise. These are akin to the sampling distribution of the sample mean $\bar{X}$ discussed in the last chapter. Unfortunately, whereas we saw there that the sample mean is an unbiased estimator of a population mean μ, there is no guarantee that the OLS estimation method will provide such 'good' estimators of regression parameters. As we noted earlier, it is necessary for a whole series of assumptions, described in Chapter 6, to be valid if the OLS estimators are to be 'good' estimators in any sense.

The measures of closeness of fit discussed in Section 4.3 will also be subject to sampling variability. For example, the R^2 calculated is an estimate of a population coefficient of determination that measures *for the whole population of households* the proportion of consumption variations that can be attributed to variations in income. Obviously, we hope that the value $R^2 = 0.691$ found provides an adequate estimate of this population measure. But again, unless further assumptions are made, there can be no guarantee that this will be so.

When dealing with aggregate time series data, as in Section 4.3, it is rather more difficult to envisage sampling distributions arising for the OLS estimators. It would be somewhat contrived to pretend that, first, another 20 years data eventually becomes available, and then, later, yet a further 20 years data and so on. Rather, we must regard the underlying economic system, that has generated the 20 observations for 1971–90, as having been capable of generating any number of possible 'realizations' for this period.[4] The sample of actual data for 1971–90 represents just one of these possible realizations – the one actually experienced. Any of the other realizations *might* have occurred, but in fact did not. A different realization would have meant a different set of observations on X and Y and hence different values for the OLS estimators. Hence, if we visualize a large number of different alternative realizations, we have a framework in which sampling distributions for the estimators will arise. Again, only if we are prepared to accept some or all of the assumptions dealt with in Chapter 6, will these sampling distributions have acceptable properties.

The fact that aggregate data such as that in Table 4.3 refers to the whole economy, yet is still treated as merely a sample rather than a population, sometimes causes students confusion. However, the above discussion should resolve such confusion. The data represents a sample because it is but one realization amongst many possible realizations.

The spurious regression problem

There is a second and often more serious reason why we should be cautious in interpreting regression statistics. Notice that we have been careful to define the coefficient of determination, R^2, as the proportion of the variation in a dependent Y variable that *can be attributed to* variations in an explanatory X variable. It can be very dangerous, particularly when dealing with time series data, to replace the words 'can be attributed to' by the words '*are caused by*'.

We have already noted that R^2, being the square of the correlation coefficient, is, strictly speaking, a measure merely of association with nothing to say about causality.[5] However, since causality is implicitly assumed at the outset in OLS regression analysis, there is a natural tendency to assume that high values for R^2 are indicative of a strong ability of the X variable to 'explain' the dependent Y variable. Unfortunately, high values for the coefficient of determination are often very easy to achieve when dealing with economic time series data, even when the causal link between two variables is extremely tenuous or perhaps non-existent.

The problem is that many economic time series exhibit persistent **trends** over time. For example, in many countries, over the postwar era from 1945 on, economic variables such as price indices, output levels or money stocks have trended consistently upwards. Clearly, if we compute coefficients of correlation and determination for any two such variables then we will obtain values fairly close to unity, even if the variables were in no way related. This is because the highest values for both variables will occur during the later part of the period and the lowest values during the earlier part. Even if there is some genuine causal link between the variables, the common trends they possess are likely to result in artificially inflated values for R and R^2. That is, much of the apparent association discovered between the two variables is **spurious**. For example, in Section 4.3 we obtained a value for R^2 of 0.992 for the data in Table 4.3. However, inspection of Table 4.3 reveals that both the variables consumption and income are trending consistently upwards during this sample period. This means that we should treat this value for R^2 with a very large pinch of salt. Much, although not all, of the 'explanation' of variations in consumption provided by our regression line (4.35) is likely to be spurious.

We shall have much to say about the problems of spurious regression results in the remainder of this book. It is a problem that has frequently been ignored by econometricians. However, during the past decade or so, considerably more attention has been devoted to dealing with it.

4.5 Nonlinear regression

Throughout this chapter so far, we have assumed that the underlying population regression line has the linear form (4.1). Our measures of closeness of fit have also been linear measures. For example, the coefficient of correlation (4.33) is a measure of the strength of the *linear* association between two variables.

Clearly, there is no reason why economic relationships should always be linear or even approximately linear. As our next example, we shall refer back to the cross-section of 25 Transvenian households of Section 4.1. In Table 4.4 we have the data on their total consumption expenditure together with data on their expenditure on food. We shall examine the relationship between these two variables. Cross-sectional relationships between expenditure on some particular commodity grouping and total expenditure are commonly known as **Engel curves**.[6]

Since expenditure on food is dependent on the total expenditure a household is able to make, rather than vice versa, we shall adopt food expenditure as the dependent Y variable and total expenditure as the explanatory X variable.

A scatter diagram of the 25 observations is shown in Figure 4.8. There appears to be some sort of positive relationship between X and Y, but it looks very unlikely that the relationship is a linear one. Although as X increases Y also rises, the relationship appears nonlinear.

Table 4.4 Household food expenditure Y

Household	X	Y
1	52.30	45.33
2	78.44	45.11
3	88.76	46.14
4	54.08	33.87
5	111.44	48.43
6	105.20	48.73
7	45.73	37.24
8	122.35	55.76
9	142.24	62.34
10	86.22	45.62
11	174.50	66.89
12	185.20	65.32
13	111.80	56.23
14	214.60	71.22
15	144.60	61.34
16	174.36	63.78
17	215.40	70.56
18	286.24	68.45
19	188.56	67.11
20	237.20	64.32
21	181.80	58.24
22	373.00	73.12
23	191.60	63.14
24	247.12	72.54
25	269.60	68.13

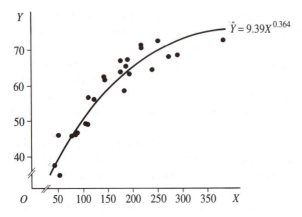

Figure 4.8 A nonlinear regression equation.

Clearly, it is not appropriate to attempt to fit a straight line to this scatter and we shall attempt the fitting of a curve. Consider the nonlinear function

$$Y = AX^\beta, \quad A > 0 \tag{4.36}$$

where A and β are constants.

The graph of (4.36) is sketched in Figures 4.9(a,b) for various ranges of β. It can be seen that there is a strong likelihood that such a function, with $0 < \beta < 1$, might be made to fit the points in our scatter quite well, if appropriate values of A and β are selected. But how are we to select these values, and can we use the method of ordinary least squares outlined earlier in this chapter?

The nonlinear function (4.36) has one very useful property: it can be transformed into a linear function simply by taking logarithms of any base. Taking natural logarithms (i.e. to base e), we have

$$\ln(Y) = \ln(A) + \beta \ln(X) \tag{4.37}$$

Equation (4.37) expresses $\ln(Y)$ as a linear function of $\ln(X)$, and we may rewrite it as

$$Y^* = \alpha + \beta X^* \tag{4.38}$$

where $Y^* = \ln(Y)$, $X^* = \ln(X)$ and $\alpha = \ln(A)$.

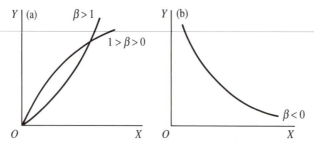

Figure 4.9 (a) and (b) Double-logarithmic functions.

We are now in a position to apply our standard *linear* regression model using the linear relationship (4.38). Working in terms of the *transformed* variables Y^* and X^*, we define a population regression equation analogous to (4.1),

$$E(Y^*) = \alpha + \beta X^* \tag{4.39}$$

and introduce a disturbance ϵ to allow for differences between Y^* and $E(Y^*)$, so that

$$Y^* = \alpha + \beta X^* + \epsilon \tag{4.40}$$

We now use the method of ordinary least squares to estimate (4.39) by a linear sample regression line of the form

$$\hat{Y}^* = \hat{\alpha} + \hat{\beta} X^* \tag{4.41}$$

where $\hat{Y}^*$ is the predicted value of $Y^* = \ln(Y)$. In fact we choose $\hat{\alpha}$ and $\hat{\beta}$ so as to minimize the sum of the squares of residuals e_i, where now

$$e_i = Y_i^* - \hat{Y}_i^*, \quad i = 1, 2, 3, \ldots, n \tag{4.42}$$

The expressions for the OLS estimators of α and β in (4.39) take the usual forms (4.16) and (4.18), except that the transformed variables X^* and Y^* replace the original variables X and Y. That is,

$$\hat{\alpha} = \bar{Y}^* - \hat{\beta} \bar{X}^* \tag{4.43}$$

where $\bar{X}^* = \sum X_i^*/n$ and $\bar{Y}^* = \sum Y_i^*/n$, and

$$\hat{\beta} = \frac{\sum x_i^* y_i^*}{\sum x_i^*} \tag{4.44}$$

where $x_i^* = X_i^* - \bar{X}^*$ and $y_i^* = Y_i^* - \bar{Y}^*$.

Table 4.5 indicates the basic calculations in terms of X^* and Y^* that are required for the computation of (4.43) and (4.44). The basic building blocks are

$$\sum x_i^* = 7.403, \quad \sum y_i^* = 1.107, \quad \sum x_i^* y_i^* = 2.694$$

so that, using (4.44), we obtain $\hat{\beta} = 0.364$.

We can also obtain, from Table 4.5, $\bar{X}^* = 4.962$ and $\bar{Y}^* = 4.046$, so that, using (4.43), $\hat{\alpha} = 2.24$. Our sample regression equation (4.41) is therefore

$$\hat{Y}^* = 2.24 + 0.364 X^* \tag{4.45}$$

or, in terms of the original variables,

$$\widehat{\ln(Y)} = 2.24 + 0.364 \ln(X) \tag{4.46}$$

Equations (4.45) and (4.46) represent our estimate of the linear population regression line (4.39). However, to see how (4.46) relates to the scatter in Figure 4.8, we must rewrite it in terms of X and Y rather than $\ln(X)$ and $\ln(Y)$. We therefore obtain

$$\hat{Y} = 9.39 X^{0.364} \quad (\ln(9.39) = 2.24) \tag{4.47}$$

Table 4.5   Basic calculation for double-logarithmic regression

Household	$X^* = \ln(X)$	$Y^* = \ln(Y)$	$X^{*2} = [\ln(X)]^2$	$Y^{*2} = [\ln(Y)]^2$	$X^*Y^* = \ln(X)\ln(Y)$
1	3.9570	3.8140	15.6578	14.5464	15.0919
2	4.3623	3.8091	19.0300	14.5093	16.6166
3	4.4859	3.8317	20.1236	14.6818	17.1887
4	3.9905	3.5225	15.9238	12.4082	14.0565
5	4.7135	3.8801	22.2170	15.0553	18.2889
6	4.6559	3.8863	21.6771	15.1033	18.0941
7	3.8228	3.6174	14.6135	13.0855	13.8284
⋮	⋮	⋮	⋮	⋮	⋮
21	5.2029	4.0646	27.0702	16.5207	21.1476
22	5.9216	4.2921	35.0651	18.4221	25.4160
23	5.2554	4.1454	27.6193	17.1840	21.7855
24	5.5099	4.2841	30.3587	18.3538	23.6051
25	5.5969	4.2214	31.3257	17.8204	23.6270
	124.04	101.14	622.81	410.32	504.52

The sample regression relationship (4.47) has in fact been sketched on the scatter diagram in Figure 4.8. We see that (4.47) is a curve that fits the scatter rather better than any straight line could.

At this point, it is useful to pause and consider exactly what we have done in fitting the curve in Figure 4.8. We have in fact used *linear* regression analysis to fit a *nonlinear* function to a scatter of points. We did this by using transformed variables $X^* = \ln(X)$ and $Y^* = \ln(Y)$. This enabled us to replace a nonlinear population relationship by the relationship (4.39), which was linear in the *transformed* variables.

We can, of course, calculate a coefficient of determination for our fitted relationship. Working again in terms of the transformed variables and using (4.31), we have

$$R^2 = \frac{(0.364)^2 7.403}{1.107} = 0.886$$

It is tempting to interpret this figure of 0.886 as telling us the proportion of the total variation in food demand Y that can be attributed to variations in total expenditure X. However, we must be more careful in our interpretation. R^2 is always a measure of the strength of the *linear* association between two variables. The linear relationship that we have estimated is between $\ln(Y)$ and $\ln(X)$, not between Y and X, and it is to this relationship that the R^2 refers. A correct interpretation of the 0.886 is therefore to say that 88.6% of variations in $\ln(Y)$ can be attributed to variations in $\ln(X)$.

Since we have fitted a curve rather than a straight line to the scatter in Figure 4.8, the interpretation we give to the OLS estimators differs from that in our previous examples. Because our population relationship is based on the function (4.36), the parameter β is in fact the elasticity of food expenditure Y with respect to total expenditure X of Transvenian households. Our estimate of this elasticity is $\hat{\beta} = 0.364$. That is, we estimate that a 1% rise in total expenditure will lead to a rise of 0.364% in food expenditure. Notice that this elasticity is considerably less than unity, as we would expect since food is a necessity rather than a luxury good.

As in Section 4.2, we can use our sample regression relationship to make predictions about Transvenian households not in our sample. Suppose, for example, household 26 is known to have a total expenditure of $X_{26} = 184.4$. Since $\ln(X_{26}) = 5.217$ we have, using (4.46), that

$$\ln(\widehat{Y_{26}}) = 2.24 + 0.364(5.217) = 4.14$$

Hence we predict that the logarithm of food expenditure for household 26 is 4.14. Our prediction for the actual food expenditure for household 26 is therefore $e^{4.14} = \$62.7$.

Exercise 4.7

The following data refers to a firm's *average* revenue P per unit of output, for varying levels of its output Q:

P	20.3	12.6	7.5	16.5	6.1	9.9
Q	100	250	750	150	1000	400

$$\sum q^2 = 647\,080, \quad \sum p^2 = 149, \quad \sum pq = -8830$$

and, if $A = \ln(P)$ and $B = \ln(Q)$,

$$\sum B = 5.78, \quad \sum A = 2.41$$
$$\sum b^2 = 4.06, \quad \sum a^2 = 1.06, \quad \sum ab = -2.07$$

(lower-case letters denote deviations from means).
(a) Use the data to estimate equations of the form $\hat{P} = \hat{\alpha} + \hat{\beta}Q$ and $\hat{P} = \hat{K}Q^{\hat{\beta}}$.
(b) Sketch both your equations on the same scatter diagram with P- and Q-axes. Comment on your results.
(c) Use the second of your equations to estimate the elasticity of demand for the firm's product.

Alternative nonlinear regression equations

The function (4.36) is known as a **double-logarithmic** function, because it can be reduced to linear form simply by taking logarithms of both sides. Obviously, however, we cannot expect a double-log function to fit closely every nonlinear scatter of points that we meet. It is normally necessary to consider a number of possible

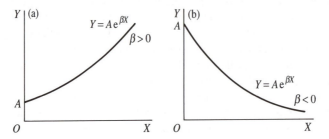

Figure 4.10 (a) and (b) Exponential functions.

nonlinear functions, before selecting one that may be appropriate for a particular scatter. There are a number of convenient possibilities.

The **exponential function** has the form

$$Y = Ae^{\beta X}, \qquad A > 0 \tag{4.48}$$

and is graphed in Figures 4.10(a,b) for positive and negative values of β. It can be reduced to convenient linear form by taking natural logarithms (remember $\ln(e) = 1$):

$$\ln(Y) = \alpha + \beta X, \qquad \alpha = \ln(A) \tag{4.49}$$

This suggests that, if either of the curves in Figures 4.10(a,b) look likely to fit our scatter then we should define a transformed variable $Y^* = \ln(Y)$ and adopt as our hypothesized population regression equation[7]

$$E(Y^*) = \alpha + \beta X \tag{4.50}$$

Linear regression analysis can now proceed, but with the normal OLS estimating formulae expressed in terms of X and Y^*.

The **semi-logarithmic function** has the form

$$Y = \alpha + \beta \ln(X) \tag{4.51}$$

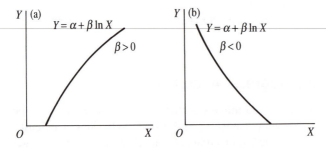

Figure 4.11 (a) and (b) Semi-logarithmic functions.

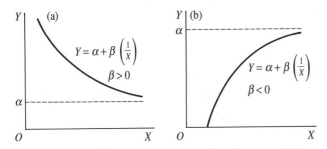

Figure 4.12 (a) and (b) Hyperbolic functions.

and is graphed in Figures 4.11(a,b) for positive and negative values of β. If either of these curves looks likely to fit a scatter then what needs to be done is to define the transformed variable $X^* = \ln(X)$ and adopt the population regression equation[8]

$$E(Y) = \alpha + \beta X^* \tag{4.52}$$

The OLS formula will now be in terms of Y and X^*.

As a final example, consider the **hyperbolic function** which has the form

$$Y = \alpha + \beta \frac{1}{X} \tag{4.53}$$

and is graphed in Figures 4.12(a,b). For appropriate scatters, we would now define the transformed variable X^* as $1/X$ and again adopt a population regression equation of the form (4.52).[9]

Clearly, when there are a number of possible nonlinear forms that might fit a particular scatter diagram, we need some criteria for determining which is the most appropriate. When the dependent variable used in the regression is the same (as, for example, it would be if we wished to compare the forms (4.51) and (4.53) above), the coefficient of determination is one possible measure we could use for discriminating purposes. Unfortunately, when the dependent variable differs, matters are not so simple. For example, suppose we fitted equations based on (4.49) and (4.51) to the same data set. The linear R^2 for Equation (4.49) would tell us the proportion of the variation in $\ln(Y)$ that could be attributed to variations in X. However, the linear R^2 relating to (4.51) would tell us the proportion of the variation in Y that could be attributed to variations in $\ln(X)$. We could not use these R^2s to tell us which relationship fitted the data best, because we would not then be comparing like with like. Other measures of the adequacy of fit are then necessary. We shall return to this problem in Chapter 12.

Determining the appropriate functional form is one aspect of what is known as the **specification problem** in econometrics. The specification problem is simply that of specifying an appropriate population relationship. When we discuss multiple regression analysis, we shall see that another aspect of this problem is that of determining the number and nature of the explanatory variables to be included in a relationship. Problems of specification and misspecification are among the most important in econometrics, but we shall defer further discussion of them until later in the text.

Exercise 4.8

For the data on average costs and outputs in Exercise 4.3, values for $B = 1/Q$ are

$$0.056 \quad 0.040 \quad 0.019 \quad 0.111 \quad 0.026 \quad 0.032$$

and, with lower-case letters again denoting deviations,

$$\sum b^2 = 0.005\ 68, \qquad \sum ab = 27.57$$

(a) Estimate $\hat{\alpha}$ and $\hat{\beta}$ in the equation $\hat{A} = \hat{\alpha} + \hat{\beta}(1/Q)$. What is the coefficient of determination for your regression?

(b) Sketch both the equation estimated in (a) and that estimated in Exercise 4.3 on the *same* scatter diagram, with A on the vertical axis and Q on the horizontal axis.

(c) Compare the coefficients of determination for the two equations and comment.

Exercise 4.9

Annual data for the UK economy, for the years 1953–64, on the percentage change in wage rates W and the percentage of the labour force unemployed U were as follows:

W	4.4	5.4	7.1	6.2	4.2	3.1	2.6	3.3	3.8	3.6	4.1	4.4
U	1.5	1.3	1.1	1.2	1.4	2.1	2.2	1.6	1.5	2.0	2.1	1.6

(a) If $\sum w^2 = 18.77$, $\sum u^2 = 1.567$ and $\sum wu = -4.45$, estimate a relationship of the form $W = \alpha + \beta U + \epsilon$. Calculate the coefficient of determination R^2 for this regression.

(b) Estimate a relationship of the form $W = \alpha + \beta N + \epsilon$, where $N = \ln(U)$, if $\sum n^2 = 0.591$ and $\sum wn = -2.86$. Calculate R^2 for this regression, and comment.

(c) In 1967, $W = 5.1$ and $U = 2.4$. Does this suggest any shift in the relationship estimated in (b)?

(In parts (a) and (b) lower-case letters, as usual, denote deviations of variables from their means.)

Appendix 4A

Notes to Chapter 4

1. Both the life-cycle hypothesis and the permanent income hypothesis of consumer behaviour suggest that consumption depends not so much on income

as on some measure of total lifetime resources. At the very least, some measure of consumer wealth needs to be included in a consumption function. We will introduce such a variable in Chapter 7 when we deal with multiple regression analysis.

2. The second-order partial derivatives are

$$\frac{\partial^2 S}{\partial \hat{\alpha}^2} = 2n, \qquad \frac{\partial^2 S}{\partial \hat{\beta}^2} = 2 \sum_i X_i^2, \qquad \frac{\partial^2 S}{\partial \hat{\alpha}\, \partial \hat{\beta}} = 2 \sum_i X_i$$

It is therefore easily verified that the second-order conditions for a minimum are met.

3. With time series data, it is no longer possible to abstract from price changes. Consumption equations must therefore be specified in real or constant price terms. That is, consumption and income data must be deflated by some general index of prices. The data in Table 4.3 is therefore the result of the deflation by a price index with 1980 base.

4. The underlying economic system is in fact represented by the population regression line (4.1), and the different possible realizations exist because, even if the income X-values were to remain unchanged, the values of the disturbance ϵ can differ from realization to realization.

5. We are at present using the words 'cause' and 'causality' in their everyday sense. In fact, as we shall see towards the end of this text, causality has a very precise (and some might say peculiar) meaning to econometricians.

6. Engel curves are named after E. Engel, an economist who performed cross-sectional studies of demand in the mid-nineteenth century.

7. Unlike in the double-log case, the elasticity of Y with respect to X is not a constant for (4.49). Rather, as in the linear case, it varies with the values of X and Y. In fact, for Equation (4.49), the elasticity is given by $(dY/dX)(X/Y) = \beta X$.

8. In the semi-log case the elasticity of Y with respect to X again varies with the values of X and Y. For Equation (4.52), the elasticity is given by $(dY/dX)(X/Y) = \beta / Y$.

9. However, in this case the elasticity of Y with respect to X is given by $(dY/dX)(X/Y) = -\beta / XY$.

5

Estimators and methods of estimation

As we have stressed in the last two chapters, population parameters are unknown, and therefore frequently have to be estimated. We saw in Chapter 3 that there are two forms of estimator: the point estimator and the confidence interval. Although in that chapter we spent more time on confidence intervals, there are many occasions where specifying a range for an unknown parameter is not enough, and we require a single number or point estimate. When we select a point estimator, obviously we want the estimate we obtain to be a 'good' estimate in some sense. The first part of this chapter is therefore spent describing the properties an estimator could have or needs to have if it is to be regarded as a 'good' estimator. Once we have defined what we mean by a 'good' estimator, the problem arises of how we should find such estimators. In the final two sections of this chapter we therefore look at various methods by which 'good' estimators can be found.

To set the scene for our discussion of the desired properties of estimators, suppose we have a population of values for a random variable X. The values of X are determined by some probability distribution, which may or may not be known. Suppose that this population has, as one of its characteristics, the parameter θ. θ might, for example, be the population mean or the population variance. Alternatively, it might be one of the parameters α or β in a two-variable regression equation. However, to keep the analysis completely general, we shall not specify what the parameter θ actually is.

Suppose θ has to be estimated from a random sample of n observations on X, which we represent as $(X_1, X_2, X_3, \ldots, X_n)$. Thus X_i is the ith sample observation. We shall use the symbol $\hat{\theta}$ for an estimator of the true θ. Such an estimator will be some expression or formula involving some or all of the X_i. That is, it will be a function of the sample observations:

$$\hat{\theta} = \hat{\theta}(X_1, X_2, X_3, \ldots, X_n) \tag{5.1}$$

For example, if $\hat{\theta}$ were simply the population mean then one possible estimator would be the sample mean, which, of course, is a function of all the X_i. That is,

$$\bar{X} = \frac{X_1 + X_2 + X_3 + \cdots + X_n}{n}$$

Note that, while we refer to formulae such as (5.1) as **estimators**, when we actually substitute sample values into such formulae, the single number we then obtain is referred to as an **estimate**.

The important point to remember is that *all estimators such as (5.1) will possess sampling distributions*. That is, since different samples will contain different X values, they will provide different values of $\hat{\theta}$. If many such samples are taken, we obtain a distribution of values for $\hat{\theta}$, with its own mean $E(\hat{\theta})$ and variance $E[\hat{\theta} - E(\hat{\theta})]$.

5.1   The small-sample properties of estimators

Properties of estimators fall into two categories: **small-sample properties** and **large-sample** or **asymptotic properties**. In this section we discuss properties whose attributes are apparent no matter what the size of the samples from which estimates are being obtained. Such properties are referred to as small-sample properties because, when possessed by an estimator, their attributes are apparent *even when the sample size is small*. In the next section we shall discuss properties whose attributes only become apparent when the sample size is large. These are the large-sample or asymptotic properties.

Unbiasedness

The first small-sample property that we might like estimators to have is that of unbiasedness. We discussed this in Chapter 3 in relation to the population mean and variance. In general, an estimator $\hat{\theta}$ is said to be an **unbiased estimator** of a parameter θ if

$$E(\hat{\theta}) = \theta \tag{5.2}$$

That is, the mean of the sampling distribution for $\hat{\theta}$ equals the parameter being estimated, as illustrated in Figure 5.1. In colloquial terms, this implies that if we take

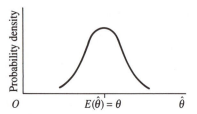

Figure 5.1 Sampling distribution for an unbiased estimator.

many samples of a fixed size then the average value of all the different $\hat{\theta}$s obtained will equal the true θ.

If an estimator is such that (5.2) is not true then it is said to be a **biased estimator**. The difference between $E(\hat{\theta})$ and θ is known as the **bias**. That is,

$$\text{Bias } (\hat{\theta}) = E(\hat{\theta}) - \theta \tag{5.3}$$

If $\hat{\theta}$ tends to overestimate θ 'on average' over many samples then the bias is **positive**. If $\hat{\theta}$ tends to underestimate θ then the bias is **negative**.

We encountered examples of biased and unbiased estimators in Chapter 3. Recall that the sample mean $\bar{X}$ was an unbiased estimator of the population mean μ, because $E(\bar{X}) = \mu$. However, the sample variance v^2, worked out using (3.4), was a biased estimator of the population variance σ^2, because $E(v^2) \neq \sigma^2$. The bias was in this case negative, since v^2 tends to underestimate σ^2.

In practice, of course, we normally take but one sample. This being the case, the fact that if we did take 'very many' samples we would get 'on average' the right answer is but cold comfort. Recall that areas under the sampling distribution in Figure 5.1 represent probabilities. Even if our estimator is unbiased, for the single sample we take there is therefore a probability of getting a value for $\hat{\theta}$ some way away from the true θ. If the variance of $\hat{\theta}$ happens to be large then we might be unlucky enough to get a value very far away from θ. Clearly, if possible, we would therefore like an estimator not only to be unbiased but also to have a small variance. That is, we would like the dispersion of its sampling distribution to be as small as possible. This leads us to our next desired property.

Efficiency

An estimator $\hat{\theta}$ is said to be an **efficient estimator** *of a parameter θ if (a) it is unbiased, that is, $E(\hat{\theta}) = \theta$, and (b) no other unbiased estimator of θ has a smaller variance.*

By seeking the efficient estimator, what we are doing effectively is minimizing the probability of obtaining an estimate 'a long way away' from the true θ. Note that, before an estimator can be efficient, it must be unbiased. For this reason, an efficient estimator is sometimes referred to as a **best unbiased estimator**.

Although efficiency is one of the most desirable properties that an estimator can possess, it turns out that *the* efficient estimator is often difficult to find. Demonstrating unbiasedness simply involves taking the expected value of an estimator and checking

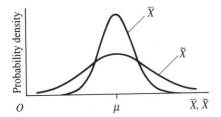

Figure 5.2 Relative efficiency.

that it equals the parameter being estimated. However, demonstrating the efficiency of an unbiased estimator involves checking that its variance is the minimum among the variances of *all* unbiased estimators. Mathematically, this is a much harder task, and for this reason the word 'efficiency' is also used in a relative sense. For example, the sample mean $\bar{X}$ is an unbiased estimator of the population mean μ. An alternative unbiased estimator of μ is

$$\tilde{X} = \tfrac{1}{2}(X_{\mathrm{L}} + X_{\mathrm{S}})$$

where X_{L} and X_{S} are the largest and smallest observations in the sample taken. However, if many samples are taken, it turns out that the variance of $\bar{X}$ is smaller than the variance of $\tilde{X}$ (their sampling distributions are illustrated in Figure 5.2).[1] $\bar{X}$ is therefore said to be **relatively more efficient** than $\tilde{X}$. What this means is that, if we estimate μ by $\bar{X}$, then there is a smaller probability of obtaining an estimate 'a long way away' from μ than there would be if we were to use the estimator $\tilde{X}$.

The difficulty, discussed above, of finding *the* efficient estimator has meant that statisticians frequently restrict their search for efficiency to a subset of all unbiased estimators. This is because it is often much easier to find the most efficient estimator amongst all *linear* unbiased estimators.

A linear estimator is one that can be expressed as a linear function of the sample observations. That is, it has the form

$$\hat{\theta} = a_1 X_1 + a_2 X_2 + a_3 X_3 + \cdots + a_n X_n \tag{5.4}$$

where the *a*s are fixed constants. For example, the sample mean $\bar{X}$ is a linear estimator of the population mean, because it can be expressed in the form

$$\bar{X} = \frac{1}{n} X_1 + \frac{1}{n} X_2 + \frac{1}{n} X_3 + \cdots + \frac{1}{n} X_n$$

There is no reason why a linear estimator should necessarily be a 'good' estimator in any sense. Since the *a*s in (5.4) could take any (possibly silly) values, such an estimator might, for example, be seriously biased. However, the advantage of linear estimators is that they are much easier to handle mathematically than nonlinear estimators, and thus it is often relatively easy to find the most efficient unbiased linear estimator. Limiting attention to such estimators leads to a third desirable small-sample property.

Best linear unbiasedness

An estimator $\hat{\theta}$ is said to be a **best linear unbiased estimator** *(BLUE) of a parameter*
θ if (a) it is a linear estimator, (b) it is unbiased and (c) no other linear unbiased
estimator has a smaller variance.

A BLUE is not necessarily the 'best' estimator, since there may well be some
nonlinear estimator with a smaller sampling variance than the BLUE. In many
situations, however, the efficient estimator may be so difficult to find that we have to
be satisfied with the BLUE (provided of course that the BLUE itself can be obtained).
Note, though, that if the efficient estimator happens to be a linear estimator then the
BLUE and the efficient estimator will be identical.

Mean square error

We have now defined three properties that we might like our estimators to have.
Essentially, we have been concerned with two aspects of estimators: their variance,
which we like to be small, and whether or not they are unbiased. However, suppose it
is not possible to find an estimator that is both unbiased and has a small variance.
Consider, for example, the two sampling distributions illustrated in Figure 5.3.

The estimator $\hat{\theta}_1$ is the efficient estimator of θ. It is therefore unbiased, but
happens to have a large variance. The estimator $\hat{\theta}_2$ is biased (slightly), but has a much
smaller variance. Which estimator should we prefer? It is true that while $\hat{\theta}_1$ is
unbiased, $\hat{\theta}_2$ tends systematically to overestimate the parameter θ (i.e. it has a small
positive bias). However, remember that areas under the curves in Figure 5.3 represent
probabilities, so that, for the single sample taken, we are far more likely to obtain an
estimate 'far away' from the true θ if we use the estimator $\hat{\theta}_1$ than if we make use of
$\hat{\theta}_2$. Might it not be wiser to put up with the small positive bias in $\hat{\theta}_2$ for the sake of its
smaller variance? That is, should we not be prepared to trade off some bias for a
smaller variance?

It is helpful at this point to define the mean square error of an estimator. Like the
variance, the mean square error relates to the dispersion of the sampling distribution
of an estimator. However, whereas the variance measures dispersion about the
expected value of an estimator, the mean square error measures dispersion about

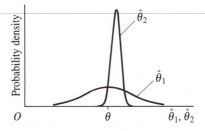

Figure 5.3 Trading off bias and variance.

the true value of the parameter being estimated. The **mean square error** (MSE) is defined as

$$\text{MSE} \, (\hat{\theta}) = \text{E}(\hat{\theta} - \theta)^2 \tag{5.5}$$

Since Var $(\hat{\theta}) = \text{E}[\hat{\theta} - \text{E}(\hat{\theta})]^2$, the variance and the MSE will only be the same if $\text{E}(\hat{\theta}) = \theta$, that is, if the estimator is unbiased. Otherwise, the relationship between MSE and variance can be shown to be[2]

$$\text{MSE} \, (\hat{\theta}) = \text{Var} \, (\hat{\theta}) + [\text{Bias} \, (\hat{\theta})]^2 \tag{5.6}$$

where the bias is given by (5.3). Thus the MSE is simply the sum of the variance and the squared bias.

From (5.6), we see that the MSE provides us with a way of formalizing the trade-off between the desire for a small bias and the desire for a small variance, mentioned above. If possible, we simply *select the estimator with the smallest mean square error*. In this way, we hope to avoid the possibility of either too large a bias or too large a variance.[3] Also, since the MSE is simply the average squared difference between the value of an estimator and the true value of the parameter, its minimization is a sensible aim in itself. Notice that if two estimators are unbiased then, since the variances and MSEs are now identical, choosing the estimator with the smaller MSE is the equivalent of selecting the more efficient estimator.

Finally, notice that in discussing the properties of this section, we have made no reference to the size of samples taken. Sample size could have been large or, more particularly, small. For this reason, all the properties discussed are what we described earlier as small-sample properties.

Exercise 5.1

A variable X has mean μ and variance σ^2. To estimate μ from a random sample of size n, three estimators are proposed:

$$\tilde{\mu} = \bar{X} + 3, \qquad \hat{\mu} = \bar{X} + \frac{80}{n}, \qquad \mu^* = \frac{n}{n+1}\bar{X}$$

where $\bar{X}$ is the sample mean. Recall that $\text{E}(\bar{X}) = \mu$ and $\text{Var} \, (\bar{X}) = \sigma^2/n$. Use Theorem 2.1 of chapter 2 for the following:
(a) Show that all three proposed estimators are biased. What is the bias in each case? If $n = 20$ and $\mu = 70$, which estimator has the largest bias?
(b) Find the variance of the sampling distribution for each estimator.

Exercise 5.2

A variable X has mean μ and variance σ^2. Two independent samples of observations on X, of sizes n and m, have sample means $\bar{X}_n$ and $\bar{X}_m$ respectively. Two possible estimators of μ are being considered:

$$\hat{\mu}_1 = \frac{1}{3}\bar{X}_n + \frac{2}{3}\bar{X}_m, \qquad \hat{\mu}_2 = \frac{n}{n+m}\bar{X}_n + \frac{m}{n+m}\bar{X}_m$$

Show that (i) both estimators are unbiased; (ii) that if $n = m$ then $\hat{\mu}_2$ is the more efficient estimator.

Exercise 5.3

Find the mean square errors of the three proposed estimators in Exercise 5.1. If $n = 20$, $\mu = 70$ and $\sigma^2 = 25$, which mean square error is the smallest?

5.2 The large-sample properties of estimators

In later chapters of this book we shall discover that, when dealing with economic data, it is rarely the case that the estimators we employ have any of the desirable small-sample properties described in the last section. In two-variable regression analysis, for example, we will frequently have to make do with estimators of α and β that only possess what we referred to earlier as *large-sample or asymptotic properties*. That is, they become 'good' estimators, and their sampling distributions take on desirable properties, only as the sample size becomes very large or tends to infinity. We therefore need to evaluate the way a sampling distribution changes as the sample size increases. To do this, and to properly understand the large-sample properties of estimators, we must first grasp the concepts of asymptotic distributions and probability limits.

Asymptotic distributions and probability limits

We shall introduce these ideas by way of an example. Suppose we have a population of values for a random variable X, which has mean μ and variance σ^2. We shall assume that the population is *non-normally distributed*. For example, the probability distribution for X might take any of the shapes illustrated in Figure 3.2. If we take a random sample, of size n, from this population, we can estimate μ by the sample mean $\bar{X}$. Let us consider the sampling distribution for $\bar{X}$.

Suppose, first, that our sample size is 'small' (e.g. $n = 10$). We saw in Theorem 3.1 that, even for such small samples, the sampling distribution for $\bar{X}$ will have mean $E(\bar{X}) = \mu$ and variance $\sigma_{\bar{X}}^2 = \sigma^2/n$. However, *for such small samples*, we can say nothing about the shape of the sampling distribution of $\bar{X}$. This is likely to reflect the shape of the parent population distribution, which may well be unknown.

However, suppose we make the size of the samples taken become gradually larger. We know from Theorem 3.2 that, as n becomes larger, the sampling distribution for $\bar{X}$ approaches a normal distribution with the above mean μ and variance σ^2/n. The larger the sample size, the better the approximation. Remember that the point about Theorem 3.2, the so-called Central Limit Theorem, is that the sampling distribution for $\bar{X}$ approaches the normal distribution *regardless of the shape of the parent population distribution*. Hence, as n becomes larger, the sampling distribution would approach normality for any of the parent distributions illustrated in Figure 3.2. This $N(\mu, \sigma^2/n)$ distribution is referred to as the **asymptotic distribution** for $\bar{X}$.

In general, the asymptotic distribution for any estimator $\hat{\theta}$ is that distribution to which the sampling distribution for $\hat{\theta}$ tends as the sample size becomes larger. Asymptotic distributions need not always have the shape of the normal distribution, although in practice, as in the above example, they frequently do. The example of the sample mean $\bar{X}$ is further illustrated in Figure 5.4, where the sampling distribution for $\bar{X}$ has a non-normal shape when the size of samples taken, n, is small, but approaches normality as n increases.

Remaining with the example of the sample mean $\bar{X}$, suppose we now make the size of the samples taken very large indeed. In fact, suppose the sample size $n \to \infty$. We can now see that the normal asymptotic distribution is not, in this case, the final shape taken by the sampling distribution for $\bar{X}$. As $n \to \infty$,

$$\text{Var}(\bar{X}) = \sigma^2/n \to 0$$

Since a zero variance implies no dispersion at all in the sampling distribution for $\bar{X}$, this implies that as $n \to \infty$ (or, in practice, as the size of samples taken becomes very large indeed), the sampling distribution for $\bar{X}$ 'collapses' onto a single value equal to the population mean μ. This is illustrated in Figure 5.5 for increasing size of samples.

When the sampling distribution of an estimator collapses onto a single value in this way, the estimator is said to **converge in probability** to that value. Thus $\bar{X}$ is said to converge in probability to μ. The value to which it converges is then referred to as the **probability limit** (written plim) of the estimator. Thus we say that the probability limit of $\bar{X}$ is μ, that is,

$$\text{plim}(\bar{X}) = \mu \tag{5.7}$$

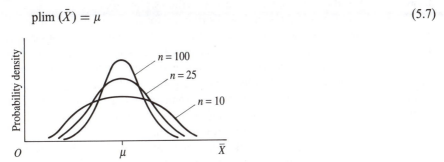

Figure 5.4 The asymptotic distribution of the sample mean.

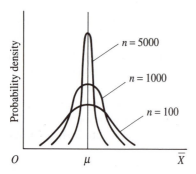

Figure 5.5 Collapse of a sampling distribution.

A number of points may be noted that should help understanding of Figure 5.5 and the concept of a probability limit. First, in Figure 5.5 we are *not* talking about a single sample the size of which is gradually being increased. *Each* curve corresponds to a separate situation in which 'very many' samples are taken of a fixed size. Secondly, since each curve represents a sampling distribution, the areas under the various curves represent probabilities, and for each curve the total area must equal unity. Hence, since the area under the curves is constant, the smaller is the dispersion of a curve, the greater must be its height.

Thirdly, when the curve has collapsed onto a single point, this means that all probability is concentrated at that point. Hence, as the sample size approaches infinity, the probability of obtaining an $\bar{X}$ exactly equal to μ, the parameter being estimated, approaches unity. In everyday terms, this means that if we take many samples of massively large size then each such sample will yield an $\bar{X}$ virtually exactly equal to μ.

We should note at this point that sampling distributions do not necessarily collapse onto a single value as in the above example. That is, the probability limit of an estimator may not in fact exist. However, in most cases such a 'collapse' does occur, so in this text we shall assume, unless stated otherwise, that an estimator $\hat{\theta}$ always has a probability limit, which we shall write as plim $(\hat{\theta})$.

In the above example the sampling distribution for $\bar{X}$ conveniently 'collapsed' onto μ, the parameter being estimated. Unfortunately, sampling distributions do not always collapse onto the right value! In fact, as we shall see in later chapters, it is often the case in regression analysis that the sampling distribution for an estimator $\hat{\theta}$ collapses on to some value that differs from the parameter θ that we are trying to estimate. That is, $\hat{\theta}$ converges in probability to some value other than the true θ. In other words, it is by no means necessarily the case that plim $(\hat{\theta}) = \theta$. This, obviously, has serious implications for the problem of estimation.

Asymptotic distributions, just like any other probability distributions, have means and variances. The mean of an asymptotic distribution is referred to as the **asymptotic mean** of the estimator, and the variance as the **asymptotic variance**. To derive the asymptotic mean of an estimator, we simply note what happens to the mean of the sampling distribution of the estimator as the sample size $n \to \infty$. Deriving the asymptotic variance of an estimator is more difficult, and we shall not pursue this here.

Some properties of probability limits

Probability limits have a number of useful properties, some of which we state here, without proof. Suppose we have a parameter θ_1 for which we have an estimator $\hat{\theta}_1$, and another parameter θ_2 for which we have an estimator $\hat{\theta}_2$. Suppose further that the probability limits of $\hat{\theta}_1$ and $\hat{\theta}_2$ both exist. It can then be shown that, for example,

$$\text{plim} \, (\hat{\theta}_1 + \hat{\theta}_2) = \text{plim} \, (\hat{\theta}_1) + \text{plim} \, (\hat{\theta}_2) \tag{5.8}$$

and

$$\text{plim} \left(\frac{\hat{\theta}_1}{\hat{\theta}_2} \right) = \frac{\text{plim} \, (\hat{\theta}_1)}{\text{plim} \, (\hat{\theta}_2)} \tag{5.9}$$

The significance of the results (5.8) and (5.9) will not become apparent until later chapters. Although we do not attempt to prove such results, an intuitive derivation of them is given in Appendix 5A to this chapter.

We are now in a position to describe the desirable large-sample or asymptotic properties of estimators. Strictly speaking, these properties can only become apparent as sample sizes tend to infinity, but, when held, the properties can be regarded as holding approximately for large samples. However, if an estimator possesses any of these properties, then attributes of the property are not apparent at all for small samples.

Asymptotic unbiasedness

An estimator $\hat{\theta}$ is said to be an **asymptotically unbiased estimator** *of a parameter θ if* $E(\hat{\theta}) \to \theta$ *as* $n \to \infty$.

That is, an estimator is asymptotically unbiased if it becomes unbiased as the sample size tends to infinity. It may well be biased for small samples, but the bias disappears as the size of samples taken becomes very large. Thus its asymptotic mean equals the parameter being estimated. Sampling distributions for an asymptotically unbiased estimator are illustrated in Figure 5.6.

In Figure 5.6 the sampling distribution obtained for $\hat{\theta}$, when the size of samples is $n = 10$, centres itself some way away from the true value of θ. That is, for $n = 10$, $\hat{\theta}$ is biased. However, as the size of samples taken is increased, the sampling distribution shifts across towards θ, so that as $n \to \infty$, the bias disappears.

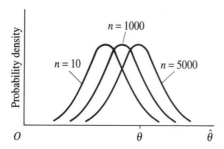

Figure 5.6 Sampling distributions for an asymptotically unbiased estimator.

We have, in fact, already encountered an example of an asymptotically unbiased estimator in Chapter 3. Recall that the sample variance v^2, given by (3.4), was a biased estimator of the population variance σ^2 because

$$E(v^2) = \frac{n-1}{n} \sigma^2 < \sigma^2$$

However, as $n \to \infty$, $(n-1)/n \to 1$, and $E(v^2) \to \sigma^2$. Thus, as the sample size increases, the bias in the estimator v^2 disappears. So v^2 is asymptotically unbiased.

Consistency

An estimator $\hat{\theta}$ is said to be a **consistent estimator** *of a parameter θ if* plim $(\hat{\theta}) = \theta$.

Recall that the probability limit of an estimator is the value onto which its sampling distribution collapses as the size of samples taken, $n \to \infty$. Thus an estimator is consistent if, as $n \to \infty$, its sampling distribution collapses onto a value equal to the parameter being estimated. Put more briefly, an estimator is consistent if it converges in probability to the parameter being estimated. Sampling distributions for a consistent estimator (that happens to be biased in small samples) are illustrated in Figure 5.7.

Notice that in Figure 5.7, as the size of the samples taken increases, the sampling distribution for $\hat{\theta}$ not only shifts across towards the true parameter value θ, as in Figure 5.6, but also becomes less and less dispersed. That is, its variance becomes smaller and smaller until 'in the limit' the distribution collapses onto θ.

Figure 5.7 illustrates a consistent estimator that is biased for small samples. However, it is quite possible for consistent estimators to be unbiased for small samples. We had such an example earlier when we noted that the sample mean $\bar{X}$ had a probability limit equal to the population mean μ. That is, plim $(\bar{X}) = \mu$. Thus $\bar{X}$ is a consistent estimator of μ, but, of course, we know that it is also unbiased in small samples.

Notice that in Figure 5.7, as the sample size gets larger and larger, both the bias and the variance of the estimator $\hat{\theta}$ become smaller and smaller. In fact, a *sufficient*

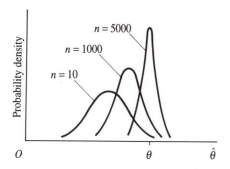

Figure 5.7 Sampling distributions for a consistent estimator.

condition for consistency is that both the variance and the bias (if it exists) of the estimator should tend to zero as n → ∞. Recalling from Equation (5.6) that the mean square error of an estimator equals the sum of the variance and the squared bias, it follows that *an estimator must be consistent if its MSE tends to zero as n* → ∞.

We saw earlier that sampling distributions do not always collapse onto 'the right value'. If the sampling distribution of an estimator $\hat{\theta}$ collapses onto a value that is *not* equal to θ, the parameter being estimated, then the estimator is said to be **inconsistent**. That is, plim $(\hat{\theta}) \neq \theta$. Sampling distributions for an inconsistent estimator are illustrated in Figure 5.8. Notice that not only is such an estimator biased in small samples, but the *bias persists*, however large the samples taken become. In fact, since areas under the curves in Figure 5.8 as usual represent probabilities, while there is at least a chance of obtaining an estimate very close to θ when the sample size is small, as the sample size becomes larger, getting a value close to θ becomes impossible, given the distributions illustrated. Unfortunately, as we shall see, we tend to meet inconsistent estimators frequently in regression analysis using economic data.

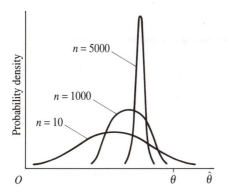

Figure 5.8 Sampling distributions for an inconsistent estimator.

Exercise 5.4

Determine which of the estimators $\tilde{\mu}$, $\hat{\mu}$ and μ^* in Exercise 5.1 are (a) asymptotically unbiased; (b) consistent. (To show consistency, you need to demonstrate that both bias and variance tend to zero as sample size tends to infinity.)

Exercise 5.5

Show that both the estimators $\hat{\mu}_1$ and $\hat{\mu}_2$ in Exercise 5.2 are consistent.

Asymptotic efficiency

Suppose that, when estimating a parameter θ, we have two possible estimators $\hat{\theta}_1$ and $\hat{\theta}_2$, sampling distributions for which are illustrated in Figures 5.9(a,b). Notice, first, that both estimators are consistent, because both have sampling distributions that collapse onto θ as the size of samples taken tends to infinity. Notice, also, that as n increases, the sampling distribution for $\hat{\theta}_1$ collapses onto θ 'more quickly' than that for $\hat{\theta}_2$. In fact, we could say that whereas the sampling distribution for $\hat{\theta}_1$ has reached the point of 'virtual collapse' by the time the sample size reaches $n = 100$, that for $\hat{\theta}_2$ does not reach this stage until the sample size is much larger.

A 'collapsed' distribution in this situation means that every sample taken would yield an estimate very close to or virtually equal to the parameter estimated. Since the size of economic data samples is often relatively small, this implies that we should prefer estimator $\hat{\theta}_1$ to estimator $\hat{\theta}_2$, because for this estimator we benefit from the property of consistency at a smaller sample size.

Suppose the sample size is sufficiently large for the sampling distributions for both estimators to have taken on the shape of their asymptotic distributions (defined earlier in this section). If the estimator $\hat{\theta}_1$ is collapsing 'more quickly' onto θ then this

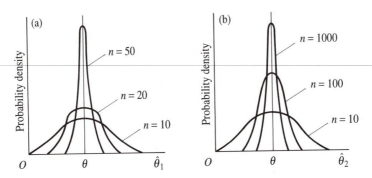

Figure 5.9 (a) and (b) Asymptotic efficiency.

implies that the variance of its sampling distribution for this size of sample must be smaller than the variance of the sampling distribution for $\hat{\theta}_2$. That is, it must have a smaller asymptotic variance. In general, the smaller the asymptotic variance of a consistent estimator, the more quickly its sampling distribution collapses onto the parameter being estimated.

An estimator $\hat{\theta}$ is said to be an **asymptotically efficient estimator** *of a parameter θ if (a) it is consistent and (b) no other consistent estimator has a smaller asymptotic variance.*

Thus the asymptotically efficient estimator is that estimator whose sampling distribution collapses most quickly onto the parameter being estimated as the size of samples taken increases. It is the estimator that converges in probability most quickly to the parameter being estimated.

As we noted earlier, frequently in regression analysis we are unable to find estimators that possess any of the small-sample properties of the last section. We are forced to rely on large-sample properties. Since sample sizes in economics are often fairly small, it therefore becomes of great importance to seek an estimator that is both consistent and *asymptotically efficient*.

5.3 A Monte Carlo experiment

In this section we shall carry out a simulated or 'Monte Carlo' experiment. Such experiments are the closest we get in econometrics to the controlled experiment of the physical scientist, and we shall make use of them occasionally in this text to emphasize important points or concepts. In this experiment we shall illustrate, first, the concept of a sampling distribution. We shall then demonstrate, for our example, the validity of the Central Limit Theorem introduced in Chapter 3. Finally, we shall illustrate the concepts of unbiasedness and consistency, discussed earlier in this chapter.

Suppose we have a non-normally distributed population of values for a random variable X. Specifically, we shall assume that X has the negative exponential distribution given by (2.18) with parameter $\theta = 0.02$. That is, X has the probability density function

$$p(X) = 0.02e^{-0.02X} \tag{5.10}$$

Our population therefore has a mean $\mu = 1/\theta = 50$ and a variance given by $\sigma^2 = 1/\theta^2 = 2500$. This population distribution is illustrated in Figure 5.10. Notice that the density function intersects the vertical axis at the point 0.02.

We shall now *simulate*, with the aid of a computer, the drawing of a random sample, size $n = 10$, from this population. First, the computer may be used to generate 10 random numbers *between 0 and 0.02*. Three such numbers, designated Y_1, Y_2 and Y_3, are illustrated in Figure 5.10. By making use of the density function in the figure, we can now generate 10 random drawings from our exponentially

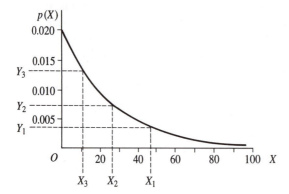

Figure 5.10 Simulating values for Y.

distributed population. Three of these, designated X_1, X_2 and X_3, corresponding to Y_1, Y_2 and Y_3, are illustrated.

In practice, the random X drawings are obtained by first inverting the density function (5.10) as follows. If

$$Y = 0.02e^{-0.02X}$$

then

$$\ln (Y) = \ln (0.02) - 0.02X$$

Hence

$$X = 50 \ln (0.02/Y) \tag{5.11}$$

The 10 random X values can now be obtained by substituting 10 random Y values (all between 0 and 0.02) into (5.11). The X values are shown (rounded to one decimal place) in the first row of Table 5.1. *They constitute a simulated random sample, of size $n = 10$, drawn from the exponentially distributed population.*

Clearly, we can generate as many samples (all of size 10) as we wish in the above manner. For example, four more are shown in Table 5.1. Moreover, for each such

Table 5.1 Simulated samples

Sample	Observations										$\bar{X}$
1	32.0	16.8	19.3	2.5	108.1	30.4	32.5	45.9	76.5	37.8	40.2
2	14.0	68.2	89.2	264.9	76.4	58.5	41.5	2.6	36.1	3.4	65.5
3	34.1	17.7	121.8	139.8	27.0	26.6	55.1	0.3	24.6	15.8	46.3
4	25.9	67.1	65.7	115.9	6.5	57.8	19.1	78.8	110.4	29.6	57.7
5	28.9	213.4	86.9	43.7	12.0	55.5	52.8	38.8	36.0	58.7	62.7

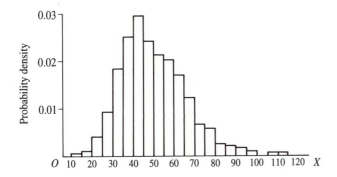

Figure 5.11 Sampling distribution of the mean with $n = 10$.

sample, we can compute the sample mean $\bar{X}$. The sample means for the 5 samples in Table 5.1 are shown in the right-hand column. Naturally, $\bar{X}$ varies from sample to sample.

In Figure 5.11 a probability histogram for the sample means $\bar{X}$ obtained from 1000 such samples (again all of size 10) has been drawn. For example, 124 of the samples proved to have a mean between 35 and 40. We have therefore translated this into a probability of 0.124. Since the 35–40 block in Figure 5.11 is 5 units wide, the probability density associated with it is $0.124/5 = 0.0248$.

The histogram in Figure 5.11 illustrates the very important concept of a sampling distribution. It represents the sampling distribution of the mean of a random sample drawn from an exponential population. Notice that the distribution is asymmetrical. In fact, it reflects the shape of the population distribution in Figure 5.10.

Theorem 3.1 stated that the sampling distribution for $\bar{X}$ had mean $E(\bar{X}) = \mu$ and variance $\sigma_{\bar{X}}^2 = \sigma^2/n$. Our population has mean $\mu = 50$ and variance $\sigma^2 = 2500$. Hence, according to the theorem, our sampling distribution should have a mean of 50 with variance $2500/10 = 250$. In fact, for our 1000 samples, $\bar{X}$ turned out to have a mean of 49.6 with a variance of 244.7. This is very close to the theorem's predictions. Our results would have been even closer to those predicted if, for example, we had taken 10 000 rather than 1000 samples.

Theorem 3.2, the Central Limit Theorem, stated that as the sample size becomes larger, the sampling distribution for $\bar{X}$ approaches the normal distribution in shape. This should be the case regardless of the shape of the parent population distribution. It should therefore be the case even for our exponentially distributed population.

In Figure 5.12 the result of drawing 1000 samples, all this time of size $n = 50$, from our exponential population is illustrated. The procedure followed is exactly the same as that above, except that each sample now involves 50 random drawings via Equation (5.11).

The distribution in Figure 5.12 is more symmetrical than that in Figure 5.11 and is roughly of normal distribution shape. According to Theorem 3.1, this distribution

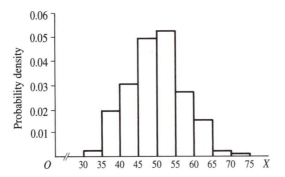

Figure 5.12 Sampling distribution of the mean with $n = 50$.

should have a mean of 50, with a variance of $\sigma^2/n = 2500/50 = 50$. Thus it is predicted to have a much smaller variance than the distribution in Figure 5.11. In fact, the distribution in Figure 5.12 turned out to have a mean of 49.8, with a variance of 53.2. Theorem 3.1 is again supported by our experiments.

In Figure 5.13 the sample size has been increased to $n = 100$. Note that the sampling distribution for $\bar{X}$ is now almost symmetrical and very similar to the normal distribution shape, as predicted by the Central Limit Theorem. It appears that, even for an exponentially distributed population, the sampling distribution of the mean approaches the normal distribution as the sample size increases. This normal distribution is the asymptotic distribution for $\bar{X}$, mentioned in the last section. According to Theorem 3.1, the distribution in Figure 5.13 should have a mean of 50 and a variance $\sigma^2/n = 2500/100 = 25$. The actual mean and variance for our 1000 samples are 49.9 and 24.8 respectively.

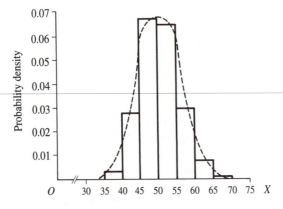

Figure 5.13 Sampling distribution of the mean with $n = 100$.

Two of the most important properties of estimators discussed in earlier sections of this chapter were *unbiasedness* and *consistency*. We saw that, theoretically at least, the sample mean $\bar{X}$ was an unbiased and consistent estimator of the population mean μ. The above simulated experiments appear to support these theoretical findings. First, even for small samples, the sampling distributions we have constructed for $\bar{X}$ appear to have a mean value that, allowing for slight experimental error, equals the population mean of 50. That is, $E(\bar{X}) = \mu$.

Secondly, consistency of $\bar{X}$ implies that as the sample size tends to infinity, the sampling distribution for $\bar{X}$ should 'collapse' onto μ, the parameter being estimated. We saw that a sufficient condition for this was that as n tended to infinity, the bias (if it exists) and the variance of the estimator should tend to zero. In the present case $\bar{X}$ is not biased, and we saw that Var $(\bar{X})$ does indeed become smaller as n is increased from 5 to 50 and then to 100. In fact, Figures 5.11 to 5.13 illustrate the first stages of the collapse of the sampling distribution for $\bar{X}$ onto the population mean $\mu = 50$.

To reinforce the above point, a further 100 samples of size $n = 1000$ were simulated. We do not present a histogram for this experiment, but merely note that all but one of these 100 samples yielded a sample mean $\bar{X}$ within the range 49.5–50.5. Thus it appears that for a sample size $n = 1000$, the sampling distribution for $\bar{X}$ is extremely narrowly dispersed about its mean of 50. That is, it has 'virtually collapsed' onto its mean value.

5.4 Methods of estimation

In Section 5.1 we spent some time describing the properties that we like our estimators to have, but we have said virtually nothing about how we obtain estimators in the first place. It is time to rectify this omission. There are, basically, three methods of obtaining estimators, and we look at each in turn.

The method of moments

If we have a population of values for a random variable X then the quantity $E(X^r)$ is known as the *r***th population moment about zero**. For example, $E(X)$, the population mean, is the **first moment about zero**, whereas $E(X^2)$ is the **second moment about zero**, and so on.

If the population mean $E(X) = \mu$ then the quantity $E(X - \mu)^r$ is known as the *r***th population moment about the mean**. For example, the population variance $E(X - \mu)^2$ is also known as the **second moment about the mean**.

It is also possible to define sample moments. Given a sample of observations $(X_1, X_2, X_3, \ldots, X_n)$, we define the *r***th sample moment about zero** as $\sum X_i^r / n$. Thus, for example, the sample mean $\bar{X} = \sum X_i / n$ is the **first sample moment about zero**. Similarly, the *r***th sample moment about the mean** is defined as $\sum (X_i - \bar{X})^r / n$. Thus, for example, the sample variance $v^2 = \sum (X_i - \bar{X})^2 / n$ is the **second sample moment about the mean**.

In the method of moments we simply estimate population moments, about zero or the mean, by the corresponding sample moments. Thus, for example, we estimate the population mean by the sample mean $\bar{X}$, and the population variance by the sample variance v^2 as defined above.

It is possible to show that, under very general conditions, *sample moments are consistent estimators of the corresponding population moments*. However, sample moments are not necessarily unbiased estimators. For example, we already know that v^2 as just defined is a biased estimator of the population variance.

We also note at this point that, just as a sample variance is a consistent estimator of a population variance, so a sample covariance $\sum(X_i - \bar{X})(Y_i - \bar{Y})/n$ can be shown to be a consistent estimator of a population covariance $E[X - E(X)][Y - E(Y)]$.

The method of least squares

We have already made use of this method of estimation in the last chapter on two-variable regression. It is, however, a quite general method of estimating population moments about zero.

Consider the rth population moment about zero, $E(X^r)$, which is generally written as μ_r. In the method of least squares we estimate μ_r by selecting the value that minimizes the sum of squares $\sum(X_i^r - \mu_r)^2$. For example, to estimate the population mean μ (which is the first moment about zero, μ_1), we select μ so as to minimize

$$S = \sum(X_i - \mu)^2 \tag{5.12}$$

To minimize (5.12) we must differentiate with respect to μ and set the resultant derivative equal to zero. This yields

$$\frac{dS}{d\mu} = -2\sum(X_i - \mu) = 0, \quad \text{or} \quad \sum X_i - n\mu = 0 \tag{5.13}$$

Solving (5.13) for μ gives the least squares estimator, denoted by $\hat{\mu}$, as

$$\hat{\mu} = \sum X_i/n$$

Since the second-order derivative $d^2S/d\mu^2 = 2\sum(1) = 2n > 0$, the sum of squares (5.12) has in fact been minimized. Thus the least squares estimator of the population mean is simply the sample mean.

Unfortunately, there can be no certainty that the method of least squares will necessarily yield estimators with any of the properties discussed earlier in this chapter. The properties of least squares estimators have to be investigated for each case.

Maximum likelihood estimation

A method of estimation that is increasingly used in econometrics is that of maximum likelihood (ML). The advantage of this method is that, unlike, for example, least squares estimators, maximum likelihood estimators (MLEs) can be shown to be consistent and asymptotically efficient under very general conditions.

To provide an intuitive grasp of the method, suppose we have a population of workers in an industry who are either in favour of or against industrial action over some issue. We wish to estimate the proportion π of such workers who are in favour. Suppose we take a random sample of say 17 workers from the industry and find that only 2 of these workers favour action.

In the light of this sample evidence, let us consider possible values for the population proportion π. It seems highly unlikely that, for example, a value of $\pi = 0.8$ (80% in favour of action) could have generated the above sample evidence of just 2 out of 17 in favour. It seems only a little more likely that the value $\pi = 0.5$ could have generated such evidence. However, it is apparent that a value $\pi = 0.1$ has a far greater 'likelihood' of generating the above sample. In everyday terms, the maximum likelihood estimator of π is the value that is 'most likely' or has the 'maximum likelihood' of generating the given sample evidence of 2 workers out of 17 being in favour of industrial action. It is the value of π that has the greatest probability of generating the sample we have actually obtained.

Since workers in the population are either for or against industrial action, the number of workers in our sample who are in favour of action must have the binomial distribution described in Section 2.1. Substituting $n = 17$ and $X = 2$ (the number in favour) into (2.7) therefore yields

$$\text{Pr} = \text{Pr (2 workers in favour in sample of 17)} = 136(\pi)^2(1 - \pi)^{15} \qquad (5.14)$$

What (5.14) tells us is that the probability of getting the sample we actually obtained depends on the unknown population proportion π. For example, if $\pi = 0.8$ then (5.14) yields the very tiny probability of $\text{Pr} = 0.285 \times 10^{-8}$. This verifies what we suggested above – that it is highly unlikely that our sample could have been generated by a population with $\pi = 0.8$.

Similarly, if $\pi = 0.5$, (5.14) yields the probability $\text{Pr} = 0.00104$, a value somewhat larger than for $\pi = 0.8$, but still very small. However, if $\pi = 0.1$, (5.14) yields a much larger probability of $\text{Pr} = 0.280$. This verifies what we also suggested above – that a value of $\pi = 0.1$ had a far greater likelihood of generating our given sample.

The MLE is simply the value of π that maximizes the probability obtained from (5.14). The function (5.14) is graphed in Figure 5.14. It can be seen that the maximum probability (maximum Pr) in fact occurs when π takes a value slightly greater than 0.1.

To find the exact value of π that maximizes (5.14), that is, the exact value of the MLE, we can simply differentiate Pr with respect to π and set the resultant derivative equal to zero. That is, using the rule for differentiating products,

$$\frac{d\text{Pr}}{d\pi} = 136[2\pi(1 - \pi)^{15} - 15\pi^2(1 - \pi)^{14}] = 0$$

It follows that

$$\pi(1 - \pi)^{14}[2(1 - \pi) - 15\pi] = 0$$

Hence, since we cannot have either $\pi = 0$ or $\pi = 1$, we have

$$2(1 - \pi) - 15\pi = 0 \qquad (5.15)$$

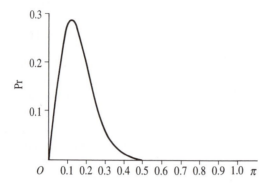

Figure 5.14 Sample likelihoods for different values of π.

Equation (5.15) can now be solved to find the value of π that maximizes (5.14). Thus, denoting the MLE of π by $\tilde{\pi}$, we have

$$\tilde{\pi} = \frac{2}{17} = 0.118$$

Rather than check the second-order condition for a maximum, we can see from Figure 5.14 that a value of 0.118 actually maximizes (5.14) rather than minimizing it.

Thus the value of π that is most likely to have generated our sample result (2 workers out of 17 in favour of industrial action) is 2/17 or 0.118. Notice that the maximum likelihood estimate of the population proportion π turns out to be the sample proportion, that is, the proportion of the *sample* that is in favour of industrial action. Thus the ML method of estimation has yielded what most people would regard as a very sensible result.

The general case

In general, an MLE is found by first deriving a **likelihood function**. This is simply a mathematical expression for the probability or likelihood of obtaining a given sample outcome. For example, in our introductory case above the likelihood function was given by (5.14).

Normally a sample outcome will consist of n known observations, which we shall denote by $(X_1, X_2, X_3, \ldots, X_n)$. If the population is characterized by a single parameter θ then the probability or likelihood L of obtaining a given sample will depend, first, on the value of θ and, secondly, on the precise observations in the sample. The likelihood function will therefore normally take the form

$$L = L(\theta, X_1, X_2, X_3, \ldots, X_n) \tag{5.16}$$

The MLE of θ is the value of θ that maximizes the likelihood function (5.16). Since the X_i are known constants, once the precise algebraic form of (5.16) has been derived, differential calculus may then be used to obtain the value of θ that maximizes L.

Very often, populations will possess more than one parameter. The probability of obtaining a given sample will then depend on the values of *all* parameters and the given sample observations. The likelihood function then takes the more general form

$$L = L(\theta_1, \theta_2, \ldots, \theta_m, X_1, X_2, \ldots, X_n) \tag{5.17}$$

where there are now m parameters in all. The MLEs of the m parameters may now be found by partially differentiating (5.17) with respect to each θ in turn and then setting all the partial derivatives obtained to zero.

Some examples may make this general procedure a little clearer.

★ A discrete-variable example

Suppose our population involves values of a discrete variable X that have the geometric probability distribution given by (2.10). That is,[4]

$$p(X) = (1 - \theta)\theta^X, \qquad 0 < \theta < 1 \tag{5.18}$$

Thus here we have a situation where the population is characterized by a single parameter θ. We wish to find the MLE of θ. Suppose we have a sample of n random observations on X, which, as usual, we write as $(X_1, X_2, X_3, \ldots, X_n)$. Using (5.18), the probability of obtaining the ith sample observation is

$$p(X_i) = (1 - \theta)\theta^{X_i}, \qquad i = 1, 2, 3, \ldots, n \tag{5.19}$$

For a random sample, the n observations will all be independent values. Hence we can write the probability of obtaining our n observations as

$$L = p(X_1)p(X_2)p(X_3) \cdots p(X_n)$$

or, using (5.19),

$$L = [(1 - \theta)\theta^{X_1}][(1 - \theta)\theta^{X_2}][(1 - \theta)\theta^{X_3}] \cdots [(1 - \theta)\theta^{X_n}] \tag{5.20}$$

Equation (5.20) gives the likelihood function in this case. The required MLE of θ is the value of θ that maximizes (5.20).

Since the X_i are known sample values, (5.20) is a function of the parameter θ only. The first-order condition for maximum L is therefore that $dL/d\theta = 0$. The differentiation of L as it stands, however, is awkward, and it is helpful if we first find the logarithm of L. That is,

$$l = \ln(L) = [\ln(1 - \theta) + X_1 \ln(\theta)] + [\ln(1 - \theta) + X_2 \ln(\theta)]$$
$$+ [\ln(1 - \theta) + X_3 \ln(\theta)] + \cdots + [\ln(1 - \theta) + X_n \ln(\theta)]$$

or

$$l = n \ln(1 - \theta) + \ln(\theta) \sum X_i \tag{5.21}$$

Since the larger $l = \ln(L)$, the larger is L, the value of θ that maximizes (5.21) must also maximize (5.20), the likelihood function. We can therefore find the MLE of θ by maximizing (5.21), the so-called **log-likelihood function**. As is often the case in ML estimation, this proves a less awkward task than maximizing the original likelihood function.

To maximize (5.21), we differentiate with respect to θ and set the resultant derivative to zero. Thus

$$\frac{dl}{d\theta} = -\frac{n}{1-\theta} + \frac{\sum X_i}{\theta} = 0$$

or

$$n\theta = (1-\theta)\sum X_i \tag{5.22}$$

Equation (5.22) may now be solved to find the MLE of θ, denoted by $\tilde{\theta}$:

$$\tilde{\theta} = \frac{\sum X_i}{n + \sum X_i} = \frac{\bar{X}}{1 + \bar{X}} \tag{5.23}$$

where $\bar{X}$, as usual, is the sample mean.[5]

Equation (5.23) may seem a strange estimator of the parameter θ. However, the mean of the geometric distribution (5.19) can be shown to be $E(X) = \theta/(1-\theta)$. Rearranging gives the true value of θ as

$$\theta = \frac{E(X)}{1 + E(X)} \tag{5.24}$$

The expression for the MLE, (5.23), can now be seen to be the sample analogue of the population relationship (5.24).

★ A continuous-variable example

If a random variable X is a continuous variable then, as we saw in Section 2.2, its probability distribution $p(X)$ is more properly called a probability density function. The reader is advised at this point to refer back and check the exact meaning of a probability density. Because we have to work in terms of probability densities, the ML procedure is a little harder to grasp when we deal with continuous variables. However, the basic idea is the same.

Suppose we have a population of values for a continuous variable X, the distribution of X being given by the negative exponential distribution (2.18). That is[6]

$$p(X) = \theta e^{-\theta X} \tag{5.25}$$

Again, we wish to find the MLE of the parameter θ. If a random sample size n is drawn from this population then, just as with discrete variables, we can form a likelihood function for the sample observations X_i:

$$L = p(X_1)p(X_2)p(X_3)\cdots p(X_n) \tag{5.26}$$

where in this case the $p(X_i)$ are given by (5.25).

Since we are now dealing with a continuous variable, we cannot regard (5.25) as giving the probability of obtaining the n sample values. Instead, (5.26) tells us the density of probability about these sample values. However, this probability density still depends on the value of the parameter θ, and it therefore makes intuitive sense to choose the value of θ that maximizes it. That is, the MLE of θ is still defined as the value of θ that maximizes the likelihood function.

Using (5.25) to substitute into (5.26), the precise form of the likelihood function in this case is

$$L = (\theta e^{-\theta X_1})(\theta e^{-\theta X_2})(\theta e^{-\theta X_3}) \cdots (\theta e^{-\theta X_n})$$

Again, however, it is more convenient to work in terms of the log-likelihood function:

$$l = \ln (L) = [\ln (\theta) - \theta X_1] + [\ln (\theta) - \theta X_2] + [\ln (\theta) - \theta X_3]$$
$$+ \cdots + [\ln (\theta) - \theta X_n]$$

or

$$l = n \ln (\theta) - \theta \sum X_i \tag{5.27}$$

As in the previous example, maximizing l is equivalent to maximizing L. Hence the MLE of θ can be obtained by differentiating (5.27) with respect to θ and setting the derivative to zero. This yields

$$\frac{dl}{d\theta} = \frac{n}{\theta} - \sum X_i = 0 \tag{5.28}$$

Solving (5.28) for θ gives the MLE as[7]

$$\theta = \frac{n}{\sum X_i} = \frac{1}{\bar{X}} \tag{5.29}$$

where $\bar{X}$ is the sample mean. Since the mean of the negative exponential distribution is $E(X) = 1/\theta$, so that the true value of $\theta = 1/E(X)$, we see that ML estimation again yields an intuitively sensible result.

★ A two-parameter example

All the maximum likelihood examples we have considered so far have involved just a single population parameter. However, as (5.17) indicates, the method can be used to estimate a number of parameters simultaneously.

As an example of the simultaneous estimation of two parameters, suppose we have a normally distributed population of values for X with mean μ and variance σ^2. We require the MLEs of μ and σ^2. The density function for X is given by (2.11), which we reproduce here:

$$p(X) = (2\pi\sigma^2)^{-0.5} \exp [-0.5(X - \mu)^2/\sigma^2]$$

Since $\ln(e) = 1$, this means that

$$\ln[p(X)] = \ln[(2\pi\sigma^2)^{-0.5}] - 0.5(X - \mu)^2/\sigma^2$$
$$= -0.5 \ln(2\pi) - 0.5 \ln(\sigma^2) - 0.5(X - \mu)^2/\sigma^2 \qquad (5.30)$$

The likelihood function for a random sample of n observations on X as usual has the form (5.26). The log-likelihood function therefore has the form

$$l = \ln(L) = \sum \ln[p(X_i)] \qquad (5.31)$$

Using (5.30), we therefore have

$$l = \sum[-0.5 \ln(2\pi) - 0.5 \ln(\sigma^2) - 0.5(X_i - \mu)^2/\sigma^2]$$
$$= -0.5n \ln(2\pi) - 0.5n \ln(\sigma^2) - 0.5(1/\sigma^2)\sum(X_i - \mu)^2 \qquad (5.32)$$

Given the sample observations, l is a function of the two parameters μ and σ^2. To maximize the log-likelihood, we therefore partially differentiate (5.32) with respect to μ and σ^2 and set the derivatives obtained to zero:

$$\frac{\partial l}{\partial \mu} = -\frac{1}{\sigma^2}\sum(X_i - \mu)(-1) = \frac{1}{\sigma^2}\sum(X_i - \mu) = 0 \qquad (5.33)$$

and[8]

$$\frac{\partial l}{\partial \sigma^2} = -\frac{0.5n}{\sigma^2} + \frac{0.5}{\sigma^4}\sum(X_i - \mu)^2 = 0 \qquad (5.34)$$

Equations (5.33) and (5.34) represent two equations in the two unknowns μ and σ^2, which may be solved to find the MLEs. First, since σ^2 must be non-zero, we obtain from (5.33)

$$\sum(X_i - \mu) = 0, \quad \text{or} \quad \sum X_i - n\mu = 0$$

Solving this equation for μ gives the MLE as

$$\tilde{\mu} = \sum X_i/n = \bar{X} \qquad (5.35)$$

Thus the maximum likelihood estimator of a population mean μ is simply the sample mean $\bar{X}$.

To solve for σ^2, we multiply (5.34) by $2\sigma^4$ to give

$$-n\sigma^2 + \sum(X_i - \mu)^2 = 0$$

Since we already know that $\tilde{\mu} = \bar{X}$, we find the MLE of σ^2 to be

$$\tilde{\sigma}^2 = \frac{\sum(X_i - \bar{X})^2}{n} = v^2 \qquad (5.36)$$

Thus the maximum likelihood estimator of a population variance σ^2 is the sample variance v^2, as defined in (3.4).

Exercise 5.6

A production line produces light bulbs, some proportion π of which turn out to be defective. A random sample of 10 bulbs from the line is inspected and found to contain one defective. Sketch the likelihood function for π, and hence obtain a maximum likelihood estimate.

Exercise 5.7

Weekly earnings are normally distributed with a variance of $16 and an unknown mean μ. Two randomly selected workers are found to have earnings (measured to the nearest dollar) of $510 and $513. Use standard normal tables to calculate the probability of obtaining this sample for values of μ equal to $500, $505, $508, $510, $512, $515 and $520. Hence sketch the likelihood function for μ and obtain a maximum likelihood estimator.

Exercise 5.8

Calls per hour to a telephone exchange have a Poisson distribution[9]

$$p(X) = \frac{\lambda^X e^{-\lambda}}{X!}, \qquad \text{with } E(X) = \lambda$$

During n randomly selected hours, the numbers of calls received by the exchange are found to be $(X_1, X_2, X_3, \ldots, X_n)$. Find an expression for the MLE of λ.

The usefulness of maximum likelihood estimation

One point should be relatively obvious from the above examples. Maximum likelihood estimation is only possible if we know the form of the probability distribution for the parent population – that is, whether it is binomial, geometric, normal, etc. However, provided we can make some reasonable assumption about the population distribution, the procedure is a powerful general method of estimating population parameters.

We saw at the beginning of this section that, generally, MLEs possess the large-sample properties of consistency and asymptotic efficiency. Unfortunately, there can be no guarantee that they possess any desirable small-sample properties. For example, in the case of the normally distributed population the ML estimator of the population variance σ^2 is the sample variance v^2, as given by (3.4). As we have pointed out on several occasions, v^2 is a biased estimator of σ^2 in small samples.

ML estimation has become increasingly popular in regression analysis. As we shall see in later chapters, economic data tends to be generated in such a way that the least squares method of the last chapter is unable to provide estimators with any of the properties, small-sample *or* large-sample, described earlier. This being the case, the fact that ML estimation provides estimators with at least the desirable large-sample properties explains the popularity of the method.

The difficulty with ML estimation is that maximizing the relevant likelihood function is not always as straightforward as in the above examples. Frequently the resultant equations that have to be solved to find the MLEs are highly nonlinear, and may not have algebraic solutions. They then have to be solved by quite complicated 'numerical methods'. Until recent years, such numerical methods were extremely time-consuming, and for this reason were normally avoided. However, nowadays, powerful computer algorithms are available for such tasks, and this has vastly increased the applicability of maximum likelihood methods.

Appendix 5A

The properties of probability limits

Suppose we have a population of values for X, from which we take a series of samples of size n. Let the sample observations be $(X_1, X_2, \ldots, X_n)$. Suppose for each such sample we compute the same two sample statistics $\hat{\theta}_1$ and $\hat{\theta}_2$, and also calculate $\hat{\theta}_1 + \hat{\theta}_2$ and $\hat{\theta}_1/\hat{\theta}_2$. We need not specify what $\hat{\theta}_1$ and $\hat{\theta}_2$ are, but both will be functions of the sample observations. Thus

$$\hat{\theta}_1 = \hat{\theta}_1(X_1, X_2, \ldots, X_n), \qquad \hat{\theta}_2 = \hat{\theta}_2(X_1, X_2, \ldots, X_n)$$

Clearly, if many samples of size n are taken, we shall obtain sampling distributions for $\hat{\theta}_1$ and $\hat{\theta}_2$, and also for $\hat{\theta}_1 + \hat{\theta}_2$ and $\hat{\theta}_1/\hat{\theta}_2$. We assume that the probability limits of $\hat{\theta}_1$ and $\hat{\theta}_2$ exist. That is, the sampling distributions of these statistics collapse onto single points as $n \to \infty$. Let these probability limits be θ_1 and θ_2. That is,

$$\text{plim}\,(\hat{\theta}_1) = \theta_1, \quad \text{plim}\,(\hat{\theta}_2) = \theta_2 \tag{5A.1}$$

In everyday language, what (5A.1) implies is that, if the sample size is sufficiently large, each and every sample will yield a value for $\hat{\theta}_1$ virtually identical to θ_1, and a value for $\hat{\theta}_2$ virtually identical to θ_2. We shall therefore write (although this is not quite correct statistically)

$$\hat{\theta}_1 = \theta_1 \quad \text{and} \quad \hat{\theta}_2 = \theta_2 \quad \text{for large samples} \tag{5A.2}$$

It follows from (5A.2) that, again for sufficiently large samples,

$$\hat{\theta}_1 + \hat{\theta}_2 = \theta_1 + \theta_2 \tag{5A.3}$$

$$\hat{\theta}_1/\hat{\theta}_2 = \theta_1/\theta_2 \tag{5A.4}$$

What (5A.3) and (5A.4) imply is that, if many samples of sufficiently large size are taken, each and every sample yields a $\hat{\theta}_1 + \hat{\theta}_2$ that is equal to $\theta_1 + \theta_2$, and a $\hat{\theta}_1/\hat{\theta}_2$ that is equal to θ_1/θ_2. In other words, the sampling distribution for $\hat{\theta}_1 + \hat{\theta}_2$ must have collapsed onto the point $\theta_1 + \theta_2$, and the sampling distribution for $\hat{\theta}_1/\hat{\theta}_2$ must have collapsed onto the point θ_1/θ_2. That is, probability limits for $\hat{\theta}_1 + \hat{\theta}_2$ and $\hat{\theta}_1/\hat{\theta}_2$ exist and, moreover,

$$\text{plim } (\hat{\theta}_1 + \hat{\theta}_2) = \theta_1 + \theta_2$$

$$\text{plim } (\hat{\theta}_1/\hat{\theta}_2) = \theta_1/\theta_2$$

But θ_1 and θ_2 are the probability limits of $\hat{\theta}_1$ and $\hat{\theta}_2$ respectively. Thus

$$\text{plim } (\hat{\theta} + \hat{\theta}_2) = \text{plim } (\hat{\theta}_1) + \text{plim } (\hat{\theta}_2)$$

and

$$\text{plim } \left(\frac{\theta_1}{\theta_2}\right) = \frac{\text{plim } (\hat{\theta}_1)}{\text{plim } (\hat{\theta}_2)}$$

These are the results concerning probability limits given in the main text of this chapter. The above is not meant to be a rigorous demonstration of the properties, but should assist the reader in gaining an intuitive understanding of them. By similar arguments, it is easy to see that, for example

$$\text{plim } (\hat{\theta}_1 \hat{\theta}_2) = \text{plim } (\hat{\theta}_1) \, \text{plim } (\hat{\theta}_2)$$

$$\text{plim } \left(\frac{1}{\hat{\theta}_1}\right) = \frac{1}{\text{plim } (\hat{\theta}_1)}$$

and so on.

Such results on probability limits can also be extended to matrices. Suppose $\hat{\mathbf{A}}$ and $\hat{\mathbf{B}}$ are matrices of sample statistics and suppose that the probability limits of these sample statistics all exist and are given by the corresponding elements in the matrices $\mathbf{A}$ and $\mathbf{B}$. Provided in each case that $\hat{\mathbf{A}}$ and $\hat{\mathbf{B}}$ are of suitable dimensions, it can be shown that, for example,

$$\text{plim } (\hat{\mathbf{A}} + \hat{\mathbf{B}}) = \text{plim } (\hat{\mathbf{A}}) + \text{plim } (\hat{\mathbf{B}})$$

$$\text{plim } (\hat{\mathbf{A}}\hat{\mathbf{B}}) = \text{plim } (\hat{\mathbf{A}}) \, \text{plim } (\hat{\mathbf{B}})$$

It is also the case that if the inverse matrix $\hat{\mathbf{A}}^{-1}$ exists then

$$\text{plim } (\hat{\mathbf{A}}^{-1}) = [\text{plim } (\mathbf{A})]^{-1}$$

Appendix 5B

Notes to Chapter 5

1. $\tilde{X}$ is obviously unbiased since,

$$\text{E}(\tilde{X}) = \frac{1}{2}\text{E}(X_L) + \frac{1}{2}\text{E}(X_S) = \frac{1}{2}\mu + \frac{1}{2}\mu = \mu$$

Its variance is

$$\text{Var}\,(\tilde{X}) = \left(\frac{1}{2}\right)^2 \text{Var}\,(X_L) + \left(\frac{1}{2}\right)^2 \text{Var}\,(X_S) = \frac{1}{4}\sigma^2 + \frac{1}{4}\sigma^2 = \frac{1}{2}\sigma^2$$

Thus $\text{Var}\,(\bar{X}) < \text{Var}\,(\tilde{X})$ for $n > 2$.

2. $\begin{aligned}[t]
\text{MSE}\,(\hat{\theta}) &= \text{E}(\hat{\theta} - \theta)^2 = \text{E}[(\hat{\theta} - \text{E}\hat{\theta}) + (\text{E}\hat{\theta} - \theta)]^2 \\
&= \text{E}(\hat{\theta} - \text{E}\hat{\theta})^2 + 2\text{E}(\hat{\theta} - \text{E}\hat{\theta})(\text{E}\hat{\theta} - \theta) + \text{E}(\text{E}\hat{\theta} - \theta)^2 \\
&= \text{Var}\,(\hat{\theta}) + 2(\text{E}\hat{\theta} - \theta)\text{E}(\hat{\theta} - \text{E}\hat{\theta}) + [\text{Bias}\,(\hat{\theta})]^2 \\
&= \text{Var}\,(\hat{\theta}) + [\text{Bias}\,(\hat{\theta})]^2
\end{aligned}$

since $\text{E}(\hat{\theta} - \text{E}\hat{\theta}) = \text{E}\hat{\theta} - \text{E}\hat{\theta} = 0$.

3. Use of the MSE criterion implies that equal weight is being given to unbiasedness and variability in the estimator. If unbiasedness is thought more important than a small variance, or vice versa, then, instead of minimizing the mean square error, a weighted sum of the variance and squared bias may be minimized. That is we minimize $W\,\text{Var}\,(\hat{\theta}) + (1 - W)[\text{Bias}\,(\hat{\theta})]^2$, where the weights W and $1 - W$ lie between 0 and 1. The greater is W, the less importance is given to unbiasedness.

4. For example, the number of customers waiting in line at a single check-out point might have a geometric distribution.

5. Since $d^2l/d\theta^2 = -n/(1 - \theta)^2 - \sum X_i/\theta^2 < 0$, the second-order condition for a maximum is met.

6. For example, the time taken to serve a customer at a check-out point might have a negative exponential distribution.

7. Since $d^2l/d\theta^2 = -n/\theta^2 < 0$, the second-order condition for a maximum is met.

8. Remember that we are differentiating with respect to σ^2, not with respect to σ. Thus the derivative of $1/\sigma^2$ is $-1/(\sigma^2)^2$.

9. The Poisson, negative exponential and geometric distributions all link together in a simple single waiting line model. If arrivals at a service desk are Poisson-distributed and serving times are exponentially distributed then the number waiting in line will have a geometric distribution.

Further reading

A readable discussion of the properties of estimators can be found in Kmenta (1986), Chapter 6. A more advanced treatment is provided by Greene (1993), Chapter 4. These texts also discuss methods of estimation. Introductory low-level material on MLE is difficult to find, but see Thomas (1993). A more advanced introduction is given by Silvey (1975), and a fuller treatment can be found in Kendall and Stuart (1973).

6 The classical two-variable regression model

In Chapter 4 we considered the use of ordinary least squares estimators in two-variable regression analysis. We stressed the fact that the OLS estimates obtained from any data set were specific to that data set. Different samples would yield different estimates. That is, the OLS estimators were subject to sampling variability and possessed sampling distributions. We emphasize again that there can be no guarantee that the OLS estimators and their sampling distributions will possess any of the desirable properties that we described in Chapter 5. There is nothing inherently praiseworthy about the OLS estimating method. There is no reason why the OLS estimators should necessarily be, for example, unbiased or consistent. This will only be the case if a number of quite stringent conditions, which we shall now examine, can be shown to hold.

6.1 The assumptions of the classical two-variable regression model

The classical two-variable model was developed at the beginning of this century for use in the physical sciences. As we shall see, many of its assumptions are inappropriate when dealing with data for the social sciences. However, it represents a useful starting-off point, both for dealing with the inferential aspects of regression analysis and for identifying the conditions under which the OLS estimating method can be considered appropriate. We shall therefore describe it in some detail.

Underlying the classical model is a population relationship of the type (4.3). The dependent Y variable is therefore linearly dependent on the explanatory X variable, but is also influenced by the disturbance ϵ. Equation (4.3) is assumed to hold for all observations in a sample of size n. We therefore have

$$Y_i = \alpha + \beta X_i + \epsilon_i \quad \text{for all } i \tag{6.1}$$

The remainder of the classical model involves a series of assumptions, first concerning the explanatory variable and secondly, concerning the disturbance.

Assumptions concerning the explanatory variable

In the classical model it is assumed that the explanatory X variable:

(IA) is non-stochastic;

(IB) has values that are fixed in repeated samples;

(IC) is such that as $n \to \infty$, its variance $\sum(X_i - \bar{X})^2/n = \sum x_i^2/n \to Q$, where Q is a fixed finite constant.

These assumptions will need some explaining. As we saw in Chapter 2, a stochastic variable is simply a variable whose values are determined by some chance mechanism and are hence subject to a probability distribution. A non-stochastic variable therefore has values that are not determined by chance. In the context of the classical model, this implies that the values of the explanatory X variable are in fact determined by an experimenter or investigator. Recall that this model was developed for the physical sciences, where laboratory experiments are possible. Under such circumstances, it is reasonable to postulate an investigator selecting values for the X variable to suit the purposes of the experiment. Assumption IA implies that the values of the X variable (e.g. the third column in Table 4.1) have been chosen in this way. Of course, in economics or any other social science it is rarely possible to conduct laboratory experiments, so this is an assumption that we will clearly have to relax later. It is, however, convenient to retain it for the present.

It should be noted at this point that, even when the X variable is non-stochastic, the same is not true of the Y variable. From (6.1), it can be seen that Y values depend not only on X values but also on values of the disturbance. Since the disturbance is outside the investigator's control, the Y variable is stochastic, deriving its stochastic nature from that of the disturbance.

Assumption IB refers to what would happen in a situation where 'very many' samples were taken. It is assumed that investigators, if repeating the experiment, choose exactly the same set of X values on each such occasion. That is, in every sample taken (i.e. experiment performed), the X values remain unchanged. Notice, however, that this does not imply that the values of the dependent Y variable also remain unchanged from sample to sample. The Y values also depend on the uncontrollable values of the disturbance ϵ, which will vary from one sample to another.

The fact that the Y values vary from sample to sample means that different samples will still yield different values for the OLS estimators. Recall that the expressions (4.16) and (4.18) for these estimators involve both the X values and the Y values. Hence sampling distributions for the OLS estimators will still exist, although they must be viewed as those arising when many samples are taken with the same set of X values.

The relevance of assumption IC will become clearer later. It implies that, if the sample size were increased, the variance $\sum x_i^2/n$ would not increase without limit. Clearly, as n increases, the sum of squares $\sum x_i^2$ must almost always increase, since we have more x_i^2s to sum over. However, this need not be true of $\sum x_i^2/n = \sum (X_i - \bar{X})^2/n$, provided the investigator takes care in the X values (s)he chooses.[1]

We can at this stage give some inkling of the importance of assumptions such as IC. As we noted in Chapter 4, many economic variables show continual upward trends over time. In such cases, as the sample size available increases and more time periods are included in the sample, the variance of X, $\sum x_i^2/n$, continually increases, so that assumptions such as IC break down. The importance of such assumptions, then, is that they rule out explanatory variables that exhibit strong trends. This will become important when we do away with our imaginary investigator and relax the assumption of a non-stochastic X variable. As we shall see later, there are considerable problems in making inferences about relationships in which the explanatory variable shows a strong trend.

Assumptions concerning the disturbance

In the classical model the disturbance ϵ is assumed to have the following properties:

(IIA) $E(\epsilon_i) = 0$ for all i;

(IIB) Var $(\epsilon_i) = E(\epsilon_i - E\epsilon_i)^2 = E(\epsilon_i^2) = \sigma^2 = $ constant for all i;

(IIC) Cov $(\epsilon_i, \epsilon_j) = E(\epsilon_i - E\epsilon_i)(\epsilon_j - E\epsilon_j) = E(\epsilon_i\epsilon_j) = 0$ for all $i \neq j$;

(IID) each ϵ_i is normally distributed.

These assumptions are best understood by referring to Figure 6.1, where the population regression line, introduced as Equation (4.1), has been drawn. X_6 is the value of the explanatory X variable belonging to the 6th observation (e.g. it is the income of the 6th household if we refer to the first example of Chapter 4).

Given assumptions IA and IB, X_6 does not vary from sample to sample. However, as we noted, the Y_6 values will vary. This is reflected by the points marked out on the X_6 line. Each such point represents the 6th observation in a different

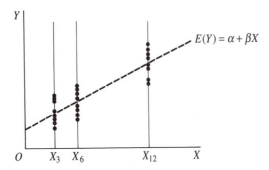

Figure 6.1 The classical regression model.

sample. Recall from Chapter 4 that disturbances represent the vertical distances of such points from the population regression line. The distances of the points on the X_6 line from the population line therefore represent different values for ϵ_6, the disturbance associated with the 6th observation. Assumption IIA simply states that the mean of such disturbances, taken over many samples, is zero. Similarly, the means of the disturbances ϵ_3, ϵ_{12} etc. associated with the fixed X_3, X_{12} etc. are also assumed to be zero. We have, in fact, already implicitly made use of this assumption in Chapter 4 when writing Equations (4.1)–(4.3). The assumption simply implies that, for any of the fixed X_i lines in Figure 6.1, the points obtained when repeated samples are taken are evenly spaced above and below the population regression line.

Assumption IIB specifies that the variance of all the ϵ_6s that would be obtained if repeated samples were taken is identical to the variance of all the ϵ_3s obtained, which in turn is identical to the variance of the ϵ_{12}s, etc. This constant variance is given the symbol σ^2. Recall that the variance is a measure of the dispersion or 'spread' of a distribution. Hence assumption IIB implies that when many samples are taken, the dispersion of the points about the population regression line in Figure 6.1 is the same for each and every X value.

When the disturbances obey assumption IIB, they are said to be **homoskedastic**. As we shall see in Chapter 10, this assumption is often invalid for economic data. It is particularly likely to break down when there is a large variation in the size of the X values. When this is the case, there is a tendency for the variance of the disturbances to increase rather than remain constant as the size of X increases. When their variance is not constant the disturbances are said to be **heteroskedastic**.

Assumption IIC states that the covariance and hence the correlation between any two disturbances is zero. When this assumption holds, the disturbances are said to be **non-autocorrelated**. The assumption implies that when repeated samples are taken, there is no tendency for samples with, for example, large positive ϵ_6s also to have large positive ϵ_3s. Negative correlations are also ruled out. Thus, for example, there must be no tendency for positive ϵ_3s to be associated with negative ϵ_{12}s. In fact, no correlations between any disturbances are permitted.

Like assumption IIB, assumption IIC is also likely to break down when we are dealing with economic data. This is particularly the case when the data is time series data, such as that in Table 4.3. With such data, there is a tendency for disturbances to 'spill over' from one period to the next. For example, with an output series as the dependent Y variable, the disturbing factor might be trade-union-induced industrial action resulting in below normal output and hence a negative disturbance. Since there is at least a possibility that industrial action in period t may also be felt in period $t + 1$, negative disturbances in period t will tend to be followed by negative disturbances in period $t + 1$. Thus there will be a positive correlation between the two disturbances, and assumption IIC cannot hold.

The assumption of non-autocorrelated disturbances is less likely to break down with annual time series data than with quarterly or monthly data. This is simply because spillover effects are likely to be of more importance between two consecutive months, or even two consecutive quarters, than they are between two years.

Assumption IID states that, for example, the ϵ_6s that would be obtained from repeated sampling are normally distributed about their mean of zero, and similarly for all the other disturbances. The main implication of this is that there is a much larger probability of obtaining 'small' disturbances than there is of obtaining 'large' disturbances. Hence in Figure 6.1 there is a greater likelihood of obtaining points close to the population regression line than there is of obtaining points far away from it.

Assumptions IIA–IID may be summed up in the statement that the ϵ_i are normally and independently distributed with zero mean and constant variance σ^2. That is,

$$\epsilon_i \text{ is NID } (0, \sigma^2) \quad \text{for all } i \tag{6.2}$$

Note that, although assumption IIC merely states that the ϵ_i are uncorrelated, the fact that (by assumption IID) they are normally distributed implies that they must also be independent. This follows from the discussion at the end of Section 2.5.

6.2 Properties of the OLS estimators

It should be clear by now that, with the possible exceptions of IIA and IID, all the assumptions of the classical model are, to a greater or lesser extent, implausible when applied to economic data. However, if the OLS estimators derived in Chapter 4 are to possess any of the desirable properties described in Chapter 5 then it is necessary that at least some of the classical assumptions should be valid. In this section we shall consider precisely which of the assumptions are required for each of the desirable properties. First, however, we derive a useful alternative expression for the OLS estimator of the slope of the population regression line, β. From (4.18),

$$\hat{\beta} = \frac{\sum x_i y_i}{\sum x_i^2} = \frac{\sum x_i (Y_i - \bar{Y})}{\sum x_i^2} = \frac{\sum x_i Y_i}{\sum x_i^2} \quad (\text{since } \bar{Y} \sum x_i = 0)$$

$$= \sum w_i Y_i \tag{6.3}$$

where

$$w_i = \frac{x_i}{\sum x_i^2} \quad \text{for all } i \tag{6.4}$$

Note that, since $\sum x_i = 0$,

$$\sum w_i = 0 \tag{6.5}$$

and hence, since $x_i = X_i - \bar{X}$,

$$\sum w_i X_i = \sum w_i x_i = 1 \quad \text{(using (6.5) and then (6.4))} \tag{6.6}$$

Using (6.3), we have

$$\hat{\beta} = \sum w_i(\alpha + \beta X_i + \epsilon_i) = \alpha \sum w_i + \beta \sum w_i X_i + \sum w_i \epsilon_i$$

Thus, using (6.5) and (6.6),

$$\hat{\beta} = \beta + \sum w_i \epsilon_i \tag{6.7}$$

Equation (6.7) is the alternative expression for $\hat{\beta}$. Since this expression involves the unknown disturbances, it is useless for computational purposes, but it is a very useful starting-off point for further theoretical development.

We now consider the properties of the OLS estimators, concentrating mainly on the properties of the slope estimator $\hat{\beta}$, because this is often of greater interest than the intercept estimator $\hat{\alpha}$.

Linearity

Only classical assumptions IA and IB are necessary if the OLS estimators are to be linear estimators. Recall that these assumptions imply that the investigator chooses the values of the X variable and that these values are held fixed for repeated samples. The X values can therefore be treated as constants, so that the investigator observes merely the Y values. The OLS estimators therefore need only be linear functions of the Y values for them to be considered linear estimators. It can easily be seen, given assumptions IA and IB, that this is the case. Since the X_i may be regarded as constants, so may the x_i. Hence the w_i in (6.4) may also be so regarded. Thus, from (6.3), $\hat{\beta}$ is a linear function of the Y_i, that is, of the sample observations. It is not difficult to show that, under the present assumptions, the OLS estimator of α is also a linear estimator.

Recall from Chapter 5 that a linear estimator is not necessarily a 'good' estimator of the parameter being estimated. However, linear estimators are easier to handle mathematically than are nonlinear estimators.

Unbiasedness

By making use of assumptions IA, IB and IIA, we can demonstrate that the OLS estimators $\hat{\alpha}$ and $\hat{\beta}$ are unbiased. That is, $E(\hat{\alpha}) = \alpha$ and $E(\hat{\beta}) = \beta$, so that the means of the sampling distributions for the OLS estimators equal the true values of α and β. We concentrate again on $\hat{\beta}$. Expanding (6.7), we have

$$\hat{\beta} = \beta + w_1\epsilon_1 + w_2\epsilon_2 + w_3\epsilon_3 + \cdots + w_n\epsilon_n \tag{6.8}$$

Taking expectations and using the fact that the w_i can be treated as constants and hence, by Theorem 2.1, can be taken outside the expectation symbol, we have

$$E(\hat{\beta}) = \beta + w_1E\epsilon_1 + w_2E\epsilon_2 + w_3E\epsilon_3 + \cdots + w_nE\epsilon_n \tag{6.9}$$

Hence, since by assumption IIA, $E(\epsilon_i) = 0$ for all i,

$$E(\hat{\beta}) = \beta \tag{6.10}$$

Thus $\hat{\beta}$ is an unbiased estimator of β. Similarly, it can be shown that the OLS estimator $\hat{\alpha}$ is an unbiased estimator of the intercept parameter α. That is, $E(\hat{\alpha}) = \alpha$.

★ Consistency

We need only make use of assumptions IA–IC and IIA to demonstrate that the OLS estimators are consistent. That is, as $n \to \infty$, their sampling distributions collapse onto the true values of α and β. Substituting for w_i in (6.7),

$$\hat{\beta} = \beta + \frac{\sum x_i\epsilon_i}{\sum x_i^2} = \beta + \frac{\sum x_i\epsilon_i/n}{\sum x_i^2/n} \tag{6.11}$$

Taking probability limits,

$$\text{plim } (\hat{\beta}) = \text{plim } (\beta) + \text{plim } \left(\frac{\sum x_i\epsilon_i/n}{\sum x_i^2/n}\right) = \beta + \text{plim } \left(\frac{\sum x_i\epsilon_i/n}{\sum x_i^2/n}\right) \tag{6.12}$$

In (6.12) we have used the property (5.8) of probability limits introduced in the last chapter and the fact that the probability limit of any constant is simply equal to that constant. It follows that

$$\text{plim } (\hat{\beta}) = \beta + \frac{\text{plim } (\sum x_i\epsilon_i/n)}{\text{plim } (\sum x_i^2/n)} \tag{6.13}$$

To obtain (6.13), we have used the property (5.9) of probability limits introduced in the last chapter.

Considering, first, the numerator of the second term on the right-hand side of (6.13),

$$\frac{\sum x_i\epsilon_i}{n} = \frac{\sum (X_i - \bar{X})(\epsilon_i - \bar{\epsilon})}{n} \quad \text{(since } \bar{\epsilon}\sum x_i = 0\text{)}$$

Hence $\sum x_i\epsilon_i/n$ is the sample covariance between X and ϵ. We saw in Section 5.4, when discussing the method of moments, that sample covariances are consistent estimators of population covariances. Hence the probability limit of $\sum x_i\epsilon_i/n$ is equal to the population covariance between X and ϵ, which is zero. The population covariance must be zero because of the assumption of non-stochastic fixed X values. Such values clearly cannot be influenced by the disturbance. More formally, $E(x_i\epsilon_i) = x_iE(\epsilon_i) = 0$.

In the denominator on the right-hand side of (6.13), $\sum x_i^2/n$ is the sample variance of the X values. Given non-stochastic X_i, to find its probability limit, we simply have to take the limit of $\sum x_i^2/n$ as the sample size n tends to infinity. However, given assumption IC, this limit is the fixed constant Q.

Equation (6.13) therefore reduces to

$$\text{plim } (\hat{\beta}) = \beta + \frac{0}{Q} = \beta$$

Thus $\hat{\beta}$ is a consistent estimator. That is, as $n \to \infty$, it converges in probability to the true value of β. It can also be shown that plim $(\hat{\alpha}) = \alpha$, so that the OLS estimator $\hat{\alpha}$ is a consistent estimator of the intercept parameter α.

Best linear unbiasedness

We have now shown that if the classical assumptions concerning the explanatory variable and the first two assumptions concerning the disturbance are valid then the OLS estimators will be both linear and unbiased. However, as we saw in the last chapter, unbiasedness alone is not a particularly reassuring property. Under what additional conditions, if any, will the OLS estimators have the minimum variance of all linear unbiased estimators? It turns out that we also require classical assumptions IIB and IIC if the OLS estimators are to be best linear unbiased. That is, the disturbances must have a constant variance and zero covariances.

A proof that the OLS estimator of the slope parameter β is BLUE under these conditions is relatively complicated and is given in Appendix 6A at the end of this chapter. The procedure followed is to start the estimation again, from scratch as it were, and actually derive the BLUE of β, building in the properties of linearity, unbiasedness and minimum variance one by one. It turns out that the expression for the BLUE, derived in this way, is identical to the expression (4.18) for the OLS estimator of β. Thus the OLS estimator must be BLUE.

An advantage of the best linear unbiased method of estimation is that when employing it we always obtain, as a by-product as it were, an expression for the variance of the estimator concerned. In the present case the variances, normally written $\sigma_{\hat{\beta}}^2$ and $\sigma_{\hat{\alpha}}^2$ are

$$\text{Var } (\hat{\beta}) = \sigma_{\hat{\beta}}^2 = \frac{\sigma^2}{\sum x_i^2} \tag{6.14}$$

and

$$\text{Var } (\hat{\alpha}) = \sigma_{\hat{\alpha}}^2 = \frac{\sigma^2 \sum X_i^2}{n \sum x_i^2} \tag{6.15}$$

where σ^2 is of course the common variance of the disturbances.

Recall that with repeated sampling, we obtain sampling distributions for the OLS estimators $\hat{\beta}$ and $\hat{\alpha}$. The variances (6.14) and (6.15) are measures of the dispersion of these distributions about their means β and α. As we shall see, knowledge of the expressions (6.14) and (6.15) will become vital once we wish to form confidence intervals for, or test hypotheses about, the population parameters β and α. The square roots of the variances (6.14) and (6.15), that is, $\sigma_{\hat{\beta}}$ and $\sigma_{\hat{\alpha}}$, are known as the **standard errors** of $\hat{\beta}$ and $\hat{\alpha}$ respectively.

Efficiency and asymptotic efficiency

If the OLS estimators are to have minimum variance, not merely among all linear unbiased estimators, but among all unbiased estimators linear or nonlinear, then it can be shown that the classical assumption IID must also hold. That is, all classical assumptions must hold, including that of normally distributed disturbances, if the OLS estimators are to be efficient. Proof of this is, however, difficult, and beyond the scope of this text.

Since efficiency is a small-sample property, the OLS estimators must be efficient regardless of sample size and remain so as the sample size tends to infinity. Hence they must also be asymptotically efficient. Thus if all classical assumptions are valid, the OLS estimators must have not only the large-sample property of consistency but also that of asymptotic efficiency. Recall from Section 3.2 that this implies that, out of all consistent estimators, the OLS estimators are the ones whose sampling distributions collapse most quickly onto β and α as the sample size becomes larger.

Normality

Assumption IID, that the disturbances are normally distributed, implies that the sampling distributions for $\hat{\alpha}$ and $\hat{\beta}$ are normal distributions. To see this, consider (6.1). Since the X_i can be regarded as fixed constants, this equation implies that each Y_i is the sum of a constant and a normally distributed disturbance. Adding a constant to a normally distributed variable does not change the shape of that variable's distribution but merely shifts the distribution along the horizontal axis. Hence each of the Y_i has a normal distribution. But the OLS estimators are linear functions of the Y_i, given assumptions IA and IB. Since, as we saw in Chapter 2, any linear function of normally distributed variables will itself have a normal distribution, it follows that the OLS estimators $\hat{\beta}$ and $\hat{\alpha}$ must also have such distributions.

Since $\hat{\beta}$ and $\hat{\alpha}$ are unbiased and have variances given by (6.14) and (6.15), we can say that if all classical assumptions hold then

$$\hat{\beta} \text{ is } N(\beta, \sigma_{\hat{\beta}}^2) \tag{6.16}$$

$$\hat{\alpha} \text{ is } N(\alpha, \sigma_{\hat{\alpha}}^2) \tag{6.17}$$

where $\sigma_{\hat{\beta}}^2$ and $\sigma_{\hat{\alpha}}^2$ are given by (6.14) and (6.15) respectively.

As we shall see shortly, (6.16) and (6.17) are of crucial importance if we wish to make inferences about the true values of the population regression parameters β and α.

Maximum likelihood estimation

Once the assumption is made that the disturbances are normally distributed, it becomes possible to apply the method of maximum likelihood to the estimation of the regression parameters α and β. Details of the derivation of MLEs are given in Appendix 6B at the end of this chapter, but two facts are noted here. First, the MLEs of α and β turn out to be identical to the OLS estimators. Thus, under classical assumptions, *the OLS estimators are maximum likelihood estimators.* That is, of all possible values that the unknown α and β might take, the ones 'most likely' to have generated a particular sample are those obtained when OLS estimates are computed.

Secondly, the ML method of estimation also yields an estimator of the other parameter in the classical two-variable model, namely the disturbance variance σ^2. As can be seen from Appendix 6B, this estimator is

$$\tilde{\sigma}^2 = \frac{\sum e_i^2}{n} \tag{6.18}$$

$\sum e_i^2$ is of course the sum of the squares of the OLS residuals. Since, from (4.13), a property of these residuals is that their sum and hence their mean is zero, (6.18) is in fact the variance of the residuals. This is logical enough, since, if we regard residuals as being estimates of the corresponding unknown disturbances, it is natural to estimate the disturbance variance by the residual variance. Since (6.18) is an MLE, it is a consistent estimator of σ^2. Unfortunately, however, it is not unbiased. As shown in Appendix 6C,

$$E(\tilde{\sigma}^2) = \frac{n-2}{n}\sigma^2 \tag{6.19}$$

Thus in small samples $\tilde{\sigma}^2$ underestimates the unknown σ^2.

6.3 Making inferences about the regression parameters

We have seen that, provided all classical assumptions hold, the OLS estimators are normally distributed as (6.16) and (6.17). It follows that

$$\frac{\hat{\beta} - \beta}{\sigma_{\hat{\beta}}} \quad \text{and} \quad \frac{\hat{\alpha} - \alpha}{\sigma_{\hat{\alpha}}} \text{ have } N(0, 1) \text{ distributions} \tag{6.20}$$

That is, they are standard normal variables. If the disturbance variance σ^2 were known, we could use (6.20) as the basis for forming confidence intervals for and testing hypotheses about the parameters α and β. Unfortunately, σ^2 is unknown, but an unbiased estimate of it is given by

$$s^2 = \frac{n}{n-2}\tilde{\sigma}^2 = \frac{\sum e_i^2}{n-2} \tag{6.21}$$

because, using (6.19),

$$Es^2 = E\left(\frac{n}{n-2}\right)\tilde{\sigma}^2 = \frac{n}{n-2}E\tilde{\sigma}^2 = \sigma^2$$

Given an unbiased estimator of σ^2, unbiased estimators of the variances of $\hat{\alpha}$ and $\hat{\beta}$ can be obtained by replacing the σ^2 in (6.14) and (6.15) by its unbiased estimator (6.21). The estimators of $\sigma^2_{\hat{\beta}}$ and $\sigma^2_{\hat{\alpha}}$ are given by

$$s^2_{\hat{\beta}} = \frac{s^2}{\sum x_i^2} \tag{6.22}$$

and

$$s^2_{\hat{\alpha}} = \frac{s^2 \sum X_i^2}{n \sum x_i^2} \tag{6.23}$$

However, when we replace $\sigma_{\hat{\alpha}}$ and $\sigma_{\hat{\beta}}$ in (6.20) by $s_{\hat{\alpha}}$ and $s_{\hat{\beta}}$, as explained in Appendix 6D, we have to switch to the Student's t distribution, so that

$$\frac{\hat{\beta} - \beta}{s_{\hat{\beta}}} \quad \text{and} \quad \frac{\hat{\alpha} - \alpha}{s_{\hat{\alpha}}} \quad \text{have Student's } t \text{ distributions with } n - 2 \text{ d.f.} \tag{6.24}$$

To clarify the above, we derive the estimated variances (6.22) and (6.23) for the first example of Chapter 4, relating to the consumption function of four-person households. For this example, we have computed

$$\hat{\alpha} = 30.71, \quad \hat{\beta} = 0.812 \tag{6.25}$$

and also the 'basic building blocks'

$$\sum x_i^2 = 166\ 258.2, \quad \sum y_i^2 = 158\ 688.5, \quad \sum x_i y_i = 135\ 068.5 \tag{6.26}$$

To obtain the estimated variances (6.22) and (6.23), we first need to use (6.21) to estimate the variance of the disturbances, σ^2. To do this, we require the sum of squared residuals, $\sum e_i^2$. This is most easily obtained by using (4.27) and (4.30). These imply $\sum y_i^2 = \hat{\beta}^2 \sum x_i^2 + \sum e_i^2$. Thus

$$\sum e_i^2 = \sum y_i^2 - \hat{\beta}^2 \sum x_i^2 \tag{6.27}$$

For reasons that will become clearer in a later chapter, it is instructive to substitute for $\hat{\beta}$ in (6.27) to obtain

$$\sum e_i^2 = \sum y_i^2 - \hat{\beta} \sum x_i y_i \tag{6.28}$$

Notice that (6.28) contains two of the 'basic building blocks' (6.26). This is what makes it such a convenient expression to use. Using (6.25) and (6.26) to substitute in (6.28), we obtain

$$\sum e_i^2 = 158\ 688.5 - 0.812(135\ 068.5) = 49\ 012.9 \tag{6.29}$$

We can now use (6.21) to obtain an estimate of σ^2. Since $n - 2 = 23$,

$$s^2 = \frac{49\ 012.9}{23} = 2131.0 \tag{6.30}$$

Given (6.30), we can now use (6.22) and (6.23) to estimate the required variances. To compute (6.23), we also require $\sum X_i^2$, which can be obtained from Table 4.2 as 832 146.8. Hence, again making use of one of the basic building blocks,

$$s_{\hat{\beta}}^2 = \frac{2131}{166\ 258.2} = 0.0128 \tag{6.31}$$

and

$$s_{\hat{\alpha}}^2 = \frac{2131(832\ 146.8)}{25(166\ 258.2)} = 426.6 \tag{6.32}$$

Taking the square roots of (6.31) and (6.32), we obtain the **estimated standard errors** of $\hat{\beta}$ and $\hat{\alpha}$ as

$$s_{\hat{\beta}} = 0.113, \qquad s_{\hat{\alpha}} = 20.65 \tag{6.33}$$

It is worth pausing at this point to reflect on what exactly the quantities computed in (6.33) actually mean. Recall that different samples of households will yield different values for the OLS estimators $\hat{\alpha}$ and $\hat{\beta}$. Repeated sampling would result in a distribution or 'spread' of different values for $\hat{\alpha}$ and $\hat{\beta}$. The true standard errors of α and β are measures of the extent of this spread. The values in (6.33) are our estimates of these true standard errors. The computational steps required to obtain them are summarized in Table 6.1.

Confidence intervals

We saw in Section 3.2 that the standard form for a confidence interval is

point estimate + (critical value)(standard error of estimate)

Since we are now dealing with the Student's t distribution, the critical values must be taken from t tables. For the parameter α, the point estimate is given by the OLS estimator $\hat{\alpha}$ and the standard error by $s_{\hat{\alpha}}$ from (6.23). Thus, for example, a 95% confidence interval for α is given by

$$\hat{\alpha} + t_{0.025} s_{\hat{\alpha}} \tag{6.34}$$

To find a 99% interval, we simply replace the critical value $t_{0.025}$ by $t_{0.005}$. Similarly, a 95% confidence interval for β is given by

$$\hat{\beta} + t_{0.025} s_{\hat{\beta}} \tag{6.35}$$

Again, to form a 99% interval, $t_{0.005}$ replaces $t_{0.025}$.

Table 6.1 Computational procedure for two-variable regression

Step 1	Compute the quantities:
	$$\sum X_i \quad \sum Y_i \quad \sum X_i^2 \quad \sum Y_i^2 \quad \sum X_i Y_i$$
Step 2	**Compute basic building blocks:**
	$$\sum x_i^2 = \sum X_i^2 - (1/n)(\sum X_i)^2$$ $$\sum y_i^2 = \sum Y_i^2 - (1/n)(\sum Y_i)^2$$ $$\sum x_i y_i = \sum X_i Y_i - (1/n)(\sum X_i)(\sum Y_i)$$
Step 3	Compute OLS estimates:
	$$\hat{\beta} = \frac{\sum x_i y_i}{\sum x_i^2}, \qquad \hat{\alpha} = \frac{\sum Y_i}{n} - \hat{\beta}\frac{\sum X_i}{n}$$
Step 4	Compute residual sum of squares and s^2:
	$$\sum e_i^2 = \sum y_i^2 - \hat{\beta}\sum x_i y_i, \qquad s^2 = \frac{\sum e_i^2}{n-2}$$
Step 5	Compute standard errors of $\hat{\alpha}$ and $\hat{\beta}$:
	$$s_{\hat{\alpha}}^2 = \frac{s^2 \sum X_i^2}{n \sum x_i^2}, \qquad s_{\hat{\beta}}^2 = \frac{s^2}{\sum x_i^2}$$

Taking again as our example the consumption function for four-person households, if we require 95% confidence intervals then, since d.f. $= n - 2 = 23$, we have $t_{0.025} = 2.069$. A 95% confidence interval for α is therefore, using (6.25) and (6.33),

$$30.71 \pm 2.069(20.65) = 30.71 \pm 42.72$$

and a 95% confidence interval for the MPC, β, is

$$0.812 \pm 2.069(0.113) = 0.812 \pm 0.234$$

Notice that the width of the above confidence intervals is quite large. For example the interval for the marginal propensity to consume, β, stretches from 0.578 to 1.046. This is a reflection of the smallness of our sample. With $n = 25$ only, we cannot expect great precision in our estimates.

Significance tests

Consider the population relationship (6.1). If $\beta = 0$ in this equation then X does not influence Y, which then has an expected value of α, from which it can only be disturbed by a non-zero ϵ. If $\beta \neq 0$, however, then this means that X does influence Y. We can therefore test whether X influences Y by setting up the null hypothesis H_0:

$\beta = 0$ and testing it against an alternative hypothesis $H_A: \beta \neq 0$. We can obtain a test statistic for this purpose from (6.24). Under H_0,

$$\hat{\beta}/s_{\hat{\beta}} \text{ has a Student's } t \text{ distribution with } n - 2 \text{ d.f.} \tag{6.36}$$

We can therefore use $\hat{\beta}/s_{\hat{\beta}}$ as a test statistic, and reject the null hypothesis $\beta = 0$ (X does not influence Y) if the absolute value of this test statistic exceeds the relevant critical value taken from Student's t tables. Effectively what we do is to consider whether the OLS estimate $\hat{\beta}$ is sufficiently different from zero for us to reject the null hypothesis that the true β is non-zero. Dividing $\hat{\beta}$ by its estimated standard error enables us to use Student's t tables to decide what is meant by 'sufficiently different'.

Again taking the example of the household consumption function from the early part of Chapter 4, $H_0: \beta = 0$ implies that a household's income does not influence its consumption. Since if β is non-zero we expect $\beta > 0$ in this case, we employ an upper tail test. That is, the alternative hypothesis is $H_A: \beta > 0$. Taking the 0.05 level of significance, the critical t value is $t_{0.05} = 1.714$ (d.f. $= n - 2 = 23$). In this case we have $\hat{\beta} = 0.812$ and $s_{\hat{\beta}} = 0.113$, so that the test statistic (6.36) takes a value of 7.19. This clearly exceeds the critical value, so we can reject the null hypothesis $\beta = 0$ at the 0.05 significance level and conclude that household income influences consumption.

It is possible to test a null hypothesis $H_0: \alpha = 0$ in a similar manner. Under this null hypothesis, we have from (6.24) that

$$\hat{\alpha}/s_{\hat{\alpha}} \text{ has a Student's } t \text{ distribution with } n - 2 \text{ d.f.} \tag{6.37}$$

(6.37) may therefore be used as a test statistic, and we reject H_0 if its absolute value exceeds the relevant critical t value.

Once the estimated standard errors $s_{\hat{\alpha}}$ and $s_{\hat{\beta}}$ have been computed, it is clearly a simple matter to test the null hypotheses $\alpha = 0$ and $\beta = 0$. The test statistics used, $\hat{\alpha}/s_{\hat{\alpha}}$ and $\hat{\beta}/s_{\hat{\beta}}$, are referred to as t **ratios**. It is customary to present sample regression equations with these t ratios placed in parentheses underneath the estimates $\hat{\alpha}$ and $\hat{\beta}$. That is, we present

$$\hat{Y} = \underset{(\hat{\alpha}/s_{\hat{\alpha}})}{\hat{\alpha}} + \underset{(\hat{\beta}/s_{\hat{\beta}})}{\hat{\beta}X} \tag{6.38}$$

Thus for the first example of the last chapter, we would present

$$\hat{Y} = \underset{(1.49)}{30.71} + \underset{(7.19)}{0.812X}$$

Once regression results are presented in this manner, one can immediately perform a quick rough test of whether or not a regression parameter is zero. For example, in (6.38), if we wish to test whether or not X influences Y ($H_0: \beta = 0$), the value of the relevant test statistic is given by the t ratio underneath $\hat{\beta}$. Suppose the required level of significance is 0.05. Provided the sample is sufficiently large (25 or more), the critical value for t is $t_{0.025} \approx 2$, assuming this time a two-tail test (the more common situation). Hence we reject $\beta = 0$, and say that X influences Y, if the absolute value of the t ratio in parentheses exceeds a value of approximately two.[2] When this happens, it is customary to say that *the estimated coefficient of X is significantly different from zero at the 0.05 level of significance.*

There are occasions when we may wish to test hypotheses other than $\beta = 0$ and $\alpha = 0$. Suppose we wished to test the hypothesis that the parameter β takes some non-zero value β^*. Under H_0, $\beta = \beta^*$, and we can see from (6.24) that the required test statistic is $(\hat{\beta} - \beta^*)/s_{\hat{\beta}}$. Under H_0 this will have a Student's t distribution with the usual $n - 2$ degrees of freedom.

For example, in our four-person household consumption function example, we might wish to test whether the MPC β of households was less than unity. We can set up a null hypothesis H_0: $\beta = 1$ and test it using the test statistic $(\hat{\beta} - 1)/s_{\hat{\beta}}$. Since the alternative has to be H_A: $\beta < 1$, we use a lower tail test.

Under H_0, the test statistic has a Student's t distribution, so we expect its value to be close to zero. Since we will reject H_0 if the OLS estimate $\hat{\beta}$ is sufficiently different from unity, we reject if the test statistic is sufficiently different from zero. Given a one-tail test and taking the 0.05 level of significance, with $n - 2 = 23$ d.f., the relevant critical t value is $t_{0.05} = 1.714$. We reject H_0 if the absolute value of the test statistic exceeds this value. For our sample, we know that $\hat{\beta} = 0.812$ and $s_{\hat{\beta}} = 0.113$. Hence the test statistic takes a value

$$\frac{\hat{\beta} - 1}{s_{\hat{\beta}}} = \frac{0.812 - 1}{0.113} = -1.66$$

Since the absolute value of the test statistic does not in this case exceed the critical t value, we cannot reject the null hypothesis $\beta = 1$. So we must conclude that, on the basis of the present sample, there is not enough evidence to say that the MPC of households is less than unity.

Exercise 6.1

The following data refers to the price of a good P and the quantity of the good supplied, S:

P	2	7	5	1	4	8	2	8
S	15	41	32	9	28	43	17	40

$\sum s^2 = 1205,$ $\sum p^2 = 55.9,$ $\sum ps = 255.4$

(lower-case letters denote deviations of variables from means).

(a) Estimate the linear OLS regression line $E(S) = \alpha + \beta P$.
(b) Estimate the standard errors of $\hat{\alpha}$ and $\hat{\beta}$.
(c) Test the hypothesis that price influences supply.
(d) Obtain a 95% confidence interval for α. Comment on your interval.

Exercise 6.2

For the data in Exercise 4.1, estimate the standard errors of $\hat{\alpha}$ and $\hat{\beta}$. Hence

(a) test the hypothesis that the price of apples affects demand;
(b) find a 99% confidence interval for the level of demand when the price of apples is zero.

Exercise 6.3

For the data in Exercise 4.2, estimate the standard errors of the OLS estimators.
    It is claimed that a rise of one percentage point in the rate of interest leads to a fall of $10 billion dollars in the demand for money. Test this claim.

Exercise 6.4

For the data in Exercise 4.6, test the hypothesis that a rise of $1 billion in national income leads to a rise of more than $0.2 billions in the demand for transactionary balances.

Prediction

In Chapter 4 we saw that we could use sample regression lines to make predictions. For example, we used Equation (4.25), an estimated household consumption function, to predict the consumption of a household with income $X_{26} = 247.3$, obtaining the predicted value $\hat{Y}_{26} = 231.5$. In this subsection we show that, provided the classical assumptions hold, it is possible to form confidence intervals for such predictions.

In general, suppose we have a population regression equation given by (4.4) that has been estimated by a sample regression equation (4.6). A new observation X_0 becomes available (this might be the income of an additional household), and we wish to predict the corresponding value of Y, that is, Y_0. Using (4.6), our predicted value will be

$$\hat{Y}_0 = \hat{\alpha} + \hat{\beta} X_0 \tag{6.39}$$

The predicted value obtained from (6.39) will not normally coincide with the true value Y_0, which is given by

$$Y_0 = \alpha + \beta X_0 + \epsilon_0 \tag{6.40}$$

The difference between (6.39) and (6.40) is termed a prediction error or **forecast error**[3] f. That is,

$$f = Y_0 - \hat{Y}_0$$

$$= (\alpha - \hat{\alpha}) + (\beta - \hat{\beta})X_0 + \epsilon_0 \tag{6.41}$$

Equation (6.41) demonstrates that forecast errors are the result of

(a) $\alpha - \hat{\alpha}$ and $\beta - \hat{\beta}$, the sampling errors in estimating the unknown parameters α and β;

(b) the disturbance ϵ_0 associated with the new value X_0.

The first of these sources of error is the result of having to estimate an unknown population regression equation. Such an error may be reduced if we increase our sample size and thus increase the precision with which we estimate α and β. The second source of forecast error is a result of the basic randomness in the relationship between X and Y. This is beyond our control.

Notice from (6.41) that f depends on $\hat{\alpha}$ and $\hat{\beta}$. Like $\hat{\alpha}$ and $\hat{\beta}$, the error in forecasting Y_0 will therefore vary from sample to sample. Since under classical assumptions $\hat{\alpha}$, $\hat{\beta}$ and ϵ_0 are all *normally distributed*, f, which is a linear function of these variables, will therefore itself be normally distributed. Since $E(\hat{\alpha}) = \alpha$, $E(\hat{\beta}) = \beta$ and $E(\epsilon_0) = 0$, it follows from (6.41) that

$$E(f) = \alpha - E(\hat{\alpha}) + [\beta - E(\hat{\beta})]X_0 + E(\epsilon_0) = 0$$

That is, the mean of the sampling distribution for f is zero. Thus under classical assumptions, OLS estimation results in *mean forecast errors that are zero*. Thus OLS predictions are *unbiased*.

The derivation of the *variance of the forecast error* is lengthy and tedious, so we shall not reproduce it here,[4] but it can be shown to be

$$\sigma_f^2 = \sigma^2 \left[1 + \frac{1}{n} + \frac{(X_0 - \bar{X})^2}{\sum x_i^2} \right] \tag{6.42}$$

where σ^2 is, as usual, the variance of the disturbances and $\bar{X}$ and $\sum x_i^2$ refer to the original n sample observations.

We can summarize the above by saying that, under classical assumptions, the forecast error has a sampling distribution of the form

$$f \text{ is } N(0, \sigma_f^2) \tag{6.43}$$

It is on the basis of (6.43) that we are able to construct a confidence interval for the unknown Y_0. It follows immediately that

$$\frac{f}{\sigma_f} = \frac{Y_0 - \hat{Y}_0}{\sigma_f} \text{ has a } N(0, 1) \text{ distribution} \tag{6.44}$$

The problem with (6.44) is that σ_f depends on the unknown parameter σ^2. However, if we replace σ^2 in (6.42) by its unbiased estimator s^2 (as given by (6.21)), we can obtain an unbiased estimator of the variance of the forecast error f given by

$$s_f^2 = s^2 \left[1 + \frac{1}{n} + \frac{(X_0 - \bar{X})^2}{\sum x_i^2} \right] \tag{6.45}$$

Replacing σ_f by s_f in (6.44), we then have that

$$\frac{Y_0 - \hat{Y}_0}{s_f} \text{ has a Student's } t \text{ distribution with } n - 2 \text{ degrees of freedom} \qquad (6.46)$$

We can now make use of the general expression for a confidence interval introduced in Section 3.2. For example, a 95% confidence interval for the forecast error $Y_0 - \hat{Y}_0$ would be

$$0 \pm t_{0.025} s_f$$

Of more direct interest is a 95% confidence interval for the unknown Y_0 that we are trying to predict. This is given by

$$\hat{Y}_0 \pm t_{0.025} s_f \qquad (6.47)$$

To obtain a 99% interval, $t_{0.025}$ in (6.47) is replaced by $t_{0.005}$.

Notice that the width of the prediction interval (6.47) depends on the variance of the forecast error as given by (6.42) and its estimate (6.45). Thus the smaller is the variance of the forecast error, the smaller becomes the width of the prediction interval and hence the more precise becomes our forecast of Y_0. Study of (6.42) indicates that the variance of the forecast error will be the smaller

(a) the smaller is the basic randomness of the relationship between X and Y, as measured by σ^2;

(b) the larger is the original sample size n;

(c) the larger is the variability in the X values for the original sample (that is, the larger is $\sum x_i^2$);

(d) the closer is X_0 to the mean of the sample X values, $\bar{X}$.

The last of the above factors implies that our forecasts of Y_0 will be more precise for values of X_0 close to $\bar{X}$. This suggests, quite reasonably, that we are able to forecast better for values of X_0 that are similar to those already experienced (i.e. similar to those in the original sample). Forecasts for values of X_0 outside our experience, that is, outside the range of sample values, are rather more uncertain. This is illustrated in Figure 6.2, where we have drawn the sample regression line (4.6). For any given value of X_0, this line yields the point predictor of Y_0 given by (6.39). For any given X_0, the upper and lower limits of the confidence interval for Y_0 are given by the two curves. Notice that the further we are from X, the wider is the 'confidence band'.

As an illustration of the construction of a prediction interval, consider again the estimated household consumption function (4.25), and suppose again that we wish to predict the consumption of an additional household with an income this time written as $X_0 = 247.3$. Substituting this value into (4.25), we obtain the point predictor of consumption $\hat{Y}_0 = 231.5$ as in Chapter 4. To compute the prediction interval (6.47), we must estimate the variance of the forecast error using (6.45). Substituting in (6.45),

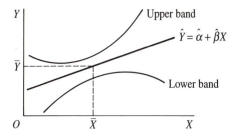

Figure 6.2 Confidence band for predictions.

we have $n = 25$, $s^2 = 2131$ from (6.30) and $\sum x_i^2 = 166\ 258.2$ from (6.26). $\bar{X} = 163.2$ from (4.19), so that $X_0 - \bar{X} = 247.3 - 163.2 = 84.1$. Thus

$$s_f^2 = 2131\left[1 + \frac{1}{25} + \frac{(84.1)^2}{166\ 258.2}\right] = 2306.9, \qquad s_f = 48.03$$

Since, with $n - 2$ d.f., $t_{0.025} = 2.069$, a 95% prediction interval is, using (6.47),

$$231.5 \pm 2.069(48.03) = 231.5 \pm 99.4 \tag{6.48}$$

We can therefore say that we are 95% confident that a household with income 247.3 will have a consumption level between 132.1 and 330.9. The prediction interval may seem rather wide, but this is a consequence of the smallness of the original sample and the fact that the income of the household, 247.3, lay some way from the sample mean $\bar{X} = 163.2$.

Notice that confidence bands such as that illustrated in Figure 6.2 may be constructed, even though we have no observations additional to our original sample. We merely have to use (6.47) to compute prediction intervals for a series of arbitrary values of X_0.

Suppose, after the construction of a confidence band, an additional observation becomes available. For example, in our household consumption example we might acquire data on the income and consumption of another household. Such an extra observation can be represented by the coordinates of an additional point on a diagram such as that in Figure 6.2. If such a point lies outside the confidence band drawn then this can be interpreted as implying that the consumption–income relationship for the new household differs from that of the households in the original sample. However, if the point lies within the confidence band then we have no evidence for suggesting this. For example, in our above numerical example we constructed the interval (6.48) for a household with income $X_0 = 247.3$. Suppose it transpired that this household actually had a consumption level $Y_0 = 124$. Since this value lies outside the prediction interval, we would have to conclude that the consumption function for this household differed from that of the households in the original sample.

Exercise 6.5

For the data in Exercise 6.1, obtain a 95% prediction interval for the quantity of the good supplied when price $P = 10$. If it transpires that S actually equals 56 when $P = 10$, what would you conclude?

6.4 Nonlinear regression again

In Section 6.2 we outlined the properties of the OLS estimators and indicated which of the classical assumptions were necessary for each property. In Section 6.3 we saw how we could make inferences about the population regression parameters, assuming that the classical assumptions held. However, it cannot be stressed too strongly that everything stated in Sections 6.2 and 6.3 is dependent on Equation (4.1) being a correct representation of the true relationship between X and Y. That is, our **specification** of the population regression equation must be correct. For example, suppose the true relationship between X and Y had a nonlinear form, such as that given by (4.51), so that the population regression equation was

$$E(Y) = \alpha + \beta \ln (X) \tag{6.49}$$

Clearly, we cannot expect the normal OLS estimators (4.16) and (4.18), which are based on a linear regression line, to provide sensible values for α and β in (6.49). Similarly, if any of the other nonlinear relationships discussed in Section 4.5 describe the true population relationship then the expressions (4.16) and (4.18) will be equally invalid estimators. Furthermore, we cannot expect the significance testing procedures of the last section to be valid if we have mis-specified the population regression line as linear.

Of course, if we are confident about the precise form of any nonlinearity in the population relationship and are able by a simple transformation to eliminate the nonlinearity, then our normal techniques can still be applied. For example, in Section 4.5, by observing the scatter in Figure 4.8, we were able to decide on a double-log form for our Engel curve for food. By working in terms of the transformed variables $X^* = \ln (X)$ and $Y^* = \ln (Y)$, we were able to convert the Engel curve to linear form and compute the sample regression equation (4.46).

If we are confident about the nonlinear specification we have chosen then not only can we satisfactorily estimate population parameters but we can also make inferences about them. For example, suppose that in the Engel curve example of Section 4.5 we wished to test the hypothesis that the elasticity of food expenditure with respect to total expenditure was less than unity. This involves testing the null hypothesis H_0: $\beta = 1$ in the double-log relationship (4.39), against the alternative H_A: $\beta < 1$. The test proceeds in similar manner to that of the last section, except that we work in terms of the transformed variables $X^* = \ln (X)$ and $Y^* = \ln (Y)$. Our estimate of the required elasticity was $\hat{\beta} = 0.364$, so that, using (6.28), (6.21) and the basic building blocks computed below (4.44), we have

$$\sum e_i^* = 1.107 - 0.364(2.694) = 0.126, \qquad s^2 = 0.126/23 = 0.00549$$

Thus, using (6.22), the estimated variance of $\hat{\beta}$ is

$$s_{\hat{\beta}}^2 = 0.005\,49/7.403 = 0.000\,742$$

The test statistic is

$$\frac{\hat{\beta} - 1}{s_{\hat{\beta}}} = \frac{0.364 - 1}{0.027} = -23.55$$

Since the absolute value of the test statistic easily exceeds a critical t value (with $n - 2 = 23$ d.f.) of $t_{0.05} = 1.714$, we reject the null hypothesis at the 0.05 level of significance. The food elasticity appears to be less than unity.

Exercise 6.6

For the data used in Exercises 4.3 and 4.8, estimate the standard errors of $\hat{\alpha}$ and $\hat{\beta}$ in the regression $\hat{A} = \hat{\alpha} + \hat{\beta}(1/Q)$. Hence test the hypothesis that the firm's *fixed* costs exceed 4000.

Exercise 6.7

For the data in Exercise 6.1, if $X = \ln(P)$ and $Y = \ln(S)$, then

$$\sum x^2 = 4.16, \qquad \sum xy = 3.02, \qquad \sum y^2 = 2.23$$

(a) Calculate $\sum X$ and $\sum Y$, and hence estimate a supply equation of the form $\hat{S} = \hat{A}P^{\hat{\beta}}$.
(b) Find a 95% confidence interval for the elasticity of supply.

Exercise 6.8

For the data in Exercise 4.7, assume that the firm's average revenue function has the form $\hat{P} = \hat{K}Q^{\hat{\beta}}$. Hence test the hypothesis that elasticity of demand for the firm's product is greater than unity.

Tests for mis-specification

Problems arise when we are uncertain how to specify the population regression equation – should it be linear or nonlinear? If it is nonlinear, what form of nonlinearity should we specify? Since, as was pointed out earlier, we cannot rely on our estimating method or our inferential procedures if we mis-specify the population regression equation, this is a serious problem. Econometricians are therefore often concerned with testing for mis-specification.

The obvious procedure in two-variable regression is to plot the equation we have estimated on the scatter diagram of the sample observations. In Figure 6.3 we present again the scatter for the observations in Table 4.4 on the food and total expenditure of our cross-section of households. This time, however, we show in Figure 6.3 the linear sample regression line we would have obtained had we employed straightforward linear regression to what is apparently a nonlinear scatter. The line is in fact

$$\hat{Y} = 38.05 + 0.124X \tag{6.50}$$

The task of computing (6.50) is left to the reader.

Recall that the distances of points in a scatter from an OLS regression equation represent the residuals, that is, the e_i. The fact that we have fitted a linear relationship to what is apparently a nonlinear scatter is reflected in the size and pattern of these residuals. There is a tendency for positive residuals (points above the line), and also for negative residuals (points below the line), to be grouped together. This is obviously a direct consequence of our mis-specifying the regression equation. The actual values of these residuals are in fact shown in Table 6.2, where the residuals have been listed according to the size of X.

When runs of largely negative residuals tend to alternate with runs of largely positive residuals, as in Table 6.2, this is symptomatic of a mis-specified population regression equation. An extreme case is illustrated by the hypothetical scatter of points in Figure 6.4. These points lie almost exactly on the nonlinear function represented by the drawn curve. However, if the solid line in the figure is fitted to these points, it is easily seen that, if we order the residuals by the size of X then the first 6 residuals are positive, the next 18 are negative and the final 8 are positive.

Similar, although less obvious patterns can arise if the mis-specification involves selecting the wrong type of nonlinear regression equation for a nonlinear scatter. Because of this, econometricians always check their specifications by analysing the

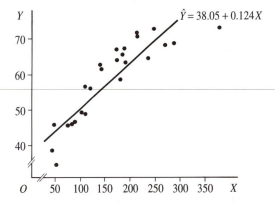

Figure 6.3 Nonlinear scatter and linear sample regression line.

Table 6.2 Residuals listed according to size of X

X value	Residual
45.73	− 6.4992
52.30	0.7738
54.08	− 10.9076
78.44	− 2.6968
86.22	− 3.1542
88.76	− 2.9501
105.20	− 2.4044
111.44	− 3.4804
111.80	4.2749
122.35	2.4930
142.24	6.5996
144.60	5.3062
174.36	4.0455
174.50	7.1381
181.80	− 2.4197
185.20	4.2375
188.56	5.6097
191.60	1.2617
214.60	6.4816
215.40	5.7221
237.20	− 3.2287
247.12	3.7577
269.60	− 3.4477
286.24	− 5.1969
373.00	− 11.3156

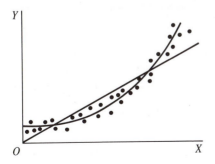

Figure 6.4 Runs of positive and negative residuals.

residuals from any fitted equations. Whenever we find a tendency for distinct patterns to arise we should suspect a mis-specified regression equation.

Residual patterns are not always as clear cut as that in Figure 6.4. However, a number of statistics can be used for testing for possible patterns in sets of residuals. The resultant tests are referred to as **tests of mis-specification**. Possibly the best known is the **Durbin–Watson statistic**, which in a moment we shall apply to the residuals of Table 6.2 and Figure 6.3. As we shall see in Chapter 10, this statistic was actually first developed as a test for autocorrelated disturbances (that is a breakdown in assumption IIC of the classical model). However, it is more suitably regarded nowadays as a test statistic for possible mis-specification. It is defined as

$$dw = \frac{\sum\limits_{i=2}^{n}(e_i - e_{i-1})^2}{\sum\limits_{i=1}^{n} e_i^2} \tag{6.51}$$

In calculating (6.51), the residuals have to be listed as in Table 6.2, according to the size of X. If this is done then, if runs of positive and negative residuals occur, the quantity in the numerator of (6.51) will be small because e_i and e_{i-1} will usually tend to be of similar magnitude and sign.[5] Hence dw will be close to zero in these circumstances. However, if the regression equation is correctly specified and the disturbances follow all the classical assumptions then, as we will show in Chapter 10, dw can be expected to take a value close to 2. Thus a value much closer to 0 than 2 could well mean a mis-specified regression equation. The calculations necessary to compute the Durbin–Watson statistic for the residuals in Table 6.2 are indicated in Table 6.3, where we have rounded the residuals shown to one decimal place. The

Table 6.3 Computation of the Durbin–Watson statistic

i	e_i	e_i^2	e_{i-1}	$e_i - e_{i-1}$	$(e_i - e_{i-1})^2$	
1	− 6.5	42.3	—	—	—	
2	0.8	0.6	− 6.5	7.3	53.3	
3	− 10.9	118.8	0.8	− 11.7	136.9	
4	− 2.7	7.3	− 10.9	8.2	67.2	$dw = \dfrac{754.6}{692.3} = 1.09$
⋮	⋮	⋮	⋮	⋮	⋮	
23	− 3.4	11.6	3.8	− 7.2	51.8	
24	− 5.2	27.0	− 3.4	− 1.8	3.2	
25	− 11.3	127.7	− 5.2	− 6.1	37.2	
		692.3			754.6	

value for *dw* is as low as 1.09, indicating the specification error that has been made in fitting a linear equation to the scatter in Figure 6.3.

In contrast, when the nonlinear equation (4.46) is fitted to this scatter and the residuals again ordered according to the size of X, the reader should verify that the Durbin–Watson statistic takes a much higher value of 1.95. This is very much closer to 2, suggesting that a specification error is now much less likely.

We shall consider the Durbin–Watson statistic in more detail in Chapter 10 when we come to discuss autocorrelation. Here we merely point out that a tendency towards runs of positive and negative residuals can sometimes be the result of something other than a mis-specified regression equation. Recall that assumption IIC of the classical model (that of non-autocorrelated disturbances) could break down because of a tendency for disturbances to spill over from one observation to another. If we regard residuals as estimates of the unknown disturbances then runs of positive and negative residuals could be interpreted as being the result of such spillover effects. In our case examination of Figure 6.3 strongly suggests mis-specification when a linear equation is fitted. However, there is an obvious danger of misinterpreting a specification error in our regression equation and wrongly suspecting a breakdown of the classical assumption of non-autocorrelated disturbances.

Clearly, there is the possibility of confusion when interpreting residual patterns. However, most econometricians would nowadays spend considerable time searching for a more appropriate specification before accepting that, for example, a very low Durbin–Watson statistic was indicative of a breakdown in assumption IIC.

Exercise 6.9

In Exercise 4.7 the data was used to estimate the OLS regression $\hat{P} = \hat{\alpha} + \hat{\beta}Q$. Find the residuals for this regression. Hence compute the Durbin–Watson statistic and comment.

6.5   Relaxation of the assumption of non-stochastic X

As we have seen the most implausible assumption of the classical model, as far as economic data is concerned, is that of a non-stochastic explanatory variable. It is very rarely the case that we are able to fix the values of our X variable and perform a controlled experiment. In this section we will relax this assumption, thus going a little way towards making the model suitable for use with typical data sets. We replace assumptions IA, IB and IC by the following:

The explanatory X variable:

(IA') is stochastic;

(IB') has values that are distributed independently of the disturbance, ϵ;

(IC') is such that plim $(\sum x_i^2/n) = Q$, where Q is a fixed finite constant.

Assumption IA' implies that the X values can no longer be regarded as fixed, but are determined by some random sampling process. This is clearly a more plausible assumption for economic data sets.

Once we adopt assumption IA' and abandon the idea that the values of X are determined by some investigator, it should be clear that in any repeated sampling process it is no longer possible to envisage the same set of X values arising in each sample. Not merely the disturbance values but also the X values will now vary from sample to sample, since they are outside the control of the investigator. Assumption IB' states that each such X value is independent of each and every disturbance value. That is, for example, when many samples are taken, the X_5 values obtained are completely uninfluenced by the ϵ_5 values obtained, or the ϵ_2 values obtained, or the ϵ_{12} values obtained, etc. The situation is similar for any other X values. The importance of this will become increasingly clear later in this section and in Chapter 8, but for now we merely note that assumption IB is a special case of assumption IB'. If the X values are fixed and unchanged from sample to sample then obviously they could not be influenced by the disturbance values.

Assumption IC' replaces IC, because, now that X is stochastic, the variance $\sum x_i^2/n$ will vary from sample to sample. However, as the size of the samples taken tends to infinity, the sampling distribution for $\sum x_i^2/n$ is assumed to collapse onto the finite number Q. The significance of this assumption, like that of assumption IB', will become clearer in the next subsection.

It may seem that, now we have relaxed the assumption of non-stochastic X, we should reformulate the classical assumptions concerning the disturbance. If the X values are no longer fixed constants, we should now only consider conditional distributions for the disturbances, i.e. those distributions we would obtain for *given* sets of values for the X variable. These distributions might differ, depending on what set of X values we are faced with. Thus it might seem necessary to reformulate, for example, assumption IIA as

(IIA') $E(\epsilon_i | X_1, X_2, X_3, \ldots, X_n) = 0$ for all i.

However, assumption IB' states that the ϵ and X values are independent. As we saw at the end of Chapter 2, marginal (i.e. unconditional) distributions and conditional distributions are identical for independent variables (recall that if P and Q are independent then $\Pr(P | Q) = \Pr(P)$). Thus the distribution of the ϵ_i is uninfluenced by the X_i values obtained. It follows that the conditional properties of the ϵ_i are identical to the marginal or unconditional properties, so that assumption IIA' reduces to IIA – that is, no reformulation is necessary. Similarly, given independence between the ϵ and X values, no reformulation of the other assumptions concerning the disturbance is necessary either.

Effect on the OLS estimators

How does our relaxation of the assumption of non-stochastic X affect the properties of the OLS estimators? First, they will remain unbiased. Consider Equation (6.8), noting that, since the w_i are functions of the X_i, they are now random variables and hence cannot be taken outside expectation signs as in Equation (6.9). Taking expectations over (6.8) now yields

$$
\begin{aligned}
E(\hat{\beta}) &= \beta + E(w_1\epsilon_1) + E(w_2\epsilon_2) + \cdots + E(w_n\epsilon_n) \\
&= \beta + E(w_1)E(\epsilon_1) + E(w_2)E(\epsilon_2) + \cdots + E(w_n)E(\epsilon_n)
\end{aligned}
\qquad (6.52)
$$

The second of the above steps follows from the fact that each ϵ_i is independent of all the X values and hence of each w_i. Since $E(\epsilon_i) = 0$ for all i, we again obtain $E(\hat{\beta}) = \beta$. Thus $\hat{\beta}$ is still an unbiased estimator of β under current assumptions. Similarly, the OLS estimator $\hat{\alpha}$ remains an unbiased estimator of the intercept parameter α.

With stochastic X, the w_i in (6.3) can no longer be treated as fixed constants. Hence $\hat{\beta}$ is no longer a linear estimator, and therefore cannot be a best linear unbiased estimator. But it can be shown that $\hat{\beta}$ *retains the property of efficiency*; that is, it still has the minimum variance of all unbiased estimators of β. The proof of this is, however, beyond the scope of this text. Similarly, under current assumptions, $\hat{\alpha}$ remains the efficient estimator of α.

As far as large-sample properties are concerned, it is not difficult to see that $\hat{\beta}$ retains the property of consistency. In Equation (6.12) the numerator in the last term still equals the population covariance between X and ϵ, which is zero by assumption IB′, while the denominator remains a fixed constant by assumption IC′. Thus (6.12) again reduces to plim $(\hat{\beta}) = \beta$. Similarly, under current assumptions, $\hat{\alpha}$ remains a consistent estimator of α.

Since the OLS estimators remain efficient under current assumptions, they also retain the large-sample property of asymptotic efficiency. That is, of all consistent estimators, the OLS estimators collapse most quickly onto the parameters α and β as the sample size tends to infinity.

It should be clear that relaxing the assumption of non-stochastic X, in the manner we have done, is not too damaging as far as the properties of the OLS estimators are concerned. The least squares estimating method appears to remain a method well worth considering. Unfortunately, even our present set of assumptions concerning the explanatory X variable are likely to be violated by many sets of economic data.

First, as we shall see in Chapter 8, assumption IB′, that of independence between the explanatory X variable and the disturbance, is often likely to break down. Secondly, assumption IC′ will often break down when we are dealing with time series data. As we saw earlier, many economic variables display strong upward trends over time, so that, as the sample size increases, the variance $\sum x_i^2 / n$ may increase without limit. With such a 'non-stationary' explanatory variable, assumption IC′ cannot hold.

Assumption IC′ is important, because non-stationary explanatory variables have, as we shall see, serious consequences for the properties of the OLS estimators and the validity of classical inferential techniques. For example, one problem that can arise with trending variables is that of spurious correlation. As we saw in Chapter 4, if two variables are trending then, even if there is no causal link between them, they are likely to be highly correlated. But the correlation is an entirely unmeaningful or spurious one. In two-variable regression, if the explanatory X variable exhibits a definite trend then it is very likely that the dependent Y variable will also do so. Even though X and Y may be causally linked, in these circumstances much of the correlation between the two is likely to be spurious. Moreover, it can be demonstrated that the standard classical inferential techniques described in Section 6.3 become inapplicable. Dealing with the problems of handling non-stationary variables will provide one of the major themes of the last third of this text.

Appendix 6A

The best linear unbiasedness of the OLS estimators

We derive from first principles the BLUE, $\bar{\beta}$, of β, concentrating, in particular, on the points in the derivation where we have to make use of the classical assumptions.

If our estimate is to be linear, we must have

$$\bar{\beta} = \sum a_i Y_i \qquad (6A.1)$$

where the a_i are constants to be determined, but may hence depend on the fixed X_i although not on the observed Y_i.

If our estimate is to be unbiased then we must have $E(\bar{\beta}) = \beta$. But

$$E(\bar{\beta}) = E(\sum a_i Y_i) = \sum a_i E(Y_i) \qquad (6A.2)$$

Since $Y_i = \alpha + \beta X_i + \epsilon_i$, if X is non-stochastic and $E(\epsilon_i) = 0$, we have

$$E(Y_i) = \alpha + \beta X_i \qquad (6A.3)$$

Substituting for $E(Y_i)$ in (6A.2) gives

$$E(\bar{\beta}) = \sum a_i(\alpha + \beta X_i) = \alpha \sum a_i + \beta \sum a_i X_i \qquad (6A.4)$$

Thus if we are to have $E(\bar{\beta}) = \beta$, it is clear from (6A.4) that we require

$$\sum a_i = 0 \quad \text{and} \quad \sum a_i X_i = 1 \qquad (6A.5)$$

If the a_i obey the restrictions (6A.5) then our estimator is unbiased.

We next derive an expression for the variance of the linear estimator (6A.1):

$$\text{Var}\,(\bar{\beta}) = \text{E}[\bar{\beta} - \text{E}(\bar{\beta})]^2 = \text{E}[\sum a_i Y_i - \text{E}(\sum a_i Y_i)]^2$$
$$= \text{E}[\sum a_i(Y_i - \text{E}(Y_i))]^2 = \text{E}(\sum a_i \epsilon_i)^2 \quad \text{(using (6A.3))}$$
$$= \text{E}[a_1^2 \epsilon_1^2 + a_2^2 \epsilon_2^2 + a_3^2 \epsilon_3^2 + \cdots + a_n^2 \epsilon_n^2$$
$$+ 2a_1 a_2 \epsilon_1 \epsilon_2 + 2a_1 a_3 \epsilon_1 \epsilon_3 + \cdots]$$
$$= a_1^2 \text{E}(\epsilon_1^2) + a_2^2 \text{E}(\epsilon_2^2) + a_3^2 \text{E}(\epsilon_3^2) + \cdots + a_n^2 \text{E}(\epsilon_n^2)$$
$$+ 2a_1 a_2 \text{E}(\epsilon_1 \epsilon_2) + 2a_1 a_3 \text{E}(\epsilon_1 \epsilon_3) + \cdots \tag{6A.6}$$

However, by assumption IIB, $\text{E}(\epsilon_i^2) = \sigma^2$ for all i, and, by assumption IIC, $\text{E}(\epsilon_i \epsilon_j) = 0$ for all $i \neq j$. Hence

$$\text{Var}\,(\bar{\beta}) = \sigma^2 \sum a_i^2 \tag{6A.7}$$

We now choose the a_i in the linear estimator (6A.1) so as to minimize the variance (6A.7) subject to the constraints (6A.5) that ensure unbiasedness. This requires the use of Lagrange multipliers.

We form the Lagrangian

$$H = \sigma^2 \sum a_i^2 - \lambda(\sum a_i) - \mu(\sum a_i X_i - 1) \tag{6A.8}$$

where λ and μ are Lagrange multipliers.

Partially differentiating H with respect to the a_i, λ and μ, equating these derivatives to zero and then rearranging eventually gives the optimal a_i as

$$a_i = \frac{x_i}{\sum x_i^2} \tag{6A.9}$$

We have omitted the details of the derivation of (6A.9) because it is lengthy and tedious and, moreover, does not involve use of any of the classical assumptions. The point is, however, that the a_i in (6A.9) are identical to the weights w_i in the expression (6.3) for the OLS estimator $\hat{\beta}$. Hence substituting these weights into (6A.1) gives

$$\bar{\beta} = \sum w_i Y_i = \sum w_i(y_i + \bar{Y}) = \sum w_i y_i \quad \text{(since } \bar{Y} \sum w_i = 0)$$
$$= \frac{\sum x_i y_i}{\sum x_i^2} = \hat{\beta}$$

Thus the best linear unbiased estimator of β is the OLS estimator.

As we noted in the main text, an advantage of the best linear unbiased method of estimation is that it also always provides us with an expression for the variance of the estimator obtained. We can obtain the variance of $\bar{\beta} = \hat{\beta}$ by substituting the optimal a_i given by (6A.9) into the expression for the variance given by (6A.7). This gives

$$\text{Var}\,(\hat{\beta}) = \text{Var}\,(\bar{\beta}) = \sigma^2 \frac{\sum x_i^2}{(\sum x_i^2)^2} = \frac{\sigma^2}{\sum x_i^2}$$

The best linear unbiased estimator of the intercept parameter α can be obtained by a similar procedure. It turns out to be identical to the OLS estimator of α, with a variance equal to (6.15).

★ Appendix 6B

Maximum likelihood estimation of regression parameters

If $Y_i = \alpha + \beta X_i + \epsilon_i$ then, given the classical assumptions, each Y_i is normally distributed with mean and variance

$$E(Y_i) = \alpha + \beta X_i \qquad (6B.1)$$

$$\text{Var } (Y_i) = \text{Var } (\epsilon_i) = \sigma^2 \qquad (6B.2)$$

Each Y_i therefore has a probability density function of the normal form

$$p(Y_i) = (2\pi\sigma^2)^{-0.5} \exp \{-[Y_i - E(Y_i)]^2/2\sigma^2\} \qquad (6B.3)$$

where $E(Y_i)$ is given by (6B.1). Thus

$$\ln [p(Y_i)] = -\frac{1}{2}\ln (2\pi) - \frac{1}{2}\ln (\sigma^2) - \frac{1}{2\sigma^2}[Y_i - E(Y_i)]^2 \qquad (6B.4)$$

Since the classical assumption IIC implies that the ϵ_i are uncorrelated and assumption IID states that they are normally distributed, they must also be independent of each other. Hence, since each of the Y_i depends on the corresponding ϵ_i, the Y_i must be independently distributed. We can therefore write the likelihood function for the Y_i in the usual form as

$$L = p(Y_1)p(Y_2)p(Y_3)\cdots p(Y_n) \qquad (6B.5)$$

Using (6B.4), the log-likelihood function for the Y_i is therefore

$$l = \sum \ln [p(Y_i)] = \frac{n}{2}\ln (2\pi) - \frac{n}{2}\ln (\sigma^2) - \frac{1}{2\sigma^2}\sum [Y_i - E(Y_i)]^2 \qquad (6B.6)$$

The normal procedure now would be to partially differentiate (6B.6) with respect to α, β and σ^2, equate the derivatives to zero and then solve to find the maximum likelihood estimators $\tilde{\alpha}$, $\tilde{\beta}$ and $\tilde{\sigma}^2$. However, in this case we can simply note that if (6B.6) is to be maximized then we must choose α and β so as to minimize the sum of squares $\sum [Y_i - E(Y_i)]^2$. That is, we must select $\tilde{\alpha}$ and $\tilde{\beta}$ so as to minimize

$$\sum (Y_i - \tilde{\alpha} - \tilde{\beta}X_i)^2 \qquad (6B.7)$$

However, this is precisely what we did in Chapter 4 when obtaining the OLS estimators. Hence the maximum likelihood estimators of the parameters α and β are identical to the ordinary least squares estimators. That is, $\tilde{\alpha} = \hat{\alpha}$ and $\tilde{\beta} = \hat{\beta}$.

An advantage of the maximum likelihood method of estimation is that it also provides us with an estimator of the third regression parameter σ^2, the variance of the disturbances. Differentiating (6B.6) with respect to σ^2 and equating to zero yields

$$\frac{\partial l}{\partial \sigma^2} = -\frac{n}{2\sigma^2} + \frac{\sum [Y_i - E(Y_i)]^2}{2(\sigma^2)^2} = 0 \tag{6B.8}$$

or

$$n = \frac{\sum [Y_i - E(Y_i)]}{\sigma^2}$$

Substituting $\tilde{\alpha}$ and $\tilde{\beta}$ for α and β in $E(Y_i)$ and solving for the MLE $\tilde{\sigma}^2$ gives

$$\tilde{\sigma}^2 = \frac{\sum e_i^2}{n} \tag{6B.9}$$

where $e_i = Y_i - \tilde{\alpha} - \tilde{\beta} X_i$ is the ith residual from the maximum likelihood regression. As shown in Appendix 6C, though, (6B.9) does not provide us with an unbiased estimator of σ^2.

Appendix 6C

The biasedness of the maximum likelihood estimator of σ^2

The maximum likelihood estimator of σ^2 is given by (6B.9). Each residual e_i can be written as

$$e_i = Y_i - \hat{Y}_i = \alpha + \beta X_i + \epsilon_i - \hat{\alpha} - \hat{\beta} X_i$$
$$= -(\hat{\alpha} - \alpha) - (\hat{\beta} - \beta)X_i + \epsilon_i \tag{6C.1}$$

Taking (6.1), summing over all observations and dividing by n, gives

$$\bar{Y} = \alpha + \beta \bar{X} + \bar{\epsilon}, \quad \text{or} \quad \alpha = \bar{Y} - \beta \bar{X} - \bar{\epsilon}$$

where $\bar{\epsilon} = \sum \epsilon_i / n$. Hence

$$\hat{\alpha} - \alpha = (\bar{Y} - \hat{\beta} \bar{X}) - (\bar{Y} - \beta \bar{X} - \bar{\epsilon}) = -(\hat{\beta} - \beta)\bar{X} + \bar{\epsilon} \tag{6C.2}$$

Substituting for $\hat{\alpha} - \alpha$ in (6C.1), we have

$$e_i = (\hat{\beta} - \beta)\bar{X} - \bar{\epsilon} - (\hat{\beta} - \beta)X_i + \epsilon_i = -(\hat{\beta} - \beta)x_i + \epsilon_i - \bar{\epsilon}$$

Hence

$$\sum e_i^2 = (\hat{\beta} - \beta)^2 \sum x_i^2 + \sum (\epsilon_i - \bar{\epsilon})^2 - 2(\hat{\beta} - \beta) \sum x_i(\epsilon_i - \bar{\epsilon}) \tag{6C.3}$$

Since $\bar{\epsilon} \sum x_i = 0$ and, from (6.7) and (6.4), $\sum x_i \epsilon_i = (\hat{\beta} - \beta) \sum x_i^2$, we can rewrite (6C.3) as

$$\sum e_i^2 = -(\hat{\beta} - \beta)^2 \sum x_i^2 + \sum (\epsilon_i - \bar{\epsilon})^2 \tag{6C.4}$$

Taking expected values of the terms on the right-hand side of (6C.4),

$$E[(\hat{\beta} - \beta)^2 \sum x_i^2] = \sigma^2 \quad \text{(using (6.14))}$$

$$E[\sum(\epsilon_i - \bar{\epsilon})^2] = (n-1)\sigma^2$$

Hence

$$E(\sum e_i^2) = -\sigma^2 + (n-1)\sigma^2 = (n-2)\sigma^2$$

Thus

$$E\left(\frac{\sum e_i^2}{n}\right) = \frac{n-2}{n}\sigma^2 \neq \sigma^2$$

The maximum likelihood estimator of σ^2 is therefore a biased estimator.

Appendix 6D

Why we use the t distribution in two-variable regression

Note first that to compute the residual sum of squares

$$\sum e_i^2 = \sum(Y_i - \hat{Y}_i)^2 = \sum(Y_i - \hat{\alpha} - \hat{\beta}X_i)^2$$

we have to replace *two* parameters α and β by their OLS estimates $\hat{\alpha}$ and $\hat{\beta}$. Moreover, recall from (4.13) that if we use the OLS estimation method then *two* restrictions $\sum e_i = 0$ and $\sum e_i X_i = 0$ are placed on the residuals. Hence, from our discussion of degrees of freedom in Chapter 3, we see the sum of squares $\sum e_i^2$ must have $n-2$ degrees of freedom.

Recall next that, from (6.2), the disturbances ϵ_i are NID$(0, \sigma^2)$ if the classical assumptions hold. Thus each ϵ_i/σ has a standard normal or N(0, 1) distribution. It follows that the quantity $(\sum \epsilon_i^2)/\sigma^2$ is the sum of n independent standard normal variables, and therefore has a χ^2 distribution with n degrees of freedom. However, if we replace the ϵ_i by the residuals e_i, we lose 2 degrees of freedom. Hence

$$\frac{\sum e_i^2}{\sigma^2} \text{ has a } \chi^2 \text{ distribution with } n-2 \text{ d.f.} \tag{6D.1}$$

We also know that, from (6.20), if all classical assumptions hold

$$\frac{\hat{\beta} - \beta}{\sigma_{\hat{\beta}}} \text{ has a N(0, 1) distribution} \tag{6D.2}$$

A Student's t distribution is the ratio of a N(0, 1) variable to the square root of a χ^2 variable divided by its degrees of freedom. Using (6D.1) and (6D.2), we can therefore say that

$$\frac{(\hat{\beta} - \beta)/\sigma_{\hat{\beta}}}{\sqrt{\sum e_i^2/\sigma^2(n-2)}} \text{ has a Student's } t \text{ distribution with } n-2 \text{ d.f.}$$

But

$$\frac{(\hat\beta - \beta)/\sigma_{\hat\beta}}{\sqrt{\sum e_i^2/\sigma^2(n-2)}} = \frac{(\hat\beta - \beta)/\sigma_{\hat\beta}}{\sqrt{s^2/\sigma^2}} = \frac{(\hat\beta - \beta)/\sigma_{\hat\beta}}{\sqrt{s_{\hat\beta}^2/\sigma_{\hat\beta}^2}} = \frac{\hat\beta - \beta}{s_{\hat\beta}}$$

Thus $(\hat\beta - \beta)/s_{\hat\beta}$ has a Student's t distribution with $n-2$ d.f. Similarly, it can be shown that $(\hat\alpha - \alpha)/s_{\hat\alpha}$ also has this distribution. Note that the degrees of freedom of these distributions are derived from the degrees of freedom associated with the residual sum of squares $\sum e_i^2$.

Appendix 6E

Notes to Chapter 6

1. $\sum x_i^2 = \sum(X_i - \bar X)^2$ will only remain unchanged as n increases if each new X_i equals $\bar X$. Otherwise, it must increase, but its rate of increase can be kept lower than the rate at which n increases.
2. Some econometricians place the estimated standard errors $s_{\hat\alpha}$ and $s_{\hat\beta}$ in parentheses beneath $\hat\alpha$ and $\hat\beta$. To perform the usual significance test, it is then necessary to divide the relevant OLS estimate by its estimated standard error and see whether the result exceeds 2.
3. Econometricians often distinguish between 'predictions' and 'forecasts'. Suppose our regression result referred to time series data on aggregate income and consumption as in Table 4.3. The equation is estimated during period $n+1$ for time periods $t = 1, 2, 3, \ldots, n$, and we are interested in consumption in, for example, period $t = n+4$. Before using our regression equation to estimate consumption in period $n+4$, it is first necessary to forecast a value for the explanatory income variable in this period. Only when we have done this can we use our equation to obtain a consumption value. The value obtained is referred to as a **forecast** (sometimes called an **ex ante forecast**). Once period $n+4$ arrives, however, we will actually know the value of income for this period. If this income value is substituted into the original regression equation, the value for consumption obtained is referred to as a **prediction** (sometimes called an **ex post forecast**).
4. It can be shown that (see e.g. Kmenta, 1986, page 250)

$$E(Y_0 - \hat Y_0)^2 = E[Y_0 - E(Y_0)]^2 + E[\hat Y_0 - E(Y_0)]^2$$

That is,

$$\sigma_f^2 = \sigma^2 + E[\hat Y_0 - E(Y_0)]^2$$

where $E[\hat Y_0 - E(Y_0)]^2$ is the variance of the predictor $\hat Y_0$ about its mean $E(Y_0)$.

It can be shown that (see Kmenta, 1986, page 235)

$$E[\hat{Y}_0 - E(Y_0)]^2 = \sigma^2 \left[\frac{1}{n} + \frac{(X_0 - \bar{X})^2}{\sum x_i^2} \right]$$

The expression (6.42) then follows.

5. The numerator of dw is

$$(e_2 - e_1)^2 + (e_3 - e_2)^2 + (e_4 - e_3)^2 + \cdots$$

Notice that the summation in the numerator is from $i = 2$ to $i = n$. This is because to include $i = 1$ would require $(e_1 - e_0)^2$. But e_0 does not exist because the sample begins at $i = 1$.

Further reading

Detailed coverage of two-variable regression can be found in Griffiths et al. (1993), Chapters 5–8. Johnston (1984) also covers the two-variable model in detail in Chapters 2 and 3, with a good section on nonlinear regression in the latter chapter. See also Greene (1993), Chapter 5.

7

The classical multiple regression model

It is rarely the case that economic relationships involve just two variables. Rather, a dependent variable Y can depend on a whole series of explanatory variables or regressors. For example, the demand for a good does not just depend on its price but also on the prices of close substitutes or complements, the general level of prices and on the resources of consumers. Thus in practice we are normally faced with relationships of the form

$$Y = \beta_1 + \beta_2 X_2 + \beta_3 X_3 + \beta_4 X_4 + \cdots + \beta_k X_k + \epsilon \tag{7.1}$$

where the X_j $(j = 2, 3, \ldots, n)$ are the explanatory variables or regressors, the β_j $(j = 1, 2, 3, \ldots, k)$ are unknown parameters and ϵ is a disturbance. The disturbance is of similar nature to that in previous chapters, reflecting the basic random nature of human responses and any other (minor) factors, other than the X_j, that might influence Y. Notice that in (7.1) we have adopted the usual notation of labelling the first regressor as X_2, the second as X_3, etc. In fact, as we shall see, it is sometimes convenient to regard the parameter β_1 as being the coefficient on a variable X_1 that always takes a value of unity. It is then possible to rewrite (7.1) as

$$Y = \beta_1 X_1 + \beta_2 X_2 + \beta_3 X_3 + \cdots + \beta_k X_k + \epsilon \tag{7.1a}$$

For the moment, though, we concentrate on the formulation (7.1), which, although it contains k parameters to be estimated, involves just $k - 1$ genuine regressors.

7.1 Ordinary least squares estimation in multiple regression

If we assume, as in two-variable regression, that $E(\epsilon) = 0$ then for given values of the X variables, taking expectations over (7.1), we have

$$E(Y) = \beta_1 + \beta_2 X_2 + \beta_3 X_3 + \beta_4 X_4 + \cdots + \beta_k X_k \tag{7.2}$$

Equation (7.2) is referred to as the **population regression equation**. It is akin to the population regression equation of two-variable regression and is unknown to any investigator. For the moment, we have conveniently given it a linear form. Unlike in two-variable regression, we cannot represent it on a two-dimensional diagram.

The β_j are population parameters. They are also sometimes known as **regression coefficients**. β_1 is referred to as the **intercept** and β_2, β_3 etc. as **regression slope parameters**. Notice that β_4, for example, measures the effect on $E(Y)$ of a unit change in X_4 when all the other explanatory variables are held constant. Similarly, β_2 measures the effect on $E(Y)$ of a unit change in X_2 when all other X variables are held constant.

Since the population regression equation is unknown, it has to be estimated from sample data. We assume that a sample of n observations is available, each observation containing values for the dependent Y variable and for each of the explanatory X variables. We shall write the values in the ith observation as

$$Y_i, X_{2i}, X_{3i}, X_{4i}, \ldots, X_{ki}$$

Thus, for example, X_{37} represents the value of X_3 in the 7th observation and X_{24} is the value taken by X_2 in the 4th observation. Similarly, Y_6 is the value of the Y variable in the 6th observation, etc.[1]

Since the population relationship (7.1) is assumed to have generated the sample data, each observation must involve a set of values that satisfy (7.1). Hence we have

$$Y_i = \beta_1 + \beta_2 X_{2i} + \beta_3 X_{3i} + \cdots + \beta_k X_{ki} + \epsilon_i \quad \text{for all } i \tag{7.3}$$

where ϵ_i is the value of the disturbance in the ith observation.

It is convenient to rewrite (7.3) in simple matrix form as

$$\mathbf{Y} = \mathbf{X}\boldsymbol{\beta} + \boldsymbol{\epsilon} \tag{7.4}$$

where

$$\mathbf{Y} = \begin{pmatrix} Y_1 \\ Y_2 \\ Y_3 \\ \vdots \\ Y_n \end{pmatrix}, \quad \mathbf{X} = \begin{pmatrix} 1 & X_{21} & X_{31} & \cdots & X_{k1} \\ 1 & X_{22} & X_{32} & \cdots & X_{k2} \\ 1 & X_{23} & X_{33} & \cdots & X_{k3} \\ \vdots & \vdots & \vdots & & \vdots \\ 1 & X_{2n} & X_{3n} & \cdots & X_{kn} \end{pmatrix}, \quad \boldsymbol{\beta} = \begin{pmatrix} \beta_1 \\ \beta_2 \\ \beta_3 \\ \vdots \\ \beta_k \end{pmatrix}, \quad \boldsymbol{\epsilon} = \begin{pmatrix} \epsilon_1 \\ \epsilon_2 \\ \epsilon_3 \\ \vdots \\ \epsilon_n \end{pmatrix}$$

Note that $\mathbf{Y}$ is an $n \times 1$ column vector containing the n sample Y values, and $\mathbf{X}$ is an

$n \times k$ matrix containing, first, a column of ones[2] and then all the sample values of the $k - 1$ X variables. Thus the fourth column of $\mathbf{X}$, for example, contains the n sample values of X_4, the seventh column the values of X_7, and so on. β is a $k \times 1$ column vector containing the β_j parameters, and ϵ is an $n \times 1$ column vector containing the disturbance values.

Let us suppose that the sample data has been used to estimate the population regression equation. We leave the method of estimation unspecified for the present, and merely assume that (7.2) has been estimated by a **sample regression equation**, which we write as

$$\hat{Y} = \hat{\beta}_1 + \hat{\beta}_2 X_2 + \hat{\beta}_3 X_3 + \hat{\beta}_4 X_4 + \cdots + \hat{\beta}_k X_k \tag{7.5}$$

where the $\hat{\beta}_j$ are estimates of the β_j, and $\hat{Y}$ is known as the **predicted value** of Y. Note that if we take the ith sample observation and substitute its X values into (7.5) then, since the $\hat{\beta}_j$ are known estimates, we obtain a predicted value of Y for the ith observation, that is, $\hat{Y}_i$. Thus, just as in two-variable regression, we obtain a predicted value of Y for each observation in the sample. These values can be written as

$$\hat{Y}_i = \hat{\beta}_1 + \hat{\beta}_2 X_{2i} + \hat{\beta}_3 X_{3i} + \cdots + \hat{\beta}_k X_{ki} \quad \text{for all } i \tag{7.6}$$

Actual sample values of Y will not coincide with predicted values of Y, and, just as in two-variable regression, the differences between the two are referred to as **residuals**. We therefore have

$$Y_i = \hat{Y}_i + e_i \quad \text{for all } i \tag{7.7}$$

where e_i is the residual corresponding to the ith observation.

Equation (7.7) is in fact identical to (4.8) for two-variable regression, but in the general case we are unable to illustrate the e_i diagrammatically. Using (7.6), we can rewrite (7.7) as

$$Y_i = \hat{\beta}_1 + \hat{\beta}_2 X_{2i} + \hat{\beta}_3 X_{3i} + \cdots + \hat{\beta}_k X_{ki} + e_i \quad \text{for all } i \tag{7.8}$$

We can also write (7.8) in matrix form as

$$\mathbf{Y} = \mathbf{X}\hat{\boldsymbol{\beta}} + \mathbf{e} \tag{7.9}$$

where $\mathbf{Y}$ and $\mathbf{X}$ are defined above and

$$\hat{\boldsymbol{\beta}} = \begin{pmatrix} \hat{\beta}_1 \\ \hat{\beta}_2 \\ \hat{\beta}_3 \\ \vdots \\ \hat{\beta}_k \end{pmatrix}, \quad \mathbf{e} = \begin{pmatrix} e_1 \\ e_2 \\ e_3 \\ \vdots \\ e_n \end{pmatrix}$$

Thus $\hat{\boldsymbol{\beta}}$ is a $k \times 1$ column vector of the $\hat{\beta}_j$ estimators, and $\mathbf{e}$ is an $n \times 1$ column vector of residuals.

There are two points to notice concerning the residuals. First, whatever method (there are a number of alternatives) we use to estimate the population regression equation (7.2), we will obtain such residuals – one for each of the sample observations. Secondly, since once (7.2) has been estimated, the $\hat{\beta}_j$ will be known, Equation (7.8) may be used to calculate these residuals. Thus, as in two-variable regression, the residuals (unlike the disturbances) are known quantities.

The best-known method of estimation in multiple regression is that of ordinary least squares. Just as in two-variable regression, we choose our sample regression line so as to minimize the sum of the squared residuals. That is, we select values for $\hat{\beta}_1, \hat{\beta}_2, \hat{\beta}_3, \ldots, \hat{\beta}_k$ in (7.5) so as to minimize

$$S = \sum e_i^2 = \sum (Y_i - \hat{Y}_i)^2 \tag{7.10}$$

where $\hat{Y}_i$ is given by (7.6).

The minimization of (7.10) involves the differentiation of S with respect to each $\hat{\beta}_j$ in turn. This is very messy in terms of ordinary algebra, so it is better at this stage to work in matrix terms. Note that $\sum e_i^2 = \mathbf{e'e}$. Thus, using (7.9), we have

$$\begin{aligned} S = \mathbf{e'e} &= (\mathbf{Y} - \mathbf{X\hat{\beta}})'(\mathbf{Y} - \mathbf{X\hat{\beta}}) \\ &= (\mathbf{Y'} - \mathbf{\hat{\beta}'X'})(\mathbf{Y} - \mathbf{X\hat{\beta}}) \\ &= \mathbf{Y'Y} - \mathbf{\hat{\beta}'X'Y} - \mathbf{Y'X\hat{\beta}} + \mathbf{\hat{\beta}'X'X\hat{\beta}} \\ &= \mathbf{Y'Y} - 2\mathbf{\hat{\beta}'X'Y} + \mathbf{\hat{\beta}'X'X\hat{\beta}} \end{aligned} \tag{7.11}$$

where the last step is possible because $\mathbf{\hat{\beta}'X'Y} = \mathbf{Y'X\hat{\beta}}$ are scalars.

We must now differentiate (7.11) with respect to the vector $\mathbf{\hat{\beta}}$ and set the result equal to zero. Such matrix differentiation yields

$$\frac{\partial S}{\partial \mathbf{\hat{\beta}}} = -2\mathbf{X'Y} + 2\mathbf{X'X\hat{\beta}} = 0 \tag{7.12}$$

Readers who are unhappy about matrix differentiation are advised to read the relevant section of Appendix I at the end of this text.

Equation (7.12) represents a set of k equations that can be written as

$$\mathbf{X'X\hat{\beta}} = \mathbf{X'Y} \tag{7.13}$$

Equations (7.13) are the normal equations in the multiple regression case, and are analogous to the equations (4.14) and (4.15) in two-variable regression. Notice for future reference that if we substitute for $\mathbf{Y}$ in (7.13) using (7.9), we obtain

$$\mathbf{X'X\hat{\beta}} = \mathbf{X'}(\mathbf{X\hat{\beta}} + \mathbf{e}) = \mathbf{X'X\hat{\beta}} + \mathbf{X'e}$$

Hence

$$\mathbf{X'e} = 0 \tag{7.14}$$

From the definitions of $\mathbf{X}$ and $\mathbf{e}$, it can be seen that (7.14) implies

$$\sum e_i = 0, \quad \sum e_i X_{2i} = 0, \quad \sum e_i X_{3i} = 0, \quad \sum e_i X_{4i} = 0 \quad \text{etc.} \tag{7.14a}$$

Thus a property of the OLS estimation method is that the resultant residuals satisfy the relationships (7.14a). Recall the similar relationships (4.13) in two-variable regression.

Provided the matrix $\mathbf{X'X}$ is non-singular, the normal equations (7.13) may be solved to yield $\hat{\boldsymbol{\beta}}$, the vector of ordinary least squares (OLS) estimators. Premultiplying (7.13) by $(\mathbf{X'X})^{-1}$ gives

$$(\mathbf{X'X})^{-1}\mathbf{X'X}\hat{\boldsymbol{\beta}} = (\mathbf{X'X})^{-1}\mathbf{X'Y}$$

Thus

$$\hat{\boldsymbol{\beta}} = (\mathbf{X'X})^{-1}\mathbf{X'Y} \qquad (7.15)$$

Equation (7.15), the expression for the OLS estimators in the multiple regression case, is probably the most well-known formula in econometrics. *Those who are uncertain about its derivation are advised to consult Appendix 7A to this chapter, where it is derived using ordinary algebra for the special case of just two explanatory variables.*

To compute the vector $\hat{\boldsymbol{\beta}}$, we have to perform the following steps:

(i) form the $k \times k$ matrix $\mathbf{X'X}$ and the $k \times 1$ matrix $\mathbf{X'Y}$;

(ii) form the $k \times k$ inverse matrix $(\mathbf{X'X})^{-1}$;

(iii) multiply the $k \times k$ matrix $(\mathbf{X'X})^{-1}$ into the $k \times 1$ matrix $\mathbf{X'Y}$.

Step (iii) above yields the $k \times 1$ vector of OLS estimates, $\hat{\boldsymbol{\beta}}$.

It is step (ii) above that involves the greatest computational effort. Even with just two explanatory X variables, $k = 3$, and we are faced with inverting a 3×3 matrix. As the number of explanatory variables increases, the computational burden involved increases exponentially. For this reason, computing (7.15) is normally a task for a computer, and is rarely undertaken by hand nowadays. Fortunately, many OLS computer packages are readily available.

The computational effort involved in obtaining OLS estimates can be reduced if we work in terms of the deviation of variables from their means. As we shall see, it turns out then that, instead of inverting a $k \times k$ matrix as in step (ii) above, we have to invert a matrix of order only $(k - 1) \times (k - 1)$. Anyone inverting, for example, 4×4 and 3×3 matrices by hand will appreciate the saving this involves.

Consider again Equation (7.8). If we sum this equation over all i and divide the result by n, we obtain

$$\bar{Y} = \hat{\beta}_1 + \hat{\beta}_2\bar{X}_2 + \hat{\beta}_3\bar{X}_3 + \cdots + \hat{\beta}_k\bar{X}_k + \bar{e} \qquad (7.16)$$

where the bars as usual denote the mean sample values of variables. However, recall that a property of the OLS estimation method is that $\sum e_i$ and hence $\bar{e}$ equal zero. Hence, if we take (7.16) away from the original (7.8), we obtain

$$y_i = \hat{\beta}_2 x_{2i} + \hat{\beta}_3 x_{3i} + \cdots + \hat{\beta}_k x_{ki} + e_i \quad \text{for all } i \qquad (7.8a)$$

where lower-case letters represent deviations of variables from their means. That is, $y_i = Y_i - \bar{Y}$ and $x_{2i} = X_{2i} - \bar{X}_2$ etc. Notice the similarity between (7.8) and (7.8a).

It is also possible to write (7.8a) in a similar form to (7.9), that is, as

$$\mathbf{y} = \mathbf{x}\hat{\boldsymbol{\beta}} + \mathbf{e} \tag{7.9a}$$

provided we define the $\mathbf{x}$, $\mathbf{y}$ and $\hat{\boldsymbol{\beta}}$ matrices as

$$
\mathbf{y} = \begin{pmatrix} y_1 \\ y_2 \\ y_3 \\ \vdots \\ y_n \end{pmatrix}, \quad
\mathbf{x} = \begin{pmatrix} x_{21} & x_{31} & x_{41} & \cdots & x_{k1} \\ x_{22} & x_{32} & x_{42} & \cdots & x_{k2} \\ x_{23} & x_{33} & x_{43} & \cdots & x_{k3} \\ \vdots & \vdots & \vdots & & \vdots \\ x_{2n} & x_{3n} & x_{4n} & \cdots & x_{kn} \end{pmatrix}, \quad
\hat{\boldsymbol{\beta}} = \begin{pmatrix} \hat{\beta}_2 \\ \hat{\beta}_3 \\ \hat{\beta}_4 \\ \vdots \\ \hat{\beta}_k \end{pmatrix}
$$

Equation (7.9a) differs from (7.9) in that the values of variables are now in deviation form, the column of ones does not appear in the $\mathbf{x}$ matrix, which is of order $n \times (k - 1)$, and $\hat{\beta}_1$ no longer appears in the $\hat{\boldsymbol{\beta}}$ vector, which is now of order $(k - 1) \times 1$. The $\mathbf{e}$ vector remains as defined previously.

The point is that, since the definition of $\mathbf{e}$ is unchanged, the sum of squared residuals is still $\mathbf{e}'\mathbf{e}$, and, using (7.9a), can be expressed in a form similar to (7.11) except that the $\mathbf{x}$ and $\mathbf{y}$ matrices replace $\mathbf{X}$ and $\mathbf{Y}$. Differentiation with respect to the redefined $\hat{\boldsymbol{\beta}}$ yields an expression similar to (7.15), except that values of variables are in deviation form. That is,

$$\hat{\boldsymbol{\beta}} = (\mathbf{x}'\mathbf{x})^{-1}\mathbf{x}'\mathbf{y} \tag{7.15a}$$

The advantage of (7.15a) over (7.15) is that the matrix $\mathbf{x}'\mathbf{x}$ that now has to be inverted is only of order $(k - 1) \times (k - 1)$ as opposed to $k \times k$. The only problem is that the new $\hat{\boldsymbol{\beta}}$ does not contain a value for $\hat{\beta}_1$. However, once $\hat{\boldsymbol{\beta}}$ is known, a value for $\hat{\beta}_1$ can be obtained by rearranging (7.16), remembering that $\bar{e} = 0$:

$$\hat{\beta}_1 = \bar{Y} - \hat{\beta}_2\bar{X}_2 - \hat{\beta}_3\bar{X}_3 - \cdots - \hat{\beta}_k\bar{X}_k \tag{7.17}$$

Summarizing, we may compute the OLS estimators in two ways. First, we can use (7.15), but this involves inverting a $k \times k$ matrix. Alternatively, we can work in terms of deviations from variable means, using (7.15a), which only requires the inversion of a $(k - 1) \times (k - 1)$ matrix. However this method also requires use of (7.17) to find $\hat{\beta}_1$.

Structure of the x′x and x′y matrices

It is instructive to look closely at the structure of the matrices $\mathbf{x}'\mathbf{x}$ and $\mathbf{x}'\mathbf{y}$, introduced in (7.15a). Remembering that lower-case letters denote deviations of values of variables from their means,

$$\mathbf{x'x} = \begin{pmatrix} \sum x_2^2 & \sum x_2 x_3 & \sum x_2 x_4 & \cdots & \sum x_2 x_k \\ \sum x_3 x_2 & \sum x_3^2 & \sum x_3 x_4 & \cdots & \sum x_3 x_k \\ \sum x_4 x_2 & \sum x_4 x_3 & \sum x_4^2 & \cdots & \sum x_4 x_k \\ \vdots & \vdots & \vdots & & \vdots \\ \sum x_k x_2 & \sum x_k x_3 & \sum x_k x_4 & \cdots & \sum x_k^2 \end{pmatrix}, \quad \mathbf{x'y} = \begin{pmatrix} \sum x_2 y \\ \sum x_3 y \\ \sum x_4 y \\ \vdots \\ \sum x_k y \end{pmatrix} \quad (7.18)$$

where, for convenience, we have omitted the i subscripts. Note that since $\sum x_2 x_3 = \sum x_3 x_2$ etc., $\mathbf{x'x}$ is a symmetric matrix. For example, with just two explanatory variables ($k = 3$), we have

$$\mathbf{x'x} = \begin{pmatrix} \sum x_{2i}^2 & \sum x_{2i} x_{3i} \\ \sum x_{3i} x_{2i} & \sum x_{3i}^2 \end{pmatrix}, \quad \mathbf{x'y} = \begin{pmatrix} \sum x_{2i} y_i \\ \sum x_{3i} y_i \end{pmatrix} \quad (7.19)$$

We shall use these expressions shortly.

In the simple case of two-variable regression ($k = 2$), the matrix products in (7.18) reduce to 1×1 quantities, and hence are scalars. That is, $\mathbf{x'x} = \sum x_{2i}^2$ and $\mathbf{x'y} = \sum x_{2i} y_i$. Hence the OLS formula (7.15a) now yields

$$\hat{\beta}_2 = \hat{\beta} = (\mathbf{x'x})^{-1} \mathbf{x'y} = (\sum x_{2i}^2)^{-1} (\sum x_{2i} y_i) = (\sum x_{2i} y_i)/(\sum x_{2i}^2)$$

and (7.17) reduces to

$$\hat{\beta}_1 = \bar{Y} - \hat{\beta}_2 \bar{X}_2$$

These are, of course, identical to the OLS estimators for two-variable regression derived in Chapter 4 as (4.18) and (4.16) respectively, except that we now refer to the single explanatory variable as X_2.

Although it is usual nowadays to perform multiple regression using a computer package, there is much to be said for computing a limited number of regressions by hand calculator first. It is only by performing the calculations ourselves that we get to know exactly what the computer is doing for us. Such knowledge is important if we are to get a good 'feel' for multiple regression and to be able to pinpoint the problem when, through no fault of the investigator, apparently strange results are obtained.

WORKED EXAMPLE 7.1

As a first example of multiple regression, refer back to the 25 households referred to in Table 4.1. Suppose, as well as having data on the income and consumption of such households, we also had data on the stocks of liquid assets they hold midway through the year in question. The augmented data set is shown in Table 7.1, where we now refer to income as X_2 instead of X, with liquid assets being the X_3 variable. It is reasonable to suppose that, in addition to the size of its income, the size of its

Table 7.1 Household consumption Y, income X_2 and liquid assets X_3

Household	Y	X_2	X_3
1	52.30	36.40	104.70
2	78.44	46.80	26.00
3	88.76	57.20	248.10
4	54.08	67.60	201.30
5	111.44	74.30	143.70
6	105.20	86.50	462.30
7	45.73	91.30	244.80
8	122.35	102.80	381.30
9	142.24	114.50	183.80
10	86.22	120.90	370.80
11	174.50	135.00	615.20
12	185.20	144.00	465.60
13	111.80	156.00	443.70
14	214.60	173.70	585.60
15	144.60	182.00	612.00
16	174.36	199.20	948.80
17	215.40	208.00	587.30
18	286.24	217.80	1034.30
19	188.56	223.20	584.60
20	237.20	234.00	934.70
21	181.80	251.00	841.30
22	373.00	260.00	1536.60
23	191.60	289.50	772.60
24	247.12	296.40	1345.60
25	269.60	312.00	704.40

liquid assets stock might also affect a household's consumption. We shall therefore hypothesize a population regression equation of the form

$$E(Y) = \beta_1 + \beta_2 X_2 + \beta_3 X_3 \tag{7.20}$$

Since $k = 3$ in (7.20), we use (7.19) to set up the matrix products $\mathbf{x'x}$ and $\mathbf{x'y}$. We have already computed some of the elements of these matrices in Chapter 4. In fact, from (4.20) and (4.21), we have, to four significant figures,

$$\sum x_{2i}^2 = 1.663 \times 10^5, \qquad \sum x_{2i} y_i = 1.351 \times 10^5 \tag{7.21}$$

We can calculate the remaining elements in a similar manner. Using Table 7.1,

$$\sum X_{2i} X_{3i} = 2\,981\,925.0, \quad \sum X_{3i}^2 = 11\,737\,267.5, \quad \sum X_{3i} Y_i = 2\,994\,882.5$$
$$\sum X_{2i} = 4080.1 \qquad \sum X_{3i} = 14\,379.1 \tag{7.22}$$

Remembering to distinguish between upper- and lower-case letters,

$$\sum x_{2i}x_{3i} = \sum X_{2i}X_{3i} - \frac{1}{n}(\sum X_{2i})(\sum X_{3i}) = 6.352 \times 10^5 \tag{7.23}$$

Similarly,

$$\sum x_{3i}^2 = 34.67 \times 10^5, \qquad \sum x_{3i}y_i = 6.469 \times 10^5 \tag{7.24}$$

We can now slot all the required elements into (7.19). This gives

$$\mathbf{x'x} = 10^5 \begin{pmatrix} 1.663 & 6.352 \\ 6.352 & 34.67 \end{pmatrix}, \qquad \mathbf{x'y} = 10^5 \begin{pmatrix} 1.351 \\ 6.469 \end{pmatrix} \tag{7.25}$$

The determinant of $\mathbf{x'x}$ is $|\mathbf{x'x}| = 17.31 \times 10^5$. Its inverse is therefore

$$(\mathbf{x'x})^{-1} = 5.777 \times 10^{-7} \begin{pmatrix} 34.67 & -6.352 \\ -6.352 & 1.663 \end{pmatrix} \tag{7.26}$$

Using (7.15a) then gives the OLS estimates of β_2 and β_3 as

$$\begin{pmatrix} \hat{\beta}_2 \\ \hat{\beta}_3 \end{pmatrix} = 5.772 \times 10^{-7} \begin{pmatrix} 34.67 & -6.352 \\ -6.352 & 1.663 \end{pmatrix} \begin{pmatrix} 1.351 \\ 6.469 \end{pmatrix} = \begin{pmatrix} 0.332 \\ 0.126 \end{pmatrix} \tag{7.27}$$

To find $\hat{\beta}_1$, we have to use (7.17) with $k = 3$. From (4.19), we have $\bar{Y} = 163.29$ and $\bar{X}_2 = 163.20$, and, using (7.22), $\bar{X}_3 = \sum X_{3i}/n = 575.16$. Thus (7.17) gives

$$\hat{\beta}_1 = 163.29 - (0.332)163.20 - (0.126)575.16 = 36.64 \tag{7.28}$$

Our OLS estimated sample regression equation is therefore

$$\hat{Y} = 36.64 + 0.332X_2 + 0.126X_3 \tag{7.29}$$

Notice that the estimated coefficient on the income variable X_2 takes a very different value from that obtained in the simple regression of Chapter 4. As we shall see, such a result is not at all unusual. It is virtually always the case that *adding extra variables to a regression equation will change the value of estimated coefficients on variables already included in the equation.*[3] It is not difficult to see why this is so. For example, in Equation (7.29) the coefficient 0.332 of X_2 represents an attempt to assess the influence on household consumption of an increase in income under the *ceteris paribus* assumption that the household's liquid assets stock remains unchanged. An examination of Table 7.1 indicates that the variables household income and household liquid assets stock tend to move together. That is, households with high X_2 also tend to have high X_3. In the simple regression (4.25) we have ignored the fact that liquid asset stocks are not constant, but vary from household to household. The coefficient 0.812 on the income variable in (4.25) therefore reflects not only the effect of income variations on consumption, but also the effect of liquid asset variations. Since these effects work in the same direction, the income coefficient in (4.25) is considerably larger than that in (7.29), which measures the effect of income variation only.

We shall return to this example later in the chapter.

WORKED EXAMPLE 7.2

A population regression line is believed to have the form

$$E(Y) = \beta_1 + \beta_2 X_2 + \beta_3 X_3 + \beta_4 X_4 \tag{7.30}$$

This equation is estimated from a random sample of size $n = 25$, for which, in terms of deviations from means,

$$(\mathbf{x}'\mathbf{x})^{-1} = \begin{pmatrix} 0.030 & 0.004 & -0.031 \\ 0.004 & 0.028 & 0.015 \\ -0.031 & 0.015 & 0.275 \end{pmatrix}, \quad \begin{aligned} \sum x_{2i}y_i &= 226.2 \\ \sum x_{3i}y_i &= 259.1, \quad \sum y_i^2 = 6733 \\ \sum x_{4i}y_i &= -48.3 \end{aligned}$$

Calculate the OLS estimates of β_2, β_3 and β_4.

In this example the matrix $\mathbf{x}'\mathbf{x}$ has already been inverted for us, and we are given the elements of $\mathbf{x}'\mathbf{y}$. Hence, using (7.15a),

$$\begin{pmatrix} \hat{\beta}_2 \\ \hat{\beta}_3 \\ \hat{\beta}_4 \end{pmatrix} = \begin{pmatrix} 0.030 & 0.004 & -0.031 \\ 0.004 & 0.028 & 0.015 \\ -0.031 & 0.015 & 0.275 \end{pmatrix} \begin{pmatrix} 226.2 \\ 259.1 \\ -48.3 \end{pmatrix} = \begin{pmatrix} 9.31 \\ 7.44 \\ -16.41 \end{pmatrix}$$

Since we do not have information on the sample means of variables, we cannot in this case compute $\hat{\beta}_1$. We shall return to this example shortly.

Closeness of fit in multiple regression

In Chapter 4 we defined, for two-variable regression, the so-called coefficient of determination, which measured the proportion of the total variation in a dependent Y variable that could be attributed to variations in the single explanatory X variable. A similar measure of closeness of fit can be defined in multiple regression.

Consider again Equation (7.7). Taking $\bar{Y}$ from each side, we have

$$Y_i - \bar{Y} = \hat{Y}_i - \bar{Y} + e_i \quad \text{for all } i \tag{7.31}$$

Thus if we measure variations in Y about its mean $\bar{Y}$, we can say that for each observation, the total variation in Y can be split up into an explained variation $\hat{Y}_i - \bar{Y}$ and a residual variation e_i. Equation (7.31) is in fact identical to (4.26) in two-variable regression.

If, again as in two-variable regression, we first square (7.31) and then sum it over all observations, we obtain

$$\sum (Y_i - \bar{Y})^2 = \sum (\hat{Y}_i - \bar{Y})^2 + \sum e_i^2 + 2 \sum e_i (\hat{Y}_i - \bar{Y}) \tag{7.32}$$

The last term on the right-hand side of (7.32) can be shown to equal zero for OLS regression:

$$\sum e_i(\hat{Y}_i - \bar{Y}) = \sum e_i(\hat{\beta}_1 + \hat{\beta}_2 X_{2i} + \hat{\beta}_3 X_{3i} + \cdots + \hat{\beta}_k X_{ki} - \hat{Y})$$
$$= \hat{\beta} \sum e_i + \hat{\beta}_2 \sum X_{2i} e_i + \hat{\beta}_3 \sum X_{3i} e_i + \cdots + \hat{\beta}_k \sum X_{ki} e_i - \bar{Y} \sum e_i$$
$$= 0 \quad \text{(using (7.14a))}$$

Thus (7.32) reduces to

$$\sum (Y_i - \bar{Y})^2 = \sum (\hat{Y}_i - \bar{Y})^2 + \sum e_i^2 \tag{7.33}$$

or

$$\text{SST} \quad = \quad \text{SSE} \quad + \text{SSR}$$

Equation (7.33) is identical to (4.27) for two-variable regression. It implies that, over all observations, our measure of the total variation in Y, SST, can again be split up into a measure of the explained variation in Y, SSE, and a residual variation, SSR. We stress, however, that, as in two-variable regression, (7.33) is only valid if the method of estimation is OLS, since the relationships (7.14a) only hold for this form of estimation.

We now define the **coefficient of multiple determination** R^2 as the proportion of the total variation in Y that can be attributed to variations in *all* the explanatory variables acting together. That is, given (7.33),

$$R^2 = \frac{\text{explained sum of squares}}{\text{total sum of squares}} = \frac{\text{SSE}}{\text{SST}} \tag{7.34}$$

Unfortunately, there is no neat formula akin to (4.31) for computing R^2 in multiple regression. However, we can still proceed as in (4.32), so that

$$R^2 = 1 - \frac{\sum e_i^2}{\sum y_i^2} \tag{7.35}$$

The residual sum of squares in (7.35) can then be computed using an extension of (6.28) that can be shown to hold for multiple regression:

$$\sum e_i^2 = \sum y_i^2 - \hat{\beta}_2 \sum x_{2i} y_i - \hat{\beta}_3 \sum x_{3i} y_i - \cdots - \hat{\beta}_k \sum x_{ki} y_i \tag{7.36}$$

We now compute the coefficient of multiple determination for the two numerical examples introduced earlier.

WORKED EXAMPLE 7.1 (continued)

First, for the household data in Table 7.1, we have already computed all the quantities required to find (7.36). Apart from $\sum y_i^2$, these are given in (7.21), (7.24) and (7.27). $\sum y_i^2$ was computed in (4.22) as 1.587×10^5.

Since $k = 3$ in this example, (7.36) becomes

$$\sum e_i^2 = \sum y_i^2 - \hat{\beta}_2 \sum x_{2i} y_i - \hat{\beta}_3 \sum x_{3i} y_i$$
$$= 10^5 [1.587 - 0.332(1.351) - 0.126(6.469)] = 3.234 \times 10^4$$

Hence, using (7.35),

$$R^2 = 1 - \frac{3.234 \times 10^4}{1.587 \times 10^5} = 0.796$$

Thus approximately 80% of the variation in household consumption can be attributed to variations in their income and liquid asset holdings.

WORKED EXAMPLE 7.2 (continued)

In our second worked example the population regression line is given by (7.30). That is, $k = 4$, so that (7.36) becomes

$$\sum e_i^2 = \sum y_i^2 - \hat{\beta}_2 \sum x_{2i} y_i - \hat{\beta}_3 \sum x_{3i} y_i - \hat{\beta}_4 \sum x_{4i} y_i$$

Substituting in the values below (7.30),

$$\sum e_i^2 = 6733 - 9.31(226.2) - 7.44(259.1) - (-16.41)(-48.3)$$
$$= 1906.8$$

Thus in this case (7.35) gives

$$R^2 = 1 - \frac{1906.8}{6733.0} = 0.717$$

Hence in this example 71.7% of variation in Y can be attributed to variations in X_2, X_3 and X_4.

At this point it is necessary to re-emphasize the warning we gave in Chapter 4 concerning the interpretation of R^2. In particular, the reader would be well advised to reread the discussion of spurious regressions in Section 4.4. Just as in two-variable regression, artificially high values of R^2 can be achieved when applying multiple regression to data time series which exhibit strong trends.

The adjusted coefficient of determination

The coefficient of determination R^2 is sometimes used as a means of comparing the closeness of fit of two estimated equations containing different numbers of explanatory variables. For example, for our 25 households in Table 7.1, we saw in Section 4.3 that $R^2 = 0.691$ for Equation (4.25), in which the only explanatory variable was disposable income. However, in this chapter we obtained $R^2 = 0.796$ when we considered an equation with both disposable income and liquid asset holdings as explanatory variables. The rise in R^2 could be regarded as evidence in favour of adding the second explanatory variable.

However, caution must be exercised when using R^2 in this way. When additional explanatory variables are included in regression equations, R^2, the proportion of the variation in Y that we can explain, cannot possibly decrease. It is virtually always possible to increase R^2 by adding extra explanatory variables, regardless of the true importance of these variables. It is therefore hardly fair to compare in this way, for example, an equation containing 3 explanatory variables with one using just 2 of them. For this reason, many econometricians make comparisons of closeness of fit using a measure referred to as 'R^2 adjusted for degrees of freedom' (i.e. adjusted for the number of X variables), which is given by

$$\bar{R}^2 = 1 - \frac{\sum e_i^2/(n-k)}{\sum y_i^2/(n-1)} \tag{7.37}$$

We will not concern ourselves with the theoretical basis of (7.37). However, note that an increase in the number of X variables included (and hence an increase in k) will reduce $\sum e_i^2$ and hence tend to increase $\bar{R}^2$. However, since $\sum e_i^2$ in (7.37) is divided by $n-k$, the increase in k tends to offset the effect of the fall in $\sum e_i^2$. When an extra variable is added to a regression equation, $\bar{R}^2$, unlike R^2, can in fact *fall* if the increase in $\sum e_i^2$ is so small that it is offset by the rise in k. Except when $R^2 = 1$, $\bar{R}^2$ will be less than R^2, and, for a given R^2, will decrease as the number of explanatory variables is increased. For these reasons, $\bar{R}^2$ is a 'fairer' measure than R^2 for comparing the closeness of fit of different estimated equations. The criterion is to include an extra variable provided it increases $\bar{R}^2$.

The Akaike information criterion

Another method of allowing for the number of explanatory variables when assessing goodness of fit is to use the **Akaike information criterion (AIC)**. This is defined as

$$\text{AIC} = \ln\left(\frac{\sum e_i^2}{n}\right) + \frac{2k}{n} \tag{7.38}$$

Again we will not concern ourselves with the theoretical basis of the AIC, but simply note that in this case the criterion is to include an extra variable only if it decreases the AIC. Like $\bar{R}^2$, the AIC depends on the residual sum of squares, $\sum e_i^2$, and the number of parameters to be estimated, k. However, a fall in $\sum e_i^2$ that occurs when an extra explanatory variable is included may not necessarily lead to a fall in the AIC. The extra variable means an increase in k, the number of parameters to be estimated, and this increases the AIC. Thus the AIC only falls if the decline in $\sum e_i^2$ is sufficient to outweigh the effect of the rise in k.

As an example of the use of both $\bar{R}^2$ and the AIC, consider our household consumption equations (4.25) and (7.29), for which we have already obtained values for the (unadjusted) R^2 of 0.691 and 0.796 respectively. Considering first (4.25), we have $\sum y_i^2 = 1.587 \times 10^5$, $\sum e_i^2 = 0.4901 \times 10^5$, with $k = 2$ for this equation. Thus, since $n = 25$, using (7.37) and (7.38),

$$\bar{R}^2 = 1 - \frac{0.4901/23}{1.587/24} = 0.678$$

$$\text{AIC} = \ln\left(\frac{49010}{25}\right) + \frac{4}{25} = 7.74$$

For Equation (7.29), in which the additional regressor, liquid asset stock, appears, $\sum e_i^2 = 0.3234 \times 10^5$ and $k = 3$, while $\sum y_i^2$ and n are unchanged. Thus

$$\bar{R}^2 = 1 - \frac{0.3234/22}{1.587/24} = 0.778$$

$$\text{AIC} = \ln\left(\frac{32340}{25}\right) + \frac{6}{25} = 7.40$$

It can now be seen that the addition of the liquid assets variable to our household consumption equation increases $\bar{R}^2$ and decreases the AIC. Thus, on both these criteria, it appears to be a variable that should be added to the equation. This confirms any tentative conclusion based on the rise in the unadjusted coefficient of determination R^2.

Other popular measures for trading off goodness of fit against extra explanatory variables include the **Schwarz criterion** and the **Amemiya criterion**. Lack of space prevents discussion of these measures, but an assessment of their relative merits, together with those of $\bar{R}^2$ and the AIC, is provided by Amemiya (1980).

Exercise 7.1

The following data refer to weekly sales Y, weekly advertising expenditure X_2 and the mean weekly income of customers X_3:

Y	302	338	362	361	422	380	408	447	495	480
X_2	14	15	26	23	30	33	33	38	42	46
X_3	32	33	35	36	40	41	44	44	47	48

When variables are in deviation form,

$$\sum y^2 = 34\,990, \quad \sum x_2^2 = 1028, \quad \sum x_3^2 = 300$$
$$\sum x_2 y = 5683, \quad \sum x_3 y = 3069$$

(a) Find $\sum x_2 x_3$.

(b) Estimate the regression equation $E(Y) = \beta_1 + \beta_2 X_2 + \beta_3 X_3$.

(c) Calculate the coefficient of determination for this regression.

(d) Calculate the adjusted coefficient of determination.

Exercise 7.2

A production function has the Cobb–Douglas form $Q = AK^\alpha L^\beta$. When natural logarithms of all variables are taken, and these transformed values are expressed in deviation terms, a sample of 60 observations yields

$$\sum q^2 = 1700, \qquad \sum k^2 = 3200, \qquad \sum l^2 = 2800$$

$$\sum kq = 1100, \qquad \sum lq = 800, \qquad \sum kl = -1500$$

(a) Use OLS to estimate the elasticities of output Q with respect to capital input K and labour input L.

(b) If $\sum \ln (Q) = 825$, $\sum \ln (K) = 771$ and $\sum \ln (L) = 648$, estimate A.

Exercise 7.3

The model $Y = \beta_1 + \beta_2 X_2 + \beta_3 X_3 + \beta_4 X_4 + \epsilon$ is to be estimated from 24 observations, for which, when the variables are measured in deviation form,

$$(\mathbf{x'x})^{-1} = \begin{pmatrix} 0.8 & 0.1 & -0.6 \\ 0.1 & 0.6 & -0.8 \\ -0.6 & -0.8 & 1.4 \end{pmatrix}, \qquad \begin{array}{l} \sum x_2 y = 21, \\ \sum x_3 y = 42, \qquad \sum y^2 = 78 \\ \sum x_4 y = 34, \end{array}$$

Obtain the OLS estimators of β_2, β_3 and β_4, and calculate the coefficient of determination.

7.2   The classical assumptions in multiple regression

Just as in two-variable regression, OLS is by far the most popular and well-known method of estimating multiple regression parameters. However, it is again important to stress that there is no guarantee that OLS estimators will in any sense be 'good' estimators. As with two-variable regression, different samples will yield different OLS estimates, so that each of the $\hat{\beta}_j$ of the previous section will possess a sampling distribution. There can be no certainty that these sampling distributions will have any of the desirable properties described in Chapter 5, unless we can make a number of further valid assumptions.

In this section we outline the assumptions of the classical multiple regression model. In most respects they represent simple extensions of the assumptions of the two-variable model listed in Section 6.1.

Underlying the classical multiple regression model is the population relationship (7.1). This relationship is assumed to have generated all n sample observations, so that Equation (7.3) holds. The matrix equivalent of Equation (7.3) is (7.4). As in two-variable regression, assumptions are made concerning explanatory variables and concerning disturbances.

Assumptions concerning the explanatory variables

It is assumed that *each* of the explanatory variables

(IA) is non-stochastic;

(IB) has values that are fixed in repeated samples;

(IC) is such that, as $n \to \infty$, the variance of its sample values $(1/n)\sum x_{ji}^2 \to Q_j$ $(j = 2, 3, \ldots, k)$, where the Q_j are fixed finite constants.

The meaning of 'non-stochastic' in this context was explained in some detail in Section 6.1. Notice that, as in two-variable regression, the dependent Y variable, which depends on the disturbance as well as the X variables, is stochastic. Assumption IB implies that if repeated samples were taken, the same set of values for the X variables would be selected in each sample. This implies that $\mathbf{X}$, as defined below (7.4), can be treated as a matrix of fixed constants as far as the sampling process is concerned. The $\mathbf{Y}$ vector of sample values will vary from sample to sample, however, since, from (7.4), this depends not only on $\mathbf{X}$ but also on the vector of disturbance values $\boldsymbol{\epsilon}$. Hence $\hat{\boldsymbol{\beta}}$, the vector of OLS estimators, which depends on both $\mathbf{X}$ and $\mathbf{Y}$, will vary from sample to sample. Thus, despite assumptions IA and IB, the OLS estimators will still possess sampling distributions.

Assumption IC is simply an extension of the corresponding assumption in two-variable regression, and rules out explanatory variables that exhibit definite trends over time. The significance of this will become clearer later, but for now can be regarded as ruling out any problems of spurious correlation.

There is a fourth assumption concerning the explanatory variables in the multiple regression model that has no equivalent in two-variable regression. It is that

(ID) there exist no exact linear relationships between the sample values of any two or more of the explanatory variables.

By assumption ID, we mean that it must not be the case that, for example, $X_{2i} = 3 + 4X_{3i}$ for all i (that is, it must not be the case that the second column in the $\mathbf{X}$ matrix equals three plus four times the third column). This would imply an exact linear relationship between the sample values of X_2 and X_3. Similarly, relationships such as $X_{3i} = 5 - 2X_{4i} + 3X_{2i}$ involving three or more X variables are also ruled out.

If assumption ID broke down, this would imply that a linear relationship existed between columns of the matrix $\mathbf{X}$. Consequently, a linear relationship between columns of the matrix $\mathbf{X'X}$ would then exist, so that this matrix would become singular. If this were the case, the matrix inverse $(\mathbf{X'X})^{-1}$ would not exist, and the formula (7.15) for the OLS estimators could not be computed. In effect, it would be impossible to solve the normal equations (7.13), and OLS estimators would simply not exist. It is extremely rare for assumption ID to break down in practice, but, as we shall see, conditions under which there exist approximate linear relationships between the X variables are not uncommon. Such relationships can have serious consequences, which we discuss in Section 9.1.

It is useful to express assumptions IC and ID in matrix terms. This can be done succinctly by stating that *we require the matrix* $\mathbf{x'x}$ *to be non-singular and to be such that, as* $n \to \infty$, $(1/n)\mathbf{x'x} \to \mathbf{Q}$ *where* $\mathbf{Q}$ *is a (non-singular) matrix of fixed constants.*

To see that this statement implies assumptions IC and ID, first note that if there are to be no linear relationships between the columns of the matrix $\mathbf{X}$ then there must be no such relationships between the columns of the matrix of deviations from means, $\mathbf{x}$. Thus assumption ID requires not only that the matrix $(\mathbf{X'X})^{-1}$ be non-singular but so must the matrix $(\mathbf{x'x})^{-1}$. The elements of $\mathbf{x'x}$ are shown in (7.18). It can be seen that the diagonal elements of the matrix $(1/n)\mathbf{x'x}$ are therefore the sample variances $(1/n)\sum x_{ji}^2$. Hence, if as $n \to \infty$, the matrix $(1/n)\mathbf{x'x} \to \mathbf{Q}$, where $\mathbf{Q}$ is a fixed matrix, then assumption IC must hold. The Q_j in assumption IC are simply the diagonal elements in $\mathbf{Q}$.

Assumptions concerning the disturbances

The assumptions concerning the disturbances in the classical multiple regression model are identical to those made in two-variable regression, namely

(IIA) $E(\epsilon_i) = 0$ for all i;

(IIB) $\text{Var}(\epsilon_i) = E(\epsilon_i^2) = \sigma^2 = \text{constant for all } i$;

(IIC) $\text{Cov}(\epsilon_i, \epsilon_j) = E(\epsilon_i\epsilon_j) = 0$ for all $i \neq j$;

(IID) each ϵ_i is normally distributed.

Thus the disturbances are normally distributed with zero means, and are homoskedastic and non-autocorrelated. Since they are normally distributed with zero covariances, this implies that they must be independently distributed. Thus, as in two-variable regression, the assumptions can be summarized by Equation (6.2).

It is also useful to summarize assumptions IIA–IID in terms of the **variance–covariance matrix of the disturbances**. Recall the $n \times 1$ vector $\boldsymbol{\epsilon}$ of disturbances. If we form the $n \times n$ matrix $\boldsymbol{\epsilon\epsilon'}$ and take expectations, we obtain the symmetric matrix

$$E(\boldsymbol{\epsilon\epsilon'}) = \begin{pmatrix} E(\epsilon_1^2) & E(\epsilon_1\epsilon_2) & E(\epsilon_1\epsilon_3) & \cdots & E(\epsilon_1\epsilon_n) \\ E(\epsilon_2\epsilon_1) & E(\epsilon_2^2) & E(\epsilon_2\epsilon_3) & \cdots & E(\epsilon_2\epsilon_n) \\ E(\epsilon_3\epsilon_1) & E(\epsilon_3\epsilon_2) & E(\epsilon_3^2) & \cdots & E(\epsilon_3\epsilon_n) \\ \vdots & \vdots & \vdots & & \vdots \\ E(\epsilon_n\epsilon_1) & E(\epsilon_n\epsilon_2) & E(\epsilon_n\epsilon_3) & \cdots & E(\epsilon_n^2) \end{pmatrix} \tag{7.39}$$

Since each disturbance has zero mean, the diagonal elements in the symmetric matrix (7.39) represent the variances of the disturbances, and the off-diagonal elements are the covariances between different disturbances. The matrix (7.39) is the **variance–covariance matrix**.

Using assumptions IIB and IIC, we see that the classical model implies that

$$E(\boldsymbol{\epsilon\epsilon'}) = \begin{pmatrix} \sigma^2 & 0 & 0 & \cdots & 0 \\ 0 & \sigma^2 & 0 & \cdots & 0 \\ 0 & 0 & \sigma^2 & \cdots & 0 \\ \vdots & \vdots & \vdots & & \vdots \\ 0 & 0 & 0 & \cdots & \sigma^2 \end{pmatrix} = \sigma^2 \mathbf{I}_n \tag{7.40}$$

where $\mathbf{I}_n$ is the $n \times n$ identity matrix.

Since assumption IIA implies $E(\boldsymbol{\epsilon}) = 0$, we can represent all four assumptions concerning the disturbance by the single statement

$$\boldsymbol{\epsilon} \text{ is NID}(\mathbf{0}, \sigma^2 \mathbf{I}_n) \tag{7.41}$$

The statement (7.41) should be read as stating that the vector of disturbances $\boldsymbol{\epsilon}$ is normally and independently distributed with mean equal to the null vector $\mathbf{0}$ and variance–covariance matrix $\sigma^2 \mathbf{I}_n$.

7.3   Properties of the OLS estimators

As in two-variable regression, the properties possessed by the OLS estimators depend very much on which of the classical assumptions are valid. In fact, the pattern followed by this section follows closely that of Section 6.2. However, we assume throughout that assumption ID holds, otherwise estimation would be infeasible. As in two-variable regression, we will concentrate mainly on the estimators of the slope parameters β_j $(j = 2, 3, \ldots, k)$ rather than the intercept parameter β_1. In applied work it is normally the slope parameters that are of the greatest interest.

Linearity

Only assumptions IA and IB are necessary if the OLS estimators are to be linear functions of the sample observations. Since the values of the X variables can be regarded as fixed constants under these assumptions, by the sample observations we mean just the Y values. Recalling the expression (7.15) for the OLS estimators, we have

$$\hat{\boldsymbol{\beta}} = (\mathbf{X}'\mathbf{X})^{-1}\mathbf{X}'\mathbf{Y} = \mathbf{CY} \qquad (7.42)$$

where, since $\mathbf{X}$ is a matrix of fixed constants, $\mathbf{C} = (\mathbf{X}'\mathbf{X})^{-1}\mathbf{X}'$ is also such a matrix. The property of linearity is implied by (7.42), since the equation can be rewritten in scalar terms as

$$\hat{\beta}_j = c_{j1}Y_1 + c_{j2}Y_2 + c_{j3}Y_3 + \cdots + c_{jn}Y_n \quad \text{for all } j$$

where the Y_i are the sample observations and the c_{ji} are the fixed constants in the jth row of the $k \times n$ matrix $\mathbf{C}$.

Unbiasedness

Assumptions IA, IB and IIA are sufficient to demonstrate the unbiasedness of the OLS estimators. The situation is thus identical to that in two-variable regression, except that we now have more than one non-stochastic regressor. Substituting (7.4) into (7.15), we have

$$\hat{\boldsymbol{\beta}} = (\mathbf{X}'\mathbf{X})^{-1}\mathbf{X}'(\mathbf{X}\boldsymbol{\beta} + \boldsymbol{\epsilon})$$
$$= (\mathbf{X}'\mathbf{X})^{-1}\mathbf{X}'\mathbf{X}\boldsymbol{\beta} + (\mathbf{X}'\mathbf{X})^{-1}\mathbf{X}'\boldsymbol{\epsilon} = \mathbf{I}\boldsymbol{\beta} + \mathbf{C}\boldsymbol{\epsilon}$$
$$= \boldsymbol{\beta} + \mathbf{C}\boldsymbol{\epsilon} \qquad (7.43)$$

where $\mathbf{C}$ is the matrix of fixed constants defined above. In scalar terms, (7.43) implies

$$\hat{\beta}_j = \beta_j + c_{j1}\epsilon_1 + c_{j2}\epsilon_2 + \cdots + c_{jn}\epsilon_n \quad \text{for all } j \qquad (7.43a)$$

where the c_{ji} again represent the jth row of $\mathbf{C}$.

Taking expectations over (7.43a), we have, since the c_{ji} are constants, by assumptions IA and IB,

$$E(\hat{\beta}_j) = \beta_j + c_{j1}E(\epsilon_1) + c_{j2}E(\epsilon_2) + \cdots + c_{jn}E(\epsilon_n) \quad \text{for all } j$$

But, by assumption IIA, $E(\epsilon_i) = 0$ for all i. Thus

$$E(\hat{\beta}_j) = \beta_j \quad \text{for all } j \qquad (7.44)$$

Hence the OLS estimators, the $\hat{\beta}_j$, are unbiased.

Alternatively, we can work in terms of matrix algebra, and take expectations over (7.43) directly:

$$E(\hat{\boldsymbol{\beta}}) = \boldsymbol{\beta} + \mathbf{C}E(\boldsymbol{\epsilon})$$

However, assumption IIA can also be written as $E(\boldsymbol{\epsilon}) = \mathbf{0}$. Hence we have

$$E(\hat{\boldsymbol{\beta}}) = \boldsymbol{\beta} \qquad (7.44a)$$

which is the matrix equivalent of (7.44).

Consistency

Assumptions IA, IB, IC and IIA are sufficient to prove the consistency of the OLS estimators, the $\hat{\beta}_j$. That is, we make use of all the classical assumptions concerning the explanatory variables and the first of the assumptions concerning the disturbance. The proof parallels that for two-variable regression, and is presented in Appendix 7B to this chapter. Here we simply recall what the property implies. If the $\hat{\beta}_j$ are consistent then, as the sample size $n \rightarrow \infty$, they converge in probability to the true β_j. That is, the sampling distributions for the $\hat{\beta}_j$ collapse onto the true β_j. Thus plim $(\hat{\beta}_j) = \beta_j$ for all j.

Best linear unbiasedness

We have seen that, given assumptions IA and IB, the OLS estimators are both linear and unbiased. For them to have the minimum variance of all such linear unbiased estimators, that is, to be BLUEs, it is necessary that classical assumptions IIB and IIC also be valid. That is, as in two-variable regression, the disturbances must be homoskedastic and non-autocorrelated.

A general matrix demonstration of BLUness in the multiple regression case is beyond the scope of this text. We shall limit ourselves to simply finding expressions for the variances and covariances of the OLS estimators. As we shall see, these expressions are of great importance if we wish to make inferences about multiple regression parameters.

Consider the symmetric $k \times k$ matrix

$$E(\hat{\beta} - \beta)(\hat{\beta} - \beta)'$$

$$= \begin{pmatrix} E(\hat{\beta}_1 - \beta_1)^2 & E(\hat{\beta}_1 - \beta_1)(\hat{\beta}_2 - \beta_2) & \cdots & E(\hat{\beta}_1 - \beta_1)(\hat{\beta}_k - \beta_k) \\ E(\hat{\beta}_2 - \beta_2)(\hat{\beta}_1 - \beta_1) & E(\hat{\beta}_2 - \beta_2)^2 & \cdots & E(\hat{\beta}_2 - \beta_2)(\hat{\beta}_k - \beta_k) \\ \vdots & \vdots & & \vdots \\ E(\hat{\beta}_k - \beta_k)(\hat{\beta}_1 - \beta_1) & E(\hat{\beta}_k - \beta_k)(\hat{\beta}_2 - \beta_2) & \cdots & E(\hat{\beta}_k - \beta_k)^2 \end{pmatrix}$$

$$(7.45)$$

Since $\beta_j = E(\hat{\beta}_j)$ for all j, we can write (7.45) as

$$E(\hat{\beta} - \beta)(\hat{\beta} - \beta)' = \begin{pmatrix} \text{Var}(\hat{\beta}_1) & \text{Cov}(\hat{\beta}_1, \hat{\beta}_2) & \cdots & \text{Cov}(\hat{\beta}_1, \hat{\beta}_k) \\ \text{Cov}(\hat{\beta}_2, \hat{\beta}_1) & \text{Var}(\hat{\beta}_2) & \cdots & \text{Cov}(\hat{\beta}_2, \hat{\beta}_k) \\ \vdots & \vdots & & \vdots \\ \text{Cov}(\hat{\beta}_k, \hat{\beta}_1) & \text{Cov}(\hat{\beta}_k, \hat{\beta}_2) & \cdots & \text{Var}(\hat{\beta}_k) \end{pmatrix}$$

$$(7.46)$$

The matrix (7.46) is known as the **variance–covariance matrix** of the vector $\hat{\boldsymbol{\beta}}$, normally written **Var** $(\hat{\boldsymbol{\beta}})$. Notice that it contains down its main diagonal the variances of the $\hat{\beta}_j$. The off-diagonal elements represent the covariances between the different $\hat{\beta}_j$ that would be obtained if many samples were taken. Clearly, we require an expression for this matrix if we are to make inferences about the true β_j.

From (7.43),

$$\hat{\boldsymbol{\beta}} - \boldsymbol{\beta} = \mathbf{C}\boldsymbol{\epsilon} = (\mathbf{X}'\mathbf{X})^{-1}\mathbf{X}'\boldsymbol{\epsilon}$$

Hence, since $(\mathbf{X}'\mathbf{X})^{-1}$ is symmetric,

$$
\begin{aligned}
\mathrm{E}(\hat{\boldsymbol{\beta}} - \boldsymbol{\beta})(\hat{\boldsymbol{\beta}} - \boldsymbol{\beta})' &= \mathrm{E}[(\mathbf{X}'\mathbf{X})^{-1}\mathbf{X}'\boldsymbol{\epsilon}][\boldsymbol{\epsilon}'\mathbf{X}(\mathbf{X}'\mathbf{X})^{-1}] \\
&= (\mathbf{X}'\mathbf{X})^{-1}\mathbf{X}'\mathrm{E}(\boldsymbol{\epsilon}\boldsymbol{\epsilon}')\mathbf{X}(\mathbf{X}'\mathbf{X})^{-1}
\end{aligned}
\tag{7.47}
$$

since $\mathbf{X}$ can be regarded as a matrix of constants.

However, $\mathrm{E}(\boldsymbol{\epsilon}\boldsymbol{\epsilon}')$ is the variance–covariance matrix of the disturbances, which, under assumptions IIB and IIC, is given by (7.40) as equal to $\sigma^2\mathbf{I}_n$. Substituting into (7.47) therefore gives

$$
\begin{aligned}
\mathbf{Var}\ (\hat{\boldsymbol{\beta}}) = \mathrm{E}(\hat{\boldsymbol{\beta}} - \boldsymbol{\beta})(\hat{\boldsymbol{\beta}} - \boldsymbol{\beta}) &= (\mathbf{X}'\mathbf{X})^{-1}\mathbf{X}'(\sigma^2\mathbf{I}_n)\mathbf{X}(\mathbf{X}'\mathbf{X})^{-1} \\
&= \sigma^2(\mathbf{X}'\mathbf{X})^{-1}\mathbf{X}'\mathbf{X}(\mathbf{X}'\mathbf{X})^{-1} \\
&= \sigma^2(\mathbf{X}'\mathbf{X})^{-1}
\end{aligned}
\tag{7.48}
$$

Equation (7.48) is our required expression for the variance–covariance matrix of the OLS vector $\hat{\boldsymbol{\beta}}$.

We shall write the element in the ith row and jth column of the *inverse matrix* $(\mathbf{X}'\mathbf{X})^{-1}$ as X^{ij}. Since $(\mathbf{X}'\mathbf{X})^{-1}$ is symmetric, it will be the case that $X^{ji} = X^{ij}$. A comparison of (7.48) with (7.46) indicates that the variance of $\hat{\beta}_j$, which we write as $\sigma^2_{\hat{\beta}_j}$, is given by

$$\sigma^2_{\hat{\beta}_j} = \mathrm{Var}\ (\hat{\beta}_j) = \sigma^2 X^{jj}, \quad j = 1, 2, \ldots, k \tag{7.49}$$

Thus, to find the variance of $\hat{\beta}_j$, we have to pick out the jth diagonal element of $(\mathbf{X}'\mathbf{X})^{-1}$ and multiply by the common variance of the disturbances, σ^2. The square root of Var $(\hat{\beta}_j)$ is known as the **standard error** of $\hat{\beta}_j$, written $\sigma_{\hat{\beta}_j}$.

Further comparison of (7.48) and (7.46) indicates that

$$\mathrm{Cov}\ (\hat{\beta}_i, \hat{\beta}_j) = \sigma^2 X^{ij} \quad \text{for all } i \neq j \tag{7.50}$$

The expressions (7.49) and (7.50) are of considerable importance for inference in multiple regression.

It is possible to obtain expressions equivalent to (7.49) and (7.50), working in terms of deviations of variables from their means. It is simply necessary to work in terms of the inverse matrix $(\mathbf{x}'\mathbf{x})^{-1}$ rather than $(\mathbf{X}'\mathbf{X})^{-1}$. A full derivation would prove repetitive, but it is not difficult to show that

$$\sigma^2_{\hat{\beta}_j} = \mathrm{Var}\ (\hat{\beta}_j) = \sigma^2 x^{jj}, \quad j = 2, 3, \ldots, k \tag{7.49a}$$

and

$$\text{Cov} (\hat{\beta}_i, \hat{\beta}_j) = \sigma^2 x^{ij} \quad \text{for } i \neq j, \quad i, j = 2, 3, \ldots, k \tag{7.50a}$$

where x^{ij} is the element in the $(i-1)$th row and $(j-1)$th column of $(\mathbf{x}'\mathbf{x})^{-1}$. The expressions (7.49a) and (7.50a) are alternatives to (7.49) and (7.50) which are often useful for computational purposes. Notice, though, that (7.49a) does not yield an expression for Var $(\hat{\beta}_1)$.

In the special case of two-variable regression $\mathbf{x}'\mathbf{x}$ in (7.18) is simply the scalar $\sum x_2^2$, so that $x^{22} = 1 / \sum x_2^2$. Thus (7.49a) just gives

$$\text{Var} (\hat{\beta}_2) = \sigma^2 / \sum x_2^2$$

This is, as expected, identical to the expression for the variance of the OLS estimator of the slope parameter in two-variable regression, obtained in Chapter 6 as (6.14).

Other properties

As in two-variable regression, if the OLS estimators are to be not merely unbiased but also *efficient* and *asymptotically efficient*, we also require that assumption IID of the classical model holds – that is, the disturbances must be normally distributed. Hence, if OLS estimators are to possess these properties, we require all of the classical assumptions to be valid. A proof of the efficiency property is, however, beyond our scope. Recall that efficiency implies that the OLS estimators have the minimum variance of *all* unbiased estimators – not merely of all linear unbiased estimators.

Normality of the disturbances has two other important consequences for OLS regression. First, it means that the sampling distributions of the OLS estimators will be normal distributions. A demonstration of this is exactly analogous to that in two-variable regression (see Section 6.2) and is left to the reader. It follows, however, that, since, given all classical assumptions, each $\hat{\beta}_j$ is unbiased with a variance given by (7.49),

$$\hat{\beta}_j \text{ is } N(\beta_j, \sigma^2 X^{ij}), \quad j = 1, 2, 3, \ldots, k \tag{7.51}$$

Such exact knowledge of the sampling distributions of the OLS estimators, the $\hat{\beta}_j$, is of vital importance in inference as we shall see in the next section.

It is often useful to express (7.51) in alternative form, working in terms of deviations of the X variables from their means. Using (7.49a) instead of (7.49), we also have

$$\hat{\beta}_j \text{ is } N(\beta_j, \sigma^2 x^{ij}), \quad j = 2, 3, \ldots, k \tag{7.51a}$$

The other consequence of assuming normally distributed disturbances is that, as in two-variable regression, the OLS estimators now also become *maximum likelihood* estimators. This property is demonstrated in Appendix 7C to this chapter. It is in fact a straightforward extension to the two-variable proof of Appendix 6B. As in two-variable regression, the ML method provides not only estimators of the β_j parameters but also an estimator of σ^2, the disturbance variance. As in two-variable regression, the MLE of σ^2 turns out to be

$$\tilde{\sigma}^2 = \frac{\sum e_i^2}{n} \tag{7.52}$$

where $\sum e_i^2$ is the sum of the squared residuals. Again, however, $\tilde{\sigma}^2$ proves to be a biased estimator of the true σ^2. In fact, it can be shown that in multiple regression

$$E(\tilde{\sigma}^2) = \frac{n-k}{n}\sigma^2 \neq \sigma^2 \tag{7.53}$$

Equation (7.53) is simply a generalization of the two-variable regression result (6.19) that was demonstrated in Appendix 6C.

Since, under classical assumptions, OLS and ML estimators of the β_j parameters are identical, it may seem at this point that ML estimation adds little to our analysis of regression equations. However, *maximum likelihood estimation becomes of real relevance when the classical assumptions break down.* For example, the method is frequently used in cases where a population regression equation is *nonlinear.* We refer briefly to this situation in Appendix 7C. It is also of great importance when the classical assumptions concerning the explanatory variables and/or those concerning the disturbances break down. As we have seen, if the classical assumptions are invalid then the OLS estimators lose some or all of their normal desirable properties. But it turns out that, under such conditions, the OLS and ML estimators *are not identical.* The ML estimators then have the great advantage that, as we noted in Section 5.3, they still possess the large-sample properties of consistency and asymptotic efficiency.

7.4 Inference in multiple regression

Provided all the classical assumptions are valid, inferences concerning the slope parameters in multiple regression can be based on the result (7.51a), which implies that for $j = 2, 3, \ldots, k$,

$$\frac{\hat{\beta}_j - \beta_j}{\sigma_{\hat{\beta}_j}} \text{ has N}(0, 1) \text{ distribution} \tag{7.54}$$

where the standard errors $\sigma_{\hat{\beta}_j}$ are given by (7.49a). We shall concentrate on the slope parameters, which are often of most interest. Inference about the intercept parameter β_1 has to be based on (7.51) with $j = 1$.

The problem with (7.54) is that the standard errors, the $\sigma_{\hat{\beta}_j}$, are unknown, since the disturbance variance σ^2 is unknown. However, an unbiased estimator of σ^2 is given by

$$s^2 = \frac{\sum e_i^2}{n-k} \tag{7.55}$$

This follows from (7.53), since $E(s^2) = [n/(n-k)]E(\tilde{\sigma}^2) = \sigma^2$. The residual sum of squares is most easily calculated by using (7.36).

Given (7.55), unbiased estimates of the variances of the OLS estimators are, using (7.49a),

$$s^2_{\hat{\beta}_j} = s^2 x^{jj}, \qquad j = 2, 3, \ldots, k \qquad (7.56)$$

However, when we replace the $\sigma_{\hat{\beta}_j}$ in (7.54) by their unbiased estimators, the $s_{\hat{\beta}_j}$, as in two-variable regression, we have to switch to the Student's t distribution. In fact, it can be shown that

$$\frac{\hat{\beta} - \beta}{s_{\hat{\beta}_j}} \text{ has a Student's } t \text{ distribution with } n - k \text{ d.f.} \qquad (7.57)$$

A demonstration of (7.57) is identical to that in Appendix 6D, except that the residual sum of squares in this case has $n - k$ degrees of freedom. Hence the resultant t distribution has $n - k$ degrees of freedom.

Inference may now be based on (7.57). For instance, a 95% confidence interval for any β_j $(j = 2, 3, \ldots, k)$ is

$$\hat{\beta}_j + t_{0.025} s_{\hat{\beta}_j} \qquad (7.58)$$

the value of $t_{0.025}$ depending on $n - k$, the number of degrees of freedom. To obtain a 99% interval, we simply replace $t_{0.025}$ by $t_{0.005}$.

Significance testing can proceed along similar lines to that undertaken in two-variable regression. To test a null hypothesis of the kind H_0: $\beta_j = 0$ $(j = 2, 3, \ldots, k)$, we simply state that, under such a null hypothesis, (7.57) implies that

$$\hat{\beta}_j / s_{\hat{\beta}_j} \text{ has a Student's } t \text{ distribution with } n - k \text{ d.f.} \qquad (7.59)$$

Hence, we may use $\hat{\beta}_j / s_{\hat{\beta}_j}$ as a test statistic and reject the null hypothesis that the variable X_j does *not* influence Y if the absolute value of this test statistic is sufficiently large. As in two-variable regression, the test statistic is often referred to as a t ratio.

WORKED EXAMPLE 7.1 (continued)

As a first numerical illustration of inference in multiple regression, we return to the data on the 25 households given in Table 7.1. First, let us note the relevant calculations that have already been made for this example. We have the inverse matrix $(x'x)^{-1}$ given by (7.26). We have the OLS estimators $\hat{\beta}_2 = 0.332$ and $\hat{\beta}_3 = 0.126$, given in (7.27). Finally, below (7.36), the residual sum of squares, $\sum e_i^2 = 3.234 \times 10^4$, is computed.

To make inferences about the true β_2 and β_3, we require the estimated standard errors $s_{\hat{\beta}_i}$ and $s_{\hat{\beta}_j}$. Using (7.55), our estimate of the disturbance variance is

$$s^2 = \frac{\sum e_i^2}{n-3} = \frac{3.234 \times 10^4}{22} = 1470$$

Taking the diagonal elements $x^{22} = 34.67(5.777 \times 10^{-7})$ and $x^{33} = 1.663(5.777 \times 10^{-7})$ from the matrix (7.26), we then have, using (7.56),

$$s_{\hat{\beta}_2}^2 = s^2 x^{22} = 1470(34.67)(5.777 \times 10^{-7}) = 0.029\,44$$

$$s_{\hat{\beta}_3}^2 = s^2 x^{33} = 1470(1.663)(5.777 \times 10^{-7}) = 0.001\,412$$

Thus the estimated standard errors of $\hat{\beta}_2$ and $\hat{\beta}_3$ are $s_{\hat{\beta}_2} = 0.172$ and $s_{\hat{\beta}_3} = 0.0376$.

Confidence intervals for β_2 and β_3 may now be found using (7.58). For example, a 95% confidence interval for β_3, the marginal propensity to consume liquid assets, is

$$\hat{\beta}_3 \pm t_{0.025} s_{\hat{\beta}_3} = 0.126 \pm 2.074(0.0376) = 0.126 \pm 0.078$$

since, with $n - k = 22$ d.f., $t_{0.025} = 2.074$.

Significance testing is equally straightforward. For example, if we wish to test whether liquid asset holdings influence consumption, we set up the null hypothesis H_0: $\beta_3 = 0$, and use as our test statistic the t ratio $\hat{\beta}_3/s_{\hat{\beta}_3}$. This has a value of $0.126/0.0376 = 3.35$, which, at the 5% level of significance with 22 d.f., must be compared with a critical t value of $t_{0.05} = 1.717$. The test statistic is clearly large enough for us to reject the null hypothesis and conclude that liquid asset holdings influence household consumption.

Similarly, to test whether income influences consumption, we have H_0: $\beta_2 = 0$, and this time a t ratio $\hat{\beta}_2/s_{\hat{\beta}_2} = 0.332/0.172 = 1.93$. Again this exceeds the critical t value, so we conclude that income also influences household consumption.

When presenting multiple regression results, it is customary, as in two-variable regression, to place t ratios in parentheses beneath the relevant estimated coefficients. We can now therefore rewrite (7.29) as

$$\hat{Y} = 36.64 + 0.332X_2 + 0.126X_3, \qquad R^2 = 0.796 \tag{7.60}$$
$$\phantom{\hat{Y} = 36.64 + }(1.93) \qquad (3.35)$$

We noted earlier in this chapter that the addition of the liquid assets variable to our household consumption function led to a substantial fall in the size of the estimated coefficient on the income variable. We also note from Equation (7.60) that the income variable has a lower t ratio than the liquid assets variable, and hence appears to be 'less significant' in the determination of household consumption. However, to anyone familiar with the life-cycle and permanent income theories of consumption, these findings should not be surprising. In these theories it is some measure of overall lifetime resources rather than current measured income that is held to be the major influence on consumption. Liquid asset holdings may well be a better indicator of these lifetime resources than is disposable income.

WORKED EXAMPLE 7.2 (continued)

For our second numerical example of inference in multiple regression, we shall again take the data below (7.30). We have already computed the OLS estimators $\hat{\beta}_2$, $\hat{\beta}_3$ and $\hat{\beta}_4$ and the residual sum of squares $\sum e_i^2 = 1906.8$ for this example. We can now estimate the standard errors of the estimators.

First, using (7.55), we have

$$s^2 = \frac{\sum e_i^2}{n-4} = \frac{1906.8}{21} = 90.8$$

Using the $(\mathbf{x'x})^{-1}$ matrix below (7.30), we see that its diagonal elements are

$$x^{22} = 0.030, \qquad x^{33} = 0.028, \qquad x^{44} = 0.275$$

Hence, using (7.56),

$$s_{\hat{\beta}_2}^2 = s^2 x^{22} = 90.8(0.030) = 2.724, \qquad s_{\hat{\beta}_2} = 1.65$$

$$s_{\hat{\beta}_3}^2 = s^2 x^{33} = 90.8(0.028) = 2.542, \qquad s_{\hat{\beta}_3} = 1.59$$

$$s_{\hat{\beta}_4}^2 = s^2 x^{44} = 90.8(0.275) = 24.97, \qquad s_{\hat{\beta}_4} = 5.00$$

We can now make inferences about the parameters β_2, β_3 and β_4. For example, using (7.58) we can form a 95% confidence interval for β_2. Since with $n - k = 21$ d.f., $t_{0.025} = 2.080$, we have

$$\hat{\beta}_2 \pm 2.080 s_{\hat{\beta}_2} = 9.31 \pm 2.080(1.65) = 9.31 \pm 3.43$$

To test whether, for example, X_3 influences Y, we set up the null hypothesis $\beta_3 = 0$ and compute the t ratio $\hat{\beta}_3/s_{\hat{\beta}_3} = 7.44/1.59 = 4.68$. Using a 5% significance level and a two-tail test, this must be compared with a critical t value of $t_{0.025} = 2.080$. We therefore reject the null hypothesis and conclude that X_3 is a significant variable in the determination of Y.

A summary of the computational steps involved in multiple regression analysis is provided in Table 7.2.

Exercise 7.4

For the data in Exercise 7.1,

(a) Compute the estimated standard errors of $\hat{\beta}_2$ and $\hat{\beta}_3$.

(b) Construct a 95% confidence interval for β_2.

(c) Test the hypothesis $\beta_3 = 0$ against an alternative $\beta_3 > 0$.

Table 7.2   Computational procedure for multiple regression

Step 1   Working in terms of deviations of variables from their means, form the $(k-1) \times (k-1)$ matrix $\mathbf{x}'\mathbf{x}$ and the $(k-1) \times n$ matrix $\mathbf{x}'\mathbf{y}$

Step 2   Invert the $\mathbf{x}'\mathbf{x}$ matrix obtaining $(\mathbf{x}'\mathbf{x})^{-1}$

Step 3   Compute the OLS estimators using

$$\begin{pmatrix} \hat{\beta}_2 \\ \hat{\beta}_3 \\ \vdots \\ \hat{\beta}_k \end{pmatrix} = (\mathbf{x}'\mathbf{x})^{-1}\mathbf{x}'\mathbf{y}, \qquad \hat{\beta}_1 = \bar{Y} - \beta_2 \bar{X}_2 - \beta_3 \bar{X}_3 - \cdots - \beta_k \bar{X}_k$$

Step 4   Compute residual sum of squares

$$\sum e_i^2 = \sum y_i - \hat{\beta}_2 \sum x_{2i} y_i - \hat{\beta}_3 \sum x_{3i} y_i - \cdots - \hat{\beta}_k \sum x_{ki} y_i$$

Step 5   Compute s^2 and the variances of the OLS estimators

$$s^2 = \frac{\sum e_i^2}{n-k} \qquad s_{\hat{\beta}_j}^2 = s^2 x^{jj} \quad (j = 2, 3, 4, \ldots, k)$$

where x^{jj} is the jth diagonal element of $(\mathbf{x}'\mathbf{x})^{-1}$

Exercise 7.5

For the data in Exercise 7.2,

(a) Compute the estimated standard errors of $\hat{\alpha}$ and $\hat{\beta}$.

(b) Test the hypotheses $\alpha < 1$ and $\beta < 1$.

Exercise 7.6

For the data in Exercise 7.3,

(a) Compute the estimated standard errors of $\hat{\beta}_2$, $\hat{\beta}_3$ and $\hat{\beta}_4$.

(b) Test whether the variables X_2, X_3 or X_4 have any influence on Y.

(c) Test the hypothesis $\beta_3 < 5$.

COMPUTER EXERCISE

Now that we are aware of the calculations involved in multiple regression, we are well equipped to start estimating equations using a computer package. Suitable packages were mentioned in Chapter 1, and it is assumed the reader has ready access to one. We shall attempt to estimate a demand equation for food using Data Set 1 on the floppy disk which contains 30 annual observations for the US economy.

The economic theory of the consumer suggests that a demand equation for food might have the form

$$Q = f(X, P, G) \qquad (7.61)$$

where Q is the quantity of food demanded by US consumers, X is the total money expenditure of consumers, P is a price index for food and G is a general price index. G is included because, although there are no obvious substitutes for food in the everyday sense, all other goods are substitutes in the general sense that they compete with food for the dollars in the consumer's total budget.[4]

Consumer theory also suggests that the above function should be *homogeneous of degree zero in its three explanatory variables*. What this means is that equiproportionate changes in total money expenditure and all prices should leave the demand for food unchanged. For example, a doubling in X, P and G should leave Q constant. If our demand equation is to have this property then it must be possible to rewrite (7.61) as

$$Q = g(X/G, P/G) \qquad (7.62)$$

Equation (7.62) implies that the demand for food depends on the *real* total expenditure of consumers, X/G, and on the *relative* price of food, P/G. It is homogeneous of degree zero because, for example, a doubling of X, P and G leaves the ratios X/G and P/G unchanged and hence has no effect on Q.

We shall estimate equations of both forms (7.61) and (7.62) but first we must decide on what functional form to use. Purely for the sake of convenience we shall work in terms of the natural logarithms of variables. This means that we will be able to interpret regression coefficients as elasticities which are the quantities of greatest interest in demand studies. Thus we will give (7.61), for example, the form

$$Q = AX^{\beta_2} P^{\beta_3} G^{\beta_4} \qquad (7.63)$$

Taking natural logarithms and adding a disturbance then gives

$$\ln(Q) = \beta_1 + \beta_2 \ln(X) + \beta_3 \ln(P) + \beta_4 \ln(G) + \epsilon \qquad (7.64)$$

where $\beta_1 = \ln(A)$. β_2, β_3 and β_4 are demand elasticities. Thus we obtain a linear regression equation to estimate. Similarly, our empirical version of (7.62) is

$$\ln(Q) = \beta_1 + \beta_2 \ln(X/G) + \beta_3 \ln(P/G) + \epsilon \qquad (7.65)$$

Another useful advantage of working in logarithmic terms is that the homogeneity property of demand equations can then be very easily expressed algebraically. For (7.64) to be homogeneous of degree zero, it is necessary for the three elasticities to sum to zero. That is, we require $\beta_2 + \beta_3 + \beta_4 = 0$. Enforcing this restriction on the regression parameters in (7.64) will yield the homogeneous equation (7.65). To show this, we simply substitute $\beta_4 = -\beta_2 - \beta_3$ into (7.64). Simple rearrangement will then yield (7.65). Thus if we estimate (7.65) we are implicitly assuming that the elasticities sum to zero.

Before we can actually estimate (7.64) or (7.65), we have to define empirical counterparts to the theoretical variables Q, X, P and G. Since we cannot add together such diverse items as, for example, bananas and sausages, we have to measure the total demand for food in monetary terms. However, since demand is a quantity variable, we shall work in constant prices and define demand as

Q = consumers' expenditure on food in 1980 prices

The other variables are easier to define. Since total expenditure X is in nominal money terms, we define it as

X = total consumers' expenditure in current prices

We obtain a price index for food by noting that

$$\text{food expenditure in constant prices} = \frac{\text{food expenditure in current prices}}{P}$$

where the price index P is known as the implicit deflator of food expenditure. P can therefore be calculated as

$$P = \frac{\text{food expenditure in current prices}}{\text{food expenditure in 1980 prices}}$$

Similarly, we define the general price index G as the implicit deflator of total consumer expenditure. That is,

$$G = \frac{\text{total consumer expenditure in current prices}}{\text{total consumer expenditure in 1980 prices}}$$

Annual observations for 1963–92 on all the necessary variables are contained in Data Set 1 on the floppy disk and also in Appendix III. The data is taken from the annual publication, *OECD National Accounts*. Transformation routines in your program will enable you to compute values for the ratio variables X/G and P/G very quickly. The routines will also enable you to form the natural logarithms of all variables.

For the moment, we shall make use only of the observations for 1965 through 1989 in Data Set 1. The remaining observations will be made use of in later chapters. The reader is expected to duplicate the regression results that follow using a multiple regression package.

A labelled version of a typical computer printout of the estimation of (7.64) by OLS is shown in Table 7.3. This printout was obtained using the computer package MICROFIT, but similar output can be obtained using the alternatives mentioned in Chapter 1. At present, we are unable to interpret all of this printout, some of it being explained in later chapters. Extracting the regression coefficients, their t ratios and

Table 7.3   Computer printout for Equation (7.66)

Ordinary Least Squares Estimation

****

Dependent variable is LN Q
25 observations used for estimation from 1965 to 1989

****

Regressor	Coefficient	Standard Error	T-Ratio[Prob]
INTER	$\hat{\beta}_1 \rightarrow$ 5.3200	1.2023$\leftarrow s_{\hat{\beta}_1}$	4.4250[.000]
LN X	$\hat{\beta}_2 \rightarrow$ .47964	.083588$\leftarrow s_{\hat{\beta}_2}$	5.7382[.000]
LN P	$\hat{\beta}_3 \rightarrow -$.15340	.10419$\leftarrow s_{\hat{\beta}_3}$	-1.4723[.156]
LN G	$\hat{\beta}_4 \rightarrow -$.40491	.17295$\leftarrow s_{\hat{\beta}_4}$	-2.3411[.029]

****

R-Squared	.94269	F-statistic F(3, 21)	115.1331[.000]
R-Bar-Squared	.93450	S.E. of Regression	.018213
Residual Sum of Squares	.0069656	Mean of Dependent Variable	12.1936
S.D. of Dependent Variable	.071161	Maximum of Log-likelihood	66.8471
DW-statistic	.66893		

****

Source: *Printout from software MICROFIT 3.0, Electronic Publishing, OUP, by H and B Pesaran.*

the coefficient of multiple determination, we can present the OLS version of (7.64) in the usual manner, with t ratios in parentheses:

$$\widehat{\ln(Q)} = 5.32 + 0.480 \ln(X) - 0.153 \ln(P) - 0.405 \ln(G), \quad R^2 = 0.943$$
$$\quad\quad (4.43) \quad (5.74) \quad\quad\quad (-1.47) \quad\quad\quad (-2.34)$$

$$(7.66)$$

The standard error of the regression given in the printout is simply what we have referred to previously as s, and is given by the square root of Equation (7.55). It is therefore the standard deviation of the residuals, and can be regarded as another measure of goodness of fit.

Equation (7.66) indicates that 94.3% of the variation in $\ln(Q)$ during our sample period can be attributed to variations in the three explanatory variables. With $n - k = 21$ d.f., the critical t values are $t_{0.05} = 1.721$ and $t_{0.025} = 2.080$. Examination of the t ratios therefore indicates that the intercept and the coefficients on $\ln(X)$ and $\ln(G)$ are significantly different from zero at the 5% level, whether we use a one-tail or a two-tail test. We can therefore tentatively conclude that the demand for food is influenced by total consumer expenditure and by the general price level. However, the coefficient on the food price variable is not significantly different from zero. This implies that, surprisingly perhaps, we are unable to detect any effect for the price of food on the demand for it.

The sign on the coefficient of the X variable is positive, as expected. Obviously, since food is a normal good, as total expenditure rises, we expect the demand for food to rise. While the food price coefficient is insignificant, its negative sign is also as expected. A rise in the price of food should lead to a fall in demand.

The expected sign on G is less obvious. Remember that the coefficient on this variable measures the effect of a rise in the general price level on the demand for food *when the other variables, the price of food and total expenditure in current prices, are held constant*. If the price of other goods rises but the price of food remains unchanged then we expect a substitution effect as consumers switch from buying other goods to buying food, which is now relatively cheaper. This suggests a positive sign on the G variable. However, a rise in the price of other goods with total money expenditure X held constant implies a fall in total real expenditure. Such a fall will mean less is spent on all goods, including food. This expenditure or income effect thus suggests a negative sign on the G variable. In practice, the sign we find on G will depend on the balance of the two effects.

Our equation, with its negative sign on G, can therefore be interpreted as implying that the expenditure effect of a general price change outweighs any substitution effect. In general, the demand for food seems to be more sensitive to real expenditure changes than to price changes.

The sizes of the estimated elasticities in (7.66) are quite small. For example, a 1% rise in total expenditure leads to only a 0.480% rise in the demand for food. However, this is to be expected as food is more a necessity than a luxury.

The three elasticities in (7.66) sum to -0.078. This is not quite the zero suggested by theory! In chapter 10 we shall actually be able to test the hypothesis that the elasticities sum to zero, but for the moment we move on and estimate Equation (7.65). Recall that in this equation we are implicitly *assuming* that the elasticities sum to zero. A typical computer printout for this regression is shown in Table 7.4. From it, we can extract

$$\widehat{\ln (Q)} = 7.74 + 0.311 \ln (X/G) - 0.180 \ln (P/G), \quad R^2 = 0.931 \quad (7.67)$$
$$\phantom{\widehat{\ln (Q)} = } (27.3) \quad (15.6) (-1.63)$$

Notice, first, that the t ratios in (7.67) indicate that, while the coefficient on real expenditure, X/G, is significantly different from zero, that on the relative price of food, P/G is not. Thus again we are unable to detect any price effects. The signs on the variables are as expected.

To make a direct comparison with (7.66), we can rewrite (7.67) as

$$\widehat{\ln (Q)} = 7.74 + 0.311[\ln (X) - \ln (G)] - 0.180[\ln (P) - \ln (G)]$$
$$= 7.74 + 0.311 \ln (X) - 0.180 \ln (P) - 0.131 \ln (G) \quad (7.68)$$

When (7.68) is written in this form, we see that it is somewhat different from (7.66). This is the consequence of 'forcing' the elasticities to sum to zero,[5] when in fact (7.66) suggested they did not quite do so.

Another consequence of enforcing the restriction on the elasticities is the decline in R^2 to 0.931 in Equation (7.67). Had the elasticities actually summed to zero, imposing the restriction that they do so would not have led to such a fall in R^2.

We shall return to this data set in later chapters. However, before leaving it for now, we must recall the words of warning issued in previous chapters regarding time series data in which variables exhibit definite trend movements. If you examine Data

Table 7.4 Computer printout for Equation (7.67)

```
                   Ordinary Least Squares Estimation
**********************************************************************
Dependent variable is LN Q
25 observations used for estimation from 1965 to 1989
**********************************************************************
Regressor      Coefficient          Standard Error      T-Ratio[Prob]
INTER             7.7404                .28379           27.2753[.000]
LN X/G             .31146               .019955          15.6082[.000]
LN P/G            -.18023               .11077           -1.6270[.118]
**********************************************************************
R-Squared                    .93106   F-statistic F( 2, 22)  148.5573[.000]
R-Bar-Squared                .92479   S.E. of Regression             .019515
Residual Sum of Squares    .0083786   Mean of Dependent Variable     12.1936
S.D. of Dependent Variable .071161    Maximum of Log-likelihood      66.5384
DW-statistic                 .64831
**********************************************************************
```

Source: *Printout from software MICROFIT 3.0, Electronic Publishing, OUP, by H and B Pesaran.*

Set 1, you will observe that all the variables Q, X, P and G move consistently upwards over the sample period. There is also a definite trend in X/G. It is virtually certain that such variables will be unable to satisfy assumption IC of the classical regression model. As we shall see in later chapters, the consequences of this are serious. For example, we have already noted previously that values of R^2 are artificially inflated in such circumstances because of the problem of spurious correlation, so we should not be over-impressed by the values in excess of 0.9 obtained above.

The reader may also have noted that the Durbin–Watson statistics for Equations (7.66) and (7.67) were as low as 0.669 and 0.648 respectively. We shall be discussing the Durbin–Watson (*dw*) statistic in detail in Chapter 10. However, recall from Section 6.4 that values for this statistic much below 2, as in this case, generally indicate that an estimated equation has been mis-specified in some way. One possible mis-specification in Equations (7.66) and (7.67) is the omission of some other variable(s) that influence the current level of the demand for food. We shall be investigating this possibility in later chapters but, for now, we will merely regard it as another reason for viewing the above estimated equations with caution.

Data Sets 2 and 3 on the floppy disk contain data on the variables defined above for the UK and Japan. The reader should estimate Equations (7.64) and (7.65) using these data sets and comment on the results.

Exercise 7.7

A demand equation has the form $Y = A X_2^{\beta_2} X_3^{\beta_3} X_4^{\beta_4}$, where Y = quantity demanded, X_2 = money income, X_3 = own-price and X_4 = general price index. The equation is estimated in logarithms, from a sample size $n = 2$ and when the logs of variables are measured in deviation terms,

$$(\mathbf{x}'\mathbf{x})^{-1} = \begin{pmatrix} 0.4 & 0.1 & 0.2 \\ 0.1 & 0.8 & -0.7 \\ 0.2 & -0.7 & 1.05 \end{pmatrix}, \qquad \mathbf{x}'\mathbf{y} = \begin{pmatrix} 20 \\ -20 \\ -18 \end{pmatrix}, \qquad \sum y^2 = 106$$

(a) Find the OLS estimators of the demand elasticities together with their estimated standard errors.

(b) Does the demand equation appear to be homogeneous of degree zero in money income and prices?

Appendix 7A

The OLS estimators with two explanatory variables

With just two explanatory variables, Equations (7.6) and (7.7) imply that the residuals are given by

$$e_i = Y_i - \hat{Y}_i = Y_i - \hat{\beta}_1 - \hat{\beta}_2 X_{2i} - \hat{\beta}_3 X_{3i} \quad \text{for all } i \tag{7A.1}$$

The sum of the squared residuals is therefore

$$S = \sum e_i^2 = \sum (Y_i - \hat{\beta}_1 - \hat{\beta}_2 X_{2i} - \hat{\beta}_3 X_{3i})^2 \tag{7A.2}$$

To minimize (7A.2), we partially differentiate S with respect to $\hat{\beta}_1$, $\hat{\beta}_2$ and $\hat{\beta}_3$ in turn and set the resultant derivatives equal to zero. This yields

$$\frac{\partial S}{\partial \hat{\beta}_1} = -2 \sum (Y_i - \hat{\beta}_1 - \hat{\beta}_2 X_{2i} - \hat{\beta}_3 X_{3i}) = 0$$

$$\frac{\partial S}{\partial \hat{\beta}_2} = -2 \sum X_{2i}(Y_i - \hat{\beta}_1 - \hat{\beta}_2 X_{2i} - \hat{\beta}_3 X_{3i}) = 0$$

$$\frac{\partial S}{\partial \hat{\beta}_3} = -2 \sum X_{3i}(Y_i - \hat{\beta}_1 - \hat{\beta}_2 X_{2i} - \hat{\beta}_3 X_{3i}) = 0$$

Rearranging these equations then gives the normal equations for the OLS estimators as

$$\sum Y_i = n\hat{\beta}_1 + \hat{\beta}_2 \sum X_{2i} + \hat{\beta}_3 \sum X_{3i} \tag{7A.3}$$

$$\sum X_{2i} Y_i = \hat{\beta}_1 \sum X_{2i} + \hat{\beta}_2 \sum X_{2i}^2 + \hat{\beta}_3 \sum X_{2i} X_{3i} \tag{7A.4}$$

$$\sum X_{3i} Y_i = \hat{\beta}_1 \sum X_{3i} + \hat{\beta}_2 \sum X_{3i} X_{2i} + \hat{\beta}_3 \sum X_{3i}^2 \tag{7A.5}$$

The three equations (7A.3), (7A.4) and (7A.5) must now be solved to find the OLS estimators $\hat{\beta}_1$, $\hat{\beta}_2$ and $\hat{\beta}_3$. If we define the following vectors and matrices:

$$\mathbf{X} = \begin{pmatrix} 1 & X_{21} & X_{31} \\ 1 & X_{22} & X_{32} \\ 1 & X_{23} & X_{33} \\ \vdots & \vdots & \vdots \\ 1 & X_{2n} & X_{3n} \end{pmatrix}, \quad \mathbf{Y} = \begin{pmatrix} Y_1 \\ Y_2 \\ Y_3 \\ \vdots \\ Y_n \end{pmatrix}, \quad \hat{\boldsymbol{\beta}} = \begin{pmatrix} \hat{\beta}_1 \\ \hat{\beta}_2 \\ \hat{\beta}_3 \end{pmatrix}$$

then it is easy to see that

$$\mathbf{X}'\mathbf{X} = \begin{pmatrix} n & \sum X_{2i} & \sum X_{3i} \\ \sum X_{2i} & \sum X_{2i}^2 & \sum X_{2i}X_{3i} \\ \sum X_{3i} & \sum X_{3i}X_{2i} & \sum X_{3i}^2 \end{pmatrix}, \quad \mathbf{X}'\mathbf{Y} = \begin{pmatrix} \sum Y_i \\ \sum X_{2i}Y_i \\ \sum X_{3i}Y_i \end{pmatrix}$$

Straightforward matrix multiplication now indicates that the matrix equation

$$\mathbf{X}'\mathbf{Y} = \mathbf{X}'\mathbf{X}\hat{\boldsymbol{\beta}} \tag{7A.6}$$

replicates Equations (7A.3), (7A.4) and (7A.5). Premultiplication of (7A.6) by $(\mathbf{X}'\mathbf{X})^{-1}$ then yields Equation (7.15) in the main text.

★ # Appendix 7B
Consistency of the OLS estimators in multiple regression

We need only make use of assumptions IA–ID and IIA of the classical model to prove the consistency of the OLS estimators. We shall concentrate here on the OLS estimators of the slope parameters, β_j ($j = 2, 3, \ldots, k$).

First, note that if we sum (7.3) over all observations and divide by n we obtain

$$\bar{Y} = \beta_1 + \beta_2\bar{X}_2 + \beta_3\bar{X}_3 + \cdots + \beta_k\bar{X}_k + \bar{\epsilon} \tag{7B.1}$$

where $\bar{\epsilon} = \sum \epsilon_i/n$. Taking (7B.1) from the original (7.3) gives

$$y_i = \beta_2 x_{2i} + \beta_3 x_{3i} + \cdots + \beta_k x_{ki} + \epsilon_i - \bar{\epsilon} \tag{7B.2}$$

We can express (7B.2) in matrix form as

$$\mathbf{y} = \mathbf{x}\boldsymbol{\beta} + \boldsymbol{\epsilon} - \bar{\boldsymbol{\epsilon}} \tag{7B.3}$$

where $\mathbf{y}$, $\mathbf{x}$ and $\boldsymbol{\beta}$ are now as defined in (7.9a). $\bar{\boldsymbol{\epsilon}}$ is an $n \times 1$ vector in which all elements are equal to $\bar{\epsilon}$. Equation (7B.3) is in fact the 'deviation' version of (7.4).

Substituting (7B.3) into (7.15a) yields

$$\hat{\boldsymbol{\beta}} = (\mathbf{x}'\mathbf{x})^{-1}\mathbf{x}'(\mathbf{x}\boldsymbol{\beta} + \boldsymbol{\epsilon} - \bar{\boldsymbol{\epsilon}})$$

$$= \boldsymbol{\beta} + (\mathbf{x}'\mathbf{x})^{-1}\mathbf{x}'(\boldsymbol{\epsilon} - \bar{\boldsymbol{\epsilon}}) \tag{7B.4}$$

Taking probability limits over (7B.4), we have

$$\text{plim } (\hat{\boldsymbol{\beta}}) = \boldsymbol{\beta} + \text{plim } (\mathbf{x}'\mathbf{x})^{-1}\mathbf{x}'(\boldsymbol{\epsilon} - \bar{\boldsymbol{\epsilon}})$$

$$= \boldsymbol{\beta} + \text{plim } \{[(1/n)\mathbf{x}'\mathbf{x}]^{-1}\}[(1/n)\mathbf{x}'(\boldsymbol{\epsilon} - \bar{\boldsymbol{\epsilon}})]$$

$$= \boldsymbol{\beta} + \text{plim } \{[(1/n)\mathbf{x}'\mathbf{x}]^{-1}\} \text{ plim } [(1/n)\mathbf{x}'(\boldsymbol{\epsilon} - \bar{\boldsymbol{\epsilon}})] \tag{7B.5}$$

To find plim $\{[(1/n)\mathbf{x}'\mathbf{x}]^{-1}\}$ in (7B.5), we first use the fact, pointed out earlier, that, for any matrix $\mathbf{A}$, plim $(\mathbf{A}^{-1}) = [\text{plim } (\mathbf{A})]^{-1}$. Thus

$$\text{plim } \{[(1/n)\mathbf{x}'\mathbf{x}]^{-1}\} = \{\text{plim } [(1/n)\mathbf{x}'\mathbf{x}]\}^{-1} \tag{7B.6}$$

Since the X variables are non-stochastic, to find plim $[(1/n)\mathbf{x}'\mathbf{x}]$, we have to take the limit (if it exists) of the matrix $(1/n)\mathbf{x}'\mathbf{x}$ as $n \to \infty$. But, by assumptions IC and ID, we know that this limit exists and equals the non-singular matrix of fixed constants $\mathbf{Q}$. Hence we can rewrite (7B.6) as

$$\text{plim } \{[(1/n)\mathbf{x}'\mathbf{x}]^{-1}\} = \mathbf{Q}^{-1} \tag{7B.7}$$

To find plim $[(1/n)\mathbf{x}'(\boldsymbol{\epsilon} - \bar{\boldsymbol{\epsilon}})]$ in (7B.5), note first that $(1/n)\mathbf{x}'(\boldsymbol{\epsilon} - \bar{\boldsymbol{\epsilon}})$ is simply the $(k-1) \times 1$ vector of sample covariances between the X variables and the disturbance. For example, the first element in this vector is

$$(1/n) \sum x_{2i}(\epsilon_i - \bar{\epsilon}) = (1/n) \sum (X_{2i} - \bar{X}_2)(\epsilon_i - \bar{\epsilon})$$

Hence the probability limit of the vector must be the vector of population covariances between X variables and disturbance. But, since the X variables are all non-stochastic with fixed values over repeated samples, all such population covariances must be zero. Hence

$$\text{plim } [(1/n)\mathbf{x}'(\boldsymbol{\epsilon} - \bar{\boldsymbol{\epsilon}})] = \mathbf{0} \tag{7B.8}$$

where $\mathbf{0}$ is the null vector.

Substituting (7B.7) and (7B.8) into (7B.5) now gives

$$\text{plim } (\hat{\boldsymbol{\beta}}) = \boldsymbol{\beta} + \mathbf{Q}^{-1}\mathbf{0} = \boldsymbol{\beta}$$

Hence each $\hat{\beta}_j$ $(j = 2, 3, \ldots, k)$ is a consistent estimator of the corresponding β_j. It can also be shown that $\hat{\beta}_1$ is a consistent estimator of the intercept parameter β_1.

★ # Appendix 7C
Maximum likelihood and multiple regression

Derivation of MLEs in multiple regression parallels the two-variable derivation of Appendix 6B. Given Equation (7.3), it follows that, under classical assumptions, each

Y_i is normally distributed, with mean and variance

$$E(Y_i) = \beta_1 + \beta_2 X_{2i} + \beta_3 X_{3i} + \cdots + \beta_k X_{ki} \tag{7C.1}$$

$$\text{Var}(Y_i) = \text{Var}(\epsilon_i) = \sigma^2 \tag{7C.2}$$

Each Y_i therefore has a probability density function as given by (6B.3), except that $E(Y_i)$ is now given by (7C.1) rather than (6B.1).

The log-likelihood function for the Y_i is therefore again given by (6B.6), which is reproduced here:

$$l = \sum \ln [f(Y_i)] = \frac{n}{2} \ln (2\pi) - \frac{n}{2} \ln (\sigma^2) - \frac{1}{2\sigma^2} \sum [Y_i - E(Y_i)]^2 \tag{7C.3}$$

with $E(Y_i)$ is again given by (7C.1).

To maximize the log-likelihood l, we must choose the β_j in (7C.1) so as to minimize the sum of squares $\sum [Y_i - E(Y_i)]^2$ in (7C.3). This means choosing the β_j so as to minimize the sum of squared residuals that result. Thus, as in two-variable regression, the MLEs of the β_j are identical to the OLS estimators. That is, $\tilde{\beta}_j = \hat{\beta}_j$ for all j.

As in the two-variable case, the ML method also yields an estimator of σ^2, the disturbance variance. Differentiation of (7C.3) with respect to σ^2 proceeds as in Appendix 6B, and we again eventually obtain the MLE as

$$\tilde{\sigma}^2 = \frac{\sum e_i^2}{n} \tag{7C.4}$$

Nonlinear estimation

Suppose we face a population relationship of the form

$$Y_i = f(X_{2i}, X_{3i}, \ldots, X_{ki}) + \epsilon_i \tag{7C.5}$$

where, although the ϵ_i obey all the classical assumptions, f is now a *nonlinear* function of the X_{ji}. For example, in two-variable regression we might have $Y_i = \beta_1 X_{2i}^{\beta_2} + \epsilon_i$. We now have, instead of (7C.1),

$$E(Y_i) = f(X_{2i}, X_{3i}, \ldots, X_{ki}) \tag{7C.6}$$

although $\text{Var}(Y_i)$ is still given by (7C.2).

ML estimation of the parameters of (7C.5) proceeds in exactly the same way as above except that $E(Y_i)$ in the likelihood function (7C.3) is now given by (7C.6). Thus the parameters in f have to be chosen so as to minimize $\sum [Y_i - E(Y_i)]^2$. In other words, as in the linear case, we must choose estimates of the parameters that *minimize the sum of squared residuals*. Thus again the ML and OLS estimators are identical. The estimators obtained are referred to as **nonlinear least squares estimators**. Deriving the small-sample properties of these least squares estimators is not a simple task. However, because they are also MLEs they can be relied on to have the large-sample properties of consistency and asymptotic unbiasedness.

Appendix 7D

Notes to Chapter 7

1. In general, if the symbol Y appears without a subscript then it is being used as a shorthand symbol for the name of the variable it represents (e.g. 'consumption' or 'income'). Similarly, if X_3, for example, appears without a second subscript then it is being used as shorthand for the name of some variable.
2. Recall Equation (7.1a). The ones could be regarded as the constant values of a variable X_1.
3. Regression coefficients will remain unchanged only if the variable being added to the equation is completely uncorrelated with the explanatory variables already present. This will very rarely be the case.
4. Note that we include total expenditure rather than income in our demand function. This is because in the economic theory of the consumer it is total expenditure that appears on the right-hand side of the consumer's budget constraint. This will not coincide with income unless saving is zero.
5. Notice that although the parameter β_4 does not appear explicitly in Equation (7.65), we still obtain an OLS estimate of it, given by the coefficient of $\ln(G)$ in Equation (7.68). This estimate $\hat{\beta}_4 = -0.131$ can also be obtained from the original estimated equation (7.67) by using $\hat{\beta}_4 = -\hat{\beta}_2 - \hat{\beta}_3 = -0.311 + 0.180 = -0.131$.

Further reading

Multiple regression is thoroughly and well covered in Judge et al. (1988). The ML approach is outlined in detail in Chapter 6 of this text. See also Greene (1993), Chapters 6 and 10, for a more advanced treatment of the classical model. Readers who feel uneasy about matrix algebra will find that Kmenta (1986), Chapter 10, reduces it to a minimum in his discussion of multiple regression.

8 Stochastic explanatory variables

We saw at the end of Chapter 6 that, even when the explanatory variable in a two-variable regression model is stochastic, the least squares estimators retain their desirable properties, provided that the explanatory variable is independent of the disturbance. In addition, we are able to proceed with the OLS inferential procedures provided this condition is met. Analogous results hold for multiple regression. It can be shown that, provided all the regressors in an equation such as (7.6) are independent of the disturbance, the OLS estimators retain such properties as efficiency and consistency. Moreover, the normal OLS inferential procedures will remain valid. The problem is that, as we shall see, the assumption of independence between X variables and disturbance frequently breaks down with economic data sets. We therefore begin this chapter by considering the consequences of such a breakdown. We then examine reasons why the breakdown might often occur.

8.1 Non-independence of explanatory variables and disturbance

For ease of exposition, we shall concentrate mainly on the two-variable regression model of Chapter 6. When the X variable and the disturbance can no longer be assumed independent in such a model, much depends on the precise nature of the relationship between them. Suppose, for example, that the explanatory variable and the disturbance are positively correlated. In Figure 8.1(a) we show the population regression line (4.1). The positive correlation assumed implies that 'large' or 'high' sample values of X (high X_i) will tend to coincide with 'large' or 'high' sample values of the disturbance (high ϵ_i). Similarly, 'small' or 'low' X_i will tend to coincide with 'small' or 'low' ϵ_i. Recall that disturbance values represent vertical distances between points in a scatter diagram, such as those depicted in Figure 8.1(a), and the population regression line. Since $E(\epsilon_i) = 0$, high disturbances mean positive disturbances or points above the population regression line. Similarly, 'low' disturbances mean points in the scatter below the underlying population line. The consequences of the positive correlation we have assumed is therefore that when sample values of X are large, we tend to get points in the scatter above the population regression line, but when X values are small, we tend to get points below the line. The result is that we obtain scatters similar to that in Figure 8.1(a).

It is important to remember that an investigator observes not the population regression line but merely the scatter of points. The population regression line remains unknown and has to be *estimated using the scatter*. Use of the OLS estimation method to fit a sample regression line to the scatter in Figure 8.1(a) is clearly likely to result in a line that is too steep and has too small an intercept. Hence a positive correlation between explanatory variable and disturbance means that the OLS estimators $\hat{\alpha}$ and $\hat{\beta}$ will tend to underestimate the intercept parameter α and overestimate the slope parameter β. That is, $\hat{\alpha}$ and $\hat{\beta}$ will be biased estimators. Moreover, increasing the sample size will simply lead to more points in the scatter above the population line for large X and more points below the line for small X. The bias will therefore persist, however large the sample taken, and, because of this, the OLS estimators are not merely biased in small samples but remain so in large samples. They therefore also lose the large-sample property of consistency.

Similar problems to the above also occur when there is a negative correlation between X variable and disturbance. This situation is depicted in Figure 8.1(b). In this case, as can be seen, the OLS estimators tend to overestimate the intercept parameter α and underestimate the slope parameter β.

In the last section of Chapter 6, we considered how the standard proofs of the unbiasedness and consistency of the OLS estimators could be modified to allow for a situation where explanatory variable and disturbance were independent. Clearly, from

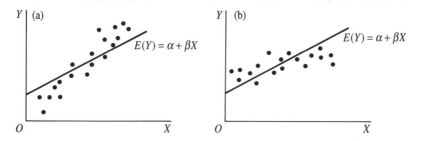

Figure 8.1 (a) Positive correlation between X and ϵ. (b) Negative correlation between X and ϵ.

the above, if X and ϵ are not independent but correlated then these proofs must break down completely in some way.

We consider first the proof that $\hat{\beta}$ is unbiased. Considering again Equation (6.8), taking expectations yielded Equation (6.52), which we reproduce here:

$$E(\hat{\beta}) = \beta + E(w_1\epsilon_1) + E(w_2\epsilon_2) + E(w_3\epsilon_3) + \cdots + E(w_n\epsilon_n) \tag{8.1}$$

Recall from (6.4) that each w_i is a function of all the X_i. Hence, when X and ϵ were independent, it was possible to separate out each of the $E(w_i\epsilon_i)$ terms and write

$$E(w_i\epsilon_i) = E(w_i)E(\epsilon_i) = E(w_i)(0) = 0 \tag{8.2}$$

It followed that $E(\hat{\beta}) = \beta$ so that $\hat{\beta}$ was unbiased.

If X and ϵ are correlated then $E(w_i\epsilon_i) \neq E(w_i)E(\epsilon_i)$, and (8.2) will no longer be true. Hence the unbiasedness proof breaks down, and $E(\hat{\beta}) \neq \beta$.

Next, consider the proof of the consistency of the OLS estimator $\hat{\beta}$. In Equation (6.13) the numerator still equals the population covariance between X and ϵ, but if these variables are correlated then this covariance can no longer be equal to zero. Hence it is no longer the case that plim $(\hat{\beta}) = \beta$, so the OLS estimator is now inconsistent.

Suppose the above correlation or lack of correlation refers to time series data. Since the assumed correlation between X and ϵ relates to a relationship between X and the 'same period' or contemporaneous value of ϵ, the situation we have just been referring to is generally known as the **contemporaneously correlated case**. The situation where X and ϵ are independent is, for obvious reasons, known as the **independence case**. We next consider a situation that arises frequently in econometrics, and which lies 'in between' the independence and contemporaneously correlated cases.

With time series data, each observation refers to a different time period. Hence, when we say X and ϵ are independent variables, we mean that any value of X must be independent not only of the contemporaneous disturbance value but also of all future and past disturbance values. This is necessary if the OLS estimators are to be unbiased. Consider the following equation, however:

$$Y_t = \alpha + \beta Y_{t-1} + \epsilon_t \tag{8.3}$$

In (8.3) we have replaced the previous i subscripts by t subscripts, since we are dealing with time series data. In this equation the right-hand-side 'X variable' is now simply the 'previous period' value of the dependent Y variable, and for this reason is referred to as a **lagged dependent variable**. As we shall see in later chapters, lagged dependent variables arise frequently in econometrics, although, of course, we rarely face equations as simple as (8.3).

If we lag (8.3) by one period, we obtain

$$Y_{t-1} = \alpha + \beta Y_{t-2} + \epsilon_{t-1} \tag{8.4}$$

It is clear from (8.4) that Y_{t-1} depends on ϵ_{t-1}. Thus, although it may be reasonable to assume that the right-hand-side variable in (8.3) is uncorrelated with the contemporaneous disturbance ϵ_t in that equation, it will not be uncorrelated with all past values of that disturbance. This has consequences for the properties of the OLS estimators.

Consider first the question of unbiasedness. Using t subscripts again, Equation (6.4) becomes

$$w_t = \frac{y_{t-1}}{\sum y_{t-1}^2}, \qquad \text{where} \quad y_{t-1} = Y_{t-1} - \bar{Y}_{t-1}$$

But

$$\bar{Y}_{t-1} = \frac{1}{n}(Y_0 + Y_1 + Y_2 + \cdots + Y_t + \cdots + Y_{n-1})$$

Thus y_{t-1} and hence w_t depend on Y_t, which, unlike Y_{t-1}, is not independent of ϵ_t. Hence, *even if Y_{t-1} and ϵ_t in (8.3) are uncorrelated,* we annot in this case separate out the $E(w_t\epsilon_t)$ terms in (8.1) as we did in (8.2). Thu $E(\hat{\beta}) \neq \beta$, and the OLS estimator of β in (8.3) is biased.

When we come to consider large samples, however, we find that the property of consistency still holds for equations such as (8.3). Since Y_{t-1} and ϵ_t have been assumed to be contemporaneously uncorrelated, the numerator in Equation (6.13) (which in the present case is plim $(\sum y_{t-1}\epsilon_t/n))$ remains zero, so that we still obtain plim $(\hat{\beta}) = \beta$. Thus in this case, although the OLS estimator of the slope parameter β is biased, the bias disappears in large samples, since the property of consistency is retained. Similar conclusions apply to the OLS estimator of the intercept parameter α.

Since in Equation (8.3), even if the right-hand-side variable may be assumed uncorrelated with the contemporaneous value of the disturbance, it will still not be independent of past values of the disturbance; this case is normally referred to as the **contemporaneously uncorrelated case**.

Summarizing the material of this section so far, when the explanatory X variable in two-variable regression is stochastic, we need to distinguish three cases:

(1) the independence case when the OLS estimators remain unbiased and consistent;

(2) the contemporaneously uncorrelated case when the OLS estimators are biased but consistent;

(3) the contemporaneously correlated case when the OLS estimators are both biased and inconsistent.

So far in this section we have considered only the consequence of a breakdown in assumption IB'. We have implicitly assumed that assumption IC' is valid. Recall that assumption IC' effectively rules out explanatory variables that exhibit continual upward trends. However, if we were attempting to estimate Equation (8.3), and the parameter β were equal to or greater than unity, then it should be clear that the variable Y *would* be trending upwards over time, given a positive initial value and a non-negative α.[1] Under such circumstances, assumption IC' cannot hold, and this has consequences for the large-sample properties of the OLS estimators. Although such large-sample theory is beyond the scope of this text, it turns out that even when X and

ϵ are independent, the standard proof of consistency breaks down when assumption IC' does not hold. This is a danger whenever lagged dependent variables appear on the right-hand side of regression equations. A breakdown in assumption IC' does not necessarily mean that the OLS estimators will be inconsistent, but what it does mean is that we can no longer automatically assume that the consistency property holds. Each case has to be examined using a large-sample theory, which is, as we have said, outside our scope. For example, in the case of Equation (8.3) it turns out that if $\beta > 1$ then the OLS estimators remain consistent. However, for the special case $\beta = 1$ they are biased downwards, even for large samples.

Since, as we have already pointed out, many econometric equations contain lagged dependent variables, we frequently find ourselves facing, at best, case (2) of the three cases listed above. In these circumstances the OLS estimators are biased, so we have to rely on large-sample properties that are guaranteed to hold only provided assumption IC' is valid. Hence if assumption IC' breaks down, and we can no longer take large-sample properties for granted, we may find ourselves in a position of being unable to make any reliable inferences at all about underlying parameters without engaging in highly complicated large-sample theory. Restricting analysis to data sets that satisfy IC' makes life considerably simpler! For the remainder of this chapter and the following two chapters, we shall do just that.

As we noted previously, if the explanatory variable is stochastic then it is rather unlikely that we will be able to assume that it is independent of the disturbance. We are likely to be faced with either case (2) or case (3) of the above. When this is so, we have to reformulate the classical assumptions concerning the disturbances along the lines indicated in Section 6.5. Since the X_i can no longer be treated as fixed constants, we have to consider conditional distributions for the disturbances – conditional on, for example, the X variable taking the set of X values we are faced with in our sample. Hence we must reformulate assumptions IIA–IID of the two-variable classical model as

> (IIA') $E(\epsilon_i \mid X_1, X_2, X_3, \dots, X_n) = 0$ for all i;
> (IIB') $\text{Var}(\epsilon_i \mid X_1, X_2, X_3, \dots X_n) = \sigma^2 = \text{const}$ for all i;
> (IIC') $\text{Cov}(\epsilon_i, \epsilon_j \mid X_1, X_2, X_3, \dots, X_n) = 0$ for all $i \neq j$;
> (IID') for given $X_1, X_2, X_3, \dots, X_n$, each ϵ_i is normally distributed.

It is only when two variables are independent that conditional and marginal distributions become identical. Hence only when X and ϵ are independent do assumptions IIA'–IID' reduce to the classical assumptions IIA–IID.

What these reformulated assumptions imply is that, for any given set of X values (including obviously the set in our sample), the expected value of each disturbance is zero, the variances of all disturbances are equal, the covariance between any two disturbances is zero and each disturbance is normally distributed.[2]

In multiple regression similar problems to the above arise once we relax the assumption of non-stochastic regressors. If the OLS estimators are to retain both the properties of unbiasedness and consistency, it is necessary that *each* stochastic explanatory variable should be independent of the disturbance. The appearance of just one lagged dependent variable among the regressors, as for example in the equation

$$Y_t = \beta_1 + \beta_2 X_{2t} + \beta_3 X_{3t} + \beta_4 Y_{t-1} + \epsilon_t \tag{8.5}$$

implies contemporaneous non-correlation but not independence between regressors and disturbance. As in the two-variable case, the OLS estimators then retain the property of consistency, but become biased in large samples. Also, if one or more of the stochastic regressors are *contemporaneously correlated* with the disturbance, the OLS estimators become *inconsistent as well as biased*. Finally, again as in two-variable regression, the appearance of definite trends over time in any regressors (e.g. $\beta_4 > 1$ in Equation (8.5) would imply a trending Y_{t-1}) means that standard regression techniques become inapplicable.

We now turn to the question of why case (3) above, namely a contemporaneous correlation between explanatory variable and disturbance in a regression equation, should occur so frequently in practice.

8.2   Errors of measurement

Economic data series are notoriously unreliable, and frequently measure concepts that differ somewhat from those of economic theory. It is therefore important that we take account of such errors of measurement. Unfortunately, it turns out that the existence of measurement errors is one of the major reasons why contemporaneous correlations between disturbance and explanatory variables should occur.

We again concentrate mainly on the two-variable case. Consider again the population relationship (6.1), which we reproduce here:

$$Y_i = \alpha + \beta X_i + \epsilon_i \quad \text{for all } i \tag{8.6}$$

Let us suppose that this relationship holds for the 'true' values of X and Y. As usual, ϵ is a disturbance obeying all the classical assumptions. It therefore has a constant variance σ^2. Suppose that, instead of measuring the true values of X and Y, we observe, for each i, X^* and Y^*, where

$$X_i^* = X_i + v_i, \quad Y_i^* = Y_i + w_i \tag{8.7}$$

The v_i and w_i represent the errors we are making in the measurement of X and Y.

We shall assume that the v_i and w_i are both normally distributed, with zero mean and constant variances σ_v^2 and σ_w^2 respectively. Since v_i has zero mean, this implies that[3]

$$E(X_i^*) = E(X_i) = X_i \quad \text{(since the } X_i \text{ are fixed)} \tag{8.8}$$

We also assume that the two errors are contemporaneously uncorrelated with each other and that both are contemporaneously uncorrelated with the disturbance ϵ.

That is,[4]

$$E(v_i w_i) = E(v_i \epsilon_i) = E(w_i \epsilon_i) = 0 \quad \text{for all } i \tag{8.9}$$

Finally, we assume that errors made in measuring X and Y in any period are uncorrelated with the corresponding errors made in any other period. That is,

$$E(v_i v_j) = E(w_i w_j) = 0 \quad \text{for all } i \neq j \tag{8.10}$$

The above assumptions are a reasonable approximation to what we are likely to face in reality.

Suppose that we are forced to estimate α and β in (8.6) using not the true values of X and Y but rather X^* and Y^*. Using (8.7), the regression equation (8.6) becomes

$$Y_i^* = \alpha + \beta X_i^* + (\epsilon_i + w_i - \beta v_i) \quad \text{for all } i \tag{8.11}$$

Lacking data on X and Y, we are forced to estimate (although we may not realize it) Equation (8.11), which includes the composite disturbances

$$\epsilon_i^* = \epsilon_i + w_i - \beta v_i \tag{8.12}$$

The problem with estimating (8.11) is that, since both X^* and the composite disturbance depend on v, they are contemporaneously correlated so that the application of OLS leads to bias. More precisely,

$$\begin{aligned}
\text{Cov } (X_i^*, \epsilon_i^*) &= E(X_i^* - EX_i^*)(\epsilon_i^* - E\epsilon_i^*) \\
&= E(X_i^* - X_i)\epsilon_i^* \quad \text{(using (8.8) and since } E(\epsilon_i^*) = 0) \\
&= E(v_i)(\epsilon_i + w_i - \beta v_i) \quad \text{(using (8.12))} \\
&= E(v_i \epsilon_i) + E(v_i w_i) - \beta E(v_i^2) \\
&= -\beta \sigma_v^2 \quad \text{(using (8.9))} \\
&\neq 0 \tag{8.13}
\end{aligned}$$

Thus X^* and the composite disturbance ϵ^* are negatively correlated if $\beta > 0$ and positively correlated if $\beta < 0$. OLS therefore yields biased estimates when applied to (8.11). Since we know from Figures 8.1(a,b) that the direction of biases depends on the nature of the correlation between explanatory variable and disturbance, the direction of the biases in this case depends on the sign of β.

Notice that it is the error in the measurement of the explanatory X variable that causes OLS bias. If X is perfectly observed then $v_i = 0$ in (8.7), the composite disturbance in (8.11) becomes $\epsilon_i + w_i$, and the correlation between it and $X^* = X$ becomes zero. Thus errors in measuring the dependent Y variable alone do not lead to OLS bias. They do have one unwelcome consequence, however. If $v_i = 0$, Equation (8.11) becomes

$$Y_i^* = \alpha + \beta X_i + (\epsilon_i + w_i) \tag{8.14}$$

Although OLS will yield unbiased estimates of α and β in (8.14), there will be a decline in efficiency as a result of the error in measuring Y. Since ϵ and w have been assumed to be uncorrelated, the composite disturbance in (8.14) will have a variance

$$\text{Var}\,(\epsilon) + \text{Var}\,(w) = \sigma^2 + \sigma_w^2$$

This is greater than the variance σ^2 for the disturbance ϵ in the original equation (8.6). Since, from (6.14) and (6.15), the variances of the OLS estimators increase as the variance of the disturbance increases, failure to measure Y properly leads to a loss of precision in the OLS estimators.

Errors in the measurement of variables have equally serious consequences for OLS estimation in multiple regression. While errors in the measurement of the dependent Y variable result only in a lack of precision, it can easily be demonstrated that errors in the measurement of any of the explanatory variables lead to bias and inconsistency in the OLS estimators.

8.3 Simultaneous equation bias

Another reason why contemporaneous correlations arise between explanatory variables and disturbances is because of the simultaneity of many economic relationships. As an example, consider the following simple model of national income determination:

$$C = \alpha + \beta Y + u, \qquad \alpha > 0, \quad 0 < \beta < 1 \tag{8.15}$$

$$Y = C + Z \tag{8.16}$$

Equation (8.15) is a simple consumption function relating consumption expenditure C to national income Y. u is a disturbance satisfying the normal classical assumptions. Equation (8.16) is an identity stating that national income is the sum of consumption expenditure and non-consumption expenditure Z. We therefore have a two-equation model determining the values of two *endogenous* variables, C and Y. The other variable, Z is assumed *exogenous*, that is, it is determined outside the model.

This division between **endogenous variables** (values of which are determined by the system we are observing) and **exogenous variables** (values of which are predetermined in some way) is a common one in econometrics, and we shall look at it in more detail towards the end of this text. At the moment, however, we shall simply concern ourselves with the estimation of the parameters α and β in the consumption function (8.15). Since the explanatory variable Y in (8.15) is endogenous (i.e. determined inside our model), it is stochastic – its values clearly cannot be fixed by any hypothetical investigator. The question is whether its values are likely to be correlated with the values of the disturbance u in any way. To answer this question, we derive the **reduced form** of the model.

The reduced form of any system of equations is obtained by solving the system for the endogenous variables, expressing these variables solely in terms of the exogenous variables and any disturbances in the system. For (8.15) and (8.16), this is most easily done by first substituting for Y in (8.15):

$$C = \alpha + \beta(C + Z) + u$$

Hence

$$C = \frac{\alpha}{1 - \beta} + \left(\frac{\beta}{1 - \beta}\right)Z + \frac{u}{1 - \beta} \tag{8.17}$$

Then substituting for C in (8.16) using (8.17), and solving for Y, gives

$$Y = \frac{\alpha}{1 - \beta} + \left(\frac{1}{1 - \beta}\right)Z + \frac{u}{1 - \beta} \tag{8.18}$$

Equations (8.17) and (8.18) constitute the reduced form of the model, expressing the endogenous C and Y in terms of the exogenous Z and the disturbance u.

What we can deduce from Equation (8.18) of this reduced form is that the income variable Y, which appears on the right-hand side of the consumption function, depends on the disturbance u in that equation. In fact, since the marginal propensity to consume, β, lies between zero and unity, we can deduce that, given the value of Z, Y and u are positively correlated. This contemporaneous correlation means that OLS estimators of the consumption function parameters will be biased and inconsistent. In fact, we have a situation analogous to that depicted in Figure 8.1(a), with OLS tending to overestimate β and underestimate α.

Since the bias in the above model arises from the fact that the consumption function is but one of two relationships that hold simultaneously, it is normally referred to as **simultaneous equation bias**. This is a problem met frequently in economics. It is the rule rather than the exception for economic relationships to be imbedded in a simultaneous set of relationships. When this is the case, endogenous variables, such as Y in the above model, almost invariably appear on the right-hand side of certain equations as explanatory variables. The reduced form will always reveal which disturbances in the model influence any particular endogenous variable. Except in certain special cases, right-hand-side endogenous variables are always found to be correlated with the disturbance in the equation in which they appear. This leads to OLS bias in the estimation of the parameters in that equation.

To reinforce the above point, consider another two-equation simultaneous equation model, this time involving a simplified wage–price spiral:

$$W = \alpha + \beta P + \gamma E + u \tag{8.19}$$

$$P = \lambda + \mu W + v \tag{8.20}$$

W and P are the percentage rates of wage and price inflation respectively, E is a measure of excess demand in the labour market, while u and v are disturbances. If E is assumed to be exogenously determined then (8.19) and (8.20) represent two equations determining two endogenous variables, W and P.

Suppose we wish to estimate the price equation (8.20), using the two-variable regression model of Chapter 6. This equation has the endogenous W as its single explanatory variable. The question is: will W be correlated with v, the disturbance in the price equation? To answer this question, we again obtain the reduced form.

To obtain the reduced form in this case, we first substitute for P in Equation (8.19). After rearrangement, this gives

$$W = \frac{\alpha + \beta\lambda}{1 - \beta\mu} + \left(\frac{\gamma}{1 - \beta\mu}\right)E + \frac{u + \beta v}{1 - \beta\mu} \tag{8.21}$$

Substituting for W in Equation (8.20) then gives, again after rearrangement,

$$P = \frac{\lambda + \alpha\mu}{1 - \beta\mu} + \left(\frac{\mu\gamma}{1 - \beta\mu}\right)E + \frac{\mu u + v}{1 - \beta\mu} \tag{8.22}$$

Equations (8.21) and (8.22) express the endogenous W and P solely in terms of the exogenous E and the disturbances u and v. They therefore constitute the reduced form of the model.

We can now see from (8.21) that W, the explanatory variable in the price equation, is dependent on v, the disturbance in that equation. In fact, since we can expect β and μ both to lie between zero and unity, it can be seen that, for given values of E and u, W will be positively correlated with v. Hence we again have a situation analogous to that in Figure 8.1(a). The application of OLS to the price equation (8.20) will result in biased and inconsistent estimators, with a tendency for μ to be overestimated and λ to be underestimated. Again, the simultaneous nature of economic relationships and the resultant appearance of an endogenous variable as a right-hand-side regressor has resulted in OLS bias.

It should be fairly obvious that the problem of simultaneity is equally as serious for multiple regression as it is in the two-variable case. For example, suppose (8.20) were replaced by

$$P = \lambda + \mu W + \kappa M + v \tag{8.20a}$$

where M is the rate of raw material price inflation and, like E, is treated as exogenous. Since M is determined outside our model, we can assume it will be independent of v, the disturbance in (8.20a). However, in estimating (8.20a), we would again be concerned about possible contemporaneous correlation between the endogenous W variable and the disturbance v. To investigate this, we need to examine the reduced form of the model represented by Equations (8.19) and (8.20a). It is left to the reader to derive the reduced form and deduce that W and v are again contemporaneously correlated. Thus we again have a problem of simultaneous equation bias in the OLS estimators.

We now take the opportunity to look, relatively briefly, at another problem that arises when we consider simultaneous systems. This is the so-called **identification problem**, which really arises prior to the estimation problem.

Consider the wage–price model described by Equations (8.19) and (8.20). We can use (8.20) to express W in terms of P:

$$W = -\frac{\lambda}{\mu} + \frac{1}{\mu}P - \frac{v}{\mu} \tag{8.23}$$

Now suppose A and B are *any* two constants. Let us multiply Equation (8.19) by A, multiply Equation (8.23) by B and then add the two equations. This gives

$$(A + B)W = A\alpha - B\frac{\lambda}{\mu} + \left(A\beta + \frac{B}{\mu}\right)P + A\gamma E + Au - \frac{B}{\mu}v$$

or

$$W = \frac{A\alpha - B\lambda/\mu}{A + B} + \left(\frac{A\beta + B/\mu}{A + B}\right)P + \left(\frac{A\gamma}{A + B}\right)E + \frac{Au - (B/\mu)v}{A + B} \tag{8.24}$$

Equation (8.24) is what is known as a **linear combination** of (8.19) and (8.23). The point about (8.24) is that it is of the same statistical form as the wage equation (8.19). That is, it has the form

$$W = \text{constant} + (\text{constant})P + (\text{constant})E + \text{disturbance}$$

Moreover, since A and B can take any values we like, this implies that our wage–price model generates an infinite number of equations such as (8.24), *which are all statistically indistinguishable from the wage equation (8.19)*. Hence, if we apply OLS or any other technique to data on W, P and E in an attempt to estimate the wage equation, we cannot know whether we are actually estimating (8.19) rather than one of the infinite number of possibilities given by (8.24). Equation (8.19) is said to be **unidentified**, and consequently there is now *no way* in which unbiased or even consistent estimators of its parameters may be obtained.

Notice that, in contrast, the price equation (8.20) cannot be confused with the linear combination (8.24), because it is a relationship involving W and P only and does not, like (8.24), contain the variable E. The price equation (8.20) is therefore said to be **identified**, and in principle it *is* possible to obtain consistent estimators of its parameters. However, as we observed above, the OLS method of estimation could not be used because of the *separate* problem of simultaneous equation bias. We shall discuss one method that might be used to estimate (8.20) in the next section.

The identification problem that arises with the wage equation (8.19) would not occur if an extra variable, *which did not appear in the wage equation*, appeared in the price equation. Suppose, for example, that the price equation was that given by (8.20a). This equation may be rewritten as

$$W = -\frac{\lambda}{\mu} - \frac{\kappa}{\mu}M + \frac{1}{\mu}P - \frac{1}{\mu}v \tag{8.25}$$

If we now took a linear combination of (8.19) and (8.25), we would obtain an equation, akin to (8.24), but which would contain both the variables E and M. In such circumstances, neither the price equation (8.20a) (which does not contain E) nor the wage equation (8.19) (which does not contain M) could be confused with the linear combination. Thus *both* equations would now be identified. However, as we have seen, OLS would still not provide unbiased or consistent estimators of the parameters of the wage equation, because of the problem of simultaneous equation bias. Other methods have to be used.

To emphasize the distinction between the problems of identification and simultaneous equation bias, consider another simple two-equation model:

$$Q = \alpha + \beta P + \gamma S + u \tag{8.26}$$

$$Q = \lambda + \mu P + \kappa C + v \tag{8.27}$$

Q is the quantity demanded and supplied of a good (it is assumed that the market always clears). P is the price of the good, S the price of a close substitute and C an index of production costs. u and v, as usual, are disturbances. The demand equation (8.26) and the supply equation (8.27) between them therefore determine the values of the endogenous variables Q and P for given values of the exogenous S and C and the disturbances.

We face no identification problems when estimating either (8.26) or (8.27). To see this, let us take a linear combination of the equations, multiplying (8.26) by A and (8.27) by B:

$$Q = \frac{A\alpha + B\lambda}{A + B} + \left(\frac{A\beta + B\mu}{A + B}\right)P + \left(\frac{A\gamma}{A + B}\right)S + \left(\frac{B\kappa}{A + B}\right)C + \frac{Au + Bv}{A + B} \tag{8.28}$$

It is clear that neither the demand equation (8.26), which does not contain C, nor the supply equation (8.27), which does not contain S, can be confused with the linear combination (8.28). Thus both equations in the model are identified, and in principle it should be possible to obtain consistent estimators of their parameters.

We do, however, face a problem of OLS bias. The endogenous variable P appears on the right-hand side of both equations in the model. If the reduced-form equation for P is obtained, it will be seen that this variable is contemporaneously correlated with the disturbances in both Equations (8.26) and (8.27).[5] Thus the application of *OLS* to either equation will lead to bias and inconsistency. Although consistent estimation is possible, some method other than OLS is again required.

Suppose now that, during the time data is collected on the above market, it happens to be the case that the variables S and C remain constant although P and Q still vary. It is now possible to write Equations (8.26) and (8.27) as

$$Q = \alpha^* + \beta P + u, \qquad \alpha^* = \alpha + \gamma \bar{S} \tag{8.29}$$

and

$$Q = \lambda^* + \mu P + v, \qquad \lambda^* = \lambda + \kappa \bar{C} \tag{8.30}$$

where $\bar{S}$ and $\bar{C}$ are the constant values of S and C.

It should be clear that now we would have an identification problem, because any linear combination of (8.29) and (8.30) will contain P and Q only. We would therefore be unable statistically to distinguish either the demand equation (8.29) or the supply equation (8.30) from the linear combination (or indeed from each other). Thus in this situation, regressing Q on P by OLS *or any other method* will always yield biased and inconsistent estimators of the model's parameters.

This situation is illustrated in Figure 8.2, where, for each i, D_i and S_i are the demand and supply curves for 'period i'. In terms of this diagram, variations in the

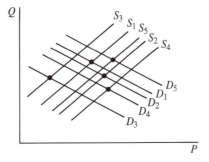

Figure 8.2 Shifting demand and supply curves.

disturbances u and v over time result in shifts in the demand and supply curves representing (8.29) and (8.30). All that the econometrician can ever observe is the intersection points of these shifting curves (one point for each data 'period'). These form a scatter. Unfortunately, any attempt to fit a line to this scatter, whether by OLS or any other means, will result in the estimation of a relationship bearing no resemblance to either demand or supply curves.[6] Figure 8.2 is the diagrammatic representation of the identification problem.

Identification problems do not just arise in two-equation models. However, in econometric models with three or more equations it is a complicated matter to investigate identification questions by examining linear combinations as above. Luckily, various general rules have been deduced for such situations. The most well-known is the so-called **order condition for identification**. We state this condition without proof.

> *A necessary condition for an equation to be identified is that the total number of restrictions placed on its parameters should be at least as great as the number of equations in the model less one.*

The restrictions referred to in the rule may be of a very simple kind, merely implying that some variable in the model does not appear in the equation of interest. For example, consider the wage–price model given by Equations (8.19) and (8.20). The variable E does not appear in the price equation (8.20). Thus it can be said that a restriction is imposed on the parameters of this equation, the restriction being that the coefficient on the variable E in Equation (8.20) is equal to zero. Similarly, in the demand–supply model given by Equations (8.26) and (8.27) restrictions are imposed on both equations. The variable C is absent from Equation (8.26) (i.e. its coefficient has been set to zero), while the variable S is absent from Equation (8.27).

Occasionally, the restrictions relevant to the above order condition may be more complex than the simple omission of a variable from an equation. For example, in the computer exercise at the end of the last chapter, we imposed the restriction that our demand equation should be homogeneous of degree zero. In the double-log formulation adopted, this implied that the coefficients (elasticities) in the demand equation should sum to zero. Restrictions of this type on equation parameters are as important in determining whether an equation is identified as is the simple omission of variables.

It should be noted that, while the order condition is a necessary condition for identification, it is not a sufficient condition. That is, if the condition *does not hold* then an equation *cannot* be identified, but the mere fact that it *does hold* is insufficient always to *ensure* identification. In certain rather special circumstances it is possible for the equation of interest to be unidentified even when the order condition is satisfied. A sufficient condition for identification does in fact exist – the so-called **rank condition**. However, the mathematics necessary to outline this condition is beyond the scope of this text.

Exercise 8.1

Use the order equation for identification to determine whether the following equations are identified:
(a) the consumption function in the model (8.15)–(8.16);
(b) the equations in the wage–price model (8.19)–(8.20);
(c) the equations in the demand–supply model (8.26)–(8.27).

Exercise 8.2

Use the order condition for identification to determine which equations in the following model are identified:

$$Y_1 = a_0 + a_1 Y_2 + a_2 X_2 + u$$
$$Y_2 = b_0 + b_1 Y_1 + b_2 Y_3 + b_3 X_2 + b_4 X_3 + v$$
$$Y_3 = c_0 + c_1 Y_2 + c_2 X_4 + w$$

We shall not discuss the identification problem in any greater detail here. However, two points are worth noting.

First, some econometricians would argue that so-called structural equations, such as the consumption function, the wage and price equations, and the demand and supply equations in the above models, are almost always unidentified. For example, as long ago as 1960, Liu argued that, realistically, economic relationships involve far more variables than are normally included in econometric equations, and that the omission of variables from equations is an essentially spurious way of achieving identification. If this is the case then the only equations worth estimating are reduced-form equations such as those above.

Secondly, although there are various rules that can be applied to determine whether or not an equation is identified, these depend on it being possible to distinguish clearly between endogenous and exogenous variables. However, it can be argued that this is never possible. For example, in the above wage–price model we assumed that the excess demand for labour could be treated as an exogenous variable.

However, in a full model of the economy the excess demand for labour would be equally as endogenous as the rates of wage and price change.

The difficulty of defining truly exogenous variables has led one group of econometricians (see e.g. Sims, 1980) to argue that all variables in a model should be treated as endogenous. This has led to the so-called **vector autoregression** approach, which we discuss briefly in Chapter 16.

8.4   Instrumental variable estimation

One of the best methods of overcoming problems of contemporaneous correlation, whether these result from measurement error or simultaneity, is that of instrumental variables. An intuitive idea of this method can be obtained if we again consider two-variable regression and the least squares normal equations (4.14) and (4.15), reproduced here:

$$\sum Y_i = n\alpha + \beta \sum X_i \tag{8.31}$$

$$\sum X_i Y_i = \alpha \sum X_i + \beta \sum X_i^2 \tag{8.32}$$

Equation (8.31) can be thought of as being derived by summing the population relationship (8.6) throughout and ignoring the last term $\sum \epsilon_i$. Similarly, we can derive (8.32) by multiplying (8.6) throughout by X_i, summing, and ignoring the last term $\sum X_i \epsilon_i$. If the X_i and ϵ_i are uncorrelated in (8.6) then $\mathrm{E} x_i \epsilon_i = 0$. Since $\mathrm{E}\epsilon_i = 0$ also, we can therefore justify the above derivation of (8.31) and (8.32), since, provided our sample is sufficiently large, $\sum \epsilon_i$ and $\sum X_i \epsilon_i$ will indeed be close to zero.[7] This is an intuitive way of seeing that solving (8.31) and (8.32) for α and β yields estimators possessing the large-sample property of consistency. However, when the X_i and ϵ_i are correlated, $\sum X_i \epsilon_i \neq 0$ even in large samples, the procedure cannot be justified, and the OLS estimators are no longer consistent.

Suppose we are faced with a correlation between the X_i and ϵ_i, but are able to find another variable Z whose values are uncorrelated with the ϵ_i. Such a variable is known in this context as an **instrument**. In obtaining the second of the normal equations, suppose we multiply (8.6) through, not by X_i as above but by Z_i. Since the Z_i and ϵ_i are uncorrelated, we are justified in ignoring the $\sum Z_i \epsilon_i$ term, provided the sample is large, so that the normal equations now become

$$\sum Y_i = n\alpha + \beta \sum X_i \tag{8.31}$$

$$\sum Z_i Y_i = \alpha \sum Z_i + \beta \sum Z_i X_i \tag{8.33}$$

Solving (8.31) and (8.33) for α and β yields estimators that are consistent, unlike the OLS estimators obtained by solving (8.31) and (8.32). The solution to (8.31) and (8.33) is, in fact,

$$\alpha^* = \bar{Y} - \beta^* \bar{X} \tag{8.34}$$

$$\beta^* = \frac{\sum z_i y_i}{\sum z_i x_i} \tag{8.35}$$

where $z_i = Z_i - \bar{Z}$ and $\bar{Z} = \sum Z_i/n$. Equations (8.34) and (8.35) are called the **instrumental variable (IV) estimators** of α and β. We have 'superscripted' them with asterisks to distinguish them from the OLS estimators (4.16) and (4.18). A rigorous demonstration of the consistency of $\beta*$ is provided in Appendix 8A.

We stress that, when we use the IV method of estimation, we are *not* simply replacing X by the instrument Z and then regressing Y on Z instead of X. However, it can be shown that IV estimation is equivalent to the following two-stage procedure.

In the first stage of this procedure we use OLS to regress X on the instrument Z, and obtain

$$\hat{X}_i = \hat{\gamma} + \hat{\delta} Z_i \quad \text{for all } i \tag{8.36}$$

where $\hat{\gamma}$ and $\hat{\delta}$ are estimated coefficients. The predicted values $\hat{X}_i$ from this regression are retained for use in the second stage.

In the second stage of the procedure we use OLS to regress Y on the $\hat{X}_i$ obtained in the first stage. This yields

$$\hat{Y}_i = \alpha* + \beta*\hat{X}_i \quad \text{for all } i \tag{8.37}$$

It can be shown that the $\alpha*$ and $\beta*$ obtained in the regression (8.37) are identical to those given by (8.34) and (8.35). In this context, the predicted value variable $\hat{X}$ is known as an **instrumental variable**. Thus IV estimation is equivalent to, not regressing the dependent Y variable on the instrument Z, but rather regressing Y on the instrumental variable $\hat{X}$.

The method of instrumental variables can also be used in multiple regression. It is then necessary to find instruments for every explanatory variable that is contemporaneously correlated with the disturbance. Each such instrument must be uncorrelated with the disturbance but correlated (preferably highly) with the corresponding explanatory variable. If any explanatory variables are already uncorrelated with the disturbance then they may serve as their own instruments.

8.5   A 'controlled experiment'

The reader should now have grasped that, theoretically at least, IV estimators are superior to OLS estimators, provided the sample is large. But does this superiority hold in practice? To examine this, we shall carry out a 'Monte Carlo' experiment similar to that of Section 5.3. As explained in Chapter 5, such experiments are usually the closest we can get in econometrics to the repeated controlled experiment of the physical scientist. We have talked at some length previously about the behaviour of regression estimators and their distributions when 'repeated samples' are taken. We shall now make use of a computer actually to generate such repeated samples.

Suppose we have a very simple economy in which the determination of income and consumption can be described by Equations (8.15) and (8.16). Let us also suppose that, when income and consumption are measured in billions of constant-price dollars, the values of the population parameters α and β in (8.15) are

$$\alpha = 7.0, \qquad \beta = 0.8 \tag{8.38}$$

The parameters α and β are, of course, unknown to any investigator. The aim of our Monte Carlo experiment is to generate 'samples' from which an econometric investigator might estimate α and β.

Given the above values of α and β, the reduced-form equations (8.17) and (8.18) become

$$C = 35 + 4Z + v \tag{8.39}$$

$$Y = 35 + 5Z + v \tag{8.40}$$

where v is a disturbance equal to $5u$ (i.e. five times the disturbance in the consumption function (8.15)).

Since Z is an exogenous variable, determined outside our model, we shall take its values as given and fixed (they might, for example, be determined by government policy and overseas spending on exports). We shall assume that the disturbance v obeys all the classical assumptions – that is, its values are normally and indepen-

Table 8.1   One possible realization for economy

Year	Z	Y	C	v
1	3.68	46.53	42.85	−1.37
2	3.87	56.20	52.33	0.37
3	4.11	47.83	43.72	−1.54
4	4.30	51.68	47.38	−0.96
5	4.66	52.16	47.50	−1.23
6	4.93	63.72	58.79	0.81
7	5.05	66.50	61.45	1.25
8	5.24	68.19	62.95	1.40
9	5.39	49.24	43.85	−2.54
10	5.65	63.51	57.86	0.05
11	6.19	56.01	49.82	−1.99
12	6.58	71.82	65.24	0.78
13	7.13	63.65	56.52	−1.40
14	7.35	66.08	58.73	−1.13
15	7.84	72.13	64.29	−0.41
16	8.07	76.42	68.35	0.21
17	8.33	67.81	59.48	−1.77
18	8.66	75.02	66.36	−0.66
19	8.72	83.41	74.69	0.96
20	8.95	87.21	78.26	1.49

dently distributed, with zero mean and constant variance $\sigma^2 = 1.2$. The parameter σ^2, like α and β, is unknown to the investigator.

What Equations (8.39) and (8.40) do is determine, for given values of Z and the disturbance v, the levels of income and consumption in our very simple economy. Let us consider a 20-year period. Suppose during these 20 years, non-consumption expenditure Z (which, remember, is exogenous) takes the values given in the second column of Table 8.1. What will happen to income and consumption during the 20 years? This will depend on the behaviour of the random disturbance v. We can generate 20 annual values for v with the help of a random number generator on a computer. The values in the last column of Table 8.1 are in fact 20 random drawings (some positive, some negative) from the required N(0, 1.2) distribution for v. Given the values for Z and v, we can now use the reduced-form equations (8.39) and (8.40) to obtain values for Y and C during the 20-year period. These are shown in the third and fourth columns of Table 8.1.

What we have in the second, third and fourth columns of Table 8.1 is one possible set of 'outcomes' for our economy during the 20-year period. That is, we have one possible 'realization'. Other realizations are also possible, because the random disturbance v could have taken totally different values from those in Table 8.1. In fact, in Table 8.2 we show a second possible realization. Notice that in Table 8.2, while the exogenous Z values are identical to those in Table 8.1, the v values

Table 8.2 A second possible realization

Year	Z	Y	C	v
1	3.68	52.66	48.98	−0.15
2	3.87	52.54	48.67	−0.36
3	4.11	51.76	47.65	−0.76
4	4.30	44.82	40.52	−2.34
5	4.66	60.06	55.40	0.35
6	4.93	57.45	52.52	−0.44
7	5.05	67.01	61.96	1.35
8	5.24	60.80	55.56	−0.08
9	5.39	77.03	71.64	−3.02
10	5.65	65.57	59.92	0.46
11	6.19	76.99	70.80	2.21
12	6.58	67.80	61.22	−0.02
13	7.13	63.42	56.29	−1.45
14	7.35	69.18	61.82	−0.52
15	7.84	76.43	68.59	0.45
16	8.07	70.32	62.25	−1.01
17	8.33	74.92	66.59	−0.35
18	8.66	79.58	70.92	0.26
19	8.72	81.33	72.61	0.55
20	8.95	82.58	73.63	0.57

differ because we have obtained them by using a computer to obtain a further 20 random drawings from the $N(0, 1.2)$ distribution for v. The second, third and fourth columns in Table 8.2 represent a second possible realization for our simple economy.

Clearly, although the Z values are kept unchanged, we could generate as many possible realizations as we like for our economy simply by generating different sets of random values for v. Suppose, however, that the realization that actually occurs and is observed by an investigator is that given by Table 8.2. Note that all the investigator observes are the values for Z, Y and C. (S)he cannot observe the values of the random disturbance v, but, on the basis of the known Z, Y and C values, wishes to estimate the α and β parameters in the consumption function (8.15).

One possible method of estimating α and β is to use OLS. We know, from the discussion in Section 8.3, that this will yield biased and inconsistent estimators because of the contemporaneous correlation between Y and the disturbance u in the consumption function, but let us suppose the investigator tries OLS anyway. Using the C and Y values from Table 8.2 and the procedures of Section 4.2, the investigator will obtain the OLS sample regression equation

$$\hat{C} = 2.83 + 0.864Y, \qquad \sum e^2 = 17.31 \tag{8.41}$$

Notice that, as might be expected, OLS overestimates the slope parameter β. We know (although the investigator does not) that, from (8.38), true $\beta = 0.8$. OLS, also as expected, underestimates the intercept parameter (from (8.38), true $\alpha = 7$). This is consistent with our analysis in Section 8.3, which suggested that OLS will *tend* to overestimate β and *tend* to underestimate α.

Suppose, however, that the investigator, aware of the bias in the OLS estimators, decides instead to use an IV method of estimation. An obvious instrument to use is non-consumption expenditure Z. Since Z is regarded as exogenously determined, it can be assumed to be uncorrelated with the disturbance u in the consumption function (8.15). Moreover, since, from (8.16), it is one of the determinants of income, it is correlated with Y, the explanatory variable in the consumption function. Thus it is a suitable instrument.

The expressions for the IV estimators are given by (8.34) and (8.35). In this case the dependent variable is C and the explanatory variable Y, so they become

$$\beta^* = \frac{\sum z_i c_i}{\sum z_i y_i}, \qquad \alpha^* = \bar{C} - \beta^* \bar{Y} \tag{8.42}$$

Using the data in Table 8.2, the investigator will obtain

$$\bar{Z} = \frac{\sum Z_i}{n} = 6.235, \qquad \bar{C} = \frac{\sum C_i}{n} = 60.377, \qquad \bar{Y} = \frac{\sum Y_i}{n} = 66.613$$

$$\sum z_i c_i = \sum (Z_i - \bar{Z})(C_i - \bar{C}) = \sum Z_i C_i - \frac{1}{n}\left(\sum Z_i\right)\left(\sum C_i\right)$$

$$= 253.4$$

$$\sum z_i y_i = \sum (Z_i - \bar{Z})(Y_i - \bar{Y}) = \sum Z_i Y_i - \frac{1}{n}\left(\sum Z_i\right)\left(\sum Y_i\right)$$

$$= 313.3$$

Substituting in (8.42), the IV estimators are therefore

$$\beta^* = \frac{253.4}{313.3} = 0.809, \qquad \alpha^* = 60.377 - 0.809(66.613) = 6.49$$

so that the investigator will obtain the IV sample regression line

$$\hat{C} = 6.49 + 0.809Y, \qquad \sum e^2 = 24.34 \tag{8.43}$$

Notice that the IV estimators are much closer to the true values of α and β than the OLS estimates in Equation (8.41). The estimate of β is in fact very close to the true value. This is despite the fact that the residual sum of squares is considerably greater for the IV estimation than for the OLS estimation. The sum of squared residuals is, of course, minimized when OLS is used, and so must necessarily rise when the method of estimation is changed.

The two sets of estimates obtained for the consumption function parameters appear, at first sight, to confirm the superiority of the IV method of estimation when there is a contemporaneous correlation between explanatory variable and disturbance. Moreover, although the superiority of IV estimators is theoretically proven only for large samples (recall that they can be shown to be consistent but not unbiased), in the above case they seem to provide better estimates than OLS even with a relatively small sample of 20. However, we should pause for thought at this point.

Recall that properties such as unbiasedness and consistency refer to the sampling distributions of estimators, not to any specific estimates actually obtained from a particular sample. The sample from which our investigator obtained OLS and IV estimates referred to only one realization out of many possible different realizations for our economy that might have occurred. Suppose, instead, that what actually happens during the 20 years is the realization summed up by the figures in Table 8.1 rather than Table 8.2. The investigator would now have been faced with a different set of sample values with which to estimate α and β. But does the apparent superiority of the IV method hold for this sample as well? In fact, the OLS sample regression line obtained from the data in Table 8.1 is

$$\hat{C} = 2.11 + 0.87Y, \qquad \sum e^2 = 16.70 \tag{8.44}$$

The IV sample regression line for Table 8.1 is

$$\hat{C} = 5.34 + 0.82Y, \qquad \sum e^2 = 23.17 \tag{8.45}$$

From (8.44) and (8.45), we see that again the IV method provides estimates closer to the true α and β than does the OLS method. In this case, however, the 'accuracy' of the IV estimates is less impressive. Indeed, for some other realization of our economy, might it not be conceivable that OLS could prove superior to IV estimation?

If we are properly to compare the performance of OLS and IV estimators in practice, it should be clear that we need to compare them over very many samples or realizations for our simple economy. Such a comparison is in fact made in Table 8.3, for 10 further possible realizations, each providing a 'sample' of 20 years' data. Each such sample has been generated in the same way as those in Tables 8.1 and 8.2. It can

Table 8.3 Further alternative realizations

	OLS estimates		IV estimates	
Realization	α	β	α^*	β^*
1	2.90	0.86	7.33	0.79
2	2.51	0.87	5.50	0.82
3	2.82	0.86	5.96	0.81
4	3.93	0.85	7.91	0.79
5	3.07	0.86	5.10	0.83
6	3.45	0.85	8.84	0.77
7	5.42	0.83	7.66	0.79
8	5.65	0.83	10.72	0.75
9	4.24	0.84	7.89	0.78
10	3.45	0.85	5.77	0.81

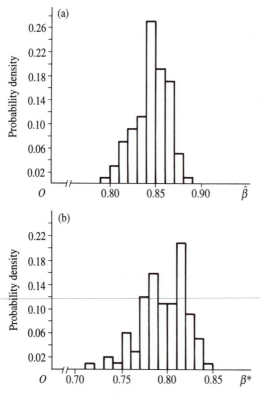

Figure 8.3 (a) Sampling distribution for $\hat{\beta}$ ($n = 20$). (b) Sampling distribution for β^* ($n = 20$).

be seen, for these realizations, that while the IV estimators are generally superior to the OLS estimators, in the sense that they normally provide estimates closer to the true α and β values, this is not necessarily always the case. For example, in realization 8 in Table 8.3 the OLS estimates are closer to the true α and β than the IV estimates. This is not, however, in conflict with the theoretical results obtained earlier. The fact that, when there is a positive correlation between Y and the disturbance, the OLS estimator of β is biased upwards simply means that there is a tendency, over many samples, for it to overestimate β. The error may be quite small in any particular sample (OLS might even underestimate β occasionally). Similarly, while over many large samples IV estimates should be superior to OLS, in a particular sample the IV estimate of β can have a large error.

Obviously we can generate as many realizations as we like using the above procedure. We can in fact obtain empirical versions of the sampling distributions for both the OLS and the IV estimators. For example, the probability histograms shown in Figures 8.3(a,b) are the sampling distributions for the OLS estimator $\hat{\beta}$ and the IV estimator β^* obtained over 100 realizations, each realization corresponding to a 20-year 'sample'.

The sampling distribution in Figure 8.3(a) illustrates well the upward bias in the OLS estimator $\hat{\beta}$ for the model we have assumed. In fact, $E(\hat{\beta}) = 0.846$, whereas we know that true $\beta = 0.8$. The bias over our 100 realizations is therefore $E(\hat{\beta}) - \beta = +0.046$. In contrast, as can be seen from Figure 8.3(b), the IV estimator

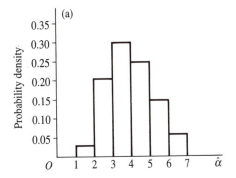

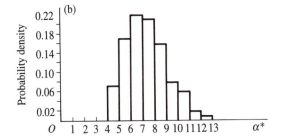

Figure 8.4 (a) Sampling distribution for $\hat{\alpha}$ ($n = 20$). (b) Sampling distribution for α^* ($n = 20$).

$\beta*$ tends to underestimate β, although the bias is less than for OLS. In fact, $E(\beta*) = 0.788$, so that the bias for $\beta*$ is -0.012. Notice, though, that the spread of the distribution for $\beta*$ is greater than that for $\hat{\beta}$. In fact, $\text{Var}(\hat{\beta}) = 0.000\,29$, whereas $\text{Var}(\beta*) = 0.000\,51$. Thus, although IV estimation is likely to give better results 'on average', there always remains the distinct possibility that, for the single realization or sample an investigator actually experiences, $\beta*$ takes a value some way from true β.

Sampling distributions for the OLS and IV estimators of the intercept parameter α are shown in Figures 8.4(a,b). Recall that the true $\alpha = 7$.

From Figure 8.4(a), we see that the OLS estimator of α is subject to the downward bias we expect in this model. $E(\hat{\alpha}) = 3.46$, so that the bias is $E(\hat{\alpha}) - \alpha = -3.54$. The IV estimator of α is also downward-biased in this case, although the bias is much smaller, as Figure 8.4(b) suggests. In fact, $E(\alpha*) = 6.91$ over our 100 realizations, so that the IV bias is only -0.09. Notice again, though, that the spread of the distribution for $\alpha*$ is much wider than for $\hat{\alpha}$. The variances are $\text{Var}(\alpha*) = 2.33$ and $\text{Var}(\hat{\alpha}) = 1.06$.

The above sampling distributions are based on 'samples' of size 20. What if we increased the sample size? The theoretical advantage of the IV method is that it

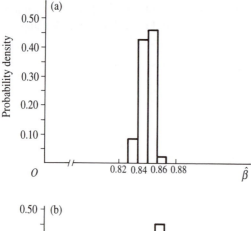

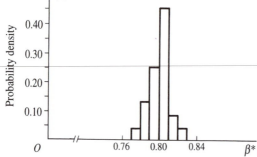

Figure 8.5 (a) Sampling distribution for $\hat{\beta}$ ($n = 100$). (b) Sampling distribution for $\beta*$ ($n = 100$).

provides consistent estimators, and this is a large-sample property. We should therefore not be too surprised that the IV estimator of β appears to be biased in samples of size 20. But we should expect this bias to disappear as the sample size is increased. On the other hand, in the present model, the OLS estimators should remain biased even for large samples.

The sampling distributions for $\hat{\beta}$ and $\beta*$ in Figures 8.5(a,b) are obtained in the same manner as those in Figures 8.3(a,b). They are again the result of 100 different realizations, but this time for each realization we have simulated a 'sample' size $n = 100$. Notice that the OLS estimator $\hat{\beta}$ still invariably overestimates the true β of 0.8. Indeed since $E(\hat{\beta}) = 0.842$ on this occasion, the bias of $+0.042$ is virtually the same as that obtained for samples of size 20. However, the bias in the IV estimator has all but disappeared now that the sample size has been increased. In fact, $E(\beta*) = 0.803$ compared with $\beta = 0.8$.

Notice also the reduction in the spread of the sampling distributions in Figures 8.5(a,b) compared with Figures 8.3(a,b). For a sample size of 100, Var $(\hat{\beta})$ and Var $(\beta*)$ fall to 0.000 028 and 0.000 13 respectively. This is to be expected, given the

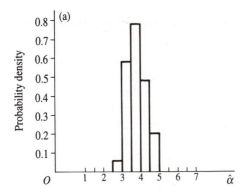

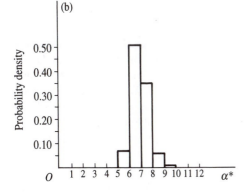

Figure 8.6 (a) Sampling distribution for $\hat{\alpha}$ ($n = 100$). (b) Sampling distribution for $\alpha*$ ($n = 100$).

increase in sample size. Moreover, since the IV estimator β^* is consistent, its sampling distribution should collapse onto the true β as the sample size tends to infinity. In Figures 8.3(b) and 8.5(b) we can see the first stages of such a collapse.

The sampling distributions for the OLS and IV estimators of α, for a sample size 100, are shown in Figures 8.6(a) and (b) respectively. Notice that the bias in the OLS estimator $\hat{\alpha}$ persists, with $E(\hat{\alpha}) = 3.57$ compared with a true $\alpha = 7$. In contrast, the bias in the IV estimator α^* has again all but disappeared, with $E(\alpha^*) = 6.98$. As in the estimation of β, the variances of the sampling distributions fall with the increase in sample size. Var $(\hat{\alpha})$ is now 0.17 and Var (α^*) is 0.64. Thus we are again witnessing the first stage of the collapse in the sampling distribution of the IV estimator.

The results of our 'controlled experiment' are fairly clear cut. When there is a contemporaneous correlation between explanatory variable and disturbance, as in the above model, the theoretical superiority of IV estimators over OLS estimators is borne out in practice for 'large' samples. Moreover, there is some evidence that this superiority holds even for smaller samples.

8.6   The problems arising with IV estimation

There are, unfortunately, practical difficulties in making use of the IV estimators (8.34) and (8.35) and their multiple regression equivalents. The major problem lies in finding suitable instruments that are both highly correlated with the relevant explanatory X variables and uncorrelated with the disturbance ϵ. Clearly, an instrument that is correlated with ϵ will result in biased estimators. Also, while a high correlation between explanatory variable and instrument is not necessary for consistency, the higher the correlation the greater the asymptotic efficiency of the resultant estimators; that is, the more quickly will their sampling distributions collapse onto the true parameter values as the sample size increases.

One possible procedure is to use a lagged value of the explanatory variable X as its instrument. For example, in the two-variable case, if

$$Y_t = \alpha + \beta X_t + \epsilon_t \tag{8.46}$$

in a time series regression then X_{t-1} is used as the instrument for X_t. If X_t and ϵ_t are contemporaneously correlated because of, for example, measurement error, then, provided successive measurement errors are uncorrelated, X_{t-1} will be uncorrelated with such composite disturbances as (8.12). Also, with time series data, X_{t-1} is likely to be highly correlated with X_t, and this makes it a suitable instrument.

Nowadays, econometricians would not normally limit their choice of instrument to a single variable. Suppose we in fact have m possible instruments, $Z_1, Z_2, Z_3, \ldots,$ Z_m, when wishing to estimate the two-variable equation (8.6), all uncorrelated with ϵ. Rather than form the instrumental variable by regressing X on any single instrument, X is regressed on all the instruments using the multiple regression techniques of the last chapter. The instrumental variable now consists of the predicted values of X

obtained from the multiple regression. That is, we take

$$\hat{X}_i = \hat{\gamma}_1 Z_{1i} + \hat{\gamma}_2 Z_{2i} + \hat{\gamma}_3 Z_{3i} + \cdots + \hat{\gamma}_m Z_{mi} \tag{8.47}$$

where the $\hat{\gamma}$s are the OLS estimated coefficients from the regression.

As we have written (8.47), the equation does not contain an intercept term. However, recall from Equation (7.1a) that the intercept in multiple regression can be regarded as the coefficient of a variable that always takes the value unity. In practice, such a variable is normally used as the first instrument Z_1. Since such a constant variable can never be correlated with a disturbance, it always makes a suitable instrument.

Notice that, since all the Z instruments are uncorrelated with the disturbance ϵ in (8.6), the $\hat{X}_i$ from (8.47), which are linear functions of the Z values, must also be uncorrelated with ϵ. This makes $\hat{X}$ a most suitable instrumental variable, since use of the OLS method to obtain (8.47) means that the correlation between $\hat{X}$ and the original Zs has been maximized. The IV estimates of α and β in (8.6) can then be regarded as obtained by using OLS to regress Y on the $\hat{X}_i$. These estimators are known as **generalized instrumental variable estimators** (GIVEs).

COMPUTER EXERCISE

In this computer exercise we shall make use of Data Set 4 on the floppy disk. The data can also be found in appendix III at the end of the text. This contains quarterly UK data for the period 1974Q1 through 1984Q4 on the two variables

$C = $ real consumer expenditure in £m at 1985 prices

$Y = $ real personal disposable income in £m at 1985 prices

We shall use this data to compute both OLS and IV estimates of the parameters in the simple consumption equation

$$C_t = \alpha + \beta Y_t + \epsilon_t \tag{8.48}$$

OLS estimators of α and β in Equation (8.48) are biased and inconsistent for the reasons involving simultaneity outlined in Section 8.3. Recall that OLS is likely to overestimate β and underestimate α. The reader should, as usual, attempt to replicate the regression equations that follow using a computer package.

OLS estimation of (8.48) using the 40 quarterly observations for 1975Q1 through 1984Q4 should yield

$$\hat{C}_t = 2160 + 0.848 Y_t, \qquad R^2 = 0.803, \qquad \text{SSR} = 8.89 \times 10^7 \tag{8.49}$$
$$\quad\;\; (0.58) \quad (12.4)$$

Values in parentheses are, as usual, t ratios.

To compute IV estimates of the parameters in (8.48), we shall use the GIVE method outlined above. Your computer package will require you to name at least two instruments for use in forming instrumental variables of the form (8.47). In the absence of any data on non-consumption expenditure, such as Z in Tables 8.1 and 8.2, we shall use income lagged one period, Y_{t-1}, as one of our instruments. As explained earlier, this will be highly correlated with Y_t, and there is no reason why it should be correlated with the disturbance ϵ_t in Equation (8.48). As a second instrument, we shall simply use a constant – in fact, a variable that always takes the value unity. The computer will therefore form instrumental variable values using (8.47) with $Z_{1t} = 1$ and $Z_{2t} = Y_{t-1}$.

Once you have specified the two instruments, GIVE estimation of (8.48), for the sample period 1975Q1 through 1984Q4, should yield a printout similar to that in Table 8.4. From the printout, we extract

$$\hat{C}_t = 3095 + 0.831 Y_t, \qquad SSR = 8.91 \times 10^7 \qquad (8.50)$$
$$\phantom{\hat{C}_t = }(0.78) \quad (11.4)$$

Although, unlike in the Monte Carlo experiment carried out earlier in this chapter, we do not know the true values of α and β in Equation (8.48), the relationship between the OLS estimates in (8.49) and the GIVE estimates in (8.50) is what we might expect. Since OLS overestimates β, we would expect the GIVE estimate of 0.831 to be lower than the OLS estimate of 0.848. Similarly, we would expect the GIVE estimate of α to exceed the OLS estimate, and this is indeed the case.

We have not quoted the R^2 statistic for the GIVE equation (8.50), because this statistic can only be given its usual interpretation when the estimation method is OLS. However, notice that the residual sum of squares in (8.50) is slightly larger than that for the OLS equation (8.49). This is to be expected, because, as we have stressed before, it is the OLS method that minimizes this sum of squares. Notice also

Table 8.4 Computer printout for Equation (8.50)

```
                          Instrumental Variable Estimation
*******************************************************************************
Dependent variable is C
List of instruments:
INTER         Y(-1)
40 observations used for estimation from 75Q1 to 84Q4
*******************************************************************************
Regressor            Coefficient           Standard Error        T-Ratio[Prob]
INTER                   3094.6                 3956.5             .78216[.439]
Y                       .83080                 .072894            11.3973[.000]
*******************************************************************************
R-Squared                    .80263    F-statistic F( 1, 38) 154.5312[.000]
R-Bar-Squared                .79744    S.E. of Regression            1531.0
Residual Sum of Squares   8.91E+07    Mean of Dependent Variable    48103.6
S.D. of Dependent Variable   3401.6
DW-statistic                 1.6373
*******************************************************************************
```

Source: *Printout from software MICROFIT 3.0, Electronic Publishing, OUP, by H and B Pesaran.*

that your computer package will give you the standard errors and t ratios for the GIVEs. Although beyond the scope of this text, it is possible to derive expressions for the variances and hence standard errors of GIVEs.

Despite the fact that most computer packages will calculate GIVE equations directly, we saw earlier that the GIVE procedure can be regarded as the outcome of two stages. It is instructive to recalculate the GIVEs by performing these two stages. The first stage is to form instrumental variables using (8.47). In our example this involves using OLS to regress the explanatory variable Y_t on Y_{t-1}, making sure we have an intercept in the equation. This should yield

$$\hat{Y}_t = 1638.6 + 0.974 Y_{t-1} \qquad (8.51)$$

The estimated standard errors and t ratios for (8.51) are of no relevance, and we have not presented them. The predicted values of Y, that is the $\hat{Y}_t$s, from (8.51) must now be saved and included in the data set. The second stage of the procedure is then to regress C_t on the $\hat{Y}_t$s, again with an intercept included. This should yield

$$\hat{C}_t = 3095 + 0.831 \hat{Y}_t, \qquad \text{SSR} = 14.7 \times 10^7 \qquad (8.52)$$
$$\phantom{\hat{C}_t = }(0.61) \quad (8.9)$$

The estimates of α and β in (8.52) are identical to those in (8.50). These are the GIVEs. Note, however, that the residual sum of squares and t ratios differ from those in (8.50). These statistics refer only to the second stage, that is, the OLS regression of C_t on $\hat{Y}_t$, and not to the GIVE regression of C_t on Y_t. The correct GIVE values for SSR and the t ratios are those attached to Equation (8.50).

We shall return to Data Set 4 in later chapters. The equation we have estimated, (8.48), represents a particularly simple Keynesian form for the consumption function, and we shall be estimating more complicated equations relating to other consumption function hypotheses. Furthermore, the reader should recall the discussion in Section 4.4, concerning the dangers of placing too much confidence in regression equations involving variables that are trending upwards. In Data Set 4, apart from seasonal fluctuations, both income and consumption move consistently upwards during our sample period. Graphical plots of C and Y over time, which your computer should provide for you, clearly indicate this. The regressions of this exercise should therefore be viewed with considerable scepticism. They have been estimated solely to illustrate the use of instrumental variables.

8.7   Estimation in simultaneous equation models

We saw in Section 8.3 that a major factor leading to correlations between stochastic regressors and disturbances was the simultaneity of many economic relationships. When estimating simultaneous equation models, such as those in Section 8.3, by the GIVE method, the choice of instruments is relatively easy. Since the exogenous variables in the model can be regarded as independent of the model disturbances they may be used as instruments. Moreover, as can always be seen from the reduced form of the model, movements in the endogenous variables are determined by changes in the exogenous variables. Thus the exogenous variable instruments should be highly correlated with any regressors they are required to act for. This makes them highly suitable instruments.

As an example, consider the demand–supply model given by Equations (8.26) and (8.27). Each equation contains on its right-hand side the endogenous price variable P, which is correlated with both disturbances. The exogenous variables S and C may be used as instruments, since they may be assumed uncorrelated with either disturbance. Thus if we wish to estimate, for example, the demand equation (8.26), the first stage in the GIVE procedure would be to regress P on the two instruments S and C, computing

$$\hat{P}_i = \hat{\gamma}_1 + \hat{\gamma}_2 S_i + \hat{\gamma}_3 C_i \tag{8.53}$$

The second stage is then to replace P in (8.26) by $\hat{P}$, using the values for $\hat{P}$ obtained in the first stage, and then regress Q and $\hat{P}$ and S to obtain the GIVE estimates. Equation (8.27) can be estimated in a similar way, this time regressing Q on $\hat{P}$ and C.

In this context, the GIVE estimators are sometimes called **two-stage least squares** (TSLS) **estimators**. TSLS is the most frequently used method of obtaining consistent estimators of parameters in a simultaneous system of relationships.[8]

Maximum likelihood methods can also be used to estimate parameters in a simultaneous equation model, provided such parameters are identified. Although the details of such methods are beyond our scope, two approaches are possible. If it is required to estimate just a single equation in the model then the method of **limited information maximum likelihood** may be used. This involves setting up a likelihood function for the endogenous variables that depends on the parameters of the reduced-form equations for the model. If, however, the aim is to estimate all equations in a model then the method of **full information maximum likelihood** is more appropriate. This method also requires the maximization of a likelihood function for the endogenous variables, but this time the function is expressed in terms of the parameters from all the structural equations. For a mainly intuitive account of these methods, see Thomas (1993).

★ Appendix 8A

Consistency of the IV estimator

We demonstrate the consistency of the IV estimator of β in Equation (8.6). If the instrument Z is uncorrelated with ϵ in (8.6), this implies that $E(z_i\epsilon_i) = 0$. Hence

$$\text{plim} \left(\sum z_i\epsilon_i/n \right) = E(z_i\epsilon_i) = 0 \tag{8A.1}$$

since $\sum z_i\epsilon_i/n$ is the sample correlation between Z and ϵ.

If Z is correlated with X then $E(z_i x_i) = $ constant $\neq 0$. Hence

$$\text{plim} \left(\sum z_i x_i / n \right) = E(z_i x_i) = \text{constant} \neq 0 \tag{8A.2}$$

Since $\sum z_i = 0$, we can write the IV estimator β^* as

$$\beta^* = \frac{\sum z_i y_i}{\sum z_i x_i} = \frac{\sum z_i Y_i}{\sum z_i x_i} = \frac{\sum z_i (\alpha + \beta X_i + \epsilon_i)}{\sum z_i x_i}$$

$$= \frac{\beta \sum z_i x_i + \sum z_i \epsilon_i}{\sum z_i x_i} = \beta + \frac{\sum z_i \epsilon_i}{\sum z_i x_i} \tag{8A.3}$$

Hence, taking probability limits,

$$\text{plim} \, (\beta^*) = \beta + \frac{\text{plim} \left(\sum z_i \epsilon_i / n \right)}{\text{plim} \left(\sum z_i x_i / n \right)} = \beta \quad \text{(using (8A.1) and (8A.2))}$$

Thus β^* is a consistent estimator of β. Similarly, α^* can be shown to be a consistent estimator of α.

Notice that, although β^* is consistent, it is not unbiased. From (8A.3),

$$\beta^* = \beta + \frac{1}{\sum z_i x_i} (z_1 \epsilon_1 + z_2 \epsilon_2 + z_3 \epsilon_3 + \cdots + z_n \epsilon_n) \tag{8A.4}$$

Since Z and ϵ are uncorrelated, it is true that $E(z_i \epsilon_i) = E(z_i) E(\epsilon_i) = 0$ for all i. Unfortunately, however, if we take expectations over (8A.4), since X and Z are correlated, we cannot write

$$E(\beta^*) = \beta + E\left(\frac{1}{\sum z_i x_i} \right) E(z_1 \epsilon_1 + z_2 \epsilon_2 + z_3 \epsilon_3 + \cdots + z_n \epsilon_n)$$

Hence we are unable to obtain $E(\beta^*) = \beta$.

Appendix 8B

Notes to Chapter 8

1. For example, if $\beta = 1$ then (8.3) becomes $\Delta Y_t = \alpha + \epsilon_t$. Thus, with $\alpha > 0$ and $E(\epsilon_t) = 0$, Y_t must trend upwards.
2. Simply reformulating the assumptions about the disturbances does not of course restore the properties of the OLS estimators.
3. It is the X_i^* that are stochastic. The true X_i are non-stochastic, but, of course, $X_i^* = X_i + v_i$, where v_i is a stochastic measurement error.
4. For example, since $E(v_i) = E(w_i) = 0$, $E(v_i w_i)$ is the covariance between v_i and w_i.
5. The reduced-form equation for P may be found by equating the right-hand sides of (8.26) and (8.27) and then solving for P. If the expression obtained for P is then substituted into either (8.26) or (8.27), the reduced-form equation for Q is found.

6. If, by some chance, the disturbances were to equal zero throughout the period when data was collected then all that could be observed would be not a scatter but a single point at the intersection of stationary demand and supply curves.

7. $\sum X_i \epsilon_i = \sum x_i \epsilon_i + \bar{X} \sum \epsilon_i$. For large samples, $\sum \epsilon_i = 0$, so $\sum X_i \epsilon_i = \sum x_i \epsilon_i$. Thus if $E x_i \epsilon_i = 0$ then $\sum X_i \epsilon_i = 0$ for large samples.

8. Another method of obtaining consistent estimators that is sometimes feasible is that known as **indirect least squares** (ILS). To obtain ILS estimators, the reduced-form equations are estimated. Since reduced-form equations contain only exogenous variables on the right-hand side, OLS will always provide consistent estimators of the reduced-form coefficients. The reduced-form coefficients are functions of the parameters in the original structural equations (see e.g. Equations (8.21) and (8.22)). Once estimates of the reduced-form coefficients have been obtained, obtaining estimates of structural parameters is therefore a matter of solving a set of equations. Unfortunately, the ILS method often breaks down because such sets of equations do not always have a single unique solution. See Thomas (1993), Chapter 8, for more details on this.

Further reading

Stochastic explanatory variables, measurement errors and instrumental variable estimation are covered in Judge et al. (1988), Chapter 13. A far more detailed treatment of simultaneity and identification than appears in this text is given by Judge et al. in their Chapters 14 and 15. See also Greene (1993), Chapter 20, and Johnston (1984), Chapter 11, for coverage of these topics at a more advanced level. The GIVE method of estimation is well treated in Stewart (1991).

9 More about multiple regression

In this chapter we first consider a problem in multiple regression that did not arise in the two-variable model of earlier chapters. Then we examine a number of useful extensions to the classical regression model.

9.1 Multicollinearity

Assumption ID of the classical model of Chapter 7 stated that there should exist no linear relationships between the sample values of the explanatory variables. We saw that, if this assumption breaks down, the matrices $\mathbf{X'X}$ and $\mathbf{x'x}$ become singular, so that their inverses do not exist. It then becomes impossible to compute the OLS estimators (7.15) or (7.15a). Under such circumstances, OLS estimators simply do not exist.

It is fairly easy to see intuitively why a breakdown in assumption ID should cause such problems. Consider a population regression equation

$$E(Y) = \beta_1 + \beta_2 X_2 + \beta_3 X_3 \tag{9.1}$$

Suppose we attempt to estimate (9.1) using a sample for which

$$X_{3i} = a + bX_{2i} \quad \text{for all } i \tag{9.2}$$

where a and b are known constants. That is, our sample is such that in each and every observation the X_3 value is the same linear function of the X_2 value. Such a relationship does not always occur – it just happens to hold for every observation in the particular sample *we* have taken. It might well not hold in another sample.

Substituting $X_3 = a + bX_2$ into (9.1) gives

$$E(Y) = \beta_1 + \beta_2 X_2 + \beta_3(a + bX_2)$$
$$= (\beta_1 + a\beta_3) + (\beta_2 + b\beta_3)X_2$$

or

$$E(Y) = \mu_1 + \mu_2 X_2, \quad \text{where} \quad \mu_1 = \beta_1 + a\beta_3, \quad \mu_2 = \beta_2 + b\beta_3 \qquad (9.1a)$$

The problem is that *as far as our sample is concerned*, Equation (9.1) has become (9.1a). Hence all we can estimate with our sample, using OLS or any other method, are the quantities μ_1 and μ_2. This will remain the case so long as all data that become available obeys (9.2). Unfortunately, however good are our estimates of μ_1 and μ_2, we will never be able to obtain estimates of β_1, β_2 and β_3. To obtain such estimates, we would have to solve the equations (from (9.1a))

$$\hat{\mu}_1 = \hat{\beta}_1 + a\hat{\beta}_3$$
$$\hat{\mu}_2 = \hat{\beta}_2 + b\hat{\beta}_3 \qquad (9.3)$$

Given the estimates $\hat{\mu}_1$ and $\hat{\mu}_2$, (9.3) represent two linear equations in the three unknowns $\hat{\beta}_1$, $\hat{\beta}_2$ and $\hat{\beta}_3$. Unfortunately, there are an infinite number of sets of values for the $\hat{\beta}$s that would satisfy such equations.[1] No estimation method can provide us with estimates of the true β values.

The situation where an exact linear relationship exists between the sample values of X variables is referred to as one of **perfect multicollinearity**. This situation virtually never arises in practice and can be disregarded. What frequently happens with real-world data, however, is that an approximate linear relationship occurs among the sample values of explanatory variables. That is, one of the columns of the matrix **X** is an approximate linear function of one or more of the other columns. In such a situation, the closer the approximation the higher the *degree* **of multi-collinearity** that is said to be present.

When a high degree of multicollinearity exists, it is still possible to apply the OLS estimation method, since the matrix $\mathbf{X'X}$ in (7.15) is non-singular and can be inverted. However, a problem *can* still arise, although it is by no means certain to.

If one of the columns of the matrix **X** is an approximate linear function of one or more of the others, then the matrix $\mathbf{X'X}$ will be close to singularity – that is, its determinant $|\mathbf{X'X}|$ will be close to zero. Since, when forming the inverse $(\mathbf{X'X})^{-1}$, we have to divide by the reciprocal of $|\mathbf{X'X}|$, this means that the elements (and particularly the diagonal elements) of $(\mathbf{X'X})^{-1}$ will be large.[2] Consequently, we see from Equation (7.49) that the variances and hence standard errors of the estimators $\hat{\beta}_j$ will tend to be large whenever there is a high degree of multicollinearity. Since there is no reason why multicollinearity should affect our estimators of these standard errors, their size will be reflected in any estimated standard errors that we compute.

This is the major possible adverse factor when multicollinearity is present – *large standard errors* and hence large estimated standard errors. One important consequence of this is that any confidence intervals for the true β_j parameters that we form (using (7.58)) may turn out to be very wide. That is, our estimates will lack precision and we will be very uncertain about true parameter values.

A further consequence of large standard errors is that t ratios will tend to be low. Recall that a t ratio $\hat{\beta}_j/s_{\hat{\beta}_j}$ is simply the ratio of an estimated regression coefficient to its estimated standard error. We use such t ratios as the test statistic for assessing hypotheses of the type $\beta_j = 0$. When t ratios are low, we find ourselves in the position of being unable to reject such hypotheses and having to reserve judgement on them. Our usual significance tests are unable to tell us whether or not explanatory variables really influence the dependent variable.

We shall stress later, however, that large standard errors and low t ratios are by no means a certain consequence of multicollinearity. For example, as can be seen from (7.49), the true standard errors depend not only on the elements of $(\mathbf{X'X})^{-1}$ but also on σ^2, the variance of the disturbances. If σ^2 is small then this can counterbalance any multicollinearity that is present.

We have already encountered one case of a somewhat reduced t ratio. Recall the 25 households of Table 7.1. In Chapters 4 and 6 we computed the simple regression of consumption on disposable income for these households. This eventually resulted in the equation below (6.38) in which the t ratio on the income coefficient was 7.19. However, when in Chapter 7 we added a liquid assets variable to our consumption equation and obtained Equation (7.60), the t ratios on the two explanatory variables were only 1.93 and 3.35. These smaller t ratios are the result of a roughly linear relationship that exists between the income and liquid assets variables. Not surprisingly, households with higher incomes tend to have larger liquid assets stocks. In fact, the correlation between the two is 0.84 for the data in Table 7.1.

The t ratios in Equation (7.60) were still large enough for us to conclude that both income and liquid assets influenced consumption. But consider the data in Table 9.1 for a further 25 households. With this data set, the correlation between income X_2 and liquid assets X_3 is as high as 0.99. Thus there is a much closer linear relationship between the two – a much higher degree of multicollinearity. The following regressions can be estimated using this data set:

$$\hat{Y} = 36.74 + 0.832X_2 \qquad\qquad R^2 = 0.735 \qquad\qquad\qquad (9.4)$$
$$\phantom{\hat{Y} = }(1.98) \quad (7.98)$$

$$\hat{Y} = 36.61 + 0.208X_3 \qquad\qquad R^2 = 0.735 \qquad\qquad\qquad (9.5)$$
$$\phantom{\hat{Y} = }(1.97) \quad (7.99)$$

$$\hat{Y} = 33.88 - 26.00X_2 + 6.71X_3 \quad R^2 = 0.742 \qquad\qquad\qquad (9.6)$$
$$\phantom{\hat{Y} = }(1.77) \quad (0.74) \quad\;\; (0.77)$$

Numbers in parentheses are, as usual, t ratios.

Equations (9.4) and (9.5) indicate that, when income X_2 or liquid assets X_3 are included alone as explanatory variables, both have high t ratios and appear to be significant determinants of consumption. Each variable on its own can explain 73–74% of the variation in Y. However, when both variables are included together as

Table 9.1 A multicollinear data set

Household	Y	X_2	X_3
1	55.7	37.2	149.4
2	99.6	45.8	183.7
3	71.8	54.6	217.6
4	107.6	61.5	247.3
5	85.6	73.3	293.9
6	94.3	83.0	333.1
7	121.0	97.3	390.6
8	80.6	101.2	403.8
9	117.4	110.3	442.0
10	185.6	117.5	469.4
11	137.3	132.6	531.1
12	187.4	144.6	577.8
13	143.5	155.4	622.4
14	108.4	168.7	675.1
15	171.6	176.6	707.5
16	206.3	188.4	754.6
17	267.3	194.2	775.3
18	185.3	208.6	832.8
19	265.8	216.5	867.6
20	211.7	233.7	936.1
21	274.2	245.1	981.0
22	213.7	262.8	1052.2
23	345.5	275.8	1104.1
24	183.3	293.8	1173.8
25	313.7	307.7	1231.7

explanatory variables in (9.6), marked changes occur. Despite the slight increase in R^2, there is a dramatic fall in the t ratios on X_2 and X_3. In fact, both t ratios are now too small for us to conclude that either of the explanatory variables are significant in the determination of Y. We are unable to tell whether it is X_2 or X_3 or both that is important.

The second point to note about Equation (9.6) is that neither of the coefficients on X_2 or X_3 make much economic sense. The estimated MPC income is negative and the estimated MPC liquid assets is 6.71! These are, however, point estimates, and are extremely imprecise. The estimated standard error of the MPC income is, in fact, as high as $s_{\hat{\beta}_2} = 34.96$. Since, with $n - 3 = 22$ d.f., $t_{0.025} = 2.074$, the 95% confidence interval for the true MPC income is

$$\hat{\beta}_2 \pm 2.074 s_{\hat{\beta}_2} = -26.00 \pm 2.074(34.96) = -26.00 \pm 72.51$$

This is a very wide interval, and, although it contains some perfectly reasonable values for the MPC, the truth is that we can have no real idea what the true value of

β_2 is. Similar comments, of course, apply to the true value of β_3, the MPC liquid assets.

Summarizing, although we know that between them variations in X_2 and X_3 can explain a substantial proportion of the variation in Y, we cannot disentangle the effects of the individual variables and assess the relative importance of each. The reason for our difficulties is the high correlation between income and liquid assets for the 25 households in Table 9.1. Intuitively, since in this data set a high-income household always has a large liquid asset stock, we cannot tell whether its high consumption level is due to its high income or to its large assets stock.

The problem with multicollinearity then is that it *can* lead to large standard errors and small t ratios. Its possible consequences may be summarized as follows.

(a) Estimates of regression equation parameters may be imprecise in the sense that large estimated standard errors mean that confidence intervals will be wide.

(b) Small t ratios mean that significance tests concerning single variables may tell us little. The danger here is that a low t ratio may cause us to drop an apparently insignificant variable from the estimating equation when in fact this variable is important in the determination of Y. Its true importance may simply be obscured by the multicollinearity that is present.

(c) It may become impossible to disentangle the individual influences of explanatory variables. This point was, of course, well illustrated by Equation (9.6) above.

(d) Specific estimates of regression parameters may have large errors, and even small changes to the data set may have a marked effect on such estimates. Large standard errors mean that the sampling distributions of the OLS estimators stretch over a very wide range. Thus, even if these estimators are unbiased, for the single sample that we take, they may unluckily take values very far away from the true parameters. This is, in fact, what has happened in Equation (9.6) above.

One fact should always be remembered when considering the possible consequences of multicollinearity. Except when it is perfect, in which case estimation is impossible, *multicollinearity does not imply any violation of the classical assumptions*. Even with a high degree of multicollinearity, the OLS estimators retain all their desired properties of efficiency, consistency etc. The OLS method is still the best method of proceeding, and its inferential aspects are still valid. The problem is that even the best method may leave much to be desired, and the inferential procedures may be uninformative.

'Testing' for multicollinearity

Statistical tests normally involve hypotheses about *population* parameters. The problem with multicollinearity is that it is a property of the particular *sample* that we are presented with rather than the population from which our sample is drawn. An alternative sample might not exhibit the same degree of collinearity between the values of explanatory variables. Since multicollinearity is a sample attribute, this means that we cannot test for it in a true statistical sense. That is why we have placed the word 'testing' in inverted commas at the start of this subsection.

When we have just two explanatory variables such as in (9.6) an obvious way to 'test' for multicollinearity is to examine the simple correlation r between the sample values of X_2 and X_3. Obviously, the greater is r the stronger the linear relationship that is present in our sample. It would be very convenient if we could specify some value for r, e.g. 0.7 or 0.9, such that values in excess of this implied a degree of multicollinearity that was likely to cause problems in our results. Unfortunately, a given degree of multicollinearity, as measured by r, will not always have the same consequences. That is why we have stressed earlier that multicollinearity *can result in high standard errors, but does not necessarily do so*.

In the case of just two explanatory variables it can be shown (see Appendix 9A) that the sampling variances for the OLS estimators $\hat{\beta}_2$ and $\hat{\beta}_3$ are given by

$$\text{Var}\,(\hat{\beta}_2) = \frac{\sigma^2}{\sum x_2^2(1-r^2)}, \qquad \text{Var}\,(\hat{\beta}_3) = \frac{\sigma^2}{\sum x_3^2(1-r^2)} \tag{9.7}$$

where $r^2 = (\sum x_2 x_3)^2 / \sum x_2^2 \sum x_3^2$ is the square of the sample correlation between X_2 and X_3.

It can be seen from (9.7) that, *other things being equal*, a rise in the value for r, that is, an increase in the degree of multicollinearity, does indeed lead to an increase in the variances and hence the standard errors of the OLS estimators. But (9.7) indicates that standard errors depend not only on r but also on two other factors. They also depend on the disturbance variance σ^2, and on $\sum x_2^2 = \sum (X_2 - \bar{X}_2)^2$ and $\sum x_3^2 = \sum (X_3 - \bar{X}_3)^2$, these latter two quantities measuring the variability in the sample values of X_2 and X_3.

It should now be clear that, even when X_2 and X_3 are highly correlated, small standard errors are still possible if either σ^2 is sufficiently low (in which case the 'fit' of the equation should be good)[3] and/or there is sufficient variability in the values of X_2 and X_3. Conversely, large standard errors may occur not because of multicollinearity but because σ^2 is large or because there is insufficient variation in the explanatory variables.

Summarizing the above, the size of standard errors in regression equations with just two explanatory variables depends on other factors in addition to the correlation r between X_2 and X_3. Thus there is no 'critical value' for r above which we can expect the consequences of multicollinearity always to be serious.

Multicollinearity can, of course, also occur in equations with more than two explanatory variables, and its consequences, as we have seen, may again be large standard errors. Assessing the degree of multicollinearity or 'testing' in the general case is more difficult, however. An obvious first step is to examine the simple correlation coefficients for each pair of explanatory variables. However, multicollinearity can also involve linear relationships between more than two X variables, and such relationships are less easy to spot. One possibility, suggested by Farrar and Glauber as long ago as 1967, is to run a series of 'test' regressions. In turn, each explanatory X variable is regressed on all the other X variables, the coefficient of determination R^2 being computed in each case. If an approximate linear relationship exists among the X variables then this should show up as a 'large' value for R^2 in at least one of the test regressions.

The problem is that, again, a given degree of multicollinearity does not always have the same consequences. With more than two explanatory variables, the equivalent of the expressions (9.7) can be shown to be

$$\text{Var}\,(\hat{\beta}_j) = \frac{\sigma^2}{\sum x_j^2(1 - R_j^2)} \tag{9.8}$$

where R_j^2 is the coefficient of multiple determination when the variable X_j is regressed on all the other explanatory variables. What (9.8) demonstrates is that the variance and hence standard error of $\hat{\beta}_j$ depend on not only R_j^2 but also σ^2 and $\sum x_j^2$.

A popular measure of multicollinearity associated with (9.8) is the **variance inflation factor** (VIF), defined as

$$\text{VIF}\,(\hat{\beta}_j) = \frac{1}{1 - R_j^2} \tag{9.9}$$

The VIF can be interpreted as the ratio of actual the variance of $\hat{\beta}_j$ to what it would have been in an ideal situation where $R_j^2 = 0$. But as (9.8) illustrates, the actual variance of $\hat{\beta}_j$ depends on other factors apart from $1/(1 - R_j^2)$.

A high degree of multicollinearity, then, may have an adverse effect on regression results, but this is by no means inevitable. The implication is that, if regression equations have low estimated standard errors and high t ratios, we should not spend too much time worrying about any multicollinearity that might be present. Remember that, even in the presence of severe multicollinearity, the OLS estimators retain all their desirable properties, and, moreover, estimated standard errors remain unbiased.

The existence of high estimated standard errors can make us *suspect* the presence of multicollinearity. Certainly, if R^2 is high and standard errors are large, as in for example Equation (9.6), then multicollinearity must be present. The high R^2 indicates that either X_2 or X_3 or both influence Y. The fact that neither variables are significant means that their true importance is being obscured by multicollinearity.

We must, however, resist the temptation to attribute all large standard errors and low t ratios to multicollinearity. An explanatory variable may have a small t ratio *simply because it is unimportant in the determination of the dependent Y variable.* Also, as we saw earlier, lack of variation in an explanatory variable can also result in a large standard error. Obviously, if a variable does not vary, we can hardly expect to be able to assess with any precision the effect of it varying.

If we are convinced that multicollinearity is the chief factor behind high standard errors and is obscuring the importance of at least some of the explanatory variables, is there anything that can be done? The answer is 'very little', apart from obtaining more data.

Consider again the expressions (9.7). More observations alone will almost certainly increase $\sum x_2^2$ and $\sum x_3^2$, and hence reduce the size of standard errors. If the extra observations increase the variability of X_2 and X_3 then so much the better. Moreover, if the result of the larger sample size is to reduce the correlation r between X_2 and X_3 then this attacks the multicollinearity deadlock directly.

If extra data is unobtainable, there are several other techniques that have been suggested for dealing with multicollinearity. However, these are outside the scope of this book, and all in fact have major drawbacks. **Ridge regressions** are an essentially mechanical and arbitrary technique, although they can lead to estimators with smaller mean square errors than the OLS estimators. The use of **principal components** has its advocates, but the results obtained by this technique are frequently very hard to interpret in a sensible economic manner.

9.2   Linear restrictions on regression parameters

In the computer exercise at the end of Chapter 7 we estimated the demand equation (7.64). Because the variables in this equation were in logarithms, their coefficients could be interpreted as elasticities, and, according to consumer theory, were expected to sum to zero. That is, they should obey the *linear restriction*

$$\beta_2 + \beta_3 + \beta_4 = 0 \tag{9.10}$$

We estimated not only (7.64) in the computer exercise but also Equation (7.65), in which the restriction (9.10) was *imposed*. That is, the estimates of the parameters were constrained to sum to zero. To do this, we substituted $\beta_4 = -\beta_2 - \beta_3$ into (7.64), and eventually obtained (7.65). Estimation of (7.65) then yielded OLS estimates $\hat{\beta}_2$ and $\hat{\beta}_3$, and an estimate of β_4 could be obtained using $\hat{\beta}_4 = -\hat{\beta}_2 - \hat{\beta}_3$.

The estimates obtained in this way are known as **restricted least squares estimates.** Equation (7.65) is referred to as the **restricted equation**, whereas the original (7.64) is known as the **unrestricted equation**.

It is possible to impose more than one restriction at a time on a regression equation. For example, suppose we have the unrestricted equation

$$Y = \beta_1 + \beta_2 X_2 + \beta_3 X_3 + \beta_4 X_4 + \beta_5 X_5 + \epsilon \tag{9.11}$$

and wish to impose the two restrictions

$$\beta_2 + \beta_3 = 1 \quad \text{and} \quad \beta_4 = \beta_5 \tag{9.12}$$

Substituting the restrictions into (9.11) gives

$$Y = \beta_1 + \beta_2 X_2 + (1 - \beta_2)X_3 + \beta_4 X_4 + \beta_4 X_5 + \epsilon \tag{9.13}$$

Rearranging (9.13) then yields a restricted equation

$$Y^* = \beta_1 + \beta_2 X_2^* + \beta_4 X_4^* + \epsilon \tag{9.14}$$

where $Y^* = Y - X_3$, $X_2^* = X_2 - X_3$ and $X_4^* = X_4 + X_5$.

In this case the restricted least squares estimates would be obtained by applying OLS to the restricted equation (9.14) to obtain directly the estimates $\hat{\beta}_1$, $\hat{\beta}_2$ and $\hat{\beta}_4$, and then using the restrictions (9.12) to obtain $\hat{\beta}_3 = 1 - \hat{\beta}_2$ and $\hat{\beta}_5 = \hat{\beta}_4$.

Exercise 9.1

Suppose

$$W_t = \beta_1 + \beta_2 P_t + \beta_3 P_{t-1} + \beta_4 U_t + \beta_5 V_t + \beta_6 W_{t-1} + \epsilon_t \tag{I}$$

where W_t = wage rate, P_t = price level, U_t = unemployment level and V_t = level of unfilled vacancies.

Show that imposing the restrictions $\beta_2 + \beta_3 = 0$, $\beta_4 + \beta_5 = 0$ and $\beta_6 = 1$ on (I) results in

$$\Delta W_t = \beta_1 + \beta_2 \, \Delta P_t + \beta_5 D_t + \epsilon_t \tag{II}$$

where $\Delta W_t = W_t - W_{t-1}$, $\Delta P_t = P_t - P_{t-1}$ and $D_t = V_t - U_t$.

Exercise 9.2

Consider the equation

$$Y = \beta_1 + \beta_2 X_2 + \beta_3 X_3 + \beta_4 X_4 + \epsilon \tag{I}$$

Show that estimation of (I) subject to the restrictions $\beta_2 + \beta_3 = 1$ and $\beta_4 = \beta_3$ is equivalent to estimation of

$$Z = \beta_1 + \beta_2 W + \epsilon \tag{II}$$

where $Z = Y - X_3 - X_4$ and $W = X_2 - X_3 - X_4$.

F testing linear restrictions

Frequently, we will not be prepared just to accept linear restrictions on regression parameters without question. For example, in the demand equation of the computer exercise in Chapter 7, we may not wish merely to accept the a priori notion of theory that the elasticities sum to zero. We may well want to test such a restriction against the data.

The most commonly used statistical test of a restriction such as (9.10) involves the estimation of both the unrestricted equation (7.64) and the restricted equation (7.65). If both these equations are estimated by OLS then, in each case, the total sum of squares in Y can be divided into the conventionally measured explained sum of squares and the residual sum of squares (see Equation (7.33)). That is, for the unrestricted equation, we have

$$\text{SST} = \text{SSE}_\text{U} + \text{SSR}_\text{U}$$

and for the restricted equation

$$\text{SST} = \text{SSE}_\text{R} + \text{SSR}_\text{R}$$

where the subscripts U and R refer to unrestricted and restricted equations respectively. Notice that $\text{SST} = \sum y^2$ is the same in both cases, because both (7.64) and (7.65) have the same dependent variable and were estimated from the same data set.

It should be clear that we are likely to be able to explain more of the variation in Y when we place no restrictions on our estimates of β_2, β_3 and β_4 than when we restrict them to sum to zero. That is, we expect to find

$$\text{SSE}_\text{R} < \text{SSE}_\text{U}, \quad \text{and hence} \quad \text{SSR}_\text{R} > \text{SSR}_\text{U} \tag{9.15}$$

However, if the restriction is valid and the elasticities do sum to zero then imposing the restriction that they do so should make little difference to our ability to explain variations in Y. Thus, if the restriction is valid, we should expect little difference between SSR_R and SSR_U – that is, there should be little deterioration in the fit of the equation when the restriction is imposed. Hence it makes sense to reject the restriction if $\text{SSR}_\text{R} - \text{SSR}_\text{U}$, the increase in the residual sum of squares that results from imposing it, is sufficiently large. The problem is that we need some criteria for deciding what we mean by 'sufficiently large'.

To resolve this problem, we make use of a property of OLS regression explained in Appendix 9B. It is shown there that the quantity SSR/σ^2 has a χ^2 distribution with $n - k$ degrees of freedom, σ^2 being the disturbance variance and k the number of β_j parameters being estimated. Thus we can say, first, that for an unrestricted equation such as (7.64),

$$\text{SSR}_\text{U}/\sigma^2 \text{ has a } \chi^2 \text{ distribution with } n - k_\text{U} \text{ d.f.} \tag{9.16}$$

where k_U is the number of parameters in the unrestricted equation (for (7.64), $k_\text{U} = 4$).

Secondly, for a restricted equation such as (7.65), we have

$$\text{SSR}_\text{R}/\sigma^2 \text{ has a } \chi^2 \text{ distribution with } n - k_\text{R} \text{ d.f.} \tag{9.17}$$

where k_R is the number of parameters in the restricted equation (for (7.65), $k_\text{R} = 3$).

Every linear restriction we impose on regression coefficients always reduces the number of β_j parameters to be estimated by one. Thus in general, if h is the number of restrictions being imposed, we have

$$h = k_\text{U} - k_\text{R}$$

It follows that, using (9.16) and (9.17), we have, subtracting one χ^2 distribution from the other,

$$(SSR_R - SSR_U)/\sigma^2 \text{ has a } \chi^2 \text{ with } h \text{ d.f.} \tag{9.18}$$

since $n - k_R - (n - k_U) = h$.

For Equations (7.64) and (7.65), h is obviously equal to 1. However, if we were testing the restrictions (9.12) that were imposed on (9.11) then $h = k_U - k_R = 2$.

If we knew the disturbance variance σ^2, we would now have a criterion for deciding whether $SSR_R - SSR_U$ is sufficiently large to reject any restriction(s) imposed. We simply compute (9.18), and, if it exceeds the relevant critical value taken from χ^2 tables, we reject the null hypothesis that the restriction(s) are valid.

The problem, of course, is that σ^2 is unknown. However, we may derive a suitable test statistic using (9.16) and (9.18). Recall that the ratio of two independent χ^2 distributions, each divided by their respective degrees of freedom, has an F distribution. Hence

$$\frac{(SSR_R - SSR_U)/h}{SSR_U/(n - k_U)} \quad \text{has an } F \text{ distribution with } [h, n - k_U] \text{ d.f.} \tag{9.19}$$

Since all quantities in (9.19) are known, we can reject the null hypothesis of valid restrictions if (9.19) exceeds the relevant critical F value. Notice that this test statistic is based on the quantity $(SSR_R - SSR_U)/SSR_U$, which is the *proportionate* increase in the sum of squared residuals.

To illustrate the use of the test statistic (9.19), we again refer back to the computer exercise in Chapter 7. The demand equation (7.66) has a residual sum of squares $SSR_U = 0.006\,97$, given in Table 7.3. When we imposed the single restriction that all elasticities summed to zero, we obtained Equation (7.67) which has a residual sum of squares $SSR_R = 0.008\,38$, given in Table 7.4. Since $h = 1$, $n = 25$ and for Equation (7.66), $k_U = 4$, the test statistic (9.22) takes a value

$$\frac{(0.008\,38 - 0.006\,97)/1}{0.006\,97/21} = 4.25$$

Because, with [1, 21] d.f., the critical F value is $F_{0.05} = 4.32$, we see that we cannot quite reject the null hypothesis of a valid restriction. The data is consistent (just) with the hypothesis that the elasticities sum to zero.

Exercise 9.3

Unrestricted estimation of Equation (I) in Exercise 9.1 yielded a residual sum of squares of 374, whereas estimation of Equation (II) yielded a residual sum of squares of 422. If the sample size is 60, test whether the restrictions imposed in (II) are rejected by the data.

Exercise 9.4

With $\sum (Y - \bar{Y})^2 = 834$ and $\sum (Z - \bar{Z})^2 = 273$, estimation of Equations (I) and (II) in Exercise 9.2, from a sample of 44 observations, yields R^2s of 0.86 and 0.42 respectively. Test whether, when imposed together, the restrictions $\beta_2 + \beta_3 = 1$ and $\beta_4 = \beta_3$ are rejected by the data.

Exercise 9.5

Show that OLS estimation of

$$Y_t = \beta_1 + \beta_2 X_t + \beta_3 X_{t-1} + \beta_4 Y_{t-1} + \epsilon_t \tag{I}$$

subject to $\beta_2 + \beta_3 + \beta_4 = 1$ is equivalent to OLS estimation of

$$Y_t - Y_{t-1} = \beta_1 + \beta_2 (X_t - X_{t-1}) + (\beta_2 + \beta_3)(X_{t-1} - Y_{t-1}) + \epsilon_t \tag{II}$$

Estimated versions of (I) and (II) yield residual sums of squares of 236 and 347 respectively, from a sample size 48. Test the validity of the restriction being imposed.

What further restriction is being tested when the equation

$$Y_t - Y_{t-1} = \beta_1 + \beta_2 (X_t - Y_{t-1}) + \epsilon_t \tag{III}$$

is estimated?

OLS estimation of (III) from the same sample as previously resulted in $\sum e_t^2 = 362$. Carry out any additional tests you think are appropriate, and suggest what equation should be estimated next.

Assessing the joint significance of explanatory variables

As we saw in the last section, multicollinearity in a regression equation can obscure the true influence of explanatory variables. For example, in Equation (9.6) neither explanatory variable had significant coefficients, despite an R^2 of 0.742. In such a situation we might wish to test whether the *combined* influence of X_2 and X_3 on Y is significant. That is, we test the hypothesis that either X_2 or X_3 or both influence the dependent variable Y. Because of the multicollinearity, we are unable to be more precise than this. Effectively, we wish to know whether the R^2 of 0.742 in (9.6) is significantly different from zero.

In such a situation we set up the null hypothesis that *none* of the explanatory variables influence Y. That is, in the general case,

$$H_0 : \quad \beta_j = 0, \quad j = 2, 3, 4, \ldots, k \tag{9.20}$$

For Equation (9.6), $k = 3$. The alternative hypothesis is that at least one of the β_j in

(9.20) is non-zero; that is, that at least one of the $k - 1$ explanatory variables influence Y. Rejection of the null hypothesis in favour of the alternative implies that the combined influence of the X variables is significant.

The hypothesis (9.20) can be interpreted as the imposing of $k - 1$ restrictions on an unrestricted equation of the form

$$Y = \beta_1 + \beta_2 X_2 + \beta_3 X_3 + \ldots + \beta_k X_k + \epsilon \tag{9.21}$$

The restricted equation is simply

$$Y = \beta_1 + \epsilon \tag{9.22}$$

To test the $h = k - 1$ restrictions, that is, to test the null hypothesis (9.20), we may use the test statistic (9.19). However, in this case (9.19) may be expressed in an interesting alternative form.

Considering the restricted equation (9.22), the absence of any explanatory variables means that the explained sum of squares SSE_R must be zero. Hence $\text{SST} = \text{SSR}_\text{R}$. It follows that (9.19) can, in this case, be expressed as

$$\frac{(\text{SST} - \text{SSR}_\text{U})/(k - 1)}{\text{SSR}_\text{U}/(n - k)} = \frac{\text{SSE}_\text{U}/(k - 1)}{\text{SSR}_\text{U}/(n - k)} \quad \begin{array}{l} \text{has an } F \text{ distribution} \\ \text{with } [k - 1, n - k] \text{ d.f.} \end{array} \tag{9.23}$$

The test statistic (9.23) is based on the ratio $\text{SSE}_\text{U}/\text{SSR}_\text{U}$, that is, on the ratio of the variation in Y that can be attributed to variation in the X variables in the unrestricted equation (9.21) to the variation in Y that cannot be so attributed. The idea of the test is that if this ratio is sufficiently large, that is, if what we can explain is sufficiently large relative to what we cannot explain, then we reject the null hypothesis that none of the X variables influence Y.

If we divide both top and bottom of the test statistic (9.23) by the total sum of squares SST, we obtain

$$\frac{\text{SSE}_\text{U}/\text{SST}(k - 1)}{\text{SSR}_\text{U}/\text{SST}(n - k)} = \frac{R^2/(k - 1)}{(1 - R^2/(n - k))} \quad \begin{array}{l} \text{has an } F \text{ distribution} \\ \text{with } [k - 1, n - k] \text{ d.f.} \end{array} \tag{9.24}$$

where R^2 is the coefficient of multiple determination obtained when estimating the unrestricted equation. Notice that the larger is R^2, the larger will be the value of the test statistic (9.24). Effectively, we reject the null hypothesis that the X variables do not influence Y if R^2 is sufficiently large.

To illustrate the use of this test statistic, refer again to the household consumption equation (9.6). We can test the null hypothesis $\beta_2 = \beta_3 = 0$ (neither income nor liquid assets influence consumption) by substituting the R^2 of 0.742 for this equation into (9.24) with $n = 25$ and $k = 3$. This gives a value for the test statistic of 31.6. With [2, 22] d.f., the critical F value is $F_{0.05} = 3.44$. We can therefore reject the null hypothesis at the 5% level of significance and conclude that at least one of the variables income and liquid assets influences consumption.

Exercise 9.6

The model $Y = \beta_1 + \beta_2 X_2 + \beta_3 X_3 + \beta_4 X_4 + \epsilon$ is to be estimated from 29 observations for which, when the variables are expressed in deviation form,

$$(\mathbf{x}'\mathbf{x})^{-1} = \begin{pmatrix} 0.5 & 0.2 & -0.5 \\ 0.2 & 0.6 & -0.8 \\ -0.5 & -0.8 & 1.25 \end{pmatrix}, \quad \begin{array}{l} \sum x_2 y = 22, \\ \sum x_3 y = 41, \quad \sum y^2 = 102 \\ \sum x_4 y = 36, \end{array}$$

(a) Compute the OLS estimates of β_2, β_3 and β_4, together with their estimated standard errors.
(b) Test the hypothesis that at least one of the variables X_2, X_3 and X_4 influences Y.

Comment on your results.

Adding or deleting explanatory variables

Frequently, in applied work econometricians find themselves considering whether to add or delete explanatory variables from estimating equations. When only one variable is involved, a decision can be made by simply considering its t ratio. When considering the addition or deletion of more than one X variable at a time, however, we may need to assess the combined influence of such variables. This will particularly be the case when the relevant variables have, maybe because of multi-collinearity, coefficients with non-significant t ratios.

Consider the two equations

$$Y = \beta_1 + \beta_2 X_2 + \ldots + \beta_k X_k + \epsilon \tag{9.25}$$

$$Y = \beta_1 + \beta_2 X_2 + \ldots + \beta_k X_k + \beta_{k+1} X_{k+1} + \ldots + \beta_q X_q + \epsilon \tag{9.26}$$

Thus (9.26) contains $q - k$ more variables than (9.25), and we are interested in the combined effect, if any, of these variables on Y. We may consider (9.25) as a restricted version of (9.26) where the $h = q - k$ restrictions imposed are

$$\beta_{k+1} = \beta_{k+2} = \ldots = \beta_q = 0 \tag{9.27}$$

We may therefore use the test statistic (9.19) to test the null hypothesis (9.27), which implies that none of the *extra* variables in (9.26) influences Y. Rejection of (9.27) implies that the combined influence of the extra variables is significant, that is, that at least one of them influences Y.

In this case the test statistic (9.19) can be written as

$$\frac{(SSR_R - SSR_U)/h}{SSR_U/(n - k)} = \frac{(SSE_U - SSE_R)/(q - k)}{SSR_U/(n - q)} \quad \begin{array}{l} \text{has an } F \text{ distribution} \\ \text{with } [q - k, n - q] \text{ d.f.} \end{array} \tag{9.28}$$

That is, it is based on the additional explanation of variations in Y, $SSE_U - SSE_R$, that is provided by the extra $q - k$ variables that appear in Equation (9.26). If this addition is sufficiently large, we reject the null hypothesis (9.27) that none of the extra variables influence Y. What is meant by 'sufficiently large' is decided by reference to the relevant critical F value.

Notice that, by dividing both numerator and denominator by SST, the test statistic (9.28) can also be written in the form

$$\frac{(SSE_U - SSE_R)/(q - k)}{SSR_U/(n - q)} = \frac{(R_U^2 - R_R^2)/(q - k)}{(1 - R_U^2)/(n - q)}$$

where R_U^2 and R_R^2 are the coefficients of determination obtained for the unrestricted and restricted equations respectively. That is, the test statistic can also be regarded as being based on the increase in the coefficient of determination R^2 that results from adding the extra variables to the estimating equation.

Exercise 9.7

The relationship $E(Y) = \beta_1 + \beta_2 X_2 + \beta_3 X_3 + \beta_4 X_4$ is estimated by OLS from 34 observations. When variables are measured in deviation form,

$$(\mathbf{x}'\mathbf{x})^{-1} = \begin{pmatrix} 1.2 & 0.3 & 0.1 \\ 0.3 & 0.6 & -0.2 \\ 0.1 & -0.2 & 0.8 \end{pmatrix}, \quad \begin{matrix} \sum x_2 y = -30, \\ \sum x_3 y = 30, \\ \sum x_4 y = 20, \end{matrix} \quad \sum y^2 = 1300$$

When Y is regressed on X_2 alone, the coefficient of determination $R^2 = 0.76$. Test the hypothesis that at least one of the variables X_3 and X_4 influences Y.

Exercise 9.8

The model of Exercise 9.7 was estimated from 40 observations for which, when variables are expressed in deviation form,

$$(\mathbf{x}'\mathbf{x})^{-1} = \begin{pmatrix} 0.8 & -0.2 & -0.2 \\ -0.2 & 1.1 & -0.5 \\ -0.2 & -0.5 & 0.7 \end{pmatrix}, \quad \mathbf{x}'\mathbf{y} = \begin{pmatrix} 25 \\ 15 \\ 20 \end{pmatrix}, \quad \sum y^2 = 525$$

(a) Test the hypotheses (i) that X_3 has no influence on Y; (ii) that X_4 has no influence on Y.
(b) Given that when Y is regressed on X_2 alone the OLS result

$$\hat{Y} = 8.33 + 11.2X_2$$

is obtained, test the hypothesis that the combined influence of X_3 and X_4 on Y is significant.

Comment on your results.

Exercise 9.9

The following equation was estimated by OLS from 56 observations for which $\sum y^2 = 243$:

$$\hat{Y} = 3.6 + 5.83X_2 + 2.74X_3 - 0.64X_4, \qquad R^2 = 0.937$$

If $\sum x_4^2 = 233$ and $\sum x_4 y = -217$, assess the combined influence of X_3 and X_4 when they are added to an equation including X_4 only. (Lower-case letters denote deviations of variables from their mean.)

Other tests for linear restrictions

The χ^2 test

The F statistic (9.19) is based on the fact that (9.16) and (9.18) both have χ^2 distributions. However, if the disturbance variance σ^2 were known, we could test linear restrictions like (9.10) or (9.12) by computing (9.18) alone. Like (9.19), (9.18) is based on the increase in the sum of squared residuals that results from imposing the restriction(s). We would again reject restrictions if this quantity were sufficiently large. This time, however, we would decide what is sufficiently large by reference to the χ^2 distribution. The restrictions would be rejected if (9.18) exceeded the relevant critical χ^2 value.

In practice, of course, σ^2 is not known. However, if we replace σ^2 in (9.18) by a consistent estimator then the statistic obtained will still have a χ^2 distribution in large samples. The MLE of σ^2, which under the null hypothesis that the restrictions are valid is $\tilde{\sigma}^2 = \text{SSR}_R/n$, is such a consistent estimate. Thus we can say that, in large samples,

$$\frac{\text{SSR}_R - \text{SSR}_U}{\text{SSR}_R/n} \text{ has a } \chi^2 \text{ distribution with } h \text{ d.f.} \qquad (9.29)$$

where, as usual, h is the number of restrictions. Restrictions may therefore be tested by comparing (9.29) with the relevant critical χ^2 value.

It is instructive to present the test statistic (9.29) in an alternative form. As an example, consider Equations (9.11) and (9.14), which is obtained from (9.11) by the imposition of the restrictions (9.12). Suppose the restricted equation (9.14) has been estimated and its residuals saved. We denote these residuals by e_R, so that $\text{SSR}_R = \sum e_R^2$. Suppose now that, instead of estimating the unrestricted equation (9.11), that is, regressing Y on X_2, X_3, X_4 and X_5, we regress e_R on these variables instead. That is, we compute the regression

$$\hat{e}_R = \hat{\delta}_1 + \hat{\delta}_2 X_2 + \hat{\delta}_3 X_3 + \hat{\delta}_4 X_4 + \hat{\delta}_5 X_5 \qquad (9.30)$$

The $\hat{\delta}$s in (9.30) are the OLS coefficients. Equation (9.30) is generally referred to as an **auxiliary regression**. The reason for computing it is that it can be shown that the *residuals from (9.30) are identical to the residuals we would have obtained had we estimated the unrestricted equation (9.11) instead.* It follows that the residual sum of squares for (9.30) is SSR_U. Moreover, since the dependent variable in (9.30) is e_R, the total sum of squares for this regression is SSR_R. This means that, in terms of statistics relating to (9.30), the test statistic (9.29) can be written as

$$\frac{SSR_R - SSR_U}{SSR_R/n} = \frac{SST - SSR}{SST/n} = nR^2 \tag{9.31}$$

where R^2 is the coefficient of determination for the auxiliary regression.

Summarizing, to carry out the large-sample χ^2 test for linear restrictions, we estimate an auxiliary equation such as (9.30) and compute nR^2 for this regression. We reject the restriction(s) if nR^2 exceeds the relevant critical χ^2 value.

As an illustration of the χ^2 test, consider again Equations (7.66) and (7.67). If the residuals from (7.67) are saved, we can test the restriction (9.10) that has been imposed on this equation. The auxiliary regression involves regressing the saved residuals on the three explanatory variables in (7.66). If this regression is computed, we should obtain $R^2 = 0.1686$. Since the sample size is $n = 25$, we have a value for the test statistic (9.29) of (using (9.31)) $nR^2 = 4.22$. Since we are testing just a single restriction, $h = 1$ and the critical χ^2 value is $\chi^2_{0.05} = 3.841$. Hence, on this occasion, at the 5% level of significance we have to reject the restriction.

Notice that the χ^2 test has given us a different result from the earlier F test of this restriction. On the F test, we (narrowly) failed to reject the restriction. This may seem a trifle inconsistent! However, it must be remembered from Chapter 3 that all statistical tests involve the possibility of error. By adopting a 5% level of significance, we have fixed the probability of type I error (that is, rejecting the restriction when it is valid) at 0.05. If, on the basis of the F test, we were to accept the restriction, we would not even know the probability of a type II error. One of the tests is clearly giving the wrong signal – but we cannot tell which. In fact, the two results are not all that different. On the F test, the restriction is close to being rejected, while, on the χ^2 test, rejection is only at the 5% level of significance. Since $\chi^2_{0.01} = 6.635$, we would be unable to reject the restriction at the 1% level of significance.

The *t* test

It is possible to test a linear restriction without actually estimating the restricted equation that incorporates it. Consider, for example, the OLS estimated equation

$$\hat{Y} = \hat{\beta}_1 + \hat{\beta}_2 X_2 + \hat{\beta}_3 X_3 \tag{9.32}$$

Suppose we wish to test the restriction that the true β_j parameters obey the restriction $\beta_2 + \beta_3 = 1$, without actually enforcing this restriction and re-estimating.

An obvious way of proceeding is to calculate the sum of the OLS estimates, $\hat{\beta}_2 + \hat{\beta}_3$, and compare this sum with 1. If the sum differs sufficiently from 1 then the restriction is rejected. However, to determine what is sufficiently different, we need to know the sampling distribution of $\hat{\beta}_2 + \hat{\beta}_3$.

Provided all the assumptions of the classical model are valid, we can say that

$$\hat{\beta}_2 + \hat{\beta}_3 \quad \text{is } N(\beta_2 + \beta_3, \ v^2) \tag{9.33}$$

where

$$v^2 = \text{Var} \ (\hat{\beta}_2 + \hat{\beta}_3) = \text{Var} \ (\hat{\beta}_2) + \text{Var} \ (\hat{\beta}_3) + 2 \ \text{Cov} \ (\hat{\beta}_2, \hat{\beta}_3) \tag{9.34}$$

It follows that

$$\frac{\hat{\beta}_2 + \hat{\beta}_3 - (\beta_2 + \beta_3)}{v} \quad \text{has an } N(0, 1) \text{ distribution} \tag{9.35}$$

Thus, under H_0: $\beta_2 + \beta_3 = 1$, we have

$$\frac{\hat{\beta}_2 + \hat{\beta}_3 - 1}{v} \quad \text{has an } N(0, 1) \text{ distribution} \tag{9.36}$$

Inference concerning $\beta_2 + \beta_3$ can be based on (9.36), provided we can estimate v^2. Notice that, as intuition suggested, (9.36) depends on the difference between $\hat{\beta}_2 + \hat{\beta}_3$ and unity.

To estimate v^2, we must estimate each part of (9.34). The variances of $\hat{\beta}_2$ and $\hat{\beta}_3$ are given as usual by (7.49a), and the covariance can be obtained using (7.50a). Thus

$$v^2 = \sigma^2(x^{22} + x^{33} + 2x^{23})$$

where x^{22}, x^{33} and x^{23} are elements of the matrix $(\mathbf{x'x})^{-1}$. σ^2 can be estimated by s^2, using (7.55) as usual. An unbiased estimator of v^2 is then given by

$$u^2 = s^2(x^{22} + x^{33} + 2x^{23}) \tag{9.37}$$

However, if we replace v in (9.36) by u then we have to switch to the Student's t distribution. Thus

$$\frac{\hat{\beta}_2 + \hat{\beta}_3 - 1}{u} \quad \text{has a Student's } t \text{ distribution with } n - k \text{ d.f.} \tag{9.38}$$

The restriction $\beta_2 + \beta_3 = 1$ is now rejected if the absolute value of the test statistic (9.38) exceeds the relevant critical t value.

Exercise 9.10

The following equation is estimated by OLS:

$$Y = \beta_1 + \beta_2 X_2 + \beta_3 X_3 + \beta_4 X_4 + \beta_5 X_5 + \epsilon$$

If no further equation is to be estimated, describe how you would test the following restrictions:

(a) $\beta_2 = \beta_3$; (b) $\beta_2 + \beta_5 = 0$; (c) $\beta_2 + \beta_3 + \beta_4 = 1$.

Exercise 9.11

Consider the estimated consumption function

$$\hat{Y} = 15 + 0.80X_2 + 0.50X_3$$

where Y = consumption, X_2 = income and X_3 = wealth. If $n = 20$, $\sum e^2 = 34$ and, when variables are measured in deviation form,

$$(\mathbf{x}'\mathbf{x})^{-1} = \begin{pmatrix} 0.02 & 0.005 \\ 0.005 & 0.03 \end{pmatrix}$$

test whether MPC income = MPC wealth.

★ 9.3 The testing of nonlinear restrictions

Consider the equation

$$Y = \beta_1 + \beta_2 X_2 + \beta_3 X_3 + \epsilon \tag{9.39}$$

Suppose we wished to estimate (9.39) subject not to a linear restriction but to the *nonlinear* restriction $\beta_2\beta_3 = 1$. In this case it is not possible to find a simple restricted equation such as (9.14) to estimate. If $\beta_2\beta_3 = 1$ then, substituting into (9.39), we obtain

$$Y = \beta_1 + \beta_2 X_2 + \frac{1}{\beta_2} X_3 + \epsilon \tag{9.40}$$

which cannot be estimated by normal OLS.[4]

·Estimation has to proceed by *minimizing the residual sum of squares* from an estimated version of (9.39) *subject to the constraint* that the estimates $\hat{\beta}_2$ and $\hat{\beta}_3$ obey the restriction $\hat{\beta}_2\hat{\beta}_3 = 1$. Such procedures are beyond the scope of this text, but powerful computer algorithms are available to perform such tasks, even for complicated restrictions. This method of estimation is known as **nonlinear least squares**.[5]

The problem with nonlinear least squares is that it does not normally yield estimators with the desired small-sample properties. However, minimizing the residual sum of squares subject to a restriction is equivalent to maximizing the likelihood function for the Y values subject to that restriction.[6] It follows that nonlinear least squares estimators are maximum likelihood estimators, and therefore do at least possess the large-sample properties of consistency and asymptotic efficiency. However, if we wish to test any nonlinear restriction imposed, we can no longer rely on any of the tests of the previous section, since these are dependent on standard OLS procedures.

For this reason, testing of nonlinear restrictions is generally based on maximum likelihood principles. There are three well-known tests: the **likelihood ratio** (LR) test, the **Wald** (W) **test** and the **Lagrange multiplier** (LM) **test**. Full consideration of these tests is beyond the scope of this text, but we shall look at each test briefly. For a more detailed introduction see Thomas (1993), Chapter 4. All three procedures result in test statistics that, in large samples, have a χ^2 distribution with h degrees of freedom, where h again refers to the number of restrictions being tested.

★ The likelihood ratio test

In the classical multiple regression model there are $k+1$ unknown parameters: the β_j $(j=1, 2, \ldots, k)$ and σ^2. ML estimation of these parameters involves maximizing a likelihood function that we can write as[7]

$$L = L(\beta_1, \beta_2, \beta_3, \ldots, \beta_k, \sigma^2, Y_1, Y_2, Y_3, \ldots, Y_n) \tag{9.41}$$

That is we choose the values for the parameters in (9.41) that maximize L, taking the sample Y values as known. Once we have obtained the MLEs, they can be substituted back into (9.41) to obtain what is known as the **maximized likelihood**. In fact, since MLEs and OLS estimators are identical in classical regression, many OLS computer packages actually print out the maximized likelihood (or its natural logarithm) as standard output for every regression computed. Notice for example that, for the regressions in Tables 7.3 and 7.4, values for the maximized log-likelihood are given on the bottom right-hand sides of the printouts.

Suppose, however that we wish to estimate the β_j parameters subject to one or more (nonlinear) restrictions of the kind $\beta_2\beta_3 = 1$. To obtain MLEs, we now have to maximize (9.41) subject to these restrictions. That is, we have a constrained maximization problem to solve. Software packages for solving such problems are nowadays readily available. Solving the above problem gives a set of **constrained MLEs** for the parameters in (9.41). These will almost certainly differ from the original **unconstrained MLEs** of the previous paragraph. These MLEs may also be substituted back into (9.41) to give the maximized likelihood for this second situation.

Intuitively, it should be clear that we will be able to obtain a higher value for the maximized likelihood when we place no limits on the set of β_j values we select than when we restrict ourselves to choosing only sets that obey the restrictions we are faced with. That is, the maximized likelihood for the unconstrained estimates, L_U, will be larger than the maximized likelihood for the constrained estimates, L_R. That is, $L_R/L_U < 1$. However, if the restrictions are valid then L_R should not be *much* less than L_U. That is, the **likelihood ratio** L_R/L_U should not be much less than unity. The idea is to reject the restrictions if the likelihood ratio is 'very much' less than unity.

Let $l_R = \ln(L_R)$ and $l_U = \ln(L_U)$. When L_R/L_U is less than unity, its logarithm $l_R - l_U$ will be negative. Thus we reject the restrictions if $l_R - l_U$ is sufficiently negative. In fact, if the restrictions are valid then it can be shown that, for large samples,

$$\text{LR} = -2(l_R - l_U) \text{ has a } \chi^2 \text{ distribution with } h \text{ d.f.} \tag{9.42}$$

where h, as usual, is the number of restrictions. We therefore reject the null hypothesis of valid restrictions if the test statistic (9.42) exceeds the relevant critical χ^2 value.

Although its greatest value is in the testing of nonlinear restrictions, there is of course no reason why the LR test should not be used to test linear restrictions. For example, we have already used the F test and one χ^2 test to test the restriction (9.10) that has been imposed on the demand equation (7.66) to yield (7.67). We may also use the LR χ^2 test. The maximized log-likelihood for the unrestricted equation (7.66) is $l_U = 66.85$ (see Table 7.3). That for the restricted equation (7.67) is $l_R = 64.54$ (see Table 7.4). The LR statistic (9.42) thus gives a value of

$$\text{LR} = -2(64.54 - 66.85) = 4.62$$

This exceeds a critical value (1 d.f.) of $\chi^2_{0.05} = 3.841$. Thus, on this test, like the earlier χ^2 test but unlike the F test, we reject the restriction at the 5% level of significance.

Exercise 9.12

The maximized likelihoods for Equations (I), (II) and (III) of Exercise 9.5 are 60.4, 51.5 and 50.3. Using the LR test, retest
(a) the restriction imposed on (I) to give (II);
(b) the restriction imposed on (II) to give (III);
(c) both restrictions together.

★ The Wald test

To understand the so-called **Wald test** it is helpful to refer back to the t test of the last section. We considered the testing of the restriction $\beta_2 + \beta_3 = 1$ on Equation (9.32). This test was based on the fact that, under classical assumptions, (9.36) holds. Suppose that, in estimating $v^2 = \text{Var}\,(\hat{\beta}_2 + \hat{\beta}_3)$, we estimate σ^2 not by s^2 but by its consistent MLE $\tilde{\sigma}^2 = \sum e_i^2/n$. That is, we estimate v^2 not by (9.37) but by

$$\tilde{v}^2 = \tilde{\sigma}^2(x^{22} + x^{33} + 2x^{23}) \tag{9.43}$$

Provided the sample size is large, we can replace v in (9.36) by $\tilde{v}$ and still say that

$$z = \frac{\hat{\beta}_2 + \hat{\beta}_3 - 1}{\tilde{v}} \quad \text{has an N(0, 1) distribution} \tag{9.44}$$

The square of a standard normal distribution is a χ^2 distribution with just one degree of freedom. It follows that

$$W = \left(\frac{\hat{\beta}_2 + \hat{\beta}_3 - 1}{\tilde{v}}\right)^2 \quad \text{has a } \chi^2 \text{ distribution with 1 d.f.} \tag{9.45}$$

It is therefore possible to test the restriction $\beta_2 + \beta_3 = 1$ by comparing (9.45) with the relevant critical χ^2 value. W in (9.45) is in fact the Wald test statistic for the restriction.[8]

The Wald test can also be used to test more than one restriction at a time. With h restrictions to test altogether, we can derive h test statistics $z_1, z_2, z_3, \ldots, z_h$ of the kind (9.44). Recall from Section 3.4 that the sum of the squares of h independent standard normal distributions has a χ^2 distribution with h degrees of freedom. Unfortunately, the zs in this case are not independent, so we cannot derive a χ^2 distribution so easily. However, although the derivation is beyond our scope, it is still possible to derive a more complicated function of the zs, W, that does have a χ^2 distribution.[9] That is,

$$W(z_1, z_2, \ldots, z_h) \text{ has a } \chi^2 \text{ distribution with } h \text{ d.f.} \tag{9.46}$$

The joint hypothesis that all h restrictions are valid is then rejected if the Wald statistic (9.46) exceeds the relevant critical χ^2 value.

The Wald test for a nonlinear restriction proceeds analogously to that for a linear restriction. Suppose, for example, we wished to test the restriction $\beta_2\beta_3 = 1$ on Equation (9.39). The idea behind a Wald test would be to estimate (9.39), compute $\hat{\beta}_2\hat{\beta}_3$ and compare its value with 1, using the sampling distribution for $\hat{\beta}_2\hat{\beta}_3$. In large samples

$$\hat{\beta}_2\hat{\beta}_3 \quad \text{has an } N(\beta_2\beta_3, \, v^2) \text{ distribution} \tag{9.47}$$

where v^2 now equals Var $(\hat{\beta}_2\hat{\beta}_3)$. Notice that (9.47) only holds for large samples, since, even though $E(\hat{\beta}_2) = \beta_2$ and $E(\hat{\beta}_3) = \beta_3$, it does not follow that $E(\hat{\beta}_2\hat{\beta}_3) = \beta_2\beta_3$ in small samples.

It follows that, under H_0: $\beta_2\beta_3 = 1$,

$$W = \left(\frac{\hat{\beta}_2\hat{\beta}_3 - 1}{v} \right)^2 \quad \text{has a } \chi^2 \text{ distribution with 1 d.f.} \tag{9.48}$$

in large samples. The problem in computing (9.48) lies in finding an expression for v^2. Since $\beta_2\beta_3$ is a nonlinear function, we cannot use the standard Theorem 2.4 to obtain an expression for its variance. A so-called Taylor approximation has to be used instead. However, if this is done and v^2 estimated then (9.48) is the Wald statistic for the nonlinear restriction $\beta_2\beta_3 = 1$. Wald statistics may also be formed for testing more than one nonlinear restriction at a time.

The details of the construction of Wald statistics are beyond our scope, but a number of regression packages will compute them as optional outputs. Their major advantage is that they *only require estimation of the unrestricted equation*. This is particularly useful when restrictions are nonlinear, since, as explained at the beginning of this section, estimation subject to restrictions is then more complicated.

★ The Lagrange multiplier test

In contrast to the Wald statistic, the **Lagrange multiplier** (LM) **test** *requires estimation of the restricted equation only.* It is therefore useful when the imposition of the restriction(s) simplifies the estimation process.[10] Recall that ML estimation of a restricted equation requires maximization of (9.41) subject to the relevant restrictions. Any such constrained optimisation problem involves the use of Lagrange multipliers – one for each restriction imposed. The values of these Lagrange multipliers measure the effect on the value of (9.41) (i.e. on the maximized likelihood) of relaxing the respective restrictions. But, if a restriction is valid, its imposition should, as we saw earlier, result in little change in the maximized likelihood. Thus the value of the Lagrange multiplier for a valid restriction should be small. The idea behind the LM test is therefore to reject restrictions if the values of the Lagrange multipliers associated with them are sufficiently large. The LM statistic itself is a somewhat complicated function of the Lagrange multipliers, and under the null hypothesis of valid restrictions can be shown to have a χ^2 distribution, again with degrees of freedom h equal to the number of restrictions imposed.

As with the LR and Wald tests, we cannot go into the details of the construction of LM statistics. Suffice it to say that when the restrictions being tested are linear, *the test can be shown to be exactly equivalent to the χ^2 test of the last section.* The LM statistic can therefore be computed as nR^2 obtained from an auxiliary regression. When restrictions are nonlinear, the auxiliary equation that has to be estimated is more complicated, but again the LM statistic can be computed as nR^2 from such a regression. We shall encounter examples of such LM statistics in the next chapter when we consider tests for autocorrelation and heteroskedasticity.

Although the LR, Wald and LM statistics all have χ^2 distributions with degrees of freedom equal to the number of restrictions being imposed, there is no reason why they should not take different values. In fact, it can be shown that in classical regression it is the case that

$$LM \leqslant LR \leqslant W$$

Thus only when the Wald test leads to a failure to reject restrictions or when an LM test does lead to a rejection will all the tests necessarily give the same result.

Choice between the tests is generally made on grounds of ease of computation. For this reason, the least popular is probably the LR test, because it requires estimation of *both* unrestricted and restricted equations. A choice between the Wald and LM tests often depends on which equation – unrestricted or restricted – is easier to estimate.

Exercise 9.13

The following equations were estimated by OLS from $n = 43$ observations:

$$Y = \beta_1 + \beta_2 X_2 + \beta_3 X_3 + \beta_4 X_4 + \beta_5 X_5 + \epsilon \tag{I}$$

$$Y - X_5 = \beta_1 + \beta_2(X_2 + X_3) + \beta_4(X_4 - X_5) + \epsilon \tag{II}$$

What restrictions have been imposed on the β parameters to give (II)?
The following information is available:

	Equation (I)	Equation (II)
Residual sum of squares	327	394
Maximized log-likelihood	−22.60	−26.32

When the residuals from the OLS estimation of (II) are regressed on the four X variables, the coefficient of determination is 0.17.

Test the restrictions imposed in (II) using (a) an F test; (b) an LR test; (c) an LM test.

9.4 Qualitative explanatory variables

Frequently in regression analysis we encounter factors that may well influence the dependent variable but which we are unable to quantify in any meaningful way. Let us suppose we were estimating a demand equation for alcoholic drink from quarterly data. We might specify an equation of the form

$$Q = \beta_1 + \beta_2 E + \beta_3 P + \epsilon \tag{9.49}$$

where Q is quantity demanded, E is the total real expenditure of consumers and P is the relative price of alcohol. Since we are using quarterly data, we suddenly realize that, for obvious reasons, expenditure on alcohol tends to be largest during the festive fourth quarter of each year. But how do we allow for a non-quantifiable factor such as this?

One way of allowing for qualitative factors is to **codify** them by assigning numerical values to different circumstances. In the above case we could define a **dummy variable** D, where D takes the value unity during the fourth quarter of each year but the value zero during all other quarters. Instead of estimating (9.49), we could then estimate

$$Q = \beta_1 + \alpha_1 D + \beta_2 E + \beta_3 P + \epsilon \tag{9.50}$$

The variable D is treated just like any other variable in the equation – it just happens to take the unusual values

$$0, 0, 0, 1, 0, 0, 0, 1, 0, 0, 0, 1, 0, \ldots$$

To interpret the parameter α_1 in (9.50), note that for the fourth quarter, when $D = 1$, the equation implies, assuming $E(\epsilon) = 0$,

$$E(Q) = (\beta_1 + \alpha_1) + \beta_2 E + \beta_3 P \tag{9.51}$$

However, during all other quarters, when $D = 0$, (9.50) implies

$$E(Q) = \beta_1 + \beta_2 E + \beta_3 P \tag{9.51a}$$

Thus α_1 measures the change in the intercept parameter that occurs in the fourth quarter. A positive value (as expected) measures, for given values of E and P, the

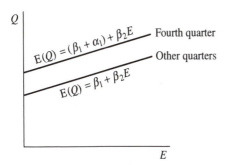

Figure 9.1 A parallel shift in the population regression line.

increase in mean alcohol expenditure that occurs during the fourth quarter. The situation is illustrated in Figure 9.1, where we have abstracted from the price variable. Equation (9.50) implies a parallel shift in the population regression equation during the fourth quarter.

Note that to estimate α_1, we need estimate Equation (9.50) only, using data for all quarters. We can test the hypothesis that $\alpha_1 = 0$ by examining its t ratio in the usual way.

Multiplicative dummies

Suppose, however, that it is not the intercept parameter that we suspect changes in the fourth quarter, but one of the other parameters in Equation (9.49). For example, we might wish to test whether β_2, the marginal propensity to consume alcohol, increases in the fourth quarter. Such a test is possible if we estimate

$$Q = \beta_1 + \beta_2 E + \alpha_2 (ED) + \beta_3 P + \epsilon \tag{9.52}$$

where D is defined as above. The variable ED is known as a **multiplicative dummy** and takes values equal to total expenditure E during the fourth quarter when $D = 1$, and values of zero in all other quarters, when $D = 0$.

During the fourth quarter, (9.52) implies

$$E(Q) = \beta_1 + (\beta_2 + \alpha_2) E + \beta_3 P \tag{9.53}$$

whereas in all other quarters it implies Equation (9.51a). Thus a different MPC exists for the fourth quarter if α_2 is non-zero. This situation is illustrated in Figure 9.2, where we have again abstracted from the price level. In this case it is the slope of the population regression equation that changes in the fourth quarter. To test for a non-zero α_2, we simply examine its t ratio when (9.52) is estimated.

A fourth-quarter change in the parameter β_3 can of course be allowed for in a similar manner. Also we could, if we wished, allow for fourth-quarter changes in both the intercept and β_2 at the same time by specifying

$$E(Q) = \beta_1 + \alpha_1 D + \beta_2 E + \alpha_2 (ED) + \beta_3 P \tag{9.54}$$

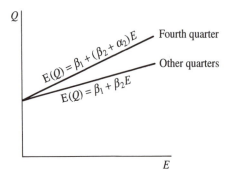

Figure 9.2 Changing the slope of the population regression line.

In principle, there is no reason why we should not allow for fourth-quarter changes in all the β_j parameters, but this is no different from estimating a separate equation using fourth-quarter data only.

Full seasonal effects

It may well be the case that we believe that the parameters in our equation are likely to vary between all quarters. For example, it may not be just the fourth quarter that is out of line with the others in our demand-for-alcohol equation. Such variations can be allowed for by defining additional dummy variables.

For example, suppose we wished to allow the intercept parameter in (9.49) to vary in all quarters. Let us define three dummy variables:

$D_2 = 1$ during second quarter, $D_2 = 0$ during other quarters

$D_3 = 1$ during third quarter, $D_3 = 0$ during other quarters

$D_4 = 1$ during fourth quarter, $D_4 = 0$ during other quarters

D_2, D_3 and D_4 are known as **seasonal dummies**. Notice that we have *not* defined a dummy D_1 for the first quarter.

Next, consider the equation

$$Q = \beta_1 + \delta_2 D_2 + \delta_3 D_3 + \delta_4 D_4 + \beta_2 E + \beta_3 P + \epsilon \qquad (9.55)$$

Given $E(\epsilon) = 0$ and the above dummy variables, (9.55) implies the demand equations

$$E(Q) = \beta_1 + \beta_2 E + \beta_3 P \qquad \text{for the first quarter}$$

$$E(Q) = (\beta_1 + \delta_2) + \beta_2 E + \beta_3 P \quad \text{for the second quarter}$$

$$E(Q) = (\beta_1 + \delta_3) + \beta_2 E + \beta_3 P \quad \text{for the third quarter}$$

$$E(Q) = (\beta_1 + \delta_4) + \beta_2 E + \beta_3 P \quad \text{for the fourth quarter}$$

Thus if we specify (9.55), we permit the intercept to vary from quarter to quarter. The significance of seasonal effects may be determined by estimating (9.55) and considering the t ratios on the δ coefficients.

As noted above, we did not define a first-quarter dummy of the type

$D_1 = 1$ during first quarter

$D_1 = 0$ during other quarters

First, it is obviously not necessary. We simply use the first-quarter intercept as the 'benchmark' from which we measure changes in the other quarters. Secondly, to include a full set of seasonal dummies would result in all estimating procedures breaking down. Since in all quarters just one dummy is unity and the others zero, it would be the case that for every observation,

$$D_1 + D_2 + D_3 + D_4 = 1$$

Thus an exact linear relationship would exist between the sample values of four of the explanatory variables in our equation. This is a case of the perfect multi-collinearity, discussed at the beginning of this chapter, under which estimation is not possible.

Seasonal variations may, of course, affect parameters other than the intercept. However, this may be allowed for by introducing multiplicative dummies for three of the four quarters.

Much time series economic data is quarterly. Often, published quarterly data will be 'seasonally adjusted'. That is, seasonal variations have been eliminated in some way or other before publication. On other occasions, such data will be 'unadjusted'. Clearly, the above seasonal dummies are for use with unadjusted data. Indeed, most econometricians prefer to work with unadjusted data and make use of seasonal dummies. This is because when seasonally adjusted data is presented, it is often unclear exactly what procedures have been followed to eliminate seasonal variations. Also, the removal of seasonal variations before estimation can lead to unpredictable distortions in any relationships between economic variables that we are seeking to uncover.

Other uses for dummy variables

Dummy variables can be used to represent qualitative factors other than seasonal effects. For example, in the UK, tobacco advertisements have been banned from television for some years. How might we allow for this when estimating a demand-for-tobacco equation? Presumably, such a ban can be expected to reduce demand. We may simply define an intercept dummy variable D, where $D=1$ for periods with TV advertising and $D=0$ for periods without such advertising. Insertion of such a dummy into an equation of the form (9.49) yields

$$Q = \beta_1 + \alpha D + \beta_2 E + \beta_3 P + \epsilon \tag{9.56}$$

where Q now represents the demand for tobacco products.

Equation (9.56) implies an intercept of β_1 when tobacco adverts are banned from TV but an intercept of $\beta_1 + \alpha$ when adverts are permitted. The effectiveness of the ban may then be assessed by examining the t ratio on α when (9.56) is estimated. Multiplicative dummies may be introduced to allow for the possible influence of advertising on the parameters β_2 and β_3.

It is not difficult to think of other 'either–or' situations that can be handled by the use of a dummy variable. For example, in a time series equation to determine the world price of oil, the existence or non-existence of OPEC might require the use of a dummy. In an agricultural output equation, abnormal weather conditions in certain years might have to be allowed for. Similarly, with a cross-sectional equation to explain variations in the earnings of employees, the sex of a worker would have to be handled by a dummy variable.

COMPUTER EXERCISE

In this exercise we shall make use of Data Set 4 on the floppy disk to illustrate the use of seasonal dummy variables. We have already made use of Data Set 4 in Section 8.6. Recall that it contains quarterly UK data for 1974Q1 through 1984Q4 on the variables

Y = real personal disposable income in £m at 1985 prices

C = real total consumers' expenditure in £m at 1985 prices

The basic equation we shall estimate is of the form

$$C_t = \beta_1 + \beta_2 Y_t + \beta_3 C_{t-1} + \epsilon_t \tag{9.57}$$

Notice that Equation (9.57) contains the lagged dependent variable C_{t-1} on the right-hand side. We shall consider in detail in Chapter 11 why lagged dependent variables should appear in regression equations. For now, however, we can simply regard C_{t-1} as reflecting the influence of habit on consumers' expenditure. That is, we argue that an important determinant of what consumers purchase in any one quarter is what they purchased in the previous quarter.

Your computer program will print out for you a plot of the variables C and Y against time. Such time paths are illustrated in Figure 9.3. It is clear that the consumption variable, in particular, exhibits a distinct seasonal pattern with pronounced peaks in the fourth quarter. It therefore appears that we should add seasonal dummies to our basic equation (9.57).

Your computer program will construct such dummies for you. Adding seasonal intercept dummies D_2, D_3, D_4, as defined earlier, to Equation (9.57) and estimating for the 40 quarters 1975Q1 through 1984Q4 should yield

$$\hat{C}_t = -1903 + 3067(D_2)_t + 3806(D_3)_t + 4845(D_4)_t + 0.306Y_t + 0.636C_{t-1}$$
$$\quad\;\; (-0.83) \quad (4.83) \qquad\;\; (6.48) \qquad\;\;\; (9.59) \qquad\;\;\; (2.95) \qquad (4.88)$$

$$\tag{9.58}$$

For Equation (9.58), $R^2 = 0.954$, and the residual sum of squares is 2.06×10^7. The signs of the coefficients of Y and C_{t-1} are as expected. As usual, numbers in

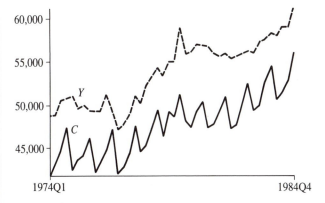

Figure 9.3 Time paths for income and consumption.

parentheses are t ratios, and it is clear that all three dummy variables have coefficients that are significantly different from zero. The intercept in our consumption equation therefore appears to vary seasonally from quarter to quarter. For example, since in the first quarter $D_2 = D_3 = D_4 = 0$, the implied consumption equation is

$$C_t = -1903 + 0.306Y_t + 0.636C_{t-1} \quad \text{(Q1)}$$

However, in the second quarter, $D_2 = 1$ and $D_3 = D_4 = 0$. Hence the implied equation for quarter two is

$$\hat{C}_t = 1164 + 0.306Y_t + 0.636C_{t-1} \quad \text{(Q2)}$$

Similarly, in the third and fourth quarters

$$\hat{C}_t = 1903 + 0.306Y_t + 0.636C_{t-1} \quad \text{(Q3)}$$

$$\hat{C}_t = 2942 + 0.306Y_t + 0.636C_{t-1} \quad \text{(Q4)}$$

Thus, for given values of income Y_t and lagged consumption C_{t-1}, consumption varies quite considerably from quarter to quarter. In fact, if we take the first quarter as a baseline then the coefficients in Equation (9.58) indicate that consumption is £3067m higher in the second quarter, £3806m higher in the third quarter and £4846m higher in the final quarter of the year. This is perhaps what one would expect, given the seasons in the UK and the fact that the fourth quarter contains the Christmas festivities.

The coefficient on the income variable in Equation (9.58) represents our estimate of the short-run *marginal propensity to consume* (MPC). A value of 0.306 for the short-run MPC may seem somewhat low, but it should be noted that this represents the *immediate* response of consumption to a change in income. The resultant rise in consumption will feed through into the next period via the lagged consumption variable in (9.58). Thus, even with no further rise in income, there will be even greater consumption in the next period.

The effect of an income rise can only be said to have been fully felt when consumption also eventually stops rising. Thus, to find the *long-run* effect of a rise in income, we have to set $C_t = C_{t-1}$ in Equation (9.58). In the first quarter, for example, this results in

$$(1 - 0.636)C_t = -1903 + 0.306Y_t$$

or

$$C_t = -5228 + 0.841Y_t \tag{9.59}$$

Long-run equations for the other quarters are similar to (9.59), but have positive intercepts. Equation (9.59) implies a long-run MPC of 0.841 – much higher than the short-run value.

9.5   Testing for parameter stability

There is no reason why the parameters of a regression equation should remain unchanged indefinitely. Yet such stability is an implicit assumption in much regression analysis. In addition, we cannot expect an estimated equation to predict or forecast satisfactorily if its parameters change over time. For this reason, we often wish to test parameters for stability.

Consider the equation

$$Y_t = \beta_1 + \beta_2 X_{2t} + \beta_3 X_{3t} + \epsilon_t \tag{9.60}$$

to be estimated from time series data. Suppose that, after the first n_1 observations or time periods of our sample, we believe that there may have been a change in at least one of the parameters β_1, β_2 and β_3. After this, there are no further changes in parameters for the remaining n_2 periods of the sample (the full sample size is $n = n_1 + n_2$).

We can test for a change in parameter values by defining the dummy variable

$$D = 0 \quad \text{for } t = 1, 2, 3, \ldots, n_1$$

$$D = 1 \quad \text{for } t = n_1 + 1, n_1 + 2, n_1 + 3, \ldots, n_1 + n_2$$

and estimating

$$Y = \beta_1 + \alpha_1 D + \beta_2 X_2 + \alpha_2(X_2 D) + \beta_3 X_3 + \alpha_3(X_3 D) + \epsilon \tag{9.61}$$

Notice that both intercept and multiplicative dummies are included in (9.61). What (9.61) implies is that during the first n_1 periods ($D = 0$), Equation (9.60) holds, whereas during the last n_2 periods ($D = 1$), we have instead

$$Y = \beta_1 + \alpha_1 + (\beta_2 + \alpha_2)X_2 + (\beta_3 + \alpha_3)X_3 + \epsilon \tag{9.62}$$

If all parameters remain unchanged throughout the sample period then this implies $\alpha_1 = \alpha_2 = \alpha_3 = 0$ in (9.61). But if this is the case then (9.61) reduces to (9.60).

Therefore a way of testing for parameter stability is to treat (9.60) as a restricted version of (9.61) and apply the test statistic (9.19) of Section 9.2. In this case the number of restrictions equals the number of parameters whose stability we are testing. Thus in the general case h in (9.19) equals k, and the degrees of freedom associated with the unrestricted equation (9.61) is $n_1 + n_2 - 2k$. Therefore (9.19) becomes

$$\frac{(\text{SSR}_R - \text{SSR}_U)/k}{\text{SSR}_U/(n_1 + n_2 - 2k)} \qquad \begin{array}{l} \text{has an } F \text{ distribution with} \\ (k, n_1 + n_2 - 2k) \text{ d.f.} \end{array} \tag{9.63}$$

For the example of (9.60) and (9.61), we have $k = 3$.

The test statistic (9.63) is often expressed in a rather different manner. The fact that we have included both intercept and multiplicative dummies in the unrestricted Equation (9.61) means that estimating this equation is, as we have seen, equivalent to estimating two separate equations: (9.60) for the first n_1 periods and (9.62) for the remaining n_2 periods. Suppose the residual sums of squares for these regressions are SSR_1 and SSR_2 respectively. It follows that

$$\text{SSR}_U = \text{SSR}_1 + \text{SSR}_2 \tag{9.64}$$

where SSR_U, remember, is the residual sum of squares when (9.61) is estimated for the whole sample instead.

When the restricted equation (9.60) is estimated for the whole sample, the result can be regarded as obtained from a pooled sample comprising both the first n_1 periods and the last n_2 periods. The residual sum of squares for this equation is therefore written as SSR_P. Thus

$$\text{SSR}_R = \text{SSR}_P \tag{9.65}$$

Using (9.64) and (9.65), we can now rewrite (9.63) as

$$\frac{[\text{SSR}_P - (\text{SSR}_1 + \text{SSR}_2)]/k}{[\text{SSR}_1 + \text{SSR}_2]/(n_1 + n_2 - 2k)} \qquad \begin{array}{l} \text{has an } F \text{ distribution with} \\ (k, n_1 + n_2 - 2k) \text{ d.f.} \end{array} \tag{9.66}$$

Summarizing, to compute the test statistic in the form (9.66), we first estimate separate regressions of the form (9.60) for the two sample subperiods, containing respectively n_1 and n_2 observations. This yields SSR_1 and SSR_2. Secondly, we estimate (9.60) for the single pooled sample and obtain SSR_P.

Notice that (9.66) is based on the proportionate increase in the sum of squared residuals that results from pooling the data. If this increase is large enough, we reject the null hypothesis of stable parameters. Whether the test statistic is large enough is decided, as usual, by comparison with the relevant critical F value. When computed in the form (9.66), the test is normally referred to as the **Chow test for parameter stability**. A numerical example of this test can be found in the computer exercise at the end of this chapter.

The Chow test for predictive failure

To carry out the above test for parameter stability, it is necessary that $n_2 > k$. That is, the second sample subperiod must be sufficiently large for it to be possible to compute the necessary regression to obtain SSR_2. If $n_2 < k$, the test cannot be performed. Alternative procedures are then necessary.

One way of proceeding would be to estimate (9.60) for the first n_1 observations and use it, in the manner of Section 6.3, to predict Y in the remaining n_2 observations.[11] This is possible because we have the values for X_2 and X_3 for the last n_2 observations. If the forecast errors are very large then the parameters in (9.60) cannot have remained unchanged.

The n_2 forecast errors can be obtained very quickly in the following way. We estimate Equation (9.60) for all $n_1 + n_2$ observations, but include n_2 'observation-specific' dummy variables. For example, a dummy variable D_1 is defined as

$$D_1 = 1 \text{ for observation } n_1 + 1 \text{ but } D_1 = 0 \text{ otherwise}$$

Similar dummies are defined for all the last n_2 observations.

The dummy variables ensure that the residuals for the last n_2 observations are all zero. That is, they ensure a perfect 'fit' for these observations. Moreover, it can be shown that *the coefficients on the dummy variables are identically equal to the forecast errors* that would be obtained if, instead, we had used (9.60) to predict Y for the last n_2 observations.[12] Clearly, if the dummy variables (and hence the forecast errors) are singly or jointly significant then this implies parameter instability.

We can test the joint significance of such dummy variables by applying the F test of Section 9.2. If (9.60) is estimated for the full $n_1 + n_2$ observations, first with and then without the dummy variables, we can regard the former regression as the unrestricted equation and the latter as the restricted equation in the test statistic (9.19). However, in this case we can express the test statistic in an alternative and instructive way.

Since when the dummies are included the last n_2 residuals all equal zero, the residual sum of squares for the unrestricted equation, SSR_U, is equal to the residual sum of squares SSR_1 that would be obtained if (9.60) were estimated for just the first n_1 observations. Moreover, the residual sum of squares for the restricted equation, SSR_R, is identical to what we termed in the last subsection SSR_P, the residual sum of squares obtained when (9.60) is estimated from the pooled sample of all $n_1 + n_2$ observations. Thus we can rewrite the test statistic (9.19) as

$$\frac{(\text{SSR}_R - \text{SSR}_U)/h}{\text{SSR}_U/(n - k_U)} = \frac{(\text{SSR}_P - \text{SSR}_1)/n_2}{\text{SSR}_1/(n_1 - k)} \quad \begin{array}{l} \text{has an } F \text{ distribution with} \\ [n_2, n_1 - k] \text{ d.f.} \end{array} \quad (9.67)$$

where $h = n_2$, because the number of restrictions being tested equals the number of observations in the period over which we forecast.

Notice that the test statistic (9.67) is based on the proportionate increase in the residual sum of squares that results from adding the extra n_2 observations to the regression. We reject a null hypothesis of parameter stability if the test statistic (9.67) exceeds the relevant critical F value. When written in the above form, the test is nowadays referred to as the **Chow test for predictive failure**.

The problem with this second Chow test is that it is based on predictions for the final n_2 observations that are made using an equation estimated for the first n_1 observations. The test statistic (9.67) really tests the null hypothesis that these predictions have a zero mean (that is, are unbiased). While stable parameters imply predictions with a zero mean, the reverse is not true. That is, it is still possible to have unbiased predictions even if the parameters are unstable. Thus, while a rejection of the null hypothesis of unbiased predictions implies unstable parameters, a failure to reject the null hypothesis does not mean the parameters are stable. A numerical example involving the second Chow test is provided in the computer exercise at the end of this chapter.

Recursive least squares

A feature of both Chow tests is that in each case we have to specify some way of dividing our data set into two subsamples. In some cases there may be some natural way to divide the data. For example, in a cross-sectional data set some of the observations might refer to males and the rest to females. The first Chow test is then a natural way to test whether regression parameters vary across the sexes. With a time series data set there may be some natural break, such as the imposition of some new economic regime, at which point we might expect a change in parameters to occur. Also, with time series data, new observations may eventually become available, and it is then natural to use the original observations for the first subsample and the new data for the second. However, often we may wish to test for parameter stability when there is no natural break in the data. Rather than select some entirely arbitrary observation in the data as the break point, many econometricians would nowadays employ a technique known as recursive least squares.

In **recursive least squares** the k parameters in a regression are first estimated for a small subsample of time series observations $t = 1, 2, 3, \ldots, m$, where $m > k$. The sample period is then extended to $t = 1, 2, 3, \ldots, m + 1$, and the equation re-estimated. The procedure is continued until estimation is over the complete data set $t = 1, 2, 3, \ldots, n$. A record of parameter estimates is kept, and the paths of these estimates over time are then plotted. Updating formulae exist that enable parameters to be re-estimated without each time inverting a fresh $\mathbf{X'X}$ matrix. For this reason, the estimates obtained are known as **recursive least squares estimates**.

A sudden break in the time pattern of recursive least squares estimates of a parameter may suggest a point at which the parameter value has changed. The significance of such a break may be tested by using a **recursive Chow test**. This is simply a version of the Chow test for predictive failure in which the original sample consists of the first m observations in the complete data set and the 'pooled sample' of the first $m + 1$ observations. This statistic can be calculated for each recursion, that is, for each successive value of m, and, if necessary, its values can be plotted against time.

Exercise 9.14

The following demand-for-money equation was estimated in logarithms from annual data for the periods 1919–57, 1919–39 and 1940–57:

$$M = \beta_1 + \beta_2 R + \beta_3 Y + \beta_4 L + \epsilon$$

where $R =$ interest rate, $Y =$ GDP and $L =$ liquid asset stock. Results were as follows $(m = M - \bar{M})$:

$$1919\text{–}57 : \quad \hat{M} = 0.003 - 0.261R + 0.530Y + 0.367L, \quad R^2 = 0.579, \sum m^2 = 0.190$$

$$1919\text{–}39 : \quad \hat{M} = 0.008 - 0.180R + 0.517Y + 0.281L, \quad R^2 = 0.697, \sum m^2 = 0.093$$

$$1940\text{–}57 : \quad \hat{M} = -0.013 - 0.419R + 0.936Y + 0.587L, R^2 = 0.479, \sum m^2 = 0.081$$

Test the hypothesis that the demand for money function has shifted between the two subperiods 1919–39 and 1940–57.

Exercise 9.15

The following demand-for-money function was estimated from 60 observations, for which $\sum (M - \bar{M})^2 = 45\,600$:

$$\hat{M} = 284 + 0.56Y - 0.43M_{-1}, \qquad R^2 = 0.841$$

When 8 further observations became available, the equation was re-estimated. The pooled data had $\sum (M - \bar{M})^2 = 50\,100$, and the re-estimated equation $R^2 = 0.818$. Carry out Chow's test for predictive failure. What do you conclude from your results?

Exercise 9.16

Application of OLS to 40 quarterly observations yielded the following consumption equation:

$$\hat{C} = 4.32 + 0.36Y + 0.53C_{-1}, \qquad \sum e^2 = 144.2$$

16 fresh quarterly observations became available. Application of OLS to the new observations only, gave

$$\hat{C} = 1.78 + 0.53Y + 0.37C_{-1} \qquad \sum e^2 = 65.9$$

When a single equation is estimated for the 56 pooled observations, the residual sum of squares for this regression is 286.8. Using a 0.01 level of significance, perform two tests for parameter stability in the consumption equation. If your two tests yield different results, explain how this can be so.

COMPUTER EXERCISE

We shall use Data Set 4 on the floppy disk to illustrate use of the Chow tests for parameter stability and predictive failure. We have already estimated the consumption equation (9.58) using this data set, but did the regression parameters remain stable throughout the sample period?

We shall (arbitrarily) split our sample into the two subperiods 1975Q1–1980Q4 and 1981Q1–1984Q4 for performing the first Chow test for parameter stability. You should find that re-estimating (9.58) for these subperiods yields residual sums of squares of $SSR_1 = 1.21 \times 10^7$ and $SSR_2 = 0.241 \times 10^7$ respectively. For the pooled data, the estimated equation (9.58) has a residual sum of squares $SSR_P = 2.06 \times 10^7$. Using the test statistic (9.66), we have $n_1 = 24$, $n_2 = 16$ and $k = 6$. The test statistic therefore takes a value

$$\frac{[2.06 - (1.21 + 0.24)]/6}{(1.21 + 0.24)/28} = 1.96$$

Since the critical value of F with $[k = 6, n_1 + n_2 - 2k = 28]$ d.f. is $F_{0.05} = 2.43$, we see that, for the above division of the sample, the equation passes the Chow test for parameter stability.

For the Chow test for predictive failure, we split the sample (again arbitrarily) into the subperiods 1975Q1–1982Q4 and 1983Q1–1984Q4. For the first subperiod, you should obtain, in this case, $SSR_1 = 1.55 \times 10^7$. For the full sample equation (9.58), we have again $SSR_P = 2.06 \times 10^7$. Using the test statistic (9.67) and this time $n_1 = 32$ and $n_2 = 8$, we obtain a value

$$\frac{(2.06 - 1.55)/8}{1.55/26} = 1.07$$

Thus since, with $[n_2 = 8, n_1 - k = 26]$ d.f., the critical F value is $F_{0.05} = 2.33$, we see that, at least for this division of the sample, Equation (9.58) passes the Chow test for predictive failure. However, as we noted above, passing this second Chow test cannot necessarily be interpreted as evidence in favour of parameter stability.

The above Chow tests have been based on entirely arbitrary subdivisions of the sample period. It is left to the reader to investigate alternative subdivisions of the sample.

A more thorough analysis of stability may be carried out using the recursive least squares procedure described earlier in this section. Recall that in this procedure Equation (9.58) has first to be estimated using a small subsample of observations from the start of our data period. OLS estimates are then recomputed for longer and longer subsamples until the whole sample period is included. The time paths of the recursive least squares estimates of the coefficients on the variables C_{t-1} and Y_t in Equation (9.58) are shown in Figures 9.4 and 9.5 respectively.

The recursive estimates, particularly that of the C_{t-1} coefficient, show some initial instability. However, this is the result of the small size of the subsamples used at the start of the recursions. Eventually, the estimates become much stabler, although there is a suggestion of a shift in parameter values after the end of 1982.

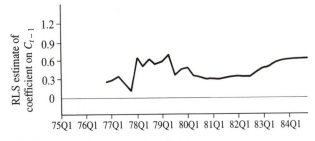

Figure 9.4 Recursive least squares estimates of coefficient on C_{t-1}.

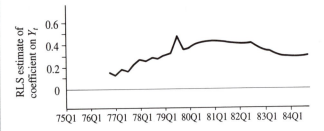

Figure 9.5 Recursive least squares estimates of coefficient on Y_t.

Recall, however, that we tested for just such a shift with the Chow predictive failure test carried out above. We failed to find any evidence of a significant change in parameter values.

Before leaving this data set for now, we should note again, as we did in Chapter 8, that both the basic series C and Y trend steadily upwards during our sample period. It is therefore virtually certain that they will fail to satisfy assumption IC of the classical model. As we have already noted, under such conditions the inferential procedures of classical regression can no longer be relied upon. We must therefore treat the results we have obtained with some caution.

Appendix 9A

Derivation of the expressions (9.7)

Recall the expression in (7.18) for the matrix $\mathbf{x'x}$. With just two explanatory variables,

$$(\mathbf{x'x})^{-1} = \begin{pmatrix} \sum x_2^2 & \sum x_2 x_3 \\ \sum x_2 x_3 & \sum x_3^2 \end{pmatrix}^{-1} = \frac{1}{D} \begin{pmatrix} \sum x_3^2 & -\sum x_2 x_3 \\ -\sum x_2 x_3 & \sum x_2^2 \end{pmatrix}$$

$$= \begin{pmatrix} x^{22} & x^{23} \\ x^{32} & x^{33} \end{pmatrix}$$

where $D = |\mathbf{x}'\mathbf{x}| = \sum x_2^2 \sum x_3^2 - (\sum x_2 x_3)^2$. Hence, using (7.49a),

$$\text{Var}(\hat{\beta}_2) = \sigma^2 x^{22} = \frac{\sigma^2 \sum x_3^2}{\sum x_2^2 \sum x_3^2 - (\sum x_2 x_3)^2} = \frac{\sigma^2}{\sum x_2^2 (1 - r^2)}$$

where r^2 is as defined in the text. Similarly,

$$\text{Var}(\hat{\beta}_3) = \frac{\sigma^2}{\sum x_3^2 (1 - r^2)}$$

Appendix 9B

Why SSR/σ^2 has a χ^2 distribution

$$\frac{\text{SSR}}{\sigma^2} = \frac{\sum e_i^2}{\sigma^2} = \sum \left(\frac{e_i - 0}{\sigma} \right)^2 \tag{9B.1}$$

Given the classical assumptions, each residual e_i is $N(0, \sigma^2)$. Thus

$$\frac{e_i - 0}{\sigma} \qquad \text{has an } N(0, 1) \text{ distribution for all } i$$

Hence (9B.1) is the sum of squares of standard normal variables. It therefore has a χ^2 distribution. The degrees of freedom are $n - k$, because in multiple regression the sum of squares $\sum e_i^2$ has $n - k$ degrees of freedom.

Appendix 9C

Notes to Chapter 9

1. Any system of linear equations that contains more variables than equations will have an infinite number of solutions. For example, in (9.4) if we select any arbitrary value for $\hat{\beta}_3$, say $\hat{\beta}_3 = k$, then we can solve for $\hat{\beta}_1$ and $\hat{\beta}_2$, obtaining

$$\hat{\beta}_1 = \hat{\mu}_1 - ak, \qquad \hat{\beta}_2 = \hat{\mu}_2 - bk$$

Since there are an infinite number of values we could choose for k, we can generate an infinite number of sets of values for $\hat{\beta}_1$, $\hat{\beta}_2$ and $\hat{\beta}_3$, all of which are solutions to the system (9.4).

2. The reader unfamiliar with the process of inverting a matrix should consult Appendix I at the end of the text.

3. If σ^2 is low then its unbiased estimate s^2 will be low. This can only be the case if the residual sum of squares is small. The smaller the residual sum of squares, the better is the fit of the equation.

4. If (9.40) is estimated simply by regressioning Y on X_2 and X_3, we will obtain

$$\hat{Y} = \hat{\beta}_1 + \hat{\beta}_2 X_2 + \hat{\beta}_3 X_3$$

where $\hat{\beta}_2$ and $\hat{\beta}_3$ are known coefficients. However, comparison with (9.40) yields *two* estimates of true β_2: $\hat{\beta}_2$ and $1/\hat{\beta}_3$. There is no reason why these estimates should turn out to be identical.

5. As with the nonlinear least squares estimators of Appendix 7C, the problem is that estimation involves the solving of nonlinear equations, which may have no algebraic solution. Purely numerical methods then have to be used.

6. The situation is as in Appendix 7C, except that maximization/minimization is now carried out subject to the restriction.

7. The precise form of the log-likelihood function is given by (7C.3).

8. The Wald statistic is a measure of the extent to which the unrestricted estimates fail to satisfy the restriction. If this measure is sufficiently large then the restriction must be invalid.

9. The function in fact has the form $W = z'C^{-1}z$, where z is a column vector of the individual z_i and C is the variance–covariance matrix of the z_i. W in this case is an overall measure of the extent to which the unrestricted estimates fail to satisfy the various restrictions being tested.

10. Suppose, for example, the unrestricted equation were

$$Y = \beta_1 + \beta_2 \left(\frac{1}{X + \beta_3} \right)$$

and the restriction to be tested $\beta_3 = 0$. Enforcing the restriction leads to a restricted equation that is much easier to estimate.

11. The required predictions are simply given by

$$\hat{Y}_i = \hat{\beta}_1 + \hat{\beta}_2 X_{2i} + \hat{\beta}_3 X_{3i}, \qquad i = n_1 + 1, \ n_1 + 2, \dots, \ n_2$$

where the $\hat{\beta}_j$ are the OLS estimates from the first n_1 observations.

12. In multiple regression, a matrix equivalent to Equation (6.42) for the variance of a forecast error can be derived. However, in practice, it is simpler merely to examine the estimated variances of the coefficients on the observation-specific dummy variables.

Further reading

Multicollinearity is well covered in Judge et al. (1988), Chapter 21, which includes a section on ridge regressions. The first part of Greene (1993), Chapter 9, also deals with multicollinearity, and includes material on principal components. See also Johnston (1984), Section 6.5.

Linear restrictions and their testing is covered in Greene, Section 7.2, and in Johnston, Section 6.1. Stewart (1991) provides an excellent coverage of the testing of nonlinear restrictions, while Greene, Chapter 11, deals with nonlinear regression models in general, as does Judge et al., Chapter 12.

A more detailed treatment of dummy variables and varying parameter models is provided by Judge et al., Chapter 10. See also Greene, Sections 8.2 and 8.3, for a more general approach.

Tests for structural changes in parameter values are well covered in Johnston, Chapter 6.2. Charemza and Deadman (1992), Section 3.6, discuss recursive least squares and also the use of recursive residuals. Greene, Section 7.5, also provides material on recursive residuals.

10 Non-spherical disturbances

Assumptions IIB and IIC of the classical multiple regression model state that the disturbances in the population relationship (7.3) are such that

$$\text{Var}\,(\epsilon_i) = \text{E}(\epsilon_i^2) = \sigma^2 = \text{constant} \quad \text{for all } i$$
$$\text{Cov}\,(\epsilon_i,\ \epsilon_j) = \text{E}(\epsilon_i \epsilon_j) = 0 \quad \text{for all } i \neq j$$

That is, first, the disturbances are **homoskedastic** (i.e. have constant variance) and, secondly, are non-autocorrelated (i.e. have zero covariances). In matrix terms, this implies that (7.39), the variance–covariance matrix of the disturbances, takes the form

$$\text{E}(\boldsymbol{\epsilon}\boldsymbol{\epsilon}') = \begin{pmatrix} \sigma^2 & 0 & 0 & \cdots & 0 \\ 0 & \sigma^2 & 0 & \cdots & 0 \\ 0 & 0 & \sigma^2 & \cdots & 0 \\ \vdots & \vdots & \vdots & & \vdots \\ 0 & 0 & 0 & \cdots & \sigma^2 \end{pmatrix} = \sigma^2 \mathbf{I}_n \tag{10.1}$$

When disturbances have the above properties, they are said to be **spherical**. If the variance–covariance matrix takes any other form, then we have what are known as **non-spherical disturbances**.

276

10.1   The general case

Let us suppose that, instead of taking form (10.1), the variance–covariance matrix is

$$E(\boldsymbol{\epsilon\epsilon'}) = V \tag{10.2}$$

where V is some $n \times n$ matrix that is *not* equal to that in (10.1).

Breakdowns in either assumption IIB or IIC could result in non-spherical disturbances. For example, suppose that, while the 'off-diagonal' terms in the matrix of (10.1) remain zero, the disturbance variances are not constant but are given by

$$\text{Var}\,(\epsilon_i) = E(\epsilon_i)^2 = \sigma_i^2 \quad \text{for all } i \tag{10.3}$$

Thus assumption IIB is no longer valid. The variance–covariance matrix (7.39) would now take the form (10.2), with the matrix V given by

$$
V = \begin{pmatrix}
\sigma_1^2 & 0 & 0 & \cdots & 0 \\
0 & \sigma_2^2 & 0 & \cdots & 0 \\
0 & 0 & \sigma_3^2 & \cdots & 0 \\
\vdots & \vdots & \vdots & & \vdots \\
0 & 0 & 0 & \cdots & \sigma_n^2
\end{pmatrix} \tag{10.4}
$$

When the disturbance variances are non-constant, as in (10.3), the disturbances are said to be **heteroskedastic**. We shall indicate the type of situations in which such disturbances might arise in the next section.

Non-spherical disturbances will also arise if classical assumption IIC breaks down. Suppose that disturbances are homoskedastic (that is, $E(\epsilon_i)^2 = \sigma^2 = \text{constant}$), but the covariances between different disturbances are no longer zero, and are given by

$$\text{Cov}\,(\epsilon_i,\ \epsilon_j) = \sigma_{ij} \quad \text{for all } i \neq j \tag{10.5}$$

This means that the off-diagonal terms in the matrices (7.39) and (10.1) are no longer zero, so that the variance–covariance matrix of the disturbances is again given by (10.2), but with V now given by

$$
V = \begin{pmatrix}
\sigma^2 & \sigma_{12} & \sigma_{13} & \cdots & \sigma_{1n} \\
\sigma_{21} & \sigma^2 & \sigma_{23} & \cdots & \sigma_{2n} \\
\sigma_{31} & \sigma_{32} & \sigma^2 & \cdots & \sigma_{3n} \\
\vdots & \vdots & \vdots & & \vdots \\
\sigma_{n1} & \sigma_{n2} & \sigma_{n3} & \cdots & \sigma^2
\end{pmatrix} \tag{10.6}
$$

When the disturbance covariances are non-zero as in (10.5), the disturbances are said to be **autocorrelated**. We shall examine the conditions under which autocorrelated disturbances might arise in Section 10.4.

We have seen that either heteroskedasticity or autocorrelation implies non-spherical disturbances, but what are the consequences of such disturbances for the standard OLS estimating procedure?

First, it is not difficult to see that the OLS estimators, given by the vector $\hat{\beta} = (X'X)^{-1}X'Y$, remain linear, unbiased and consistent. The reader should refer back to Section 7.3 and verify that to demonstrate these properties, we did not require the validity of classical assumptions IIB and IIC. The form of the variance–covariance matrix of the disturbances is therefore not relevant as far as these properties are concerned.

Unfortunately, although the OLS estimators themselves remain unbiased when disturbances are non-spherical, *this is not true of the OLS expressions used for estimating the variances and standard errors of these estimators*. The reader should again refer back to Section 7.3, recall what is meant by the variance–covariance matrix (7.46) of the OLS $\hat{\beta}$ vector and revise the derivation of Equation (7.48). This equation states that the variance–covariance matrix of $\hat{\beta}$ is given by

$$\textbf{Var}\,(\hat{\beta}) = \sigma^2(X'X)^{-1} \tag{10.7}$$

Recall that the diagonal elements of (10.7) give the variances of the OLS estimators, the $\hat{\beta}_j$. We then obtain estimates of these variances by replacing σ^2 in (10.7) by its estimate s^2, given by (7.55).

The reader will realize that the derivation of (10.7) involves the use of (10.1) and hence the assumption of spherical disturbances. We now derive an expression for **Var** $(\hat{\beta})$ when disturbances are non-spherical, that is, when either assumption IIB or IIC breaks down.

In Chapter 7 we began with Equation (7.43), which implies

$$\hat{\beta} - \beta = (X'X)^{-1}X'\epsilon$$

It followed that

$$\textbf{Var}\,(\hat{\beta}) = E(\hat{\beta} - \beta)(\hat{\beta} - \beta)' = E[(X'X)^{-1}X'\epsilon][\epsilon'X(X'X)^{-1}]$$
$$= (X'X)^{-1}X'E(\epsilon\epsilon')X(X'X)^{-1} \tag{10.8}$$

In Chapter 7 we substituted (10.1) into (10.8), and eventually obtained (10.7) as the expression for the variance–covariance matrix. However, with non-spherical disturbances, we must substitute not (10.1) but (10.2) into (10.8). This gives

$$\textbf{Var}\,(\hat{\beta}) = (X'X)^{-1}X'VX(X'X)^{-1} \tag{10.9}$$

where V is again the variance–covariance matrix of the disturbances, whatever form that happens to take. Thus (10.9) not (10.7) is the correct expression for the variance–covariance matrix of the OLS estimators when disturbances are non-spherical. For example, it is the diagonal elements of this matrix that give the variances of the OLS estimators, not the diagonal elements of (10.7).

Clearly, if the disturbances are non-spherical, whether this be because of heteroskedasticity or autocorrelation, then, if we use (10.7) as the basis for estimating the variances of the $\hat{\beta}_j$, our estimates will be incorrect. Thus *the normal OLS formula (10.7) gives biased estimates of the variances of the OLS estimators*.

This is the most serious consequence of non-spherical disturbances for the OLS estimating procedure. The consequences are serious, because we use the estimated variances and standard errors obtained from (10.7) to form confidence intervals and test hypotheses. If our estimated standard errors are biased then we can no longer rely on our usual inferential procedures. *These become invalid, and can give misleading results*.

As we have seen, the OLS estimators themselves remain linear and unbiased in the presence of non-spherical disturbances. However, they are no longer best linear unbiased. That is they no longer have the minimum variance of all linear unbiased estimators. With non-spherical disturbances, the BLUE of the parameter vector β can in fact be shown to be

$$\beta^* = (\mathbf{X}'\mathbf{V}^{-1}\mathbf{X})^{-1}\mathbf{X}'\mathbf{V}^{-1}\mathbf{Y} \tag{10.10}$$

where $\mathbf{V}$ is again the matrix in (10.2).

We shall not attempt to derive (10.10) for the general case, but in the following sections we will derive its equivalent for certain special cases. Equation (10.10) is usually referred to as the **generalized least squares** (GLS) **estimator** of β, to distinguish it from $\hat{\beta}$, the OLS estimator.

In practice, the problem with the GLS estimator (10.10) is that its use requires knowledge of the variance–covariance matrix $\mathbf{V}$. This is normally unknown, and has to be estimated from the sample data. If $\mathbf{V}$ in (10.10) is replaced by an estimated matrix $\hat{\mathbf{V}}$, the resultant estimators are referred to as **feasible least squares** (FLS) **estimators**.

We may summarize the consequences for OLS estimation of non-spherical disturbances as follows:

(1) The OLS estimators remain linear, unbiased and consistent.

(2) The normal formulae for the variances of the OLS estimators are no longer unbiased. It follows that the usual OLS inferential procedures become invalid.

(3) Although the OLS estimators remain linear and unbiased, they are no longer BLUEs. Thus they are no longer efficient estimators. Since this lack of efficiency exists regardless of the sample size, it follows that, although still consistent, they are no longer asymptotically efficient.

The reader should note that (2) and (3) above are *separate* consequences. Consequence (3) does *not* follow from consequence (2), as students often seem to believe. It has to be demonstrated separately.

10.2 Heteroskedasticity

As noted above, heteroskedasticity implies that assumption IIB of the classical model is replaced by Equation (10.3). That is, the disturbance variance is no longer a

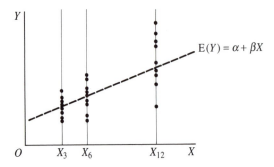

Figure 10.1 Heteroskedastic disturbances.

constant. To understand precisely what this means, it is useful to revert to the simple two-variable regression model for a moment. Consider Figure 10.1, which is akin to Figure 6.1. In Figure 10.1 we have drawn the population regression line. Recall that, for example, X_6 is the 6th observation on the single explanatory variable, and is assumed to be fixed in repeated samples. Points on the line through X_6 refer to different samples that, although having identical X_6 values, have different Y_6 values. The vertical distances of these points from the line represent the ϵ_6s, the disturbance values associated with the 6th observation. These vary from sample to sample. The variance of ϵ_6 measures the dispersion of points on the X_6 line about the population regression line. Similarly, for example, Var (ϵ_{12}) measures the dispersion about the population regression line of points on the line through X_{12}.

In Figure 6.1 the dispersion of points about the population regression line was the same, regardless of the X value concerned. This reflected the fact that Figure 6.1 represented a situation where Var (ϵ_i) was a constant for all observations. Heteroskedasticity implies that the variances of the ϵ_i, and hence the dispersions of points about the population line, varies from X value to X value. For example, in Figure 10.1 the variances and hence the dispersions become larger as the value of X increases.

Heteroskedasticity tends to occur when there is a large variation in the size of the sample X values. For example, suppose we take the population regression line in Figure 10.1 to refer to a simple cross-sectional consumption function for households, as we did in Chapters 4 and 6. X_i and Y_i then refer to the income and consumption respectively of household i. If, as is quite likely, there is a large variation in the incomes of households in our sample then X_3 in Figure 10.1 can be regarded as referring to a 'very-low-income' household, whereas X_{12} refers to a 'very-high-income" household. The low-income household has little scope for consuming much more or much less than its expected consumption level as given by the population regression line. It cannot consume much less without falling below subsistence level. It cannot consume much more, because it does not have the resources to spend any more than its current income. The disturbances for such a household are therefore always likely to be fairly close to zero, and this is reflected by the small dispersion in the points on the line through X_3 in Figure 10.1. That is, Var (ϵ_3) is 'small'.

The high-income household with income X_{12}, however, is subject to no such constraints. It is likely to have the resources to consume well above its current income if it wishes, and has no concerns about falling below subsistence levels. This is reflected in the much wider dispersion shown in Figure 10.1 for the points on the line through X_{12}. That is, Var (ϵ_{12}) is considerably larger than Var (ϵ_3).

Such large variations in the size of an explanatory variable are usually held to be most likely in cross-sectional data. In time series data sets each observation refers to an interval of the same length, whether this be a month, a quarter or a year. There is therefore less variability in the magnitude of variables, and so less likelihood of heteroskedasticity arising. However, if a data set spans a very long time period, so that the sizes of variables differ markedly, then heteroskedasticity may still occur. It is also the case that, over long time periods, the accuracy with which economic variables are measured may improve considerably, and this too can lead to heteroskedasticity.

Although it is natural to think of heteroskedasticity taking the form where Var (ϵ_i) rises as X_i rises, this need not always be the case. For example, published cross-sectional data often refer to grouped means. Typically, households in a cross-section might be classified according to their income levels, and the only information available on relevant variables might refer to their mean values for various classes. Suppose, for example, we believed that for individual households, the following cross-sectional relationship held between the demand for alcoholic drink, Q, and the level of disposable income, D:

$$Q_i = \alpha + \beta D_i + \epsilon_i \quad \text{for all } i \tag{10.11}$$

where Var $(\epsilon_i) = \sigma^2 = $ constant. The ϵ_i are therefore homoskedastic, and let us assume that they also obey the other classical assumptions.

The problem is that we cannot estimate (10.11), because we do not have data on individual households, but only on the mean values of alcohol demand and disposable income for each class.

For a class containing m households, the relationship between the class means can be obtained by summing (10.11) over all households and then dividing by m. This gives

$$\bar{Q} = \alpha + \beta \bar{D} + \epsilon \tag{10.12}$$

where $\bar{Q}$ and $\bar{D}$ are the mean values of demand and income for the class and

$$\epsilon = \frac{\sum \epsilon_i}{m} = \frac{1}{m}\epsilon_1 + \frac{1}{m}\epsilon_2 + \frac{1}{m}\epsilon_3 + \cdots + \frac{1}{m}\epsilon_m \tag{10.13}$$

If we attempt to estimate (10.12), using the class means as the basic data, we have a problem because, as we now show, the variance of ϵ depends on the class size.

Using Theorem 2.4 and assuming the ϵ_i can be treated as independent, we have from (10.13)

$$\text{Var}(\epsilon) = \frac{1}{m^2}\text{Var}(\epsilon_1) + \frac{1}{m^2}\text{Var}(\epsilon_2) + \frac{1}{m^2}\text{Var}(\epsilon_3) + \cdots + \frac{1}{m^2}\text{Var}(\epsilon_m)$$

$$= \frac{1}{m^2}m\sigma^2 = \frac{\sigma^2}{m} \tag{10.14}$$

Thus the larger the number in the class, the smaller is Var (ϵ). Equation (10.14) therefore implies that if the number in the class varies from class to class, and we attempt to estimate (10.12) using data on class means, then the disturbances in our equation will be heteroskedastic.

In typical distributions of income, most households will have incomes belonging to the classes in the middle of the range. This means that, in this situation, Var (ϵ) will not generally increase as the value of the explanatory variable increases, but will take its highest values at the lowest and highest income values.

Consequences of heteroskedasticity

We have already seen that, given any form of non-spherical disturbances, including heteroskedastic disturbances, the OLS estimators remain linear, unbiased and consistent. However, we also saw that in these circumstances the OLS estimators were no longer BLUEs; that is, they were no longer the most efficient linear unbiased estimators. We will now show, intuitively, why in the case of heteroskedasticity this should be so.

For simplicity, consider again the case of two-variable regression, and suppose that heteroskedasticity takes the form where Var (ϵ_i) increases as the value of the single explanatory variable X rises. In Figure 10.2 a **sample regression line** is shown fitted to a scatter of points. Recall that sample residuals are the *known* vertical distances of points in a scatter from such a sample regression line. With the assumed form of heteroskedasticity, the dispersion of the *unknown* disturbances increases as the size of X increases. Treating the known residuals as estimates of the unknown disturbances, we have therefore made the dispersion of points about the regression line increase as X increases in Figure 10.2.

Recall that OLS minimizes $\sum e_i^2$, the sum of the squared residuals. In this process, each squared residual is given equal weight in deciding the values of the OLS estimators. That is, each e_i is regarded as providing equally valid information about where the unknown population regression line lies. However, with a scatter such as

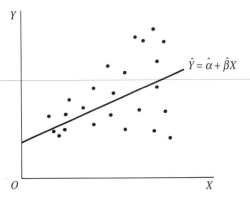

Figure 10.2 Scatter suggesting heteroskedastic disturbances.

that in Figure 10.2, this is not an especially sensible procedure. Points far from the sample line (i.e. 'large' residuals) give less useful information about the location of the population line than do points near the sample line. Moreover, the squared values of 'large' residuals are likely to dominate the sum of squared residuals. A more sensible procedure would be to give most weight to 'small' residuals when deciding on the location of the true population regression line. For this reason, the OLS method, which assigns equal weight to all residuals, does not provide the most efficient linear unbiased estimators when disturbances are heteroskedastic.

We also saw in the last section that, when disturbances are non-spherical, the normal formulae for estimating the variances of the OLS estimators become biased, thus invalidating the standard OLS inferential procedures. It is instructive to examine why this should be so in the case of heteroskedasticity. We consider again the two-variable case and concentrate on the variance of $\hat{\beta}$, the estimator of the slope parameter.

We have, using (6.7),

$$\hat{\beta} - \beta = \sum w_i \epsilon_i, \quad \text{where} \quad w_i = x_i / \sum x_i^2 \tag{10.15}$$

The variance of $\hat{\beta}$ is

$$\begin{aligned}
\text{Var}(\hat{\beta}) &= E[\hat{\beta} - E(\hat{\beta})]^2 \\
&= E[(\hat{\beta} - \beta)^2] \quad \text{(since } \hat{\beta} \text{ is unbiased)} \\
&= E[(\sum w_i \epsilon_i)^2] \quad \text{(using (10.15))} \\
&= E[(w_1 \epsilon_1 + w_2 \epsilon_2 + \cdots + w_n \epsilon_n)^2] \\
&= E[w_1^2 \epsilon_1^2 + w_2^2 \epsilon_2^2 + \cdots + w_n^2 \epsilon_n^2 + w_1 w_2 \epsilon_1 \epsilon_2 + w_1 w_3 \epsilon_1 \epsilon_3 + \cdots] \\
&= w_1^2 E(\epsilon_1^2) + w_2^2 E(\epsilon_2^2) + \cdots + w_n^2 E(\epsilon_n^2) \\
&\quad + w_1 w_2 E(\epsilon_1 \epsilon_2) + w_1 w_3 E(\epsilon_1 \epsilon_3) + \cdots]
\end{aligned} \tag{10.16}$$

If the disturbances are non-autocorrelated then, by classical assumption IIC, $\text{Cov}(\epsilon_i, \epsilon_j) = E(\epsilon_i \epsilon_j) = 0$ for all $i \neq j$, so that all the 'cross-product' terms in (10.16) are zero. Equation (10.16) therefore becomes

$$\text{Var}(\hat{\beta}) = w_1^2 E(\epsilon_1^2) + w_2^2 E(\epsilon_2^2) + \cdots + w_n^2 E(\epsilon_n^2) \tag{10.17}$$

With homoskedastic disturbances, $\text{Var}(\epsilon_i) = E(\epsilon_i^2) = \sigma^2$ for all i, so that (10.17) becomes

$$\begin{aligned}
\text{Var}(\hat{\beta}) &= w_1^2 \sigma^2 + w_2^2 \sigma^2 + \cdots + w_n^2 \sigma^2 \\
&= \sigma^2 \sum w_i^2 \\
&= \sigma^2 \sum \left(\frac{x_i}{\sum x_i^2} \right)^2 = \frac{\sigma^2}{\sum x_i^2}
\end{aligned} \tag{10.18}$$

Equation (10.18) is, of course, the standard OLS formula for $\text{Var}(\hat{\beta})$. If, however, disturbances are heteroskedastic, so that their variances are given by

Equation (10.3), that is, $E(\epsilon_1^2) = \sigma_i^2$, then substituting into (10.17), the variance of $\hat{\beta}$ becomes

$$\text{Var}(\hat{\beta}) = w_1^2\sigma_1^2 + w_2^2\sigma_2^2 + \cdots + w_n^2\sigma_n^2$$
$$= \sum w_i^2\sigma_i^2$$
$$= \sum \left(\frac{x_i}{\sum x_i^2}\right)^2 \sigma_i^2 = \frac{\sum x_i^2\sigma_i^2}{(\sum x_i^2)^2} \tag{10.19}$$

The expression (10.19) for Var $(\hat{\beta})$ when disturbances are heteroskedastic is clearly different from the standard formula (10.18). Formula (10.19) is, in fact, the version of the general-case expression (10.9) that is valid for the special case of two-variable regression with heteroskedastic disturbances.

In the present case it is possible to say something about the bias that occurs when heteroskedasticity is present and we use (10.18) instead of the correct (10.19) to estimate the variance of $\hat{\beta}$. In fact, it can be shown (see e.g. Kmenta, 1986, page 278) that if σ_i^2 and x_i^2 are positively correlated then the standard formula (10.18) will tend to underestimate the true variance and standard error of $\hat{\beta}$. In such circumstances confidence intervals for β will be misleadingly narrow, suggesting more precision in our estimates than is justified. Also, since t ratios will be artificially high, there will be a greater probability of the explanatory X variable appearing 'significant' when, in fact, it has no influence on Y.

Since $x_i = X_i - \bar{X}$, a positive correlation between σ_i^2 and x_i^2 will occur when the disturbance variance is highest for values of X_i that are furthest away from the central value $\bar{X}$. In the last subsection, we encountered one situation where this was likely to occur – that where the basic data used in a regression referred to class means. When dealing with such data, then, the apparent statistical importance of explanatory variables must be viewed with caution.

A final consequence of heteroskedastic disturbances is that the OLS estimators are no longer maximum likelihood estimators. If Var $(\epsilon_i) = \sigma_i^2$ for all i, rather than a constant σ^2, then the likelihood function for the sample observations, given in Appendix 6B, takes a different and more complicated form. Consequently, the expressions obtained for $\tilde{\alpha}$ and $\tilde{\beta}$ when the likelihood function is maximized are also different, and hence are no longer the same as the expressions for the OLS estimators.

10.3 Detecting and dealing with heteroskedasticity

One method of attempting to detect heteroskedastic disturbances is to look for patterns in the residuals obtained from fitted equations. Although heteroskedasticity is a property of the disturbances, since the disturbances are unknown, we have to treat residuals as estimates of the disturbances and examine their patterns. For example, if in two-variable regression we observed a scatter of points about a sample regression line similar to that in Figure 10.2, with the dispersion of *residuals* increasing as X increases, we would strongly suspect heteroskedastic *disturbances* with Var (ϵ_i) increasing with X.

Alternative ways of studying residual patterns are to plot the residuals e_i, or their absolute value $|e_i|$, directly against X_i. However, since Var $(\epsilon_i) = E(\epsilon_i^2)$, it can be argued that the squared residuals, e_i^2, provide a better guide to the variance of the disturbances, so that a preferable approach is to plot e_i^2 against X_i. Some typical plots are illustrated in Figure 10.3. The first plot again suggests that Var (ϵ_i) may increase with X_i. The second shows no apparent relationship between e_i^2 and X_i, suggesting that the disturbances may be homoskedastic. The third plot suggests heteroskedastic disturbances, but with Var (ϵ_i) taking its largest values at the more extreme values for X_i.

The advantage of plotting e_i^2 directly against an explanatory variable, as in Figure 10.3, rather than examining scatters such as in Figure 10.2, is that this procedure can also be used in multiple regression. In multiple regression the disturbance variance might be related to the size of any of the explanatory variables. However, to cover all possibilities, e_i^2 can be plotted against each such X variable in turn.

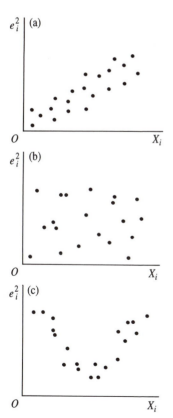

Figure 10.3 Alternative residual patterns.

Inspection of residual patterns is inevitably somewhat subjective, and can sometimes give a false impression as to whether or not heteroskedasticity is present. Statistical tests provide a more objective method of proceeding. A number of such tests exist.

The Goldfeld–Quandt test

This is a well-known procedure in multiple regression for testing a null hypothesis of homoskedastic disturbances against an alternative hypothesis that the variance of the disturbances *increases* as the values of one of the explanatory variables increase. It presupposes that we are able to identify the relevant explanatory variable. The test proceeds as follows.

(a) Observations are ranked according to the size of X_j, the variable to which the disturbance variance is linked. That is, the data set is reordered so that the first observation is that with the largest X_j value and the last observation is that with the smallest X_j value.

(b) The reordered sample is now split into two equally sized subsamples by omitting c 'central' observations. The two subsamples will therefore each contain $\frac{1}{2}(n - c)$ observations if n is the original sample size. One such subsample will contain the $\frac{1}{2}(n - c)$ largest values for X_j and the other the $\frac{1}{2}(n - c)$ smallest values.

(c) Separate OLS regressions are now run for each subsample, and the residual sum of squares retained for each regression.

(d) If disturbances are homoskedastic then Var (ϵ_i) should be the same for both subsamples; that is, the ratio of the two disturbance variances should be unity. The idea behind the Goldfeld–Quandt test is to proxy this ratio by the ratio of the residual sums of squares obtained from the two regressions.[1] The null hypothesis of homoskedasticity is rejected if this ratio is sufficiently larger than unity. In fact, under the null hypothesis that Var $(\epsilon_i) = \sigma^2$, we know that

$$\frac{\sum e_1^2}{\sigma^2} \text{ and } \frac{\sum e_2^2}{\sigma^2} \text{ have } \chi^2 \text{ distributions with } \frac{1}{2}(n - c) - k \text{ d.f.}$$

where $\sum e_1^2$ is the residual sum of squares from the subsample containing the larger X_j values and $\sum e_2^2$ is the residual sum of squares from the subsample containing the smaller X_j values. It follows from the definition of an F distribution that, under homoskedasticity,

$$\frac{\sum e_1^2}{\sum e_2^2} \text{ has an } F \text{ distribution with } [\tfrac{1}{2}(n - c) - k, \ \tfrac{1}{2}(n - c) - k] \text{ d.f.} \qquad (10.20)$$

Thus the null hypothesis of homoskedasticity is rejected if the ratio of the residual sums of squares exceeds the relevant critical value taken from F tables.[2]

A difficulty with the above test is in deciding on the value of c, the number of central observations omitted from the regressions. Observations are omitted to make it easier to discriminate between the disturbance variances for the two subsamples. However, if too many observations are omitted, the power of the test is reduced because so few observations are left to run the regressions. Judge et al. (1988) suggest $c = 4$ when the total sample size is 30, rising to $c = 10$ for a sample of 60.

The White test

This test is based on a more formal approach to the type of search for residual patterns illustrated in Figure 10.3. For example, in two-variable regression, instead of merely plotting e_i^2 against X_i we actually estimate, by OLS, equations of the form

$$e_i^2 = \alpha_1 + \alpha_2 X_i + u_i \tag{10.21}$$

$$e_i^2 = \alpha_1 + \alpha_2 X_i + \alpha_3 X_i^2 + u_i \tag{10.22}$$

and so on. Remember the e_i are the residuals obtained from the OLS regression of Y on the single explanatory variable X. If the coefficients of either X or any of its powers turn out to be significantly different from zero on the usual t test then this implies that Var (ϵ_i) varies with X_i, so that heteroskedasticity is present.[3]

In multiple regression, White (1980) suggests that the e_i^2 should be regressed on all the explanatory variables, together with their squares and cross-products. Thus, with two explanatory variables, where

$$E(Y_i) = \beta_1 + \beta_2 X_{2i} + \beta_3 X_{3i} \tag{10.23}$$

we would estimate

$$e_i^2 = \alpha_1 + \alpha_2 X_{2i} + \alpha_3 X_{3i} + \alpha_4 X_{2i}^2 + \alpha_5 X_{3i}^2 + \alpha_6 X_{2i} X_{3i} + u_i \tag{10.24}$$

Significance of any of the regressors in (10.24) would suggest heteroskedastic disturbances, as would a high value for R^2, the coefficient of multiple determination. White is in fact able to show that in large samples of size n, under the null hypothesis of homoskedastic disturbances, a test statistic equal to nR^2, calculated from the OLS estimation of (10.24), has a χ^2 distribution with degrees of freedom equal to the number of regressors excluding the intercept. If this test statistic exceeds the relevant critical χ^2 value, we conclude that heteroskedasticity is present.

Lagrange multiplier tests

Consider again the case of two explanatory variables. Using (10.23), it is possible, simply by defining new parameters, to write White's equation (10.24) as

$$e_i^2 = \alpha^* + \beta^* [E(Y_i)]^2 + u_i \tag{10.25}$$

Equation (10.25) can be used as a basis for testing for what is known as **dependent-variable heteroskedasticity**, where

$$\text{Var}\,(\epsilon_i) = E(\epsilon_i^2) = \alpha + \beta[E(Y_i)]^2 \tag{10.26}$$

Thus, if $\beta = 0$ in (10.26), disturbances are homoskedastic. Otherwise, Var (ϵ_i) varies with the expected magnitude of the dependent Y variable.

Since we do not have data on $E(Y_i)$, we replace $E(Y_i)$ in (10.25) by $\hat{Y}_i$, the predicted value from the OLS estimation of (10.23). Thus we actually estimate not (10.25) but

$$e_i^2 = \alpha^* + \beta^* \hat{Y}_i^2 + u_i \tag{10.27}$$

Clearly, if $\beta = 0$ in (10.26), we can expect the R^2 taken from (10.27) to be small. In fact, under the null hypothesis of homoskedasticity ($\beta = 0$), it can be shown that, in large samples, nR^2 obtained from the OLS estimation of (10.27) has a χ^2 distribution with 1 d.f. Thus we reject the null hypothesis if the value of this test statistic exceeds the relevant critical χ^2 value.

The above can, in fact, be shown to be an example of the Lagrange multiplier (LM) tests referred to at the end of Section 9.3. Breusch and Pagan (1979) have developed another such LM test. Suppose that

$$\text{Var}\,(\epsilon_i) = f(k + \alpha_2 Z_{2i} + \alpha_3 Z_{3i} + \cdots) \tag{10.28}$$

where the Zs are variables that we suspect affect the disturbance variance. They may include some of the explanatory variables in the equation being estimated, but might also include other variables that are thought to influence Var (ϵ_i). f can be any function. For example, we might have

$$\text{Var}\,(\epsilon_i) = \exp\,(k + \alpha_2 Z_{2i} + \alpha_3 Z_{3i} + \cdots)$$

If the αs are all zero in (10.28) then the disturbances are homoskedastic.

Now consider the regression

$$e_i^2/\hat{\sigma}^2 = \beta_1 + \beta_2 Z_{2i} + \beta_3 Z_{3i} + \cdots + u_i \tag{10.29}$$

where $\hat{\sigma}^2 = \sum e_i^2/n$. If the αs are all zero in (10.28), we can expect R^2 and the explained sum of squares obtained from the estimation of (10.29) to be small. Breusch and Pagan show that in large samples, provided the ϵ_i disturbances in the original equation are normally distributed, then under the null hypothesis of homoskedasticity, one-half of the explained sum of squares from the OLS estimation of (10.29) has a χ^2 distribution with degrees of freedom equal to the number of regressors (excluding intercept) in (10.29).

The big advantage of the Breusch–Pagan test is the generality of the alternative hypothesis given by (10.28). We do not need to know the functional form involved. However, the test requires specification of the factors that are thought to influence Var (ϵ_i), that is, the Zs in (10.28). If this is not feasible then the LM test based on (10.26) may still be used. A disadvantage of both LM tests is that they are large-sample tests. The Goldfeld–Quandt test is valid for small samples, but is only suitable for the case where Var (ϵ_i) is related to just one explanatory variable.

Dealing with heteroskedasticity

Before we outline the main approaches to dealing with heteroskedasticity, a word of caution is in order. All the above tests deal with OLS residuals, whereas true heteroskedasticity is a property of the disturbances. Positive results in any test indicate that the residuals from a fitted equation appear heteroskedastic. However, such results do not necessarily imply genuine heteroskedasticity. For example, suppose the true underlying relationship is

$$Y_i = \beta_1 + \beta_2 X_{2i} + \beta_3 X_{3i} + \epsilon_i \tag{10.30}$$

but we actually estimate

$$Y_i = \beta_1 + \beta_2 X_{2i} + u_i \tag{10.31}$$

That is, we specify our equation incorrectly, leaving out a variable X_3.

If it were the case that X_3 varied more widely in, for example, the second half of our sample data than it did in the first, this would mean that residuals from Equation (10.31) might well appear to exhibit heteroskedasticity. We might, for example, observe a residual pattern such as that in Figure 10.2. This is because the residuals from (10.31) would reflect the behaviour of the missing X_3 variable. However, the factor behind the observed residual pattern would not be genuine heteroskedasticity of the disturbances in (10.30), but rather the fact that we had specified our estimating equation wrongly.

It is also the case that if the underlying population regression line is nonlinear but we estimate a linear equation such as (10.30), the residuals from such an equation may exhibit heteroskedasticity. This can occur even if the disturbances in the true relationship have a constant variance. For example, it is sometimes the case that if residuals from a linear equation are heteroskedastic, re-estimation of the equation in logarithmic terms will solve the problem. We shall consider the consequences of mis-specifying a population regression equation, in these and other circumstances, in Chapter 12.

Heteroskedasticity consistent estimation

If we are satisfied that any apparent heteroskedasticity is not the consequence of an incorrect specification then we must attempt to deal with the problem in some other way. As we have pointed out, the OLS estimators retain the properties of unbiasedness and consistency when disturbances are heteroskedastic. Although the estimators are no longer efficient, the most serious problem with the OLS procedure is that the normal formulae for estimating the variances of estimators are biased and incon-sistent. One way of dealing with heteroskedasticity is therefore to retain the OLS approach but make use of the correct expression for the variance–covariance matrix of the estimators, that is, the matrix (10.9).

Equation (10.9), however, involves the unknown matrix **V**, which in the case of heteroskedasticity takes the form (10.4). White (1980) suggests that the diagonal elements in (10.4) should be estimated by the square of the corresponding OLS residual. That is, we estimate Var $(\epsilon_i) = E(\epsilon_i^2) = \sigma_i^2$ by e_i^2 for all i. The e_i are simply the residuals obtained from the OLS estimation of the population regression equation.

In simple two-variable regression, for example, the true variance of the slope estimator $\hat{\beta}$ is given by (10.19). The White estimator of this variance would be obtained by replacing σ_i^2 by e_i^2 in (10.19).

The White estimators for the variance of $\hat{\beta}$ in two-variable regression and for the variance–covariance matrix (10.9) in multiple regression have the large-sample property of consistency. They are therefore referred to as **heteroskedasticity consistent estimators**. If these estimators are employed, instead of the usual OLS expression (10.7), for purposes of inferences then confidence intervals and hypothesis tests will be valid for large samples, even in the presence of heteroskedasticity.

Weighted least squares

If efficient rather than merely unbiased estimators are required under heteroskedasticity then estimation must be by some form of GLS rather than OLS. The GLS estimator is given by (10.10) in the multiple regression case. It involves the unknown matrix **V**, which, for the case of heteroskedasticity, takes the form (10.4). Although, in practice, **V** has to be estimated, we shall assume for the moment that its elements are known.

Rather than use (10.10) directly, GLS estimators are normally computed by first applying an appropriate transformation to the basic data series and then *applying OLS to the transformed data*. To illustrate this procedure, we consider the case of a single explanatory variable, although what follows can easily be generalized for multiple regression. Suppose we wish to estimate

$$Y_i = \beta_1 + \beta_2 X_{2i} + \epsilon_i \tag{10.32}$$

where the ϵ_i are heteroskedastic, so that Var $(\epsilon_i) = \sigma_i^2$ for all i.

The crucial point to note is that, if we *transform* the disturbance ϵ_i by dividing it by σ_i, we obtain a new disturbance $\epsilon_i^* = \epsilon_i/\sigma_i$, which has, for all i, a constant variance of unity. That is,

$$\text{Var}\,(\epsilon_i^*) = \text{Var}\,(\epsilon_i/\sigma_i) = (1/\sigma_i^2)\,\text{Var}\,(\epsilon_i) = (1/\sigma_i^2)\sigma_i^2 = 1 \tag{10.33}$$

In (10.33) we have used Theorem 2.1, since the σ_i are constants.

Equation (10.33) implies that if we transform Equation (10.32) by dividing it throughout by σ_i, we obtain an equation involving the transformed disturbance ϵ_i^*, which is homoskedastic:

$$Y_i/\sigma_i = \beta_1(1/\sigma_i) + \beta_2(X_{2i}/\sigma_i) + \epsilon_i^* \tag{10.34}$$

We can rewrite (10.34) as

$$Y_i^* = \beta_1 X_{1i}^* + \beta_2 X_{2i}^* + \epsilon_i^* \tag{10.35}$$

where $X_{1i}^* = 1/\sigma_i$ and Y_i^* and X_{2i}^* are transformations of the original Y and X_2 variables given by Y_i/σ_i and X_{2i}/σ_i respectively.

Since ϵ_i^* in (10.35) is homoskedastic rather than heteroskedastic then, provided none of the other classical assumptions are violated, *application of OLS to the transformed equation (10.35)* will yield efficient estimators β_1^* and β_2^* of the parameters in the original equation (10.32). *These estimators are the GLS estimators in the present case.* Moreover, any estimated variances and standard errors of β_1^* and β_2^*, obtained from the estimation of (10.35), will no longer be biased, since (10.35) does not violate any of the classical assumptions.

Notice that to estimate (10.35), multiple regression techniques must be employed, because this equation contains *two* explanatory variables, and the intercept term must be suppressed.

To obtain the GLS estimators β_1^* and β_2^*, the sum of the squares of the residuals $e_i^* = Y_i^* - \beta_1^* X_{1i}^* - \beta_2^* X_{2i}^*$, obtained from OLS estimation of (10.35), is minimized. But, given the definitions of Y_i^*, X_{1i}^* and X_{2i}^*, it follows that

$$e_i^* = \frac{Y_i - \beta_1^* - \beta_2^* X_{2i}}{\sigma_i} = \frac{e_i}{\sigma_i} \quad \text{for all } i$$

where $e_i = Y_i - \beta_1^* - \beta_2^* X_{2i}$. The e_i are *the residuals from the GLS estimation of the original equation (10.32).* Thus the GLS estimators are in fact obtained by minimizing $\sum e_i^* = \sum (e_i/\sigma_i)^2$.

We can now see that, whereas OLS minimizes the straightforward 'unweighted' residual sum of squares, $\sum e_i^2$, for the original equation (10.32), GLS in fact minimizes a weighted residual sum of squares

$$\sum (e_i/\sigma_i)^2 = \sum \lambda_i e_i^2 \tag{10.36}$$

where the weights are given by $\lambda_i = 1/\sigma_i^2$. That is, the weight attached to each e_i is given by the reciprocal of the corresponding disturbance variance σ_i^2. For this reason, in this context, the GLS estimators are sometimes referred to as **weighted least squares** (WLS) **estimators.**

We saw in our discussion of Figure 10.2 that OLS estimators lack efficiency because they treat each residual as giving equal information about the location of the population regression line. When heteroskedasticity is present, it makes more sense to give a smaller weight to 'large' residuals. This is just what WLS does, using as weights the reciprocal of the corresponding Var (ϵ_i). The larger is Var (ϵ_i), the greater is the likelihood of obtaining a 'large' residual and the smaller the weight assigned. We can now see intuitively why WLS estimators are efficient.

The problem with the weighted least squares procedure is that the disturbance variances σ_i^2 are normally unknown and therefore need to be estimated. For some very large cross-sectional samples, this may be possible, and we can then replace the σ_i in the GLS/WLS procedure by estimated values. The resultant estimators are examples of the feasible least squares (FLS) estimators mentioned in Section 10.1. The difficulty is that FLS estimators, unlike the WLS/GLS estimators, are no longer unbiased, although they are consistent.

Making assumptions about the form of heteroskedasticity

If the sample size is too small to obtain reasonable estimates of each σ_i then some assumption has to be made about how σ_i is determined. Considering again the two-variable case (10.32), suppose, for example, that we suspect that

$$\text{Var}(\epsilon_i) = kX_{2i} \quad \text{for all } i \tag{10.37}$$

where k is a constant. Thus the variance of the disturbance increases with the value of X_2. If we transform (10.32) by dividing throughout by the square root of X_{2i}, we obtain

$$Y_i/\sqrt{X_{2i}} = \beta_1(1/\sqrt{X_{2i}}) + \beta_2\sqrt{X_{2i}} + \epsilon_i/\sqrt{X_{2i}} \tag{10.38}$$

Like (10.34), (10.38) contains a homoskedastic disturbance, since

$$\text{Var}(\epsilon_i/\sqrt{X_{2i}}) = (1/X_{2i})\,\text{Var}(\epsilon_i) = k \quad \text{(using (10.37))}$$

Thus (10.38), like (10.34), can also be written as

$$Y_i^* = \beta_1 X_{1i}^* + \beta_2 X_{2i}^* + \epsilon_i^* \tag{10.39}$$

but where now $Y_i^* = Y_i/\sqrt{X_{2i}}$, $X_{1i}^* = 1/\sqrt{X_{2i}}$, $X_{2i}^* = \sqrt{X_{2i}}$ and $\epsilon_i^* = \epsilon_i/\sqrt{X_{2i}}$, which is homoskedastic.

In this case the GLS/WLS estimators would be obtained by applying OLS to Equation (10.39), that is, regressing $Y/\sqrt{X_2}$ on $1/\sqrt{X_2}$ and $\sqrt{X_2}$ with the intercept suppressed.

Provided we know beforehand the form of the heteroskedasticity that is present, we can often proceed in the above manner. The trick is to find a transformation that turns the heteroskedastic disturbance into a homoskedastic one. In general, suppose

$$\text{Var}(\epsilon_i) = \sigma_i^2 = k\lambda_i \quad \text{for all } i \tag{10.40}$$

where k is a constant and λ is some function either of the size of the single explanatory variable X_2, or maybe even of some other variable Z that is not included in the regression itself. For example, we might have $\lambda_i = X_{2i}$ or $\lambda_i = X_{2i}^2$ or $\lambda_i = 1/X_{2i}$. Alternatively, if estimating regressions involving group means, as in the last section, it might be the case that $\lambda_i = 1/Z_i$, where Z_i is the number in group i.

If we now transform Equation (10.32) by dividing throughout by $\sqrt{\lambda_i}$, we obtain

$$Y_i/\sqrt{\lambda_i} = \beta_1(1/\sqrt{\lambda_i}) + \beta_2(X_{2i}/\sqrt{\lambda_i}) + \epsilon_i/\sqrt{\lambda_i} \tag{10.41}$$

Equation (10.41) can always be expressed in the form (10.35) if we define $Y_i^* = Y_i/\sqrt{\lambda_i}$, $X_{1i}^* = 1/\sqrt{\lambda_i}$, $X_{2i}^* = X_{2i}/\sqrt{\lambda_i}$ and $\epsilon_i^* = \epsilon_i/\sqrt{\lambda_i}$. The disturbance in (10.41) is again homoskedastic, since now

$$\text{Var}(\epsilon_i^*) = \text{Var}(\epsilon_i/\sqrt{\lambda_i}) = (1/\lambda_i)\,\text{Var}(\epsilon_i) = k \quad \text{(using (10.40))}$$

The GLS/WLS estimators are always obtained by regressing, using OLS, the transformed variable $Y*$ on the transformed variables X_1^* and X_2^*, however these are defined. The intercept normally has to be suppressed in such equations.[4]

The above procedures can easily be extended to multiple regression. For example, suppose we wished to estimate

$$Y_i = \beta_1 + \beta_2 X_{2i} + \beta_3 X_{3i} + \epsilon_i$$

but suspected that Var $(\epsilon_i) = kX_{3i}$. If the above equation is divided throughout by $\sqrt{X_{3i}}$ then an equation with a homoskedastic disturbance is obtained.

Exercise 10.1

The following equation is to be estimated:

$$Y_i = \beta_1 + \beta_2 X_{2i} + \beta_3 X_{3i} + \beta_4 X_{4i} + \epsilon_i$$

The disturbance ϵ_i is believed to be heteroskedastic. How would you proceed (i) if Var $(\epsilon_i) = kX_{2i}^4$; (ii) if Var $(\epsilon_i) = k_1 X_{3i}^2 + k_2 X_{4i}^2$; (iii) if Var $(\epsilon_i) = kX_{4i}^2$.

Notice that to obtain equations such as (10.41), we do not need to know the value of the parameter k in (10.40). However, we do require knowledge of the function λ. In practice, some idea of the shape of this function might be found by first estimating Equation (10.32) using OLS. The OLS residuals can then be used to regress e_i, $|e_i|$ or e_i^2 on various powers and functions of X_2.[5]

The problem is that if the function λ has to be determined then this involves estimating at least one extra parameter. For example, if (10.40) takes the form $\sigma_i^2 = kX_{2i}^\gamma$ then the parameter γ has to be estimated before embarking on the transformation procedure. The resultant estimators of regression equation parameters are the feasible least squares estimators for this case.

Unfortunately, as we noted earlier, FLS estimators are not unbiased, although they are consistent. In such a situation an alternative is to adopt the maximum likelihood approach, which will also yield consistent estimators. In fact, if the parameter γ is known, it can be shown that WLS/GLS estimators are identical to MLEs (see e.g. Thomas, 1993, Chapter 4). However, when γ has to be estimated as well, the ML method produces different estimators of the regression parameters. These estimators are consistent and asymptotically efficient.

COMPUTER EXERCISE

In this exercise we make use of Data Set 5 on the floppy disk. The data can also be found in appendix III at the end of the text. This data refers to a cross-section of 50 UK households, and contains data on the following variables:

$E =$ average hourly earnings (£) of the head of household
$A =$ 'age of household'
   $=$ time (years) spent by household head in full-time employment
$S =$ 'schooling of household'
   $=$ time (years) spent by household head in full-time education

We shall estimate a model much used in the study of household earnings:

$$\ln (E) = \beta_1 + \beta_2 A + \beta_3 S + \epsilon \tag{10.42}$$

Notice that (10.42) is of the exponential form, and is a generalization of Equation (4.49). This function has the advantage that the parameters β_2 and β_3 can be interpreted as the 'returns' to age, A, and schooling, S. Partially differentiating (10.42) with respect to A and with respect to S gives

$$\beta_2 = \frac{1}{E}\frac{\partial E}{\partial A}, \qquad \beta_3 = \frac{1}{E}\frac{\partial E}{\partial S}$$

Thus, for example, β_3 measures the proportionate increase in earnings that results from an extra year's schooling.

You should find that estimation of (10.42) by OLS yields

$$\widehat{\ln (E)} = 1.20 + 0.028A + 0.123S, \qquad R^2 = 0.396 \tag{10.43}$$
$$\quad\ \ (6.10) \quad (4.72) \qquad (3.54)$$

Both the coefficients of A and S have significant t ratios. They suggest rates of return of about 3% and 12% to age and schooling respectively. The R^2 of 0.396 may appear a little low, but is in fact quite respectable for cross-sectional data. Remember that the high R^2s obtained from time series data are generally the artificial result of common trends in the data. Of more concern is the possibility of heteroskedasticity in the residuals of (10.43), particularly since the age variable A shows a wide variation in value over the cross-section, ranging from zero to over 40.

A plot of the squared residuals from (10.43) against A is shown in Figure 10.4. Although no clear relationship is evident, it does seem that e_i^2 rises as A increases. We can examine this possibility more formally by using the Goldfeld–Quandt test of the last section.

Ordering the data by the size of A and then omitting 8 central observations leaves 21 observations in the two subsamples. OLS estimation of Equation (10.42) for each subsample should yield the residual sums of squares $\sum e_1^2 = 12.50$ and

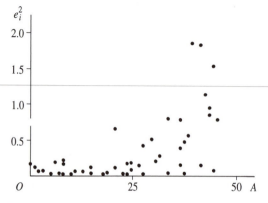

Figure 10.4 Residual pattern for Equation (10.43).

$\sum e_2^2 = 0.712$. The Goldfeld–Quandt statistic (10.20) therefore takes a value of 17.56, compared with a critical F value, using [18,18] d.f., of $F_{0.05} = 2.22$. The null hypothesis of homoskedasticity is therefore strongly rejected.

It is unwise to rely on just one test for heteroskedasticity, so we will carry out the other tests mentioned in the last section. For the White test, the residuals from Equation (10.43) must be saved and then squared. If the squared residuals are regressed on A, A^2, S, S^2 and AS, as required by the White test, you should obtain

$$\hat{e}^2 = 0.015 - 0.016A + 0.0008A^2 + 0.148S - 0.020S^2 - 0.0011AS$$
$$\quad (0.07) \quad (-1.03) \quad (2.65) \qquad (1.75) \quad (-1.84) \quad (-0.66)$$

A number of coefficients, particularly that of A^2, have significant t ratios in the above equation, and $R^2 = 0.495$. The White test statistic is therefore $nR^2 = 24.75$. This easily exceeds the critical χ^2 value of (with 5 d.f.) $\chi^2_{0.05} = 11.07$. Again, the null hypothesis of homoskedasticity is rejected.

For the LM test for dependent-variable heteroskedasticity, the fitted values from (10.43), the $\widehat{\ln(E_i)}$, must be saved and squared as well as the residuals. You should then obtain

$$\hat{e}^2 = -0.193 + 0.102 \, [\widehat{\ln(E)}]^2, \qquad R^2 = 0.191$$
$$\quad (-1.18) \quad (3.37)$$

The LM test statistic is therefore $nR^2 = 9.55$, compared with a critical χ^2 value (with 1 d.f.) of $\chi^2_{0.05} = 3.84$. Again, we find evidence of heteroskedasticity.

Finally, for the Breusch–Pagan test, we require the residual sum of squares from (10.43), which is $\sum e_i^2 = 16.02$. Thus $\sigma^2 = 16.02/50 = 0.32$. The Breusch–Pagan equation is

$$\frac{\hat{e}^2}{\hat{\sigma}^2} = -0.435 + 0.060A - 0.012S, \qquad \text{SSE} = 36.85$$
$$\qquad (-1.07) \quad (4.94) \quad (-0.16)$$

Thus the Breusch–Pagan test statistic takes a value of $0.5(\text{SSE}) = 18.43$. This compares with a critical χ^2 value of (with 2 d.f.) $\chi^2_{0.05} = 5.99$. Yet again, we reject the null hypothesis of homoskedasticity.

Your computer program will almost certainly give values for some of the above test statistics as part of its standard regression output, but it is instructive to perform the tests step by step. All our tests suggest clearly that we have a heteroskedasticity problem in the estimation of Equation (10.43). Thus, while our OLS estimators may be unbiased, they are almost certainly not efficient. Also, more worryingly, we can have no confidence in our estimated standard errors and t ratios. One approach to the problem is to compute White's heteroskedasticity consistent estimates of the true standard errors, as described in the previous section. The t ratios on the coefficients in Equation (10.42) can then be recalculated. Your program will almost certainly have a facility for doing this. You should, in fact, obtain

$$\widehat{\ln(E)} = 1.20 + 0.028A + 0.123S \qquad\qquad\qquad (10.44)$$
$$\qquad\quad (9.60) \quad (4.23) \quad (4.87)$$

The t ratios in (10.44) are still highly significant, that on S being markedly larger than in (10.43). We can therefore be fairly confident about the importance of age and schooling on hourly earnings.

The problem that remains with (10.44) is that the estimated coefficients have been obtained by OLS, which we know is inefficient under heteroskedasticity. However, we can see from a number of the tests performed above that the variance of the residuals appears to increase as the variable A increases. This suggests that we try FLS estimation methods based on the transformations described at the end of the last section. For example, if we divide (10.42) throughout by the square root of A, OLS estimation yields

$$\frac{\widehat{\ln(E)}}{\sqrt{A}} = \underset{(13.57)}{1.19(1/\sqrt{A})} + \underset{(8.17)}{0.033\sqrt{A}} + \underset{(3.24)}{0.074(S/\sqrt{A})} \tag{10.45}$$

Notice that (10.45) does not contain an intercept, so we have not quoted a value for R^2, since this statistic can only be given its normal interpretation when the estimation is standard OLS with intercept included. The reader should test (10.45) for heteroskedasticity, using the above tests. The results are a considerable improvement on (10.43).

The t ratios on $1/\sqrt{A}$ and $\sqrt{A}$ are somewhat larger than those found previously. However, this is merely a reflection of the fact that, since the range of values for A is large, we should expect, for example, $E/\sqrt{A}$ and $1/\sqrt{A}$ to be highly correlated. The relationship is therefore partly artificial or 'spurious'. The estimated coefficients in (10.45) are not, in fact, very dissimilar to those in (10.43). They suggest a return to age of again about 3%, but a lower return to schooling of about 7%.

10.4 Autocorrelation

As noted in Section 10.1, autocorrelation occurs when assumption IIC of the classical model, that Cov $(\epsilon_i, \epsilon_j) = 0$ for all $i \neq j$, is replaced by Equation (10.5). That is, the covariances and correlations between different disturbances are no longer all non-zero.

Autocorrelation is held to occur most frequently when estimating equations using time series data. It is then also referred to as **serial correlation**. With time series data, there may be a tendency for random shocks or disturbances to 'spill over' from one time period to the next. For example, if the dependent variable in a regression equation was the output of an industry, and the industry experienced some industrial action by its workforce in quarter $t - 1$, this might push output below its normal level. The disturbance ϵ_{t-1} in this quarter would therefore be negative. In the following quarter, t, there is at least a probability of the industrial action continuing and the disturbance in quarter t, ϵ_t, also being negative. Thus the correlation between ϵ_t and ϵ_{t-1} is no longer non-zero, so that we have

$$\text{Cov}(\epsilon_t, \epsilon_{t-1}) \neq 0 \tag{10.46}$$

Equation (10.46) is clearly a violation of classical assumption IIC. Other random shocks might arise because of abnormal weather conditions, for example, severe floods or extremely cold weather. In general, autocorrelation is also likely to occur with time series data because of the 'inertia' or 'momentum' in many economic time series. Many series such as GNP, unemployment or the general price level move cyclically with self-sustaining upswings being followed by downswings. Observations in one period are then likely to be dependent on observations in the previous period. It is also the case that raw data is often manipulated to produce the published series. For example, monthly observations on the price level may be averaged to provide a single quarterly observation. This averaging process produces a 'smoother' series, ironing out very-short-term fluctuations, but it can also lead to serial correlation in disturbances.

The consequences of autocorrelation in the disturbances of a regression equation were outlined in Section 10.1, when we considered non-spherical disturbances in general terms. The OLS estimators remain unbiased and consistent, but are *no longer BLUE or asymptotically efficient*. More seriously, *the normal OLS formulae for estimating the variances of the estimators become biased*, thus invalidating the usual OLS inferential procedures.

The first-order autoregressive process

Perhaps the most popular way of modelling serially correlated disturbances has been to replace the classical assumptions concerning the disturbances ϵ_t by the model

$$\epsilon_t = \rho \epsilon_{t-1} + u_t \tag{10.47}$$

where ρ is a parameter lying between 1 and -1 and u_t is a further disturbance that does obey the classical assumptions. That is, u_t is normally distributed, with

$$E(u_t) = 0$$
$$\text{Var}(u_t) = E(u_t^2) = \sigma_u^2 = \text{constant} \quad \text{for all } t$$
$$\text{Cov}(u_t, u_{t-s}) = E(u_t u_{t-s}) = 0 \quad \text{for all } t \text{ and all } s \neq 0$$

Notice that when discussing autocorrelation, it is customary to replace i subscripts by t subscripts, because autocorrelation is normally associated with time series data.

The **autoregressive process** (10.47) is designated **first-order** because it contains values of ϵ_t lagged by just one period. It implies that the disturbance in period t is influenced by the disturbance in the previous period, ϵ_{t-1}. An alternative might be, for example, the **second-order** process

$$\epsilon_t = \rho_1 \epsilon_{t-1} + \rho_2 \epsilon_{t-2} + u_t \tag{10.48}$$

Referring to the first-order process (10.47), we can distinguish three separate cases.

(1) $\rho = 0$. This implies that $\epsilon_t = u_t$, so that ϵ_t, like u_t, obeys all the classical assumptions, including non-autocorrelation. Thus *a special case of (10.43) is*

that of no autocorrelation. This will prove convenient later when we come to test for autocorrelation.

(2) $\rho > 0$. This case is normally referred to as **positive autocorrelation**. It implies that positive values of ϵ_{t-1} will tend to be followed by positive values of ϵ_t and that negative values of ϵ_{t-1} will tend to be followed by negative values of ϵ_t. Thus in such a situation we will tend to experience 'runs' over time of positive disturbances followed by 'runs' of negative disturbances. This fits in well with the idea discussed above of disturbances spilling over from one period to the next.

(3) $\rho < 0$. This is the case of **negative autocorrelation**. It implies that positive ϵ_{t-1} will tend to be followed by negative ϵ_t, and vice versa. In such a case successive disturbances will tend to alternate in sign over time. This case is usually held to be less likely to occur with economic data.

Although in the first-order process the usual classical assumptions concerning the disturbances are *initially* abandoned in favour of (10.47), we now show that (10.47) implies that all classical assumptions, with the exception of non-autocorrelation, *are* in fact satisfied after all. Thus (10.47) implies *only* the violation of assumption IIC.

Substituting in (10.47) for ϵ_{t-1} and then ϵ_{t-2},

$$\epsilon_t = \rho(\rho\epsilon_{t-2} + u_{t-1}) + u_t$$
$$= \rho^2\epsilon_{t-2} + \rho u_{t-1} + u_t$$
$$= \rho^2(\rho\epsilon_{t-3} + u_{t-2}) + \rho u_{t-1} + u_t$$
$$= \rho^3\epsilon_{t-3} + \rho^2 u_{t-2} + \rho u_{t-1} + u_t$$
$$= u_t + \rho u_{t-1} + \rho^2 u_{t-2} + \rho^3\epsilon_{t-3}$$

If we continue this process indefinitely, substituting for ϵ_{t-3}, ϵ_{t-4}, and so on, we eventually obtain

$$\epsilon_t = u_t + \rho u_{t-1} + \rho^2 u_{t-2} + \rho^3 u_{t-3} + \rho^4 u_{t-4} + \cdots \tag{10.49}$$

where, since $-1 < \rho < 1$, the last term in (10.49), which involves ϵ, is so small that it can be ignored.

What (10.49) implies is that the regression disturbance ϵ_t depends on present and past values of the u_t disturbance in (10.47). Since ρ lies between 1 and -1, the influence of previous periods continually decreases the further back in time we go.

Equation (10.49) may be used to deduce the properties of ϵ_t. Clearly,

$$E(\epsilon_t) = E(u_t) + \rho E(u_{t-1}) + \rho^2 E(u_{t-2}) + \rho^3 E(u_{t-3}) + \cdots$$

Thus, since $E(u_t) = 0$ for all t, we have

$$E(\epsilon_t) = 0 \quad \text{for all } t \tag{10.50}$$

Given the properties of u_t, (10.49) may also be used to show, via some straightforward but rather tedious algebra, first that the variance of ϵ_t is given by

$$\sigma^2 = \sigma_u^2/(1 - \rho^2) = \text{constant} \tag{10.51}$$

Thus the regression equation disturbance has a constant variance, and hence is homoskedastic.

Secondly, (10.49) may be used, together with the properties of u_t, to find the covariances between the ϵ_t. For example, it can be shown that

$$\text{Cov}\,(\epsilon_t, \epsilon_{t-1}) = \rho\sigma^2 \tag{10.52}$$

and in general that

$$\text{Cov}\,(\epsilon_t, \epsilon_{t-s}) = \rho^s\sigma^2 \quad \text{for all } s \neq 0 \tag{10.53}$$

Notice that, since $-1 < \rho < 1$, the larger is s, that is, the further apart in time are two disturbances, the smaller is the covariance between them. This fits in well with the notion of disturbances spilling over from one period to another, since we might expect the effect of such a disturbance to wear off gradually as time passes.

Finally, since all the u_t in (10.49) are normally distributed, it follows that ϵ_t must also be normally distributed, since it is a linear function of normally distributed variables.

We have now shown that the first-order process (10.47) implies that the regression equation disturbance ϵ_t is normally distributed, with zero mean and constant variance $\sigma^2 = \sigma_u^2/(1 - \rho^2)$, but with non-zero covariances given by (10.53). It therefore obeys all the classical assumptions except that of non-auto-correlation. This makes it a particularly convenient way of modelling autocorrelation if we believe that none of the other classical assumptions have been violated.

Notice also that, since from (10.52) the covariance between two successive disturbances is given by $\rho\sigma^2$, the correlation between them must be

$$\frac{\text{Cov}\,(\epsilon_t, \epsilon_{t-1})}{\sqrt{\text{Var}\,(\epsilon_t)}\sqrt{\text{Var}\,(\epsilon_{t-1})}} = \frac{\text{E}(\epsilon_t\epsilon_{t-1})}{\sqrt{\text{E}(\epsilon_t^2)}\sqrt{\text{E}(\epsilon_{t-1}^2)}} = \frac{\rho\sigma^2}{\sqrt{\sigma^2}\sqrt{\sigma^2}} = \rho \tag{10.54}$$

Thus the parameter ρ in the first-order process (10.47) can be interpreted as the correlation between successive disturbances. For this reason, ρ is often referred to as the (first-order) **autocorrelation coefficient**.

Consequences of a first-order autoregressive process

We listed the consequences of any form of autocorrelation in the disturbances of a regression equation at the end of the last subsection. These consequences must necessarily hold for a first-order process. In particular, the normal formulae for the variances of the OLS estimators become biased in the presence of such a process. However, it is instructive to examine precisely why this should be so for this particular case.

Consider the case of two-variable regression where

$$Y_t = \alpha + \beta X_t + \epsilon_t \tag{10.55}$$

but ϵ_t follows the first-order process given by (10.47). As usual, we shall concentrate on the variance of $\hat\beta$, the OLS estimator of β.

Since $\hat\beta$ is unbiased, we have

$$\begin{aligned}
\text{Var}(\hat\beta) &= \text{E}[(\hat\beta - \beta)^2] \\
&= \text{E}[(\sum w_t \epsilon_t)^2] \quad \text{(using (10.15))} \\
&= \text{E}(w_1 \epsilon_1 + w_2 \epsilon_2 + w_3 \epsilon_3 + \cdots + w_n \epsilon_n)^2
\end{aligned} \tag{10.56}$$

Recall from (6.4) that $w_i = x_i / \sum x_i^2$. We can therefore write (10.56) as

$$\text{Var}(\hat\beta) = \frac{1}{(\sum x_i^2)^2} \text{E}(x_1 \epsilon_1 + x_2 \epsilon_2 + x_3 \epsilon_3 + \cdots + x_n \epsilon_n)^2 \tag{10.57}$$

For simplicity, consider the case where $n = 3$. Equation (10.57) can then be written as

$$\begin{aligned}
\text{Var}(\hat\beta) &= \frac{1}{(\sum x_i^2)^2} \text{E}(x_1^2 \epsilon_1^2 + x_2^2 \epsilon_2^2 + x_3^2 \epsilon_3^2 + 2x_1 x_2 \epsilon_1 \epsilon_2 + 2x_2 x_3 \epsilon_2 \epsilon_3 + 2x_1 x_3 \epsilon_1 \epsilon_3) \\
&= \frac{1}{(\sum x_i^2)^2} [x_1^2 \text{E}(\epsilon_1^2) + x_2^2 \text{E}(\epsilon_2^2) + x_3^2 \text{E}(\epsilon_3^2) + 2x_1 x_2 \text{E}(\epsilon_1 \epsilon_2) \\
&\quad + 2x_2 x_3 \text{E}(\epsilon_2 \epsilon_3) + 2x_1 x_3 \text{E}(\epsilon_1 \epsilon_3)]
\end{aligned}$$

Under a first-order process, $\text{E}(\epsilon_i^2) = \sigma^2 = \text{constant}$, where σ^2 is given by (10.51). Also, using (10.53), $\text{E}(\epsilon_1 \epsilon_2) = \text{E}(\epsilon_2 \epsilon_3) = \rho \sigma^2$ and $\text{E}(\epsilon_1 \epsilon_3) = \rho^2 \sigma^2$. Thus we have

$$\begin{aligned}
\text{Var}(\hat\beta) &= \frac{\sigma^2}{(\sum x_i^2)^2} (\sum x_i^2 + 2\rho x_1 x_2 + 2\rho x_2 x_3 + 2\rho^2 x_1 x_3) \\
&= \frac{\sigma^2}{\sum x_i^2} \left(1 + 2\rho \frac{x_1 x_2}{\sum x_i^2} + 2\rho \frac{x_2 x_3}{\sum x_i^2} + 2\rho^2 \frac{x_1 x_3}{\sum x_i^2} \right)
\end{aligned} \tag{10.58}$$

Notice that the term outside the parentheses in (10.58), $\sigma^2 / \sum x_i^2$, is the normal OLS formula for the variance of $\hat\beta$. Thus, when disturbances follow a first-order autoregressive process, the true expression for $\text{Var}(\hat\beta)$ is not given by the normal OLS formula but by that formula multiplied by the quantity in parentheses in (10.58). Hence the normal formula will provide a biased estimate of the true variance.

The direction of the bias will depend on whether the term in parentheses is greater than or less than unity. As we have noted, $\rho > 0$ for most economic data. If the X variable follows an upward or downward trend, as is also likely with economic series, the product of any two $x_i = X_i - \bar X$ terms will be positive, so that, with $\rho > 0$, the term in brackets in (10.58) will exceed unity. Thus in these very common situations the normal OLS formula for Var $(\hat{\beta})$, that is, $\sigma^2/\sum x_i^2$, will *underestimate* the true variance. Although we have concentrated on the case $n=3$, the same conclusion holds regardless of the value of n.

Moreover, there is a further problem with the OLS expression for Var $(\hat{\beta})$. To estimate Var $(\hat{\beta})$, we must first estimate Var $(\epsilon_i)=\sigma^2$. The estimate s^2 is based on the sum of squares of the OLS residuals. Unfortunately, in the presence of a first-order process with $\rho>0$, s^2 tends to underestimate the true σ^2.

The combination of the above biases means that in two-variable regression *the variance and standard error of the OLS estimator $\hat{\beta}$ may be seriously underestimated by the normal OLS procedures.* Thus confidence intervals will be too narrow, giving a misleading impression of precision in the estimate of $\hat{\beta}$. Also, t ratios will be too large, so that the X variable may appear to be 'significant' when in reality it has no influence on Y.

Also, since the sum of squares of the OLS residuals gives a false impression of the true value of Var $(\epsilon_i)=\sigma^2$, this means that R^2, the coefficient of determination, will give a misleading impression of the ability of the explanatory X variable to explain Y in (10.55). In effect, since $\sum e_t^2$ is too small, R^2 tends to be 'too high'.

10.5   Detecting and dealing with autocorrelation

Clearly, the consequences of autocorrelation can be severe, so its detection is an important matter. We have seen that in time series data autocorrelation typically results both in sequences over time of positive disturbances and in sequences of negative disturbances. Since we cannot observe the disturbances, we cannot search for such patterns. However, if we treat the known residuals as estimates of the unknown disturbances, we can search for residual patterns that suggest autocorrelation in the underlying disturbances. The best way to do this is to plot the residuals from a fitted regression line against time. For example, in Figure 10.5(a) we show a residual pattern that is strongly suggestive of positive autocorrelation.

In Figure 10.5(a) a sequence of positive residuals is followed by a sequence of negative residuals, which in turn is followed by another sequence of positive residuals. Such a pattern is highly suggestive, and *could* be the result of autocorrelation in the underlying disturbances, with the observed pattern arising because of the 'spillover' effects mentioned earlier. On the other hand, in Figure 10.5(b) there is no obvious pattern to the residuals and no immediate suggestion of autocorrelation. We say the pattern in Figure 10.5(a) 'could' be the result of autocorrelated disturbances, because there are other factors that could also give rise to sequences of positive and negative residuals. We shall discuss such factors shortly.

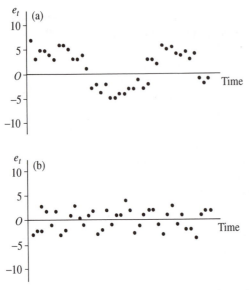

Figure 10.5 (a) Positive autocorrelation in residuals. (b) Non-autocorrelated residuals.

Testing for autocorrelation

However suggestive residual patterns may be, it is still possible that, for example, a sequence of positive residuals could occur by chance. Statistical tests are therefore necessary to decide whether a pattern is truly unusual. It is to some of these that we now turn.

The Durbin–Watson test

This is by far the most well-known test for the presence of autocorrelated disturbances. We introduced the Durbin–Watson statistic in Section 6.4, when considering the problem of specifying the appropriate functional form for a regression equation, and it is now time to look at it in detail. The statistic is defined as

$$dw = \frac{\sum_{t=2}^{n}(e_t - e_{t-1})^2}{\sum_{t=1}^{n} e_t^2} \tag{10.59}$$

and may be used to test for the presence of a *first-order* autoregressive scheme. Notice that the summation in the numerator of (10.59) is from $t=2$ to $t=n$ because use of the lagged e_{t-1} involves the loss of one observation. The numerator in (10.59) can be written as

$$\sum e_t^2 + \sum e_{t-1}^2 - 2\sum e_t e_{t-1}$$

Since $\sum e_t^2 \approx \sum e_{t-1}^2$, the numerator can also be written as

$$2\sum e_t^2 - 2\sum e_t e_{t-1} = 2(\sum e_t^2 - \sum e_t e_{t-1})$$

The Durbin–Watson statistic can therefore be written as

$$dw \approx \frac{2(\sum_{t=2}^{n} e_t^2 - \sum_{t=2}^{n} e_t e_{t-1})}{\sum_{t=1}^{n} e_t^2} \qquad (10.60)$$

Since the summations in the numerator and denominator of (10.60) differ by only one term, we can regard the two summations of e_t^2 as approximately equal. We therefore have

$$dw \approx 2(1 - \hat{\rho}) \qquad (10.61)$$

where $\hat{\rho} = \sum e_t e_{t-1} / \sum e_t^2$ is an estimator, based on the OLS residuals, of ρ, the autocorrelation coefficient (10.54).[6]

We can use (10.61) to give us an idea of the likely values of dw corresponding to different values of ρ. For example, if $\rho = 0$ and autocorrelation is not present then we can expect $\hat{\rho} \approx 0$, so that the Durbin–Watson statistic should take a value close to 2. If, on the other hand, ρ takes its maximum value of unity, in which case we have the severest possible kind of positive autocorrelation, then we can expect $\hat{\rho} \approx 1$ and, from (10.61), a value of dw close to zero. Finally, with $\rho = -1$ and perfect negative autocorrelation, we can expect $\hat{\rho} \approx -1$ and a value of dw close to 4.

It should be clear that the value of the Durbin–Watson statistic is a guide to whether autocorrelation is present or not. Values far away from 2 imply that it is present. However, dw, like all sample statistics, is subject to sampling variability, and it is possible to obtain a value different from 2 even in the absence of autocorrelation. The important question is: how far from 2 must dw be before we can safely reject the null hypothesis H_0: $\rho = 0$ and conclude that autocorrelation is present?

The problem is that, given H_0: $\rho = 0$, the sampling distribution for dw depends on the sample size n, the number of explanatory variables in the regression equation, k', and on *the values taken by those explanatory variables*. Because of this 'critical values' for dw actually depend on the precise sample taken. However, tables are available that give upper and lower *bounds* for any required critical value. These bounds depend on n and k', but are valid for any sample values. Such tables are given in Appendix IV at the end of this text.

The Durbin–Watson test of the null hypothesis of no autocorrelation H_0: $\rho = 0$, against the alternative of positive autocorrelation, H_A: $\rho > 0$, is illustrated in Figure 10.6. The upper and lower bounds d_U and d_L on the true critical value are taken from the tables for the dw statistic. They depend on n, k' and the level of significance

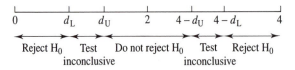

Figure 10.6 The Durbin–Watson test.

selected for the test. The test criterion has the form

$$\text{Reject } H_0 \text{ if } dw < d_L \qquad \text{Do not reject } H_0 \text{ if } dw > d_U$$

Thus, if the statistic is below d_L, it is sufficiently smaller than 2 for us to believe that positive autocorrelation is present. Notice that the test has an inconclusive region. If dw lies between d_L and d_U then the test is inconclusive.

If we wish to test for negative autocorrelation then use is made of the symmetry about 2 of the dw distribution. The alternative hypothesis is now H_A: $\rho < 0$, and the test criterion is

$$\text{Reject } H_0 \text{ if } dw > 4 - d_L \qquad \text{Do not reject } H_0 \text{ if } dw < 4 - d_U$$

Thus a value of dw in excess of $4 - d_L$ is sufficiently larger than 2 to suggest negative autocorrelation. Again, there is an inconclusive region.

To illustrate the use of the Durbin–Watson statistic, consider Equation (7.66). This apparently impressive demand-for-food equation has an R^2 of 0.943 and significant coefficients on two of its regressors. However, the computer printout given by Table 7.3 shows a value of the Durbin–Watson statistic for this regression of $dw = 0.669$. This is considerably below 2, and suggests we test for first-order autocorrelation in the residuals. Using the table in Appendix IV, with $k' = 3$ and $n = 25$, the upper and lower limits of dw are $d_L = 1.12$ and $d_U = 1.66$, assuming a 0.05 level of significance. Hence for this equation, $dw < d_L$, which implies we have a problem with the residuals. This equation is not quite as impressive as it first seemed.

Disadvantages of the Durbin–Watson statistic

Although widely used and part of the standard output of virtually all regression programs, the dw statistic has major disadvantages. The least serious of these is the inconclusive region. For large samples, this becomes narrow, and for small samples Durbin and Watson (1971) suggest methods of finding exact critical values for a given sample. More seriously, the Durbin–Watson test is a test for first-order autocorrelation only. It does not test, for example, for a second-order process such as (10.48). Neither, for example, could it detect fourth-order autocorrelation of the kind

$$\epsilon_t = \rho \epsilon_{t-4} + u_t \tag{10.62}$$

With quarterly data, particularly if it is not seasonally adjusted, it can be argued that disturbances in a regression equation are more likely to follow (10.62) than a first-order process.

Another serious disadvantage of the *dw* statistic is that *it can be shown to be biased towards 2 when a lagged dependent variable is included among the regressors of an equation.* For example, if

$$Y_t = \beta_1 + \beta_2 X_{2t} + \beta_3 Y_{t-1} + \epsilon_t \tag{10.63}$$

and ϵ_t followed a first-order autoregressive process, then it is very likely that the Durbin–Watson statistic would fail to detect the autocorrelation.[7] This is a particularly severe defect, because, as we shall see in the next chapter, the presence of autocorrelated disturbances in an equation such as (10.63), containing a lagged dependent variable, has serious consequences. In fact, under such circumstances, the OLS estimators are not merely biased in small samples but lose the property of consistency. Durbin (1970) devised an alternative test for such a situation, but this too is a test for first-order autocorrelation only.[8]

The Lagrange multiplier test

This is a test developed by Breusch (1978) and Godfrey (1978) that is not restricted to first-order autocorrelation and *remains valid in the presence of lagged dependent variables.* It is an LM test of the kind described in Section 9.3, and is far more generally applicable than the Durbin–Watson test. We shall present an intuitive explanation of the test.

Suppose we are estimating Equation (10.55) and suspect that the disturbance ϵ_t may be subject to autocorrelation of any order up to, for example, the third. That is, we model ϵ_t as

$$\epsilon_t = \rho_1 \epsilon_{t-1} + \rho_2 \epsilon_{t-2} + \rho_3 \epsilon_{t-3} + u_t \tag{10.64}$$

The LM test in this case is a test of H_0: $\rho_1 = \rho_2 = \rho_3 = 0$ in the third-order process (10.64). Rejection of H_0 implies that *some form* of autocorrelation of *up to* the third order is present. Tests for higher-order autocorrelation would simply involve adding extra lagged terms to (10.64).

Substituting (10.64) into (10.55) gives

$$Y_t = \alpha + \beta X_t + \rho_1 \epsilon_{t-1} + \rho_2 \epsilon_{t-2} + \rho_3 \epsilon_{t-3} + u_t \tag{10.65}$$

Suppose the ϵ disturbances were known. We could then actually estimate (10.65) by OLS, regressing Y_t on X_t, ϵ_{t-1}, ϵ_{t-2} and ϵ_{t-3}. Under H_0, (10.65) becomes

$$Y_t = \alpha + \beta X_t + u_t \tag{10.66}$$

which may also be estimated. We could now treat (10.65) and (10.66) as unrestricted and restricted equations respectively, and apply the F test of Section 9.2 to test the null hypothesis, H_0 above, that the coefficients of the lagged variables in (10.65) are all zero.

In practice, of course the ϵ_t are unknown. They have to be replaced by the corresponding OLS residuals e_t, obtained from the estimation of (10.66), if such a test is to be performed. Because of this, an LM test rather than the F test is employed. Since the restrictions are linear, this is equivalent to the large-sample χ^2 test in terms of nR^2, also described in Section 9.2. In this case the auxiliary equation is

$$e_t = \alpha + \beta X_t + \rho_1 e_{t-1} + \rho_2 e_{t-2} + \rho_3 e_{t-3} + u_t \tag{10.67}$$

Notice that in (10.67) the e_t have replaced the unknown ϵ_t that appear in (10.65). Under the null hypothesis of no autocorrelation, H_0: $\rho_1 = \rho_2 = \rho_3 = 0$, the statistic nR^2 taken from the estimation of (10.67) will have, in large samples, a χ^2 distribution with 3 degrees of freedom. Hence if the value of nR^2 exceeds the relevant critical χ^2 value then this is evidence of autocorrelation.

The LM test for higher than third-order autocorrelation is analogous to the above. If we wish to test for up to pth-order autocorrelation then lagged residuals up to e_{t-p} are added to (10.67), and the χ^2 test statistic then has p degrees of freedom.

To illustrate the use of the LM test, we will again make use of Equation (7.66). We have already seen that the Durbin–Watson test indicates first-order autocorrelation in the residuals of this equation. Let us see what the LM test for first-order autocorrelation suggests.

Your computer program will probably have an option for computing LM statistics, but it will be instructive to proceed as follows in this case. Save the residuals e_t from the OLS equation (7.66). The LM statistic for first-order autocorrelation can then be obtained by running the regression

$$e_t = \alpha_1 + \alpha_2 \ln X + \alpha_3 \ln P + \alpha_4 \ln G + \delta e_{t-1} + u_t$$

for the period 1966–89 (one observation is lost because of the e_{t-1} variable). The R^2 from this regression is 0.475. The LM statistic therefore has a value $nR^2 = 24 \times 0.475 = 11.4$. This exceeds the critical χ^2 value of (with 1 d.f.) $\chi^2_{0.05} = 3.841$. The LM test also suggests that we have first-order autocorrelation in the residuals of Equation (7.66). As an exercise, the reader should now test for up to second-order autocorrelation using the LM test. The LM statistic should take a value of about 13 compared with $\chi^2_{0.05} = 5.99$.

Moving average disturbances

As we noted earlier, the LM tests for autocorrelation are valid even in the presence of lagged dependent variables. They have the further advantage that they can be used to test for patterns of serial correlation rather different from those we have considered so far. Suppose the disturbance in Equation (10.55) is given by

$$\epsilon_t = u_t + \theta_1 u_{t-1} + \theta_2 u_{t-2} + \cdots + \theta_m u_{t-m} \tag{10.68}$$

where u_t is a further disturbance that obeys all the classical assumptions.

The disturbance ϵ_t in (10.68) is known as an **mth-order moving average disturbance**. Since both ϵ_t and ϵ_{t-1} depend on past values of u_t, they must be autocorrelated. Disturbance patterns such as (10.68) arise quite frequently in economic models. Indeed, we shall see in the next chapter that quite simple models can result in a first-order moving average disturbance of the form

$$\epsilon_t = u_t + \theta_1 u_{t-1} \tag{10.69}$$

It turns out that the appropriate LM test for an mth-order moving average disturbance is identical to the LM test for an mth-order autoregressive scheme. That is, the LM statistics described above can also be used to test a null hypothesis that all the θs in moving average schemes such as (10.68) are zero. This dual nature of the LM tests makes them particularly valuable.

Dealing with autocorrelated residuals

Since the disturbances in a population regression equation are unobservable, all tests for autocorrelation, including those above, deal with the residuals from a fitted sample equation. When discussing heteroskedasticity, we saw that patterns in residuals might not necessarily reflect the behaviour of the true disturbances. This is also the case when residual patterns suggest autocorrelation. In fact, with time series data, autocorrelated residuals are, *much more often than not*, an indication of some error in the way we have specified the regression equation rather than genuine autocorrelation in the disturbances.

Suppose, for example, we are faced with the unknown population relationship (10.30), but again actually estimate (10.31), making the error of leaving out X_3. The disturbance in (10.31) is $u_t = \beta_3 X_{3t} + \epsilon_t$. Now suppose that X_3 follows a clear trend upwards or downwards. X_{3t} and X_{3t-1} will then be highly correlated for all t, and this autocorrelation will be reflected in the 'false' disturbances u_t. If (10.31) is estimated in error then the residuals from this equation will be autocorrelated, even though the true disturbances in (10.30) are not. Since many explanatory variables in economics show strong trends, this situation is likely to occur very frequently.

We will consider the consequences of specification errors such as the above in Chapter 12. However, it should be obvious that in the above situation *the correct procedure is to include the missing X_3 variable in the regression equation* rather than deal with the 'false' autocorrelation in the residuals from (10.31).

Another situation that can give rise to 'false' autocorrelation in the residuals is *the choice of the wrong functional form for the regression equation*. As we saw in Section 6.4, when we first introduced the Durbin–Watson statistic, estimating a linear equation when the true relationship is nonlinear can also result in sequences of positive and negative residuals. The likelihood of this happening is just as great in multiple regression as it is with simple two-variable regression.

It cannot be stressed strongly enough that, when faced with autocorrelated *residuals*, the first thing to do is to *consider alternative likely specifications for the regression equation*. These should include trying alternative functional forms and if necessary including additional variables. We shall see when we come to discuss 'data mining' in Chapter 12 that this can also lead to problems, but it is preferable to attempting to treat a 'false' autocorrelation problem.

Alternative estimating procedures

If *genuine* autocorrelation is believed to be present in the disturbances of a regression equation, then the generalised least squares estimation method described in Section 10.1 provides a basis for attempting to deal with it. However, we should perhaps attach a health warning to the procedures described in this section. They should be adopted only when all attempts at respecifying the regression equation have failed to produce non-autocorrelated residuals.

For simplicity, we assume that the regression disturbance follows the first-order process (10.47). Given (10.51) and (10.53), the variance–covariance matrix of disturbances (10.2) therefore takes the form

$$V = \sigma^2 \begin{pmatrix} 1 & \rho & \rho^2 & \cdots & \rho^{n-1} \\ \rho & 1 & \rho & \cdots & \rho^{n-2} \\ \rho^2 & \rho & 1 & \cdots & \rho^{n-3} \\ \vdots & \vdots & \vdots & & \vdots \\ \rho^{n-1} & \rho^{n-2} & \rho^{n-3} & \cdots & 1 \end{pmatrix} \tag{10.70}$$

If ρ is known then (10.70) can be substituted into (10.10), and the resultant GLS estimators will be best linear unbiased. However, as in the case of heteroskedasticity, rather than using (10.10), it is computationally more convenient to compute the GLS estimators by *first* transforming the basic data series and *then* applying *ordinary least squares* to the transformed data.

We shall consider two-variable regression with a first-order process, although the following can easily be generalized to deal with multiple regression and/or higher-order processes. We therefore have

$$Y_t = \alpha + \beta X_t + \epsilon_t \tag{10.71}$$

where

$$\epsilon_t = \rho \epsilon_{t-1} + u_t \tag{10.72}$$

Lagging Equation (10.71) by one period and multiplying throughout by the autocorrelation coefficient ρ gives

$$\rho Y_{t-1} = \rho \alpha + \rho \beta X_{t-1} + \rho \epsilon_{t-1} \tag{10.73}$$

If we now take (10.73) from (10.71), we obtain

$$Y_t - \rho Y_{t-1} = \alpha(1 - \rho) + \beta(X_t - \rho X_{t-1}) + \epsilon_t - \rho \epsilon_{t-1} \tag{10.74}$$

which we may write as

$$Y_t^* = \alpha^* + \beta X_t^* + u_t \tag{10.75}$$

where $\alpha^* = \alpha(1 - \rho)$, $Y_t^* = Y_t - \rho Y_{t-1}$ and $X_t^* = X_t - \rho X_{t-1}$, and u_t appears in the first-order process (10.72).

Since u_t, the disturbance in (10.75), obeys all the classical conditions by assumption, OLS may be applied to this equation. That is, we first transform the data series, constructing the new variables Y_t^* and X_t^*, and regress Y_t^* on X_t^*.

The estimators obtained from applying OLS to (10.75) are not quite the same as the GLS estimators obtained by substituting (10.70) into (10.10). This is because in forming the new variables $Y*$ and $X*$ we lose one observation. That is, the first observation on, for example, $Y*$ is $Y_2^* = Y_2 - Y_1$. However, if the first observations on Y and X are transformed to give $Y_1^* = (1 - \rho^2)Y_1$ and $X_1^* = (1 - \rho^2)X_1$, and $Y*$ then regressed on $X*$ for all n observations, the resultant estimators are identical to the GLS estimators (this is known as the Prais–Winsten (1954) correction).

Exercise 10.2

Suppose the equation $Y_t = \beta_1 + \beta_2 X_{2t} + \epsilon_t$ is to be estimated, but the disturbance follows a second-order autoregressive process

$$\epsilon_t = \rho_1 \epsilon_{t-1} + \rho_2 \epsilon_{t-2} + u_t$$

How would you transform Y_t and X_{2t} before estimation?

If the equation to be estimated was instead

$$Y_t = \beta_1 + \beta_2 X_{2t} + \beta_3 X_{3t} + \epsilon_t$$

how would you proceed now?

The major problem with the above GLS procedures is that they presuppose a knowledge of the autocorrelation coefficient ρ. In practice, ρ, like all parameters, is unknown and has to be estimated. A number of ways of doing this have been suggested – some simple, some more complicated. An obvious method is to estimate the *population* autocorrelation coefficient of the *disturbances* (see Equation (10.54)) by the *sample* autocorrelation coefficient of the *residuals*. That is, we estimate ρ by

$$\hat{\rho} = \sum e_t e_{t-1} / \sum e_t^2 \tag{10.76}$$

An alternative procedure suggested by Durbin (1970) is to rewrite Equation (10.74) as

$$Y_t = \alpha(1 - \rho) + \rho Y_{t-1} + \beta X_t - \rho \beta X_{t-1} + u_t \tag{10.77}$$

Application of OLS to (10.77) will then yield an estimator of ρ as the coefficient on Y_{t-1}.

Given an estimate of ρ, obtained by either of the above two methods, the estimate may then be used instead of the true ρ in the above GLS procedures.

The problem with estimates such as (10.76) is that they are based on the OLS residuals, which, if autocorrelation is present, may not be particularly good estimates of the corresponding disturbances. Other more complicated procedures have been suggested for estimating both ρ and the regression parameters simultaneously. Examples are the Cochrane–Orcutt (1949) iterative procedure and the Hildreth–Lu (1960) grid-search procedure. We shall not spend time on the details of these procedures. In the past they have been much overused, but they are part of the standard package in most multiple regression computer programs.

If ρ has to be estimated, as is normally the case, then the resultant estimators are no longer GLS estimators but examples of the feasible least squares estimators, first mentioned in Section 10.1. Unlike the GLS estimators, these FLS estimators are not unbiased but they can be shown to be consistent. They are also asymptotically efficient if the Cochrane–Orcutt or Hildreth–Lu procedures are followed.

In the absence of knowledge about ρ, maximum likelihood methods may also be employed to estimate ρ and the regression parameters simultaneously. However, the likelihood function is complicated in this case by the fact that when a first-order process is present in the disturbances, the sample values of Y can no longer be regarded as independent of one another. We shall therefore not discuss ML estimation, but simply note that the MLEs are asymptotically equivalent to the FLS estimators discussed above.

In the early part of this section we tested the residuals from the estimated demand equation (7.66) for autocorrelation. Both tests we employed suggested that the residuals from this equation were, in fact, serially correlated. However, we will resist the temptation to rush off and employ, for example, the Cochrane–Orcutt or Hildreth–Lu procedures for dealing with autocorrelation mentioned above. As we stressed earlier, all such methods must be treated with great scepticism. As we have seen, autocorrelated residuals are more frequently the result of mis-specified regression equations rather than genuine autocorrelation. If this is the case then the appropriate procedure is to examine alternative specifications of our equation. In later chapters we will do just that for the demand equation (7.66).

10.6 Autoregressive conditional heteroskedasticity

With time series data, it is possible for serial correlation to occur in the variance of the disturbance rather than in the disturbance itself. Given Equation (10.55), the outcome of a given value for X_t is uncertain because of the existence of the disturbance ϵ_t. That is, for given X_t, we have

$$E(Y_t) = \alpha + \beta X_t, \quad \text{but} \quad \text{Var}(Y_t) = \text{Var}(\epsilon_t) = \sigma^2 \neq 0$$

The uncertainty in Y_t is reflected in its non-zero variance σ^2.

A 'large' disturbance in one period, resulting in an unusual value for Y in that period, is likely to result in greater uncertainty as measured by σ^2 in the next period. We can capture this possibility by making σ^2 vary with the disturbance in the previous period:

$$\sigma_t^2 = \sigma^2 + \gamma \epsilon_{t-1}^2 \tag{10.78}$$

Equation (10.78) is known as a first-order **autoregressive conditional heteroskedasticity** (ARCH) process.

Many studies, particularly those involving speculative prices, have encountered ARCH effects, and it is important to be aware of such possibilities. The first-order process (10.78) may be tested for by saving the residuals e_t from the OLS estimation of (10.55) and then regressing e_t^2 on e_{t-1}^2 and examining R^2. Under the null hypothesis $H_0: \gamma = 0$, that is, no ARCH effect, it can be shown that in large samples nR^2 has a χ^2 distribution with one degree of freedom. We therefore reject H_0 if this test statistic exceeds the relevant χ^2 value.

For example, if we perform this test using the residuals, saved previously, from the demand equation (7.66) then the above test statistic takes a value of 1.42. Thus we can find no evidence of ARCH effects in this equation. If ARCH effects were believed to be present then estimation would have to be by ML methods that are outside the scope of this test.

Appendix 10A

Notes to Chapter 10

1. Recall that an unbiased estimator of a disturbance variance is given by $\sum e^2/(n-2)$.
2. It is possible to perform this test with 'higher' and 'lower' subsamples of different size. If the higher subsample is of size n_1 and the lower subsample of size n_2 then the Goldfeld–Quandt test statistic takes the form

$$\frac{\sum e_1^2/(n_1 - k)}{\sum e_2^2/(n_2 - k)} \text{ has an } F \text{ distribution with } [n_1 - k, n_2 - k] \text{ d.f.}$$

3. An alternative is to regress e_i on various functions of X_i. This is the basis of the Glejser (1969) test. A further possibility is to regress $\ln(e_i^2)$ on $\ln X_i$. This is the basis for the Park (1966) test for 'multiplicative' heteroskedasticity of the kind Var$(\epsilon_i) = kX_i^\gamma$.
4. A popular assumption often made is that (10.40) takes the form Var$(\epsilon_i) = kX_{2i}^2$. Equation (10.32) must now be divided throughout by X_{2i}, giving an estimating equation

$$Y/X_{2i} = \beta_2 + \beta_1(1/X_{2i}) + \overset{*}{\epsilon_i} \tag{I}$$

This may be estimated by simple two-variable regression *with* an intercept but notice that the intercept in (I) corresponds to the slope coefficient in (10.32) while the slope coefficient in (I) is the intercept in (10.32).
5. If the White, Park or Glejser (see Note 3) tests have been used to detect the heteroskedasticity then some knowledge of the λ function may already be available.
6. A consistent estimator of Cov$(\epsilon_t, \epsilon_{t-1})$ in (10.54) is given by the covariance of the sample residuals, $\sum e_t e_{t-1}/n$. Similarly, a consistent estimator of Var(ϵ_t) = Var(ϵ_{t-1}) is given by the variance of the sample residuals, $\sum e_t^2/n$. The estimator ρ then follows from the form of (10.54).

7. Equation (10.63) can be written as

$$Y_t = \beta_1 + \beta_2 X_{2t} + \beta_3 Y_{t-1} + u_t + \rho \epsilon_{t-1} \tag{I}$$

Lagging (10.63) by one period, we see that Y_{t-1} and ϵ_{t-1} are correlated. Thus, when (I) above is estimated, part of the effect of ϵ_{t-1} will be captured by Y_{t-1} and not by the residuals. The residuals will tend to reflect u_t alone, which is non-autocorrelated by assumption. Thus the Durbin–Watson test, which is based on these residuals, is likely to suggest non-autocorrelation.

8. The Durbin h statistic is given by

$$h = (1 - 0.5\ dw)\sqrt{n/(1 - ns_\beta^2)}$$

where dw is the value of the Durbin–Watson statistic and s_β^2 is the estimated variance of the OLS estimator of the coefficient on the lagged dependent variable. In the absence of serial correlation, h has a standard normal distribution in large samples.

Further reading

Non-spherical disturbances and generalized least squares are covered in Judge et al. (1988), Chapter 8, with a more advanced treatment in Greene (1993), Chapter 13. Judge et al., Chapter 9, also has extensive material on heteroskedasticity and autocorrelation. Again, a more advanced treatment of these topics is provided by Greene, Chapters 14 and 15. See also Johnston (1984), Chapter 8. ARCH processes are covered in Greene, Section 15.9.

11 Estimating dynamic models

Frequently, when dealing with time series data, an econometrician finds that it is necessary to include lagged values of variables in an estimating equation. For example, we might find ourselves faced with an equation such as

$$Y_t = \alpha + \beta_0 X_t + \beta_1 X_{t-1} + \beta_2 X_{t-2} + \epsilon_t \tag{11.1}$$

That is, Y depends not only on the current value of X but also on past or lagged values.

There are a number of reasons why lags appear in econometric equations. First, they may arise for technological reasons. For example, it takes time for a firm to adjust its capital stock in response to a rise in the demand for its product. New plant cannot be brought into existence rapidly except at great cost. Such costs of adjustment may be lower if the response is delayed. Secondly, psychological factors can also give rise to lags. A household, because of habit or inertia, may not change its consumption level immediately in response to a change in its income. Alternatively, it may also require the income change to persist (that is, be 'permanent' rather than 'transitory') before it alters its consumption. Thirdly, lags can arise because of imperfect information. Economic agents require time to gather relevant information, and this delays the making of decisions. There are also occasions when institutional factors can result in lags. Firms may be contractually obliged to supply a certain level of output, even though cost conditions would indicate a reduction in supply.

The lag pattern in Equation (11.1) is often referred to as a **distributed lag** pattern. In (11.1) the maximum lag length is two periods, but in practice, particularly with quarterly or monthly data, the maximum lag length could be much larger, and even infinite.

11.1 Some basic ideas

Distributed lags such as that in Equation (11.1) imply that the long-run response of Y to a change in X is different from the immediate short-run response. For example, suppose X has remained constant at the level $X=A$ for at least two periods, so that $X_t = X_{t-1} = X_{t-2} = A$. From (11.1), we have, assuming $E(\epsilon_t) = 0$,

$$E(Y_t) = \alpha + \beta_0 A + \beta_1 A + \beta_2 A = \alpha + (\textstyle\sum \beta_j)A \tag{11.2}$$

Equation (11.2) gives the constant **long-run** or **equilibrium level** of $E(Y)$ corresponding to $X=A$. $E(Y)$ will remain at this level until X changes.

Suppose, however, that, at period $t+1$, X rises to $A+1$, and remains at this new level for at least two periods. Using (11.1), we now have

$$
\begin{aligned}
E(Y_{t+1}) &= \alpha + \beta_0 X_{t+1} + \beta_1 X_t + \beta_2 X_{t-1} \\
&= \alpha + \beta_0 (A+1) + \beta_1 A + \beta_2 A \\
&= \alpha + \beta_0 + (\textstyle\sum \beta_j)A
\end{aligned}
\tag{11.3}
$$

Similarly,

$$E(Y_{t+2}) = \alpha + \beta_0 + \beta_1 + (\textstyle\sum \beta_j)A \tag{11.4}$$

$$E(Y_{t+3}) = \alpha + \beta_0 + \beta_1 + \beta_2 + (\textstyle\sum \beta_j)A = \alpha + \textstyle\sum \beta_j + (\textstyle\sum \beta_j)A \tag{11.5}$$

For all periods after $t+3$, $E(Y)$ remains unchanged at the level given by (11.5), provided there is no further change in X. Hence (11.5) gives the new long-run equilibrium value of $E(Y)$ corresponding to $X=A+1$.

A comparison of (11.3) with (11.2) indicates that the immediate **short-run** or **impact effect** on $E(Y)$ of a one-unit change in X is given by the parameter β_0 in the distributed lag equation (11.1). β_0 is sometimes referred to as an **impact multiplier**. This is obviously not the full effect of a change in X, though, since, as (11.4) and (11.5) indicate, $E(Y)$ continues to rise until period $t+1$, when it reaches its new equilibrium value. A comparison of (11.5) with (11.2) indicates that the eventual overall **long-run effect** on $E(Y)$ of a one-unit change in X is given by $\sum \beta_j$, the sum of the β coefficients in the distributed lag equation (11.1). This sum, $\sum \beta_j$, is sometimes referred to as a **long-run** or **equilibrium multiplier**.[1]

From (11.2), the long-run or equilibrium relationship between X and Y can be seen to be

$$E(Y) = \alpha + (\textstyle\sum \beta_j)X \tag{11.6}$$

For any given *constant* value of X, (11.6) tells us the equilibrium or long-run value that $E(Y)$ will eventually attain.

Notice that Equations (11.2)–(11.5) trace the movement in E(Y) as it moves over time from its original equilibrium value to the new equilibrium value, following the change in X. For this reason, Equation (11.1) is referred as a **dynamic model**.

Similar analyses will hold for any maximum lag length in equations such as (11.1). In general, if

$$Y_t = \alpha + \beta_0 X_t + \beta_1 X_{t-1} + \beta_2 X_{t-2} + \cdots + \beta_m X_{t-m} + \epsilon_t \qquad (11.7)$$

then the impact effect of a change in X is again given by β_0 and the long-run effect by $\sum \beta_j$, where the summation is now over all βs in (11.7). Similarly, the long-run equilibrium relationship between E(Y) and X will again be given by (11.6).

It should be stressed that when we talk of long-run effects above, we are comparing one equilibrium position with another. The long run in this context need not involve a large number of years or even days. Equilibrium might be reached very quickly. For example, for Equation (11.1), equilibrium and the 'long run' is reached after just two periods. However, if the maximum lag length m in Equation (11.7) is very large or even infinite then the equilibrium may never be reached.

Notice that a long-run equilibrium relationship such as (11.6) does not have to be estimated directly at all. It certainly does not have to be estimated from a lengthy 'run' of time series data. Rather, a 'short-run' relationship such as (11.1) can be estimated and its coefficients used to deduce the implied long-run relationship. This may be convenient, because the economic systems we observe are rarely if ever in equilibrium, however lengthy is our sample period. For example, suppose we estimated (11.1) by

$$\hat{Y} = 15 + 0.4X_t + 0.7X_{t-1} + 0.2X_{t-2} \qquad (11.8)$$

The sum of the β coefficients is estimated by (11.8) to be 1.3, so, using (11.6), the implied long-run relationship is estimated by

$$\hat{Y} = 15 + 1.3X \qquad (11.9)$$

If all the β_j in equations such as (11.7) are positive, a useful way of summarizing the lag structure is to find the **mean lag**, given by

$$\text{mean lag} = \sum(j\beta_j)/\sum\beta_j \qquad (11.10)$$

Equation (11.10) is a weighted average of the individual lags in (11.7), with weights given by the relative sizes of the βs. For Equation (11.8), for example,

$$\text{mean lag} = 0\left(\frac{0.4}{1.3}\right) + 1\left(\frac{0.7}{1.3}\right) + 2\left(\frac{0.2}{1.3}\right) = 0.846 \text{ periods}$$

Thus 'on average' a change in X takes 0.846 periods before it affects Y.

Estimating distributed lags such as that given by (11.7) is not as simple as it may appear. If m is small, as in (11.1), then the straightforward application of OLS will yield efficient estimators of the βs. However, if the maximum lag length is large, so that there are a large number of lagged regressors, then degrees-of-freedom problems make estimation impracticable unless the sample size is large. Even for large samples, since the various lagged values of X are likely to be multicollinear there may be serious problems in determining precise estimates of the β coefficients. This may make it impossible to determine the correct length of the distributed lag (i.e. to determine m), if this has to be attempted by considering which of the βs are significantly different from zero on the usual t test.

For the above reasons, distributed lags are rarely estimated by the straightforward use of OLS. As we shall see shortly, other procedures have to be followed if equations such as (11.7) are to be estimated.

11.2 Adjustment lags

Let Y^* be the **optimal** or **desired level** of some variable Y. Suppose Y^* depends on some single explanatory variable X and a disturbance:

$$Y_t^* = \alpha + \beta X_t + \epsilon_t \tag{11.11}$$

For example, Y^* could be a firm's desired capital stock, which might be a function of its output. Alternatively, Y^* could be a household's optimal utility-maximizing level of demand for a good, which, at given prices, might depend on its disposable income. We assume that ϵ_t is a 'well-behaved' disturbance in the sense that it obeys all the classical assumptions.

Desired or optimal Y may not be the same as actual Y. Because of inertia, habit or the costs involved, actual Y may not be immediately adjusted to its optimal level Y^*, following a change in X. Suppose Y^* and Y are related as follows:

$$Y_t - Y_{t-1} = \theta(Y_t^* - Y_{t-1}), \qquad 0 < \theta < 1 \tag{11.12}$$

That is, if the desired level of Y in period t differs from the actual value in the previous period, Y_{t-1}, then actual Y is adjusted upwards or downwards towards desired Y in period t, so that $Y_t - Y_{t-1}$ is non-zero. However, in general, the adjustment is only partial, since actual Y is not moved 'all the way' to Y^* in period t. The extent of the adjustment depends on the value of the **adjustment parameter** θ. At one extreme, $\theta = 0$ and, from (11.12), $Y_t = Y_{t-1}$, so that no adjustment takes place at all. At the other extreme, $\theta = 1$ and, from (11.12), $Y_t = Y_t^*$, so that adjustment in the current period is total. Generally, θ lies between these extremes, the greater its value the greater being the extent of the adjustment. θ in fact measures the proportion of any discrepancy between Y_t^* and Y_{t-1} that is eliminated in the current period.

The above model is referred to as the **partial adjustment model** or sometimes as the **stock adjustment model**. The model was extremely popular during the 1960s because of the ease with which it can be estimated. If (11.11) is substituted into (11.12), we obtain

$$Y_t = \alpha\theta + \beta\theta X_t + (1 - \theta)Y_{t-1} + v_t \tag{11.13}$$

where the disturbance $v_t = \theta\epsilon_t$.

The advantage of (11.13) over (11.11) is that it does not involve the unobservable variable Y^*, and may therefore be estimated. If, as we have assumed, the disturbance in (11.11) is well behaved then that in (11.13) will also obey all classical assumptions, so OLS may be used for estimation. However, recall from Section 8.1 that the presence of the lagged dependent variable Y_{t-1} in (11.13) means that the OLS estimators will be *consistent but not unbiased*.

Suppose, for example, that (11.13) is estimated by

$$\hat{Y}_t = 24 + 0.54X_t + 0.40Y_{t-1} \tag{11.14}$$

Comparison with (11.13) now yields estimates $\hat{\theta} = 0.6$, $\hat{\beta} = 0.54/\hat{\theta} = 0.9$ and $\hat{\alpha} = 24/0.6 = 40$. Thus we estimate the underlying relationship (11.11) by

$$Y_t^* = 40 + 0.9X_t$$

and the adjustment parameter in (11.12) as 0.6. That is, 60% of any difference between desired and actual Y is made up in the current period.

Since in (11.13) Y_t is dependent on its own lagged value, this type of lag is referred to as an **autoregressive lag**. In the last section we discussed distributed lags. There is, in fact, a very close link between such autoregressive lags and a certain kind of distributed lag. If we substitute in (11.13) for Y_{t-1}, we obtain, ignoring the disturbance for the moment,

$$\begin{aligned} Y_t &= \alpha\theta + \beta\theta X_t + (1-\theta)[\alpha\theta + \beta\theta X_{t-1} + (1-\theta)Y_{t-2}] \\ &= \alpha\theta + \alpha\theta(1-\theta) + \beta\theta X_t + \beta\theta(1-\theta)X_{t-1} + (1-\theta)^2 Y_{t-2} \end{aligned} \tag{11.15}$$

If we use (11.13) to continue substituting into (11.15) for Y_{t-2}, then Y_{t-3}, then Y_{t-4}, etc., we eventually obtain

$$Y_t = \alpha^* + \beta\theta X_t + \beta\theta(1-\theta)X_{t-1} + \beta\theta(1-\theta)^2 X_{t-2} + \beta\theta(1-\theta)^3 X_{t-3} + \cdots \tag{11.16}$$

Provided $1 - \theta < 1$, the final term in (11.16), involving a lagged value of Y, eventually becomes so small that it can be ignored, and

$$\alpha^* = \alpha\theta + \alpha\theta(1-\theta) + \alpha\theta(1-\theta)^2 + \cdots \tag{11.17}$$

Equation (11.17) is an infinite geometric series with first term $\alpha\theta$ and common ratio $1 - \theta$. It is therefore convergent, so that α^* is finite and in fact equal to[2]

$$\alpha^* = \frac{\alpha\theta}{1 - (1-\theta)} = \alpha$$

Thus the intercept in (11.16) is, in fact, the same as that in the original (11.11).

Notice that (11.16) contains a distributed lag of the kind (11.7), except that the maximum lag in this case is infinite. Also, since $0 < 1 - \theta < 1$, in this case the coefficients of the current and lagged values of X decline geometrically as the lag length increases. That is, the greater the lag, the smaller the effect on Y. For example, since (11.14) implies $\hat{\theta} = 0.6$, $\hat{\alpha} = 40$ and $\hat{\beta} = 0.9$, using (11.16) it must also imply the distributed lag

$$Y_t = 40 + 0.54X_t + 0.216X_{t-1} + 0.086X_{t-2} + \cdots$$

The geometric lag in (11.16) is sometimes referred to as a **Koyck distributed lag**. Since the autoregressive lag model (11.13) implies a distributed lag, such models are also referred to as **autoregressive distributed lag** (ADL) models.

Obviously, since (11.13) implies (11.16), the reverse must also be true. In fact, (11.13) can easily be retrieved from (11.16) by applying a so-called **Koyck transformation**. If (11.16) is lagged one period and multiplied throughout by $1 - \theta$, we obtain

$$(1 - \theta)Y_{t-1} = \alpha(1 - \theta) + \beta\theta(1 - \theta)X_{t-1} + \beta\theta(1 - \theta)^2 X_{t-2}$$
$$+ \beta\theta(1 - \theta)^3 X_{t-3} + \cdots \tag{11.18}$$

Subtracting (11.18) from the original (11.16), cancelling out terms and rearranging will now yield the autoregressive lag equation (11.13).

The above gives the clue to a method of estimating distributed lag equations such as (11.7). If the coefficients β_j in (11.7) are assumed to follow some pattern, then the number of independent parameters that have to be estimated can be reduced to manageable proportions. For example, in (11.16) they are assumed to decline geometrically. That is, each $\beta_j = \beta\theta(1 - \theta)^j$, so that, apart from α, only two parameters β and θ have to be estimated. As we have seen, this can be done by estimating the autoregressive equation (11.13).

Estimation of the geometric lag may not, however, be quite as simple as it may seem. Careful attention has to be paid to the stochastic specification of equations. In the above model we included a well-behaved disturbance ϵ_t in Equation (11.11). This resulted in a similar disturbance v_t in (11.13), so that this equation could then be estimated by OLS. However, we ignored the disturbance when successively substituting into (11.13) to obtain the distributed lag formulation (11.16). The reader should verify that if we include disturbances when substituting into (11.13), we eventually obtain in (11.16) a disturbance

$$u_t = v_t + (1 - \theta)v_{t-1} + (1 - \theta)^2 v_{t-2} + \cdots \tag{11.19}$$

The disturbance (11.19) is of the moving average kind (10.68), and hence is autocorrelated. Thus if the disturbance in the autoregressive equation (11.13) is well behaved then the disturbance in the distributed lag equation (11.16) will be autocorrelated. This is a further reason for preferring to estimate the parameters α, β and θ in the partial adjustment model via Equation (11.13) rather than via Equation (11.16).

Suppose, however, we *begin* by specifying the geometric distributed lag equation (11.16), adding to it a disturbance u_t, which we assume is well behaved. If we now use the Koyck transformation, as above, to obtain the autoregressive equation (11.13), we find that it contains a disturbance

$$v_t = u_t - (1 - \theta)u_{t-1} \tag{11.20}$$

It is the disturbance (11.20) that is now of moving average kind and hence is autocorrelated. Estimating (11.13) now becomes considerably more difficult, because this equation now contains both a lagged dependent variable and an autocorrelated disturbance. We shall examine the estimation difficulties that arise from this combination of problems in the next section. For the moment, we merely stress that the method adopted for estimating an ADL model depends very much on the stochastic specification of that model.

COMPUTER EXERCISE I

In the exercise at the end of Chapter 7 we used Data Set 1 to estimate the demand for food equation (7.67). Although we obtained a high coefficient of determination R^2, we discovered in Section 10.5 that both the Durbin–Watson and the LM test statistics strongly suggested autocorrelation in the residuals of this equation.

Suppose we reinterpret Equation (7.67) as giving the equilibrium long-run demand for food, Q^*, that exists when consumers are fully adjusted to any changes in real expenditure X/G and relative price P/G. That is

$$\ln (Q^*)_t = \beta_1 + \beta_2 \ln (X/G)_t + \beta_3 \ln (P/G)_t + \epsilon_t \tag{11.21}$$

Actual demand for food, Q, may differ from equilibrium demand because of habit or the inertia of consumers. Let us specify a logarithmic version of the partial adjustment model (11.12) to relate Q to Q^*:

$$\ln (Q)_t - \ln (Q)_{t-1} = \theta[\ln (Q^*)_t - \ln (Q)_{t-1}] \tag{11.22}$$

Substituting for $\ln (Q^*)_t$ in (11.22) now gives

$$\ln (Q)_t = \beta_1\theta + \beta_2\theta \ln (X/G)_t + \beta_3\theta \ln (P/G)_t + (1 - \theta) \ln (Q)_{t-1} + u_t \tag{11.23}$$

where $u_t = \theta\epsilon_t$. Equation (11.23) suggests that the problem with our estimated equation (7.67) may have been the fact that we failed to include the lagged dependent variable $\ln (Q)_{t-1}$ among its regressors. Recall from our discussion in Section 10.5 that a frequent cause of autocorrelated residuals is not so much genuine autocorrelation as the omission of relevant regressors. Our poor dw and LM statistics may be the result of a mis-specified regression equation. Such an omission of lagged dependent variable(s) is an example of what is sometimes referred to as a **dynamic mis-specification**.

If you re-estimate Equation (7.67) with the variable $\ln (Q)_{t-1}$ added, using the same sample period, 1965–1989, you should obtain

$$\widehat{\ln (Q)}_t = \underset{(4.31)}{4.34} + \underset{(2.75)}{0.142 \ln (X/G)_t} - \underset{(-2.18)}{0.197 \ln (P/G)_t} + \underset{(3.47)}{0.478 \ln (Q)_{t-1}}$$

$$\tag{11.24}$$

Note that the coefficient of ln $(Q)_{t-1}$ in (11.24) is significantly different from zero, with a t ratio well in excess of 3. It implies a value of $\hat{\theta} = 0.522$ in Equation (11.22), suggesting that about 52% of any difference between the actual and equilibrium demand for food is eliminated within a year. This is not an unreasonable figure. We can also estimate the long-run elasticities β_2, β_3 in Equation (11.21). Comparison of (11.24) and (11.23) indicates we should estimate $\beta_2\theta$ by 0.142. Given our estimate of θ, this indicates that we should estimate the long-run real expenditure elasticity as $\hat{\beta}_2 = 0.272$. Similarly, we can estimate the long-run relative price elasticity as $\hat{\beta}_3 = -0.377$.

Unfortunately, the autocorrelation we observed in the residuals of Equation (7.67) remains in Equation (11.24). Your computer will provide autocorrelation statistics as part of its standard output. You should obtain for this equation a value for the *dw* statistic of 1.15 and for the Breusch–Godfrey LM statistic for first-order autocorrelation a value of 6.42 compared with a critical value of $\chi^2_{0.05} = 3.84$. Although these figures are an improvement on those for Equation (7.67), they still indicate strongly autocorrelated residuals. Remember also that the *dw* statistic is biased towards 2 in these circumstances because of the presence of the lagged dependent variable Q_{t-1}. Yet its value is still very low. It appears that we cannot solve our specification problem with Equation (7.67) merely by introducing partial adjustment.

More complicated lag structures

A major problem with the geometric distributed lag (11.16) is that the size of the coefficients in the lag structure decline continually as the lag on the explanatory X variable is increased. The lag patterns for various values of the parameter θ are illustrated in Figure 11.1. Notice that the greater the value of θ, the more rapid the 'rate of decay' as the lag is increased. In practice, however, such lag structures may be

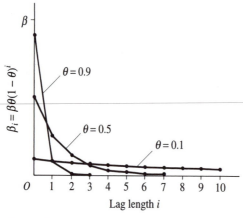

Figure 11.1 Geometric lag coefficients.

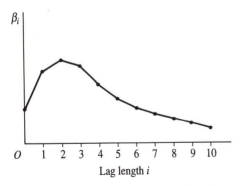

Figure 11.2 An inverted-U lag distribution.

inappropriate. It is often the case that a change in X does not have the maximum effect on Y until a number of periods have passed. The coefficients in equations such as (11.7) may follow an 'inverted U' distribution, as illustrated in Figure 11.2, rising to a peak after a few periods and only then starting to decline.

There are a number of ways in which lag structures similar to that in Figure 11.2 can be modelled. For example, a simple generalization of the partial adjustment equation (11.13) is

$$Y_t = \alpha + \beta_0 X_t + \beta_1 X_{t-1} + \gamma Y_{t-1} + v_t \tag{11.25}$$

Successive substitution in (11.25) for Y_{t-1}, Y_{t-2}, etc. will now eventually yield, provided $0 < \gamma < 1$,

$$Y_t = \alpha^* + \beta_0 X_t + \mu X_{t-1} + \gamma \mu X_{t-2} + \gamma^2 \mu X_{t-3} + \cdots + u_t \tag{11.26}$$

where $\mu = \gamma \beta_0 + \beta_1$, $\alpha^* = \alpha/(1 - \gamma)$ and

$$u_t = v_t + \gamma v_{t-1} + \gamma^2 v_{t-2} + \cdots$$

For appropriately chosen values of γ, β_0 and β_1, (11.26) will yield a distributed lag equation with the largest coefficient being that of X_{t-1}, the coefficients declining geometrically thereafter. Notice, though, that the disturbance in (11.26) is again of moving average form.

Alternatively, (11.13) may be replaced by

$$Y_t = \alpha + \beta X_t + \gamma_1 Y_{t-1} + \gamma_2 Y_{t-2} + v_t \tag{11.27}$$

Again, successive substitution in (11.27) for Y_{t-1}, Y_{t-2}, etc. will lead, eventually, to an equation involving an infinite distributed lag. In fact, it can be shown that *any* infinite distributed lag can be approximated by an ADL equation of the form

$$\begin{aligned} Y_t = {} & \alpha + \beta_0 X_t + \beta_1 X_{t-1} + \beta_2 X_{t-2} + \cdots + \beta_L X_{t-L} \\ & + \gamma_1 Y_{t-1} + \gamma_2 Y_{t-2} + \cdots + \gamma_M Y_{t-M} + v_t \end{aligned} \tag{11.28}$$

provided the values of the maximum lag lengths L and M are appropriately chosen. In practice, small values of L and M have to be used, unless the sample is very large.

The above **rational lags**, of which the geometric lag is a special case, were first used by econometricians in the late 1960s and 1970s.[3] Like the simple distributed lags of the last section, they imply that a change in X has different short- and long-run effects on Y. For example, in (11.28) the short-run impact effect of a unit change in X, that is, the short-run multiplier, is given by the parameter β_0. To find the eventual long-run effect of a unit change in X, however, we have to set

$$Y_t = Y_{t-1} = Y_{t-2} = \cdots = Y_{t-M} = Y^* = \text{constant}$$

and

$$X_t = X_{t-1} = X_{t-2} = \cdots = X_{t-L} = X^* = \text{constant}$$

in (11.28). That is, we assume that X remains constant for sufficiently long for all previous changes in X to have had their full effect on Y, so that Y has also become constant. Substituting in (11.28), assuming $E(v_t) = 0$ and then taking expectations gives

$$E(Y) = \frac{\alpha}{1 - \sum \gamma_j} + \frac{\sum \beta_j}{1 - \sum \gamma_j} X \tag{11.29}$$

as the long-run or equilibrium relationship between X and Y. The long-run effect on Y of a unit change in X, that is, the long-run multiplier, is therefore $(\sum \beta_j)/(1 - \sum \gamma_j)$.

As with the geometric lag, care has to be taken with the stochastic specification of any rational lag model. It must always be remembered that if the disturbance in the distributed lag version of the model obeys all classical assumptions then the disturbance in the autoregressive equation (11.28) will be autocorrelated. This is a consequence of the transformations that have to be applied to express the original model in autoregressive form.

Polynomial lags

Polynomial lags were developed by Almon (1965) to approximate inverted U-shaped or even more complicated lag distributions that have a finite rather than an infinite maximum lag. Consider again the finite distributed lag (11.7) and suppose we wish to approximate a lag distribution such as that in Figure 11.3. A maximum lag length of $m = 8$ therefore seems appropriate, so that (11.7) becomes

$$Y_t = \alpha + \beta_0 X_t + \beta_1 X_{t-1} + \beta_2 X_{t-2} + \cdots + \beta_8 X_{t-8} + \epsilon_t \tag{11.30}$$

The Almon idea is to approximate the relationship between the β coefficients in (11.30) by a polynomial of suitable degree. We shall restrict ourselves to second-order polynomials. A curve drawn through the points in Figure 11.3 can be approximated by[4]

$$\beta_i = k_0 + k_1 i + k_2 i^2 \tag{11.31}$$

where the ks are constants. We can use (11.31) to express each of the βs in terms of

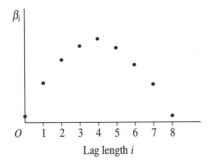

β_i

O 1   2   3   4   5   6   7   8

Lag length i

Figure 11.3 A polynomial lag distribution.

the ks:

$$\beta_0 = k_0$$
$$\beta_1 = k_0 + k_1 + k_2$$
$$\beta_2 = k_0 + 2k_1 + 4k_2 \tag{11.23}$$
$$\vdots$$
$$\beta_8 = k_0 + 8k_1 + 64k_2$$

Substituting these expressions for the βs into (11.30) gives

$$Y_t = \alpha + k_0 X_t + (k_0 + k_1 + k_2)X_{t-1} + (k_0 + 2k_1 + 4k_2)X_{t-2}$$
$$+ \cdots + (k_0 + 8k_1 + 64k_2)X_{t-8} + \epsilon_t \tag{11.33}$$

Equation (11.33) can be rearranged as

$$Y_t = \alpha + k_0 \sum X_{t-i} + k_1 \sum i X_{t-i} + k_2 \sum i^2 X_{t-i} + \epsilon_t \tag{11.34}$$

where the summations are from $i=0$ to $i=8$ in each case. If we now define three new variables

$$W_{1t} = \sum X_{t-i}, \qquad W_{2t} = \sum i X_{t-i}, \qquad W_{3t} = \sum i^2 X_{t-i}$$

it is possible to rewrite (11.34) as

$$Y_t = \alpha + k_0 W_{1t} + k_1 W_{2t} + k_3 W_{3t} + \epsilon_t \tag{11.35}$$

Equation (11.35) may be estimated by OLS, once the variables W_1, W_2 and W_3 have been created from the original data on X. Once estimates of the ks have been obtained by this method, the original β coefficients in (11.30) can be estimated using the relationships (11.32).

What the polynomial approximation has done is to reduce the number of parameters that have to be estimated from nine in Equation (11.30) to just four in Equation (11.35). There is a similar reduction in the number of explanatory variables in the estimating equation. The procedure can therefore substantially reduce any multicollinearity problems that might arise in the estimation of Equation (11.30). In general, with a second-order polynomial, for a maximum lag length m, the number of parameters to be estimated will be reduced from $m+1$ to 4. If the sample size is relatively small, this can be an important saving in degrees of freedom.

A further important advantage of polynomial lags is that, unlike rational lags, they do not require any transformations that result in the disturbance violating classical assumptions. For example, if the disturbance in (11.30) is non-autocorrelated then so must be that in the estimating equation (11.35).

Notice that to apply the above procedure, the maximum lag length m has to be decided in advance. Also, although we have assumed a second-order polynomial above, in practice the order of the polynomial must also be decided in advance. For example, if it were decided to use a third-order polynomial then the βs would be approximated not by (11.31) but by

$$\beta_i = k_0 + k_1 i + k_2 i^2 + k_3 i^3$$

and the constructed variable $W_{4t} = \sum i^3 X_{t-i}$ included in (11.35). Both the maximum lag length and the degree of the polynomial are normally decided by experimentation.[5]

COMPUTER EXERCISE II

In this exercise we shall illustrate the Almon lag technique, using Data Set 4 on the floppy disk. Recall that this quarterly data refers to UK consumer expenditure, and we last used it to estimate Equation (9.58) in the section on dummy variables. Equation (9.58) contains the lagged dependent variable C_{t-1}, and could therefore be interpreted in terms of the partial adjustment model. The coefficient of C_{t-1} suggests an adjustment parameter θ of 0.364, implying that about 36% of any difference between actual and optimal consumption is made up in each quarter.

The reader should first re-estimate (9.58), and verify that neither the Durbin–Watson statistic (2.07) nor the LM statistic (0.64) suggest any problem of first-order autocorrelation in the residuals of this equation. Remember, though, that the dw statistic is biased towards 2 because of the presence of C_{t-1} in (9.58), and therefore cannot be trusted. Moreover, with quarterly data, fourth-order is as likely as first-order autocorrelation. However, your computer package should also compute for you the LM statistic for up to fourth-order autocorrelation. Verify that its value is 5.07, compared with $\chi^2_{0.05} = 9.49$. So there is no problem with this type of autocorrelation either.

Although Equation (9.58) seems quite satisfactory, its specification does impose a geometric lag on the income variable, implying, as we have explained, declining weights on Y_t, Y_{t-1}, Y_{t-2} and so on. It is possible that with quarterly data, the response of consumption to an income change only reaches its maximum after a few quarters have passed. That is, a more suitable lag pattern could be the inverted U shape of Figure 11.2. To investigate this possibility we make use of the Almon lag technique of the last subsection.

We shall approximate the lag pattern for disposable income Y by a second-order polynomial and use a maximum lag length of six quarters. The transformation routines in your regression package will enable you to calculate, for the periods 1976Q3 through 1984Q4, the equivalents of W_1, W_2 and W_3, below (11.34). Remembering to include the seasonal dummy variables, you should obtain the Almon lag equation

$$\hat{C}_t = 4627 + 0.577W_{1t} - 0.372W_{2t} + 0.050W_{3t} + \text{dummies} \qquad (11.36)$$
$$\quad\ (1.48) \quad (5.53) \qquad (-3.41) \qquad (2.80)$$

with a coefficint of determination $R^2 = 0.915$, slightly less than that for Equation (9.58).

If the consumption equation is written as

$$C_t = \alpha + \beta_0 X_t + \beta_1 X_{t-1} + \beta_2 X_{t-2} + \cdots + \beta_6 X_{t-6} + \text{dummies} + \epsilon_t$$

we can now use (11.31) and the coefficients of the Ws in (11.36) to deduce the implied lag pattern for the income variable. In fact,

$$\beta_0 = 0.577$$
$$\beta_1 = 0.577 - 0.372 + 0.050 = 0.255$$
$$\beta_2 = 0.577 - 2(0.372) + 4(0.050) = 0.033$$
$$\beta_3 = 0.577 - 3(0.372) + 9(0.050) = -0.089$$
$$\beta_4 = 0.577 - 4(0.372) + 16(0.050) = -0.111$$
$$\beta_5 = 0.577 - 5(0.372) + 25(0.050) = -0.033$$
$$\beta_6 = 0.577 - 6(0.372) + 36(0.050) = 0.145$$

This polynomial lag structure is illustrated in Figure 11.4, together with the geometric lag structure implied by Equation (9.58). There is no suggestion of an inverted-U shape, the polynomial equation in fact suggesting an even larger immediate response to a change in income. Notice also that the third-, fourth- and fifth-order lag coefficients are improbably negative.

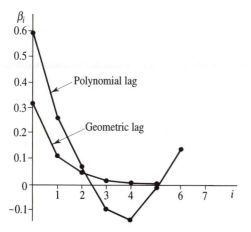

Figure 11.4 Polynomial versus geometric lag.

The autocorrelation statistics for the polynomial lag equation (11.36) are poor. The Durbin–Watson statistic is as low as 0.74, while the first- and fourth-order LM statistics exceed their 5% critical values. This suggests that a second-order polynomial lag represents a serious dynamic mis-specification of the equation. In this instance the simple geometric lag of Equation (9.58) seems markedly superior.

11.3 Problems in the estimation of dynamic models

Consider, for example, the dynamic model (11.14). If the value of Y in any period is known then, for a given constant value of X, it is possible to trace the time path of Y through all future periods. For example, if $X_t = 30 = $ constant for all t and $Y_0 = 50$ then, using (11.14),

$$Y_1 = 24 + 0.54X_1 + 0.40Y_0 = 60.2$$
$$Y_2 = 24 + 0.54X_2 + 0.40Y_1 = 64.28$$
$$Y_3 = 24 + 0.54X_3 + 0.40Y_2 = 65.91$$

and so on.

Similarly, if we take the general ADL equation (11.28), it is again possible to trace the time path of Y for a given fixed value of X, provided we have sufficient 'starting' values of Y.

The interesting question now arises of what the time paths implied by dynamic models look like. We have stressed in earlier chapters that classical regression techniques were not designed to cope with variables that were 'non-stationary' in the sense that they exhibited upward or downward trends over time. If explanatory variables exhibit such trends then classical assumption IC' will be violated. In such a case, as we pointed out in Section 8.1, normal large-sample statistical theory is no longer valid. We can no longer rely on our estimators possessing the usual large-sample properties, and standard classical inferential procedures can no longer be applied.

Under what conditions will the time paths implied by dynamic models violate classical assumptions? For the simple first-order autoregressive model (11.13), it is not difficult to see that if the value of $1 - \theta$ were to equal or exceed unity then the time path of Y would be unstable in the sense that, for a given value of X, Y would increase over time without limit rather than tending towards some equilibrium value. This can easily be verified by setting the coefficient of Y_{t-1} in Equation (11.14) equal to 1.2 rather than 0.4.

If Y_t in the first-order autoregressive model (11.13) increases without limit in this way then so must Y_{t-1}. But Y_{t-1} is one of the regressors in (11.13), so classical assumption IC' has indeed been violated.

Since $1 - \theta > 1$ implies $\theta < 0$, it could be argued that, in the context of the partial adjustment model (11.12), such instability is virtually ruled out in this case.

However, the first-order model (11.13) can exist independently of the partial adjustment model, and, moreover, in attempting to approximate more complex distributed lags, econometricians frequently find themselves estimating higher-order ADL models of the type (11.28).

It is possible to show that, for given values of X_t, X_{t-1}, X_{t-2} etc., the nature of the time path for Y implied by the more general equation (11.28) depends on the roots μ_i $(i = 1, 2, \ldots, M)$ of the equation

$$\mu^M - \gamma_1 \mu^{M-1} - \gamma_2 \mu^{M-2} - \gamma_3 \mu^{M-3} - \cdots - \gamma_{M-1}\mu - \gamma_M = 0 \qquad (11.37)$$

where the γ are the coefficients on lagged values of Y in Equation (11.28) and M is the maximum lag on Y in that equation. The implied time path of Y will be unstable if any of the roots μ_i of (11.37) are greater than or equal to unity in absolute value.[6]

The consequences of an unstable time path for Y in the general case are the same as for the first-order case. When estimating ADL equations such as (11.28), conventional large-sample theory cannot be applied so that the usual OLS inferential procedures may become invalid even in large samples.

For the reasons outlined at the beginning of this chapter, econometricians frequently estimate models involving complicated autoregressive lag structures. The above discussion indicates that, when estimation is undertaken, close attention needs to be paid to the dynamic properties of such models and to whether the time paths of variables violate classical assumptions.

Autocorrelation and lagged dependent variables

We saw in the last section that if the disturbance in a distributed lag equation is well behaved, in the sense that it obeys all the classical assumptions, then, when an appropriate transformation is applied to obtain the autoregressive version of the model, this results in a moving-average-type disturbance that is autocorrelated. For example, if a well-behaved disturbance is added to the geometric distributed lag (11.16) and the Koyck transformation applied then we eventually obtain

$$Y_t = \alpha\theta + \beta\theta X_t + (1 - \theta)Y_{t-1} + v_t \qquad (11.38)$$

where v_t is a first-order moving average disturbance of the form

$$v_t = u_t - (1 - \theta)u_{t-1} \qquad (11.39)$$

and u_t is the disturbance in the original distributed lag equation.

The fact that v_t in (11.38) is autocorrelated has important implications for estimation. In the absence of autocorrelation, we saw in Section 8.1 that the appearance of a lagged dependent variable among the regressors of an equation merely means that the OLS estimators lose the property of unbiasedness. They retain the large-sample property of consistency. In the absence of a lagged dependent variable, we saw in Section 10.4 that an autocorrelated disturbance alone merely means that the OLS estimators lose the property of efficiency. They remain both unbiased and consistent. However, the *combination* of autocorrelated disturbance and lagged dependent variable results in the OLS estimators becoming *both biased and inconsistent*.

To see this intuitively, note that, from (11.38) and (11.39), Y_{t-1} depends on v_{t-1} and hence on u_{t-1}. But because of the form of the disturbance (11.39), v_t depends on u_{t-1}. Hence Y_{t-1} and v_t are related. But Y_{t-1} is one of the regressors in (11.38). Thus in this equation we have a contemporaneous correlation between right-hand-side variable and disturbance. We know from Section 8.1 that in these circumstances OLS provides estimators that are not only biased but also inconsistent.

Autocorrelation in the disturbance has similar consequences whenever lagged dependent variables appear on the right-hand side of an estimating equation. That is why we stressed in the last section that careful attention should be paid to the stochastic specification of autoregressive equations of any order. While such equations do not necessarily suffer from serial correlation (for example, the partial adjustment equation (11.13) has a well-behaved disturbance), the consequences of autocorrelation are so serious in these circumstances that the possibility of it being present must always be carefully tested for.[7]

The simplest way to obtain consistent estimators of the parameters in, for example, Equation (11.38), which *does* possess an autocorrelated disturbance, is to use the instrumental variable methods described in Section 8.4. X_t can serve as its own instrument, and the obvious instrument for Y_{t-1} is X_{t-1}. X_t and X_{t-1} are, by assumption, uncorrelated with v_t in (11.38), while X_{t-1} will be highly correlated with Y_{t-1}.[8] Alternatively, if the GIVE procedure is used then a composite instrumental variable can be formed out of current and lagged values of X.

Unfortunately, instrumental variable estimators, although consistent, are unlikely to be very efficient, because X_t will normally be highly correlated with its lagged values. An alternative approach to estimation of α, β and θ is based on the distributed lag form (11.16), which was assumed to contain a well-behaved disturbance. Equation (11.16) can be written as

$$Y_t = \alpha + \beta[\theta X_t + \theta(1-\theta)X_{t-1} + \theta(1-\theta)^2 X_{t-2}$$
$$+ \theta(1-\theta)^3 X_{t-3} + \cdots] + u_t \tag{11.40}$$

or

$$Y_t = \alpha + \beta Z_t + u_t \tag{11.41}$$

where

$$Z_t = \theta X_t + \theta(1-\theta)X_{t-1} + \theta(1-\theta)^2 X_{t-2} + \cdots \tag{11.42}$$

If θ were known, the variable Z_t could be constructed out of the data on X, provided the infinite series (11.42) was truncated after a finite number of terms. OLS could then be applied to (11.41) to obtain estimates of α and β. But θ, of course, is not known, and in practice alternative versions of the Z series have to be constructed using different possible values for θ. Each such version can then be used in the estimation of (11.41). In fact, a 'grid search' can be carried out, initially using values of $\theta = 0.1, 0.2, 0.3, \ldots$, and that version of (11.41) with the largest explained sum of squares selected to provide the estimates of α and β. If necessary, once an approximate value of θ is obtained, a finer grid search may be performed. For example, if θ were found to be in the range 0.2–0.3, the second grid search would be over $\theta = 0.21, 0.22, 0.23, \ldots$.

The major problem with the above procedure is that, particularly for values of θ around 0.5, the necessary truncation of (11.42) can lead to an inaccurate Z series and biased estimates. However, Klein (1958) devised a procedure that overcomes this problem and provides maximum likelihood estimates.

11.4 A Monte Carlo study

In this section we illustrate the consequences of lagged dependent variables by means of two simulation studies, each involving the following simple ADL model:

$$Y_t = \beta_1 + \beta_2 X_t + \beta_3 Y_{t-1} + v_t \tag{11.43}$$

with

$$\beta_1 = 3, \qquad \beta_2 = 0.3, \qquad \beta_3 = 0.6$$

X is exogenous and v is a disturbance. The β parameters are unknown to any econometric investigator. First, we consider the OLS estimation of this model when the disturbance v obeys all classical assumptions. Then, in a second study we assume that v is of moving average form and hence is autocorrelated.

First, let us assume that v is normally and independently distributed, with zero mean and variance $\sigma^2 = 1.5$. We can simulate 'observations' from the above model in the following manner.

Since the variable X is exogenous, we can select its values ourselves, independently of the behaviour of Y. A sequence of such values,[9] for periods $t = 1, 2, 3, \ldots$ is given in the second column of Table 11.1. Simulated values for v can be obtained from a computer in the usual way. Such values are given in the fourth column of Table 11.1. To obtain simulated values of Y, we require what is referred to as a 'starting value' for Y. We assume that $Y_0 = 55$. A starting value is required because of the presence of the lagged dependent variable.[10]

Given this value for Y_0, we can now obtain the simulated values for Y_t by successive substitution in (11.43). These values are shown in the fifth column of Table 11.1. For example, Y_1 is given by

$$Y_1 = 3 + 0.3X_1 + 0.6Y_0 + v_1$$
$$= 3 + 0.3(56.1) + 0.6(55) - 1.12 = 51.71$$

Once Y_1 has been obtained, we can use (11.43) to obtain Y_2. That is,

$$Y_2 = 3 + 0.3X_2 + 0.6Y_1 + v_2$$
$$= 3 + 0.3(63.6) + 0.6(51.71) + 0.66 = 53.77$$

Table 11.1 Simulation of Y values

t	X_t	Y_{t-1}	v_t	Y_t
1	56.1	55.0	−1.12	51.7
2	63.6	51.7	0.66	53.8
3	60.5	53.8	0.42	53.8
4	57.2	53.8	1.10	53.6
5	57.8	53.6	−0.37	52.1
6	58.1	52.1	0.05	51.7
7	61.2	51.7	−0.82	51.6
8	63.1	51.6	−2.14	50.7
9	63.8	50.7	0.32	52.9
10	66.1	52.9	1.85	56.4
11	73.4	56.4	−0.31	58.6
12	76.8	58.6	−0.14	61.0
13	78.3	61.0	0.52	63.6
14	70.1	63.6	0.48	62.7
15	65.3	62.7	−0.04	60.2
16	59.2	60.2	−0.37	56.5
17	57.4	56.5	0.16	54.3
18	56.8	54.3	0.98	53.6
19	56.1	53.6	0.64	52.6
20	54.3	52.6	−1.10	49.8
21	53.7	49.8	−0.22	48.8
22	53.0	48.8	0.14	48.3
23	53.1	48.3	−0.67	47.2
24	61.1	47.2	0.83	50.5
25	67.6	50.5	−0.42	53.2
26	69.2	53.2	1.73	57.4
27	73.8	57.4	0.64	60.2
28	71.5	60.2	−0.02	60.6
29	70.8	60.6	−0.31	60.3
30	69.1	60.3	−0.53	59.4
31	69.2	59.4	1.61	61.0
32	68.1	61.0	0.04	60.1
33	67.0	60.1	−0.33	58.8
⋮	⋮	⋮	⋮	⋮

Similarly,

$$Y_3 = 3 + 0.3(60.5) + 0.6(53.77) + 0.42 = 53.83$$

and so on.

Clearly, given the values for X and v, we can carry on in this manner, generating as many Y values as we wish. To generate a sample of size $n = 20$, for example, we could take the first 20 rows from a table such as Table 11.1. However, if we do this then it is possible that our 'sample' will be unduly influenced by the arbitrary value we selected for Y_0. It is therefore preferable to take 20 rows from further down the table, for example rows 11–30, by which time the influence of Y_0 will have become minimal.

Let us now put ourselves in the place of the applied econometrician, who, of course, does not know the values of the parameters in (11.43) but has to estimate them from a random sample. Suppose (s)he has available the above sample contained in rows 11–30 in Table 11.1. Remember the sample will consist of the X and Y values but not the values of the disturbance, which remain unknown to any investigator. Applying OLS to this sample in fact yields

$$\hat{\beta}_1 = 3.18, \quad \hat{\beta}_2 = 0.324, \quad \hat{\beta}_3 = 0.570$$

Comparing these estimates with the true values below Equation (11.43), we see that the econometrician underestimates β_3 and overestimates β_1 and β_2.

This result may seem to confirm the theoretical result, first mentioned in Section 8.1, that the presence of a lagged dependent variable in a regression equation leads to OLS bias in small samples. However, it must be remembered that bias refers to what would happen 'on average' if 'very many' samples all of the same size were taken. For example, a second sample of size 20 could lead to very different results from those just obtained.

We shall concentrate on the parameter β_3. The probability histogram in Figure 11.5 refers to values for the OLS estimator of β_3 in Equation (11.43) obtained from 200 simulated samples, all of size $n = 20$. Each such sample was generated in a similar manner to that in Table 11.1, with the same set of X values and the same starting Y_0 value. The remaining Y values vary from sample to sample because of the different disturbance values generated by the computer.

It can be seen from Figure 11.5 that the OLS estimator $\hat{\beta}_3$ is indeed biased. Most of its distribution lies to the left of 0.6. In fact, $E(\hat{\beta}_3) = 0.572$ compared with the true value $\beta_3 = 0.6$, so there is a downward bias of 0.028.

Our discussion in Chapter 8 indicated that in these circumstances any bias in the OLS estimators should decline as the sample size increases. In fact, the OLS estimators are consistent even in the presence of a lagged dependent variable. We can check this by simulating samples of size $n = 100$ rather than 20. The results for

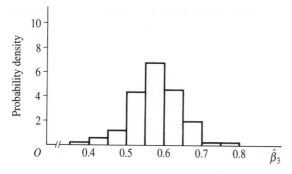

Figure 11.5 Sampling distribution for $\hat{\beta}_3$ ($n = 20$).

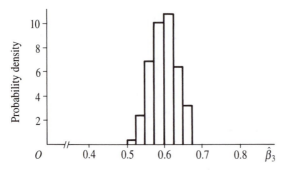

Figure 11.6 Sampling distribution for $\hat{\beta}_3$ ($n = 100$).

200 such samples are summarized in Figure 11.6 again for the OLS estimator $\hat{\beta}_3$. It can be seen that for samples of this size the bias is much reduced. This time $E(\hat{\beta}_3) = 0.594$, so that there is a small downward bias of only 0.006. Notice also that the dispersion of the $\hat{\beta}_3$ distribution is also much reduced in Figure 11.6 compared with the distribution in Figure 11.5. The respective variances are, in fact, 0.0108 and 0.0012 respectively. This reflects the consistency of the $\hat{\beta}_3$ estimator. Its sampling distribution is collapsing onto the true value of β_3, as expected.

In our second simulation study we retain Equation (11.43) with the same parameter values, but assume that the disturbance v, instead of being well behaved, is of the moving average form

$$v_t = u_t + 0.6u_{t-1} \tag{11.44}$$

where u_t is normally and independently distributed with zero mean and variance $\sigma_u^2 = 1.1.$[11]

We now have a model in which a lagged dependent variable is combined with an autocorrelated disturbance. As we saw in the last section, this combination, in theory at least, results in OLS estimators that are not merely biased but inconsistent. We shall see if this is confirmed by our simulation study.

Samples for the model comprising (11.43) and (11.44) can be generated in a manner similar to that in Table 11.1, with one small variation. The computer is used

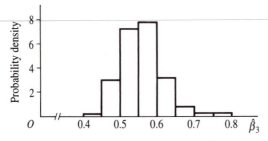

Figure 11.7 Sampling distribution for $\hat{\beta}_3$ ($n = 20$ and moving average disturbance).

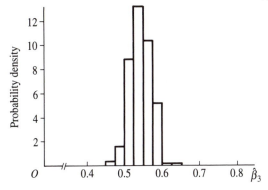

Figure 11.8 Sampling distribution for $\hat{\beta}_3$ ($n = 100$ and moving average disturbance).

to generate a time series of values for u_t rather than the disturbances v_t that appear in Equation (11.43). These values are then fed into (11.44) to give the required values of v_t.

The probability histogram in Figure 11.7 refers to the values of the OLS estimator $\hat{\beta}_3$ obtained from 200 samples of size $n = 20$. In each sample the same values for Y_0 and X are used as in the previous study. As can be seen from Figure 11.7, $\hat{\beta}_3$ tends to underestimate the true value of $\beta_3 = 0.6$. $E(\hat{\beta}_3) = 0.558$, so there is a bias of -0.042, considerably larger than that found when v_t was a well-behaved disturbance.

With the present model, however, the bias shows no tendency to disappear if we increase the size of the samples taken. Figure 11.8 shows the distribution for $\hat{\beta}_3$ obtained from 200 simulations with sample size $n = 100$. $E(\hat{\beta}_3) = 0.554$, virtually unchanged from that obtained from the smaller samples. With this model, there is no suggestion of the $\hat{\beta}_3$ distribution collapsing onto the true β_3 as the sample size tends to infinity. Indeed, if anything, Figure 11.8 suggests that $\hat{\beta}_3$ may converge in probability to a value below 0.55. The combination of lagged dependent variable and autocorrelated disturbance results in the OLS bias persisting even in large samples.

11.5   The formation of expectations

Econometricians frequently have to model expectations. The future is never known with certainty, and expectations about such variables as the general price level, the rate of interest and even disposable income have key roles to play in economic decision making. Consider a model where Y depends not so much on the actual value of X but on its expected value X^*:

$$Y_t = \alpha + \beta X_t^* + \epsilon_t \tag{11.45}$$

The classic interpretation of X_t^* is that it could represent permanent income in the Friedman (1957) sense. Y_t might then be consumer expenditure or the demand for money. Actual X differs from expected or permanent X. Since the latter is unobservable, we have to specify how it is determined. The **adaptive expectations hypothesis** specifies that

$$X_t^* - X_{t-1}^* = \phi(X_t - X_{t-1}^*), \qquad 0 < \phi < 1 \tag{11.46}$$

Thus expected X is linked to actual X by a simple *learning process*. In each period X_t is compared with its previously expected value X_{t-1}^*. If the actual value exceeds the expected value then the latter is adjusted upwards in the next period, so that X_t^* exceeds X_{t-1}^*. If the actual value is lower than the previously expected value then expectations are adjusted downwards, and X_t^* is smaller than X_{t-1}^*. The extent of the adjustment depends on the value of ϕ, the adjustment parameter. The greater is ϕ the fuller is the adjustment.

Equation (11.46) is often rewritten as

$$X_t^* = \phi X_t + (1 - \phi) X_{t-1}^* \tag{11.47}$$

Thus expected X is a weighted average of actual X and previously expected X. At one extreme, if $\phi = 1$ then $X_t^* = X_t$, so that expected X is always fully adjusted to actual X. At the other extreme, if $\phi = 0$ then $X_t^* = X_{t-1}^*$, and there is no adjustment, since expected X remains unchanged regardless of how much it might differ from actual X. Normally, of course, ϕ is expected to lie between zero and unity.

Notice that successive substitution in (11.47) for X_{t-1}^*, X_{t-2}^*, etc. gives

$$\begin{aligned}
X_t^* &= \phi X_t + \phi(1 - \phi) X_{t-1} + (1 - \phi)^2 X_{t-2}^* \\
&= \phi X_t + \phi(1 - \phi) X_{t-1} + \phi(1 - \phi)^2 X_{t-2} + (1 - \phi)^3 X_{t-3}^* \\
&\vdots \\
&= \phi X_t + \phi(1 - \phi) X_{t-1} + \phi(1 - \phi)^2 X_{t-2} + \phi(1 - \phi)^3 X_{t-3} \\
&\quad + \phi(1 - \phi)^4 X_{t-4} + \cdots
\end{aligned} \tag{11.48}$$

Equation (11.48) clearly demonstrates how current and past levels of X influence expected X under the adaptive expectations hypothesis. In the determination of X_t^*, most weight is given to the current level X_t and, since $1 - \phi$ lies between zero and unity, successively smaller weights to the past levels $X_{t-1}, X_{t-2}, X_{t-3}$, etc. In fact, the coefficients in (11.48) form an infinite but convergent geometric series with common ratio $1 - \phi$.

Substitution of (11.48) into (11.45) now yields

$$\begin{aligned}
Y_t = \alpha + \beta\phi X_t + \beta\phi(1 - \phi) X_{t-1} + \beta\phi(1 - \phi)^2 X_{t-2} \\
+ \beta\phi(1 - \phi)^3 X_{t-3} + \cdots + \epsilon_t
\end{aligned} \tag{11.49}$$

Thus the adaptive expectations hypothesis implies that Y is related to actual X via a geometric distributed lag of the kind encountered in Section 11.2.

Estimation of the adaptive expectations model is obviously handicapped by the fact that X^* is unobservable. While (11.49) involves only actual X, its estimation involves all the usual multicollinearity and degrees-of-freedom problems associated with infinite distributed lags. The geometric lag (11.49) has to be approached by applying the Koyck transformation described in Section 11.2. That is, we lag (11.49) by one period, multiply throughout by $1 - \phi$ and then subtract the result from (11.49) to obtain

$$Y_t = \alpha\phi + \beta\phi X_t + (1 - \phi)Y_{t-1} + v_t \tag{11.50}$$

where $v_t = \epsilon_t - (1 - \phi)\epsilon_{t-1}$. Since (11.50) involves only the observable variables X and Y, it may be estimated. However, as we stressed in Section 11.2, care must always be taken over the stochastic specification of distributed lag models. In this case, if the original equation (11.45) is correctly specified then we can assume that the disturbance ϵ_t in that equation is well behaved. But if that is the case then, as usual, the Koyck transformation results in an autocorrelated disturbance v_t in the autoregressive equation (11.50). As a consequence, OLS, as explained above, will yield biased and inconsistent estimators when applied to (11.50). Estimation of the adaptive expectations model has to proceed by one of the alternative methods described at the end of Section 11.3.

Notice that there is a fundamental problem of interpretation with equations such as (11.50). Apart from the disturbance, this equation is of the same form as the partial adjustment estimating equation (11.13). Both equations contain X and lagged Y as regressors. Suppose, again, that we obtain, by some suitable estimation method, Equation (11.14). In Section 11.2 we interpreted this equation in terms of a partial adjustment model with adjustment parameter $\theta = 0.6$. But we could just as easily have interpreted it in terms of the adaptive expectations model (11.50). Equation (11.14) would then imply $\alpha = 40$ and $\beta = 0.9$ in Equation (11.45) rather than in Equation (11.11), and an adjustment parameter $\phi = 0.6$ in (11.46). The difficulty is that, without some a priori information about which is the appropriate model, we cannot tell whether the lagged dependent variable in our estimated equation arises because of 'adjustment lags' or because of 'exceptional lags'. Although it is possible to specify a more general model incorporating both partial adjustment and adaptive expectations, the economic interpretation of autoregressive distributed lag models is always a difficult matter.

Rational expectations

Until the mid-1960s, the adaptive expectations model proved very popular with applied econometricians. However, the mechanical and backward-looking nature of the model eventually provoked much criticism. First, it is not difficult to show that if a variable X grows at a fixed positive rate through time then economic agents are being irrational if they form expectations about the variable in an adaptive manner. Their expectation of X always turns out to be lower than the actual value that occurs (see e.g. Thomas, 1993, p. 127). Yet agents are assumed never to attempt to adjust for such errors and to carry on forming expectations according to (11.46).

A more general criticism of adaptive expectations is that they imply a fixed relationship between expectations and past values of relevant variables. A change in government policy regime cannot affect the past value of variables, and hence, under adaptive expectations, can have no effect on the expectations of economic agents. However, such agents are being irrational if they do not allow for changes in government policy when formulating their expectations. This was the basis of the Lucas (1976) critique of economic policy evaluation.

Consider again Equation (11.45), where Y depends on expected X. In a **rational expectations** model it is assumed, first, that the structure of the relevant economic system is such that there exists, at time $t - 1$, a unique mathematical expectation of the value of variable X at time t. We denote this expectation by $E_{t-1}(X_t)$. For example, we might have

$$E_{t-1}(X_t) = a_0 + a_1 X_{t-1} + b_1 Z_{1t-1} + b_2 Z_{2t-1} + b_3 Z_{3t-1} + \cdots \qquad (11.51)$$

where the Zs are exogenous variables that influence X. The magnitude of the a and b parameters in (11.51) could be affected by the nature of whatever government policy regime is in operation. Since current values of variables are unknown at time $t - 1$, we have included only lagged variables on the right-hand side of (11.51).

Under rational expectations, it is assumed that economic agents possess complete knowledge of the economic system and put this knowledge to the best possible use when forming their expectations. They therefore know not only the structure of Equation (11.51), but (unlike the econometrician) also the values of its parameters. Their expectation of X at time t, X_t^* in Equation (11.45), is therefore set equal to the $E_{t-1}(X_t)$ of Equation (11.51). That is,

$$X_t^* = E_{t-1}(X_t) \qquad (11.52)$$

Actual X may not turn out to be the same as expected X of course. That is, economic agents may make a **prediction error**, so that

$$X_t = X_t^* + u_t \qquad (11.53)$$

If expectations are rational in the above sense, the prediction error u_t in (11.53) must satisfy certain properties. First, its expected value must be zero. If prediction errors were systematically positive or negative then agents would adjust their forecasting methods accordingly. Secondly, the prediction error must be uncorrelated with any information available when the prediction is made. If not, this would imply that the forecaster has not made use of all available information. Since all available information is summed up in the value of X_t^*, this implies that u_t must be uncorrelated with X_t^*. The prediction error must, in fact, be totally random in the sense that the forecaster is unable to predict what it will be.[12] Otherwise useful information is not being utilized and this is contrary to the rational expectations hypothesis.

These implied properties of the prediction error enable tests of the rational expectations hypothesis to be carried out. However, we shall merely point out how Equation (11.45) would be estimated given rational expectations. The difficulty is that the econometrician, although assumed to know the form of (11.51), unlike economic agents does not know its parameters. The $E_{t-1}(X_t)$ in (11.51) is also unknown. However, if we replace $E_{t-1}(X_t)$ by X_t in (11.51) and estimate

$$\hat{X}_t = \hat{a}_0 + \hat{a}_1 X_{t-1} + \hat{b}_1 Z_{1t-1} + \hat{b}_2 Z_{2t-1} + \hat{b}_3 Z_{3t-1}$$

then the predicted values $\hat{X}_t$ from this equation may be used instead of $E_{t-1}(X_t)$ in the estimation of the original (11.45). Notice that this two-stage procedure is, in fact, the same as a GIVE estimation of the equation

$$Y_t = \alpha + \beta X_t + \epsilon_t$$

with X_{t-1} and lagged values of the Zs acting as instruments. The resultant estimators of α and β will therefore be consistent.

The above estimation procedure for rational expectations models was first developed by McCallum (1976). For further work along these lines, see the papers by Meullbauer (1983) on consumption and by Cuthbertson and Taylor (1986, 1988) on the demand for money.

Appendix 11A

Notes to Chapter 11

1. The effect on $E(Y)$ of a unit change in X after two periods is easily seen to be a change of $\beta_0 + \beta_1$. This quantity is sometimes referred to as an **interim multiplier**.

2. Recall that the sum to infinity of a geometric series is $a/(1-r)$, where a is the first term and r is the common ratio. In (11.17) we have $a = \alpha\theta$ and $r = 1 - \theta$.

3. Rational lags were first developed by Jorgenson (1963), and used in the study of the investment behaviour of firms.

4. The rule that has to be followed is that the degree of the polynomial used should be at least one more than the number of turning points in the curve that is being approximated.

5. It is possible to 'tie down' the lag structure by imposing the 'end-point restrictions' that $\beta_0 = 0$ and $\beta_m = 0$. However, this procedure has been found to result in biased estimates of the β coefficients.

6. This includes not only the cases $\mu_i > 1$ and $\mu_i < -1$, but also certain complex roots.

7. When checking the residuals of an ADL model for autocorrelation, it is important to recall from Chapter 10 that the Durbin–Watson statistic is biased towards 2 in the presence of lagged dependent variables.

8. An alternative instrument for Y_{t-1} would be Y_{t-2}.

9. The X values chosen fluctuate about a constant mean of 65. This ensures a trendless series.

10. If X were to remain constant at its average value of 65 then setting $Y_t = Y_{t-1}$ in

(11.43) indicates a static equilibrium value for Y of 56.25. We have selected a starting value Y_0 close to this value.

11. From (11.44), Var $(v_t) =$ Var $(u_t) + 0.36$ Var $(u_{t-1}) = 1.36\sigma_u^2$. Thus if $\sigma_u^2 = 1.1$ then Var $(v_t) = 1.496$, virtually identical to its value in the previous simulations.

12. For example, the prediction error must not be serially correlated; otherwise, it would be possible to predict future errors from past errors.

Further reading

Judge et al. (1988) contains a good chapter (17) on distributed lags. A more advanced treatment is provided by Greene (1993), Chapter 18. Johnston (1984), Chapter 9, provides a fuller treatment of Almon polynomial lags than is provided in this text. Cuthbertson et al. (1992), Chapter 6, consider rational expectations, as does Maddala (1988), Chapter 10.

12 Choosing the appropriate model

Until now, we have almost always assumed that an investigator has some clear a priori idea about the form or specification of the equation (s)he intends to estimate. In practice, this is rarely the case. For example, theory almost never has anything to say about the functional form of economic relationships, and frequently there will be some doubt about which or how many variables should be included in our equation.

We begin this chapter, therefore, by examining the consequences of selecting the 'wrong' equation to estimate. It turns out that these consequences can be so serious that investigators are frequently forced to use their sample data to help them decide what is an appropriate equation to estimate. This in itself can have serious consequences, which are examined in Section 12.2. In Section 12.3 we introduce readers to an approach to selecting appropriate equations that has become increasingly popular during the past 15 years, the so-called general-to-specific approach. It will be argued that this approach goes some way to overcoming many of the problems outlined in Sections 12.1 and 12.2. Finally, we attempt to use this approach in two computer exercises.

12.1 The consequences and detection of errors of specification

In our description and analysis of the classical regression model we have paid little attention to the form of the equation actually being estimated. That is, we have simply assumed that the expected value of the dependent Y variable is a linear function of a known number of regressors or explanatory variables (see e.g. Equation (7.2)). But suppose we estimate the 'wrong' equation. That is, suppose we *mis-specify* the population regression equation. Clearly, any assumptions we make about non-stochastic X variables or about the disturbance in our relationship can be of little help or relevance if, in the first place, we have made a **specification error** in the equation we are estimating.

There are two types of error we can make when specifying a population regression equation of the kind (7.2). First, we could include the 'wrong' X variables in the equation. Secondly, we could choose an incorrect functional form (for example, we may assume the population regression line is linear when in fact it is nonlinear).

We consider, first, situations where we estimate an equation containing the 'wrong' explanatory variables. Suppose, for example, that the 'true' population relationship is

$$Y = \beta_1 + \beta_2 X_2 + \beta_3 X_3 + \epsilon, \qquad \beta_2 \neq 0, \qquad \beta_3 \neq 0 \tag{12.1}$$

but we estimate

$$Y = \beta_1 + \beta_2 X_2 + u \tag{12.2}$$

That is, we omit a 'relevant' explanatory variable, X_3, from our estimating equation. X_3 is relevant, because it does in fact influence Y.

The disturbance in a regression equation is included to represent all influences on Y apart from those of the X variables actually present. If we estimate (12.2), therefore, we are forcing the disturbance u in that equation to represent the omitted variable X_3 as well as any purely random factors. In fact, $u = \beta_3 X_3 + \epsilon$, where ϵ, is the 'true' disturbance in (12.1). But suppose X_3 happens to be correlated with X_2. This implies that the disturbance in (12.2) is correlated with the variable X_2, which is a regressor in that equation. But we have seen in Section 8.1 that the consequence of such a contemporaneous correlation between explanatory variable and disturbance is that OLS estimators become *biased* and *inconsistent*. In this context, such bias is referred to as **omitted variable bias**.

The direction of the biases resulting from the omission of a relevant variable depend

(a) on the direction of the correlation between X_2 and X_3;

(b) on the sign of β_3, the coefficient of X_3, in (12.1).

Since $u = \beta_3 X_3 + \epsilon$, if $\beta_3 > 0$ and the correlation between X_2 and X_3 is positive, the correlation between X_2 and u in (12.2) will be positive. As we saw in Section 8.1, such a positive correlation between explanatory variable and disturbance leads to OLS tending to overestimate β_2 and underestimate β_1. However, if $\beta_3 < 0$ and the correlation between X_2 and X_3 is positive then OLS will tend to underestimate β_2 and overestimate β_1. If there is a negative correlation between X_2 and X_3 then the direction of the above biases will be reversed.

Such OLS bias is the usual consequence of the omission of relevant variable(s) from a regression equation. It will occur whenever an omitted variable is correlated with one or more of the X variables included in the equation. The only occasion on which the omission of a relevant variable will not cause bias is in the rare case where it is totally uncorrelated with any of the included X variables. For example, if X_2 and X_3 happened to be uncorrelated in (12.1) then X_2 and u would be uncorrelated in (12.2), and the source of the bias would have disappeared.

Next consider a situation where (12.1) is again the 'correct' equation, but this time we estimate

$$Y = \beta_1 + \beta_2 X_2 + \beta_3 X_3 + \beta_4 X_4 + v \tag{12.3}$$

That is, instead of omitting a relevant variable, we include an 'irrelevant' variable, X_4, which does not actually influence Y.

This situation is easier to analyse than that where a variable has been omitted. Since (12.3) is merely a special case of the 'correct' equation (12.1) with $\beta_4 = 0$, none of the classical assumptions are being violated if we estimate (12.3). Thus OLS will yield *unbiased* and *consistent* estimators when applied to (12.3). Since $\beta_4 = 0$, its OLS estimator will simply have an expected value of zero. That is, $E(\hat{\beta}_4) = 0$.

Despite the fact that the inclusion of an irrelevant variable does not lead to bias, the OLS estimators are unlikely to remain efficient. If the included irrelevant variable is correlated with any of the other X variables in the equation then an unnecessary element of multicollinearity will have been introduced into the estimation process. This will lead to the standard errors on the coefficients of, for example, X_2 and X_3 in Equation (12.3) being larger than they would have been had the irrelevant variable X_4 been omitted. Thus applying OLS to (12.3) will lead to less efficient estimators than when OLS is applied to (12.1).

We have considered the consequences, first, of omitting a relevant explanatory variable and, secondly, of including an irrelevant explanatory variable. But what if we make both kinds of specification error at the same time? Suppose, for example, that the 'correct' equation is again (12.1), but this time we estimate

$$Y = \beta_1 + \beta_2 X_2 + \beta_4 X_4 + w \tag{12.4}$$

In this case we have omitted the relevant X_3 but included the irrelevant X_4; that is, we have included the 'wrong' explanatory variable. As we saw above, the more serious of the two errors is the former. If the omitted X_3 is at all correlated with X_2 and/or X_4 then OLS estimators will be biased and inconsistent.

The consequences of omitting a relevant variable are so serious that it is important that we are able to detect such an omission. *One of the best aids to detection is a visual examination of the residuals from the estimated equation.* Figures 12.1 and 12.2 show plots of residuals against time. In Figure 12.1 negative residuals in the early part of the sample period are followed by positive residuals in the later part. This strongly suggests the omission of a relevant explanatory variable that possesses a strong trend element over time. In Figure 12.2 the residuals follow a cyclical pattern, suggesting the omission of a relevant variable that itself exhibits cycles.

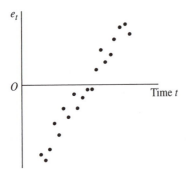

Figure 12.1 Trending residuals.

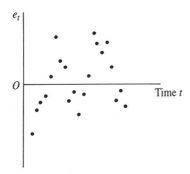

Figure 12.2 Cyclical pattern in residuals.

In both Figures 12.1 and 12.2 omission of a relevant variable has resulted in runs of positive and negative residuals. Such residual patterns can be detected by use of any of the tests for autocorrelation described in Chapter 11. As we stressed in that chapter, these tests are nowadays regarded more as ways of testing the specification of an equation than as tests for autocorrelated disturbances. That is, autocorrelated *residuals*, such as we have in Figures 12.1 and 12.2, are more often an indication of a mis-specified estimating equation than of autocorrelated *disturbances*.

Often, in practice, mis-specification will occur because of the incorrect omission of one or more lagged values of either the dependent Y variable or the explanatory X variables. This form of specification error is generally referred to as a **dynamic mis-specification**. That is, we have mis-specified the manner in which the Y variable moves over time in response to changes in the X variables. The consequences of a dynamic mis-specification are identical to that of the omission of any relevant regressor.

The second kind of specification error mentioned at the beginning of this section is that of an incorrect functional form. The most obvious situation is where the true population regression equation is nonlinear but we adopt a linear estimating equation. For example, suppose the true regression equation is

$$E(Y) = AX_2^{\beta_2} X_3^{\beta_3} \tag{12.5}$$

but we attempt to estimate

$$E(Y) = \beta_1 + \beta_2 X_2 + \beta_3 X_3 \tag{12.6}$$

The parameters β_2 and β_3 in (12.5) are elasticities. However, if we estimate (12.6), the OLS estimator $\hat{\beta}_2$, for example, is simply an estimate of the change in $E(Y)$ per unit change in X_2. Clearly, this will be a biased estimator of the elasticity[1] β_2. In general, not surprisingly, we cannot expect to obtain unbiased estimators of population regression equation parameters if we specify an incorrect population regression equation in the first place.

We saw in Section 6.4 that in two-variable regression an incorrect functional form is likely to show up in a residual pattern possibly similar to that in Table 6.2 or Figure 6.4. Similarly, in multiple regression, mis-specification of the functional form is also likely to result in runs of positive and negative residuals. Thus, just as with the case of omitted variables, this form of mis-specification can often be detected either by a visual examination of the residuals or by a study of the autocorrelation statistics for the estimated equation. This is another reason why a low value for the Durbin–Watson statistic, for example, is more likely to be indicative of some form of mis-specification than of first-order autocorrelation in the disturbances.

As we saw in Section 10.3, significant values for the statistics designed to test for heteroskedasticity can also be indicative not of genuine heteroskedasticity but of some form of mis-specification. Indeed, *any systematic pattern in the residuals* of a regression equation should be regarded as suggestive of the possibility of mis-specification.

Testing for normality of the disturbances

Recall that assumption IID in the classical regression model stated that the disturbances had to be normally distributed about their zero mean. The assumption is necessary if the inferential aspects of classical regression (t test, F tests etc.) are to be valid in small samples.[2] It is therefore a vital part of the specification of the classical model, and should therefore always be tested.

Normality in the disturbances is usually tested for by considering the third and fourth moments of the OLS residuals. Recall that the second moment of the residuals about their zero mean is $\sum e_i^2/n$. We give this moment the symbol μ_2. Similarly, the third and fourth such moments are given by $\mu_3 = \sum e_i^3/n$ and $\mu_4 = \sum e_i^4/n$.

The moments of the residuals are regarded as estimates of the moments of the unknown disturbances. Under a null hypothesis of normally distributed disturbances, the third and fourth moments of the disturbances should take certain specified values.[3] Thus if the moments of the residuals depart sufficiently far from these values then the hypothesis of normal disturbances must be rejected. The Jarque–Bera (1980) statistic is based on the extent of such departures, and is defined as

$$JB = n\left[\frac{\mu_3^2}{6\mu_2^3} + \frac{(\mu_4/\mu_2 - 3)^2}{24}\right] \tag{12.7}$$

By applying the Lagrange multiplier principle of Section 9.3, it is possible to show that, under the null hypothesis of normally distributed disturbances, the test statistic (12.7) has a χ^2 distribution with 2 degrees of freedom. We therefore reject the null hypothesis of normality if JB exceeds the relevant critical χ^2 value. We shall make use of the Jarque–Bera test in the computer exercises at the end of this chapter.

Linear versus log-linear regressions

A choice the applied econometrician often has to make is whether to estimate an equation in linear or log-linear form. Suppose, for example, we are uncertain whether the true population relationship has the form (12.5) or (12.6). That is, we must choose between taking a logarithmic transformation of (12.5) and estimating

$$\ln (Y) = \beta_1 + \beta_2 \ln (X_2) + \beta_3 \ln (X_3) + u \tag{12.5a}$$

or simply estimating

$$Y = \beta_1 + \beta_2 X_2 + \beta_3 X_3 + v \tag{12.6a}$$

Since (12.5a) and (12.6a) have different dependent variables, we cannot just estimate each equation and choose the functional form that yields the largest R^2. However, it is possible to scale the Y variable in such a way that it becomes possible to compare the residual sums of squares obtained from the OLS estimation of (12.5a) and (12.6a). The procedure, developed by Zarembka (1968), is based on the work of Box and Cox (1964).

The first step in the procedure is to obtain the geometric mean of the sample Y values. That is,

$$\tilde{Y} = (Y_1 Y_2 Y_3 \cdots Y_n)^{1/n} = \exp \left(\frac{1}{n} \sum \ln Y_i \right) \tag{12.8}$$

The second step is to transform the sample Y values by dividing each of them by the above geometric mean. That is, we form

$$Y_i^* = Y_i / \tilde{Y} \quad \text{for all } i$$

The final step in the procedure is to estimate the log-linear equation (12.5a), but with $\ln (Y^*)$ replacing $\ln (Y)$ as the dependent variable, and to estimate the linear equation (12.6a), but with Y^* replacing Y as the dependent variable. The X variables are left unchanged in each case. The residual sums of squares for the two regressions can now be shown to be directly comparable, and the equation with the lower sum can be said to have the better fit.

If we wish to know whether our preferred specification is significantly better than the alternative then the following test may be performed. Let SSR_2 be the larger of the residual sums of squares obtained and SSR_1 the smaller. It can be shown that, under the null hypothesis of no difference between the two equations in terms of goodness of fit, the test statistic

$$(\tfrac{1}{2} n) \ln \left(\frac{SSR_2}{SSR_1} \right) \text{ has a } \chi^2 \text{ distribution with 1 d.f.} \tag{12.9}$$

As an illustration of the above procedure, consider Data Set 1 on the floppy disk, that is, the data on the US demand for food, which we have already used in Chapters 7, 9 and 11. In Chapter 7, for example, we estimated the log-linear demand-for-food equation (7.66) over the period 1965–89 and obtained a coefficient of multiple determination $R^2 = 0.943$. But what if, instead, we had simply regressed demand Q on total expenditure X, the price of food P, and the general price index G? The reader should verify that the coefficient of determination for this *linear* demand equation is only $R^2 = 0.829$.

Unfortunately, as noted above, the R^2s for the log-linear and linear demand equations are not comparable. In the former case R^2 measures the proportion of variations in ln (Q) that can be explained, while in the linear case it measures the proportion of variations in Q that can be explained. We cannot then claim that the double-log function provides the better fit simply because it has a higher R^2.

To carry out the above Zarembka procedure, we require the geometric mean of the Q values. The output for the log-linear demand regression will give you the mean of the dependent variable ln (Q) as

$$\frac{1}{n}\sum \ln (Q_i) = 12.19$$

Thus the geometric mean of the Qs is (using (12.8) with Q replacing Y)

$$\tilde{Q} = \exp (12.19) = 196\,811$$

We can now carry out the second step in the Zarembka procedure and transform the Q variable by dividing its values by the geometric mean, thus forming $Q_i^* = Q_i/\tilde{Q}$ for all i.

The final step is now to rerun the log-linear regression with ln (Q^*) replacing ln (Q) and to rerun the linear regression with Q^* replacing Q. This should yield the comparable residual sums of squares, $SSR_1 = 0.006\,97$ and $SSR_2 = 0.020\,53$ respectively. This indicates that the log-linear equation does indeed have the better fit. To test whether the log-linear fit is significantly better, we can compute the test statistic (12.9). This yields a value of

$$(\tfrac{1}{2}n) \ln \left(\frac{SSR_2}{SSR_1}\right) = 12.5 \ln (2.945) = 13.5$$

This value well exceeds the critical value $\chi^2_{0.05} = 3.841$. Hence we can say with some confidence that the log-linear fit is superior at the 0.05 level of significance.

Tests of mis-specification

It is instructive to draw attention to a distinction often made nowadays between **tests of specification** and **tests of mis-specification**, or **diagnostic tests**. In a test of specification there is a clearly defined alternative hypothesis. For example, suppose we wished to test for the presence of a second-order autocorrelated scheme in the disturbances of a multiple regression equation. If the LM test for second-order autocorrelation were used for this purpose then it would be regarded as a test of *specification*, since we would be testing the null hypothesis of non-autocorrelated disturbances against a clear alternative. Similarly, if we suspected a specific variable, on which we have data, had been left out of a regression equation, a test of specification would be to include the variable and examine the *t* ratio that appeared on its coefficient.

In contrast, in a test of mis-specification (a diagnostic test) we have no clearly defined alternative hypothesis. We might be worried about unspecific omitted variables, incorrect functional form or even genuine autocorrelation in the disturbances. If tests such as the LM tests for autocorrelation are used in these circumstances, then we would be conducting tests for *mis-specification*.

Similarly, tests designed originally to detect heteroskedasticity in the disturbances are often nowadays used as tests for general mis-specification. This is because distinct patterns in the variance of the residuals from a fitted equation may well be an indication not of genuine heteroskedasticity but of some mis-specification in the equation.

The Jarque–Bera test for normality of the disturbances introduced above is also sometimes regarded as a test of mis-specification. It is useful for detecting what are known as 'outliers' among the data observations. An outlier refers to an observation with a very large residual, that is, a case where the predicted value of the dependent variable is very different from the actual value. The presence of a substantial number of such outliers suggests there is some important aspect of the underlying data generating process that our model is not capturing. In other words, we have mis-specified our model in some way. Since the existence of a number of large residuals is not consistent with a normally distributed set of residuals, this deficiency in the specification of the model can be detected by the Jarque–Bera test. We shall return to the problem of outliers in Chapter 16.[4]

A test for general mis-specification

A commonly used general set of tests for mis-specification, which are not based directly on an examination of residuals, are the RESET tests (regression error specification tests) based on the work of Ramsey (1969).

Suppose, again, that we estimate Equation (12.2) in a situation where we suspect that the 'true' population relationship is (12.1). If we had a clear idea of the identity of the potential omitted regressor X_3 then the obvious test for specification error would be to estimate (12.1) and examine the *t* ratio on the coefficient of X_3 in this equation. If the coefficient on X_3 proves significant then, obviously, we are committing a specification error if we estimate (12.2).

Suppose, however, that either we do not have data on X_3 or, maybe, have no real idea what the identity of X_3 might be. Provided we can find some 'proxy' variable to represent the unknown X_3, this proxy could be included in (12.1) instead of X_3, and we could proceed as above. In the RESET test such proxies are based on the predicted value of Y, obtained from the OLS estimation of (12.2). That is, we first estimate

$$\hat{Y} = \hat{\beta}_1 + \hat{\beta}_2 X_2 \tag{12.10}$$

Ramsey suggests the use of various powers of the $\hat{Y}$s retained from (12.10) as proxies for X_3, that is $\hat{Y}^2$, $\hat{Y}^3$ etc. Thus to carry out the RESET test, we next estimate equations such as

$$Y = \beta_1 + \beta_2 X_2 + \delta_1 \hat{Y}^2 + \delta_2 \hat{Y}^3 + \epsilon \tag{12.11}$$

The significance of the δ coefficients on the proxy variables can then be tested using the standard F test for additional explanatory variables, described in Section 9.2. If only one proxy, $\hat{Y}^2$, is included then the significance of its coefficient may be assessed by the normal t test.

If one or more of the δ coefficients in (12.11) prove to be significantly different from zero then this is evidence of omitted variable error. Note, though, that, since the Y variables could be acting as proxies for more than one omitted variable, the test can be regarded as a general one for the omission of one or more relevant variables.

The RESET test can also be regarded as a test for functional form mis-specification. Consider, for the moment, the case of simple two-variable regression where the population regression equation is nonlinear. For example, it might take any of the forms (4.36), (4.51) or (4.53). Using Taylor's theorem (see e.g. Chiang, 1984, pp. 256–60), it can be shown that any such nonlinear equation can be approximated by

$$E(Y) = \beta_1 + \beta_2 X_2 + \beta_3 X_2^2 + \beta_4 X_2^3 + \cdots \tag{12.12}$$

where the βs depend on the mean of X_2. Thus adopting a linear population regression equation when the true relationship is nonlinear can be seen to be akin to omitting relevant variables X_2^2, X_2^3 etc.

To test a two-variable linear regression equation for functional form mis-specification now becomes a matter of testing the coefficients on the powers of X_2 in (12.12) to see whether they are significantly different from zero, using the normal t and F tests. If one or more prove to be significantly non-zero then the hypothesis of a linear regression equation must be rejected.

In multiple regression the population regression equation could be nonlinear in any or all the explanatory variables. The above approach then becomes infeasible, since the number of powers and cross-products of the explanatory X variables that need to be included becomes too large. However, suppose we were estimating (12.1) but suspected that the true regression line was nonlinear. Estimating (12.1) would yield

$$\hat{Y} = \hat{\beta}_1 + \hat{\beta}_2 X_2 + \hat{\beta}_3 X_3 \tag{12.13}$$

The square of $\hat{Y}$ obtained from (12.13) depends both on the squares of X_2 and X_3 and on their cross-product $X_2 X_3$. Similarly, higher powers of $\hat{Y}$ will be functions of higher powers and cross-products of X_2 and X_3. Hence, instead of attempting to estimate a multiple regression equivalent of (12.12), we can estimate the multiple regression equivalent of (12.11). That is, we add to Equation (12.1), as extra explanatory variables, the powers of $\hat{Y}$ obtained from (12.13). Values for the coefficients of the powers of $\hat{Y}$ that prove significantly different from zero could then be regarded as evidence of a nonlinear population regression equation.

We have now seen that significant coefficients on the powers of $\hat{Y}$ in equations such as (12.11) can be regarded as indicating either omitted relevant variables or a mis-specified functional form. Thus the RESET test of this subsection can be regarded as a test of general *mis-specification*. When we apply it, the null hypothesis is that of a correct specification but we have no definite alternative hypothesis in mind. Rejection of the null hypothesis merely indicates that the equation has been mis-specified in some way or other. We shall make use of the RESET test in the computer exercises at the end of this chapter.

The Hausman test for contemporaneous correlation

As we have seen, the consequences of omitting relevant variables are serious because of the near certainty that their omission will lead to a contemporaneous correlation between the disturbance and the included regressors in an estimating equation. This suggests that we should check the specification of an equation by testing for such a contemporaneous correlation. This is the idea behind the Hausman (1978) test.

Consider the two-variable regression equation

$$Y_i = \alpha + \beta X_i + \epsilon_i \tag{12.14}$$

We set up the null and alternative hypotheses

H_0: no contemporaneous correlation between X and ϵ;

H_A: non-zero contemporaneous correlation between X and ϵ.

Rejection of H_0 could be the result of a specification error resulting from omitted variable(s).[5]

To obtain an intuitive understanding of the Hausman test, we consider two estimators of the parameter β in (12.14), the OLS estimator (4.18) and the simple IV estimator (8.35). Recall that to compute the IV estimator β^*, we require an instrument Z that is uncorrelated with ϵ in (12.14).

Under H_0, the OLS estimator $\hat{\beta}$ and the IV estimator β^* are both consistent estimators of β. However, under H_A, whereas the IV estimator β^* remains a consistent estimator, the OLS estimator $\hat{\beta}$ is inconsistent. This suggests that we should reject H_0 if, in large samples, there is a big enough difference between β^* and $\hat{\beta}$.

We can derive an expression for the difference between β^* and β as follows. For OLS estimation of (12.14),

$$Y_i = \hat{\alpha} + \hat{\beta} X_i + e_i \quad \text{for all } i \tag{12.15}$$

Summing (12.15) over all observations and dividing by n gives (remember that the sum of the OLS residuals, the e_i, is zero)

$$\bar{Y} = \hat{\alpha} + \hat{\beta}\bar{X} \tag{12.16}$$

Taking (12.16) from (12.15) now yields

$$y_i = \hat{\beta}x_i + e_i \quad \text{for all } i \tag{12.17}$$

If we now substitute for y_i in the expression (8.35) for the IV estimator of β, we obtain

$$\beta^* = \frac{\sum z_i y_i}{\sum z_i x_i} = \frac{\sum z_i(\hat{\beta}x_i + e_i)}{\sum z_i x_i} = \hat{\beta} + \frac{\sum z_i e_i}{\sum z_i x_i}$$

Thus

$$\beta^* - \hat{\beta} = \frac{\sum z_i e_i}{\sum z_i x_i} \tag{12.18}$$

What (12.18) indicates is that β^* and $\hat{\beta}$ can only be the same if $\sum z_i e_i$ is zero. Thus, to test whether the two estimators are significantly different (in which case we reject H_0 above), we need to test whether, in large samples, the OLS residuals from (12.15) are uncorrelated with the instrument Z used in the computation of β^*.

The required test may be carried out by estimating the OLS regression

$$\hat{Y}_i = \hat{\alpha} + \hat{\beta}X_i + \hat{\gamma}Z_i \tag{12.19}$$

That is, we regress Y on *both* X and its instrument Z. If $\hat{\gamma}$ in (12.19) turns out to be significantly different from zero then this indicates a correlation between Z and the OLS residuals from (12.15). In this circumstance we would reject H_0 above and conclude that there was a contemporaneous correlation between regressor and disturbance in Equation (12.14).

The intuitive reasoning behind the test is straightforward. If Z were omitted from (12.19), the residuals obtained would simply be the OLS residuals, the e_i from (12.15). The coefficient of Z in (12.18) will only prove to be significantly different from zero if it is correlated with these residuals.

In practice, the Hausman test is generally performed in the context of multiple regression, and the OLS estimators of *all* parameters in the equation are compared not with simple IV estimators but with GIVE estimators of the kind described in Section 8.6. However, the test proceeds in a similar manner. Suppose, for example, that we are faced with

$$Y_i = \beta_1 + \beta_2 X_{2i} + \beta_3 X_{3i} + \epsilon_i \tag{12.20}$$

and suspected an omitted variable problem. If we have available a set of instruments $Z_1, Z_2, \ldots, Z_m$ ($m > 3$) that are uncorrelated with ϵ in (12.20) then the first stage of the GIVE process is to form the instrumental variables $\hat{X}_2$ and $\hat{X}_3$ by regressing X_2 and X_3 in turn on all the instruments. The Hausman test then proceeds by the estimation of

$$Y_i = \beta_1 + \beta_2 X_2 + \beta_3 X_3 + \gamma_2 \hat{X}_2 + \gamma_3 \hat{X}_3 \tag{12.21}$$

The F test of Section 9.2 is now used to test for the joint significance of the coefficients on the instrumental variables $\hat{X}_2$ and $\hat{X}_3$ in (12.21). If the F statistic

(9.19)/(9.28) exceeds its critical value then the hypothesis of no contemporaneous correlation between X_2 and/or X_3 and the disturbance in (12.20) has to be rejected.

As an illustration of the Hausman test, we shall again make use of Data Set 1. The log-linear demand equation (7.66) had a residual sum of squares $\mathrm{SSR_R} = 0.006\,97$. As instruments for the three regressors in this equation we shall use their lagged values, that is, $\ln(X_{t-1})$, $\ln(P_{t-1})$ and $\ln(G_{t-1})$. The first stage of the Hausman test is therefore to regress each of the regressors $\ln(X)$, $\ln(P)$ and $\ln(G)$ in turn on all the instruments, saving the fitted values $\widehat{\ln(X)}$, $\widehat{\ln(P)}$ and $\widehat{\ln(G)}$. We can then estimate for 1965–89

$$\widehat{\ln(Q)} = 6.13 + 0.827 \ln(X) - 0.726 \ln(P) + 0.207 \ln(G)$$
$$(6.29)\quad(3.47)\qquad\quad(-3.93)\qquad\quad(0.51)$$

$$-0.403\,\widehat{\ln(X)} + 0.759\,\widehat{\ln(P)} - 0.713\,\widehat{\ln(G)} \qquad\qquad (12.22)$$
$$(-1.63)\qquad\quad(3.70)\qquad\quad(-1.66)$$

The above is the present-case equivalent of Equation (12.21). The t ratios on the instrumental variables in (12.22) are quite high and the residual sum of squares for this equation is $\mathrm{SSR_U} = 0.003\,30$. Computing the test statistic (9.28), treating Equation (12.22) as the unrestricted equation and the original (7.66) as the restricted equation, yields a value of 6.67. This exceeds a critical F value (with [3, 18] d.f.) of $F_{0.05} = 3.16$. Equation (7.66) therefore fails the Hausman test. There appears to be a contemporaneous correlation between regressors and disturbance in this equation. This may well be the result of an omitted variable problem.

12.2 Data mining

We saw in the previous section that the consequences of specification errors can be extremely serious. Since an investigator can never be certain of the correct specification for an estimating equation, it is therefore almost inevitable that (s)he will turn to whatever data is available and use such data as an aid in determining what seems to be an appropriate specification. In particular, the data may well be used to decide which variables should be included in an estimating equation and what lags, if any, should be placed on these variables. This, however, can be shown to have a major effect on how we should interpret, for example, any t tests carried out on the equation specification eventually selected.

In previous chapters, when carrying out significance tests of any kind, we have been content to decide on a level of significance, look up the relevant critical value from the appropriate table, and reject a given null hypothesis at the stated level of significance if the relevant test statistic lies in the rejection region. It is time now to look at this process more carefully and maybe adopt a less unquestioning attitude.

Recall from Section 3.3 that the level of significance of a test is the probability of a type I error, that is, the probability of rejecting a null hypothesis H_0 when it is, in fact, true. In regression analysis the simplest test is the t test of $H_0 : \beta_j = 0$, where β_j is a regression coefficient, and the most common level of significance used is probably 0.05. We shall therefore concentrate on this t test and the 0.05 level of significance. Rejection of the above H_0 implies that the corresponding explanatory variable or regressor is 'significant' at the 0.05 level in the determination of the dependent variable Y.

In this context the level of significance is the probability of finding a regressor 'significant' when in fact it does not influence Y. If the regressor does not really influence Y, there is still a possibility that, purely by chance, we shall find the variable 'significant' by the usual t test. The probability that this will happen is 0.05, or 1 in 20.

Suppose, however, that we have as many as 20 possible regressors, $X_1, X_2, \ldots, X_{20}$, all completely unrelated, that we suspect might influence the dependent Y. Suppose, furthermore, that we computed 20 simple regressions, one for each regressor, of the form

$$\hat{Y} = \hat{\beta}_{1p} + \hat{\beta}_{2p}X_p \tag{12.23}$$

X_p being the pth 'candidate' regressor.

Recall that each such regressor has a 1 in 20 chance of appearing significant at the 0.05 level, even if it does not affect Y. It follows that *we can expect one of the 20 regressors to appear 'significant', by chance, even if none of them actually influence Y.* The temptation in such a situation is to conveniently consign the 19 unsuccessful regressors to the trash can and concentrate on the single 'significant regressor', maybe presenting a paper claiming that it has been demonstrated that this variable has an important influence on Y!

The above is an example of a rather extreme case of what is commonly referred to as **data mining**. However, while the above case is extreme, it has to be admitted that procedures akin to the above have been followed by many 'applied econometricians' in the past 40 years, mainly because of the need to determine the correct specification for estimating equations. For example, if the dependent variable Y in (12.23) were consumer expenditure, candidate regressors could include various definitions of income, various categories of consumer wealth, various interest rates, various measures of the rate of inflation, etc. The final equation presented would probably contain more than one 'significant' regressor and have an impressively high coefficient of determination R^2, but how much confidence could be placed in it if it was the result of a data mining procedure?

Such procedures are clearly unsatisfactory. At the very least, we might expect equations obtained in the above manner to be tested against new data before they are presented as 'evidence' in support of some 'theory'. That is, equations, carefully constructed to describe one data set, need to be exposed to further data that was *unavailable when the equation was constructed* if we are to place any confidence in them. Unfortunately, economic data is so scarce, with samples inevitably being so small, that to some extent the two processes of formulating and testing equations are bound to overlap. That is, some preliminary data 'exploration' is probably inevitable given the need to avoid specification errors. We must therefore consider the process more deeply.

Suppose we had just two possible regressors for use in Equation (12.23), and computed the following regressions from a sample size 25:

$$\hat{Y} = 25.2 + 26.3X_1 \qquad\qquad\qquad (12.24)$$
$$\phantom{\hat{Y} = }(2.34)\ (1.12)$$

and

$$\hat{Y} = 14.2 + 37.4X_2 \qquad\qquad\qquad (12.25)$$
$$\phantom{\hat{Y} = }(1.78)\ (2.33)$$

Figures in parentheses are, as usual, t ratios.

Since the critical t value with $n - 2 = 23$ d.f. is $t_{0.05} = 1.714$, it is clear that, using the conventional procedure (and a one-tail test), X_1 is not 'significant' but X_2 is 'significant at the 0.05 level'. But to what extent are we justified in presenting just Equation (12.25) and claiming that X_2 has been shown to influence Y? Can we say that X_2 is more likely to influence Y than X_1? Given that we have performed a little data mining, can we say anything definite at all?

The answer to the last question is 'yes'. We can claim that X_2 influences Y, but the level of significance at which we can say this is not 0.05 but something higher. That is, if we 'reject H_0' and claim X_2 influences Y, the probability that we are in error exceeds the stated nominal level of significance of 0.05.

To see this and to gain some idea what the true level of significance might be, let us assume that the two regressors X_1 and X_2 in Equations (12.24) and (12.25) are independent of each other and that in fact neither really influences Y. If we are using the above 0.05 nominal level of significance then, since X_1 does not influence Y, we have

Pr $(X_1$ appears significant by chance$) = 0.05$

Pr $(X_1$ does not appear significant$) = 0.95$

Similarly, since X_2 does not influence Y, we have

Pr $(X_2$ does not appear significant$) = 0.95$

Since we have assumed that X_1 and X_2 are independent, it follows that

Pr (neither X_1 nor X_2 appear significant) $= 0.95 \times 0.95 = 0.9025$

Hence

Pr (at least one of X_1, X_2 appear significant) $= 1 - 0.9025 = 0.0975$

What we have now demonstrated is that if neither X_1 nor X_2 influences Y, and we estimate equations of the type (12.24) and (12.25), then the probability of us still finding a 'significant' variable by this procedure and incorrectly claiming that that variable influences Y is 0.0975. That is, the probability of a type I error and hence the level of significance for this procedure is not 0.05 but 0.0975. Thus if we obtain, for example, (12.25) and wish to claim that X_2 influences Y, we must admit to a 0.0975 probability of error and not a 0.05 probability. If we wish to limit the probability of a type I error to 0.05, that is, make the *true* significance level 0.05, then we must only claim significance for a variable when its t ratio exceeds some value considerably greater than $t_{0.05} = 1.714$.

To find the correct critical value for t, corresponding to a **true** significance level of 0.05, in the above case, suppose the stated or **nominal** significance level needs to be α. The probability of neither X_1 nor X_2 appearing 'significant' and having a t ratio in excess of $t_{0.05} = 1.714$ is now $(1 - \alpha)^2$ rather than $(0.95)^2$. Hence the true significance level is

$$\alpha^* = 1 - (1 - \alpha)^2 \tag{12.26}$$

If we wish the true significance level to be 0.05 then we must solve the equation

$$0.05 = 1 - (1 - \alpha)^2$$

This yields a value of $\alpha = 0.0253$. Thus we should find a variable significant at the 0.05 level only if its t ratio exceeds $t_{0.0253}$. With $n - 2 = 23$ d.f., this gives a value of about 2.07 rather than 1.714.

The above analysis can easily be extended to the case where we have c independent candidate regressors in all and compute c regressions of the type (12.23). If none of the c regressors actually influence Y then the probability of finding at least one regressor with a t value in excess of $t_{0.05}$, that is, the true level of significance, is in this case

$$\alpha^* = 1 - (1 - \alpha)^c \tag{12.27}$$

Thus if we test 10 regressors, with a nominal level of significance of $\alpha = 0.05$, then the true significance level is $\alpha^* = 0.401$. That is, there is a probability as high as 0.4 that we will incorrectly conclude that one of the regressors influences Y.

In practice, when attempting to 'explain' variations in a dependent Y variable, we may well 'find' more than one nominally significant regressor and hence eventually arrive at a 'preferred equation' containing several such right-hand-side variables. Lovell (1983) provided a 'rule of thumb' for finding the true significance level in the case where k regressors are selected out of a total of c possible candidates. The Lovell expression for the true level of significance in this case is

$$\alpha^* = 1 - (1 - \alpha)^{c/k} \tag{12.28}$$

where α is again the nominal significance level. A short-cut approximation to (12.28) is, in fact,

$$\alpha^* = (c/k)\alpha \tag{12.29}$$

Thus if we select, for example, $k = 2$ regressors out of a possible $c = 10$, with a nominal 0.05 significance level, then Lovell's short-cut expression indicates a true significance level of about 0.25.

The above calculations rest on the assumption that all the candidate regressors can be treated as independent variables. However, in practice, as Lovell points out, the set of regressors suspected of influencing Y are unlikely to be independent. For example, if we are attempting to explain consumers' expenditure then different measures of consumer wealth are very likely to be correlated. For non-independent regressors, true significance levels may be lower in each case than is suggested by (12.28) and (12.29). For example, in our detailed numerical example above, where $k = 1$ and $c = 2$, we could no longer obtain Pr (neither regressor appears significant) by taking 0.95×0.95 if the two candidate regressors were correlated.

Lovell, however, also points out that performing the t test requires an estimate of the disturbance variance σ^2. Since a data mining process is almost certain to result in an underestimate of σ^2, t ratios are likely to be overestimated, and this means that in the case of independent regressors true significance levels will be higher than that indicated by (12.28) and (12.29). Since two such errors may well roughly 'cancel out', Lovell maintains that (12.28) and (12.29) will still act as a good rule of thumb for true significance levels, even when candidate regressors are correlated.

The data mining problem described in this section is, to some extent, an inevitable consequence of the fact that researchers rarely have any a priori knowledge of what is the 'correct' or 'best' empirical model. The consequences of specification errors can be so serious that at least some preliminary research effort has to be devoted to choosing the 'best' model. In the next section we consider in some detail the problem of deciding on the best approach to selecting an appropriate model.

12.3 Alternative approaches to selecting the 'best' model

Until perhaps 15 years ago, the traditional approach to economic modelling was to begin by formulating the simplest equation or model that was consistent with the relevant economic theory. Such a model was then estimated and various tests performed to determine whether it was satisfactory. By 'satisfactory' in this context it was meant that an equation should have, for example, a high R^2. In addition, its coefficients should have significant t ratios and have signs that were consistent with theory. Also, to be satisfactory, it should have residuals that showed no evidence of autocorrelation or heteroskedasticity.

For example, in the analysis of consumer expenditure C the simplest possible consumption function

$$C = \alpha + \beta Y + \epsilon \tag{12.30}$$

where Y is a measure of disposable income, might initially be estimated.

If such an initial equation proved 'unsatisfactory' in any way then the normal procedure was to 'improve' it in some manner. Extra explanatory variables might be tried in the equation, any that prove significant being added to the model to improve the overall fit. Alternatively, if the residuals proved autocorrelated then the equation might be re-estimated using maybe the Cochrane–Orcutt procedure mentioned in Section 10.5. For example, if the above consumption function proved unsatisfactory then a consumer wealth variable might be added to (12.30). Alternatively, lagged consumption might be included on the right-hand side of (12.30), justified maybe by a belief in the operation of some partial adjustment mechanism in the determination of consumer expenditure. If these additions did not result in a satisfactory equation then further variations might be tried. Such procedures meant that, although the initial model estimated might be very simple, the final model arrived at could be quite complicated. Such an approach has therefore been named the **simple-to-general approach**.

A number of major criticisms can be made of the simple-to-general approach. First, it should be clear from the brief description of the procedure given above that it is open to the accusation of data mining. Since often only the final 'general' model is presented by the investigator, we can have no idea of how many variables were actually tried in the model or how many preliminary regressions were estimated. Hence we can have no idea of what the true significance level is for any of the tests performed on the presented or 'preferred' model. In fact, it is often impossible to judge the worth of the final preferred model in any sensible way.

A further serious criticism of the simple-to-general approach is that revisions to the initial simple model tend to be carried out in an essentially arbitrary manner and often simply reflect the investigator's preconceived notions. These a priori notions are rarely abandoned, and no serious effort is made to consider alternatives. The data are simply 'mined' until some equation is uncovered that can be reconciled with the investigator's a priori beliefs. It is therefore quite possible for two 'applied econometricians', researching the same area and using the same data set, to come to radically different 'conclusions'. To quote Gilbert (1986), 'many so-called researchers are concerned merely to illustrate the theories that they believe independently and are determined to support, come what may'. No serious effort is being made to find the 'correct' equation, and 'research' proceeds in an arbitrary and haphazard manner.

During the past 20 years, an alternative approach to econometric investigation has been developed that is termed **general-to-specific**. This approach is very much associated with the London School of Economics, and particularly with Professor D. F. Hendry. The approach involves a far more systematic examination of various economic hypotheses, and avoids the worst excesses of data mining.

The basic idea behind the general-to-specific approach is to *start* with a very general and maybe quite complicated model that contains, 'nested' within it as special cases, a series of simpler models. These simpler models should represent all the alternative economic hypotheses that require consideration. An example should make this clearer.

In the computer exercises in Chapters 7, 9 and 11, we have been estimating demand equations for food using Data Set 1. We argued that the demand for food, Q, depended on total nominal consumer expenditure, X, the price of food, P, and the general price index, G (representing all other prices). However, it can be plausibly argued that it will take time for changes in X, P or G to have their full effect on the demand for food. Consumers typically are creatures of habit, and suffer from inertia.

We might therefore adopt as our 'general' equation the following:

$$q_t = \alpha_1 + \alpha_2 q_{t-1} + \beta_1 x_t + \beta_2 x_{t-1} + \gamma_1 p_t + \gamma_2 p_{t-1}$$
$$+ \delta_1 g_t + \delta_2 g_{t-1} + \epsilon_t \qquad (12.31)$$

where we have used lower-case letters to denote the natural logarithms of variables. If we were dealing with annual data, as in Data Set 1, then the one-period lags introduced into (12.31) could be regarded as adequately covering the possibility of lagged consumer responses.

Prior to estimation, we have no precise idea of how the demand for food is actually determined, but can envisage a number of economically sensible possibilities. For example, Q may be determined in a simple 'static' manner:

$$q_t = \alpha_1 + \beta_1 x_t + \gamma_1 p_t + \delta_1 g_t + \epsilon_t \qquad (12.32)$$

Alternatively, since food is such a basic necessity, demand for it may be unaffected by any food price variations in our sample, but still affected by total expenditure and general price changes. Such changes may, however, affect food demand with a short lag:

$$q_t = \alpha_1 + \beta_1 x_t + \beta_2 x_{t-1} + \delta_1 g_t + \delta_2 g_{t-1} + \epsilon_t \qquad (12.33)$$

Another possibility is that (12.32) is an adequate specification of the long-run or equilibrium demand for food, but in the short run demand is subject to a partial adjustment mechanism of the kind described in Section 11.2. That is,

$$q_t = \alpha_1 + \alpha_2 q_{t-1} + \beta_1 x_t + \gamma_1 p_t + \delta_1 g_t + \epsilon_t \qquad (12.34)$$

Notice that Equations (12.32)–(12.34) are all *special cases* of the general model (12.31). That is, *they can all be obtained by placing restrictions on the parameters of (12.31)*. Equation (12.32) is obtained by imposing the four restrictions $\alpha_2 = \beta_2 = \gamma_2 = \delta_2 = 0$ on (12.31). Equation (12.33) results from imposing $\alpha_2 = \gamma_1 = \gamma_2 = 0$, and Equation (12.34) implies $\beta_2 = \gamma_2 = \delta_2 = 0$.

When equations are special cases of a general model in this sense, they are said to be **nested** within the general model. Note that it is perfectly possible for a model to be nested within another model that is itself nested within an even more general third model. For example, Equation (12.32) above is clearly a special case of Equation (12.34), which is itself nested within the general model (12.31). Similarly, consider the model

$$q_t = \alpha_1 + \alpha_2 q_{t-1} + \beta_1 (x_t - g_t) + \gamma_1 (p_t - g_t) + \epsilon_t \qquad (12.35)$$

Equation (12.35) can be obtained from (12.34) by imposing the single restriction that $\beta_1 + \gamma_1 + \delta_1 = 0$. It is therefore also nested within (12.34). If variables are defined in logarithmic terms, so that β_1, γ_1 and δ_1 are elasticities then (12.35) implies that demand for food is homogeneous of degree zero, as predicted by theory. In (12.35), $x_t - g_t = \ln (X/G)_t$ and $p_t - g_t = \ln (P/G)_t$ are the logarithms of real total expenditure and the relative price of food respectively. Notice that the restriction imposed on (12.34) to obtain (12.35) was not of the simple kind, such as $\alpha_2 = 0$, that merely results in a variable being excluded from the model. Rather, it involved a linear relationship between three parameters. Such restrictions are equally as important as the more simple kind in generating nested models.

The relationship between the above models is illustrated in Figure 12.3. It is important to realize that different models or equations are not necessarily nested within each other. For example, Equations (12.33) and (12.34) above are **non-nested** models, because neither can be obtained from the other by the imposition of a restriction. This is reflected by the fact that they appear in different 'branches' of the structure in Figure 12.3. Both models are, however, nested within the general model (12.31), of course.

In practice, a general-to-specific investigation of the demand for food would commence with an initial equation such as (12.31). In general, it is important that the initial model should

(a) have nested within it all competing hypotheses or theories concerning the phenomenon under investigation;

(b) be able to explain existing data and be able to satisfy various tests for mis-specification.

The above two criteria may well in fact be linked. For example, if an important theory has been overlooked, and consequently a relevant variable has been omitted from the initial general equation, then that equation is likely to fail many of the tests for mis-specification described in the first section of this chapter. In fact, the initial equation is generally exposed to a whole battery of such diagnostic tests to ensure, for example, that functional form has not been mis-specified, that variables have not been omitted, or that lag lengths are not too short.

Once the general-to-specific practitioner is satisfied with the specification of the general model, a so-called **simplification search** is carried out, in which simpler special cases are tested against the general model. Since special cases are obtained by

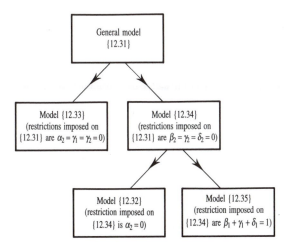

Figure 12.3 Nested models.

placing restrictions on the parameters of the general model, the F test for such restrictions, described in Section 9.2, may be employed for this purpose. If the restrictions involved are nonlinear then the maximum likelihood tests described in Section 9.3 are used. In addition to F tests on the restrictions implied by the nested models, tests of mis-specification are also continually performed. That is, for example, a simpler model would not be preferred to a more general one if the imposition of its restrictions led to a serious deterioration in autocorrelation test statistics. Regular diagnostic testing is therefore part and parcel of the simplification search.

Ideally, the simplification search should be carried out in a systematic and, if possible, in a sequential manner. That is, we should proceed from the general model to simpler and simpler special cases, with each special case being nested within the previous special case.

The simplification search, or **testing-down procedure**, as it is sometimes called, only changes direction or reaches a conclusion when, eventually, the restriction(s) implied by a model are rejected by the data. Thus, for example, if the restrictions $\beta_2 = \gamma_2 = \delta_2$ implied by Equation (12.34) above were not rejected by the data, then, as suggested by Figure 12.3, we would proceed to estimate (12.32) and (12.35) or some other model nested within (12.34). If, however, the restrictions implied by (12.34) were rejected by the F test then we would not estimate any special case of (12.34). To do so would involve serious specification error, because if any of β_2, γ_2 or δ_2 are non-zero then relevant variable(s) are being omitted from (12.34). Rather, in such a situation we would revert to the general model (12.31) or one of its special cases that is not rejected by the data. That is, in terms of Figure 12.3, we would abandon the right-hand branch of the structure and explore the left-hand branch.

The Hendry general-to-specific approach is particularly useful in a situation where there is little doubt about which explanatory variables should be included in an equation, but considerable doubt about the lag structures that should be assigned to each such variable. Economic theory often has much to say about long-run equilibrium relationships, but rarely anything about the short-run dynamics of how an equilibrium is approached. Dynamic factors can often only be uncovered by allowing actual data to determine the appropriate lag structure. In such a situation the simplification search involves the gradual elimination of apparently unimportant lagged variables and thus a testing down to an empirically determined suitable lag structure.

Problems arise with the general-to-specific approach when we are faced with making a choice between non-nested models. In such a situation none of the standard tests is applicable. For example, suppose that neither Equation (12.33) nor Equation (12.34) above can be rejected when tested against the general model (12.31). We could not now use the normal F test to choose between (12.33) and (12.34), because neither can be obtained from the other by the imposition of restriction(s).

One possible way of choosing between non-nested equations is on goodness-of-fit grounds. The adjusted coefficient of determination $\bar{R}^2$ and the Akaike criterion, described at the end of Section 7.1, are examples of measures that could be used for this purpose. More importantly, a number of statistical tests have also been suggested for choosing between non-nested models, and we now briefly consider some of these.

Tests for non-nested models

Suppose we wish to choose between the following models/hypotheses:

$$H_0: \ Y = \beta_1 + \beta_2 X + \beta_3 Z + u \tag{12.36}$$

$$H_1: \ Y = \alpha_1 + \alpha_2 X + \alpha_3 W + v \tag{12.37}$$

Since neither model is nested within the other, we cannot F-test one against the other.

In all the hypothesis testing situations we have encountered so far, we have formulated a null hypothesis H_0 and an alternative hypothesis H_A that covered all possibilities other than H_0. This meant that rejection of H_0 automatically implied acceptance of H_A. We now face a different situation. Because H_0 and H_1 above are non-nested, rejection of H_0 does not necessarily imply acceptance of H_1, since H_1 does not cover all possibilities other than H_0. It is therefore possible for us to end up rejecting *both* H_0 and H_1. Also, as we shall see shortly, it is conceivable that we will be unable to reject either H_0 or H_1.

One method of approach is to nest H_0 and H_1 artificially in a general model. A suitable general model in the above case would be

$$Y = \gamma_1 + \gamma_2 X + \gamma_3 Z + \gamma_4 W + \epsilon \tag{12.38}$$

The models H_0 and H_1 may now be F-tested against (12.38) in the usual way. Such tests are sometimes referred to as **encompassing F tests**.

This approach has been further developed by Mizon and Richard (1986). Its drawback is that the artificial general model (12.38) may not make much sense from an economic viewpoint. This would be the case if H_0 and H_1 reflected conflicting or even mutually exclusive economic theories. If the general model is implausible then this destroys the whole basis of the procedure. Note that, as foreseen above, the F tests could result in the rejection of both models. Also, if the variables W and Z were highly collinear, we could end up not rejecting either H_0 or H_1. This is because in these circumstances the omission of either variable from the general model is unlikely to cause the fit of the equation to deteriorate much.

An alternative approach has been pioneered by Davidson and MacKinnon (1981). Suppose we nest H_0 and H_1 above in the general model

$$Y = (1 - \mu)(\beta_1 + \beta_2 X + \beta_3 Z) + \mu(\alpha_1 + \alpha_2 X + \alpha_3 W) + \epsilon \tag{12.39}$$

If $\mu = 0$ in (12.39) then it reduces to H_0, and if $\mu = 1$ then it reduces to H_1. This suggests that we should test H_0 by testing $\mu = 0$. The problem is that while we can estimate quantities like $\mu\alpha_1$, $\mu\alpha_2$ and $(1 - \mu)\beta_1$ by applying OLS to (12.39), we cannot unscramble an estimate of μ itself. That is, μ is not identified.

Davidson and MacKinnon suggest that to estimate μ, we first apply OLS to the model H_1 to obtain

$$\hat{Y} = \hat{\alpha}_1 + \hat{\alpha}_2 X + \hat{\alpha}_3 W \tag{12.40}$$

The predicted values from (12.40) may now be used instead of $\alpha_1 + \alpha_2 X + \alpha_3 W$ in the estimation of (12.39). That is, we estimate

$$Y = (1 - \mu)\beta_1 + (1 - \mu)\beta_2 X + (1 - \mu)\beta_3 Z + \mu \hat{Y} + \epsilon \qquad (12.41)$$

Davidson and MacKinnon show that if the model H_0 is valid then the t ratio on the OLS estimator of μ in (12.41) should be distributed as N(0, 1) in large samples. We therefore reject model H_0 if this t ratio is sufficiently large. Intuitively, this makes sense, because if $\hat{Y}$ based on H_1 has some explanatory power beyond that of X and Z, the variables in H_0, then H_0 cannot be the true model. Notice, though, that rejecting H_0 does not necessarily mean that we accept H_1. Rather, as indicated by setting $\mu \neq 0$ in (12.39), we reject H_0 in favour of some unspecified combination of H_0 and H_1.

If we wish to test the model H_1 then the above procedure must be repeated with the role of H_0 and H_1 reversed. That is, we first estimate

$$\hat{Y} = \hat{\beta}_1 + \hat{\beta}_2 X + \hat{\beta}_3 Z \qquad (12.42)$$

and then make use of $\hat{Y}$ from (12.42) to estimate

$$Y = \lambda \hat{Y} + (1 - \lambda)\alpha_1 + (1 - \lambda)\alpha_2 X + (1 - \lambda)\alpha_3 W + \epsilon \qquad (12.43)$$

The model H_1 is now rejected if the OLS estimate of λ in (12.43) is significantly different from zero. The above tests are referred to as **J tests** because they involve the joint estimation of parameters.

Notice that as with the encompassing F tests, J tests can result either in rejection of both models or a failure to reject either model. This is implicit in the nature of non-nested models. We shall make use of the J test in one of the computer exercises at the end of this chapter.

Additional tests for non-nested models exist, but are beyond the scope of this text. (For a survey of such tests, see McAleer and Peseran (1986).)

Data mining and the general-to-specific approach

The charge of data mining has been levelled at the general-to-specific methodology. Using this methodology, we begin with a large 'overparameterized' general model that contains (including lagged values) a large number of variables. We then test down to a preferred smaller model, chiefly by eliminating those variables with low t ratios. Is this not data mining? The short answer is 'yes'. However, at least the data mining is there for all to see and it is carried out in a systematic manner that avoids its worst excesses.

In the reporting of a general-to-specific investigation both the initial general model and *all the steps involved*, in moving from nested model to nested model until the preferred small model is obtained, are presented. In contrast, in the typical published paper using a simple-to-general approach it is normally impossible for a reader to have the remotest idea of all the steps and procedures followed before the final model is selected.

In the general-to-specific approach, since the number of steps taken to move to the final model is known to the reader, it is possible to obtain some idea of the true as opposed to the nominal significance levels that should be attached to, for example, any t tests carried out on the final model. In general, if the models are properly nested within one another and k steps are required to get to the final model then, if at each stage the *nominal* significance level is α, the *true* significance level of tests on the final model can be shown to be

$$\alpha^* = 1 - (1 - \alpha)^k$$

(see T. W. Anderson (1966), as quoted in Maddala, 1988, p. 425). Similarly, the true significance level of the jth test in the sequence will be

$$\alpha^* = 1 - (1 - \alpha)^j$$

When choices have to be made between non-nested models, matters become more complicated. Also, there are times when it is possible to move from the general model to the final model by alternative sequences of steps. True levels of significance may then be less clear. It is also the case that at the start of an investigation some decision has to be made about what the initial general model should be. For example, how is the maximum lag length to be determined? Some preliminary exploration of the data, prior to the simplification search, is necessary.

However, as we pointed out earlier, given the size of sample normally available to the econometrician, some data mining is almost certainly inevitable. This is particularly the case when short-run lag structures, about which theory says nothing, have to be determined. Supporters of the general-to-specific approach are well aware of possible accusations of data mining. For this reason, they place great stress on the need for final models to be tested against *new data* that was not available when the model was chosen. To be regarded as in any way satisfactory, a model must be able to provide adequate *out-of-sample forecasts*. General-to-specific practitioners claim, with some justification, that their models are more likely to achieve such forecasts than are models derived using a simple-to-general methodology.

Recall also that one of the factors that originally led to data mining procedures was the fear of serious specification errors, resulting from the omission of relevant variables. Providing the general model includes all relevant variables at the outset (as it is, of course, designed to do), and the simplification search is carried out correctly, no danger of omitted variable bias should arise in a general-to-specific sequence. It is true that because of the deliberate overparameterization of the general model, irrelevant variables are almost certainly likely to be present during the early stages of testing down. However, as we saw in the first section of this chapter, this type of error is less serious than omitted-variable error. Also, any resultant lack of efficiency in estimators should gradually disappear as the simplification search proceeds and irrelevant variables are dropped from the equation.

12.4 Selecting models: some important criteria

Supporters of the general-to-specific approach believe that it is important that the models they eventually select observe certain criteria. These have been outlined by Hendry and Richard (1983).

First, it is important that a model be **data-coherent**. That is, the model should be able to explain adequately existing data. However, it is not enough that an equation should have, for example, a high R^2 or a low residual sum of squares. Residuals from a data-coherent model should be completely random. That is, they should, for example, be non-autocorrelated and homoskedastic. If not then the implication is that some important and systematic factor has been omitted from the model. For example, unsatisfactory autocorrelation statistics would suggest an omitted relevant variable. This is why, as we pointed out earlier, tests for mis-specification are as important during the testing-down process as any tests of restrictions imposed.

Secondly, it is important that all regressors should be **exogenous**. There are different degrees of exogeneity, which we shall consider briefly later in this text, but what this criterion effectively means is that regressors should not be contemporaneously correlated with the disturbance in our equations. As we saw in Section 8.1, such correlations lead to OLS estimators being biased and inconsistent. The Hausman test for contemporaneous correlation, considered in Section 12.1, is clearly of importance here.

Thirdly, a satisfactory model should have **constant parameters** and be able to forecast well outside the sample period used to estimate it. As we have pointed out, equations arrived at by the general-to-specific approach are open to the accusation of being the result of data mining. It is therefore vital to test them against data that was not available when they were constructed. The Chow tests for parameter stability and predictive failure, together with recursive least squares techniques, described in Section 9.5, are often among the tools used to assess whether a model meets this criterion.

Fourthly, the functional forms used in a model should be **data-admissible**. This means that we should not adopt a functional form that results in a model predicting values for the dependent variable that are inadmissible. For example, a linear equation, explaining the price of alcohol, might predict a negative price for values of the explanatory variables that, although sensible, are some way outside existing sample values. Such silly predictions might be avoided by the selection of an appropriate nonlinear functional form.

Fifthly, and this is one of the most important criteria, models should be **consistent with economic theory**, or, at any rate, with at least one of any competing theories. Since economic theory generally refers to the long run, this implies that preferred models should have sensible long-run interpretations. There is a possible conflict here, because it is possible that while a model may have satisfactory statistical properties, it may be unsatisfactory from an economic viewpoint.

Sixthly, a preferred model should, if at all possible, **encompass** all models previously presented by investigators concerning the phenomenon of interest. By this, we mean that a model should not just be able to explain existing data. It should also be able to explain why previous models could or could not do so. In particular, if different researchers using different models have come to different conclusions, a preferred model should be able to explain why this is the case. The importance of this criterion is that, unless new models are always encompassing, research progress in the area of interest will be non-systematic, and any advances are likely to be of an utterly haphazard nature. A new model should not supersede a previous model unless it can do all the previous model could do and more.

Finally, models satisfying the above criteria should be **parsimonious**. This means that a simple explanation of the data should always be preferred to a more complicated explanation. In a regression context, this implies that, other things being equal, an equation with few variables should always be preferred to an equation with more variables. As Milton Friedman (1953) pointed out, 'A hypothesis is important if it explains much by little.' The real world is a complicated place, and we can only expect to model its most important aspects. Unimportant aspects must remain unmodelled and represented by the disturbance term in the preferred equation.

Models should ideally satisfy all the above criteria. However, even if we find such a model, we should beware of regarding it as the 'correct' model. Any model can only at best be an approximation to what is termed the true **data generating process**. Reality is very complex, and, moreover, there is always the possibility that the real world might change. We should therefore always be attempting to adapt and, whenever possible, improve our models. To quote Hendry and Richard, our preferred model can only be a 'tentatively adequate conditional data representation'. We should always be prepared to revise it.

12.5 Computer Exercises

COMPUTER EXERCISE I

In this exercise, we shall again make use of Data Set 1, previously used in Chapters 7, 9 and 11, involving annual observations on the US demand for food. On this occasion, however, we will make a start at employing the general-to-specific approach to estimating an acceptable demand for food equation, taking as our initial general model Equation (12.31). A first attempt at using this approach can be made now, but Chapter 13 will need to be studied before the exercise can be satisfactorily completed.

Estimation of (12.31) for the years 1965–1989 should yield, with lower-case letters denoting natural logarithms,

$$\hat{q}_t = 1.80 + 0.577q_{t-1} + 0.571x_t - 0.337x_{t-1}$$
$$\quad\;\;(1.87)\;\;(4.10)\qquad(3.09)\quad\;(-1.82)$$

$$-0.350p_t + 0.486p_{t-1} - 0.459g_t + 0.039g_{t-1} \qquad\qquad (12.44)$$
$$(-2.15)\quad\;(4.63)\qquad(-1.36)\quad\;\;(0.14)$$

$$R^2 = 0.986, \qquad \sum e^2 = 0.001\,66, \qquad dw = 1.95$$

$$z_{11} = 0.02, \qquad z_2 = 0.28, \qquad z_3 = 2.04, \qquad z_4 = 0.45, \qquad z_5 = 1.14$$

Table 12.1 Computer printout for Equation (12.44)

```
Ordinary Least Squares Estimation
*******************************************************************
Dependent variable is LNRF
25 observations used for estimation from 1965 to 1989
*******************************************************************
Regressor      Coefficient      Standard Error    T-Ratio[Prob]
INTER          1.8045           .96291            1.8740[.078]
LNRF1          .57710           .14062            4.1038[.001]
LNNTE          .57125           .18462            3.0942[.007]
LNNTE1         -.33661          .18489            -1.8206[.086]
LNPF           -.34995          .16286            -2.1488[.046]
LNPF1          .48558           .10480            4.6335[.000]
LNGP           -.45867          .33785            -1.3576[.192]
LNGP1          .038644          .26908            .14361[.887]
*******************************************************************
R-Squared              .98636      F-statistic F(7,17)          175.6449[.000]
R-Bar-Squared          .98075      S.E. of Regression           .0098741
Residual Sum of Squares .0016575   Mean of Dependent Variable   12.1936
S.D. of Dependent Variable .071161 Maximum of Log-likelihood    84.7933
DW-statistic           1.9515
*******************************************************************
```

Diagnostic Tests

```
*****************************************************************************
  Test Statistics          LM Version                  F Version
*****************************************************************************
A: Serial Correlation    CHI-SQ( 1) = .018293[.892]   F( 1,16) = .011716[.915]
B: Functional Form       CHI-SQ( 1) = .42276[.516]    F( 1,16) = .27522[.607]
C: Normality             CHI-SQ( 2) = 2.0354[.361]       Not applicable
D: Heteroskedasticity    CHI-SQ( 1) = .45379[.501]    F( 1,23) = .42521[.521]
E: Predictive Failure    CHI-SQ( 3) = 3.4231[.331]    F( 3,17) = 1.1410[.361]
*****************************************************************************
```

A: Lagrange multiplier test of residual serial correlation
B: Ramsey's RESET test using the square of the fitted values
C: Based on a test of skewness and kurtosis of residuals
D: Based on the regression of squared residuals on squared fitted values
E: A test of adequacy of predictions (Chow's second test)

KEY TO VARIABLES

$LNRF = q_t$ $LNRF1 = q_{t-1}$ $LNNTE = x_t$ $LNNTE1 = x_{t-1}$
$LNPF = p_t$ $LNPF1 = p_{t-1}$ $LNGP = g_t$ $LNGP1 = g_{t-1}$

Source: *Printout from software MICROFIT 3.0, Electronic Publishing, OUP, by H and B Pesaran.*

Figures in parentheses are, as usual, t ratios. z_{11} above is the LM statistic for first-order autocorrelation and z_2 is the RESET statistic, described earlier in this chapter, using just the square of the fitted values. z_3 is the Jarque–Bera statistic for normality in the residuals, also described earlier in this chapter, and z_4 is the LM statistic for heteroskedasticity described in Chapter 10.3. z_5 is the Chow test statistic for predictive failure, described in Section 9.5. We have used the observations in Data Set 1 for the years 1990–92 in the computing of this last statistic. Recall that ability to predict well 'out of sample' is an important attribute of a satisfactory model. $z_{11}, \ldots, z_5$, or similar diagnostic statistics, are standard output from most modern regression packages. A MICROFIT printout showing the basic regression result and most of these statistics is presented in Table 12.1.

The LM statistics z_{11} and z_4 are distributed as χ^2 with 1 degree of freedom, and so have critical values of $\chi^2_{0.05} = 3.841$. z_2, the RESET statistic, has an F distribution with [1,16] d.f., with a critical value $F_{0.05} = 4.49$. z_3, the normality statistic, is distributed as χ^2 with 2 degrees of freedom, and therefore has a critical value of $\chi^2_{0.05} = 5.991$. z_5, the Chow statistic, has an F distribution with [3,17] d.f. and a critical value of $F_{0.05} = 3.20$. None of these statistics exceed their critical values, and the Durbin–Watson statistic takes a value close to 2. The reader should also confirm, using LM statistics, that there is no sign of higher-order autocorrelation in the residuals of (12.44).

As explained earlier, diagnostic statistics can be regarded as tests of mis-specification in this context, so that their values can be regarded as confirmation that we have an appropriate functional form and are justified in omitting lags of more than one period from the equation. However, the reader should also verify that the addition of second-order lags (i.e. the variables $q_{t-2}, x_{t-2}, p_{t-2}$ and g_{t-2}) to (12.44) leads to no improvement in the explanatory power of the equation. This may be verified by estimating an equation including such second-order lags and applying the F-test statistic (9.28) for additional explanatory variables, or its equivalent (9.19). Note also that the addition of second-order lags leads to a value for z_3, the normality statistic, well in excess of its critical value of 5.991.

Earlier in this chapter we used the Hausman test for contemporaneous correlation to assess the specification of the static demand equation (7.66). The reader should apply this test to the general model (12.44). You will need 8 instruments in all for the test. Use the intercept, one-period-lagged values of q_t, x_t, p_t and g_t, and two-period-lagged values of x_t, p_t and g_t. You should find that (12.44) passes the Hausman test, confirming that it is a reasonable specification.

In Section 12.1 we also used the Zarembka version of the Box–Cox procedure to demonstrate that with this data set for the simple static demand model, a double-log specification provided a superior fit to a linear specification. The reader should verify that this superiority still holds when first-order lags are introduced into the equation as in (12.44). This will confirm the findings of the above diagnostic tests that the double-log specification of (12.44) is satisfactory.

A whole series of diagnostic tests, then, suggests no problems of specification with the general model (12.44). We will now begin a simplification search. We have already suggested, earlier in this chapter, a number of simpler models that are nested within (12.44). The relationship between these models was illustrated in Figure 12.3. Our next step is therefore to test such models against the general model (12.44).

First, estimation of Equation (12.34), the simple partial adjustment model, yields

$$\hat{q}_t = 3.94 + 0.423q_{t-1} + 0.216x_t - 0.186p_t - 0.055g_t \qquad (12.45)$$
$$\quad\;\; (3.31)\;\; (2.59) \qquad\;\; (1.72)\quad (-2.00)\quad (-0.27)$$

$$R^2 = 0.957, \qquad \sum e^2 = 0.005\,21, \qquad dw = 1.09$$

$$z_{11} = 7.72, \qquad z_2 = 4.13, \qquad z_3 = 0.82, \qquad z_4 = 0.36, \qquad z_5 = 0.15$$

What is immediately striking about (12.45) is the sharp deterioration in the autocorrelation statistics z_{11} and dw compared with (12.44). There is now clear evidence of first-order autocorrelation in the residuals, and moreover the RESET statistic z_2 is now close to its critical value. This suggests we have made a serious specification error in omitting the lagged variables x_{t-1}, p_{t-1} and g_{t-1} from (12.44).

We can test the three restrictions placed on (12.44) to obtain (12.45), using the F-test statistic (9.19) and the residual sums of squares obtained for (12.44) and (12.45). In this case we have

$$\frac{(\mathrm{SSR_R} - \mathrm{SSR_U})/h}{\mathrm{SSR_U}/(n-k)} = \frac{(0.005\,21 - 0.001\,66)/3}{0.001\,66/(25-8)} = 12.1$$

Since, with [3,17] d.f., the critical F value is $F_{0.05} = 3.20$, we see that the restrictions are strongly rejected by the data.

It is clear that the nested model (12.45) has to be rejected when compared with the general model (12.44). The simplification search in this particular direction therefore terminates. There is no point in carrying on and estimating equations of the forms (12.32) or (12.35), which are nested within (12.45). Note that we did, in fact, estimate Equation (12.32) in Chapter 7 (see Equation (7.66)) and Equation (12.35) in Chapter 11 (see Equation (11.24)). However, since (12.45) is rejected against the general model, we now see that these models must also be rejected. Thus, although when we estimated them in earlier chapters, equations such as (11.24) looked superficially attractive, with high R^2s etc., they, in fact, represent a highly inadequate description of the data set. We must revert to the general model and look for other models nested within it.

Reverting to the general model (12.44), suppose we estimate the special case (12.33), which is also nested in (12.44). This should yield, over the same sample period,

$$\hat{q}_t = 5.28 + 0.917x_t - 0.435x_{t-1} - 0.871g_t + 0.316g_{t-1} \qquad (12.46)$$
$$\quad\;\; (4.35)\;\; (2.89)\quad (-1.36) \qquad (-3.89)\qquad (1.52)$$

$$R^2 = 0.944, \qquad \sum e^2 = 0.006\,83, \qquad dw = 0.89$$

$$z_{11} = 6.66, \qquad z_2 = 6.97, \qquad z_3 = 0.43, \qquad z_4 = 3.67, \qquad z_5 = 0.19$$

Again there is a deterioration in the autocorrelation and RESET statistics, suggesting specification problems with (12.46). Moreover, if we F-test the three restrictions necessary to obtain this equation, we obtain a value for the test statistic (9.19) as high as 17.7. These restrictions are therefore very strongly rejected by the data. Thus the simplification search in this direction must also end, and we must again revert to the general model.

Until now, we have been rather haphazard in our selection of special cases, and have paid no attention to the signs and statistical significance of the coefficients on variables in our models. In practice, this kind of information can be very useful in indicating which direction a simplification search should take. For example, one thing of interest in the general model (12.44) is that both the general price variables have coefficients that are not significantly different from zero. This suggests that, statistically at least, the obvious first step in a simplification search should have been to omit the general price variables g_t and g_{t-1}. However, we shall delay undertaking a rigorous simplification search until we have covered the material of the next chapter.

COMPUTER EXERCISE II

In this exercise we return to Data Set 4, which contains UK data on personal disposable income and consumption. We now examine this data set using the general-to-specific approach. Since this data is quarterly rather than annual, it is wise to allow for more than one-period lags. We shall therefore tentatively adopt a second-order ADL model with seasonal dummy variables as our general model. Estimation of such a model in logarithms for the period 1975Q1 through 1984Q4 should yield

$$\hat{c}_t = 0.015 + 0.045D_2 + 0.086D_3 + 0.106D_4 + 0.498c_{t-1} + 0.417c_{t-2}$$
$$\quad (0.03) \quad (2.57) \quad\quad (7.57) \quad\quad (10.96) \quad\quad (3.25) \quad\quad (2.52)$$
$$+ 0.272y_t + 0.253y_{t-1} - 0.447y_{t-2} \quad\quad\quad\quad\quad\quad (12.47)$$
$$\quad (2.02) \quad\quad (1.65) \quad\quad (-3.32)$$

$$R^2 = 0.966, \quad \sum e^2 = 0.006\,605, \quad dw = 1.86$$

$$z_{14} = 2.88, \quad z_2 = 0.42, \quad z_3 = 8.28, \quad z_4 = 0.14, \quad z_5 = 0.56$$

In Equation (12.47) lower-case letters denote the natural logarithms of variables. D_2, D_3 and D_4 are seasonal dummy variables for the second, third and fourth quarters. z_{14} is now the LM statistic for up to *fourth*-order autocorrelation. This is more appropriate than the first-order statistic, since we are dealing with quarterly data. Its critical value (with 4 d.f.) is $\chi^2_{0.05} = 9.488$. The other diagnostic statistics are as defined in the previous exercise. z_5, the Chow statistic, has been calculated using the last 8 quarters, 1983Q1–1984Q4, for predictive purposes.

Most of the diagnostic statistics associated with (12.47) are satisfactory. The exception is z_3, the Jarque–Bera statistic for normality, to which we will return shortly.

With quarterly data, it is possible that higher-order lags should be included in the general model. It is therefore suggested that the reader experiment by including up to fourth-order lags in Equation (12.47). You should find that this yields a residual sum of squares $\sum e^2 = 0.005\,915$, smaller than that for (12.47). However, if you compute the F statistic (9.19), it should become apparent that the additional lagged variables do not add significant explanatory power to the equation. In addition, their inclusion leads to an even greater value for the z_3 normality statistic. It appears, then, that higher-order lags are of little or no importance in our model.

In previous chapters (see, for example, the computer exercise in Section 9.4), we have always used linear rather than log-linear equations when using Data Set 4. The reader should apply the Zarembka procedure of Section 12.1 and compare Equation (12.47) with the corresponding linear model. You should find that the fit of the log-linear model is just marginally superior and that problems with the z_3 statistic are just as apparent with the linear model.

As we noted in Section 12.1, the Jarque–Bera statistic for normality is very useful for picking up 'outliers', that is, observations with large residuals. Your regression package should have a facility for printing plots of residuals against time. Such a plot for the residuals from Equation (12.47) is shown in Figure 12.4. The two horizontal bands are at distance s from the zero mean, where s is the standard deviation of the residuals. If the residuals were indeed normally distributed, we would expect about two-thirds of them to lie within these bands. We can see that we do have a problem with outlying observations during 1979Q2 and 1979Q3. Without these outliers, s would, in fact, be considerably smaller.

It is apparent from the residuals that actual consumption markedly exceeded its predicted value in 1979Q2, but was considerably smaller than predicted in 1979Q3. In the absence of any indication of why this should be so, we must either live with it or, somewhat arbitrarily, include dummy variable(s) to allow for these aberrations.[6] We shall adopt the former course, remembering that when disturbances are non-normally distributed, our testing procedures are only valid asymptotically. With only 40 observations, we must therefore be cautious in interpreting test results.

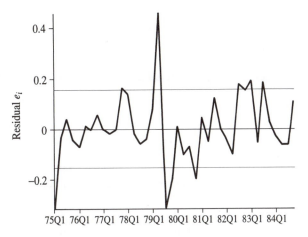

Figure 12.4 Residual plot for Equation (12.47).

We will now test two special cases of Equation (12.47). First, we will estimate a log-linear version of the partial adjustment model (9.58). You should obtain

$$\hat{c}_t = 0.242 + 0.061D_2 + 0.077D_3 + 0.098D_4 + 0.593c_{t-1} + 0.375y_t \quad (12.48)$$
$$\quad\;\; (0.49) \quad (4.52) \qquad (6.12) \qquad (9.17) \qquad (4.46) \qquad (3.15)$$

$$R^2 = 0.952, \qquad \textstyle\sum e^2 = 0.009\,43, \qquad dw = 2.10$$

$$z_{14} = 6.22, \qquad z_2 = 0.05, \qquad z_3 = 0.29, \qquad z_4 = 0.01, \qquad z_5 = 0.97$$

There are no problems with the diagnostic statistics in (12.48), and indeed the z_3 statistic is now satisfactory. Unfortunately, there is a marked rise in the residual sum of squares. If you use the F statistic (9.19) to test the three restrictions (dropping of c_{t-2}, y_{t-1} and y_{t-2}) that have been imposed on (12.47) to give (12.48), you will obtain a value of 4.4. This clearly exceeds a critical F value ([3,31] d.f.) of $F_{0.05} = 2.91$. Thus the partial adjustment model (12.48) has to be rejected against the general model, despite its satisfactory diagnostic statistics.

Even a brief glance at the data series for c_t and y_t in Data Set 4 will reveal that both trend continually upward during our sample period. We have pointed out the dangers of computing regressions for such trending variables on several occasions already in this text (see e.g. Section 4.4). In a first attempt to avoid such problems as spurious correlation, we shall adopt, as our second special case nested within (12.47), a model involving only changes in the variables c_t and y_t. It is often the case that the one-period change in a trending variable shows no continual movement upwards or downwards. Use the data transformation routines in your computer program to construct the variables

$$\Delta c_t = c_t - c_{t-1} = \ln\,(C)_t - \ln\,(C)_{t-1}$$
$$\Delta y_t = y_t - y_{t-1} = \ln\,(Y)_t - \ln\,(Y)_{t-1}$$

You will find that, unlike c_t and y_t, Δc_t and Δy_t show no definite trend over time. Variables such as Δc_t and Δy_t are normally referred to as **first differences** of the original c_t and y_t.

As a first-differenced special case nested within (12.47), we estimate

$$\widehat{\Delta c_t} = -\,0.058 + 0.046D_2 + 0.091D_3 + 0.109D_4 - 0.465\,\Delta c_{t-1}$$
$$\quad\;\; (-7.91)\;\; (2.73) \qquad (11.79) \qquad (14.75) \qquad (-3.54)$$

$$\qquad\qquad\qquad\qquad + 0.239\,\Delta y_t + 0.476\,\Delta y_{t-1} \qquad\qquad (12.49)$$
$$\qquad\qquad\qquad\qquad\quad (2.08) \qquad\quad (4.05)$$

$$R^2 = 0.936, \qquad \textstyle\sum e^2 = 0.006\,661, \qquad dw = 1.94$$

$$z_{14} = 3.19, \qquad z_2 = 0.78, \qquad z_3 = 10.18, \qquad z_4 = 0.18, \qquad z_5 = 0.48$$

The model (12.49) may be obtained from the general model (12.47) by imposing two restrictions. First, the coefficients of c_{t-1} and c_{t-2} must sum to unity, and, secondly, the sum of the coefficients of y_t, y_{t-1} and y_{t-2} must be zero. Notice that imposing two linear restrictions reduces the number of regressors by two. This is a quite general rule. Whenever a linear restriction is imposed on an equation, the number of explanatory variables is reduced by one.

The diagnostic statistics for (12.49) show only slight deterioration from those of the general model (12.47). The fall in R^2 is simply a reflection of the change of dependent variable from c_t to Δc_t. We are now attempting to explain variations in the change in consumption – a rather harder task than explaining variations in its level. There is, in fact, very little change in $\sum e^2$ in (12.49) compared with (12.47). If you compute the F statistic (9.19) to test the two restrictions imposed, you will obtain a value of only 0.13. This is considerably less than the critical F value ([2,31] d.f.) of $F_{0.05} = 3.31$. The restrictions imposed in the estimation of (12.49) appear to be data-acceptable.

All the explanatory variables in (12.49) have coefficients with t ratios in excess of 2. These coefficients are thus all significantly different from zero. In fact the critical t value, using 33 d.f., is only $t_{0.05} = 1.69$. Thus since, apart from the normality statistic, its diagnostic statistics are satisfactory, we could accept (12.49) as a suitably parsimonious version of the general model and end our specification search. There are no variables we should drop from (12.49) and no obvious further restrictions to impose. However, recall that an important criterion of a satisfactory model was that it should make economic sense. Unfortunately, as we shall see in the next chapter, models in differences such as (12.49) can have unacceptable economic properties. We shall therefore be returning to this data set again later in the text.

Appendix 12A

Notes to Chapter 12

1. Since (12.6) is a linear equation, the elasticities of Y with 1. spect to X_2 and X_3 are not constants. For example, the elasticity with respec^t X_2 is given by $(X_2/Y)\beta_2$, which depends on the values of Y and X_2.
2. Recall that for large samples, the tests will be asymptotically valid even if the disturbances are not normally distributed.
3. The third moment about the mean is a measure of the **skewness** or symmetry of a distribution, while the fourth moment is sometimes regarded as a measure of **kurtosis** or peakedness.
4. It should be noted that the various diagnostic tests described in this section are not independent of one another. For example, the failure of any one diagnostic test means that the others become less reliable.
5. It could also be the result of what we referred to in Section 8.3 as simultaneous equation bias. That is, (12.14) could be but one equation in a simultaneous system of equations in which X is endogenous. The precise cause of the contemporaneous correlation does not have to be specified.
6. One possibility would be to define a dummy variable D, taking the value $D=1$ in 1979Q2, $D = -1$ in 1979Q3 and $D=0$ in all other quarters. The reader should verify that including such a dummy does indeed solve the problem with the z_3 normality statistic.

Further reading

Kmenta (1986), Chapter X, has a clear treatment of specification errors. For a more advanced approach, see Johnston (1984), Section 6.6, and Greene (1993), Section 8.4 and also Chapter 11. Charemza and Deadwood (1993), Chapter 2, is excellent on data mining.

Gilbert (1986) provides a readable discussion of the different approaches to model selection, and the criteria for selecting models. See also Cuthbertson et al. (1992), Chapter 4, and Charemza and Deadwood, Chapter 4. Charemza and Deadwood, Chapter 8, also discuss non-nested models and encompassing. A more advanced account of the general-to-specific approach is given by Hendry himself (1983, 1987).

13 Handling non-stationary time series

In previous chapters we have referred on several occasions to the potential problems that arise when classical regression techniques are applied to variables that exhibit consistent trends over time. It is time now to address these problems more directly. We therefore begin this chapter by defining precisely what we mean by stationary and non-stationary time series. We then briefly review the difficulties that arise when we have to deal with non-stationary series, and begin to examine the procedures that have to be followed if we are to circumvent such difficulties. In particular, we introduce the concept of the error correction model. This is a dynamic-type model that has become increasingly popular in recent years and has provided the applied econometrician with a vital tool for facing up to non-stationary series.

13.1 Stationary and non-stationary stochastic processes

Consider a family of random variables $X_1, X_2, X_3, X_4, X_5, \ldots$, where the subscripts refer to successive time periods. In general, each such variable has its own probability distribution, and together they make up what is known as a **stochastic process**. Suppose that for each period, the relevant variable takes a particular value. We then have a **time series** of observations, each observation referring to a different variable.

Although a time series is a particular realization of the stochastic process, for convenience, we will use the terms stochastic process and time series synonymously. We refer to the above process/time series as X_t $(t = 1, 2, 3, \ldots)$.[1]

In general, each X_t will have its own mean $E(X_t)$ and variance Var (X_t). Also, non-zero covariances may exist between different X_t. There is no reason why these means, variances and covariances should be the same for each X_t. That is, they may not necessarily remain constant over time. For example, if $E(X_t)$ continually increases over time then a time path of X_t is likely to look something similar to that in Figure 13.1(a). Alternatively, if $E(X_t)$ does remain constant but Var (X_t) increases over time then we are likely to observe a time path for the series similar to that in Figure 13.2.

We are now in a position to give precise definitions of the terms 'stationary' and 'non-stationary' time series. A time series X_t is said to be **stationary** if

(a) $E(X_t) = \text{constant}$ for all t $\qquad\qquad\qquad\qquad\qquad$ (13.1)

(b) $\text{Var}(X_t) = \text{constant}$ for all t $\qquad\qquad\qquad\qquad\qquad$ (13.2)

(c) $\text{Cov}(X_t, X_{t+k}) = \text{constant}$ for all t and all $k \neq 0$ $\qquad\quad$ (13.3)

The above is in fact a definition of what is termed **'weak stationarity'**, but since in this text it is not necessary to distinguish between different types of stationarity, we shall adopt Equations (13.1)–(13.3) as our definition of stationarity.

A time series is therefore said to be **stationary** *if its mean, variance and covariances remain constant over time.* Thus these quantities would remain the same whether observations for the time series were, for example, from 1975 to 1985 or from 1985 to 1995. A time series is **non-stationary** if it fails to satisfy any part of the above definition. For example, it should be clear that time series trending consistently upwards or downwards, such as those illustrated in Figures 13.1(a,b), are almost certain not to satisfy (13.1), since their mean values appear to change over time. In addition, however, the time series illustrated in Figure 13.2 is also likely to be non-stationary, since, although its mean may be constant, its variance appears to be increasing over time, in contravention of Equation (13.2).

Equation (13.3) needs further explanation. It implies that the covariance, and hence the correlation, between any two values for X depends only on the difference apart in time between the two values, but does not vary with time itself. Thus, for

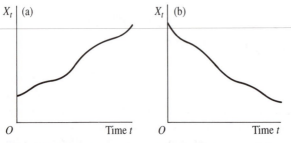

Figure 13.1 (a) Upward trend in X. (b) Downward trend in X.

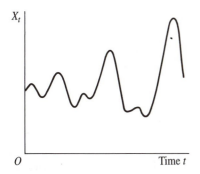

Figure 13.2 Variance increasing with time.

example, $\mathrm{Cov}\,(X_t, X_{t+4})$ remains constant over time, so that

$$\mathrm{Cov}\,(X_{10}, X_{14}) = \mathrm{Cov}\,(X_{13}, X_{17}) = \mathrm{Cov}\,(X_{16}, X_{20}), \quad \text{etc.}$$

However, although $\mathrm{Cov}\,(X_t, X_{t+6})$ also remains constant over time, so that

$$\mathrm{Cov}\,(X_{10}, X_{16}) = \mathrm{Cov}\,(X_{13}, X_{19}) = \mathrm{Cov}\,(X_{16}, X_{22}), \quad \text{etc.}$$

it may well not be the case that $\mathrm{Cov}\,(X_t, X_{t+4}) = \mathrm{Cov}\,(X_t, X_{t+6})$.

Notice that only if a time series X_t is stationary in the above sense can we be justified in viewing the observed values $X_1, X_2, X_3, X_4, \ldots$ as a sample of observations on a *single* variable X, which could therefore be included in a classical regression equation.

The simplest example of a stochastic process is where the X_t are all identically and independently distributed, with zero mean and constant variance. That is,

$$X_t = u_t, \quad \text{where} \quad u_t \text{ is IID}(0, \sigma^2) \tag{13.4}$$

A process such as $X_t = u_t$ in (13.4) is, in this context, often referred to as **white noise**. Since X_t has constant mean and variance with zero covariances (all X_t are independent), a white noise process is stationary by definition.

Another simple stochastic process is the so-called **random walk**, where X_t is determined by the process

$$X_t = X_{t-1} + u_t \tag{13.5}$$

where u_t is white noise.

Taking expectations of both sides of (13.5) gives $\mathrm{E}(X_t) = \mathrm{E}(X_{t-1})$, which implies that the mean of the process is constant. To check whether the variance is constant over time, suppose the initial value of X is given as X_0. Using (13.5), we then have

$$X_1 = X_0 + u_1$$
$$X_2 = X_1 + u_2 = X_0 + u_1 + u_2$$
$$X_3 = X_2 + u_3 = X_0 + u_1 + u_2 + u_3$$

and, in general,

$$X_t = X_0 + u_1 + u_2 + u_3 + \cdots + u_t$$

Since X_0 is a given constant and the u_t are independent, with a constant variance σ^2, it follows, using Theorem 2.4, that $\text{Var}(X_t) = t\sigma^2$. Thus $\text{Var}(X_t)$ is not a constant, but increases with time t. Hence X_t in this case is not a stationary series.

Notice, however, that the *first difference* of X_t is stationary, since, from (13.5),

$$\Delta X_t = X_t - X_{t-1} = u_t \tag{13.6}$$

where u_t is white noise. As we shall see later and in the next chapter, if an economic time series is non-stationary, it is often possible to reduce it to a stationary series by first differencing.

If a constant is added to (13.5) then we have what is known as a **random walk with drift**:

$$X_t = \alpha + X_{t-1} + u_t \tag{13.7}$$

Equation (13.7) also represents a non-stationary series. In this case the first difference $\Delta X_t = \alpha + u_t$, so the X_t series 'drifts' upwards or downwards, depending on the sign of the non-zero α.

The random walk (13.5) is, in fact, a special case of the so-called **first-order autoregressive (AR) process**

$$X_t = \phi X_{t-1} + u_t \tag{13.8}$$

It is not difficult to show that the stochastic process (13.8) will be stationary if the parameter ϕ lies between 1 and -1. It will be non-stationary[2] either if $\phi > 1$ or if $\phi < -1$.

Equation (13.8) in turn is but a special case of the general *k*th-order **AR process**

$$X_t = \phi_1 X_{t-1} + \phi_2 X_{t-2} + \phi_3 X_{t-3} + \cdots + \phi_k X_{t-k} + u_t \tag{13.9}$$

The conditions under which the stochastic process (13.9) is stationary are more difficult to obtain, and we shall not state them here (but see Appendix 14A).

As will become clear in the next section, it is of great importance in econometrics to be able to determine whether or not a given time series is stationary. However, we defer consideration of this problem until the next chapter.

13.2 Non-stationary variables and the classical model

In Chapter 7, when we introduced the classical multiple regression model, we saw that one of the assumptions (IC) that had to be made about the explanatory variables was that as $n \to \infty$, their variances, the $\sum x_{ji}^2/n$, should tend to fixed finite constants.

When we relaxed the assumption of non-stochastic regressors, we replaced this requirement with assumption IC', which required that the probability limit of these variances should equal fixed finite constants.

The large-sample theory, on which the inferential procedures of regression analysis normally depend, breaks down if assumptions such as IC/IC' are invalid. For example, the standard proof of the consistency of the OLS estimators breaks down, and the sampling distributions of these estimators take a non-standard form. Hence we can no longer make use of the t distribution, and all our normal confidence interval formulae and hypothesis testing procedures therefore become invalid.

We have pointed out in earlier chapters that assumptions IC or IC' cannot hold for variables that trend constantly upwards or downwards, as do many economic time series. Previously, we have used the term 'non-stationary' as a vague synonym for trending. However, we have now presented above a rigorous distinction between stationary and non-stationary variables. It turns out, in fact, that standard large-sample theory breaks down whenever any of the explanatory variables in a regression equation is non-stationary in the sense defined above. *The classical regression model was devised to handle relationships between stationary variables. It should not be applied to non-stationary series.* Since so many economic variables are non-stationary, this clearly places severe restrictions on their analysis by standard regression methods. For example, in earlier chapters, we have analysed the demand for food data in Data Set 1. But the fact that these time series almost certainly fail to satisfy the above definition of stationarity means that we can place little reliance on our results thus far.

A problem associated with non-stationary variables, and frequently faced by econometricians when dealing with time series data, is the **spurious regression** or **spurious correlation problem**. If at least one of the explanatory variables in a regression equation is non-stationary in the sense that it displays a distinct trend, it is very likely the case that the dependent variable in the equation will display a similar trend. For example, in most industrialized economies during the period since World War II, many economic variables such as expenditures, incomes and prices have trended continually upwards. As we have pointed out in earlier chapters, when both dependent variable and regressor(s) in an equation are trend-dominated, we are likely to obtain highly 'significant' regression coefficients and high values for the coefficient of determination R^2, even if the trending variables are completely unrelated. Such results are completely **spurious** – that is, entirely the result of chance, unauthentic and meaningless. A good example was provided by Hendry (1980), who pointed out the strong but obviously spurious correlation between rainfall and the UK inflation rate. Even in cases where there is a causal link of some kind between trending variables, the significance of regression coefficients will be artificially increased by the common trends, and much of the apparent correlation discovered will be spurious.

Academic debate concerning spurious or 'nonsense' correlations dates back to Yule (1926). The first significant recent contribution to the discussion was that of Granger and Newbold (1974). In a simulation study, these authors examined spurious relationships between two independent but non-stationary variables X and Y. They, in fact, estimated regression equations of the kind

$$\hat{Y}_t = \hat{\alpha} + \hat{\beta}X_t$$

where X_t and Y_t were both independently and separately generated by random walk processes of the kind (13.5). More often than not, the conventional t test applied to this regression resulted in the rejection of the hypothesis $\beta = 0$, while the R^2 for the equation was frequently quite high. This was despite the fact that X and Y were completely independent variables. An apparent indicator of such spurious correlation (confirmed theoretically by Phillips, 1986) was a particularly low level for the Durbin–Watson statistic, combined with an acceptable R^2.

The spurious results found by Granger and Newbold refer to a case where two variables are stationary with respect to their means but non-stationary with respect to their variances. When time series also have means that are rising over time (that is, they show distinct trends), spurious regression problems will obviously be compounded.

The problems of non-stationary variables and spurious regressions have plagued econometric research since its infancy. Indeed, until recently, many so-called applied econometricians conveniently turned a blind eye to these difficulties and happily accepted the spuriously inflated t ratios and R^2s that they obtained. It is only in recent years that serious efforts have been made to tackle the problems involved.

At one time, a popular rough and ready method of tackling the problem of spurious correlations was to first difference all variables before estimation, that is, work in terms of their rate of change. For example, suppose

$$Y_t = \beta_1 + \beta_2 X_t + \epsilon_t \tag{13.10}$$

where ϵ_t is a disturbance. If X and Y were both trend-dominated variables then we would hesitate to estimate (13.10) directly because of the problem of spurious correlation. However, lagging by one period gives

$$Y_{t-1} = \beta_1 + \beta_2 X_{t-1} + \epsilon_{t-1} \tag{13.11}$$

Subtracting (13.11) from (13.10), we have the equation in first differences

$$\Delta Y_t = \beta_2 \Delta X_t + v_t \tag{13.12}$$

where $v_t = \epsilon_t - \epsilon_{t-1}$, $\Delta Y_t = Y_t - Y_{t-1}$ and $\Delta X_t = X_t - X_{t-1}$.

As we noted earlier, the effect of first-differencing a non-stationary variable in this manner is often to remove the non-stationarity. For example, output in many industrialized economies trends upwards, but this is not normally the case for the annual change in output. Similarly, many non-stationary economic variables become stationary on first-differencing. This is especially the case if we work in terms of the logarithms of variables, because the first difference then becomes the proportional rate of growth. This is because

$$\ln(Y_t) - \ln(Y_{t-1}) = \ln\left(\frac{Y_t}{Y_{t-1}}\right) \approx \frac{Y_t - Y_{t-1}}{Y_{t-1}} \tag{13.13}$$

Provided the change in Y is relatively small, so that Y_t does not differ too much from Y_{t-1}, the approximation in (13.13) will be a good one.[3]

For economic variables, the proportionate or percentage growth rate is far more likely to remain roughly constant over time than is the absolute growth rate $Y_t - Y_{t-1}$. It follows that the equation in first differences, (13.12), particularly if it is expressed in logarithmic terms, is likely to involve stationary variables only, so that it might seem that classical regression analysis could now proceed straightforwardly. We, in fact, adopted such an approach at the end of the second computer exercise of the last chapter. Unfortunately, there are a number of problems with this procedure.

First, if the relationship (13.10) is valid and its disturbance ϵ_t is non-autocorrelated then the disturbance u_t in (13.12) is of first-order moving average form, and therefore autocorrelated. This clearly complicates the estimation process.

Secondly, and more importantly, if (13.12) is estimated then *important information concerning the levels of variables may have been ignored, and attention is directed only at the short-run relationship between X and Y.*

Clearly, estimated versions of (13.12) will provide us with no information about the parameter α. However, they also have nothing to say about the long-run relationships between variables. To see why they ignore information on the levels of variables, suppose we regard (13.10) as a valid representation of the 'equilibrium relationship' between X and Y. That is, for a given value of X, the equilibrium value of Y is (ignoring the disturbance for the moment), $\beta_1 + \beta_2 X$. At the end of period $t - 1$, one of three situations could exist.

(a) Y equals its equilibrium value, i.e. $Y_{t-1} = \beta_1 + \beta_2 X_{t-1}$;

(b) Y is below its equilibrium value, i.e. $Y_{t-1} < \beta_1 + \beta_2 X_{t-1}$;

(c) Y is above its equilibrium value, i.e. $Y_{t-1} > \beta_1 + \beta_2 X_{t-1}$.

Suppose that during the succeeding period t the variable X changes. If during period $t - 1$, situation (a) held, then there would be a resultant change in Y, which we will refer to as ΔY_t. Note that there is no reason why ΔY_t should be given by Equation (13.12). ΔY_t would only be given by this equation if the variables were to satisfy their equilibrium relationship at the end of period t as well as at the end of period $t - 1$. This need not necessarily be the case.

Suppose now that, at the end of period $t - 1$, situation (b) above held, but we experienced the same change in the variable X. Since Y was previously below its equilibrium value, it has some catching up to do. Consequently, the change in Y during period t is likely to exceed the above ΔY_t. Similarly, if situation (c) above had held at the end of period $t - 1$, some reining back in the variable Y is to be expected. Consequently, in this case the change in Y during period t is likely to be less than the above ΔY_t.

Summarizing, we can say that the change in Y during period t will depend not only on the change in X during period t, but also on the relationship between X and Y at the end of the previous period. Specifically, it will also depend on the extent of any disequilibrium between the levels of X and Y during period $t - 1$. This is what we meant when we stated that equations such as (13.12) ignored any information concerning the levels of X and Y.

Working in terms of first differences also leads quite frequently to equations with unsatisfactory long-run properties. For example, it is rarely the case, when estimating equations such as (13.12), that we fail to find a significant intercept term. That is, we tend to end up with equations of the form

$$\Delta Y_t = \hat{\alpha} + \hat{\beta}_2 \, \Delta X_t, \qquad \hat{\alpha} \neq 0 \qquad\qquad (13.14)$$

Consider a situation where X remains constant. If a static equilibrium for the model exists then Y should eventually become constant at its 'long-run' equilibrium value. But if X is constant then $\Delta X_t = 0$, so that (13.14) implies $\Delta Y_t = \hat{\alpha} \neq 0$. Thus Y, depending on the sign of $\hat{\alpha}$, either continues to rise indefinitely or continues to fall. That is, (13.14) implies that no static equilibrium can exist between X and Y. Since much of economic theory concerns the determination of static equilibria, equations such as (13.14) are generally inconsistent with whatever underlying theory is relevant. Such a criticism, in fact,

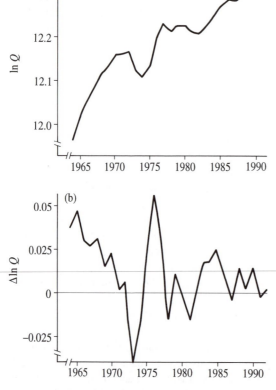

Figure 13.3 (a) Time path for $\ln(Q)$. (b) Time path for $\Delta \ln(Q)$.

applies to the last equation estimated in the second computer exercise of Chapter 12. If income remains constant, we do not expect consumption to continue changing indefinitely.

Simple first-differencing does not then provide a satisfactory solution to the problem of non-stationary variables. However, a way forward that allows for the above problems is provided by the use of error correction models, which we discuss in the next section.

COMPUTER EXERCISE I

The graphics options in your computer regression package should enable you to obtain plots of variables against time. First, using Data Set 1 on the floppy disk, examine the time paths of the variables food demand Q, total expenditure X, the price of food P and the general price index G. Look also at the time paths for real

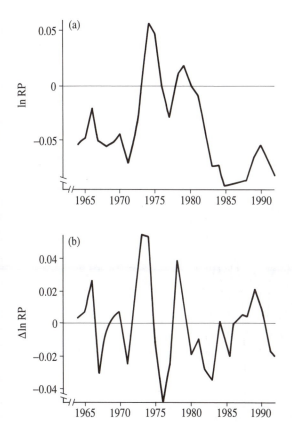

Figure 13.4 (a) Time path for $\ln (RP)$. (b) Time path for $\Delta \ln (RP)$.

total expenditure $RE = X/G$, and the relative price of food $RP = P/G$. Note that, with the exception of RP, which appears to have a slight downward trend, the variables trend continually upwards over our sample period. They clearly appear to be non-stationary. The natural logarithms of the time series exhibit a similar pattern. For example, the time paths of $\ln(Q)$ and $\ln(RP)$ are illustrated in Figures 13.3(a) and 13.4(a) respectively.

Now form first differences of the six variables and their logarithms. Examine the time paths of the first-differenced series. The trends are now much less marked, and in many cases appear to have disappeared altogether. That is, these time series appear to be stationary. For example, the time paths of $\Delta \ln(Q)$ and $\Delta \ln(RP)$ are illustrated in Figures 13.3(b) and 13.4(b). Patterns such as those exhibited by $\ln(Q)$ and $\Delta \ln(Q)$ in Figure 13.3 are typical of many economic time series.

Next examine the time paths of the variables disposable income Y and consumer expenditure C in Data Set 4. Both these variables and their logarithms also trend upwards over time, but, as we saw in Section 9.4, exhibit a strong seasonal pattern. For example, the time path of $\ln(C)$ is shown in Figure 13.5(a).

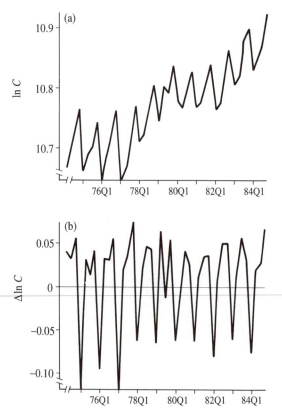

Figure 13.5 (a) Time path for $\ln(C)$. (b) Time path for $\Delta \ln(C)$.

However, the first differences of these variables show no upward trend. Although the seasonal pattern can still be seen, first-differencing again appears to have produced trendless series. For example, the time path of $\Delta \ln (C)$ is shown in Figure 13.5(b).

The visual examination of time paths is a very rough and ready way to search for stationarity. More rigorous tests than this are obviously necessary, and in the next chapter we shall present some.

13.3 Error correction models

The concept of an **error correction model** (ECM) dates back at least to the paper by Sargan (1964) on wages and prices in the UK. However, the current popularity of these models owes much to their association with the work of Hendry and his promotion of the general-to-specific approach to econometric modelling outlined in the last chapter. ECMs have a number of useful properties, but perhaps their most important use is in providing econometricians with a possible approach to dealing with the problems of non-stationary time series and spurious correlation.

A simple first-order ECM

Suppose that the long-run or equilibrium relationship between two variables X and Y is

$$Y_t = KX_t^{\beta_1} \tag{13.15}$$

where K and β_1 are constants. For example, Y might be the demand for a good and X its price under *ceteris paribus* conditions. β_1 is therefore the long-run elasticity of Y with respect to X. Using lower-case letters to denote the natural logarithms of variables, we may rewrite (13.15) as

$$y_t = \beta_0^* + \beta_1 x_t \tag{13.16}$$

where $\beta_0^* = \ln (K)$. When Y takes its equilibrium value with respect to X, Equation (13.16) holds.[4] However economic systems are rarely in equilibrium. When Y takes a value different from its equilibrium value, the difference between the left- and right-hand sides of (13.16), that is,

$$y_t - \beta_0^* - \beta_1 x_t \tag{13.17}$$

measures the extent of disequilibrium between the two variables. This quantity is, in fact, known as a **disequilibrium error**. It will, of course, take a zero value when X and Y are in equilibrium.

Since, as we noted above, X and Y will rarely be in equilibrium, what the applied econometrician usually observes is a short-run or disequilibrium relationship involving lagged values of X and Y. Suppose this takes the form

$$y_t = b_0 + b_1 x_t + b_2 x_{t-1} + \mu y_{t-1} + \epsilon_t, \qquad 0 < \mu < 1 \tag{13.18}$$

For simplicity, we have included only first-order lags in (13.18). In practice, second- or higher-order lags could appear. Notice that (13.18) implies that Y takes time to adjust fully to variations in X. This is consistent with the idea that Y is not always at its equilibrium value relative to X. Indeed, if $b_2 = 0$ in (13.18), the equation would reduce to a simple partial adjustment model.

The main problem in estimating the parameters of (13.18) is that it involves the levels of variables that may be non-stationary. We would hesitate to apply classical techniques for fear of encountering spurious regression problems. Let us, however, rearrange (13.18). Subtracting y_{t-1} from each side gives

$$y_t - y_{t-1} = b_0 + b_1 x_t + b_2 x_{t-1} - (1 - \mu) y_{t-1} + \epsilon_t \tag{13.19}$$

Adding and subtracting $b_1 x_{t-1}$ from the right-hand side of (13.19) then yields

$$y_t - y_{t-1} = b_0 + b_1 x_t - b_1 x_{t-1} + b_1 x_{t-1} + b_2 x_{t-1} - (1 - \mu) y_{t-1} + \epsilon_t$$

or

$$\Delta y_t = b_0 + b_1 \Delta x_t + (b_1 + b_2) x_{t-1} - \lambda y_{t-1} + \epsilon_t \tag{13.20}$$

where $\lambda = 1 - \mu$. We now **reparameterize** (13.20) as follows:

$$\Delta y_t = b_0 + b_1 \Delta x_t - \lambda (y_{t-1} - \beta_1 x_{t-1}) + \epsilon_t \tag{13.21}$$

where we define a new parameter $\beta_1 = (b_1 + b_2)/\lambda$. We can also further reparameterize (13.21) as

$$\Delta y_t = b_1 \Delta x_t - \lambda (y_{t-1} - \beta_0 - \beta_1 x_{t-1}) + \epsilon_t \tag{13.22}$$

where $\beta_0 = b_0/\lambda$ is a second new parameter.

We have obtained (13.22) simply by rearranging the original disequilibrium relationship (13.18) and defining two new parameters β_0 and β_1. Equation (13.22) is therefore just another way of writing (13.18). However, it can be interpreted in an interesting new way. Suppose, for the moment, we regard the parameters β_0 and β_1 as identical to the parameters β_0^* and β_1 in the equilibrium relationship (13.16) (the reason why we have distinguished between β_0 and β_0^* until now will become clear shortly). From (13.17), we now see that the term in parentheses in Equation (13.22) can be regarded as the disequilibrium error from period $t = 1$. Thus (13.22) can be interpreted as stating that the current change in Y depends on the change in X and on the extent of disequilibrium in the previous period. Equation (13.22) therefore meets the criticism of the simple first-differenced equation (13.12) of the previous section in that *it allows for any previous disequilibrium in the levels of X and Y.* The value of Y is, in fact, being corrected for any previous disequilibrium or error. Equation (13.22) is therefore referred to as a **first-order error correction model**. It is a first-order model because we only introduced first-order lags into the disequilibrium relationship (13.18). Notice that the extent to which any disequilibrium in period $t - 1$ is compensated for in period t depends on the size of the parameter λ. Since λ lies between zero and unity, only part of any disequilibrium is made up for in the current period.

Notice also that the disturbance in (13.22) is identical to that in (13.18), so that, if it is non-autocorrelated in (13.18), it will remain so in (13.22). Thus Equation (13.22) meets the other criticism of the first-differenced equation (13.12): it contains a well-behaved disturbance.

The parameters in (13.22) have a clear interpretation. We have already discussed λ, which is an adjustment parameter. β_1 appears in the equilibrium relationship (13.15), being the *long-run* elasticity of Y with respect to X. We shall return to β_0 shortly. b_1 appears in the short-run disequilibrium relationship (13.18), and clearly reflects the *immediate* response of Y to a change in X. It is therefore the *short-run* elasticity.

Error correction models do not have to be expressed in logarithmic form, but it is convenient to do so for several reasons. Not only does this mean that parameters can be interpreted as elasticities, but also, because of the approximation (13.13), first-differenced variables such as Δy_t and Δx_t can be regarded as *proportionate changes*. As we have argued previously, for economic variables such changes, unlike y_t and x_t, are likely to form stationary series, and are therefore suitable for inclusion in classical regression equations.

In addition, the approximation (13.13) makes it possible to demonstrate an important property of ECMs. Our model implies that *the parameter β_0^* in the equilibrium relationship (13.16) depends on the long-run growth rates in X and Y.* We shall now demonstrate this.

Suppose that the long-run trend growth rate in X is θ. That is,

$$\Delta x_t = \theta, \quad \text{or} \quad x_t = x_{t-1} + \theta \tag{13.23}$$

Substituting for x_t in the equilibrium or long-run relationship (13.16) yields

$$y_t = \beta_0^* + \beta_1(x_{t-1} + \theta) = \beta_0^* + \beta_1 x_{t-1} + \beta_1\theta = y_{t-1} + \beta_1\theta \tag{13.24}$$

Hence $\Delta y_t = \beta_1\theta$. Thus if X grows at a long-run rate θ then Y must grow at a long-run rate $\beta_1\theta$. Remember that β_1 is the long-run elasticity of Y with respect to X.

What we have done in Equations (13.23) and (13.24) is define a long-run equilibrium in which X and Y grow at constant proportionate rates θ and $\beta_1\theta$ respectively. If our model is to be internally consistent then, under such long-run growth rates, the error correction model (13.22) (which is just a reparameterized version of the disequilibrium relationship (13.18)) should reduce to the equilibrium relationship (13.16). Substituting $\Delta x_t = \theta$ and $\Delta y_t = \beta_1\theta$ in (13.22) gives

$$\beta_1\theta = b_1\theta - \lambda(y_t - \beta_1\theta - \beta_0 - \beta_1 x_t + \beta_1\theta) \tag{13.25}$$

Solving (13.25) for y_t, we have

$$y_t = \frac{\lambda\beta_0 - \theta(\beta_1 - b_1)}{\lambda} + \beta_1 x_t \tag{13.26}$$

What we have now shown is that in long-run equilibrium the error correction model (13.22) reduces to (13.26). For our model to be consistent, we require (13.26) to be identical to the equilibrium relationship (13.16). A comparison of (13.26) and (13.16), however, indicates that for this to be the case, we require

$$\beta_0^* = \frac{\lambda\beta_0 - \theta(\beta_1 - b_1)}{\lambda} \tag{13.27}$$

Thus the parameter β_0^* in the equilibrium relationship (13.16) depends on θ, the long-run growth rate in X. If the long-run elasticity β_1 exceeds the short-run elasticity b_1 then the parameter β_0^* will, in fact, vary inversely with the growth rate.

Notice that (13.27) implies that $\lambda\beta_0^* = \lambda\beta_0 - \theta(\beta_1 - b_1)$. This only reduces to $\beta_0^* = \beta_0$ either if the long-run growth rate in X, θ, is zero, or if the short- and long-run elasticities b_1 and β_1 are identical. Thus, while it is permissible to interpret the β_1 in the error correction model (13.22) as being identical to the β_1 in the equilibrium relationship, we cannot in general regard β_0 and β_0^* as identical. Rather, the relationship between them is given by (13.27).

It may seem strange that a parameter in a long-run relationship should depend on rates of growth. However, remember that the long-run relationship we are discussing is an equilibrium relationship, so it is not surprising that its parameter should depend on the nature of the equilibrium that is being postulated. For example, suppose (13.15) and (13.16) referred to a long-run relationship between consumption Y and income X that was one of proportionality. The elasticity β_1 would then be unity and K would be the long-run average propensity to consume. Thus we see from (13.27) that β_0^* and hence K will fall as the growth rate in income rises. This is a relationship that has, in fact, been observed empirically. Countries with higher economic growth rates do tend to have lower average propensities to consume.

Notice that without prior knowledge of the long-run parameters, we cannot estimate the above ECM in the form (13.22). This is because without knowing β_0 and β_1, we cannot construct the disequilibrium error $y_{t-1} - \beta_0 - \beta_1 x_{t-1}$. In the absence of such knowledge, to estimate the ECM, we must first multiply out the term in parentheses to obtain

$$\Delta y_t = \lambda\beta_0 + b_1 \Delta x_t - \lambda y_{t-1} + \lambda\beta_1 x_{t-1} + \epsilon_t \tag{13.28}$$

Δy_t can now be regressed on $\Delta x_t, y_{t-1}$ and x_{t-1}, estimates of all short- and long-run parameters then being obtained.

Some more complicated ECMs

The error correction models estimated by econometricians in practice tend to be more complicated than (13.28). For example, with quarterly data, higher-order lags are likely to appear in the disequilibrium relationship (13.18). Introducing second-order lags, we might have

$$y_t = b_0 + b_1 x_t + b_2 x_{t-1} + b_3 x_{t-2} + \mu_1 y_{t-2} + \mu_2 y_{t-2} + \epsilon_t \tag{13.29}$$

It is, however, still possible to rearrange and then reparameterize (13.29) to obtain an ECM. First, adding and subtracting the term $(b_1 + b_2 + b_3)x_{t-1}$ from the right-hand side of (13.29) yields

$$y_t = b_0 + b_1 \Delta x_t - b_3 \Delta x_{t-1} + (b_1 + b_2 + b_3)x_{t-1} + \mu_1 y_{t-1} + \mu_2 y_{t-2} + \epsilon_t$$

$$(13.30)$$

Taking y_{t-1} from either side and then adding and subtracting $\mu_2 y_{t-1}$ from the right-hand side of (13.30), we have

$$\Delta y_t = b_0 - \mu_2 \Delta y_{t-1} + b_1 \Delta x_t - b_3 \Delta x_{t-1}$$
$$- (1 - \mu_1 - \mu_2)y_{t-1} + (b_1 + b_2 + b_3)x_{t-1} + \epsilon_t \qquad (13.31)$$

Finally, (13.31) may be reparameterized to give

$$\Delta y_t = -\mu_2 \Delta y_{t-1} + b_1 \Delta x_t - b_3 \Delta x_{t-1} - \lambda(y_{t-1} - \beta_0 - \beta_1 x_{t-1}) + \epsilon_t \qquad (13.32)$$

where $\lambda = 1 - \mu_1 - \mu_2$, $\beta_0 = b_0/\lambda$ and $\beta_1 = (b_1 + b_2 + b_3)/\lambda$ are new parameters.

Equation (13.32) is an ECM that relates Δy_t to lagged values of itself, current and lagged values of Δx_t, and the extent of departure in the previous period from the long-run equilibrium relationship (13.16). To estimate (13.32), it is again necessary to multiply out the disequilibrium error term and rewrite the equation as

$$\Delta y_t = \lambda\beta_0 - \mu_2 \Delta y_{t-1} + b_1 \Delta x_t - b_3 \Delta x_{t-1} - \lambda y_{t-1} + \lambda\beta_1 x_{t-1} + \epsilon_t \qquad (13.33)$$

β_1 in (13.33) can again be interpreted as the long-run elasticity, with the relationship between β_0^* and β_0 again depending on rates of growth. In a similar manner, by adding further lags to the disequilibrium relationship (13.29), other ECMs may be constructed. For example, if third-order lags were introduced into (13.29) then we would obtain an ECM similar to (13.33), but having the additional regressors Δy_{t-2} and Δx_{t-2}. Fourth-order lags would result in the further addition of Δy_{t-3} and Δx_{t-3}, and so on.

It is possible, of course, for more than two variables to enter into an equilibrium relationship. For example, (13.16) could be generalized to

$$y_t = \beta_0^* + \beta_1 x_t + \beta_2 z_t \qquad (13.34)$$

A first-order disequilibrium relationship could then take the form

$$y_t = b_0 + b_1 x_t + b_2 x_{t-1} + c_1 z_t + c_2 z_{t-1} + \mu y_{t-1} + \epsilon_t \qquad (13.35)$$

A reparameterization of (13.35) is the ECM

$$\Delta y_t = b_1 \Delta x_t + c_1 \Delta z_t - \lambda(y_{t-1} - \beta_0 - \beta_1 x_{t-1} - \beta_2 z_{t-1}) + \epsilon_t \qquad (13.36)$$

where $\lambda = 1 - \mu$, $\beta_0 = b_0/\lambda$, $\beta_1 = (b_1 + b_2)/\lambda$ and $\beta_2 = (c_1 + c_2)/\lambda$. The term in parentheses in (13.36) can be interpreted in terms of the extent of departure from the equilibrium relationship (13.34).

It is also possible to have alternative ECM parameterizations of the same disequilibrium relationship. For example, we have already seen that the relationship (13.29) can be reparameterized as the ECM (13.32). However, an alternative reparameterization of (13.29) is

$$\Delta y_t = (\mu_1 - 1)\,\Delta y_{t-1} + b_1\,\Delta x_t + (b_1 + b_2)\,\Delta x_{t-1}$$
$$- \lambda(y_{t-2} - \beta_0 - \beta_1 x_{t-2}) + \epsilon_t \qquad (13.37)$$

where $\lambda = 1 - \mu_1 - \mu_2$, $\beta_0 = b_0/\lambda$ and $\beta_1 = (b_1 + b_2 + b_3)/\lambda$ as before, but the coefficients of the rate-of-change regressors are defined differently from (13.32). Whereas Equation (13.32) expresses Δy_t in terms of the rates of change in X and Y and the extent of disequilibrium one period previous, (13.37) includes the disequilibrium error from two periods previous. Since (13.32) and (13.37) are really the same equation arranged in different ways, either could be fitted to the same data set with identical results. Choice between them would depend on which parameterization had the most sensible economic interpretation.

13.4   The advantages of the ECM approach

We have already noted how an error correction model avoids the problems associated with simple first-difference models such as (13.12). In particular, the inclusion of disequilibrium terms in ECMs ensures that no information on the levels of variables is ignored. As we also noted earlier, since ECMs are formulated in terms of first differences, which typically eliminate the trends from variables, they can play an important role in dealing with potential problems relating to spurious correlation. In addition, as we shall see in the next chapter, provided an ECM is correctly formulated, its disequilibrium error term can also be regarded as a stationary variable. It follows that, provided our sample is sufficiently large, ECMs can be estimated by classical regression methods. The presence of lagged variables in the models means that we have to rely on the large-sample properties of our estimators, and this is feasible provided we are dealing with stationary variables.

The increasing use of ECMs in applied work has been inextricably linked with the rising popularity of the Hendry general-to-specific methodology discussed in the last chapter. Well-known examples are the work of Davidson et al. (1978) and of Hendry and Ericsson (1991). For a fairly straightforward introduction to the approach, see Gilbert (1986). A more sophisticated treatment is that of Hendry himself (1987).

The ease with which ECMs can be fitted into the general-to-specific approach is one of their major advantages. For example, it is easy to see that the simple ECM (13.22) is nested within the ECM (13.32). Similarly, any high-order ECM will have nested within it simpler ECMs as special cases.

The general-to-specific methodology could thus be regarded as a search for the most parsimonious ECM that best fits the given data set. However, there is rather more to it than this. In the testing-down procedure general-to-specific practitioners are usually quite sanguine about dropping any differenced variables such as Δx_t, Δx_{t-1} or Δy_{t-1} in (13.33), provided this is justified statistically by the appropriate F test and does not lead to problems with the diagnostic statistics. This is because the dropping of any differenced variables among the regressors of an ECM has implications merely for the short-run dynamics of the model, about which economic theory normally suggests nothing. It has no implications for the underlying equilibrium relationship, about which theory often has something quite definite to say. For example, dropping the variable Δx_{t-1} from the ECM (13.33) implies imposing the restriction $b_3 = 0$ on the equivalent disequilibrium relationship (13.29). This places a restriction upon the manner in which the variable Y approaches its equilibrium value, given by (13.16), but has no implication for the equilibrium relationship itself. In contrast, general-to-specific workers would be far more cautious about dropping any of the lagged level variables in an ECM, even if this appeared to be justified statistically. For example, dropping the variable x_{t-1} from the ECM (13.33) implies that β_1 in the equilibrium relationship (13.16) is zero. This obviously has serious implications for the underlying model. If statistical considerations strongly suggest dropping a level variable in an ECM then a major rethink about the underlying economic process is in order.

This clear distinction between short- and long-run effects is itself a further advantage of the ECM approach. Since, as noted above, theory normally involves hypotheses about long-run relationships, the clear distinguishing of long-run parameters in ECMs makes these models ideally suited for assessing the validity of such hypotheses.

One further major advantage of the ECM representation of disequilibrium relationships is claimed by general-to-specific researchers. The explanatory variables in equations such as (13.18) are likely to be highly collinear in most time series data. Thus, even if the variables are non-stationary, we are likely to face problems if we attempt to estimate the disequilibrium relationship in this form. Typically, standard errors will tend to be large because of the multicollinearity problem. In (13.28), the ECM reparameterization of (13.18), however, the variables x_t and x_{t-1} have been replaced by Δx_t and x_{t-1}. With typical time series data, it is a fact that the correlation between Δx_t and x_{t-1} is normally much smaller than that between x_t and x_{t-1}. Thus problems of multicollinearity are greatly reduced if we estimate (13.28) rather than (13.18).

There are similar advantages in estimating the ECM (13.33) rather than (13.29). In (13.33) the variables Δx_t, Δx_{t-1} and x_{t-1} have replaced x_t, x_{t-1} and x_{t-2}. In practice, this alone will reduce problems of collinearity, but, in addition, note that the differenced terms in x in (13.33) can be rewritten as

$$b_1\, \Delta x_t - b_3\, \Delta x_{t-1} = (b_1 - b_3)\, \Delta x_t + b_3\, \Delta^2 x_t$$

where $\Delta^2 x_t = \Delta x_t - \Delta x_{t-1}$. This means that it is also possible to further reparameterize the ECM (13.33), replacing the variables Δx_t and Δx_{t-1} by Δx_t and $\Delta^2 x_t$. This has the advantage of further reducing problems of multicollinearity, since, in typical time series data, Δx_t and $\Delta^2 x_t$ are likely to be far less highly correlated than Δx_t and Δx_{t-1}.

In general, an ECM representation of a disequilibrium relationship will always reduce problems of multicollinearity. Indeed, general-to-specific practitioners claim that the regressors in an ECM are often almost orthogonal – that is, correlations between any two variables are virtually zero. This has one further important consequence. In the testing-down procedure it is an advantage if one can be confident that high standard errors can be taken at their face value and are not the result of multicollinearity. If this is the case then low t ratios in an estimated ECM can be regarded as an adequate and reliable criterion for the omission of variables. This makes the testing-down procedure clearer cut, and facilitates the finding of a suitably parsimonious final equation.

Exercise 13.1

When expressed in natural logarithms, the long-run or equilibrium relationship between Y, X and Z is given by (13.34). The observed disequilibrium relationship, however, is (13.35), which can be expressed in the error correction form (13.36).

(a) Express the ECM (13.36) in a form suitable for estimation.

(b) What restrictions have to be placed on the estimating equation to ensure that

    (i)   long-run elasticities with respect to X and Z are equal?

    (ii) short-run elasticities with respect to X and Z are equal?

    (iii) long run elasticities sum to unity?

    (iv) the model reduces to partial adjustment form with $b_2 = c_2 = 0$?

(c) For each of the above restrictions, determine what error correction model should be estimated if the restriction is imposed.

(d) The following equations were estimated by OLS from $n = 44$ observations (figures in parentheses are t ratios):

$$\widehat{\Delta y_t} = 1.61 + 0.213 \,\Delta x_t + 0.826 \,\Delta z_t + 0.624 x_{t-1} + 0.572 z_{t-1} - 0.707 y_{t-1}, \quad \text{(I)}$$
$$(4.83)\ (0.823)\qquad(4.215)\qquad(2.872)\qquad(3.734)\qquad(3.436)$$

$$\text{SSR} = 0.006\,32$$

$$\widehat{\Delta y_t} = 1.57 + 0.224 \,\Delta x_t + 0.818 \,\Delta z_t + 0.434(x_{t-1} - z_{t-1}) - 0.593(y_{t-1} - z_{t-1}),$$
$$(4.41)\ (0.812)\qquad(3.562)\qquad(2.137)\qquad\qquad(2.241)$$

$$\text{SSR} = 0.007\,93 \quad \text{(II)}$$

$$\widehat{\Delta y_t} = 1.62 + 0.218 \,\Delta x_t + 0.834 \,\Delta z_t + 0.612(x_{t-1} + z_{t-1}) - 0.721 y_{t-1}, \quad \text{(III)}$$
$$(4.94)\ (0.831)\qquad(4.322)\qquad(3.837)\qquad\qquad(3.525)$$

$$\text{SSR} = 0.006\,43$$

$$\widehat{\Delta y_t} = 2.04 + 0.338(\Delta x_t + \Delta z_t) + 0.621(x_{t-1} + z_{t-1}) - 0.713y_{t-1}, \quad \text{(IV)}$$
$$\quad (4.98) \quad (2.237) \qquad\qquad (3.741) \qquad\qquad (3.262)$$

$$\text{SSR} = 0.007\ 31$$

$$\widehat{\Delta y_t} = 1.95 + 0.428(x_t + z_t) - 0.642y_{t-1}, \qquad\qquad \text{SSR} = 0.009\ 54 \quad \text{(V)}$$
$$\quad (5.23) \quad (2.332) \qquad (2.824)$$

By carrying out suitable F and t tests, decide which of the above equations you prefer as an adequate parsimonious description of the data. Express your preferred equations in error correction form, and comment on the short- and long-run behaviour implied. If X and Z both grow at a long-run proportionate rate of g per period, what is the long-run relationship between Y, X and Z?

Exercise 13.2

The long-run equilibrium relationship between X and Y is given in logarithmic form by (13.16). The disequilibrium relationship observed is (13.29), which can be expressed in the error correction form (13.32). Express the ECM in a form suitable for estimation.

The following equations were estimated by OLS from 56 observations (figures in parentheses are t ratios):

$$\widehat{\Delta y_t} = 0.513 + 0.344\ \Delta x_t - 0.202\ \Delta x_{t-1} + 0.194\ \Delta y_{t-1} + 0.394x_{t-1} - 0.418y_{t-1},$$
$$\quad (2.371)\ (5.731) \qquad (0.762) \qquad\quad (0.701) \qquad\quad (2.484) \qquad (2.382)$$

$$\text{SSR} = 0.008\ 58 \quad \text{(I)}$$

$$\widehat{\Delta y_t} = 0.651 + 0.331\ \Delta x_t + 0.418x_{t-1} - 0.431y_{t-1}, \qquad \text{SSR} = 0.009\ 42 \quad \text{(II)}$$
$$\quad (3.164)\ (6.073) \qquad (2.573) \qquad (2.466)$$

$$\widehat{\Delta y_t} = 1.054 + 0.223x_t - 0.384y_{t-1}, \qquad\qquad\qquad \text{SSR} = 0.011\ 34 \quad \text{(III)}$$
$$\quad (3.722)\ (3.065) \quad (2.721)$$

$$\widehat{\Delta y_t} = 0.524 + 0.341\ \Delta x_t - 0.233\ \Delta x_{t-1} + 0.165\ \Delta y_{t-1} - 0.425(y_{t-1} - x_{t-1}),$$
$$\quad (2.578)\ (5.674) \qquad (0.783) \qquad\quad (0.713) \qquad\quad (3.769)$$

$$\text{SSR} = 0.008\ 73 \quad \text{(IV)}$$

$$\widehat{\Delta y_t} = 0.606 + 0.345\ \Delta x_t - 0.431(y_{t-1} - x_{t-1}), \qquad \text{SSR} = 0.009\ 55 \quad \text{(V)}$$
$$\quad (2.788)\ (6.024) \qquad (3.812)$$

(a) Use Equation (I) above to obtain estimates of the parameters: (i) in the long-run relationship (13.16); (ii) in the disequilibrium relationship (13.29).

(b) What restrictions are being placed on short-run and/or long-run parameters when Equations (II)–(V) are estimated?

(c) Carrying out whatever tests you consider appropriate, decide on a final preferred equation. Comment on the short- and long-run behaviour implied by this equation. If X grows at a long-run rate of $100g\%$ per period, what is the long-run relationship between X and Y?

13.5 Outstanding problems

It should be clear from the material in this and the last chapter that the Hendry general-to-specific methodology, combined with the use of error correction models, represents a considerable advance over more traditional econometric approaches. However, there remain a number of outstanding problems that need to be addressed. First, for example, the use of ECMs implies the existence of some underlying long-run equilibrium relationship between the variables being investigated. How can we be sure, when dealing with time series data, that such a relationship really exists? Might not any observed correlations, even apparently strong ones, be entirely spurious?

Secondly, if we adopt the Hendry general-to-specific approach, can we be confident that this will inevitably lead us to an error correction model as our final preferred equation? It would much simplify the testing-down procedures if we could be certain of this.

Finally, even if we eventually test down to an ECM, can we be certain that all the variables in our preferred model are stationary? Remember that classical regression techniques are inapplicable when applied to non-stationary variables. It turns out that the answers to all these questions are interlinked, and it is to dealing with such problems that we turn in the next chapter.

13.6 Computer exercises

COMPUTER EXERCISE II

We have estimated demand equations using the annual US series in Data Set 1 on the floppy disk on several previous occasions, notably in Section 12.5. So far, however, we have only used variables in 'level' form. But we have seen that the levels of the variables Q, X, P and G exhibit definite upward trends, and are almost certainly non-stationary. This casts considerable suspicion on most of the results we have obtained previously.

In this exercise we shall again apply the general-to-specific approach to Data Set 1, but, unlike in Section 12.5, this time making use of the error correction type models just described. We begin by estimating a reparameterized version of the general model (12.44), which is merely an extension to three explanatory variables of the ECM (13.36). The implied long-run equilibrium relationship is therefore, again using lower-case letters to denote logarithms,

$$q_t = \beta_0^* + \beta_1 x_t + \beta_2 p_t + \beta_3 g_t \tag{13.38}$$

Estimating the ECM with no restrictions on its coefficients, for the same period 1965 through 1989 as for Equation (12.44), should yield

$$\widehat{\Delta q_t} = 1.80 + 0.571\,\Delta x_t - 0.350\,\Delta p_t - 0.459\,\Delta g_t$$
$$\phantom{\widehat{\Delta q_t} = }(1.87)\quad(3.09)\qquad(-2.15)\qquad(-1.36)$$

$$-0.423 q_{t-1} + 0.235 x_{t-1} + 0.136 p_{t-1} - 0.420 g_{t-1} \tag{13.39}$$
$$(-3.01)\qquad(2.43)\qquad(0.90)\qquad(-2.44)$$

$$R^2 = 0.855, \qquad \sum e^2 = 0.001\,66, \qquad dw = 1.95$$
$$z_{11} = 0.02, \qquad z_2 = 1.23, \qquad z_3 = 2.04, \qquad z_4 = 1.49, \qquad z_5 = 1.14$$

The z statistics in (13.39) are as defined in Section 12.5, where their critical values are also given. Notice first that the residual sum of squares and many of the values of the diagnostic statistics in (13.39) are identical to those obtained for the general model (12.44) of the last chapter.[5] This is because, just as Equation (13.36) above is simply a reparameterization of Equation (13.35), so Equation (13.39) is no more than a reparameterization of the general model (12.44). They are effectively the same equation. As a simple arithmetic exercise, the reader is invited to obtain (13.39) by rearranging (12.44).

Although (13.39) and (12.44) are really the same equation, notice that the R^2 for (13.39) of 0.855 is considerably less than the 0.986 obtained for (12.44). This is because, as we noted in Chapter 12, it is far easier to explain variations in a trending variable such as q_t than it is to explain variations in a variable such as Δq_t, from which the trend has, apparently, been eliminated. However, the R^2 in (13.39) probably means rather more than that for (12.44), since, now that we are working largely in first differences, problems of spurious correlation will, we hope, be absent.

We have already tested the general model (12.44) for possible mis-specification, so that, since (13.39) is no more than a rearrangement of (12.44) with similar diagnostic statistics, we can take it as our general model for this exercise.

Of the individual variables in (13.39), $\Delta x_t, \Delta p_t, q_{t-1}, x_{t-1}$ and g_{t-1} have coefficients that are significantly different from zero (with $n - k = 17$ d.f, the critical t value is $t_{0.05} = 1.74$). Δg_t, the change in the general price index, and p_{t-1}, the lagged food price, have insignificant coefficients, although the t ratio on Δg_t is -1.36.

It is the insignificance of the coefficient on p_{t-1} that has the more serious implication, since this suggests that in the long run the relative price of food has no influence on the demand for it. However, food is obviously a very basic necessity, so that, over the relative price ranges in our sample, the demand for it may well be eventually unaffected by its price. Dropping p_{t-1} from the equation, as the first stage of a simplification search, yields

$$\widehat{\Delta q_t} = 2.33 + 0.624\ \Delta x_t - 0.464\ \Delta p_t - 0.194\ \Delta g_t$$
$$(3.05)\quad(3.58)\qquad(-4.57)\qquad(-1.17)$$

$$-0.494 q_{t-1} + 0.257 x_{t-1} - 0.311 g_{t-1} \qquad\qquad (13.40)$$
$$(-4.26)\qquad(2.77)\qquad(-2.57)$$

$$R^2 = 0.848, \qquad \sum e^2 = 0.001\ 736, \qquad dw = 1.91$$
$$z_{11} = 0.06, \qquad z_2 = 1.08, \qquad z_3 = 2.53, \qquad z_4 = 1.48, \qquad z_5 = 1.07$$

There is no deterioration in the diagnostic statistics in (13.40) compared with (13.39). We do not need to F-test the simple restriction imposed to omit p_{t-1}, since this variable had an insignificant coefficient in (13.39).

Notice that the rate of change in general prices, Δg_t, still has an insignificant coefficient in (13.40). However, the three short-term elasticities in (13.40), that is, the coefficients on the rate-of-change variables, sum to 0.034, which is close to zero. This suggests that, as the next step in our simplification search, instead of omitting Δg_t, we impose the restriction that these elasticities sum to zero. This would imply that the demand for food is homogeneous of degree zero in total expenditure and prices in the short run. Imposing this restriction involves replacing the three rate-of-change variables by the rate of change in real expenditure, $\Delta x_t - \Delta g_t$, and the rate of change in relative prices,[6] $\Delta p_t - \Delta g_t$. You should find that this results in

$$\widehat{\Delta q_t} = 2.38 + 0.657(\Delta x_t - \Delta g_t) - 0.463(\Delta p_t - \Delta g_t)$$
$$(3.29)\quad(5.46)\qquad\qquad(-4.68)$$

$$-0.496 q_{t-1} + 0.255 x_{t-1} - 0.307 g_{t-1} \qquad\qquad (13.41)$$
$$(-4.39)\qquad(2.83)\qquad(-2.62)$$

$$R^2 = 0.847, \qquad \sum e^2 = 0.001\ 743, \qquad dw = 1.93$$
$$z_{11} = 0.03, \qquad z_2 = 1.01, \qquad z_3 = 3.30, \qquad z_4 = 1.42, \qquad z_5 = 1.14$$

Again there are no problems with the diagnostic statistics. The imposition of the restriction has left the residual sum of squares virtually unchanged. We can F-test the restriction imposed, using the test statistic (9.19), treating (13.40) as the unrestricted equation and (13.41) as the restricted equation. This yields a value of just 0.07, compared with a critical value, using [1,18] d.f. of $F_{0.05} = 4.41$. Imposing short-run homogeneity on the demand for food is clearly data-acceptable.

Examination of Equation (13.41) suggests that one further restriction, and hence one further simplification, might be made. The coefficients of x_{t-1} and g_{t-1} are of opposite sign and of roughly similar absolute value. This suggests that they be replaced by a single variable, the lagged change in real expenditure, $x_{t-1} - g_{t-1}$. Such a restriction implies that the demand for food is homogeneous not merely in the short run but also in the long run. Imposing the restriction results in

$$\widehat{\Delta q_t} = 2.99 + 0.581(\Delta x_t - \Delta g_t) - 0.374(\Delta p_t - \Delta g_t)$$
$$\quad\;\;(4.42)\quad (4.87)\qquad\qquad\quad (-4.10)$$

$$\quad\;\; -0.364 q_{t-1} + 0.101(x_{t-1} - g_{t-1}) \qquad\qquad\qquad (13.42)$$
$$\quad\;\;\;\;(-3.96)\qquad (3.00)$$

$$R^2 = 0.820, \qquad \sum e^2 = 0.002\,05, \qquad dw = 1.81$$
$$z_{11} = 0.22, \qquad z_2 = 0.50, \qquad z_3 = 1.51, \qquad z_4 = 1.25, \qquad z_5 = 1.31$$

There is again no obvious deterioration in the diagnostic statistics for (13.42) compared with (13.41). If we F-test the single restriction imposed on (13.41) to obtain (13.42), the value of the test statistic (9.19) is 3.36. This compares with a critical value, using $[1,19]$ d.f., of $F_{0.05} = 4.38$, so the restriction is not rejected by the data. This restriction, however, comes a little closer to being rejected than the previous restrictions imposed.

We have now reached the end of our simplification search, since there are no obvious further restrictions that can be imposed on equation (13.42). We have therefore tested down from the general error correction model (13.39), which contained eight variables including the intercept, to the more parsimonious error correction model (13.42) which contains just five variables. We must now test (13.42) against the general model. Three restrictions have been imposed in all to obtain (13.42) (note that each linear restriction imposed reduces the number of variables by one). Testing the combined effect of imposing these restrictions gives a value for the F-test statistic of 1.33 compared with a critical value, with $[3,17]$ d.f., of $F_{0.05} = 3.20$. Hence Equation (13.42) cannot be rejected against the general model.

Although the z_5 statistic for Equation (13.42) indicates that the model passes the second Chow test for predictive failure, we can investigate parameter stability more thoroughly by employing the recursive least squares technique described in Section 9.5. In Figure 13.6 we illustrate the time paths of the recursive least squares estimated coefficients on the explanatory variables in (13.42). Notice that after initial instability (resulting from small subsample sizes), all the estimates become stable over time. This is particularly the case for the coefficients on the lagged level variables q_{t-1} and $x_{t-1} - g_{t-1}$, which relate to the underlying long-run relationship. We appear to have uncovered a relatively stable relationship.

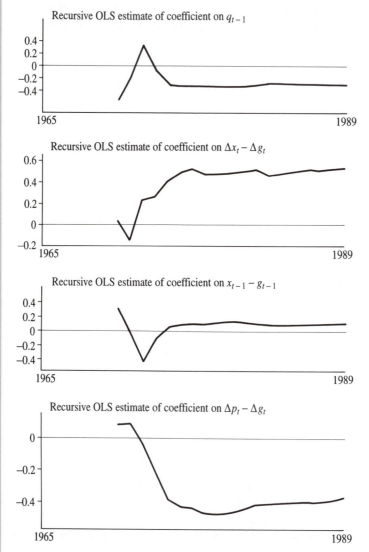

Figure 13.6 Recursive least squares estimates.

Before interpreting (13.42) from an economic viewpoint, we can rewrite it in the error correction form

$$\widehat{\Delta q_t} = 0.581(\Delta x_t - \Delta g_t) - 0.374(\Delta p_t - \Delta g_t)$$
$$- 0.364[q_{t-1} - 8.21 - 0.277(x_{t-1} - g_{t-1})] \qquad (13.43)$$

The term in square brackets in (13.43) is clearly the disequilibrium error, reflecting the extent of departure from the long-run relationship. We can see that 36.4% of any disequilibrium present in period $t-1$ is corrected for in the current period. The long-run demand-for-food relationship implied is

$$q_t = \beta_0^* + 0.277(x_t - g_t) \tag{13.44}$$

where we shall derive β_0^* shortly. As noted earlier, this data set suggests that in the long run the demand for food is independent of its price and depends only on the level of real income. The long-run real income elasticity is 0.277, well below unity, as is to be expected for a basic necessity.

The demand for food is also homogeneous of degree zero in the short run. However, in the short run, demand depends not only on real total expenditure but also on relative prices, with elasticities of 0.581 and 0.374 respectively. Notice that the short-run real expenditure elasticity is actually greater than the long-run elasticity. It appears that the initial response of demand to change in prices and total expenditure is greater than that in the long run when basic forces of habit and necessity take over and demand to some extent reverts to earlier patterns.

To obtain β_0^* in (13.44), suppose that, in the long run, real income grows at a rate θ, but relative prices remain unchanged. That is,

$$\Delta x_t - \Delta g_t = (x_t - g_t) - (x_{t-1} - g_{t-1}) = \theta$$

and

$$\Delta p_t - \Delta g_t = 0$$

Since the long-run total expenditure elasticity of demand is 0.277, the demand for food therefore grows at a rate

$$\widehat{\Delta q_t} = q_t - q_{t-1} = 0.277\theta$$

Substituting these values into (13.43) gives

$$0.277\theta = 0.581\theta - 0.364[q_t - 8.21 - 0.277(x_t - g_t)]$$

Thus

$$q_t = 8.21 - 0.835\theta + 0.277(x_t - g_t)$$

The long-run demand equation for food is therefore

$$Q = K(X/G)^{0.277}$$

where $K = e^{8.21 - 0.835\theta}$ depends on the long-run growth rate in real total expenditure, X/G. For example, with a long-run growth rate of 4% per annum, $\theta = 0.04$ and $K = e^{8.177} = 3557$. The long-run relationship is then

$$Q = 3557(X/G)^{0.277}$$

and β_0^* in (13.44) is 8.18. If, however, $\theta = 0$ then $K = e^{8.21} = 3678$, and the long-run relationship is

$$Q = 3678(X/G)^{0.277}$$

and $\beta_0^* = 8.21$, as indicated by the disequilibrium error in (13.43). Thus, as usual in error correction models, the implied equilibrium relationship depends on long-run growth rates.

This exercise illustrates the usefulness of combining the concept of an error correction model with the general-to-specific approach. We have tested down to a final model (13.42) that was not only statistically satisfactory (i.e., in the terminology of Section 12.4, it was data-coherent), but also has sensible economic properties.

This data set also demonstrates the superiority of the general-to-specific methodology over the simple-to-general approach described earlier. We adopted a simple-to-general approach to analysing this data set in Chapters 7, 9 and 11. It led to a number of promising-looking equations, which we now see have to be rejected against the general model used in this and the last chapter. There is, in fact, almost certainly no way in which the simple-to-general approach could have uncovered the model (13.42) that we have finally selected.

Data Sets 2 and 3 on the floppy disk also involve data for the demand for food, but this time for Japan and the United Kingdom. The reader should try applying the general-to-specific/error correction model approach to these data sets.

COMPUTER EXERCISE III

In this exercise we return to Data Set 4 on UK consumption, last examined in Section 12.5, where we considered special cases of the general model (12.47). Here we will attempt to combine the general-to-specific approach of Section 12.5 with the notion of an error correction model.

In fact, we can immediately reparameterize the general model (12.47) into an ECM. Since, apart from the seasonal dummies, (12.47) is exactly analogous to (13.29), it can be reparameterized as an ECM of the type (13.32)/(13.33). Estimating over the period 1975Q1 through 1984Q4, you should obtain (lower-case letters denoting logarithms)

$$\widehat{\Delta c_t} = 0.015 + 0.045D_2 + 0.086D_3 + 0.106D_4 - 0417\,\Delta c_{t-1}$$
$$\quad (0.03) \quad (2.57) \quad\quad (7.57) \quad\quad (10.96) \quad (-2.52)$$

$$\quad + 0.272\,\Delta y_t + 0.447\,\Delta y_{t-1} - 0.085c_{t-1} + 0.078y_{t-1} \quad\quad\quad (13.45)$$
$$\quad\quad (2.02) \quad\quad\quad (3.32) \quad\quad (-0.51) \quad\quad (0.51)$$

$$R^2 = 0.937, \quad \sum e^2 = 0.006\,605, \quad dw = 1.86$$
$$z_{14} = 2.88, \quad z_2 = 0.54, \quad z_3 = 8.28, \quad z_4 = 0.10, \quad z_5 = 0.56$$

Comparison of (13.45) with (12.47) reveals that they are indeed simply rearrangement of the same equation. Apart from R^2, the diagnostic statistics are identical, and R^2 differs merely because of the change in dependent variable.

The big problem with (13.45) is that, as can be seen from their t ratios, the coefficients of the level variables c_{t-1} and y_{t-1} are not significantly different from zero. As we noted earlier, dropping level variables from an ECM has serious implications for long-run behaviour. Indeed, dropping these variables from the equation leads us straight back to Equation (12.49), which was a model in differenced variables only. As we saw towards the end of Section 13.2, such models imply that no static equilibrium between variables can exist. Few economists would regard (12.49) as a plausible model.

One other possibility that could be considered is a simple first-order ECM of the type (13.22)/(13.28). This is also nested within the general model (12.47)/(13.45). Estimation of such a model over the same sample period will yield

$$\widehat{\Delta c_t} = 0.241 + 0.061D_2 + 0.076D_3 + 0.098D_4$$
$$\quad\quad (0.48) \quad (4.35) \quad\quad (5.96) \quad\quad (9.05)$$

$$\quad +0.352\,\Delta y_t - 0.428c_{t-1} + 0.396y_{t-1} \quad\quad\quad\quad (13.46)$$
$$\quad\quad (2.40) \quad\quad (-2.80) \quad\quad (2.83)$$

$$R^2 = 0.910, \quad \sum e^2 = 0.009\,40, \quad dw = 2.01$$
$$z_{14} = 7.18, \quad z_2 = 0.06, \quad z_3 = 0.24, \quad z_4 = 0.002, \quad z_5 = 1.13$$

All the diagnostic statistics are quite satisfactory in (13.46). Although z_{14}, the LM statistic for up to fourth-order autocorrelation, has risen compared with (13.45), it is still below its critical value (4 d.f.) of $\chi^2_{0.05} = 9.488$. Morever, the coefficients of the level variables c_{t-1} and y_{t-1} now have significant t ratios, so we can be certain that a static equilibrium is feasible with this model. Unfortunately, the dropping of the lagged difference terms has led to a sharp rise in the residual sum of squares. Not surprisingly, since Δc_{t-1} and Δy_{t-1} had significant t ratios in (13.45), you will find that if you F-test their omission, (13.46) has to be rejected against (13.45).

We seem to have reached something of an impasse with Data Set 4. A general-to-specific approach has led to a model (Equation (12.49)) that has implausible economic properties. While the model (13.46) makes sense economically (that is, it is consistent with a long-run static equilibrium), statistically it has to be rejected against our general model. We shall pay yet more visits to this data set.

Appendix 13A

Notes to Chapter 13

1. When the variables in a stochastic process refer to successive time intervals, the intervals should, strictly speaking, be regarded as stretching back into the indefinite past as well as into the future.
2. This can easily be verified by selecting a starting value for X, X_0, setting the disturbance u_t to zero, and examining the time path of X_t for alternative values

of ϕ. If ϕ lies between 1 and -1 then the time path for X converges to zero; otherwise, it diverges.

3. For example, if $Y_{t-1} = 153$ and $Y_t = 165$ then the proportionate rate of change is $(Y_t - Y_{t-1})/Y_{t-1} = 0.078$ (or 7.8%). For these values, $\ln(Y_t/Y_{t-1}) = 0.076$. The approximation is even better for smaller rates of change.

4. The equilibrium relationship referred to here could be of the type described in Section 11.1. That is, we refer to a situation where X remains constant sufficiently long for Y to have converged to a constant equilibrium value. Such an equilibrium is known as a **static** or **steady-state equilibrium**. However, as we shall see shortly, (13.16) could also refer to a long-run growth equilibrium in which X grows at a constant rate sufficiently long for Y to converge to a similar constant growth path.

5. The statistics z_2 and z_4 differ because they involve predicted values for the dependent variables. Equations (12.44) and (13.39) have different dependent variables.

6. Note that

$$\Delta x_t - \Delta g_t = x_t - x_{t-1} - (g_t - g_{t-1}) = x_t - g_t - (x_{t-1} - g_{t-1})$$
$$= \ln(X_t/G_t) - \ln(X_{t-1}/G_{t-1}) = \Delta \ln(X_t/G_t)$$

where X_t/G_t is real total expenditure. Similarly,

$$\Delta p_t - \Delta g_t = \Delta \ln(P_t/G_t)$$

Further reading

Stochastic processes are well covered in Pindyck and Rubinfeld (1991), Chapters 14–16. Cuthbertson et al. (1992), Chapter 4, discuss dynamic modelling and the combination of error correction models with the general-to-specific approach. See also Gilbert (1986) for this. For a more advanced treatment of error correction models, see Banerjee et al. (1993), Chapter 2. The famous paper by Davidson et al. (1978), one of the first uses of ECMs in the literature and the first to employ the general-to-specific approach, is still well worth examining.

14 Testing for stationarity

In Section 13.5 we listed three outstanding questions that need to be answered if the general-to-specific approach of Chapter 12 is to be combined successfully with the error correction models of Chapter 13. Could we be sure that the long-run relationships underpinning ECMs actually exist? Could we be confident that preferred models would always be of ECM form? How could we tell if all the variables in an ECM were stationary? It is now time to tackle these problems. In this chapter we begin with the third question of how we should test for stationarity.

14.1 Informal procedures

We defined stationarity at the beginning of Chapter 13. We stressed that classical regression techniques may well become invalid if applied to variables that do not meet this definition of stationarity. It is therefore of considerable importance to be able to determine whether an economic time series is stationary or not. Faced with such time series, the obvious first action is to view their time paths through time as we did in Section 13.2 for the variables in Data Sets 1 and 4. A stationary time series, such as that illustrated in Figure 14.2(a), tends to return frequently to its mean and to fluctuate around it in a seemingly random manner. However, a non-stationary series, such as that in Figure 14.1(a), usually appears to have different mean values at different periods of time.

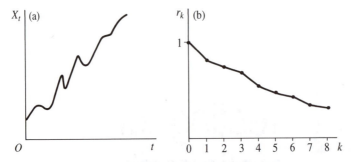

Figure 14.1 (a) Trending time series. (b) Correlogram for a trending time series.

Unfortunately, the examination of time paths can often be inconclusive and even misleading, so more objective procedures and tests are necessary. One well-known procedure is to examine the **sample autocorrelations**, which for a time series X_t are defined as

$$r_k = \frac{\sum (X_t - \bar{X}_t)(X_{t-k} - \bar{X}_{t-k})}{\sqrt{\sum (X_t - \bar{X}_t)^2 \sum (X_{t-k} - \bar{X}_{t-k})^2}}, \quad k = 1, 2, 3, 4, \ldots \tag{14.1}$$

Thus r_4, for example, is the correlation between X_t and X_{t-4}, its value four time periods previously.

As k increases, sample autocorrelations decline towards zero. However, the 'rate of decay' is likely to be much more rapid for a stationary series than for a non-stationary series. Figures 14.1 and 14.2 should help to make this clear.

In Figure 14.1(a) the time series X_t shows random fluctuations about a strong upward trend. The time series is clearly non-stationary. Because of the strong trend, the higher X_t is, the higher tends to be X_{t-1}, its value in the previous period. Thus r_1, the correlation between X_t and X_{t-1}, will be close to unity. The correlation between X_t and X_{t-2} is also likely to be high, although not as high as r_1, because the link between X_t and X_{t-2} is slightly more obscured by the random variations in the series. As k increases, r_k will decay gradually to zero as successive autocorrelations become more and more obscured by the random factors.

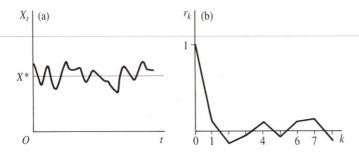

Figure 14.2 (a) Stationary time series. (b) Correlogram for a stationary time series.

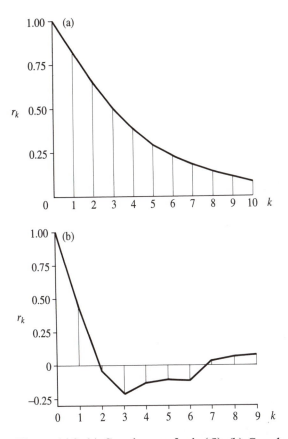

Figure 14.3 (a) Correlogram for ln (Q). (b) Correlogram for Δ ln (Q).

A plot of r_k against k is known as a **correlogram**. A typical correlogram for a strongly trending variable such as that in Figure 14.1(a) is shown in Figure 14.1(b). r_k declines gradually as k increases. $r_0 = 1$, since this is simply the correlation of X_t with itself.

In Figure 14.2(a) the time series X_t exhibits random fluctuations about a constant value X^*. It is, in fact, stationary. There is now no reason why X_t should be correlated with any of its previous values. Thus all r_k for $k > 0$ are likely to be close to zero: some negative, others positive. A typical correlogram for a stationary variable is shown in Figure 14.2(b). In contrast to Figure 14.1(b), r_k falls rapidly to around zero as k increases.

The correlograms for stationary and non-stationary variables are therefore likely to be very different, and this is obviously of help in deciding whether time series are stationary. For example, readers should use their regression packages to look at the correlograms for the logarithms of the time series for the variables Q, X, P and G in Data Set 1. We examined the time paths for these series in the last chapter, and all

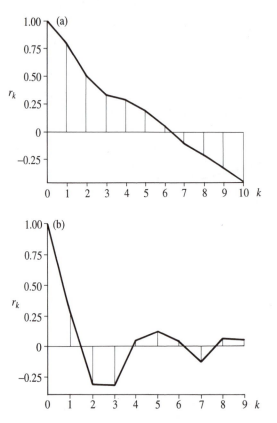

Figure 14.4 (a) Correlogram for ln (RP). (b) Correlogram for Δ ln (RP).

trend strongly upward. The correlograms for all these series also suggest non-stationarity. The correlogram for ln (Q) is shown in Figure 14.3(a).

Look also at the correlograms for the first differences of the logarithms of these variables. Since, as we noted in the last chapter, the first difference of the logarithms is a good approximation for the proportionate rate of change, there is a good chance that it will prove stationary for many economic time series. You should find that, as illustrated in Figure 14.3(b), the log-difference of Q does indeed appear stationary, but this is not the case for the log-differences of X, P and G. However, construct the variables RE = X/G (real total expenditure) and RP = P/G (the relative price of food), and examine the correlograms for the logarithms and log-differences of these time series. These log-differences appear to be stationary. For example, the correlograms of ln (RP) and Δ ln (RP) are shown in Figures 14.4(a,b).

Unfortunately, correlogram patterns are not always so clear cut as some of those just examined, and often leave the question of stationarity unresolved. Econometricians have therefore spent much time in recent years devising formal statistical tests for stationarity, and it is to these we now turn.

14.2   Statistical tests for stationarity

Suppose it is possible to model an economic time series by the first-order autoregressive (AR) process (13.8), to which we add an intercept α:

$$X_t = \alpha + \phi X_{t-1} + u_t \tag{14.2}$$

For economic time series, we can assume that the parameter ϕ will be positive.[1] It therefore follows from our discussion in the last chapter that X_t will be non-stationary if the parameter ϕ equals or exceeds unity. The time series (14.2) will only be stationary if $\phi < 1$. The obvious way of proceeding is therefore to apply OLS to (14.2) and look at $\hat{\phi}$, the estimate of ϕ obtained.[2] We can then t-test the null hypothesis H_0: $\phi = 1$ against the alternative hypothesis H_A: $\phi < 1$ in the usual way. If $s_{\hat{\phi}}$ is the estimated standard error of $\hat{\phi}$ then the required test statistic is

$$TS = \frac{\hat{\phi} - 1}{s_{\hat{\phi}}} \tag{14.3}$$

Rejection of H_0 implies that we have a stationary series.[3]

There are, unfortunately, a number of problems with such a procedure. First, we know from Section 8.1 that the presence of the lagged dependent variable in (14.2) means that the OLS estimator $\hat{\phi}$ will be biased in small samples. In fact, it can be demonstrated that $\hat{\phi}$ is biased downwards. Therefore the obvious test statistic (14.3) cannot be trusted, and if we use it, we may well conclude that $\phi < 1$ and X_t is stationary when it is not.

Secondly, if H_0: $\phi = 1$ is true and the process non-stationary then standard *large*-sample distribution results are invalid. We cannot rely on the test statistic (14.3) being normally distributed, even in large samples.[4] The distribution of the test statistic is non-standard and in fact not even symmetrical.

These problems were first faced up to by D. A. Dickey and W. F. Fuller (see e.g. Dickey and Fuller, 1979). First, let us take X_{t-1} away from each side of (14.2) and rewrite it as

$$\Delta X_t = \alpha + \phi^* X_{t-1} + u_t, \qquad \phi^* = \phi - 1 \tag{14.4}$$

Note that testing H_0: $\phi = 1$ against H_A: $\phi < 1$ in Equation (14.2) is exactly the same as testing H_0: $\phi^* = 0$ against H_A: $\phi^* < 0$ in (14.4). The reason for the switch from (14.2) to (14.4) will become clear shortly. The test required is known as a **unit-root test**, since in its original form H_0 is $\phi = 1$.

In terms of (14.4), we reject *non*-stationarity ($\phi^* = 0$) if the OLS estimate of ϕ^*, that is, $\hat{\phi}^*$, is *sufficiently negative*. The obvious test statistic to use is the standard t ratio $\hat{\phi}^*/s_{\hat{\phi}*}$ where $s_{\hat{\phi}*}$ is the estimated standard error of ϕ^*. The problem is that the downward bias in $\hat{\phi}$ noted above is reflected in $\hat{\phi}^*$, and, moreover, under the null hypothesis of non-stationarity, the t ratio has a non-standard distribution, even in large samples. This means that normal t tables cannot be used to obtain critical values for the t ratio. However, econometricians, led by Dickey and Fuller, have performed extensive simulation studies to tabulate the large-sample distribu-

Table 14.1 Critical values for t_1^*

Critical values of t_1^*	Sample size n					Usual t value $(n=\infty)$
	25	50	100	500	∞	
0.01 level of sig.	− 3.75	− 3.58	− 3.51	− 3.44	− 3.43	− 2.33
0.05 level of sig.	− 3.00	− 2.93	− 2.89	− 2.87	− 2.86	− 1.65
0.10 level of sig.	− 2.63	− 2.60	− 2.58	− 2.57	− 2.57	− 1.28

Source: Fuller (1976), p. 373.

tion of the t ratio under the null hypothesis that $\phi^* = 0$. Because of the downward bias, the t ratio is distributed not about zero, as it would be if the OLS estimator $\hat{\phi}^*$ were unbiased, but about a value that is less than zero.

In this situation we shall give the t ratio the symbol t_1^*. t_1^* is referred to as the **Dickey–Fuller** (DF) **statistic**. Some of the Dickey–Fuller critical values for t_1^* are given in Table 14.1, together with values taken from standard t tables. Notice that, in order to reject the null hypothesis of non-stationarity, the t_1^* statistic has to be *more* negative than would be suggested by the usual t tables.[5]

As an illustration of the above test (known as the **Dickey–Fuller** (DF) **test for a unit root**), we consider the time series for the relative price of food constructed from the US data in Data Set 1. That is, we consider $RP = P/G$, where P and G are indices of the price of food and the general price level. Recall that in the last section the correlogram for ln (RP) indicated non-stationarity, but that for Δ ln (RP) suggested a stationary series. OLS estimation of the equivalent of Equation (14.4) using the natural logarithm of RP over the sample period 1966 through 1989 yields

$$\Delta \widehat{\ln (RP)}_t = - 0.0066 - 0.190 \ln (RP)_{t-1} \qquad (14.5)$$
$$\phantom{\Delta \widehat{\ln (RP)}_t =} (-1.05) \quad (-1.49)$$

$$R^2 = 0.09, \qquad z_{11} = 4.30, \qquad z_{12} = 5.41$$

z_{11} and z_{12} are the LM statistics for first- and up to second-order autocorrelation, to which we shall refer presently.

The coefficient of ln (RP)$_{t-1}$ in (14.5) is $\hat{\phi}^* = -0.190$. This estimate of ϕ^* is certainly negative, but its t ratio, the t_1^* statistic, is only -1.49. Examination of the critical values in Table 14.1 indicates that this is not negative enough to reject the hypothesis of non-stationarity.

In the above test we have assumed that the time series ln (RP)$_t$ can be modelled as a first-order AR process of the type (14.2) with a disturbance that is white noise. But what if this is not a sensible assumption? Suppose the disturbance is not white noise or suppose the time series is, in fact, the result of a higher-order process? Either of these possibilities is likely to show up as an autocorrelation problem in the residuals of the OLS estimated version of (14.4). Unfortunately, the above Dickey–Fuller test is invalid in these circumstances.

Two approaches have been suggested for tackling this problem. First, we can modify the actual testing procedure by generalizing Equation (14.2). Secondly, it is possible to retain Equation (14.2) but adjust the DF statistic to allow for auto-correlated residuals. The first approach leads to the augmented Dickey–Fuller test, which we now consider.

In practice, we will not know what order of process is most suitable for modelling our time series. To get round this difficulty, let us generalize (14.2) into the rth-order process

$$X_t = \alpha + \phi_1 X_{t-1} + \phi_2 X_{t-2} + \cdots + \phi_r X_{t-r} + u_t \tag{14.6}$$

Just as it is possible to reparameterize (14.2) to (14.4), it is also possible to reparameterize (14.6) to obtain

$$\Delta X_t = \alpha + \phi^* X_{t-1} + \phi_1^* \, \Delta X_{t-1} + \phi_2^* \, \Delta X_{t-2} + \cdots + \phi_{r-1}^* \, \Delta X_{t-r+1} + u_t \tag{14.7}$$

where $\phi^* = \phi_1 + \phi_2 + \cdots + \phi_r - 1$ and the other ϕ_j^*s are also functions of the original ϕs in (14.6). The reparameterization is performed for the case $r=3$ in Appendix 14A at the end of this chapter. Notice that if (14.6) is a second-order process then one differenced term ΔX_{t-1} appears on the right-hand side of (14.7). If (14.6) is a third-order process then two differenced terms ΔX_{t-1} and ΔX_{t-2} appear, etc. Of course, if we have a first-order process then no differenced terms are included, and (14.7) reduces to (14.4).

The great advantage of the formulation (14.7) is that, as shown in Appendix 14A, testing the rth-order process (14.6) for stationarity is equivalent to testing whether or not $\phi^*=0$ in (14.7). That is, *just as for (14.2) and (14.4), the null hypothesis of non-stationarity becomes* H$_0$: $\phi^* = 0$, which we can test against an alternative hypothesis H$_A$: $\phi^* < 0$. Thus, if we can reject H$_0$ in favour of H$_A$ then this again implies a stationary process.

The obvious way of testing H$_0$: $\phi^*=0$ in this situation is to apply OLS to (14.7) and examine the t ratio on the estimate $\hat{\phi}^*$. If this is sufficiently negative, we reject H$_0$ in favour of stationarity. Again, however, the downward bias of OLS and the non-standard large-sample distribution for the t ratio means that we cannot use the usual t tables. Fortunately, it is again possible to use the critical values summarized in Table 14.1 for the first-order case. The t ratio in this case will therefore again be given the symbol t_1^*.

This test for stationarity in the general case is normally referred to as an **augmented Dickey–Fuller** (ADF) **test**, because the regressor in the original equation (14.4) has been 'augmented' by extra 'differenced terms' in Equation (14.7). The testing equation (14.7) is known as an **augmented Dickey–Fuller equation**, and the t_1^* statistic is now referred to as an **augmented Dickey–Fuller** (ADF) **statistic**. It is sometimes written as ADF(k), where k is the number of differenced terms included on the right-hand side of (14.7).

A problem with the ADF test is that, as already noted, we do not know beforehand what order of AR process bests fits the time series we are studying. That is, we do not know how many differenced terms to include on the right-hand side of (14.7). In practice, the usual approach followed is to include as many differenced terms in (14.7) as are necessary to produce non-autocorrelated OLS residuals. The LM tests for autocorrelation are usually used for this purpose. That is, a poor value for an LM statistic is regarded as indicating a need for extra differenced terms to be included. More differenced terms may be needed either because the order of the original equation was mis-specified or to allow for a disturbance term that is not white noise, but is genuinely autocorrelated.

Referring back to Equation (14.5), where we modelled the time series ln (RP) from Data Set 1 as a first-order process, the LM statistics in this case do suggest a possible mis-specification. $\chi^2_{0.05}$ critical values for z_{11} and z_{12} are (with 1 and 2 d.f.) 3.84 and 5.99 respectively.

Modelling ln (RP) as a second-order AR process, for example, implies the addition of just one differenced term to Equation (14.5). This yields

$$\Delta \widehat{\ln (RP)}_t = -0.0091 - 0.288 \ln (RP)_{t-1} + 0.445 \, \Delta \ln (RP)_{t-1} \tag{14.8}$$
$$(-1.54) \quad (-2.28) \qquad\qquad (2.19)$$

$$R^2 = 0.26, \quad z_{11} = 1.54, \quad z_{12} = 1.55$$

In (14.8) the LM statistics are now both well below their critical values, so there is no longer any suggestion of autocorrelated residuals. However, the coefficient of ln (RP)$_{t-1}$ in (14.8) has changed only slightly from its value in (14.5). Remember that we reject the hypothesis of non-stationarity if this coefficient is significantly *negative*. Its t ratio (which is an ADF(1) statistic) is -2.28, and again has to be compared with the critical values in Table 14.1. This confirms that we cannot reject non-stationarity.

Like many economic time series, ln (RP) seems then to be non-stationary. However, as we have repeatedly noted, the first difference of an economic series is frequently stationary. We therefore now test $\Delta \ln (RP)_t = \ln (RP)_t - \ln (RP)_{t-1}$ for stationarity. The Dickey–Fuller tests proceed as for ln (RP). First, we attempt to model $\Delta \ln (RP)$ as a first-order AR process. Estimation of the required Dickey–Fuller regression, for the sample period 1966 through 1989 gives

$$\Delta^2 \widehat{\ln (RP)}_t = -0.0003 - 0.7181 \, \Delta \ln (RP)_{t-1} \tag{14.9}$$
$$(-0.07) \quad (-3.46)$$

$$R^2 = 0.35, \quad z_{11} = 3.26, \quad z_{12} = 3.32$$

Since we are testing $\Delta \ln (RP)_t$ for stationarity, it is now the second difference $\Delta^2 \ln (RP)_t = \Delta \ln (RP)_t - \Delta \ln (RP)_{t-1}$ that appears on the left-hand side of (14.9). Also, we now reject the null hypothesis of non-stationarity if the estimated coefficient on $\Delta \ln (RP)_{t-1}$ is sufficiently negative. The value of the t_1^* statistic is again given by the t ratio on this coefficient. The value $t_1^* = -3.46$ must again be compared with the critical values in Table 14.1. We see that we are able to reject the null hypothesis of non-stationarity. Hence, since the LM statistics for (14.9) suggest no problems of autocorrelation in the residuals, we can conclude that the first difference of ln (RP) is stationary. However, to confirm this finding we can also estimate an augmented Dickey–Fuller regression

$$\Delta^2 \widehat{\ln (\text{RP})}_t = -0.0007 - 1.022 \, \Delta \ln (\text{RP})_{t-1} + 0.420 \, \Delta^2 \ln (\text{RP})_{t-1} \quad (14.10)$$
$$\quad\quad (-0.15) \quad (-4.23) \quad\quad\quad\quad (2.09)$$

$$R^2 = 0.46, \quad z_{11} = 0.40, \quad z_{12} = 0.59$$

The t_1^* statistic now takes a value -4.23, and reference to Table 14.1 reinforces our conclusion that $\Delta \ln (\text{RP})$ is stationary. Thus our Dickey–Fuller tests appear to confirm what the correlograms for ln (RP) and $\Delta \ln (\text{RP})$ suggested in the last section.

   A problem with the augmented Dickey–Fuller test is that it involves the inclusion of extra differenced terms in the testing equation. This results in a loss of degrees of freedom and a resultant reduction in the power of the testing procedure. An alternative has been suggested by Phillips and Perron (1988), who retain the first-order (14.4) as the testing equation, but devise a procedure for adjusting the DF statistic to allow for autocorrelation in the residuals from the equation. These tests are, however, outside the scope of this text.

   The Dickey–Fuller and augmented Dickey–Fuller tests are the best-known and most popular tests for stationarity. However, other statistical tests for stationarity also exist. For example, Sargan and Bhargava (1983) suggest that use be made of the Durbin–Watson statistic defined in Section 10.5. If X_t is regressed on a constant alone, that is, we compute

$$\hat{X}_t = \hat{\alpha} + e_t$$

then, if X_t is non-stationary, the residuals e_t obtained from this regression should also be non-stationary. If we model these as a first-order AR process then non-stationarity should result in a value close to zero for the Durbin–Watson statistic.[6] Tests based on this approach have not, however, proved as popular as the Dickey–Fuller tests.

Some useful terminology

A time series is said to be **integrated of order** d, written as $\text{I}(d)$, if, after being differenced d times, it becomes a stationary series. Thus, as we have noted, many economic series are integrated of order one, that is, are $\text{I}(1)$, because they become stationary on first differencing. However, if a series X_t and its first difference ΔX_t are non-stationary but the second difference $\Delta^2 X_t = \Delta X_t - \Delta X_{t-1}$ is stationary then the series is $\text{I}(2)$. For example, in economics some price series are $\text{I}(2)$. Some economic variables, such as certain interest rates, are integrated of order zero. That is, they are $\text{I}(0)$, because their time series are stationary without the need for any differencing. Some time series, however, never become stationary, however many times they are differenced. Such series are said to be non-integrated. We shall encounter one type of non-integrated series in Section 14.3.

Some words of warning

The Dickey–Fuller tests performed above may give the misleading impression that determining whether a series is stationary or not is a precise procedure. Unfortunately, this is not the case. Simulation studies have shown the tests to *lack power*. We discussed the power of tests in Chapter 3. Power measures the ability of a test to detect a false null hypothesis. In the present case this means *the power to detect stationarity*. Lack of such power implies that a time series may be stationary, yet the Dickey–Fuller tests may fail to detect this. This has been found to be particularly the case when time series, although stationary, are close to being non-stationary. That is, if ϕ^* in the above tests is negative but very close to zero then the usual tests will often fail to reject H_0: $\phi^* = 0$ in favour of H_A: $\phi^* < 0$.

In addition, it must be remembered that the critical values given in Table 14.1 have been obtained by simulation experiments, and are therefore only approximate. Also, it is sometimes unclear how many 'differenced terms' should be included on the right-hand sides of equations such as (14.7). Since the number of differenced terms included can seriously affect the value of the ADF statistics, this is a further source of uncertainty.

Dickey–Fuller tests should therefore be applied judiciously and with care, their results being interpreted cautiously. Other sources of information, such as the correlogram for the time series, should not be ignored. Even then, it may sometimes be the case that the order of integration of a time series is unclear. For example, it is often uncertain whether price series are I(1) or I(2).

14.3 Deterministic versus stochastic trends

Consider the following first-order process:

$$X_t = \alpha + \beta t + \phi X_{t-1} + u_t, \qquad \alpha \neq 0 \tag{14.11}$$

where u_t is again white noise and t is a time trend.

Two kinds of trend can appear in Equation (14.11). First, if $\phi = 1$ and $\beta = 0$ then

$$\Delta X_t = \alpha + u_t \tag{14.12}$$

so that X_t clearly trends upwards or downwards, depending on the sign of α. Such a trend is known as a **stochastic trend**. Secondly, if $\beta \neq 0$ and $\phi = 0$ then

$$X_t = \alpha + \beta t + u_t \tag{14.13}$$

X_t again trends upwards or downwards, this time according to the sign of β. Such a trend is known as a **deterministic trend**. If both $\beta \neq 0$ and $\phi = 1$ then both stochastic and deterministic trends are present.[7]

A stochastic trend can be removed by first-differencing, since ΔX_t is then trendless, as (14.12) indicates. X_t is then referred to as a **difference stationary process**. A deterministic trend cannot be removed by first-differencing, since this does not remove t from the process. If X_t is subject to such a trend then it is said to be a **trend stationary process.**[8]

The Dickey–Fuller tests of the previous section test only for the non-stationarity of a stochastic trend. If we set $\beta = 0$ then Equation (14.11) becomes the simple first-order AR process (14.2), and the DF test can be applied. The problem is that deterministic trends provide just as much of a difficulty for classical regression techniques as do stochastic trends. For example, both types of trend can cause spurious regression problems. We therefore need to be as wary of deterministic trends in our data as we are of stochastic trends. Dickey and Fuller suggest that we should allow for the possibility of deterministic trends in the following way. We can rewrite (14.11) as

$$\Delta X_t = \alpha + \beta t + \phi^* X_{t-1} + u_t \tag{14.14}$$

where again $\phi^* = \phi - 1$. If (14.14) is estimated by OLS then we can use the F test of Section 9.2 to test the joint hypothesis $\beta = \phi^* = 0$. Failure to reject this hypothesis would imply that X_t is subject to a stochastic trend only, since $\beta = 0$ means the absence of a deterministic trend and $\phi^* = 0$ (that is, $\phi = 1$) implies stochastic non-stationarity.[9] Normal F tables cannot, however, be used for this test, because under the null hypothesis of a stochastic trend the F statistic has a non-standard distribution. It must therefore be compared with critical values obtained by Dickey–Fuller from simulation experiments. Some such values are shown in Table 14.2. Note that they are much larger than conventional critical F values. Alternatively, it is possible to test for a deterministic trend alone by examining the t ratio on the time trend in Equation (14.14). Unfortunately, just as $\hat{\phi}^*$ is biased

Table 14.2 Critical values for Dickey–Fuller F statistic

Sample size	Level of significance		
	0.01	0.05	0.10
25	10.61	7.24	5.91
50	9.31	6.73	5.61
100	8.73	6.49	5.47
500	8.34	6.30	5.36
∞	8.27	6.25	5.34
$F(2, \infty)$	4.61	3.00	1.92

Source: Dickey and Fuller (1981), p. 1063.

downwards under the null hypothesis of non-stationarity, so $\hat{\beta}$, the coefficient on the time trend in (14.14), is biased upwards. Therefore its t ratio cannot be compared with values from normal t tables. However, critical values for this t ratio have also been provided by Dickey and Fuller, although we do not present them here.

If one wishes to test for a stochastic trend in this situation, then the DF test of the last section can be adopted for application to (14.14). That is, we test the null hypothesis of non-stationarity, H_0: $\phi^* = 0$, by examining, as before, the t ratio on the OLS estimate $\hat{\phi}^*$. However, the presence of the time trend in (14.14) results in an even greater downward bias in $\hat{\phi}^*$ than for Equation (14.4). The t ratio (which we shall refer to as t_2^* in these circumstances) therefore has to be compared with the critical values in Table 14.3 rather than those in Table 14.1. Notice that these critical values are even more negative than those in Table 14.1. Thus in this situation the t ratio has to be even more negative than previously if we are to reject the null hypothesis of non-stationarity. This reflects the greater downward bias in $\hat{\phi}^*$.

The possibility of deterministic trends being present in data series complicates applied work. For example, we saw in the last chapter that one of the attractions of error correction models was the fact that they worked largely in terms of first differences which could be assumed to be stationary. However, if trends are deterministic then simple differencing will not eliminate them. Fortunately, the work of Nelson and Plosser (1982) suggests that most economic time series are subject to stochastic rather than deterministic trends. Not all econometricians agree with this, however. For example, Cochrane (1988) provides evidence to suggest that real GDP in the US has followed a deterministic trend.[10] More generally, Perron (1989) claims that the evidence in favour of stochastic rather than deterministic trends may be the result of the presence of important structural breaks in many time series. Such breaks might affect either the intercept or the slope of a trend function. For example, the great Stock Market Crash and subsequent Depression had a once and for all effect on the level of GDP in North American economies. Perron maintains that the

Table 14.3 Critical values for t_2^*

	Sample size n					
Critical values of t_2^*	25	50	100	500	∞	Usual t value $(n = \infty)$
0.01 level of sig.	− 4.38	− 4.15	− 4.04	− 3.98	− 3.96	− 2.33
0.05 level of sig.	− 3.60	− 3.50	− 3.45	− 3.42	− 3.41	− 1.65
0.10 level of sig.	− 3.24	− 3.18	− 3.15	− 3.13	− 3.12	− 1.28

Source: Fuller (1976), p. 373.

Dickey–Fuller tests are biased towards non-rejection of unit roots if the data are characterized by stationary fluctuations about a trend that experiences a structural change.

In practice, distinguishing between deterministic and stochastic trends is therefore not always easy. This is but one aspect of the fact stressed earlier that *tests for stationarity are not precise tools.* For example, Dickey–Fuller tests based on Equation (14.14) are just as lacking in power as those based on (14.4). Indeed, on many occasions it is unclear whether to use (14.4) or (14.14) as the testing equation.[11]

As an example, let us estimate the equivalent of Equation (14.14) for the ln (RP) time series from Data Set 1. That is, we add a time trend to Equation (14.5). This should yield

$$\Delta \widehat{\ln(RP)}_t = 0.0039 - 0.000\,76t - 0.232\ \ln(RP)_{t-1} \qquad (14.15)$$
$$\phantom{\Delta \widehat{\ln(RP)}_t =} (0.33)\ \ (-1.03)\qquad (-1.73)$$

$$R^2 = 0.14, \qquad z_{11} = 4.40, \qquad z_{12} = 6.06$$

Notice that the coefficient of the time trend t in (14.15) has a small t ratio, suggesting the absence of any deterministic trend. Moreover, testing the joint hypothesis $\beta = \phi^* = 0$, using the test statistic (9.19) as suggested above, yields an F value of only 1.64. This is considerably less than the critical values in Table 14.2, which suggests that ln (RP) may be subject to a stochastic but not a deterministic trend.

The value of the t_2^* statistic is given by the t ratio on the coefficient of ln $(RP)_{t-1}$ in (14.15). The value is only -1.73, and comparison with the critical values in Table 14.3 indicates that this is not sufficiently negative for us to reject the hypothesis of non-stationarity. This is a similar result to that obtained with Equation (14.5).

Like Equation (14.5), however, the LM statistics for (14.15) suggest autocorrelated residuals and possible mis-specification. To allow for this, we can again try modelling ln (RP) by higher-order AR processes. Just as in the absence of a time trend, this involves adding a sufficient number of lagged difference terms to (14.15) to achieve satisfactory residuals. For example,

$$\Delta \widehat{\ln(RP)}_t = -0.0005 - 0.000\,61t - 0.317\ln(RP)_{t-1} + 0.426\,\Delta\ln(RP)_{t-1}$$
$$\phantom{\Delta \widehat{\ln(RP)}_t =}(-0.05)\ (-0.90)\qquad(-2.42)\qquad\qquad(2.08)$$

$$R^2 = 0.29, \qquad z_{11} = 2.07, \qquad z_{12} = 2.07$$

The LM statistics are now satisfactory, and in this case the F value for the joint hypothesis $\beta = \phi^* = 0$ takes a value of 2.97. This is again considerably less than the values in Table 14.2, confirming that ln (RP) appears to be subject to a stochastic rather than a deterministic trend. The t_2^* statistic is again the t ratio on ln $(RP)_{t-1}$. The value of -2.42 is more negative than that in Equation (14.15), but we still cannot reject the hypothesis of non-stationarity. We can now refer back to

Equations (14.9) and (14.10) and recall that first-differencing ln (RP) removes its stochastic trend. That is, $\Delta \ln (RP)$ appears to be a stationary series.

COMPUTER EXERCISE

In earlier exercises we have made use of six US economic time series constructed out of the basic series in Data Set 1. These were expenditure on food in constant prices Q, consumer expenditure in current prices X, a price index for food P, a general price index G, consumer expenditure in constant prices X/G and the relative price of food P/G. The Dickey–Fuller tests carried out above and the relevant correlograms suggested that the logarithm of the relative price of food $RP = P/G$ was integrated of order one, or I(1). That is, this time series became stationary after first-differencing just once. The reader should now examine the remaining five series.

Your computer software may well quote DF and ADF stastistics as an optional output, specifying in each case the order of the AR process being used to model the time series. However, it is instructive initially to obtain these statistics 'the long way round' by actually estimating Dickey–Fuller and augmented Dickey–Fuller regressions. Do this for the logarithm of the general price index ln (G) and its first difference $\Delta \ln (G)$, experimenting with the number of 'differenced terms' on the right-hand side until you obtain non-autocorrelated residuals. You should find that both these series are non-stationary. Their correlograms seem to confirm this. However, if you difference for a second time and form $\Delta^2 \ln (G)_t = \Delta \ln (G)_t - \Delta \ln (G)_{t-1}$, you should find a stationary series, apparently confirmed by the relevant correlogram. Thus ln (G) is integrated of order two, that is, it is I(2), since it has to be differenced twice before becoming stationary. Notice that, since $\Delta \ln (G)$ is the proportionate change in G, it is, in fact, the inflation rate. Thus we can say that the inflation rate appears to be I(1), since its first difference $\Delta^2 \ln (G)$ is stationary.

Examine the logarithms of the other time series listed above using whatever short-cut facilities your software offers. You should find that consumer expenditure in current prices, ln (X), is fairly clearly I(2). The orders of integration of the other series are not always so clear, however. Expenditure on food in constant prices, ln (Q), is almost certainly I(1), but the price of food, ln (P), could be either I(1) or I(2). Consumer expenditure in constant prices, ln (X/G), appears to be I(1). Given the previous findings for ln (X) and ln (G), does this last result surprise you?

Next, look again at Data Set 4, involving quarterly series on UK consumption C and disposable income Y. Estimate Dickey–Fuller and augmented Dickey–Fuller equations for ln (C) and ln (Y). You will have to include seasonal dummy variables to get sensible results. You should find both ln (C) and ln (Y) to be non-stationary, as was suggested when we examined their time paths in Chapter 13. However, the Dickey–Fuller tests indicate that $\Delta \ln (C)$ and $\Delta \ln (Y)$ are stationary. That is, ln (C) and ln (Y) are both integrated of order 1.

14.4 Some properties of integrated processes

In this section we point out some properties of integrated processes, knowledge of which will be of help in the next chapter. First, it should be clear that the sum of a stationary series and a non-stationary series must be non-stationary. For example, if we were to sum the two series in Figures 14.1(a) and 14.2(a) then the resultant series would contain a trend similar to that in Figure 14.1(a). The variance of the non-stationary series will always dominate the variance of the stationary series. Similarly, the difference between a non-stationary series and a stationary series will be non-stationary.

Secondly, if $x_t = \alpha + \beta y_t$, where α and β are constants, it should be intuitively clear that if y_t is stationary then x_t will be stationary. On the other hand, if y_t is non-stationary then x_t will be non-stationary.

In general, if two time series are integrated of different orders then any linear combination of the series will be integrated at the higher of the two orders of integration. For example, suppose x_t is I(1) but y_t is I(3). Consider the linear combination

$$z_t = \alpha x_t + \beta y_t \qquad (14.17)$$

If we difference z_t just once then we obtain

$$\Delta z_t = \alpha \Delta x_t + \beta \Delta y_t \qquad (14.18)$$

In (14.18), since x_t is I(1), Δx_t must be I(0). Also, since y_t is I(3), Δy_t must be I(2). Thus Δz_t is the sum of a stationary and a non-stationary series, and hence cannot yet be stationary. However, if we difference (14.18) a further two times (making three times in all), we obtain

$$\Delta^3 z_t = \alpha \Delta^3 x_t + \beta \Delta^3 y_t \qquad (14.19)$$

In (14.19) $\Delta^3 x_t$ is I(0), since differencing a stationary series (Δx_t) merely leaves it stationary. Also, since y_t is I(3), $\Delta^3 y_t$ must also be I(0). Thus $\Delta^3 z_t$ is the sum of two stationary series, and so must itself be stationary. Thus z_t has to be differenced three times before it becomes stationary. That is, it is I(3), the higher of the two orders of integration present. Generally, if the higher of the two orders of integration in a linear combination is d then the linear combination has to be differenced d times before it becomes stationary. That is, it is I(d). This result can easily be extended to more than two variables.

It may seem from the above that if we have two series x_t and y_t of the same order of integration then any linear combination such as (14.17) should also be integrated of that same order. For example, if x_t and y_t are both I(1), it would appear that z_t in (14.17) should also be I(1), since it has to be differenced once to turn it into the sum of two stationary series. This is indeed almost always the case. However, as we shall see in the next chapter, there are certain special cases where a linear combination of two I(d) variables turns out to be integrated of order less than *d.* In particular, *it is possible for a linear combination of* I(1) *variables to be integrated of order zero.*

★ # Appendix 14A

Unit roots and stationarity

Consider the general rth-order AR process given by Equation (14.6) reproduced here:

$$X_t = \alpha + \phi_1 X_{t-1} + \phi_2 X_{t-2} + \phi_3 X_{t-3} + \ldots + \phi_r X_{t-r} + u_t \tag{14A.1}$$

Introducing the **lag operator** L, where $LY_t = Y_{t-1}, L^2 Y_t = Y_{t-2}$ etc., we can rewrite equation (14A.1) as

$$(1 - \phi_1 L - \phi_2 L^2 - \phi_3 L^3 - \cdots - \phi_r L^r)X_t = \alpha + u_t$$

Now consider the polynomial equation

$$1 - \phi_1 L - \phi_2 L^2 - \phi_3 L^3 - \cdots - \phi_r L^r = 0 \tag{14A.2}$$

where the ϕs, remember, are given parameters. Equation (14A.2) is an equation in L, and it is possible to show that *the stochastic process (14A.1) will only be stationary if the roots of this equation are all greater than unity in absolute value.* Otherwise, it will be non-stationary. Thus, for example, if just one root of (14A.2) were equal to 1 or -1, or if just one root lay between 1 and -1, then the process would be non-stationary.

As an illustration, take the first-order process

$$X_t = \alpha + \phi X_{t-1} + u_t \tag{14A.3}$$

We can write this as

$$(1 - \phi L)X_t = \alpha + u_t$$

The polynomial equation now takes the simple form $1 - \phi L = 0$, and has the single solution $L = 1/\phi$. For (14A.3) to be stationary, this root must exceed unity in absolute value. Hence stationarity requires that $-1 < \phi < 1$.

As a more complicated but numerical example consider the third-order process

$$X_t = 2 + 3.9 X_{t-1} + 0.6 X_{t-2} - 0.8 X_{t-3} + u_t \tag{14A.4}$$

In this case the polynomial equation is

$$1 - 3.9 L - 0.6 L^2 + 0.8 L^3 = 0 \tag{14A.5}$$

Equation (14A.5) can (fortunately) be factorized to give

$$(1 - 0.4L)(1 + 0.5L)(1 - 4L) = 0$$

The roots in this case are $L = 2.5$, $L = -2$ and $L = 0.25$. Since one of the roots is less than unity in absolute value, it follows that the process (14A.4) must be non-stationary.

Augmented Dickey–Fuller equations

Consider the general third-order process

$$X_t = \alpha + \phi_1 X_{t-1} + \phi_2 X_{t-2} + \phi_3 X_{t-3} + u_t \tag{14A.6}$$

The associated polynomial equation is

$$1 - \phi_1 L - \phi_2 L^2 - \phi_3 L^3 = 0 \tag{14A.7}$$

We now reparameterize (14A.6) into the form (14.7) in the main text. Taking X_{t-1} from either side of (14A.6) and then rearranging gives

$$\Delta X_t = \alpha + (\phi_1 + \phi_2 + \phi_3 - 1) X_{t-1} - (\phi_2 + \phi_3) X_{t-1} + \phi_2 X_{t-2} + \phi_3 X_{t-3} + u_t$$

Adding and subtracting $\phi_3 X_{t-2}$ from the right-hand side now gives

$$\Delta X_t = \alpha + (\phi_1 + \phi_2 + \phi_3 - 1) X_{t-1} - (\phi_2 + \phi_3)\,\Delta X_{t-1} - \phi_3\,\Delta X_{t-2} + u_t$$

Reparameterizing we then have

$$\Delta X_t = \alpha + \phi^* X_{t-1} + \phi_1^*\,\Delta X_{t-1} + \phi_2^*\,\Delta X_{t-2} + u_t \tag{14A.8}$$

where $\phi^* = \phi_1 + \phi_2 + \phi_3 - 1$, $\phi_1^* = -(\phi_1 + \phi_2)$ and $\phi_2^* = -\phi_3$. We now have the third-order process (14A.6) in the form of an augmented Dickey–Fuller equation (i.e. in the form (14.7) in the main text).

We know that (14A.6) will be non-stationary if any of the roots of the polynomial equation (14A.7) are less than or equal to one in absolute value. We now show that a root $L = 1$ (i.e. a *unit root*) implies $\phi^* = 0$ in (14A.8).

If a unit root exists then it must be possible to write (14A.7) in the form

$$(1 + \lambda L + \mu L^2)(1 - L) = 0$$

where λ and μ are dependent on the ϕs in (14A.7). Hence (14A.6) can be written as

$$(1 + \lambda L + \mu L^2)(1 - L) X_t = \alpha + u_t$$

But $(1 - L)X_t = X_t - X_{t-1} = \Delta X_t$. Hence a unit root implies that we can write (14A.6) as

$$(1 + \lambda L + \mu L^2)\,\Delta X_t = \alpha + u_t$$

or as

$$\Delta X_t = \alpha - \lambda\,\Delta X_{t-1} - \mu\,\Delta X_{t-2} + u_t \tag{14A.9}$$

If we now compare (14A.9) with (14A.8) we see that a unit root indeed implies that the coefficient of X_{t-1} in (14A.8) must be zero, that is, that $\phi^* = 0$.

The augmented Dickey–Fuller procedure tests the null hypothesis of non-stationarity, that is, $H_0: \phi^* = 0$, against the alternative hypothesis $H_A: \phi^* < 0$. Just as $\phi^* = 0$ implies non-stationarity, $\phi^* < 0$ can be shown to imply stationarity. Also, if we can reject $\phi^* = 0$ in favour of $\phi^* < 0$ then obviously we can also reject $\phi^* > 0$ (which would imply a root of (14A.7) that was less than unity in absolute value).

More than one unit root

There remains the possibility that Equation (14A.7) has two unit roots. If this is the case then it must be possible to further factorize (14A.7) into

$$(1 - \theta L)(1 - L)(1 - L) = 0$$

where θ will depend on λ and μ. This implies that the process (14A.6) can be written as

$$(1 - \theta L)(1 - L)(1 - L)X_t = \alpha + u_t$$

or

$$(1 - \theta L)\,\Delta^2 X_t = \alpha + u_t \tag{14A.10}$$

where $\Delta^2 X_t = \Delta X_t - \Delta X_{t-1}$. Thus the third-order process (14A.6) can then be written as

$$\Delta^2 X_t = \alpha + \theta\,\Delta^2 X_{t-1} + u_t \tag{14A.11}$$

Equation (14A.11) implies that not only X_t but also ΔX_t is non-stationary. This is the implication of having two unit roots. However, the second difference $\Delta^2 X_t$ will be stationary as long as $\theta < 1$ in (14A.11).

Appendix 14B

Testing for unit roots

Dickey and Fuller consider three possible testing equations that might be employed in the search for unit roots:

$$X_t = \phi X_{t-1} + u_t \tag{14B.1}$$

$$X_t = \alpha + \phi X_{t-1} + u_t \tag{14B.2}$$

$$X_t = \alpha + \beta t + \phi X_{t-1} + u_t \tag{14B.3}$$

Each of the above specifications can be converted into 'augmented Dickey–Fuller form' by subtracting X_{t-1} from either side and adding 'differenced terms' to the right-hand side. We considered (14B.2) and (14B.3) in Sections 14.2 and 14.3 respectively in the main text.

While (14B.2) and (14B.3) are the specifications normally adopted by researchers, one point should not be lost sight of. Dickey and Fuller present critical values for the t ratio on the OLS estimator of $\phi^* = \phi - 1$, for all three of the above testing equations. However, the simulation studies performed to obtain these critical values are all carried out using (14B.1) with $\phi = 1$ as the true underlying data generating process, regardless of whether (14B.1), (14.B2) or (14B.3) is used as the testing equation. Thus, if either (14B.2) or (14B.3) is used, the implication is that a specification error is being made. If (14B.1) is in fact the true model then this is a further reason for mistrusting the standard t test regarding ϕ or ϕ^*.

What must be appreciated, however, is that, even when both the true model and the testing equation can be represented by (14B.1), there are major differences between the cases $\phi = 1$ (non-stationary process) and $\phi < 1$ (stationary process). We shall illustrate these differences by means of two Monte Carlo simulation studies.

First, we consider the stationary case. Suppose an investigator wishes to test H_0: $\phi = 0.6$ in (14B.1), and adopts the obvious test statistic

$$TS = \frac{\hat{\phi} - 0.6}{s_{\hat{\phi}}} \tag{14B.4}$$

where $\hat{\phi}$ is the OLS estimator of ϕ and $s_{\hat{\phi}}$ is its estimated standard error. Under H_0, (14B.4) is expected to have a standard normal distribution in large samples. However, in small samples the downward bias in the OLS estimator $\hat{\phi}$ means that its distribution can be expected to be centred around a value that is less than zero. We shall investigate these expectations in our first simulation study.

Under H_0, $\phi = 0.6$ in (14B.1), and we assume u_t is normally distributed, with zero mean and variance $\sigma^2 = 2$. We can simulate disturbance values $u_1, u_2, u_3, u_4, \ldots$ on a computer in the usual way. Given a starting value for X, which we take as $X_0 = 0$, it is now a straightforward matter to simulate samples for X of any required size by successively substituting into (14B.1) the values for X_0, X_1, X_2, X_3, X_4 etc.

First, we simulate samples of size $n = 20$, computing for each such sample the OLS regression

$$\hat{X}_t = \hat{\phi} X_{t-1} \tag{14B.5}$$

and a value for the test statistic (14B.4). The distribution for (14B.4) obtained from 500 such samples is illustrated in Figure 14B.1. We see that, as expected, it is centred about a value below zero. In fact the mean value of the test statistic over the 500 samples is -0.17. This reflects the small-sample bias in the OLS estimator $\hat{\phi}$.

In Figure 14B.2 we show the sampling distribution for the test statistic (14B.4) obtained by simulating a further 500 samples, this time of size $n = 200$. The mean value of the test statistic (14B.4) is, on this occasion, -0.002, virtually equal to

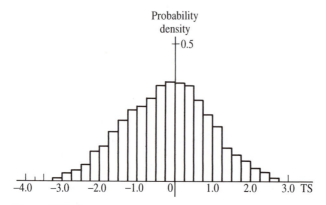

Figure 14B.1

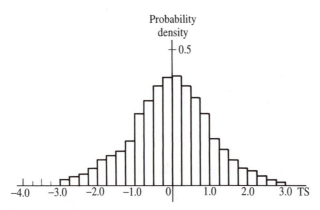

Figure 14B.2

zero, as expected. The distribution is now symmetrical and, again as expected, of roughly normal shape. Thus the test statistic (14B.4) does indeed appear to have an asymptotic normal distribution.

In our second simulation study we consider the non-stationary case where the null hypothesis is $H_0 : \phi = 1$. The obvious test statistic for an investigator to use is now

$$TS = \frac{\hat{\phi} - 1}{s_{\hat{\phi}}}$$

(14B.6)

Again, we first simulate samples of size $n = 20$. The distribution of (14B.6) obtained from 500 such samples is illustrated in Figure 14B.3. As in the stationary case it is centred about a point below zero, again reflecting the bias in the OLS estimator $\hat{\phi}$. The mean value of the test statistic is this time -0.35, even more negative than in the stationary case.

The result of simulating 500 samples of size $n = 200$ is illustrated in Figure 14B.4. In this case the distribution of the test statistic (14B.6) is still centred about a point below zero. In fact, the mean value of the test statistic (14B.6) is -0.49, even more negative than that found for small samples. Thus *there is no suggestion of a*

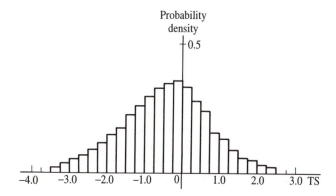

Figure 14B.3

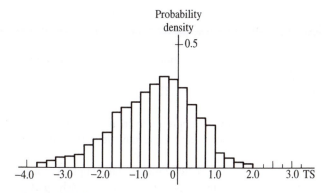

Figure 14B.4

normal distribution centred about zero. This confirms that if the data generating process is non-stationary then, even in large samples, we cannot compare the test statistic with values taken from standard t tables.

Appendix 14C

Notes to Chapter 14

1. A negative value for ϕ would imply that X_t takes alternate negative and positive values. This is implausible for an economic time series.

2. An alternative version of the Dickey–Fuller test, in fact, omits the intercept in (14.2). In practice, however, it is generally reckoned safer to include the intercept.

3. Rejection of $H_0 : \phi = 1$ in favour of $H_A : \phi < 1$ means that we can also safely reject $\phi > 1$.

4. For a stationary process ($\phi < 1$ in (14.2)), test statistics of the kind (14.3) are asymptotically normally distributed. For example, to test $H_0: \phi = 0.6$, we can treat the test statistic $(\hat{\phi} - 0.6)/s_{\hat{\phi}}$ as normally distributed in large samples and compare it with critical values from the standard normal distribution. See also the Monte Carlo studies in Appendix 14B.

5. If the intercept term is omitted from (14.2) and (14.4) then the critical values are different to those in Table 14.1. In practice, it is safer to include the intercept. See also Appendix 14B.

6. Recall from Section 10.5 that values of the dw statistic range between 0 and 4. If the autoregressive parameter ϕ (or ρ in Section 10.5) is zero then dw can be expected to take a value close to 2. However, if $\phi = 1$ then we expect a value of $dw = 0$. Values significantly greater than zero hence imply $\phi < 1$.

7. If $\beta \neq 0$ and $\phi \neq 0$ but $\phi < 1$ then the process will still be stochastically stationary, but will have a deterministic trend.

8. Such a trend can only be removed by regressing X_t on a time trend. The residuals from this regression will then be stationary. They will represent X_t 'purged' of its deterministic trend.

9. Equation (14.14) then reduces to $\Delta X_t = \alpha + u_t$. That is, X_t becomes a random walk with drift.

10. This suggests that it may occasionally be appropriate to include time trends in error correction models to deal with any deterministic trends that are present.

11. In fact, all Dickey–Fuller tests were constructed under the assumption that the true model includes neither intercept nor time trend. See the early part of Appendix 14B.

Further reading

The surveys by Permon (1991) and Holden and Thompson (1992) provide good introductions to stationarity testing. See also Charemza and Deadman, Chapter 5, and Holden and Permon, Chapter 3 in Rao (1994). For an advanced approach, see Banerjee et al. (1993), Chapter 4. A good introduction to the question of structural breaks is provided by Perron's Chapter 4 in Rao (1994).

Cointegration and the estimation of error correction models

We saw in Chapter 13 that the use of an error correction model involved the implicit assumption that some long-term relationship existed between the variables in the model. It is time now to see how we might test such assumptions. Note that it is not enough to show that the variables in the hypothesized long-run relationship are highly correlated. We saw in Chapter 13 that if such variables were non-stationary then even high correlations between them may be entirely spurious. Initially, we restrict the discussion to the case of two-variable models.

15.1 Cointegration between two variables

Consider the simple ECM discussed in Section 13.3, in particular the equilibrium relationship (13.16) reproduced here,[1]

$$y_t = \beta_0 + \beta_1 x_t \tag{15.1}$$

and the disequilibrium error given by (13.17), which we write as

$$u_t = y_t - \beta_0 - \beta_1 x_t \tag{15.2}$$

Notice, for future reference, that the disequilibrium error u_t is a linear combination of x_t and y_t.

Engle and Granger (1987) pointed out that, if the long-term relationship (15.1) underlying the ECM actually exists, then over time the disequilibrium error (15.2) should 'rarely drift far from zero' and 'often cross the zero line'. That is 'equilibrium

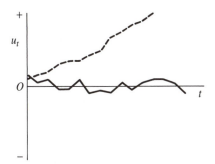

Figure 15.1 Disequilibrium errors.

will occasionally occur, at least to a very close approximation'. Thus the time path of the disequilibrium error should look rather like the solid line in Figure 15.1, fluctuating regularly about zero. For example, it would be a very strange sort of long-term equilibrium if the 'extent of disequilibrium' given by (15.2) followed the broken line in Figure 15.1 and never showed any tendency to return to zero. To quote Engle and Granger again, such an equilibrium concept would have no 'practical implications'.[2] In effect, what Engel and Granger were saying was that, if a long-run relationship such as (15.1) exists, then *disequilibrium errors such as (15.2) should form a stationary time series and have a zero mean,* that is, u_t should be I(0) with $E(u_t) = 0$.

As we have frequently stressed, many economic time series are I(1), only becoming stationary on first-differencing. Suppose x_t and y_t, the variables in the long-run relationship (15.1), are both I(1). As we saw at the end of the last chapter, we would normally expect any linear combination of x_t and y_t, such as the disequilibrium error, to be I(1), that is, only to become stationary *after* first-differencing. But we see from the above discussion that if x_t and y_t are linked together in a (linear) long-term relationship then we will find something unusual occurring. There will be a linear combination of x and y, that given by the disequilibrium error (15.2), that will not be I(1) but will instead be stationary I(0). Moreover, in the two-variable case, provided the coefficient on one of the variables is normalized to equal unity, *this stationary linear combination will be unique.*[3]

To see that the stationary linear combination will be unique, consider any other linear combination with the y_t normalized to equal unity:

$$v_t = y_t - \mu_0 - \mu_1 x_t \tag{15.3}$$

Let $\delta_0 = \mu_0 - \beta_0$ and $\delta_1 = \mu_1 - \beta_1$, where, remember, β_0 and β_1 appear in the disequilibrium error (15.2). Substituting into (15.3) gives

$$v_t = y_t - \beta_0 - \beta_1 x_t - \delta_0 - \delta_1 x_t$$
$$= u_t - \delta_0 - \delta_1 x_t \tag{15.4}$$

In (15.4) we know that u_t is I(0) but, since x_t is I(1), the linear combination v_t must be I(1). The only way in which v_t could be I(0) with $E(v_t) = 0$ is if δ_0 and δ_1 are both zero. But then $v_t = u_t$. Thus u_t must be unique.

Summarizing the above, we can say that a unique long-run relationship between two time series x_t and y_t can be said to exist if (a) both the time series x_t and y_t are I(1), that is, become stationary on first differencing, and (b) there is some linear combination of x_t and y_t that is I(0), that is, stationary. When this is the case, we can be certain that any correlation over time between x_t and y_t is not spurious.

When the conditions (a) and (b) above hold, statisticians say that the time series x_y and y_t are **cointegrated**. Thus cointegration is the statistical equivalent of the existence of a long-run economic relationship between I(1) variables. Notice that both x_t and y_t must be I(1) if they are to be cointegrated. If one of these variables were I(1) and the other I(0) then the linear combination of them given by the disequilibrium error could not be stationary.[4]

15.2   Testing for cointegration between two variables

Given the above, it is not difficult to see how we might test for cointegration and the existence of a long-term relationship between x_t and y_t. First, we must establish that the time series x_t and y_t are both[5] I(1). We can seek to do this by using the DF and ADF tests of the last chapter. If x_t and y_t are indeed I(1) then, secondly, we must find some way of testing whether the disequilibrium errors u_t in (15.2) are I(0). If this is the case then a long-term relationship exists.

The problem is that, since we do not know the parameters β_0 and β_1 in the hypothesized equilibrium relationship (15.1), the disequilibrium errors (15.2) are unknown. Because of this, the most common test for cointegration involves first using OLS to *estimate* the equilibrium relationship (15.1) and then using the *residuals* from this regression as estimates of the unknown disequilibrium errors. That is, we first use OLS to compute

$$\hat{y}_t = \hat{\beta}_0 + \hat{\beta}_1 x_t \tag{15.5}$$

Equation (15.5) is known as the **cointegrating** or **static regression**. We then estimate the u_t in (15.2) by the residuals from (15.5):

$$e_t = y_t - \hat{\beta}_0 - \hat{\beta}_1 x_t \tag{15.6}$$

where $\hat{\beta}_0$ and $\hat{\beta}_1$ are OLS estimates of the true β_0 and β_1.

We now test the e_t in (15.6) for stationarity using the Dickey–Fuller and augmented Dickey–Fuller tests of the last chapter. Stationary residuals imply that x_t and y_t are cointegrated. However, since OLS residuals have zero mean, and we do not expect them to have a deterministic trend, both intercept and time trend are normally excluded from the Dickey–Fuller regression.[6] Thus we estimate equations of the type (14.7), but involving the e_t:

$$\Delta e_t = \phi^* e_{t-1} + \phi_1^* \, \Delta e_{t-1} + \phi_2^* \, \Delta e_{t-2} + \cdots + u_t \qquad (15.7)$$

The null hypothesis H_0: $\phi^* = 0$ is, as usual, tested against H_A: $\phi^* < 0$, with as many lagged differenced terms included on the right-hand side of (15.7) as are necessary to produce non-autocorrelated residuals. Rejection of $\phi^* = 0$ implies stationarity of the residuals e_t, which, in turn, implies cointegration between x_t and y_t.

The problem with applying DF and ADF tests (sometimes called Engle–Granger tests in this context) is that we have to apply them to the residuals from the cointegrating regression (15.5) rather than to the true disequilibrium errors (15.2). Since OLS minimizes the sum of the squared residuals, it naturally seeks out a sample regression line that has stationary residuals. For example, OLS will not select a line that results in a pattern of residuals similar to that suggested by the broken line in Figure 15.1. Consequently, the downward bias in the OLS estimate of ϕ^* is even greater than in normal tests for stationarity. Thus the t ratio on the OLS estimate $\hat{\phi}^*$ has to be even more negative than the critical values used in normal DF and ADF tests before the null hypothesis of non-stationary residuals can be rejected.

In simulation experiments Engle and Granger examined a number of alternative methods of testing the e_t for stationarity. It transpired that critical values for the test statistics considered tended to depend on the model used to simulate the data. However, the experiments suggested that the tests for which critical values were least model-sensitive were the augmented Dickey–Fuller tests. These tests were also found to have the greatest power of the various tests considered. However, because of the increased downward bias in the OLS estimate of ϕ^*, mentioned above, critical values different from those in Tables 14.1 and 14.3 have to be used when using ADF tests to test for cointegration. In Table 15.1 some specimen critical values for cointegration tests, based on the work of MacKinnon (1991), are presented.

A second test considered by Engle and Granger is also sometimes used. This makes use of the Durbin–Watson statistic in the manner described towards the end of

Table 15.1   Critical values for two-variable cointegration ADF test

Sample size	Level of significance		
	0.01	0.05	0.10
25	− 4.37	− 3.59	− 3.22
50	− 4.12	− 3.46	− 3.13
100	− 4.01	− 3.39	− 3.09
∞	− 3.90	− 3.33	− 3.05

Source: Based on MacKinnon (1991).

Section 14.2 on stationarity. It therefore assumes that the disequilibrium errors and their estimates, the e_t from (15.6), can be modelled as a first-order process. In this context the test is known as the **cointegrating regression Durbin–Watson** (CRDW) **test**. Simulation experiments suggest that, at the 0.05 level of significance with a sample size of 100, the hypothesis of stationary residuals should be rejected if the dw statistic exceeds about 0.38. However, unlike the ADF statistic, the CRDW statistic can only be relied upon if the disequilibrium errors (proxied by the e_t) are, as assumed, generated by a first-order AR process.

More words of warning

Just as in the last chapter, strong words of warning need to be issued at this point. The cointegrating ADF tests are known to lack power. That is, they can quite frequently fail to reject the hypothesis of non-stationary e_t (H_0: $\phi^* = 0$ in (15.7)), even when x_t and y_t are in fact cointegrated. This is particularly the case when ϕ^* is close to zero, that is, when we are at the borderline between stationarity and non-stationarity. Also, it is again the case that the critical values we use are obtained from simulation experiments, and are therefore only approximate. Thus the results of cointegration tests have to be viewed with great caution.

Superconsistency

It may seem very strange that OLS should be used in the estimation of the cointegration regression (15.5). This is, after all, an attempt to estimate the long-term relationship (15.1). Since, in fact, we actually observe a short-term relationship involving, almost certainly, lagged values of x_t and y_t, it would appear that we are committing a serious specification error in omitting such variables from OLS estimation of (15.1). However, Stock (1987) demonstrated that, *provided x_t and y_t are cointegrated*, the OLS estimators $\hat{\beta}_0$ and $\hat{\beta}_1$ will *still be consistent*. In addition, Stock was able to demonstrate that the sampling distributions of $\hat{\beta}_0$ and $\hat{\beta}_1$ collapse onto their true values at an even faster rate in this situation than in the case where all classical assumptions are valid. That is, they converge in probability to their true values more quickly in the non-stationary case than in the stationary case! They are therefore very asymptotically efficient.

Intuitively, it is possible to understand the superconsistency result, with a little thought. If x_t and y_t are cointegrated then, for the *true* values of β_0 and β_1 in (15.1), $y_t - \beta_0 - \beta_1 x_t$ is I(0). However, if $\hat{\beta}_0 \neq \beta_0$ and/or $\hat{\beta}_1 \neq \beta_1$ then the OLS residuals, the e_t, would be non-stationary (only *one* linear combination of x_t and y_t can be stationary), and hence would have a large sample variance. Moreover, because the e_t are non-stationary, this variance would increase rapidly as the sample size increased. For $\hat{\beta}_0 = \beta_0$ and $\hat{\beta}_1 = \beta_1$, the sample variance of the e_t will be very much smaller and increase much more slowly as the sample size increases. Since the OLS estimates minimize the sample variance of the residuals, OLS is therefore very good at 'finding' estimates very close to the true β_0 and β_1, provided the sample size is large enough.

The Stock result is a remarkable one. It indicates that simple static regressions between I(1) variables will not necessarily give spurious results and that dynamic mis-specifications do not necessarily have serious consequences. However, *it is a large-sample result*. In small samples the OLS estimators of β_0 and β_1 in (15.1) are biased because of the omission of lagged values of x_t and y_t from the regression. Banerjee et al. (1986) show that this bias can be substantial and is related to $1 - R^2$, where R^2 is the coefficient of determination for the cointegrating regression. Thus a high R^2 is very desirable for static regressions of the kind (15.5).

COMPUTER EXERCISE I

To illustrate the ADF tests for cointegration between two variables, first we will again make use of Data Set 1. Recall that in the computer exercise at the end of Section 14.3 we found that the variables $\ln(Q)$ and $\ln(X/G)$, the logarithms of food expenditure in constant prices and of total consumer expenditure in constant prices, both appeared to be I(1). They are therefore both candidates for inclusion in a long-run relationship concerning the demand for food. We shall therefore test to see whether $\ln(Q)$ and $\ln(X/G)$ are cointegrated.

Using the data for 1966 through 1992, the static or cointegrating regression for these variables is

$$\widehat{\ln(Q)}_t = 7.79 + 0.309 \ln(X/G)_t, \qquad R^2 = 0.94, \qquad dw = 0.88 \qquad (15.8)$$

If $\ln(Q)$ and $\ln(X/G)$ are cointegrated then the residuals from this regression should form a stationary series, that is, be I(0).

Notice that we have not quoted any estimated standard errors or t ratios for the regression (15.8). Although, assuming cointegration, the OLS estimators themselves are consistent, *this is not the case for their estimated standard errors* as usually computed. Because the variables in the regression are I(1), the distributions of the OLS estimators are non-standard. The estimated standard errors cannot be used for significance testing, so that there is little point in reporting them. Notice, though, that we have reported the R^2 for the regression since, as noted previously, this gives a guide to the extent of the small-sample bias in the OLS estimators. Since we do have a small sample, the high R^2 is reassuring as far as it goes.

With the exception of the Durbin–Watson statistic, no diagnostic statistics have been reported for Equation (15.8) either. In this situation they are simply not relevant. For example, since no lagged variables are included in the regression, the residuals are almost certain to be autocorrelated. However, this is unimportant, except that the mis-specification may contribute to the small-sample bias. What matters is whether the residuals are stationary. The Durbin–Watson statistic is reported since, in this context, it is the CRDW statistic described above. Its value is sufficiently larger than zero to suggest that the residuals from the regression may indeed be stationary. However, recall that the CRDW test is only an appropriate test for cointegration when the residuals follow a first-order AR process.

To test for stationarity in the residuals e_t from Equation (15.8) (that is, to test for cointegration between $\ln(Q)$ and $\ln(X/G)$), we apply the DF and ADF tests, suppressing intercept and time trend in all regressions. The DF regression for the e_t saved from Equation (15.8) is

$$\widehat{\Delta e_t} = -0.473e_{t-1}, \qquad z_{11} = 9.77, \qquad z_{12} = 9.84 \qquad (15.9)$$
$$\phantom{\widehat{\Delta e_t} = }(-2.91)$$

z_{11} and z_{12} are LM statistics for first- and up to second-order autocorrelation.

The DF statistic is the t ratio on e_{t-1}. Its value is -2.91, which we have to compare with the critical values in Table 15.1. It can be seen that the DF statistic is not negative enough for us to reject the hypothesis of non-stationarity. While this might suggest that $\ln(Q)$ and $\ln(X/G)$ are not cointegrated, the LM statistics suggest autocorrelation in the residuals and that we have adopted too simple a specification. Adding Δe_{t-1} to (15.9) yields the ADF equation:

$$\widehat{\Delta e_t} = -0.714e_{t-1} + 0.601\,\Delta e_{t-1}, \qquad z_{11} = 1.31, \qquad z_{12} = 4.12 \qquad (15.10)$$
$$\phantom{\widehat{\Delta e_t} = }(-4.67) \qquad\quad (3.82)$$

Δe_{t-1} has a substantial t ratio, and the autocorrelation statistics are now satisfactory, since, with 1 and 2 d.f., critical values are $\chi^2_{0.05} = 3.84$ and 5.99 respectively. Therefore it does not appear necessary to add further differenced terms to the right-hand side of (15.10). The ADF statistic is -4.67, which is more negative than the critical values in Table 15.1. On the basis of (15.10), we can reject the hypothesis of non-stationary e_t. That is, $\ln(Q)$ and $\ln(X/G)$ appear to be cointegrated. You can verify that adding a second differenced term Δe_{t-2} to (15.10) does not alter this finding.

We are therefore justified in claiming that a long-run relationship exists in our data between the logarithms of food expenditure and total consumer expenditure. Recall that in the computer exercise in Section 13.6 we concluded by estimating an error correction model of the demand for food that assumed just such a long-run relationship. We can now be reasonably confident that such an assumption was valid and that the relationship we estimated was not a purely spurious one.

As a second exercise in cointegration analysis, we return to Data Set 4 on quarterly UK consumption C and disposable income Y. We test whether the logarithms of these variables are cointegrated. Because these series are not seasonally adjusted, we include seasonal dummy variables in the static or cointegrating regression.[7] For the sample period 1975Q1 to 1984Q4, you should obtain

$$\widehat{\ln(C)_t} = 1.22 + 0.011D_2 + 0.032D_3 + 0.064D_4 + 0.875\ln(Y)_t \qquad (15.11)$$
$$R^2 = 0.923, \qquad dw = 1.17$$

You can now test for cointegration between $\ln(C)$ and $\ln(Y)$ by examining the residuals saved from (15.11). With quarterly data, you will find that the residuals are best modelled by a higher than first-order AR process. A typical

ADF regression is

$$\widehat{\Delta e_t} = \underset{(-2.46)}{-0.421e_{t-1}} - \underset{(-1.87)}{0.277\,\Delta e_{t-1}}, \qquad z_{11} = 0.01, \qquad z_{14} = 1.91 \qquad (15.12)$$

z_{11} and z_{14} are the LM statistics for first- and up to fourth-order autocorrelation.

The ADF statistic, the t ratio on e_{t-1}, is only -2.46. Comparison with the values in Table 15.1 indicates that the residuals from (15.11) are not stationary. You should confirm that adding further differenced terms to the right-hand side of (15.12) does not alter this conclusion. We are unable to demonstrate cointegration between $\ln(C)$ and $\ln(Y)$.

The result just derived suggests that no long-run relationship exists between UK consumption and income. However, we must remember the words of caution given earlier regarding cointegration tests. The Engle–Granger tests are not precise, and, in particular, lack power. They can fail to detect a long-run relationship even when one exists. All we can say is that, with our data set, our tests fail to detect cointegration.

It must also be pointed out that long-run relationships concerning consumption may well involve more than just an income variable. For example, the life-cycle hypothesis of consumer behaviour places great stress on consumer wealth as a determinant of consumption. Interest rates may also have a role to play. If the long-run relationship, in fact, involves more than just two variables then we should not be too surprised at our failure to find cointegration between consumption and income alone. We shall have something to say about the possibility of cointegration between more than two variables later in this chapter.

In the second computer exercise of Section 13.6, we found difficulty in obtaining, via the general-to-specific approach, a satisfactory model of UK consumption behaviour. The statistical model we eventually arrived at did not appear to be capable of a static long-run equilibrium. This was because the level variables in the ECM (13.45) had coefficients that were statistically no different from zero. We can now see one possible reason for our difficulty. It may well be that no such long-run relationship between income and consumption alone exists. The problems we encountered may have been the result of our failure to include other variables such as consumer wealth or interest rates in our analysis.

15.3   The estimation of two-variable ECMs

The third of the questions posed in Section 13.5 related to whether we could be certain that the testing-down process implied by the general-to-specific procedure would necessarily lead us to an error correction model. We can now give an answer to this question. Engle and Granger showed in their 1987 article that, provided two time series x_t and y_t are cointegrated, the short-term disequilibrium relationship between them can always be expressed in the error correction form

$$\Delta y_t = \text{lagged}\,(\Delta y, \Delta x) - \lambda u_{t-1} + \epsilon_t, \qquad 0 < \lambda < 1 \tag{15.13}$$

where u_t is the disequilibrium error or extent of departure from the long-run relationship (15.1) and λ is a short-run adjustment parameter, identical in nature to that in the ECMs of Chapter 13. This is the so-called **Granger representation theorem**, and is one of the most important results in cointegration analysis. It implies that when using the general-to-specific approach, and provided we are dealing with cointegrated variables, we can reasonably concentrate on ECMs when testing down to a parsimonious preferred equation.

Intuitively, we can see why the Granger representation theorem should hold. If x_t and y_t are cointegrated so that the disequilibrium errors, the u_t of (15.2), are stationary, as illustrated by the solid line in Figure 15.1, then this implies that there must be some force always pulling the u_t back towards zero and preventing them increasing without limit. Previous departures from equilibrium must be continually being corrected, otherwise the u_t could differ substantially from zero. But this is exactly what is implied by an error correction model.

Notice also that if (15.13) is to be a sensible equation to estimate then all its variables must be integrated of the same order. The differenced terms are I(0), so it follows that the disequilibrium errors need to be I(0). Thus cointegration of x_t and y_t is necessary if an error correction model is to exist. In addition, though, the Granger theorem demonstrates that cointegration is not only a necessary but also a sufficient condition for an error correction representation to exist.

It should be noted that the precise lags on the differenced terms in the disequilibrium relationship (15.13) are not specified by the theorem. Thus the changes in x and y are not necessarily lagged by just a single period. It is also possible that more than one differenced term in Δx and/or Δy could appear in (15.13). In addition, since Δx_{t-1} is an I(0) variable, so must be Δx_t. Thus it is quite permissible to include the unlagged difference in x in the ECM.[8]

The Engle–Granger two-stage procedure

Although, when x_t and y_t are cointegrated, we can be confident that the simplification search in a general-to-specific investigation should lead to an ECM of some kind, Engle and Granger (1987) suggest a way of short-cutting such searches. They suggest that estimation should take place in two stages.

In the first stage the long-run parameters are estimated. This is achieved simply by estimating the cointegrating regression (15.5). If x_t and y_t are indeed cointegrated then we know from the Stock result of the last section that the OLS estimators of the long-run parameters β_0 and β_1 will be consistent.

Assuming cointegration, in the second stage of the Engle–Granger procedure the residuals from the cointegrating regression, the e_t in Equation (15.6), are used as estimates of the true disequilibrium errors, the u_t, in (15.13). That is, we rewrite (15.13) as

$$\Delta y_t = \text{lagged } (\Delta y_t, \Delta x_t) - \lambda e_{t-1} + \epsilon_t \tag{15.14}$$

The second stage of the procedure therefore consists in estimating (15.14), with the appropriate lags on the differenced variables being determined by experimentation. It is at this stage that estimates of λ and other short-run parameters are obtained. It is also permissible to include in (15.14) the first differences of other I(1) variables that do not appear in the long-run relationship. These variables will affect y only in the short run.

Since all the variables in (15.14) are now known to be stationary, it may be estimated by OLS. Indeed, Engle and Granger were able to show that the estimates of short-run parameters obtained in this second stage are not merely consistent. They are also as asymptotically efficient as they would have been had the true disequilibrium errors, the u_t, been used in (15.14) instead of their estimates, the e_t. It is also the case that the estimated standard errors in this second stage are consistent estimators of the true standard errors.

COMPUTER EXERCISE II

As an illustration of the Engle–Granger procedure, we estimate an ECM of the US demand for food, using again Data Set 1. We have, in fact, already performed stage one when we estimated the cointegrating regression (15.8). This equation gives us our long-run relationship between food expenditure Q and real total expenditure X/G. For stage two, we will therefore use the residuals e_t from this regression in a version of (15.14), involving log-differenced variables in Q and X/G:

$$\Delta \widehat{\ln(Q)}_t = 0.514 \, \Delta \ln(Q)_{t-1} + 0.451 \, \Delta \ln(X/G)_t$$
$$\quad\quad\quad (3.19) \quad\quad\quad\quad\quad (3.56)$$

$$\quad\quad\quad\quad\quad -0.258 \, \Delta \ln(X/G)_{t-1} - 0.636 e_{t-1} \tag{15.15}$$
$$\quad\quad\quad\quad\quad (-2.04) \quad\quad\quad\quad (-4.22)$$

$$\sum e^2 = 0.003 \, 14, \quad dw = 2.21$$

$$z_{11} = 1.10, \quad z_2 = 0.03, \quad z_3 = 1.22, \quad z_4 = 0.93, \quad z_5 = 0.34$$

Equation (15.15) is estimated for 1967 through 1992, because of the need to include the lagged residuals e_{t-1}.

The diagnostic statistics for (15.15) are as defined in Chapters 12 and 13, and are all satisfactory.[9] The error correction term e_{t-1} has the correct sign and has a highly significant t ratio. Additional difference terms with longer lags prove to have statistically insignificant coefficients when added to (15.15).

As we noted above, there is no reason why the differences of other I(1) variables should not be added to an ECM such as (15.15). Obvious candidates in this case are log-differences in the relative price of food, P/G. For example,

$$\Delta \widehat{\ln (Q)}_t = 0.364 \, \Delta \ln (Q)_{t-1} + 0.397 \, \Delta \ln (X/G)_t - 0.149 \, \Delta \ln (X/G)_{t-1}$$
$$\quad (1.82) \qquad\qquad (2.69) \qquad\qquad (-0.89)$$

$$\qquad\qquad - 0.285 \, \Delta \ln (P/G)_t + 0.111 \, \Delta \ln (P/G)_{t-1} - 0.456 e_{t-1} \qquad (15.16)$$
$$\qquad\qquad (-2.13) \qquad\qquad (0.75) \qquad\qquad (-2.69)$$

$$\sum e^2 = 0.002 \, 49, \qquad dw = 2.21$$

$$z_{11} = 3.81, \qquad z_2 = 0.61, \qquad z_3 = 1.57, \qquad z_4 = 0.88, \qquad z_5 = 0.67$$

There is a marked reduction in the residual sum of squares in (15.16) compared with (15.15), and $\Delta \ln (P/G)$ has a significant t ratio and a correct sign. But the lagged differences in $\ln (X/G)$ and $\ln (P/G)$ both have insignificant coefficients. Dropping these variables gives

$$\Delta \widehat{\ln (Q)}_t = 0.246 \, \Delta \ln (Q)_{t-1} + 0.289 \, \Delta \ln (X/G)_t$$
$$\quad (1.63) \qquad\qquad (3.33)$$

$$\qquad\qquad - 0.332 \, \Delta \ln (P/G)_t - 0.502 e_{t-1} \qquad (15.17)$$
$$\qquad\qquad (-3.09) \qquad\qquad (-3.40)$$

$$\sum e^2 = 0.002 \, 61, \qquad dw = 1.91$$

$$z_{11} = 0.01, \qquad z_2 = 0.52, \qquad z_3 = 1.06, \qquad z_4 = 0.74, \qquad z_5 = 0.69$$

Equation (15.17) is an ECM in which the short-run demand elasticities with respect to total real expenditure and relative price are 0.289 and 0.332 respectively. In the long run, however, demand is independent of relative price, while the expenditure elasticity falls slightly to the 0.309 in the equilibrium relationship (15.8).

Alternative approaches

The Engle–Granger procedure has been criticized on the grounds of the small-sample bias present in the OLS estimation of the cointegrating equation (15.5). This bias carries over into the estimates of the disequilibrium errors and hence into the second-stage estimates of the short-run parameters obtained from (15.14). The presence of such bias has led some investigators to use the cointegrating regression as merely a means of testing for cointegration and to adopt other methods of estimating the long-run parameters. One such possibility is to use an ADL equation of the kind described in Chapter 11. For example, if an equation such as (11.28) is estimated then estimates of the long-run parameters can be obtained from (11.29). Suppose the estimates of β_0 and β_1 in (15.1) obtained in this way are $\tilde{\beta}_0$ and $\tilde{\beta}_1$. Alternative estimates of the disequilibrium errors can then be constructed using

$$w_t = y_t - \tilde{\beta}_0 - \tilde{\beta}_1 x_t \qquad (15.18)$$

The w_t from (15.18) may now be substituted into (15.13) instead of the residuals

from the cointegrating regression. The second stage of the Engle–Granger procedure can then be carried out in the usual way.

A problem with ADL or 'dynamic' estimation of the long-run parameters relates
to whether it is justifiable to treat all regressors in the ADL equation as exogenous.
OLS would not be appropriate if, for example, the current value of X in (11.28) were
correlated with the disturbance in that equation. It is also not clear how long the lags
in the ADF equation should be. It is probably better to include too many lags than too
few to avoid omitted variable bias, but this may result in degrees of freedom
difficulties, particularly since this approach is usually adopted for small samples.

It is left to the reader to use Data Set 1 to estimate a long-run demand-for-food
relationship using an ADL equation including the variables $\ln(Q)$ and $\ln(X/G)$. Use
lags of up to three periods. You should obtain estimates for the long-run parameters
β_0 and β_1 of 7.82 and 0.306 respectively, very similar to those in (15.8). The second
stage of the Engle–Granger procedure then leads to an equation very similar to
(15.17).

The problem of small-sample bias in the Engle–Granger first stage led Banerjee
et al. (1986) to suggest that it may be preferable to carry out the estimation of long-
and short-run parameters in a single step. If we substitute the true disequilibrium
errors (15.2) into (15.13) we obtain

$$\Delta y_t = \lambda \beta_0 + \text{lagged} \ (\Delta y, \Delta x) - \lambda y_{t-1} + \lambda \beta_1 x_{t-1} + \epsilon_t \tag{15.19}$$

OLS may now be applied to (15.19), with the lag structure on the differenced
variables again being determined by experimentation. Although y_{t-1} and x_{t-1} are
I(1) variables, OLS can still be applied, since, assuming cointegration, there is a
linear combination of x_{t-1} and y_{t-1} that is I(0). The existence of such a linear
combination can be checked by testing the residuals from (15.19) for stationarity.
There is some evidence from simulation studies that the small-sample properties of
estimates obtained in this way are superior to those of the two-stage Engle–Granger
estimates.

We have, in fact, already estimated versions of (15.19) in Chapter 13 when we
used the general-to-specific approach to test down to the model (13.42). In a sense, we
have therefore come full circle.

For the sake of comparison, let us re-estimate (13.42) over the sample period
1967 through 1992 used in the estimation of Equation (15.17). In the notation of this
chapter, you should obtain

$$\Delta \widehat{\ln(Q)}_t = 3.30 + 0.563 \ \Delta \ln(X/G)_t - 0.352 \ \Delta \ln(P/G)_t$$
$$\phantom{\Delta \widehat{\ln(Q)}_t = } (3.37) \ \ (4.31) (-3.42)$$

$$-0.411 \ln(Q)_{t-1} + 0.119 \ln(X/G)_{t-1} \qquad (15.20)$$
$$(-3.26) \phantom{\ln(Q)_{t-1} + 0.1} (2.91)$$

$$\sum e^2 = 0.002 \ 44, \qquad dw = 1.62$$

$$z_{11} = 1.57, \qquad z_2 = 0.33, \qquad z_3 = 1.29, \qquad z_4 = 0.74, \qquad z_5 = 0.74$$

Notice that although there are definite similarities between the model estimated by the Engle–Granger procedure (Equations (15.8) and (15.17)) and the model (15.20), there are differences too. Both models imply a long-run relationship between the demand for food and real total expenditure that is independent of relative prices. Moreover, both models suggest that relative prices may be important in the short run. However, there are differences, particularly in the estimates of short-run elasticities and of the adjustment parameter attached to the disequilibrium error. These differences seem to be the result of the appearance of the lagged $\Delta \ln(Q)_t$ term appearing in the Engle–Granger model but not in the general-to-specific model.

The differences between the models illustrate an important point. *There can be no guarantee that the two approaches, Engle–Granger and general-to-specific, will lead to the same model.* This is particularly the case in a small sample such as we have here.

COMPUTER EXERCISE III

The models (15.17) and (15.20) are non-nested, so we cannot attempt to choose between them by means of the usual F tests. However, we can test them against each other by making use of the J test for non-nested models described in Section 12.3.

To perform the J tests, we need the predicted values of the dependent variables for Equations (15.17) and (15.20). To test the Engle–Granger model (15.17), add the predicted values saved from Equation (15.20) to Equation (15.17), and re-estimate. You should obtain a t ratio as high as 1.94 on the predicted values from (15.20). It appears that the general-to-specific model (15.20) has some explanatory power beyond the regressors in the Engle–Granger model.

To test the general-to-specific model (15.20), add the predicted values saved from Equation (15.17) to the model (15.20), and re-estimate. On this occasion, you should obtain a t ratio of only 1.45 on the predicted values. This is below a critical t value of $(n - k = 19 \text{ d.f.})$ $t_{0.05} = 1.73$. The Engle–Granger model does not appear to have anything significant to add to the general-to-specific model. On balance then, we marginally prefer the general-to-specific model.

15.4 The multivariate case

In the preceding sections we have restricted discussion to situations involving just two variables. However, it is obvious that long-run economic relationships often contain more than two variables. For example, we might hypothesize that in the long run

$$z_t = \beta_0 + \beta_1 w_t + \beta_2 x_t + \beta_3 y_t \tag{15.21}$$

where w, x, y and z are all I(1) variables.

If a long-run relationship such as (15.21) exists then we can argue, just as in the two-variable case, that the disequilibrium errors arising from (15.21) should be I(0).That is,

$$u_t = z_t - \beta_0 - \beta_1 w_t - \beta_2 x_t - \beta_3 y_t \qquad (15.22)$$

should form a stationary time series, again similar to the solid line in Figure 15.1.

From the above, it may seem that the idea and implications of cointegration, described in Section 15.1, carry over quite easily to the multivariate case. In general, we can say that a set of variables $w, x, y, z, \ldots$ is cointegrated if (a) each such variable is integrated of order unity and (b) there exists some linear combination of the variables that is integrated of order zero (i.e. is stationary). If a long-run relationship between variables exists then they must be cointegrated in this sense.

Unfortunately, in the multivariate case there is a major complicating factor that does not arise when we consider just two variables. While it is certainly true by definition that if a set of variables is cointegrated then there must be some linear combination of them that is stationary, it is no longer possible to demonstrate as we did in Section 15.1 that the stationary linear combination is unique. In the multivariate case *there may be more than one stationary linear combination* linking cointegrated variables. This, on reflection, should not be surprising. If we have, for example, four economic variables, there is no reason why they should not be linked together by more than one long-run relationship.

To see how this possibility fits in with the above notion of cointegration, suppose u_t in (15.22) has been found to be stationary. This could indeed imply a long-run relationship between all four variables w, x, y and z. However, another possibility is that z, w and x, y form two cointegrated pairs of variables. That is, a long-run relationship of the form

$$z_t = \alpha_0 + \alpha_1 w_t \qquad (15.23)$$

links z_t and w_t, while a long-run relationship of the form

$$x_t = \gamma_0 + \gamma_1 y_t \qquad (15.23a)$$

links x_t and y_t. The disequilibrium errors from such relationships must be stationary. That is,

$$v_{1t} = z_t - \alpha_0 - \alpha_1 w_t \qquad (15.24)$$

and

$$v_{2t} = x_t - \gamma_0 - \gamma_1 y_t \qquad (15.25)$$

must both be I(0).

Since v_{1t} and v_{2t} are both stationary, we know from Section 14.4 that any linear combination of them will also be stationary. For example,

$$v_t = v_{1t} + v_{2t} = z_t - \alpha_0 - \gamma_0 - \alpha_1 w_t + x_t - \gamma_1 y_t \qquad (15.26)$$

will also be I(0).

But v_t, like u_t in (15.22), is a linear combination of the four variables w, x, y and z. Thus we have a situation where more than one linear combination of the four variables is stationary. It follows that the finding of a stationary linear combination of w, x, y and z could mean *either* a single relationship between all four variables *or* two relationships between pairs of the variables *or* even both. Thus, while the existence of a *single* long-run relationship between more than two I(1) variables implies the variables are cointegrated, the reverse is not necessarily true. Cointegration implies the existence of *at least one* long-run relationship between the variables.

At this stage it is useful, for future reference, to introduce a frequently used term in cointegration analysis. If a linear combination of variables such as (15.22) is stationary then the coefficients in this relationship form what is known as a **cointegrating vector**. For example, for (15.22), the cointegrating vector is $(1, -\beta_0, -\beta_1, -\beta_2, -\beta_3)$. Similarly, the cointegrating vector corresponding to the stationary v_t in (15.26) is $(1, -\alpha_0 - \gamma_0, -\alpha_1, 1, -\gamma_1)$. We may therefore summarize the above discussion by saying that if more than two I(1) variables are cointegrated then there may be more than one cointegrating vector.

Testing for cointegration in the general case

To test for cointegration in the multivariate case, one possibility is to proceed very much as in the two-variable case. For example, if we wish to test whether four variables w, x, y and z are cointegrated then the first step is to estimate a cointegrating or static regression of the kind

$$z_t = \hat{\beta}_0 + \hat{\beta}_1 w_t + \hat{\beta}_2 x_t + \hat{\beta}_3 y_t + e_t \tag{15.27}$$

The residuals e_t from this regression can then be tested for stationarity using the usual DF and ADF tests.[10] If they are found to be stationary then we conclude that the variables are cointegrated. In effect, we will have found a linear combination of them that is I(0).[11]

The DF and ADF tests are again based on equations such as (15.7). There is, however, an additional complication. Because of the usual downward bias in the OLS estimator of ϕ^* in (15.7), its t ratio cannot be compared with values from normal t tables. The required critical values have again been determined from simulation experiments. However, it has been found that the size of these critical values is very much influenced by the underlying process generating the data. In particular their size is dependent on the number of parameters, m, being estimated in the cointegrating regression. Some specimen critical values, again based on the work of MacKinnon (1991), are presented in Table 15.2 for varying sample sizes and values of m. For example, if our sample size were $n = 50$ and the cointegrating regression were Equation (15.27), so that $m = 4$, then we would reject the null hypothesis of *non-cointegration* at the 0.05 level of significance if the ADF statistic were more negative than -4.32.

As an example, we consider again Data Set 1. In Section 15.2 we found that logarithms of the variables Q, real expenditure on food, and X/G, total real expenditure, were cointegrated for this data set. We now introduce the logarithm of the relative price of food, P/G, another I(1) variable, and test for cointegration

Table 15.2   Critical values for multivariate cointegration ADF test

Sample size	$m=3$ Significance level			$m=4$ Significance level			$m=6$ Significance level		
	0.01	0.05	0.10	0.01	0.05	0.10	0.01	0.05	0.10
25	−4.92	−4.10	−3.71	−5.43	−4.56	−4.15	−6.36	−5.41	−4.96
50	−4.59	−3.92	−3.58	−5.02	−4.32	−3.98	−5.78	−5.05	−4.69
100	−4.44	−3.83	−3.51	−4.83	−4.21	−3.89	−5.51	−4.88	−4.56
∞	−4.30	−3.74	−3.45	−4.65	−4.10	−3.81	−5.24	−4.70	−4.42

Source: Based on MacKinnon (1991).

between all three variables. The cointegrating regression estimated over the years 1965 through 1992 is

$$\widehat{\ln(Q)}_t = 7.78 + 0.309 \ln(X/G)_t - 0.174 \ln(P/G)_t, \qquad R^2 = 0.947 \quad (15.28)$$

If we now use the residuals e_t from (15.28) to estimate DF and ADF equations, we obtain, for example,

$$\widehat{\Delta e_t} = -0.547 e_{t-1} + 0.473 \, \Delta e_{t-1}, \qquad z_{11} = 0.97, \qquad z_{12} = 1.50 \quad (15.29)$$
$$\quad (-3.78) \qquad\quad (2.95)$$

The ADF statistic is, as usual, the t ratio on e_{t-1}, and is -3.78. However, this is not more negative than the critical values in Table 15.2, so we are unable to say that the variables $\ln(Q)_t$, $\ln(X/G)_t$ and $\ln(P/G)_t$ are cointegrated.

Notice that we have not quoted any estimated standard errors for the cointegrating regression (15.28). This is because, as in the two-variable case, they do not provide consistent estimates of the true standard errors when the regression involves I(1) variables. This has the unfortunate consequence that they cannot be used for significance testing. That is, *we cannot make use of them to help decide what variables should be included in a cointegrating regression.* We have to decide what variables to include either on a priori grounds or on the basis of the cointegration tests themselves. For example, although the t ratio on $\ln(P/G)_t$ in (15.28) is in fact very low, we cannot use this as justification for dropping this variable from the cointegrating regression. Rather, it seems appropriate to exclude $\ln(P/G)_t$ simply because, as we saw earlier, $\ln(Q)_t$ and $\ln(X/G)_t$ on their own pass the cointegration test.

Similarly, it is not possible to make use of the normal F tests to test any restrictions on parameters in the cointegrating equation that may be suggested by theory. For example, in Equation (15.28) the restriction that demand elasticities should sum to zero has been imposed. But, unfortunately, we cannot test this restriction in the usual way.

★ 15.5 Estimation in the multivariate case

In the general multivariate case estimation of both long-run relationships and ECMs is seriously complicated by the possibility that I(1) variables may be linked by more than one cointegrating vector.

If we can be certain that there is just a *single* cointegrating vector then estimation can still proceed by the Engle–Granger two-stage method. For example, if four variables w, x, y and z prove to be cointegrated then the long-run relationship between them could be estimated by the cointegrating regression (15.27). In these circumstances OLS estimation would again provide superconsistent estimators of the long-run parameters. The residuals from such a regression could still be used as estimates of true disequilibrium errors in the second-stage of the estimation of error correction models. In this case the Granger representation theorem implies that the short-run behaviour of all four variables can be modelled by ECMs, each equation containing the single disequilibrium error from the long-run relationship.

The above, however, as in the two-variable case, is a large-sample procedure. In small samples there is again substantial bias in the first-stage OLS estimates of the long-run parameters. It should be noted that in the multivariate case the R^2 for the cointegrating regression can no longer be relied on as an indicator of the extent of this bias. This is because R^2 always increases when more regressors are included in an equation. Thus a high R^2 does not suggest small biases in the multivariate case.

Unfortunately, if I(1) variables are linked by more than one cointegrating vector then the Engle–Granger procedure is no longer applicable. The OLS estimation of the cointegrating regression no longer provides consistent estimates of any of the cointegrating vectors. To see this, suppose, for example, we have estimated (15.21) by (15.27) and found the four variables w, x, y and z to be cointegrated. How do we interpret the $\hat{\beta}$s in the cointegrating regression (15.27). They could be estimates of the cointegrating vector associated with (15.21). But, equally well, they could be estimates of a cointegrating vector associated with (15.26). They might even be estimates of some fairly meaningless linear combination of these cointegrating vectors. We can have no sensible idea of what has been estimated. In fact, we have an identification problem similar to that discussed in Section 8.3.

The inapplicability of the Engle–Granger procedure in the multivariate case means that other methods of estimation have to be employed. Johansen (1988) suggests a maximum likelihood approach. To give some intuitive insight into the Johansen method, it is helpful for the moment to revert to the two-variable case. Suppose that two I(1) variables x and y are determined by the following ADL equations with a maximum lag of two periods:

$$y_t = b_{11}y_{t-1} + b_{12}x_{t-1} + b_{13}y_{t-2} + b_{14}x_{t-2} + \epsilon_{1t} \tag{15.30}$$

$$x_t = b_{21}y_{t-1} + b_{22}x_{t-1} + b_{23}y_{t-2} + b_{24}x_{t-2} + \epsilon_{2t} \tag{15.31}$$

We can rewrite (15.30) and (15.31) as

$$\Delta y_t = (b_{11} - 1)\,\Delta y_{t-1} + b_{12}\,\Delta x_{t-1}$$
$$- (1 - b_{11} - b_{13})y_{t-2} + (b_{12} + b_{14})x_{t-2} + \epsilon_{1t} \tag{15.32}$$

and

$$\Delta x_t = b_{21} \, \Delta y_{t-1} + (b_{22} - 1) \, \Delta x_{t-1}$$
$$+ (b_{21} + b_{23})y_{t-2} - (1 - b_{22} - b_{24})x_{t-2} + \epsilon_{2t} \tag{15.33}$$

It should be clear that we could reparameterize (15.32) and (15.33) into error correction form. The problem is that estimation will run into spurious regression problems unless x_t and y_t are cointegrated.

Equations (15.32) and (15.33) can be written in matrix form as

$$\Delta z_t = B_1 \, \Delta z_{t-1} + B_2 z_{t-2} + \epsilon_t \tag{15.34}$$

where

$$\Delta z_t = \begin{pmatrix} \Delta y_t \\ \Delta x_t \end{pmatrix}, \quad B_1 = \begin{pmatrix} b_{11} - 1 & b_{12} \\ b_{21} & b_{22} - 1 \end{pmatrix},$$

$$B_2 = \begin{pmatrix} -(1 - b_{11} - b_{13}) & b_{12} + b_{14} \\ b_{21} + b_{23} & -(1 - b_{22} - b_{24}) \end{pmatrix}, \quad \epsilon_t = \begin{pmatrix} \epsilon_{1t} \\ \epsilon_{2t} \end{pmatrix}$$

It is now possible to distinguish three possibilities concerning the matrix B_2. First, if all its elements are zero, which implies it has a rank of zero, then Δz_t depends only on past values of itself. That is, no error correction mechanisms are operating, and hence no long-run relationship exists between x and y. Thus x and y are not cointegrated.

Secondly, if the rank of B_2 is two, so that its rows are linearly independent, then it can be shown to follow from the Granger representation theorem mentioned earlier that both x and y are stationary variables, so that the question of cointegration does not arise. In fact, this would contradict our earlier assumption that x and y are I(1).

Finally, if the rank of B_2 is unity, so that one of the rows of B_2 is linearly dependent on the other, then it can be shown that B_2 can be written in the form

$$B_2 = \alpha \beta' \tag{15.35}$$

where α is a 2×1 column vector and β' is a 1×2 cointegrating row vector, whose elements consist of the parameters in a long-run equilibrium relationship between x and y. Thus if the rank of B_2 is unity then x and y are cointegrated.

To understand this third case, where one of the rows of B_2 is linearly dependent on the other, suppose the second row is a constant multiple k of the first row. That is,

$$b_{21} + b_{23} = -k(1 - b_{11} - b_{13})$$

and

$$-(1 - b_{22} - b_{24}) = k(b_{12} + b_{14})$$

Equation (15.33) can then be rewritten as

$$\Delta x_t = b_{21} \, \Delta y_{t-1} + (b_{22} - 1) \, \Delta x_{t-1}$$
$$- k(1 - b_{11} - b_{13})y_{t-2} + k(b_{12} + b_{14})x_{t-2} + \epsilon_{2t} \tag{15.36}$$

We may now reparameterize (15.32) and (15.36) as

$$\Delta y_t = (b_{11} - 1)\, \Delta y_{t-1} + b_{12}\, \Delta x_{t-1} - (1 - b_{11} - b_{13})(y_{t-2} - \beta x_{t-2}) + \epsilon_{1t}$$
$$(15.37)$$

and

$$\Delta x_t = b_{21}\, \Delta y_{t-1} + (b_{22} - 1)\, \Delta x_{t-1} - k(1 - b_{11} - b_{13})(y_{t-2} - \beta x_{t-2}) + \epsilon_{2t}$$
$$(15.38)$$

where

$$\beta = \frac{b_{12} + b_{14}}{1 - b_{11} - b_{13}}$$

From (15.32) and (15.36), it can be seen that the vectors α and β' in (15.35) are

$$\alpha = \begin{pmatrix} 1 \\ k \end{pmatrix}, \qquad \beta' = (-(1 - b_{11} - b_{13}), \quad b_{12} + b_{14})$$

The cointegrating vector β' implies a long-run equilibrium relationship

$$-(1 - b_{11} - b_{13})y_t + (b_{12} + b_{14})x_t = 0$$

or, normalizing the coefficient on y_t,

$$y_t = \beta x_t \qquad (15.39)$$

where β is as defined above.

If we now examine Equations (15.37) and (15.38), we see that they are of error correction form, containing the disequilibrium errors associated with the long-run relationship (15.39). It can also be seen that the elements of α determine the relative size of the adjustment coefficients on the error correction terms in (15.37) and (15.38).

In the two-variable case estimating the long-run equilibrium relationship involves estimating the single cointegrating vector β'. The multivariate case can be approached in a similar way. If we have m variables that are all I(1) then we have m equations similar to (15.30) and (15.31), each containing lagged values of all m variables. These equations can again be expressed in the form (15.34), that is,

$$\Delta z_t = B_1 \Delta z_{t-1} + B_2 z_{t-2} + \epsilon_t \qquad (15.40)$$

except that B_1 and B_2 are now both $m \times m$ matrices and ϵ_t now contains m disturbances.

In the general case the rank of B_2 is at most m. As in the two-variable case, if the rank of B_2 is zero then the m variables are not cointegrated. Again as in the two-variable case, if the rank of B_2 takes its maximum value (this time m) then all the variables are I(0), so the question of cointegration does not arise. Unlike with two variables, however, in the multivariate case there are a number of possibilities between these extremes. The rank of B_2 (that is, the number of independent rows in the matrix) could take any value between 1 and $m - 1$. It turns out that if the rank of

$\mathbf{B}_2$ is r, where $0 < r < m$, then the matrix $\mathbf{B}_2$ can again be expressed in the form (15.35), that is,

$$\mathbf{B}_2 = \boldsymbol{\alpha}\boldsymbol{\beta}'$$

but with $\boldsymbol{\alpha}$ and $\boldsymbol{\beta}$ now both $m \times r$ matrices. The columns of the matrix $\boldsymbol{\beta}$ (that is the rows of $\boldsymbol{\beta}'$) form r cointegrating vectors. *Each* such vector can be used to form a linear combination of the m variables that is stationary. *Each* such stationary linear combination represents a long-run relationship between some or all of the m cointegrated variables. As a result, it is possible to express each of the m equations in (15.40) in error correction form with the disequilibrium errors from *all* the long-run relationships appearing in *every* such equation. The elements of the matrix $\boldsymbol{\alpha}$ determine the relative sizes of the various adjustment coefficients.

If the m variables in (15.40) are cointegrated, it means that, in principle, the m equations in (15.40) can be estimated without any worries about spurious regression problems. However, standard methods of estimation are not applicable, and a maximum likelihood method has to be used. The Johansen procedure, mentioned earlier, both determines the number of cointegrating vectors and provides estimates of these vectors together with estimates of the adjustment parameters in the matrix $\boldsymbol{\alpha}$. The details of the Johansen method are beyond the scope of this text. However, the method proceeds by first testing the hypothesis $r = 0$, that is, that there are no cointegrating vectors. If this hypothesis cannot be rejected, the procedure stops because the variables are not cointegrated. If, however, $r = 0$ can be rejected, it is then possible to test the hypothesis that there is at most 1 cointegrating vector ($r \leqslant 1$). If this hypothesis is also rejected then the hypotheses $r \leqslant 2, r \leqslant 3, \ldots$ may be tested in sequence until a hypothesis cannot be rejected. If, for example, we are able to reject $r \leqslant r^* - 1$ but not $r \leqslant r^*$ then the implication is that there are r^* cointegrating vectors. Maximum likelihood estimates of the r^* vectors can then be obtained.

The Johansen procedure therefore provides estimates of all cointegrating vectors in the multivariate case. Moreover, unlike the Engle–Granger method, it provides a framework for testing restrictions on the parameters in the implied long-run relationships. However, awkward problems of interpretation remain. Suppose we are interested in a particular long-run relationship between more than two variables – this might be, for example, a demand-for-money function or an equation determining consumer expenditure. What if we find more than one cointegrating vector in our data? Which vector do we regard as providing the parameters in our long-run relationship? How do we interpret the other cointegrating vectors? Do they all necessarily have an economic meaning anyway, or are some of them merely a description of the behaviour of the various time series in our data set?

Another difficult interpretational problem arises when we model short-run behaviour via error correction models. As the above analysis indicates, when there is more than one cointegrating vector, the disequilibrium errors associated with *each* such vector normally appear in the equations for every variable in the system. This implies that, unless the relevant elements in the $\boldsymbol{\alpha}$ matrix are zero, variables are error-correcting for departures from more than one equilibrium relationship, or perhaps even for departures from some linear combination of such relationships. The economic interpretation of this is not at all clear. Addressing such problems is one of the major current tasks of econometric theoreticians.

15.6   An overview

There can be little doubt that the development of cointegration analysis has had a marked and almost certainly permanent effect on the way most econometricians approach the estimation of time series equations. It represents a vital new tool in the applied worker's armoury. Few would now estimate a time series equation without first checking the order of integration of its variables. It is generally accepted that regressions in the levels of non-stationary variables can only be meaningful if the variables are cointegrated. Thus cointegration tests are a valuable means of distinguishing between meaningful and spurious regressions.

However, it is also true that cointegration analysis is not the panacea for all the problems of time series regression that some may originally have hoped. The lack of power in the Dickey–Fuller cointegration tests is a severe handicap in their use. It is probably unwise to be guided solely by the results of unit-root tests when formulating and estimating dynamic models. For example, if a sensible error correction model can be estimated with a highly significant disequilibrium error, it may be silly to reject it because of an inability to demonstrate cointegration via Dickey–Fuller tests. Indeed, Banerjee et al. (1993) suggest that, as well as basing tests for cointegration on the residuals from static regressions, we should also consider tests on the coefficients attached to error correction terms in dynamic equations. That is, for example, we should test $H_0: \lambda = 0$ in equations such as (13.22). Rejection of H_0 implies a significant error correction term and hence that the variables are cointegrated. The problem with this approach is that, under H_0, the variables are not cointegrated, so that the standard t test is not applicable. The t ratio for the OLS estimator of λ is not asymptotically normally distributed. Unfortunately, little is yet known about the power of these tests or indeed of the Johansen tests described in the last section.

As we have seen, the interpretational problem arising when more than one cointegrating vector is detected by the Johansen procedure is another reason why overreliance on cointegration techniques alone is unwise. A priori knowledge has sometimes been used to help decide which of a number of cointegrating vectors can be identified with the long-run relationship of interest. It may seem sensible to select that vector that provides long-run elasticities most in accord with the values suggested by economic theory. However, this ad hoc approach seems to have little to recommend it.

Additional problems also arise when time series data is quarterly and subject to a distinct seasonal pattern. Although this topic is beyond our scope, seasonality, like trends, can be either deterministic or stochastic in nature. While deterministic seasonality can be handled using dummy variables as described in Section 9.4, this is not the case for stochastic seasonality. Stochastic seasonality has to be dealt with by differencing procedures akin to but more complicated than those for dealing with stochastic trends. The literature on seasonal cointegration is expanding rapidly, but many difficulties remain unresolved.

Given the above problems, it may be that the best overall strategy for modelling time series is to follow a general-to-specific approach but to be guided by the results of cointegration analysis, which can give valuable information about the form of long-run relationships. Cointegration can anyway tell us nothing about short-run responses, and these have to be modelled separately. The general-to-specific approach has the advantage that, provided the general model is rigorously tested for mis-specifications, the possibility of any dynamic mis-specifications appearing in the final model is much reduced. Recall, though, the criteria for a satisfactory model that we listed in Section 12.4. In the simplification search of a general-to-specific study, criteria such as theoretical consistency, parameter constancy and eventual parsimony are equally as important as goodness of fit and general data coherence. It would make little sense, for example, to accept a model that was inconsistent with any generally known economic theory just because its variables were statistically cointegrated.

Critics of the general-to-specific approach point out that it may involve the estimation of 'unbalanced' equations, that is, equations in which the dependent variable is not of the same order of integration as the regressors. In such cases standard inferential procedures cannot be relied upon. Typically, the dependent variable may be a first difference and hence I(0), but at least some of the regressors may be level variables and hence I(1). However, provided the I(1) variables cointegrate to form an I(0) linear combination, the equation will still 'balance' in the sense that both right- and left-hand sides involve only I(0) quantities.[12] When this is the case, *t* ratios can be shown to have asymptotically normal distributions, so that standard inference can be applied provided the sample is relatively large. Banerjee et al. (1993) argue that the general-to-specific approach is particularly effective, because the inclusion of several variables all with a number of lags increases the probability of finding a cointegrated set of regressors.

Appendix 15A

A fresh data set

COMPUTER EXERCISE IV

In this appendix we make use of Data Set 6 on the floppy disk to bring together the approaches and techniques of the last four chapters. The data can also be found in Appendix III at the end of this book. This data set involves quarterly seasonally adjusted data from 1972Q1 through 1989Q4 for the Federal Republic of (West) Germany. It contains series for the narrow money supply in billions of current Deutsche marks, GNP in billions of current Deutsche marks, a consumer price index (1985 = 100), and the Central Bank discount rate. We shall use this data to model the demand for money.

Monetary theory suggests that the real demand for money, M, depends on a 'scale variable' such as real GNP, Y, and an opportunity cost or rate-of-interest variable, R. We can form the variable M by deflating the money series on the disk by the price index. This yields the money supply in constant 1985 prices.[13] Similarly, we can form Y by deflating the GNP series by the price index. This gives GNP in constant 1985 prices. For the opportunity cost variable, we use $R = 1 + I/100$, where I is the above discount rate in percentage terms. This is the customary way to define the opportunity cost variable in econometric studies.[14] For example, it means that an increase in the interest rate from 5% to 7% represents a proportionate increase in opportunity cost of roughly 0.02 rather than 0.4 which is the proportionate increase in the original I variable. We shall work in terms of $\ln(M)$, $\ln(Y)$ and $\ln(R)$.

First, we examine our three series and attempt to ascertain their order of integration. The time paths and correlograms of $\ln(M)$, $\ln(Y)$ and $\ln(R)$ are shown in Figures 15A.1, 15A.2 and 15A.3 respectively. Those for $\ln(M)$ and $\ln(Y)$ strongly suggest that these variables are not stationary. The time paths trend upwards, and the autocorrelations decay only slowly. The time path of $\ln(R)$ shows no obvious trend, following a cyclical pattern. Its correlogram follows neither an I(0) pattern nor an I(1) pattern.

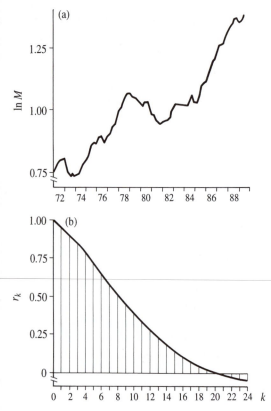

Figure 15A.1 (a) Time path for $\ln(M)$. (b) Correlogram for $\ln(M)$.

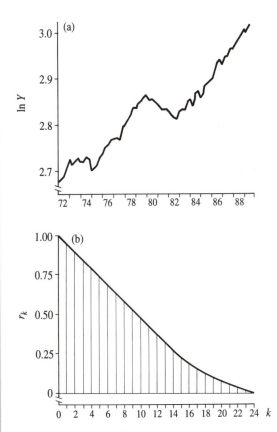

Figure 15A.2 (a) Time path for ln (Y). (b) Correlogram for ln (Y).

DF and ADF statistics for the level variables, based on equations such as (14.7), including both intercept and trend, are shown in Table 15A.1. They need to be compared with the critical values in Table 14.3. Those for ln (M) and ln (Y) clearly suggest non-stationarity. Those for ln (R) give conflicting results, depending on how

Table 15A.1   Stationarity tests for ln (M), ln (R) and ln (Y)

Statistic	Sample	ln (M)	ln (Y)	ln (R)
DF	72Q2–89Q4	−0.81	−1.35	−1.64
ADF(1)	72Q3–89Q4	−1.42	−1.26	−2.51
ADF(2)	72Q4–89Q4	−1.40	−1.10	−3.72*
ADF(3)	73Q1–89Q4	−2.06	−1.57	−2.83
ADF(4)	73Q2–89Q4	−2.08	−2.38	−2.90

* Reject non-stationarity at 5% level.

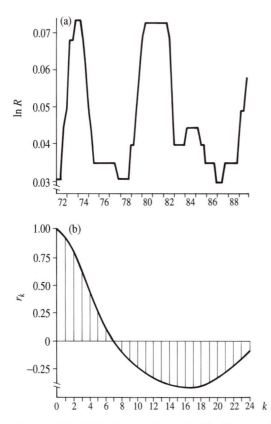

Figure 15A.3 (a) Time path for $\ln(R)$. (b) Correlogram for $\ln(R)$.

many differenced variables are included on the right-hand side of the ADF regression. However, closer study of the regressions for $\ln(R)$ indicates that the residuals are seriously autocorrelated except in the case of the ADF(2) regression, which is

$$\Delta \widehat{\ln(R)}_t = 0.008 - 0.002t - 0.141 \ln(R)_{t-1} + 0.311 \, \Delta \ln(R)_{t-1}$$
$$\quad\quad (3.26) \quad (-0.79) \quad (-3.72) \quad\quad\quad (2.80)$$

$$+0.432 \, \Delta \ln(R)_{t-2} \quad\quad (15A.1)$$
$$(3.75)$$

$$z_{11} = 0.68, \quad z_{14} = 4.94$$

where z_{11} and z_{14} as usual are the LM statistics for first- and up to fourth-order autocorrelation.

If further differenced terms are added to (15A.1), they prove to have low t ratios, and the autocorrelation statistics deteriorate markedly. The t ratio on $\ln(R)_{t-1}$ (the ADF(2) statistic) just exceeds the 0.05 critical values in Table 14.3 in absolute terms. This evidence, together with the time path in Figure 15A.3, suggests that we can regard $\ln(R)$ as a stationary I(0) variable.

Since $\ln(M)$ and $\ln(Y)$ are clearly non-stationary, we now examine their first differences. Time paths and correlograms for the differences in these variables are shown in Figures 15A.4 and 15A.5. These clearly suggest stationarity, with no obvious trends in the time paths and with the sample autocorrelations decaying rapidly to zero.

DF and ADF statistics for $\Delta\ln(M)$ and $\Delta\ln(Y)$ are shown in Table 15A.2. These are based on ADF regressions excluding a time trend[15] and therefore need to be compared with the critical values in Table 14.1. Those for $\Delta\ln(M)$ consistently suggest stationarity. The DF and lower-order ADF values for $\Delta\ln(Y)$ also strongly suggest stationarity. The reader should verify that the extra differenced terms that have to be included in the ADF regression for $\Delta\ln(Y)$ to obtain the higher-order ADF statistics have low t ratios and result in poor autocorrelation statistics. It therefore appears that $\Delta\ln(Y)$, like $\Delta\ln(M)$, is a stationary variable.

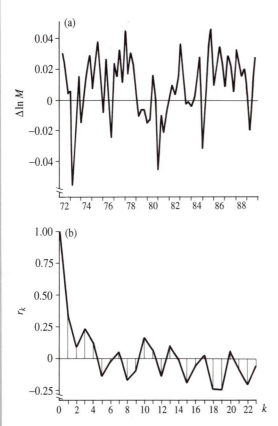

Figure 15A.4 (a) Time path for $\Delta\ln(M)$. (b) Correlogram for $\Delta\ln(M)$.

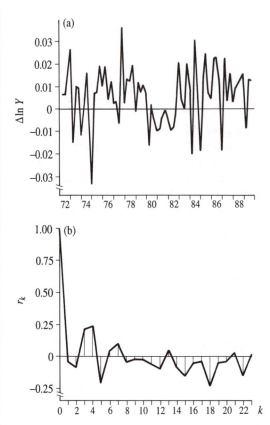

Figure 15A.5 (a) Time path for $\Delta \ln(Y)$. (b) Correlogram for $\Delta \ln(Y)$.

Table 15A.2 Stationarity tests for $\Delta \ln(M)$ and $\Delta \ln(Y)$

Statistic	Sample	$\Delta \ln(M)$	$\Delta \ln(Y)$
DF	72Q3–89Q4	−5.91*	−8.58*
ADF(1)	72Q4–89Q4	−4.85*	−6.34*
ADF(2)	73Q1–89Q4	−3.20*	−3.98*
ADF(3)	73Q2–89Q4	−2.95*	−2.84
ADF(4)	73Q3–89Q4	−3.64*	−2.93*

* Reject non-stationarity at 5% level.

Of our three basic data series, $\ln(M)_t$ and $\ln(Y)_t$ appear to be I(1), whereas $\ln(R)_t$ seems to be I(0). This suggests that we look for a possible long-run relationship between $\ln(M)_t$ and $\ln(Y)_t$ and test for cointegration between these variables. The static or cointegrating regression estimated for the full 1972Q1–

1989Q4 period is

$$\widehat{\ln(M)}_t = -3.45 + 1.56 \ln(Y)_t, \qquad R^2 = 0.954, \qquad dw = 0.34 \qquad (15A.2)$$

To test for cointegration, we need to examine the residuals from (15A.2) for stationarity, estimating equations of the type (15.7). You will find that two differenced terms need to be included on the right-hand side of your equation to obtain satisfactory autocorrelation statistics:

$$\widehat{\Delta e_t} = -0.276 e_{t-1} + 0.149 \, \Delta e_{t-1}(-3.87) + 0.310 \, \Delta e_{t-2} \qquad (15A.3)$$
$$\quad\;\; (-3.87) \qquad (1.31) \qquad\qquad\qquad (2.69)$$

$$z_{11} = 0.003, \qquad z_{14} = 5.46$$

The ADF statistic is the t ratio on the e_{t-1} variable in (15A.3). The value of -3.86 has to be compared with the values in Table 15.1. It can be seen that, at least at the 0.05 level of significance, we can reject the hypothesis of non-stationary residuals in Equation (15A.3). Thus $\ln(M)$ and $\ln(Y)$ appear to be cointegrated.

We shall now use the Engle–Granger two-stage procedure to estimate the short-run relationship between the money supply and GNP. That is, we estimate error correction models of the type (15.14), using the residuals from (15A.2) as estimates of the disequilibrium errors. Initially, we include lagged differences of up to the third order in $\ln(M)$ and $\ln(Y)$. You should obtain, for the sample period 1973Q1 through 1989Q4,

$$\widehat{\Delta \ln(M)}_t = 0.479 \, \Delta \ln(M)_{t-1} + 0.184 \, \Delta \ln(M)_{t-2} + 0.140 \, \Delta \ln(M)_{t-3}$$
$$\qquad\qquad\;\; (4.00) \qquad\qquad\qquad (1.48) \qquad\qquad\qquad (1.05)$$

$$\qquad +0.619 \, \Delta \ln(Y)_t - 0.029 \, \Delta \ln(Y)_{t-1} - 0.547 \, \Delta \ln(Y)_{t-2}$$
$$\qquad\quad (3.64) \qquad\qquad (-0.18) \qquad\qquad (-3.46)$$

$$\qquad +0.222 \, \Delta \ln(Y)_{t-3} - 0.215 e_{t-1} \qquad\qquad\qquad\qquad (15A.4)$$
$$\qquad\quad (1.28) \qquad\qquad (-3.03)$$

$$\sum e^2 = 0.014\,72, \qquad dw = 2.02$$

$$z_{14} = 3.98, \qquad z_2 = 2.28, \qquad z_3 = 0.83, \qquad z_4 = 1.50, \qquad z_5 = 0.47$$

The z statistics in (15A.4) are as defined earlier. To compute the Chow statistic z_5, we have used the 16 observations 1986Q1 through 1989Q4 for predictions.

There is no reason why we should not include differenced terms in other variables in (15A.4), provided they are of the correct order of integration. An obvious possibility is $\Delta \ln(R)$. The interest rate variable was found to be I(0), so we were unable to include it in the cointegrating regression (15A.2). However, there is no reason why it should not have a short-run effect on the demand for money.

You will find that either $\Delta \ln(R)_t$ or $\Delta \ln(R)_{t-1}$ proves to have a significant t ratio if added to (15A.4). However, the inclusion of the unlagged difference results in the coefficient on the disequilibrium term e_{t-1} losing significance and problems arising with the autocorrelation statistics. It is therefore preferable to include $\Delta \ln(R)_{t-1}$. If, in addition, you omit those difference terms in $\ln(M)$ and $\ln(Y)$ that have insignificant t ratios, you should obtain

$$\Delta \widehat{\ln (M)}_t = 0.373 \; \Delta \ln (M)_t + 0.686 \; \Delta \ln (Y)_t - 0.246 \; \Delta \ln (Y)_{t-2}$$
$$(3.42) \qquad\qquad (4.55) \qquad\qquad (-1.62)$$

$$+0.440 \; \Delta \ln (Y)_{t-3} - 1.165 \; \Delta \ln (R)_{t-1} - 0.144 e_{t-1} \qquad (15A.5)$$
$$(3.04) \qquad\qquad (-2.81) \qquad\qquad (-2.52)$$

$$\sum e^2 = 0.013\,81, \qquad dw = 2.26$$

$$z_{14} = 3.88, \qquad z_2 = 0.59, \qquad z_3 = 0.50, \qquad z_4 = 1.81, \qquad z_5 = 0.59$$

Equation (15A.5) is our final preferred demand-for-money equation obtained by the Engle–Granger two-stage procedure. All the diagnostic statistics are satisfactory, and the disequilibrium error term e_{t-1} is correctly signed with a significant t ratio. We shall return to (15A.5) shortly.

It is also possible to estimate a demand-for-money equation from this data set by a general-to-specific approach, estimating short- and long-run parameters together. It is suggested that the reader now adopts this approach, using the following general model in error correction form:

$$\Delta \widehat{\ln (M)}_t = k + \sum_{i=1}^{3} \alpha_i \; \Delta \ln (M)_{t-i} + \sum_{i=0}^{3} \beta_i \ln (Y)_{t-i} + \sum_{i=0}^{3} \gamma_i \ln (R)_{t-i}$$
$$+ a \ln (M)_{t-1} + b \ln (Y)_{t-1} + c \ln (R)_{t-1} + \epsilon_t \qquad (15A.6)$$

You should find all the diagnostic statistics for this equation to be satisfactory and the residual sum of squares to be 0.010 47, somewhat lower than for Equation (15A.5). It is then a relatively simple matter to test down to the following equation, estimated for 1973Q1 through 1989Q4:

$$\Delta \widehat{\ln (M)}_t = -0.740 + 0.138 \; \Delta \ln (M)_{t-1} + 0.445 \; \Delta \ln (Y)_t - 0.521 \; \Delta \ln (Y)_{t-2}$$
$$(-3.20) \quad (1.31) \qquad\qquad (2.88) \qquad\qquad (3.63)$$

$$-1.34 \; \Delta \ln (R)_t - 0.217 \ln (M)_{t-1} + 0.350 \ln (Y)_{t-1} - 0.770 \ln (R)_{t-1}$$
$$(-3.83) \qquad\qquad (-3.13) \qquad\qquad (3.30) \qquad\qquad (-4.16)$$
$$(15A.7)$$

$$R^2 = 0.592, \qquad \sum e^2 = 0.011\,12, \qquad dw = 1.86$$

$$z_{14} = 2.01, \qquad z_2 = 4.37, \qquad z_3 = 1.22, \qquad z_4 = 0.08, \qquad z_5 = 0.70$$

Equation (15A.7) is our final preferred equation obtained using the general-to-specific approach. The value obtained for R^2 may appear somewhat low, but remember that we are attempting to explain *quarterly changes*. This is never an easy task, and R^2s of this magnitude are quite common with this type of data.

It should be immediately apparent that there are clear differences between (15A.7) and (15A.5), obtained by the Engle–Granger two-stage procedure. Not only are the lags on the differenced variables different, but (15A.7) includes the lagged level variable $\ln (R)_{t-1}$. The disequilibrium term e_{t-1} in (15A.5) excluded this variable because we found it to be I(0) in our stationarity tests. But, in (15A.7),

$\ln(R)_{t-1}$ has a t ratio as high as -4.16, strongly suggesting a long-run interest rate effect.

Since (15A.5) and (15A.7) are non-nested models, we cannot use the usual F test to choose between them. In terms of goodness of fit, (15A.7) appears superior, with $\sum e^2 = 0.011\ 12$, compared with $\sum e^2 = 0.013\ 81$ for (15A.5). However, (15A.5) is more parsimonious, containing just six regressors compared with eight (including intercept) in (15A.7). Use of the Akaike information criterion, described at the end of Section 7.1, for comparing the two equations yields a value of $\text{AIC} = -8.48$ for (15A.7) and $\text{AIC} = -8.33$ for (15A.5). Thus (15A.7) appears superior on this criterion.

We can also use the J test for non-nested models, described in Section 12.3, to test (15A.5) and (15A.7) against each other. If we save the predicted values from (15A.5) and include them as an extra regressor in the model (15A.7), they prove to have a t ratio of only 1.44. Thus there is no justification for rejecting (15A.7) against (15A.5). However, if the predicted values are saved from (15A.7) and included as an extra regressor in (15A.5), they prove to have a t ratio as high as 4.16. Thus we clearly have to reject the model (15A.5) in favour of (15A.7).

The model (15A.7), obtained by a general-to-specific simplification search, appears to out-perform the model (15A.5), obtained by the Engle–Granger two-stage method. But why did the two approaches lead to such different equations? The reason appears to lie in the fact that, over our sample period, the interest-rate variable $\ln(R)_t$ was I(0) or stationary. As strongly suggested by theory, there may well exist a long-run equilibrium relationship between the *three* variables $\ln(M)_t$, $\ln(Y)_t$ and $\ln(R)_t$. Unfortunately, because *for our sample period* $\ln(R)_t$ was I(0), our long-run cointegration analysis was unable to detect its influence. However, when modelling short-run behaviour in our general-to-specific approach, we found the level variable $\ln(R)_{t-1}$ to have a significantly non-zero coefficient. That is, $\ln(M)_t$ appeared to be error-correcting toward a long-run relationship that *did* contain an interest-rate variable. We were thus able to detect the possible existence of a long-run relationship involving $\ln(R)_t$ from the short-run behaviour of $\ln(M)_t$.

The stability of demand-for-money functions has important implications for the efficacy of monetary policy. While Equation (15A.7) successfully passes the Chow test for predictive failure (test statistic z_5 above), a more detailed stability analysis can be performed by making use of the recursive least-squares procedure described at the end of Section 9.5. Recall that with recursive least squares, Equation (15A.7) is first estimated for a small subset of observations at the start of the sample period. The OLS estimates are then recalculated using updating formulae, as the subset of observations is gradually expanded until it includes the whole of the sample period. The time paths of the recursive OLS estimates of the coefficients on the level variables $\ln(M)_{t-1}$, $\ln(Y)_{t-1}$ and $\ln(R)_{t-1}$ are shown in Figures 15A.6(a), (b) and (c) respectively.

The initial instability of the recursive estimates is simply a reflection of the small number of observations used in estimation at the start of the procedure. The coefficients of $\ln(M)_{t-1}$ and $\ln(R)_{t-1}$ eventually become stable. The coefficient on $\ln(Y)_{t-1}$, however, is rather less stable. It is left to the reader to examine the

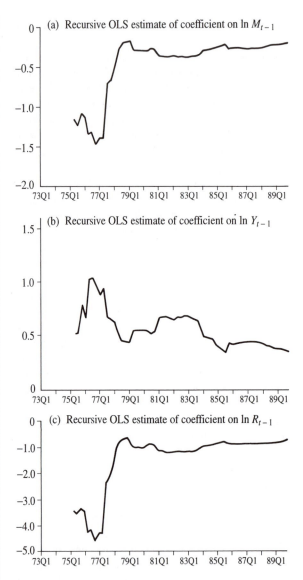

Figure 15A.6 Recursive OLS estimates for (a) $\ln(M)_{t-1}$, (b) $\ln(Y)_{t-1}$ and (c) $\ln(R)_{t-1}$.

recursive OLS estimates of the coefficients on the differenced variables in Equation (15A.7).

Finally, we can obtain estimates of both short- and long-run demand-for-money elasticities from Equation (15A.7). The short-run income elasticity is 0.445, rising to a high 1.61 in the long run. To obtain interest-rate elasticities, we have to multiply short- and long-run coefficients by the rate of interest itself.[16] At a rate of interest of $I = 0.05$, the short-run elasticity is -0.067, rising to -0.18 in the long run.

Appendix 15B

Notes to Chapter 15

1. For ease of notation in this chapter, we omit the asterisk on β_0. However, this parameter could still depend on long-run growth rates.

2. Engle and Granger are clearly referring to what economists would call a 'stable' equilibrium rather than an 'unstable' equilibrium.

3. For example, if the linear combination $2 + 5x + 10y$ is stationary then we can obtain an infinite number of stationary linear combinations simply by multiplying $2 + 5x + 10y$ by various constants. But there will only be one such linear combination in which the coefficient on y is unity, namely that obtained by multiplying $2 + 5x + 10y$ by 0.1 to give $0.2 + 0.5x + y$. The coefficient on y has now been 'normalized'.

4. The normal definition of cointegration is more general than we have given. In general, two time series are said to be cointegrated of order d, b, written $CI(d, b)$ if (a) they are both integrated of order d and (b) if there exists some linear combination of them that is integrated of order $d - b$ where $b > 0$. The case of most interest to economists, however, is the one described in the main text with $d = 1$ and $b = 1$.

5. There is no reason why a long-run relationship could not exist between $I(0)$ variables. The question of cointegration would not then arise. However, neither would the problem of spurious correlation.

6. It is possible that one of the variables in the static regression (15.5) could be subject to a deterministic trend. If this is the case, a time trend should be added to (15.5). An exactly equivalent procedure is to omit intercept and time trend from (15.5) but instead include them in the Dickey–Fuller regression (15.7).

7. The cointegration of seasonally varying time series raises questions that are beyond the scope of this text. The approach we have adopted must be regarded as a rough and ready way of dealing with the problem.

8. A question then arises during estimation concerning the exogeneity of Δx_t. It may not be plausible to regard this variable as contemporaneously uncorrelated with the disturbance in the error correction model.

9. We have not quoted a value for the coefficient of determination, because, in the absence of an intercept in (15.15), R^2 cannot be given its usual interpretation.

10. Any of the four variables w, x, y and z may be used as the dependent variable in (15.27). In small samples DF and ADF statistics may differ according to which regression is run. If the statistics are close to their critical values, it is therefore wise to try different variables on the left-hand side of the cointegrating regression.

11. Recall, though, that this does not necessarily mean that we have 'found' a long-run relationship between all four variables. The cointegrating vector(s) that exist may simply be linear combinations of relationships such as (15.24) and (15.25).

12. It is also the case when estimating cointegrating or static regressions that what matters is that the equations should balance. For example, consider a static regression

$$z_t = \alpha + \beta x_t + \gamma y_t$$

where z_t is I(1) but x_t and y_t are both I(2). This may seem to be an unbalanced equation. However, just as two I(1) variables can cointegrate to form an I(0) linear combination, so two I(2) variables can cointegrate to form an I(1) linear combination. Thus if x_t and y_t do cointegrate in this way then the above equation can still balance. For example in Data Set 1 we found that although the logarithms of the price of food and the general price index were I(2), the logarithm of the relative price of food, $\ln(P/G)$, was I(1). A possible cointegrating regression would therefore be

$$\ln(Q)_t = \beta_0 + \beta_1 \ln(X/G)_t + \beta_2 \ln(P)_t + \beta_3 \ln(G)_t + u_t$$

Although $\ln(Q)$ and $\ln(X/G)$ are I(1), whereas $\ln(P)$ and $\ln(G)$ are I(2), the equation still balances, because $\ln(P)$ and $\ln(G)$ cointegrate to form an I(1) variable.

13. Since we are dealing with a narrow money aggregate, it is reasonable to assume that the supply of money is 'demand-determined'. Thus we can interpret our money *supply* series as representative of the *demand* for money.

14. Demand-for-money equations are normally estimated in double-log form, with the variable $\ln(R) = \ln(1 + I/100)$ among the regressors. Since $\ln(1 + I/100) \approx I/100$, this is equivalent to including the interest rate itself, rather than its logarithm, in the equation. The coefficient of $\ln(R)$ cannot then, however, be regarded as the interest elasticity. The interest elasticity is given by the coefficient on $\ln(R)$ *times* the interest rate $I/100$.

15. When testing the level variables for stationarity, the F test of Section 14.3 indicates that $\ln(M)_t$ and $\ln(Y)_t$ are subject to a stochastic but not a deterministic trend.

16. See Footnote 14.

Further reading

There are now a number of good introductory surveys of cointegration techniques. See for example Holden and Thompson (1992), Cuthbertson et al. (1992), Chapter 5, and Rao (1994), Chapters 2 and 3. Charemza and Deadman (1992), Chapter 6, provides an accessible introduction to the Johansen maximum likelihood techniques. For an advanced treatment, see Banerjee et al. (1993), Chapters 5, 7 and 8.

16 Further topics

16.1 Vector autoregression

In the last few chapters we have paid much attention to the Hendry general-to-specific approach to econometric investigation and the use of cointegration analysis in determining the form of long-run relationships. However, although the Hendry approach is becoming increasingly popular, particularly with UK econometricians, it should not be thought that this is the only approach to empirical work. One well-known alternative is based on the work of C. Sims (1980), and involves the estimation of what are known as **vector autoregressions** (VARs).

The Sims methodology is based on a reaction against the traditional econometric approach to tackling multi-equation simultaneous models. We looked at some simple simultaneous equation models in Section 8.3 and discussed the problems of estimating them. A key element to the approach adopted there was the division of variables into those which were endogenous to the model and those which could be treated as exogenous. Given that such a division was feasible, consistent estimation of any equation in a model was then possible, provided that equation was identified. One of the major ways in which an equation becomes identified is via the absence from it of one of the variables in the model. For example, in the simple wage–price model of (8.19) and (8.20), the price equation (8.20) was identified because it *did not* contain the variable E. The omission of a variable from an equation can be regarded as the placing of a 'zero-restriction' on its parameters. That is, the parameter on the omitted variable is restricted to being zero.

During the 1970s, the ideas of the last paragraph were applied to the building of large-scale macroeconomic models of a number of western economies. Examples are the Treasury Model in the UK and the Wharton Model in the US. Unfortunately, these models, which often contained hundreds of equations, failed in their main purpose – that of providing governments with adequate economic forecasts. It was this perceived failure that led to Sim's 1980 questioning of traditional econometric practice.

We have already noted in Section 8.3 that Liu, as early as 1960, had questioned the use of zero restrictions to achieve the identification of equations. Sims, in fact, viewed the theoretical restrictions imposed on simultaneous equation models as essentially arbitrary and 'incredible'. Sims also regarded with great scepticism the endo–exogenous division of variables that was necessary if these models were to be estimated. In practice, such a distinction tends to be arbitrary and may simply depend on the size of the model. For example, in the wage–price model of Section 8.3 we treated E, excess demand in the labour market, as an exogenous variable in the wage equation (8.19). But, in a macro-model of the whole economy, E has to be regarded as endogenous, and hence is likely to be correlated with the disturbance in the wage equation.

In the Sims approach the division between endogenous and exogenous variables is abandoned. Effectively, all variables are treated as endogenous. Furthermore, initially at least, no zero-restrictions are placed on the parameters of equations in the model. Thus each equation has exactly the same set of regressors. This leads to the formulation of a general VAR model of the following kind:

$$\mathbf{z}_t = \sum_{i=1}^{k} \mathbf{A}_i \mathbf{z}_{t-i} + \boldsymbol{\epsilon}_t \tag{16.1}$$

where $\mathbf{z}_t$ is a column vector of observations at time t on all the variables in the model. $\boldsymbol{\epsilon}_t$ is a column vector of random disturbance values, which may be contemporaneously correlated with one another but are assumed to be non-autocorrelated over time. The $\mathbf{A}_i$ are matrices of parameters, all of which are non-zero.

The form of (16.1) will be better understood if we express a three-equation model, with a maximum lag of $k=2$ periods, in terms of ordinary algebra. Equation (16.1) then takes the form

$$w_t = a_{11}w_{t-1} + a_{12}x_{t-1} + a_{13}y_{t-1} + b_{11}w_{t-2} + b_{12}x_{t-2} + b_{13}y_{t-2} + \epsilon_{1t}$$
$$x_t = a_{21}w_{t-1} + a_{22}x_{t-1} + a_{23}y_{t-1} + b_{21}w_{t-2} + b_{22}x_{t-2} + b_{23}y_{t-2} + \epsilon_{2t} \tag{16.2}$$
$$y_t = a_{31}w_{t-1} + a_{32}x_{t-1} + a_{33}y_{t-1} + b_{31}w_{t-2} + b_{32}x_{t-2} + b_{33}y_{t-2} + \epsilon_{3t}$$

In (16.2) the vectors $\mathbf{z}_t$ and $\boldsymbol{\epsilon}_t$ are given by

$$\mathbf{z}_t = \begin{pmatrix} w_t \\ x_t \\ y_t \end{pmatrix}, \quad \boldsymbol{\epsilon}_t = \begin{pmatrix} \epsilon_{1t} \\ \epsilon_{2t} \\ \epsilon_{3t} \end{pmatrix}$$

and, since $k=2$, there are two 3×3 matrices $\mathbf{A}_i$:

$$\mathbf{A}_1 = \begin{pmatrix} a_{11} & a_{12} & a_{13} \\ a_{21} & a_{22} & a_{23} \\ a_{31} & a_{32} & a_{33} \end{pmatrix}, \quad \mathbf{A}_2 = \begin{pmatrix} b_{11} & b_{12} & b_{13} \\ b_{21} & b_{22} & b_{23} \\ b_{31} & b_{32} & b_{33} \end{pmatrix}$$

Notice that in (16.2) and in the more general (16.1) each variable in the VAR model depends on all the other variables, with exactly the same lag structure applied to each variable in all equations.[1] That is, no zero-restrictions are imposed, and all the a and b parameters are, initially at least, non-zero. Notice that no current values for any variables appear on the right-hand side of any equation. If we were to add such current variables, we would turn, for example, (16.2) into a simultaneous equation model in which x, y and z were all endogenous. In fact, a VAR can be regarded as the reduced form of a structural model in which *no* variables are exogenous.[2]

In practice, intercept terms, seasonal dummy variables and maybe deterministic time trends might be added to (16.1) and (16.2). Another practical problem relates to the number of variables to be included and the maximum lag length to be employed. For example if we have a seven-equation model with a maximum lag length of four periods then each equation will have a total of 28 regressors. With relatively small sample sizes, precise estimation then becomes impossible. Because of this problem, variables frequently have to be excluded from the model and a limit has to be placed on the length of lags. In practice, sufficient lags have to be included to ensure non-autocorrelated residuals in all equations. Otherwise, the combination of autocorrelation and lagged dependent variables would lead to estimation problems.

The VAR formulation has a number of advantages. For example, because all regressors are lagged variables, they can be assumed to be contemporaneously uncorrelated with the disturbance. Thus each equation can be consistently estimated by OLS.[3] VARs are also very easy to use for forecasting. For example suppose we wish to forecast w_{t+1} in the VAR (16.2). Using the first equation in this model,

$$\hat{w}_{t+1} = \hat{a}_{11}w_t + \hat{a}_{12}x_t + \hat{a}_{13}y_t + \hat{b}_{11}w_{t-1} + \hat{b}_{12}x_{t-1} + \hat{b}_{13}y_{t-1} \tag{16.3}$$

where $\hat{w}_{t+1}$ is the required forecast and the $\hat{a}$s and $\hat{b}$s are estimated coefficients.

The point about (16.3) is that to obtain $\hat{w}_{t+1}$, we require only current and past values of the variables in the model, and these are generally readily available.[4] This is in contrast to the normal econometric forecasting situation. A traditional equation for w_t might, for example, take the form

$$\hat{w}_t = \hat{k}_1 x_t + \hat{k}_2 y_t + \hat{k}_3 w_{t-1} \tag{16.4}$$

where the $\hat{k}$s are estimated coefficients. In (16.4) current values of x and y are included on the right-hand side. This means that before a forecast for w_{t+1} can be made, we require knowledge of x_{t+1} and y_{t+1}. Future values of these variables must first be forecast, so that our forecast for w_{t+1} will be heavily dependent on how well we can forecast x_{t+1} and y_{t+1}.

VARs are also used for policy analysis. By this, we mean the analysis of the effect of random shocks on the various variables in the model.[5] Random shocks are represented by sudden changes in the disturbances. The problem is that, as we noted earlier, the various disturbances (or 'innovations' in VAR terminology) in the model are contemporaneously correlated. Therefore it makes no sense to change one without changing the others. For example, if one of the equations in a model referred to the money supply, we could not analyse the effect on the system of a random shock to this equation (representing maybe a sudden government decision to print more money) without introducing random shocks in the other equations.

To get round this problem, VAR researchers transform their models into ones that involve **orthogonal innovations**. By this, we mean that the transformed model contains disturbances that are contemporaneously *uncorrelated*. This is most easily explained by considering a simple two-equation VAR:

$$x_t = a_1 x_{t-1} + b_1 y_{t-1} + \epsilon_{1t}, \qquad \text{Var}(\epsilon_{1t}) = \text{E}(\epsilon_{1t}^2) = \sigma_1^2 \qquad (16.5)$$

$$y_t = a_2 x_{t-1} + b_2 y_{t-1} + \epsilon_{2t}, \qquad \text{Var}(\epsilon_{2t}) = \text{E}(\epsilon_{2t}^2) = \sigma_2^2 \qquad (16.6)$$

Suppose $\text{Cov}(\epsilon_{1t}, \epsilon_{2t}) = \text{E}(\epsilon_{1t}\epsilon_{2t}) = k \neq 0$; that is, ϵ_{1t} and ϵ_{2t} are correlated. To transform the model into one with orthogonal innovations, we multiply (16.5) by k/σ_1^2 and subtract the resultant equation from (16.6). This gives

$$y_t = \frac{k}{\sigma_1^2} x_t + \left(a_2 - a_1 \frac{k}{\sigma_1^2}\right) x_{t-1} + \left(b_2 - b_1 \frac{k}{\sigma_1^2}\right) y_{t-1} + u_t \qquad (16.7)$$

where $u_t = \epsilon_{2t} - (k/\sigma_1^2)\epsilon_{1t}$. Equations (16.5) and (16.7) constitute the transformed model. The disturbances in these equations, ϵ_{1t} and u_t, are uncorrelated, because

$$\text{Cov}(\epsilon_{1t}, u_t) = \text{E}(\epsilon_{1t} u_t) = \text{E}(\epsilon_{1t}\epsilon_{2t}) - \frac{k}{\sigma_1^2} \text{E}(\epsilon_{1t}^2)$$

$$= k - k = 0$$

In larger VARs the transformations required to produce orthogonal innovations are obviously more complicated, but the required model can always be obtained by premultiplying (16.1) by an appropriate matrix.

Now that the innovations are orthogonal, it is possible to introduce a random shock into one equation in the transformed model without the need to introduce related shocks into other equations. Thus equations in the model can be used separately for policy evaluation. This procedure has, however, come in for considerable criticism. There is evidence that the results of such policy analysis may be sensitive to the ordering of the equations in the VAR. This affects the transformations necessary to obtain orthogonal innovations. More importantly, as pointed out by Cooley and LeRoy (1985), it is not possible to give a clear unambiguous meaning to the orthogonal innovations of the transformed model.

VAR models are sometimes termed 'atheoretical' since they are not based on any economic theory. Since initially no restrictions are placed on any of the parameters in any of the equations in the model, in effect 'everything causes everything'. However, inference is performed on the estimated model, so that coefficients that are not significantly different from zero may eventually be dropped.

This may lead to models that are consistent with quite specific theories. Such inference is normally carried out using what are termed **causality tests**.

Testing for causality

Causality in econometrics is a somewhat different concept to that in everyday philosophical use. It refers more to the ability to predict. Econometricians refer to **Granger causality** (see Granger, 1969), which is defined as follows.

*X is said to be a **Granger cause** of Y if present Y can be predicted with greater accuracy by using past values of X rather than not using such past values, all other information being identical.*

The problem with this definition is not so much that it does not correspond to everyday notions but that it involves the somewhat vague concept of 'all other information'. In practice, this has to mean any information in the model that is deemed relevant.

The two best known tests for Granger causality are the **Granger test** and the **Sims test**. The Granger test may be illustrated by considering the following equation:

$$y_t = \alpha_0 + \alpha_1 y_{t-1} + \alpha_2 y_{t-2} + \alpha_3 y_{t-3} + \beta_1 x_{t-1} + \beta_2 x_{t-2} + \beta_3 x_{t-3} + \epsilon_t \qquad (16.8)$$

A longer lag length can be used if it is considered appropriate. Given the above definition, if $\beta_1 = \beta_2 = \beta_3 = 0$ then x does not Granger-cause y. On the other hand, if any of the β coefficients are non-zero then x does Granger-cause y.

The hypothesis $\beta_1 = \beta_2 = \beta_3 = 0$ may be tested using the F test of Section 9.2. It is simply necessary first to estimate (16.8) as it stands and then to estimate a restricted equation from which the x variables have been omitted. The F statistic can then be calculated from the residual sums of squares obtained for the two equations.

In the context of the VAR models introduced earlier, this test might be applied to, for example, y_{t-1} and y_{t-2} in the first of Equations (16.2). That is, H_0: $a_{13} = b_{13} = 0$ would be F-tested. Failure to reject H_0 in this case would imply that y did not Granger-cause w and would lead to the dropping of the y variables from the equation. VAR models can therefore be simplified in this way so that, although they are initially completely atheoretical, they eventually may take a form supportive of one theory rather than another.

The Sims test for causality

Another well-known test for Granger causality is that of Sims, which makes use of the fact that in any general notion of causality the future cannot cause the present. Suppose that as above we wish to determine whether x Granger-causes y. In the Sims test, instead of estimating (16.8), we estimate

$$\begin{aligned} x_t = \gamma_0 + \gamma_1 x_{t-1} + \gamma_2 x_{t-2} + \gamma_3 x_{t-3} + \delta_1 y_{t+3} + \delta_2 y_{t+2} + \delta_3 y_{t+1} \\ + \delta_4 y_{t-1} + \delta_5 y_{t-2} + \delta_6 y_{t-3} + \epsilon_t \end{aligned} \qquad (16.9)$$

Notice that in (16.9) x rather than y is the dependent variable and *leading* values of y, that is, $y_{t+1}, y_{t+2}, y_{t+3}$, are included. If x Granger-causes y then we expect some relationship between x and leading values of y. Thus it should not be the case that $\delta_1 = \delta_2 = \delta_3 = 0$. Notice that non-zero values for any of δ_1, δ_2 and δ_3 cannot be interpreted as implying that causation runs from the leading values of y to x. The future cannot cause the present. Non-zero δs must imply that causation runs from x to the leading y values. Therefore if we F-test H_0: $\delta_1 = \delta_2 = \delta_3 = 0$, rejection of H_0 must imply that x is a Granger cause of y. To carry out the test, we simply estimate (16.9) as it stands and then estimate a restricted equation with the leading y values omitted.

It is unclear which of the two tests for causality is superior, although the Sims test has the disadvantage that, because of the need to include leading values, it uses up more degrees of freedom. In practice, most researchers employ both tests.

One practical difficulty in testing for causality concerns the lag length to be used. In fact, varying the maximum lag length often leads to different test results. It is almost certainly best to include as many lags as are necessary to ensure non-autocorrelated residuals. Otherwise, the combination of autocorrelation and lagged dependent variables will invalidate the F tests.

COMPUTER EXERCISE I

In this exercise we will employ the Granger and Sims tests to examine the direction of causality between UK disposable income Y and UK consumer expenditure C, using the quarterly series for 1974Q1 through 1984Q4 in Data Set 4 on the floppy disk. We shall test whether Y Granger-causes C.

The question of whether income 'causes' consumption is not as straightforward as it sounds. Both the major theories of the consumption function – the life-cycle hypothesis and the permanent income hypothesis – suggest that current consumption depends not so much on current disposable income as on some measure of total lifetime resources. Indeed Hall (1978) presents a rational expectations version of the life-cycle hypothesis that suggests that changes in consumption are entirely random and not related to income changes at all.

Using a maximum lag of three quarters, we first apply the Granger test and estimate a version of (16.8) using data for 1974Q4 through 1984Q4. The observations for the first three quarters of 1974 are required for the lagged values:

$$\hat{C}_t = -3686 + 0.520C_{t-1} + 0.543C_{t-2} + 0.049C_{t-3} + 0.312Y_{t-1}$$
$$\phantom{\hat{C}_t =} (-1.71) \quad (2.69) \qquad (2.76) \qquad (0.25) \qquad (2.28)$$

$$-0.296Y_{t-2} - 0.100Y_{t-3} + \text{seasonal dummy variables} \qquad (16.10)$$
$$(-1.99) \qquad (-0.70)$$

$$R^2 = 0.962, \qquad \sum e^2 = 1.72 \times 10^7, \qquad z_1 = 0.39, \qquad z_4 = 1.69$$

z_1 and z_4 are the LM statistics for first- and up to fourth-order autocorrelation. To apply the Granger test for causality, re-estimate (16.10) with the lagged y variables omitted. You should find that this results in an increase in the residual sum of squares to $\sum e^2 = 2.24 \times 10^7$. The F statistic (9.19) yields a value of 3.1, which exceeds the critical value (with [3,31] d.f.) of $F_{0.05} = 2.91$. Thus the test suggests that Y Granger-causes C.

To apply the Sims test, we estimate a version of (16.9), this time using data for 1974Q4 through 198Q1. The observations for the last three quarters of 1984 are required to form three leading values of C:

$$\hat{Y}_t = -2204 - 0.386C_{t-1} + 0.535C_{t-2} - 0.025C_{t-3}$$
$$\quad (-0.67)\ (-1.36) \quad\quad (1.98) \quad\quad (-0.09)$$

$$+\ 0.522Y_{t-1} + 0.276Y_{t-2} - 0.263Y_{t-3}$$
$$\quad (2.81) \quad\quad (1.34) \quad\quad (-1.31)$$

$$+\ 0.530C_{t+1} + 0.035C_{t+2} - 0.106C_{t+3} \quad\quad (16.11)$$
$$\quad (2.00) \quad\quad (0.14) \quad\quad (-0.48)$$

$$R^2 = 0.950, \quad \sum e^2 = 2.05 \times 10^7, \quad z_1 = 0.002, \quad z_4 = 4.41$$

Dropping the leading values for C from (16.11) should result in an increase in $\sum e^2$ to 2.58×10^7. The F statistic (9.19) takes a value of 2.14, whereas the critical value for F (with [3,25] d.f.) is $F_{0.05} = 2.99$. Thus dropping the leading C values is not rejected by the data. Unlike the Granger test, the Sims test therefore suggests that Y does not Granger-cause C!

Our tests suggest that it is unclear whether or not Y Granger-causes C. The reader should now see whether causation runs the other way. It seems likely that this may be so, since, in aggregate data, C is a major component of GDP, which in turn largely determines disposable income Y. Apply the Granger and Sims test to the data to determine whether C Granger-causes Y.

16.2   Exogeneity

We introduced the distinction between endogenous and exogenous variables in Section 8.3, when discussing simultaneous equation systems. Generally speaking, endogenous variables are those variables whose values are determined inside or by the model or system of equations being studied. Exogenous variables, on the other hand, are variables whose values are determined outside the model or system being studied. This somewhat vague definition of exogeneity has not satisfied modern econometricians, and nowadays various degrees of exogeneity are frequently defined and discussed. In particular, econometricians tend to ask the question 'exogenous for what purpose?' It is well to be familiar with some of the terminology in use.

To illustrate some of the concepts and distinctions involved, consider the following two-equation model, in which, for simplicity of exposition, we have dispensed with intercept terms:

$$y_t = \alpha_1 x_t + u_t \tag{16.12}$$

$$x_t = \alpha_2 y_t + \beta_2 y_{t-1} + v_t \tag{16.13}$$

The disturbances u_t and v_t in (16.12) and (16.13) are assumed to be serially uncorrelated and to be uncorrelated with each other.

The above model jointly determines the *current* values of x and y for any given *past* value of y_t and for given values of the disturbances, that is, for given y_{t-1}, u_t and v_t. Notice that, unlike the two-equation models of Section 8.3, the model contains no 'exogenous' variables. Instead, the role of exogenous variable(s) is played by the **lagged endogenous variable** y_{t-1}. For example, to find a reduced form, we have to solve (16.12) and (16.13) for x_t and y_t, expressing these variables in terms of their lagged values and the disturbances.

The reduced form of the above model is most easily formed by first substituting for x_t in (16.12) and solving for y_t to obtain

$$y_t = \left(\frac{\alpha_1 \beta_2}{1 - \alpha_1 \alpha_2}\right) y_{t-1} + \frac{\alpha_1 v_t + u_t}{1 - \alpha_1 \alpha_2} \tag{16.14}$$

Secondly, substituting for y_t in (16.13) yields

$$x_t = \left(\frac{\beta_2}{1 - \alpha_1 \alpha_2}\right) y_{t-1} + \frac{v_t + \alpha_2 u_t}{1 - \alpha_1 \alpha_2} \tag{16.15}$$

The reduced-form equations differ slightly from those of Section 8.3, in that they contain a lagged endogenous variable rather than exogenous variables on the right-hand side. In general, both lagged endognous and exogenous variables may appear as regressors in reduced-form equations. For example, if an exogenous variable z appeared in either (16.12) or (16.13) then, in addition to the lagged endogenous variable y_{t-1}, this variable would also appear in both reduced-form equations.

We now use the model (16.12)/(16.13) and its reduced form (16.14)/(16.15) to illustrate some of the distinctions that econometricians make between different degrees of exogeneity. We concentrate on the variable x_t in Equation (16.12). Its coefficient α_1 is therefore the **parameter of interest**.

First note that, in the model as it stands, x_t in Equation (16.12) is correlated with the disturbance u_t in that equation. We can see this from the reduced-form equation (16.15). In fact, we have what we referred to in Section 8.1 as the contemporaneously correlated case. In such a situation x_t can in no way be described as exogenous. It is endogenous, being jointly determined with y_t, and the OLS estimate of α_1 in (16.12) will be biased and inconsistent.

We now point out and distinguish between cases where x_t in Equation (16.12) is said to be **predetermined** for this equation and cases where x_t is said to be **strictly**

exogenous. Suppose that the parameter α_2 in Equation (16.13) is zero. The reduced-form Equation (16.15) then becomes

$$x_t = \beta_2 y_{t-1} + v_t \tag{16.16}$$

It can be seen from (16.16) that x_t is now no longer contemporaneously correlated with u_t, the disturbance in (16.12). However, it is not totally independent of u_t. From (16.12), u_{t-1} affects y_{t-1}, which in turn influences x_t via Equation (16.13), provided β_2 is non-zero. Thus x_t is *not influenced by present and future values of u_t but is influenced by a past value of u_t*. When this is the case, x_t is said to be **predetermined** in Equation (16.12). In fact, we have the second of the three cases outlined in Section 8.1, that is, the contemporaneously uncorrelated case. In this situation we know that the OLS estimator of α_1 in (16.12) will be biased in small samples but consistent.

Suppose now that not only $\alpha_2 = 0$ in (16.13) but also $\beta_2 = 0$. x_t is now not only independent of present and future values of u_t *but also of past values*. It is independent of u_{t-1} because, although u_{t-1} still affects y_{t-1}, the link between y_{t-1} and x_t via Equation (16.13) has been broken since $\beta_2 = 0$. In this situation x_t is said to be **strictly exogenous** in Equation (16.12). We now have what in Section 8.1 we termed the independence case, and the OLS estimator of α_1 in (16.12) is unbiased as well as consistent.

A somewhat different distinction between degrees of exogeneity is that made by Engle, Hendry and Richard (1983). Consider again the model (16.12)/(16.13) and again treat α_1 as the parameter of interest. It is of interest because we wish to estimate its magnitude, or because we wish to make use of it to forecast future values of y_t using Equation (16.12), or because we wish to make use of it in policy simulations.

Suppose we wish merely to obtain a consistent and asymptotically efficient estimate of α_1. All that is necessary for this is that $\alpha_2 = 0$ in Equation (16.13). We saw that, in this circumstance, x_t and u_t were contemporaneously uncorrelated in Equation (16.12). Thus OLS estimation of (16.12) will provide the desired estimate of α_1. In the Engle–Hendry–Richard terminology, x_t is then said to be **weakly exogenous** for the estimation of α_1.

Suppose, however, that we also wish to make use of our estimate of α_1 to forecast future values of y_t for a given set of future values of x_t. Under what circumstances is it possible to use Equation (16.12) independently of Equation (16.13) to do this? If it is simply the case that $\alpha_2 = 0$ but $\beta_2 \neq 0$ in (16.13) then we cannot arbitrarily select any set of future x_t values. Once we select, for example, x_{t+1}, this gives us a forecast of y_{t+1} using an estimated version of Equation (16.12). But, if $\beta_2 \neq 0$ in Equation (16.13), this implies a definite value for x_{t+2} via this equation. There is a 'feedback' effect of y on x. We cannot select any value we wish for x_{t+2}. In other words, *we cannot use Equation (16.12) for forecasting purposes in isolation from Equation (16.13)*. To be able to do this, it is necessary that the parameter $\beta_2 = 0$ as well as $\alpha_2 = 0$ in Equation (16.13). This would rule out the above feedback effect. In Engle–Hendry–Richard terminology, when $\alpha_2 = \beta_2 = 0$, x_t is said to be **strongly exogenous** in Equation (16.12).

It may seem that the obvious way to test for weak or strong exogeneity is to estimate Equation (16.13) and then test whether the parameters α_2 and β_2 are indeed zero. But it will often be the case that we will not know the exact specification of Equation (16.13). That is, while we may be confident about the form of an equation such as (16.12), we may have little knowledge of other equation(s) in the model. Other methods of testing for exogeneity must then be employed.

To test whether x_t is weakly exogenous in Equation (16.12), it is simply necessary to test whether x_t and the disturbance u_t are contemporaneously uncorrelated, using the Hausman test of Section 12.1.[6] However, to test whether x_t is strongly exogenous, we also need to check for any feedback between y_{t-1} and x_t. This can be done by testing for Granger causality in the manner of the last section. For x_t to be strongly exogenous in (16.12), it is necessary that y_{t-1} should not Granger-cause x_t. Otherwise, a feedback effect would exist.

Engle, Hendry and Richard also distinguish a situation where x_t in Equation (16.12) is not only strongly exogenous but **superexogenous**. This relates to the Lucas (1976) critique of economic policy evaluation. Suppose it was wished to use Equation (16.12) not simply for forecasting, but for a simulation analysis of the effect of various governmental policy changes. Lucas argued that the structure of many econometric equations cannot remain unchanged under different government policy regimes. Economic agents are conscious of policy changes, and are likely to vary their behaviour in response to such changes. For example, the manner in which they form their expectations concerning the future value of key economic variables will not be invariant to policy changes. Hence it is quite possible that the *true* value of the parameter α_1 might change in response to government policy. Under such circumstances, we could hardly use a version of (16.12), estimated under one policy regime, to analyse the effect of policy changes under another regime.

In the special circumstances where a parameter such as α_1 in (16.12) *does* remain invariant to government policy changes, the estimated relationship between x_t and y_t *can* be used for policy simulations. In Engle–Hendry–Richard terminology, x_t in Equation (16.12) is then said to be superexogenous.

16.3   Influential observations and robust estimators

Data sets can sometimes contain individual observation(s) that have a disproportionate influence on the sample regression equation that is fitted to them. This is particularly the case if the method of estimation is ordinary least squares. The problem is most easily illustrated in the case of two-variable regression.

Consider the scatter diagram in Figure 16.1. Most of the observations appear to lie close to some underlying linear population regression line, but one observation is far removed from the remainder. This observation is certain to have a large residual, whatever method is used to fit a line to the scatter. However, if the method of

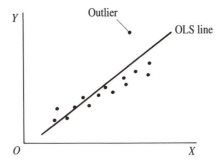

Figure 16.1 An outlier.

estimation is OLS then, since OLS minimizes the sum of the *squares* of the residuals, such large residuals have a major influence on the OLS line that is fitted. In Figure 16.1, for example, the OLS line fitted to the scatter has been 'dragged' towards the outlying observation. If this unusual point were removed from the scatter then an OLS line fitted to the remaining points would be considerably different from that illustrated.

One obvious way to detect 'outliers' such as that in Figure 16.1 is to apply OLS in the usual way and examine the residuals from this regression. Outliers should then show up as observations with unusually large residuals. A limitation of this approach, however, is that, since the OLS line is 'dragged' towards the outlying observation (as in Figure 16.1), this disguises the fact that we have an outlier. This is a particular danger in multiple regression when it is not possible to display the data set in a simple scatter diagram.

A better way to detect outliers is to investigate each observation at a time, running an OLS regression with the relevant observation *excluded*, and testing whether the prediction error for that observation is significantly large. This can be most easily done by including an **observation-specific dummy variable**. For example, to investigate the *i*th observation in a data set, we define a dummy taking a value of unity for the *i*th observation and zero for all other observations. If we include this dummy in the OLS regression, its coefficient will equal the required prediction error. To test the prediction error for significance, we can examine its *t* ratio. This *t* ratio is often referred to as a **Studentized residual**.

Outliers of the above kind are an example of what are termed **influential observations**. However, outliers are not the only kind of such observation. An outlier is an observation with an unusual value for the dependent variable. But explanatory variables can also take unusual values. Consider the scatter in Figure 16.2, in which one observation has an *X* value radically different from all other *X* values. The OLS line fitted to the full scatter is illustrated in the figure. It should be obvious that the unusual observation will have a major influence both on the line that is fitted and on any measures of goodness of fit associated with the line. The OLS line fitted in the absence of the unusual observation would have very different properties.

Observations such as that illustrated in Figure 16.2 are known as **leverage points**. They are best detected by considering each observation at a time and then

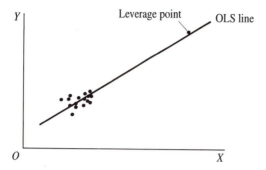

Figure 16.2 A leverage point.

running OLS regressions first with the observation included and then with it excluded. If there is any major difference in the OLS estimates and their associated statistics then this suggests a possible leverage point.

The obvious question arises of what should be done once an unusual observation has been detected. If the observation can be connected with some unusual circumstance such as a hurricane then the observation could be discarded or the unusual circumstance could be allowed for by including a dummy variable. Otherwise, however, excluding unusual observations from the data set will almost certainly be a mistake. A problem with economic data sets is often that variables of interest do not vary sufficiently for us to be able to assess their influence. That is, observations are often not unusual enough! The occasional unusual observation therefore enriches the data set, and may well reflect some aspect of economic behaviour that enables the specification and statistical properties of an equation to be improved.

For these reasons, most econometricians like to retain unusual observations in their data sets. However, because OLS is so sensitive to such observations, other methods of estimation are sometimes employed. We now turn briefly to these methods.

Robust estimators

OLS is a method of estimation specifically tailored to suit the assumptions of the classical regression model. Consequently it is particularly sensitive to violation of the classical assumptions. It is therefore sometimes wise to make use of estimation methods, which, while not the equal of OLS under classical assumptions, are less sensitive to such violations. Estimators of this type are referred to as **robust estimators**.

Many of these robust estimators are designed specifically to be insensitive to violations in assumption IID of the classical model – that which requires the disturbances to be normally distributed. Recall that the consequence of such a violation (assuming all other assumptions remain valid) was that the OLS estimators lost the property of efficiency, although they remained best linear unbiased. Unfortunately, for some non-normally distributed disturbances, the OLS estimators, although still BLUE, are very much less efficient than certain nonlinear unbiased estimators. This may reflect a distribution of the disturbances that is non-normal in the sense that it is 'fat-tailed'. That is, there is a greater probability of getting disturbances that are very different from zero than there is when the distribution is normal. It is in these situations that econometricians consider making use of robust estimators that are less sensitive than OLS to the occasional outlier in the data set.

A simple example of robust estimation is the **least absolute residual** (LAR) **method,** also known as the **mean absolute deviation** (MAD) **method**. In this case estimators of regression line parameters are chosen so as to minimize the sum of the absolute values of the residuals rather than the sum of their squares as in OLS. If this method is adopted then large residuals have less influence on the sample regression equation that is fitted to the data.

LAR estimators can be regarded as special cases of two more general types of robust estimator. First, M estimators are those that minimize a weighted sum of the absolute values of the residuals. That is, we minimize

$$S^* = \sum w_i |e_i| \tag{16.17}$$

OLS is a special case of the M estimators in which the weights in S^* are set equal to the absolute values of the residuals. We then have $S^* = \sum e_i^2$. Normally, however, the weights in S^* are chosen so that they do not increase in size as $|e_i|$ increases. One possibility is to set each weight equal to unity. We then have the above LAR estimator. Alternatively, the weights can be made a declining function of the $|e_i|$.

The LAR estimator is also a special case of the L_p estimator. In an L_p estimator what is minimized is the sum of the absolute residuals raised to the power p. That is, we minimize

$$S' = \sum |e_i|^p \tag{16.18}$$

The value of p in S' is usually given a value between 1 and 2. With $p = 1$ we have the LAR estimator, whereas with $p = 2$ we have the OLS estimator. The smaller the value chosen for p, the less influence is given to outlying observations.

Robust estimators can also involve the squares of the residuals as well as their absolute values. For example, **bounded influence estimators** minimize a weighted sum of the squared residuals where the weights are selected so that they limit or bound an outlying observation's influence on the estimators. Details of the selection of the weights, however, lie beyond our scope.

16.4   Qualitative dependent variables

We saw in Section 9.4 how it was often very useful to be able to include dummy variables among the explanatory variables of a regression equation to represent qualitative factors. However, dummy variables can also be used as dependent variables. For example, we might be interested in whether or not a household possesses an automobile. We could therefore define the qualitative dependent variable

$D_i = 1$ if ith household owns an automobile

$D_i = 0$ if ith household does not own an automobile

Whether a household owns an automobile will depend on a number of factors: its income, its age, its size, its location etc. However, for simplicity of exposition, let us assume that D_i is a linear function of just one variable X_{2i}, the income of household i. That is,

$$D_i = \beta_1 + \beta_2 X_{2i} + \epsilon_i \quad \text{for all } i \tag{16.19}$$

where ϵ_i, as usual, is a disturbance. Assuming $E(\epsilon_i) = 0$, we then have, for given X_{2i},

$$E(D_i) = \beta_1 + \beta_2 X_{2i} \tag{16.20}$$

The expected value of qualitative variables such as D_i has an interesting interpretation. Let $P_i = \Pr(D_i = 1)$. Since D_i can only take the value 0 or 1, it follows that $\Pr(D_i = 0) = 1 - P_i$. Thus

$$E(D_i) = 1 . \Pr(D_i = 1) + 0 . \Pr(D_i = 0) = 1 . P_i + 0 . (1 - P_i) = P_i \tag{16.21}$$

That is, $E(D_i)$ is simply the probability that household i owns an automobile. We can therefore rewrite (16.20) as

$$P_i = \beta_1 + \beta_2 X_{2i} \quad \text{for all } i \tag{16.22}$$

Equation (16.22) is referred to as the **linear probability model**. Given estimates of β_1 and β_2, it enables us to estimate the probability that a household with given income X_{2i} will possess an automobile.

The linear probability model could be estimated by OLS. However, this raises a number of problems. First, the disturbances cannot be normally distributed. In fact, they must have a binomial distribution. Using (16.19),

if $D_i = 1$ then $\epsilon_i = 1 - \beta_1 - \beta_2 X_{2i}$

if $D_i = 0$ then $\epsilon_i = -\beta_1 - \beta_2 X_{2i}$

Thus ϵ_i takes only the above two values with probabilities P_i and $1 - P_i$ respectively.

More importantly, the disturbance is heteroskedastic. That is, $\text{Var}(\epsilon_i)$ is not a constant. In fact, if $E(\epsilon_i) = 0$,

$$\text{Var}(\epsilon_i) = E(\epsilon_i^2) = P_i(\text{value of } \epsilon_i \text{ when } D_i = 1)^2$$
$$+ (1 - P_i)(\text{value of } \epsilon_i \text{ when } D_i = 0)^2$$
$$= P_i(1 - \beta_1 - \beta_2 X_{2i})^2 + (1 - P_i)(-\beta_1 - \beta_2 X_{2i})^2 \tag{16.23}$$

However, from (16.22), $\beta_1 + \beta_2 X_{2i} = P_i$. Hence

$$\text{Var}(\epsilon_i) = P_i(1 - P_i)^2 + (1 - P_i)P_i^2$$
$$= P_i(1 - P_i) \tag{16.24}$$

Thus, since its variance depends on P_i, which varies from household to household as income varies, the disturbance is heteroskedastic. This means that, although OLS estimation of (16.20) will yield unbiased estimators of β_1 and β_2, these estimators will not be BLUE. Moreover, estimated standard errors will now be biased, so the standard OLS inferential procedures will be invalid.

It is possible to deal with the heteroskedasticity problem by adapting the weighted average regression technique described in Section 10.3. However, the non-normality of the disturbance means that the usual t tests etc. still cannot be relied upon in small samples.

There is, moreover, a further problem with the linear probability model. Suppose we estimate (16.22) by a sample regression equation

$$\hat{P}_i = \hat{\beta}_1 + \hat{\beta}_2 X_{2i} \tag{16.25}$$

It is quite possible for (16.25) to yield values of $\hat{P}_i$, that is, estimates of the probability that a household possesses an automobile, that lie outside the range 0 to 1. Figure 16.3 illustrates the problem. Since D_i can take the values 0 or 1 only, a scatter diagram in this situation will consist of just two horizontal rows of points. OLS will fit a line to these points similar to the one drawn in Figure 16.3. Such a line will have a negative intercept, so that for low levels of income X_{2i}, it will yield negative $\hat{P}_i$. Also, for sufficiently high levels of income, this sample regression line can yield probabilities in excess of unity.

Figure 16.3 also indicates that the coefficient of determination, R^2, for the linear probability model is likely to be low. In fact, it is obvious that no straight line could fit the scatter in Figure 16.3 well. R^2 is not a good measure of equation performance when the dependent variable is a qualitative dummy.

A further problem arises when fitting a straight line to scatters such as that in Figure 16.3. A linear function implies that a given rise in income always results in the same rise in P_i, regardless of the level of income. For example, if our line has a slope $\beta_2 = 0.2$, and we measure income in thousands of dollars, then a rise in income from 10 to 11 will result in an increase in the probability that a household owns an automobile of 0.2. This may be reasonable, but, with a linear function, it is also the case that a rise in income from 19 to 20 will increase the probability by that same 0.2. In practice, we might expect that the probability of owning an automobile would

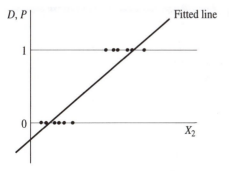

Figure 16.3 The linear probability model.

increase quite rapidly at low levels of income but that there would come a point when further income rises had little effect.

One approach to combating the problems of the linear probability model is to define a **latent variable** $Y*$ given by

$$Y_i^* = \beta_1 + \beta_2 X_{2i} + \epsilon_i \qquad (16.26)$$

In our example of automobile ownership $Y*$ might be an unobservable index of the willingness, ability or desire to own an automobile. Thus, instead of (16.20) in the linear probability model, we now have

$$E(Y_i^*) = \beta_1 + \beta_2 X_{2i} \qquad (16.27)$$

where X_2 is again household income. In practice, we might add additional explanatory variables to (16.27). Obvious examples are household location, social status, age etc.

It is necessary to link the unobservable $Y*$ to the observable dummy variable D given above. We can do this simply by specifying

$$D_i = 1 \quad \text{if } Y_i^* > 0$$
$$D_i = 0 \quad \text{if } Y_i^* < 0$$

Zero is therefore a threshold value for the index $Y*$. If $Y*$ rises above zero for a household then that household becomes an automobile owner.

Unlike in the linear probability model $P_i = \Pr(D_i = 1)$ is not now given by (16.22). To obtain an expression for P_i, note that

$$\begin{aligned} P_i = \Pr(D_i = 1) &= \Pr(Y_i^* > 0) \\ &= \Pr(\beta_1 + \beta_2 X_{2i} + \epsilon_i > 0) \quad \text{(using (16.26))} \\ &= \Pr[\epsilon_i > -(\beta_1 + \beta_2 X_{2i})] \end{aligned} \qquad (16.28)$$

If the ϵ_i distribution is symmetrical with $E(\epsilon_i) = 0$ then

$$\Pr[\epsilon_i > -(\beta_1 + \beta_2 X_{2i})] = \Pr(\epsilon_i < \beta_1 + \beta_2 X_{2i})$$

Thus we obtain

$$P_i = \Pr(D_i = 1) = \Pr(\epsilon_i < \beta_1 + \beta_2 X_{2i}) \qquad (16.29)$$

Equation (16.29) implies that P_i depends on the manner in which the ϵ_i are distributed.[7] If the ϵ_i are assumed to be normally distributed then a model known as the **probit model** results. However, the probability (16.29) is somewhat complicated to work out in this case, and most researchers prefer to represent Equation (16.29) by the so-called **logistic function**. This leads to the **logit model**.

The logit model

If a logistic function is used in (16.29) then we have

$$P_i = \frac{1}{1 + \exp[-(\beta_1 + \beta_2 X_{2i} + \epsilon_i)]} \quad \text{for all } i \qquad (16.30)$$

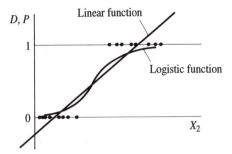

Figure 16.4 The logistic function.

Equation (16.30) constrains P_i to lie between 0 and 1 as required, because, given $\beta_2 > 0$, as $X_{2i} \to \infty, P_i \to 1$, and as $X_{2i} \to -\infty, P_i \to 0$. Equation (16.30) is compared with (16.22) of the linear probability model in Figure 16.4.

It is easy to see that

$$1 - P_i = \frac{\exp\left[-(\beta_1 + \beta_2 X_{2i} + \epsilon_i)\right]}{1 + \exp\left[-(\beta_1 + \beta_2 X_{2i} + \epsilon_1)\right]}$$

so that[8]

$$\ln\left(\frac{P_i}{1 - P_i}\right) = \beta_1 + \beta_2 X_{2i} + \epsilon_i \tag{16.31}$$

The quantity $P_i/(1 - P_i)$ is known as the **odds ratio** and its natural logarithm as the **logit**. For example, if the probability of a household possessing an automobile is 0.75 then the odds ratio is $0.75/0.25 = 3/1$, or odds of three to one that a car is possessed. Obviously, it is a simple matter to generalize (16.31) by including additional explanatory variables. In general,

$$\ln\left(\frac{P_i}{1 - P_i}\right) = \beta_1 + \beta_2 X_{2i} + \beta_3 X_{3i} + \cdots + \beta_k X_{ki} + \epsilon_i \tag{16.32}$$

Notice that in the logit model (16.31), P_i is not linearly related to X_{2i} as in the linear probability model. This is clear from Figure 16.4, and, in fact, differentiation of (16.31) with respect to X_{2i} yields

$$\frac{dP_i}{dX_{2i}} \frac{1}{P_i} + \frac{dP_i}{dX_{2i}} \frac{1}{(1 - P_i)} = \beta_2$$

Hence

$$\frac{dP_i}{dX_{2i}} = \beta_2 P_i (1 - P_i) \tag{16.33}$$

Equation (16.33) implies that as P_i rises towards unity, its response to a unit change in income X_{2i} becomes smaller and smaller. Thus the logit model avoids the problem of linearity implicit in the linear probability model.

Estimation of the logit model

Estimation of the logit model (16.32) is not straightforward. Actual values of P_i are equal to either 1 or 0 (for example, if a household owns a car then $P_i = \Pr(D_i = 1) = 1$, and if a household does not own a car $P_i = 0$). Hence the logit, given by the left-hand side of (16.32), either equals $\ln(1/0)$ or $\ln(0/1)$, neither of which is defined.

If the sample available is large then one possible approach is to first group the data. In our automobile example we might classify households according to their income. We can then estimate P_i by the proportion of households in group i who own an automobile. This enables us to calculate the logit for group i, while for X_{2i} we can use the mean income of households in group i. Like the linear probability model, however, the logit model is heteroskedastic, so that a weighted least squares procedure is necessary if efficient estimators are to be obtained.

If it is not feasible to group the data then a maximum likelihood estimation approach has to be adopted. This will provide consistent estimators of the β coefficients in (16.31) and (16.32). Suppose the sample is random and contains m households that possess an automobile out of a total of n. If we number the automobile owning households as $1, 2, 3, \ldots, m$ then the log-likelihood function takes the form

$$l = \sum_{i=1}^{m} \ln(P_i) + \sum_{i=m+1}^{n} \ln(1 - P_i) \tag{16.34}$$

where the P_i are given by (16.30). For a given sample, the likelihood function depends on β_1 and β_2 in (16.31), or, in the general case, on all the βs in (16.32), and therefore may be maximized with respect to these coefficients. However, the equations obtained when the derivatives of the log-likelihood function are set equal to zero are nonlinear, and have to be solved by numerical methods. Computer algorithms for this are readily available, and there are a number of 'canned' computer packages for the ML estimation of logit models. Such packages will also provide estimated standard errors for regression coefficients.

Once equations such as (16.31) and (16.32) have been estimated, the MLEs of the β coefficients can be substituted into Equation (16.30) or its multiple regression equivalent, and estimated probabilities obtained for any values of the explanatory variables.

Closeness of fit

As with the linear probability model, measures such as R^2 are inappropriate as measures of goodness of fit for logit models. Alternative measures based on the ML estimation process have been proposed. Suppose we place the restriction

$$\beta_2 = \beta_3 = \cdots = \beta_k = 0 \tag{16.35}$$

on the logit equation (16.32). In normal OLS regression we would F-test such a restriction using the test statistic (9.19). Recall, though, that this is effectively a test of the size of R^2, and, as we have noted, R^2 is not an appropriate measure for logit models.

A suitable alternative is to use an LR test similar to that described in Section 9.3. First (16.32) is estimated by ML and the maximized likelihood found. Next, the restrictions (16.35) are imposed to give the restricted equation

$$\ln\left(\frac{P_i}{1 - P_i}\right) = \beta_1 + \epsilon_i \tag{16.36}$$

Equation (16.36) is now also estimated by ML and the maximized likelihood for this restricted equation found. The restrictions (16.35) may then be tested using the test statistic (9.42), with degrees of freedom equal to the number of explanatory variables in the model.

McFadden (1974) has suggested an alternative to R^2 as a measure of goodness of fit for logit models, based on the above test. The McFadden pseudo-R^2 is defined as

$$\text{pseudo-}R^2 = 1 - l_U/l_R \tag{16.37}$$

where l_U and l_R are the maximized likelihoods for Equations (16.32) and (16.36) respectively. Since l_R is always less than l_U, like the normal R^2 the pseudo-R^2 must always lie between 0 and 1. Unfortunately, the pseudo-R^2 does not have the interpretation 'explained variation/total variation' that the normal R^2 has for OLS regression. Most researchers therefore simply rely on the likelihood ratio test for assessing closeness of fit.

COMPUTER EXERCISE II

In this exercise we will make use of the series in Data Set 5 on the floppy disk to estimate a linear probability model and a logit model. Data Set 5, previously used in Section 10.3, contains data on the years of full-time schooling S, the age A and the hourly earnings E of a cross-section of 50 households. Also in the data set is information on the newspaper-reading habits of the household. The dummy variable D is defined as

$D_i = 1$ if household i reads a 'quality' newspaper

$D_i = 0$ if household i does not read a 'quality' newspaper

We wish to investigate the extent to which the schooling, age and earnings of a household influence the type of newspaper it reads. We begin by estimating a linear probability model with D as the dependent variable and S, A and E as regressors. Recall that predicted values from such a model can be interpreted as probabilities. Application of OLS should yield

$$\hat{P}_i = -0.041 + 0.104S_i + 0.0028A_i + 0.0102E_i, \qquad R^2 = 0.379 \tag{16.38}$$
$$\phantom{\hat{P}_i =} (-0.30) \quad (4.03) \qquad (0.58) \qquad (1.59)$$

The t ratio on the age variable is very low in (16.38), and dropping this variable gives

$$\hat{P}_i = 0.015 + 0.0993S_i + 0.0123E_i, \quad R^2 = 0.374 \tag{16.39}$$
$$(0.16) \quad (4.07) \qquad (2.29)$$

The coefficient of the earnings variable now apparently becomes significantly different from zero. We appear to have found evidence that reading habits are influenced both by the schooling and the earnings of households. Although the R^2 may seem low, remember that it is not an appropriate measure of closeness of fit in this context.

Equation (16.39) could be used to estimate probabilities for households of any schooling and earnings. For example, for a household with years of schooling $S_i = 3$ and hourly earnings $E_i = 5$, we have

$$\hat{P}_i = 0.015 + 0.0993(3) + 0.0123(5) = 0.374$$

Thus we would estimate the probability of such a household reading a quality newspaper as 0.374.

We must not, however, forget the limitations of the linear probability model. It is quite possible for (16.39) to predict a probability outside the range 0 to 1. For example $S_i = 7$ and $E_i = 40$ yields a probability $P_i = 1.202$.

Remember too that the disturbances in the linear probability model are heteroskedastic, so that although the coefficient estimates in (16.39) remain unbiased, there is some loss of efficiency and, more importantly, we cannot trust the t ratios. Instead of adopting a weighted least squares approach, however, we shall estimate a logit model. As noted earlier, there are a number of canned computer packages for estimating such models.

First, estimate a version of (16.32) in which the explanatory variables are schooling S, age A and earnings E. You should obtain

$$\ln\left(\frac{P_i}{1 - P_i}\right) = -3.05 + 0.569S_i + 0.022A_i + 0.052E_i, \quad l = -23.33$$
$$(-2.91) \quad (3.06) \qquad (0.69) \qquad (1.26)$$
$$\tag{16.40}$$

Figures in parentheses are asymptotic t ratios and l is the maximized log-likelihood for the equation. Dropping the apparently unimportant age variable results in

$$\ln\left(\frac{P_i}{1 - P_i}\right) = -2.56 + 0.521S_i + 0.067E_i, \quad l = -23.57 \tag{16.41}$$
$$(-3.57) \quad (3.10) \qquad (1.84)$$

There is little decline in the log-likelihood in (16.41) compared with (16.40), and the coefficients of both the schooling and earnings variables are now significantly different from zero on one-tail tests.

The log-likelihood for a model of the type (16.36) is $l_R = -34.62$. Taking the log-likelihood for (16.41) as l_U, this gives a value for the likelihood ratio statistic of

$$LR = -2(l_R - l_U) = 22.1$$

With $h = 2$ degrees of freedom, the critical $\chi^2_{0.05} = 5.99$. Thus Equation (16.41) easily passes the likelihood ratio goodness-of-fit test. The value of McFadden's pseudo-R^2 is only about 0.3, however. Although we cannot give this any precise interpretation, it does suggest that possibly there are factors other than schooling and earnings that influence the reading of quality newspapers.

The advantage of the model (16.41) over (16.39) is that, being a logit equation, it yields predicted probabilities that always lie between 0 and 1. For example, consider a household with $S_i = 7$ and $E_i = 40$. The linear probability model (16.39) yielded a predicted probability of 1.202 for such a household. For the logit model (16.41), however, we have

$$\widehat{\ln\left(\frac{P_i}{1 - P_i}\right)} = -2.56 + 0.521(7) + 0.067(40) = 3.767$$

so that $\hat{P}_i = 0.977$.

Appendix 16A

Notes to Chapter 16

1. We have, in fact, already encountered VARs when considering the Johansen technique for testing for cointegration in the last chapter. For example, Equations (15.30) and (15.31) represent a two-variable VAR.
2. As we shall see in the next section, simultaneous equation models do not have to contain exogenous variables. When this is the case, the reduced form is found by solving the model for the endogenous variables in terms of their lagged values.
3. However, if the disturbances (16.2) were correlated with one another then OLS would not yield efficient estimators. Efficient estimation would require a technique known as SURE (seemingly unrelated regression estimation). See, for example, Kmenta (1986).
4. To obtain a forecast of w_{t+2}, using the VAR (16.2), requires values for w_{t+1}, x_{t+1} and y_{t+1}. However, for these values, we may use the forecasts made by the three equations in (16.2) for period $t + 1$. Similarly we may forecast w_{t+3} by using the forecasts already obtained for periods $t + 1$ and $t + 2$. Such forecasts are referred to as **dynamic forecasts**.
5. In traditional econometric models policy analysis involves studying the effect of varying certain exogenous variables that are assumed to be under government control. Since VARs contain no such exogenous variables, such an approach is impossible in the present context. VAR advocates would maintain that so-called

policy variables are, in fact, endogenous, with the government merely responding to economic events.

6. We have, in fact, rather simplified the situation by assuming at the outset that the disturbances u_t and v_t in Equations (16.12) and (16.13) are uncorrelated. Correlations between u_t and v_t would mean that x_t and v_t in (16.12) were correlated even if $\alpha_2 = 0$. Testing for weak exogeneity, in fact, frequently involves testing for correlations between disturbances.

7. More precisely, it depends on the so-called **cumulative distribution** for ϵ_i.

8. If

$$P_i = \frac{1}{1 + \exp(-\alpha)}$$

where $\alpha = \beta_1 + \beta_2 X_{2i} + \epsilon_i$, then

$$1 - P_i = 1 - \frac{1}{1 + \exp(-\alpha)} = \frac{1 + \exp(-\alpha) - 1}{1 + \exp(-\alpha)} = \frac{\exp(-\alpha)}{1 + \exp(-\alpha)}$$

Hence $P_i/(1 - P_i) = 1/\exp(-\alpha) = \exp(\alpha)$, so that $\ln[P_i/(1 - P_i)] = \alpha$.

Further reading

For further material on VARs and causality testing, see Judge et al. (1988), Chapter 18, and Charemza and Deadman (1992), Chapter 6. Charemza and Deadman also provide an accessible introduction to exogeneity in their Chapter 7.

Robust estimators are covered in greater detail in Judge et al. (1988), Chapter 22. Qualitative dependent variable models are also covered in Judge et al., Chapter 19. For an advanced and more general treatment, see Greene (1993), Chapters 21 and 22.

I

Introduction to matrix algebra

AI.1 Matrices and vectors

A **matrix** is simply a two-dimensional array of numbers. Each individual number is known as a **scalar**. In this text we represent all matrices by bold-faced capital letters. For example, suppose

$$
\mathbf{A} = \begin{pmatrix}
a_{11} & a_{12} & a_{13} & \cdots & a_{1n} \\
a_{21} & a_{22} & a_{23} & \cdots & a_{2n} \\
a_{31} & a_{32} & a_{33} & \cdots & a_{3n} \\
\cdot & \cdot & \cdot & & \cdot \\
\cdot & \cdot & \cdot & & \cdot \\
\cdot & \cdot & \cdot & & \cdot \\
a_{m1} & a_{m2} & a_{m3} & \cdots & a_{mn}
\end{pmatrix}
$$

$\mathbf{A}$ is a matrix consisting of m rows and n columns of numbers or scalars. It is therefore known as an $m \times n$ matrix. m and n are known as the **dimensions** of the matrix. Alternatively, $\mathbf{A}$ can be said to be of **order** $m \times n$. It is customary to represent the scalar in the ith row and jth column of the matrix $\mathbf{A}$ by the symbol a_{ij}. Thus a_{46}, for example, is the scalar in the 4th row and 6th column of $\mathbf{A}$. As can be seen from Chapter 7, in econometrics matrices are useful for representing data sets involving observations on two or more variables. Each row in the matrix can represent a separate observation on the variables in the data set while each column in the matrix can represent the observations on a particular variable.[1] In fact, matrices are useful when any two-way classification of data is required.

A matrix consisting of just one column is known as a **column vector**. In this text we represent vectors by bold-faced lower-case letters. For example, if

$$
\mathbf{a} = \begin{pmatrix} a_1 \\ a_2 \\ a_3 \\ a_4 \\ a_5 \\ a_6 \\ a_7 \end{pmatrix} \qquad \text{and} \qquad \mathbf{b} = \begin{pmatrix} 5 \\ -3 \\ 7 \\ 1 \\ 2 \end{pmatrix}
$$

then **a** is a 7×1 column vector and **b** is a 5×1 column vector.

Similarly, a matrix consisting of a single row is known as a **row vector**. For example, if

$$
\mathbf{x}' = (x_1 \quad x_2 \quad x_3 \quad \ldots \quad x_8); \qquad \text{and} \qquad \mathbf{y}' = (3 \quad -12 \quad 5 \quad -7)
$$

then **x**′ is a 1×8 row vector and **y**′ is a 1×4 row vector.

A matrix consisting of all zeros is known as a **null matrix**, and is given the symbol **O**. Similarly, a vector containing only zeros is known as a **null vector**, and given the symbol **o** or **o**′.

There are various rules for manipulating vectors and matrices, which we now introduce. Some of these rules may seem somewhat arbitrary, but it must be remembered that matrix algebra is, above all, a form of shorthand and the rules have been formulated so as to make this shorthand as powerful and useful as possible.

AI.2 Basic definitions and operations

Matrix equality

We have seen that the scalar in the ith row and jth column of a matrix **A** is written as a_{ij}. Similarly, for example, the element in the ith row and jth column of a matrix **B** is normally written b_{ij}. Two matrices can be said to be equal if and only if each scalar in one matrix equals the corresponding scalar in the other matrix. That is,

$$
\mathbf{A} = \mathbf{B} \text{ if and only if } a_{ij} = b_{ij} \text{ for all } i \text{ and all } j \tag{AI.1}
$$

Scalar multiplication

There are occasions when it is necessary to multiply all scalars in a matrix by some other constant or scalar. To distinguish this operation from matrix multiplication, which we discuss presently, it is referred to as **scalar multiplication**. If μ is any constant then to form a matrix $\mathbf{C} = \mu\mathbf{A}$, we use

$$c_{ij} = \mu a_{ij} \quad \text{for all } i \text{ and all } j \tag{AI.2}$$

That is, each scalar in $\mathbf{C}$ is obtained by multiplying the corresponding scalar in $\mathbf{A}$ by the constant μ. For example, if

$$\mathbf{A} = \begin{pmatrix} 4 & 1 & 3 \\ 3 & -2 & 0 \\ 1 & 4 & -5 \end{pmatrix} \quad \text{and} \quad \mu = 3$$

then

$$\mathbf{C} = 3 \begin{pmatrix} 4 & 1 & 3 \\ 3 & -2 & 0 \\ 1 & 4 & -5 \end{pmatrix} = \begin{pmatrix} 12 & 3 & 9 \\ 9 & -6 & 0 \\ 3 & 12 & -15 \end{pmatrix}$$

Matrix addition

Matrices are added simply by adding the corresponding scalars. Hence if the matrix $\mathbf{P} = \mathbf{A} + \mathbf{B}$ then the scalars in $\mathbf{P}$ are given by

$$p_{ij} = a_{ij} + b_{ij} \quad \text{for all } i \text{ and all } j \tag{AI.3}$$

For example, if

$$\mathbf{A} = \begin{pmatrix} 3 & 1 \\ 5 & -3 \\ 2 & -4 \end{pmatrix} \quad \text{and} \quad \mathbf{B} = \begin{pmatrix} 4 & -3 \\ -2 & 2 \\ 5 & -1 \end{pmatrix}$$

then

$$\mathbf{P} = \mathbf{A} + \mathbf{B} = \begin{pmatrix} 3 & 1 \\ 5 & -3 \\ 2 & -4 \end{pmatrix} + \begin{pmatrix} 4 & -3 \\ -2 & 2 \\ 5 & -1 \end{pmatrix} = \begin{pmatrix} 7 & -2 \\ 3 & -1 \\ 7 & -5 \end{pmatrix}$$

Notice that matrices can only be added if they have the same dimensions. For example, it is not possible to add a 3×5 matrix to a 4×2 matrix. The sum of such matrices is *not defined*.

Subtraction of matrices is carried out in a similar manner. For example, if $\mathbf{Q} = \mathbf{A} - \mathbf{B}$ then

$$q_{ij} = a_{ij} - b_{ij} \quad \text{for all } i \text{ and all } j$$

It should be relatively obvious that the order in which matrices are added or subtracted is not important. That is, for example,

$$\mathbf{A} + \mathbf{B} + \mathbf{C} = \mathbf{B} + \mathbf{A} + \mathbf{C} = \mathbf{C} + \mathbf{B} + \mathbf{A} \quad \text{etc.} \tag{AI.4}$$

and

$$A - B + C = A + C - B = -B + A + C \quad \text{etc.} \tag{AI.4a}$$

Matrix multiplication

Suppose we have two matrices

$$A = \begin{pmatrix} a_{11} & a_{12} & a_{13} & a_{14} \\ a_{21} & a_{22} & a_{23} & a_{24} \\ a_{31} & a_{32} & a_{33} & a_{34} \end{pmatrix} \quad \text{and} \quad B = \begin{pmatrix} b_{11} & b_{12} \\ b_{21} & b_{22} \\ b_{31} & b_{32} \\ b_{41} & b_{42} \end{pmatrix}$$

The **matrix product P = AB** is defined in what will seem at first a somewhat arbitrary and strange manner. The reason for this will become apparent shortly. The scalar in the *ith row* and *jth column* of the matrix **P** is obtained by multiplying the *ith row* in the matrix **A** into the *jth column* of the matrix **B**. For example, to form the scalar p_{32}, we multiply the third row of **A** into the second column of **B** as follows:

$$p_{32} = a_{31}b_{12} + a_{32}b_{22} + a_{33}b_{32} + a_{34}b_{42} \tag{AI.5}$$

That is, we take each scalar in the third row of **A**, multiply it by the corresponding scalar in the second row of **B**, and add the resultant products.

Similarly, to form the scalar p_{21}, multiply the second row of **A** into the first column of **B**. That is,

$$p_{21} = a_{21}b_{11} + a_{22}b_{21} + a_{23}b_{31} + a_{24}b_{41} \tag{AI.6}$$

In this way, all the scalars in the matrix product **P = AB** can be obtained. Since there are three rows in **A** and two columns in **B**, the matrix product **AB** will be of dimensions or order 3×2.

A further example, this time numerical, should make this clearer. Suppose

$$A = \begin{pmatrix} 5 & 3 & -4 \\ -2 & 6 & -2 \\ 4 & -1 & 5 \\ 7 & -3 & 0 \\ 0 & 8 & -5 \end{pmatrix} \quad \text{and} \quad B = \begin{pmatrix} 4 & -6 & 7 & -1 \\ 2 & 0 & -4 & 3 \\ -3 & 0 & 8 & 2 \end{pmatrix}$$

and again we wish to form the matrix product **P = AB**.

To obtain, for example, the scalar p_{24}, we multiply the second row of **A** into the fourth column of **B**, and obtain

$$p_{24} = -2(-1) + 6(3) - 2(2) = 16$$

Similarly, for example,

$$p_{31} = 4(4) - 1(2) + 5(-3) = -1$$

All the scalars in the matrix product **AB** may be found in this way. Since there are 5 rows in **A** and 4 columns in **B**, the matrix product **AB** will be of order 5×4. It is, in fact,

$$P = AB = \begin{pmatrix} 5 & 3 & -4 \\ -2 & 6 & -2 \\ 4 & -1 & 5 \\ 7 & -3 & 0 \\ 0 & 8 & -5 \end{pmatrix} \begin{pmatrix} 4 & -6 & 7 & -1 \\ 2 & 0 & -4 & 3 \\ -3 & 0 & 8 & 2 \end{pmatrix}$$

$$= \begin{pmatrix} 38 & -30 & -9 & -4 \\ 10 & 12 & -54 & 16 \\ -1 & -24 & 72 & 3 \\ 22 & -42 & 61 & -16 \\ 31 & 0 & -72 & 14 \end{pmatrix}$$

There are a number of points to be stressed concerning matrix multiplication. First, matrices can only be multiplied together if they are **conformable**. That is, we can only form the matrix product **AB** *if the number of columns in* **A** *equals the number of rows in* **B**. For example, suppose **A** is a 3×3 matrix and **B** a 2×4 matrix defined as follows:

$$A = \begin{pmatrix} 2 & 6 & 3 \\ 5 & -1 & 0 \\ 1 & -5 & 2 \end{pmatrix}, \quad B = \begin{pmatrix} -1 & 0 & 5 & 2 \\ 3 & 2 & -4 & -1 \end{pmatrix}$$

To form a matrix product **AB** from the above matrices, we need to multiply the rows of **A** into the columns of **B**. In this case, however, the number of scalars in each row of **A** is 3, whereas the number of scalars in each column of **B** is only 2. The normal procedure for forming a matrix product cannot be followed, and the matrix product **AB** *does not exist*. The matrices **A** and **B** are not conformable.

The easiest way of checking for conformability is simply to write down the dimensions of the relevant matrices side by side. For example, suppose **X** is of order 3×5 and **Y** is of order 5×2:

$$\begin{array}{ccc} X & Y & = & Z \\ (3 \times 5) & (5 \times 2) & & (3 \times 2) \end{array}, \qquad \begin{array}{ccc} Y & X & = & ? \\ (5 \times 2) & (3 \times 5) & & (\text{——}) \end{array}$$

The matrix product $XY = Z$ can be formed because the 'middle numbers' in the dimensions of **X** and **Y** are both equal to 5. This means that the number of columns in **X** equals the number of rows in **Y**, so these matrices are conformable when multiplied in this way, and result in a 3×2 matrix product.

Notice, however, that it is not possible to form the matrix product **YX**, because the 'middle numbers' in the dimensions are not equal. There are 2 columns in **Y** but 3 rows in **X**. If we attempt to multiply the matrices together in this way, we find they are not conformable, so that the matrix product **YX** does not exist.

When two matrices are conformable, it is a simple matter to determine the dimensions of the matrix product that results after multiplication. One simply writes down the dimensions of the two matrices in the order in which they are to be multiplied. The dimensions of the matrix product can then be obtained by 'striking out' the middle numbers. For example, in the above case the matrix product $\mathbf{Z} = \mathbf{XY}$ is of order 3×2. Similarly,

$$
\begin{array}{cccccccc}
\mathbf{A} & \mathbf{B} & = & \mathbf{C} & , & \qquad \mathbf{U} & \mathbf{V} & = & \mathbf{W} \\
(2 \times 7)(7 \times 4) & & (2 \times 4) & & & (3 \times 3)(3 \times 6) & & (3 \times 6) \\
\mathbf{L} & \mathbf{M} & = & \mathbf{N} & , & \qquad \mathbf{E} & \mathbf{F} & = & \mathbf{G} \\
(3 \times 4)(4 \times 2) & & (3 \times 2) & & & (2 \times 12)(12 \times 3) & & (2 \times 3)
\end{array}
$$

Only when two matrices $\mathbf{A}$ and $\mathbf{B}$ are **square** (that is, they have an equal number of rows and columns) is it possible to form both the matrix product $\mathbf{AB}$ and the matrix product $\mathbf{BA}$. However, it must be stressed that, in general, $\mathbf{AB}$ will *not* be the same matrix as $\mathbf{BA}$. For example, suppose

$$
\mathbf{A} = \begin{pmatrix} 2 & 3 \\ 4 & 1 \end{pmatrix} \quad \text{and} \quad \mathbf{B} = \begin{pmatrix} 5 & 1 \\ 2 & 2 \end{pmatrix}
$$

It is easily found that

$$
\mathbf{AB} = \begin{pmatrix} 16 & 8 \\ 22 & 6 \end{pmatrix}, \quad \text{but} \quad \mathbf{BA} = \begin{pmatrix} 14 & 16 \\ 12 & 8 \end{pmatrix}
$$

Thus, although it is the case that in normal scalar algebra $ab = bc$, *a similar property does not normally hold for matrices.* That is, in general, $\mathbf{AB} \neq \mathbf{BA}$.

When a matrix product $\mathbf{AB}$ is found, the customary terminology is to say that matrix $\mathbf{B}$ has been **premultiplied** by matrix $\mathbf{A}$. On the other hand, if $\mathbf{BA}$ also exists then, when it is formed, we say that $\mathbf{B}$ has been **postmultiplied** by $\mathbf{A}$. From what has just been said, it is obvious that premultiplying by a matrix of whatever form has totally different results from postmultiplying by that same matrix.

It should be clear that since vectors are just matrices containing either a single row or a single column, vectors and matrices can be multiplied together using the normal rules. For example, if

$$
\mathbf{A} = \begin{pmatrix} 3 & 1 \\ 1 & -2 \\ 0 & 6 \end{pmatrix} \quad \text{and} \quad \mathbf{z}' = (-2 \quad 1 \quad -3)
$$

then

$$
\mathbf{z}'\mathbf{A} = (-2 \quad 1 \quad -3) \begin{pmatrix} 3 & 1 \\ 1 & -2 \\ 0 & 6 \end{pmatrix} = (-5 \quad -22)
$$

However, the matrix product $\mathbf{Az}'$ does not exist.

Similarly, if

$$\mathbf{B} = \begin{pmatrix} -2 & 3 & 0 & -6 \\ 1 & 2 & -1 & 3 \end{pmatrix} \quad \text{and} \quad \mathbf{x} = \begin{pmatrix} 3 \\ -1 \\ 0 \\ 2 \end{pmatrix}$$

then

$$\mathbf{Bx} = \begin{pmatrix} -2 & 3 & 0 & -6 \\ 1 & 2 & -1 & 3 \end{pmatrix} \begin{pmatrix} 3 \\ -1 \\ 0 \\ 2 \end{pmatrix} = \begin{pmatrix} -21 \\ 7 \end{pmatrix}$$

but the matrix product **xB** does not exist.

Exercise AI.1

Consider the following matrices and vectors.

$$\mathbf{A} = \begin{pmatrix} 8 & 4 & 2 \\ 3 & 1 & 0 \\ 2 & 5 & 3 \end{pmatrix}, \quad \mathbf{B} = \begin{pmatrix} 6 & 3 & 7 \\ 4 & 5 & -3 \\ 6 & -2 & 1 \end{pmatrix}, \quad \mathbf{x} = \begin{pmatrix} -2 \\ 6 \\ -1 \end{pmatrix}, \quad \mathbf{y} = (1 \ 1 \ 2 \ -1)$$

$$\mathbf{C} = \begin{pmatrix} 2 & -2 & 1 & -4 \\ -5 & 0 & 2 & 3 \\ 2 & -1 & 4 & 0 \end{pmatrix}, \quad \mathbf{D} = \begin{pmatrix} -3 & 2 & 1 \\ 0 & 4 & -2 \end{pmatrix}, \quad \mathbf{E} = \begin{pmatrix} 1 & 1 \\ -2 & 0 \end{pmatrix}$$

(a) *When possible*, form the following matrix products:

    AC, AB, BA, Ax, DA, yC, Dx, DE, BD, DB

(b) Form the matrix products **(AB)D** and **A(BD)**, and verify that they are the same. (This result is quite general, and holds for any three conformable matrices.)

(c) Show that **D(A + B) = DA + DB**. (This result is also quite general.)

The transposition of matrices and vectors

The **transpose** of a matrix is obtained by simply interchanging columns and rows. That is, for example, the first row in the original matrix becomes the first column in the transposed matrix. Similarly, the second row becomes the second column, and so on. The transpose of a matrix **A** is generally written as **A'**. Thus if

$$\mathbf{A} = \begin{pmatrix} -1 & 0 & 2 & 3 \\ 2 & 6 & -3 & 1 \\ 4 & 1 & 1 & 2 \end{pmatrix} \quad \text{then} \quad \mathbf{A'} = \begin{pmatrix} -1 & 2 & 4 \\ 0 & 6 & 1 \\ 2 & -3 & 1 \\ 3 & 1 & 2 \end{pmatrix}$$

In general, the scalar in the ith row and jth column of $\mathbf{A}$ becomes the scalar in the jth row and ith column of the transposed matrix $\mathbf{A}'$. In other words,

$$a_{ij} = a'_{ji} \quad \text{for all } i \text{ and all } j \tag{AI.7}$$

Notice that the transpose of an $m \times n$ matrix must be of order $n \times m$.

Vectors may also be transposed. The transpose of a $1 \times n$ row vector is simply an $n \times 1$ column vector. Similarly, the transpose of an $n \times 1$ column vector is a $1 \times n$ row vector. In fact, this is why we have attached a prime sign to symbols representing row vectors above. Any row vector can be regarded as the transpose of a column vector containing the same scalars. Thus if $\mathbf{x}$ is an $n \times 1$ column vector then $\mathbf{x}'$ will be a $1 \times n$ row vector.

A matrix $\mathbf{A}$ that remains unchanged after transposition (i.e. $\mathbf{A}' = \mathbf{A}$) is known as a **symmetric matrix**. Such matrices must be square (otherwise their order would be changed by transposition), and have the property that

$$a_{ij} = a_{ji} \quad \text{for all } i \text{ and all } j \tag{AI.8}$$

For example, the following matrices are symmetric:

$$\mathbf{A} = \begin{pmatrix} 4 & -2 & 0 \\ -2 & 1 & 3 \\ 0 & 3 & -5 \end{pmatrix}, \quad \mathbf{B} = \begin{pmatrix} 1 & 5 & -4 & -2 \\ 5 & 2 & 0 & -1 \\ -4 & 0 & -1 & 2 \\ -2 & -1 & 2 & 3 \end{pmatrix}$$

Exercise AI.2

For the matrices in Exercise AI.1 form the transposed matrices $\mathbf{A}'$, $\mathbf{B}'$ and $\mathbf{D}'$, and show that $(\mathbf{AB})' = \mathbf{B}'\mathbf{A}'$ and that $(\mathbf{DAB})' = \mathbf{B}'\mathbf{A}'\mathbf{D}'$. (These results are quite general, and hold for any conformable matrices.)

AI.3 Matrix algebra as a shorthand

The definition of matrix multiplication introduced in the last section may seem rather strange and arbitrary. However, it is adopted for the very good reason that, given such a definition, matrix algebra becomes a very good mathematical shorthand. Consider, for example, the following simultaneous system of m equations in the n variables $x_1, x_2, x_3, \ldots, x_n$; the as and bs are constants:

$$a_{11}x_1 + a_{12}x_2 + a_{13}x_3 + \cdots + a_{1n}x_n = b_1$$
$$a_{21}x_1 + a_{22}x_2 + a_{23}x_3 + \cdots + a_{2n}x_n = b_2$$

$$\vdots$$

$$a_{m1}x_1 + a_{m2}x_2 + a_{m3}x_3 + \cdots + a_{mn}x_n = b_m$$

Suppose we define an $m \times n$ matrix $\mathbf{A}$ with, as usual, a_{ij} representing the scalar in ith row and jth column. If we also define column vectors $\mathbf{x}$ of order $n \times 1$ and $\mathbf{b}$ of order $m \times 1$, so that

$$\mathbf{x} = \begin{pmatrix} x_1 \\ x_2 \\ x_3 \\ \vdots \\ x_n \end{pmatrix}, \quad \mathbf{b} = \begin{pmatrix} b_1 \\ b_2 \\ \vdots \\ b_m \end{pmatrix} \tag{AI.9}$$

then the above system of equations can be expressed in matrix algebra shorthand as

$$\mathbf{Ax} = \mathbf{b} \tag{AI.10}$$

Application to (AI.10) of the rules for handling matrices described above will replicate the given equation system. In Chapter 7 we represent the normal equations for the classical OLS multiple regression procedure in just such a manner.

As a further example of the use of matrix algebra as shorthand, consider the sum of squares

$$S = x_1^2 + x_2^2 + x_3^2 + \cdots + x_n^2 \tag{AI.11}$$

If we define a column vector $\mathbf{x}$ as in (AI.9) then the sum of squares (AI.11) may be written simply as

$$S = \mathbf{x}'\mathbf{x} \tag{AI.12}$$

where $\mathbf{x}'$ is the row vector obtained by transposing $\mathbf{x}$.

Exercise AI.3

Consider the following systems of equations:

(a) $3x_1 + 2x_2 - 4x_3 = 15$
     $2x_1 - 3x_2 + 2x_3 = -8$
     $4x_1 - 2x_2 - 3x_3 = 6$

(b) $a + 2b = 11$
     $2a - 3c = 3$
     $-b + 2c = -2$

If the systems are to be expressed in the form $\mathbf{Ax} = \mathbf{b}$, how must $\mathbf{A}$, $\mathbf{x}$ and $\mathbf{b}$ be defined in each case?

AI.4 The inverse matrix

Consider the system of equations (AI.10) with $m = n$, so that we have the same number of equations as variables. Suppose we wish to solve such a system of equations. The interesting question now is whether it is possible to find some matrix, which we would write as $\mathbf{A}^{-1}$, such that we can premultiply each side of (AI.10) by $\mathbf{A}^{-1}$, obtaining

$$\mathbf{A}^{-1}\mathbf{Ax} = \mathbf{A}^{-1}\mathbf{b}, \quad \text{or} \quad \mathbf{x} = \mathbf{A}^{-1}\mathbf{b} \tag{AI.13}$$

Given such a matrix, we could then use the normal rules of matrix multiplication to form the product $\mathbf{A}^{-1}\mathbf{b}$, which, by (AI.13), would be identical to the column vector $\mathbf{x}$. The scalars in $\mathbf{x}$ would then represent the solution to the equation system.

Before we answer the above question, we must first define the **identity matrix**. This special square matrix has the scalars in its 'main diagonal' equal to unity, with all its other scalars equal to zero. It is normally given the symbol $\mathbf{I}$. For example, the 5×5 identity matrix takes the form

$$\mathbf{I} = \begin{pmatrix} 1 & 0 & 0 & 0 & 0 \\ 0 & 1 & 0 & 0 & 0 \\ 0 & 0 & 1 & 0 & 0 \\ 0 & 0 & 0 & 1 & 0 \\ 0 & 0 & 0 & 0 & 1 \end{pmatrix}$$

The identity matrix has one crucial property. If any matrix $\mathbf{A}$ of suitable dimensions is premultiplied or postmultiplied by $\mathbf{I}$ then it is left unchanged. That is,

$$\mathbf{IA} = \mathbf{AI} = \mathbf{A} \tag{AI.14}$$

For example,

$$\begin{pmatrix} 1 & 0 & 0 \\ 0 & 1 & 0 \\ 0 & 0 & 1 \end{pmatrix} \begin{pmatrix} 3 & 1 & -5 & 2 \\ 0 & -2 & -1 & 3 \\ -4 & 11 & 0 & 6 \end{pmatrix} = \begin{pmatrix} 3 & 1 & -5 & 2 \\ 0 & -2 & -1 & 3 \\ -4 & 11 & 0 & 6 \end{pmatrix}$$

Notice that the identity matrix plays a role in matrix algebra very similar to the number 1 in ordinary scalar algebra. Just as in ordinary algebra $1A = A1 = A$, so in matrix algebra (AI.14) holds.

We are now in a position to define the so-called **inverse matrix**. The inverse of a square matrix $\mathbf{A}$ is defined as that matrix, normally written as $\mathbf{A}^{-1}$, for which

$$\mathbf{AA}^{-1} = \mathbf{A}^{-1}\mathbf{A} = \mathbf{I} \tag{AI.15}$$

where $\mathbf{I}$ is the identity matrix. Notice that only square matrices have inverses and that the inverse matrix $\mathbf{A}^{-1}$ is also square, otherwise it would be impossible to form both the matrix products $\mathbf{AA}^{-1}$ and $\mathbf{A}^{-1}\mathbf{A}$.

The inverse matrix is analogous to the reciprocal of ordinary scalar algebra. In ordinary algebra the reciprocal of a scalar A is $1/A$, which is also written as A^{-1}. Thus $AA^{-1} = A^{-1}A = 1$. However, in matrix algebra, $\mathbf{A}^{-1}$ is never written as $1/\mathbf{A}$. It is not possible to 'divide' one matrix $\mathbf{A}$ by another matrix $\mathbf{B}$. Rather, in matrix algebra the analogous procedure to division is to premultiply or postmultiply $\mathbf{A}$ by the inverse of $\mathbf{B}$. That is, we form $\mathbf{B}^{-1}\mathbf{A}$ or $\mathbf{AB}^{-1}$. Indeed, if $\mathbf{A}$ is a square matrix, both these matrix products may be formed, but, as we stressed earlier, they will not normally be the same.

Now that we have defined the inverse matrix, it should be clear that, provided we can first *find* $\mathbf{A}^{-1}$, we can indeed solve systems of linear equations by the procedure outlined in (AI.13). It is to the problem of finding the inverse of a matrix that we turn next. However, we first need to introduce the concept of a determinant.

AI.5 Determinants

All square matrices $\mathbf{A}$ have associated with them a scalar quantity (i.e. a number) known as the **determinant** of the matrix and denoted either by det $(\mathbf{A})$ or by $|\mathbf{A}|$. Thus if

$$\mathbf{A} = \begin{pmatrix} 0 & -3 & 1 \\ 3 & 1 & 2 \\ 4 & 10 & -3 \end{pmatrix} \quad \text{then} \quad \det(\mathbf{A}) = |\mathbf{A}| = \begin{vmatrix} 0 & -3 & 1 \\ 3 & 1 & 2 \\ 4 & 10 & -3 \end{vmatrix}$$

In this case $|\mathbf{A}|$ is referred to as a determinant of order 3, since the matrix $\mathbf{A}$ is of order 3×3. In general, the determinant of an $n \times n$ matrix will obviously be of order n.

Evaluation of determinants of order 2

The determinant of a 2×2 matrix is defined and evaluated as follows:

$$|\mathbf{A}| = \begin{vmatrix} a_{11} & a_{12} \\ a_{21} & a_{22} \end{vmatrix} = a_{11}a_{22} - a_{12}a_{21} \tag{AI.16}$$

It is therefore obtained by taking the cross-multiplication of the scalars in the main diagonal and subtracting the cross-multiplication of the scalars in the 'reverse diagonal', as indicated by the arrows. For example,

$$\begin{vmatrix} 3 & -1 \\ -2 & 4 \end{vmatrix} = (3)(4) - (-1)(-2) = 10$$

Minors and cofactors

Before we undertake the evaluation of larger determinants, it is necessary to define the terms 'minor' and 'cofactor'. If the ith row and jth column of a square matrix are deleted, we obtain the so-called submatrix of the scalar a_{ij}. The determinant of this submatrix is known as its **minor**, and we denote it by m_{ij}. For example, let us strike out the first row and second column of a (3×3) matrix:

$$\begin{pmatrix} a_{11} & a_{12} & a_{13} \\ a_{21} & a_{22} & a_{23} \\ a_{31} & a_{32} & a_{33} \end{pmatrix}$$

yielding the submatrix

$$\begin{pmatrix} a_{21} & a_{23} \\ a_{31} & a_{33} \end{pmatrix}$$

The minor of a_{12} (the scalar at the intersection of the struck-out row and column) is the determinant of this submatrix, and is given by

$$m_{12} = \begin{vmatrix} a_{21} & a_{23} \\ a_{31} & a_{33} \end{vmatrix} = a_{21}a_{33} - a_{23}a_{31}$$

Similarly, consider the matrix

$$\mathbf{A} = \begin{pmatrix} -4 & 0 & 2 \\ 1 & -3 & 1 \\ -2 & 1 & 0 \end{pmatrix} \tag{AI.17}$$

The minor of the scalar in the second row and third column of $\mathbf{A}$, that is, m_{23}, is obtained by striking out this row and column and then evaluating the determinant of the resultant submatrix. That is,

$$m_{23} = \begin{vmatrix} -4 & 0 \\ -2 & 1 \end{vmatrix} = -4$$

Similarly, the scalar in the first row and first column of $\mathbf{A}$ has a minor

$$m_{11} = \begin{vmatrix} -3 & 1 \\ 1 & 0 \end{vmatrix} = -1$$

All scalars in a matrix will obviously have minors.

The **cofactor** of any scalar in a matrix is closely related to the minor. The cofactor of the scalar a_{ij} in the matrix $\mathbf{A}$ is defined as

$$c_{ij} = (-1)^{i+j} m_{ij} \tag{AI.18}$$

where m_{ij} is the relevant minor. Thus a cofactor is simply a minor with an appropriate sign attached to it. If $i+j$ is an odd number then the minor is given a negative sign to become the cofactor. If $i+j$ is an even number, however, then the cofactor and the minor are identical. For example, taking the matrix $\mathbf{A}$ in (AI.17), the scalar a_{23} has a minor $m_{23} = -4$. Since in this case $i+j = 5$, the cofactor of a_{23} is $c_{23} = -m_{23} = +4$. However, the scalar a_{11} has $i+j = 2$, so that its cofactor is identical to its minor. That is, $c_{11} = m_{11} = -1$.

Evaluation of determinants of order 3

The determinant of a 3×3 matrix $\mathbf{A}$ can be evaluated in a number of alternative ways, all of which yield an identical result. We may take *any row or column* of scalars from the matrix, multiply each scalar by its respective cofactor, and sum the resultant products. The sum obtained is defined as the determinant of the matrix.

For example, to find the determinant of the matrix $\mathbf{A}$ of (AI.17), we could 'expand' using the first row. This would give

$$|\mathbf{A}| = a_{11}c_{11} + a_{12}c_{12} + a_{13}c_{13}$$
$$= a_{11}m_{11} - a_{12}m_{12} + a_{13}m_{13} \tag{AI.19}$$

Since in this case

$$m_{11} = \begin{vmatrix} -3 & 1 \\ 1 & 0 \end{vmatrix} = -1, \quad m_{12} = \begin{vmatrix} 1 & 1 \\ -2 & 0 \end{vmatrix} = 2, \quad m_{13} = \begin{vmatrix} 1 & -3 \\ -2 & 1 \end{vmatrix} = -5$$

we have $|\mathbf{A}| = (-4)(-1) - (0)(2) + (2)(-5) = -6$ as the value of the determinant. Alternatively, we could expand by, for example, the second column. This gives

$$|\mathbf{A}| = a_{12}c_{12} + a_{22}c_{22} + a_{32}c_{32}$$
$$= -a_{12}m_{12} + a_{22}m_{22} - a_{32}m_{32} \tag{AI.20}$$
$$= -(0)\begin{vmatrix} 1 & 1 \\ -2 & 0 \end{vmatrix} + (-3)\begin{vmatrix} -4 & 2 \\ -2 & 0 \end{vmatrix} - (1)\begin{vmatrix} -4 & 2 \\ 1 & 1 \end{vmatrix}$$
$$= -(0)(2) + (-3)(4) - (1)(-6) = -6$$

Notice that whether we expand by the first row or the second column, we obtain the same value for the determinant. In fact, it is not difficult to show that the same value is obtained no matter what row or column we expand by. Notice also that when a matrix is expanded and expressed in terms of various minors, as in (AI.19) and (AI.20), the products that are formed *alternate in sign*. In fact, the following equation demonstrates the pattern of the signs that have to be attached to various minors to obtain cofactors

$$\begin{pmatrix} c_{11} & c_{12} & c_{13} \\ c_{21} & c_{22} & c_{23} \\ c_{31} & c_{32} & c_{33} \end{pmatrix} = \begin{pmatrix} m_{11} & -m_{12} & m_{13} \\ -m_{21} & m_{22} & -m_{23} \\ m_{31} & -m_{32} & m_{33} \end{pmatrix} \tag{AI.21}$$

Exercise AI.4

(a) Evaluate the following determinant, first by any row and then by any column, verifying that you get the same answer in each case:

$$\begin{vmatrix} -1 & 3 & 2 \\ 4 & -3 & 1 \\ 2 & 1 & -3 \end{vmatrix}$$

(b) Evaluate the following determinants:

$$\begin{vmatrix} 3 & -1 \\ 1 & 2 \end{vmatrix}, \quad \begin{vmatrix} 4 & 1 & 2 \\ 2 & 2 & 2 \\ -1 & 3 & -1 \end{vmatrix}, \quad \begin{vmatrix} 4 & 0 & 0 \\ -3 & 1 & -2 \\ -1 & 2 & 5 \end{vmatrix}, \quad \begin{vmatrix} -3 & 1 & 4 \\ 0 & 0 & 0 \\ 2 & -3 & 6 \end{vmatrix}$$

Evaluation of higher-order determinants

Determinants of 4×4 matrices and higher-order determinants can also be evaluated in terms of minors and cofactors. Now, however, if we take any scalar in the matrix and strike out its row and column, we obtain a 3×3 submatrix. The minor m_{ij} is obtained by taking the determinant of this submatrix. Since the determinant is of order 3, it has to be evaluated by the method of the last subsection. The cofactor of the scalar a_{ij} is then again obtained by using (AI.18). The pattern of signs that have to be allocated to minors to obtain cofactors is therefore a simple extension of (AI.21):

$$
\begin{pmatrix}
c_{11} & c_{12} & c_{13} & c_{14} \\
c_{21} & c_{22} & c_{23} & c_{24} \\
c_{31} & c_{32} & c_{33} & c_{34} \\
c_{41} & c_{42} & c_{43} & c_{44}
\end{pmatrix}
=
\begin{pmatrix}
m_{11} & -m_{12} & m_{13} & -m_{14} \\
-m_{21} & m_{22} & -m_{23} & m_{24} \\
m_{31} & -m_{32} & m_{33} & -m_{34} \\
-m_{41} & m_{42} & -m_{43} & m_{44}
\end{pmatrix}
\qquad \text{(AI.22)}
$$

The determinant of a 4×4 matrix $\mathbf{A}$ can be evaluated in a way exactly analogous to the evaluation of a determinant of order 3. We may take any row or column and multiply its scalars by their respective cofactors. The sum of the resultant products is defined as the determinant of the matrix. For example, expanding by the first row, we have

$$
\begin{aligned}
|\mathbf{A}| &= a_{11}c_{11} + a_{12}c_{12} + a_{13}c_{13} + a_{14}c_{14} \\
&= a_{11}m_{11} - a_{12}m_{12} + a_{13}m_{13} - a_{14}m_{14}
\end{aligned}
\qquad \text{(AI.23)}
$$

Notice that when the determinant is expressed in terms of its minors, as in (AI.23), the products formed again alternate in sign, following the pattern of (AI.22). Each minor, of course, is itself a determinant of order 3, which has to be evaluated.

Higher-order determinants can be defined in an exactly analogous way to third- and fourth-order determinants. The sign pattern in (AI.22) simply has to be extended downwards and to the right. However, as the size of the determinant increases, the amount of computation required to evaluate it increases exponentially. We have seen that evaluating a third-order determinant requires us to first evaluate three second-order determinants. We have also seen that evaluating a fourth-order determinant requires first evaluating four third-order determinants. Similarly, evaluating a fifth-order determinant would require first evaluating five fourth-order determinants, and so on! Clearly, it is impracticable to work out determinants of order greater than 3 or 4 by hand. Fortunately, computer software suitable for the task is readily available.

AI.6 Finding the inverse matrix

The inverse of an $n \times n$ matrix $\mathbf{A}$ was defined by (AI.15). Now that we are familiar with the concept of a determinant, we are in a position to find the inverse matrix $\mathbf{A}^{-1}$.

First, we form from **A** a new matrix by replacing each scalar a_{ij} by its cofactor c_{ij}. If the resultant matrix is transposed, we obtain what is known as the **adjoint** of **A**. That is,

$$
\text{adj (A)} = \begin{pmatrix}
c_{11} & c_{21} & c_{31} & \cdots & c_{n1} \\
c_{12} & c_{22} & c_{32} & \cdots & c_{n2} \\
c_{13} & c_{23} & c_{33} & \cdots & c_{n3} \\
\vdots & \vdots & \vdots & & \vdots \\
c_{1n} & c_{2n} & c_{3n} & \cdots & c_{nn}
\end{pmatrix}
\tag{AI.24}
$$

Because of a certain special property of determinants,[2] it is possible to show that

$$
\text{A[adj (A)]} = \text{[adj (A)]A} = \begin{pmatrix}
|A| & 0 & 0 & \cdots & 0 \\
0 & |A| & 0 & \cdots & 0 \\
0 & 0 & |A| & \cdots & 0 \\
\vdots & \vdots & \vdots & & \vdots \\
0 & 0 & 0 & \cdots & |A|
\end{pmatrix} = |A|I
\tag{AI.25}
$$

where **I** is the $n \times n$ identity matrix. Assuming $|A| \neq 0$, we can now multiply (AI.25) throughout by the scalar quantity $1/|A|$ to obtain

$$
A(1/|A|)[\text{adj (A)}] = (1/|A|)[\text{adj (A)}]A = I
\tag{AI.26}
$$

Comparison of (AI.26) with (AI.15) indicates that the inverse matrix A^{-1} must be given by

$$
A^{-1} = \frac{1}{|A|}[\text{adj (A)}] = \frac{1}{|A|} \begin{pmatrix}
c_{11} & c_{21} & c_{31} & \cdots & c_{n1} \\
c_{12} & c_{22} & c_{32} & \cdots & c_{n2} \\
c_{13} & c_{23} & c_{33} & \cdots & c_{n3} \\
\vdots & \vdots & \vdots & & \vdots \\
c_{1n} & c_{2n} & c_{3n} & \cdots & c_{nn}
\end{pmatrix}
\tag{AI.27}
$$

Recalling the meaning of scalar multiplication, we see that the inverse of a matrix **A** can be formed by taking its adjoint matrix and multiplying all its scalars by $1/|A|$, that is, dividing each such scalar by the determinant of **A**.

Notice that the above procedure is possible only if $|A| \neq 0$. If $|A| = 0$ then the matrix **A** is said to be **singular** and *does not have an inverse*.

A matrix has only one inverse. That is, A^{-1}, if it exists, is unique. To see this, suppose another matrix **B** exists such that $AB = I$. Then

$$
A^{-1} = A^{-1}I = A^{-1}AB = B
$$

Thus **B** must be identical to A^{-1}.

As an example, we shall find the inverse of the matrix (AI.17). We have already found the determinant of this matrix to be $|\mathbf{A}| = -6$. Computing all its cofactors yields its adjoint matrix as

$$\text{adj}(\mathbf{A}) = \begin{pmatrix} -1 & 2 & 6 \\ -2 & 4 & 6 \\ -5 & 4 & 12 \end{pmatrix}$$

Thus, using (AI.27), the inverse matrix is

$$\mathbf{A}^{-1} = \begin{pmatrix} \frac{1}{6} & -\frac{1}{3} & -1 \\ \frac{1}{3} & -\frac{2}{3} & -1 \\ \frac{5}{6} & -\frac{2}{3} & -2 \end{pmatrix} \tag{AI.28}$$

It is left to the reader to verify that both $\mathbf{A}\mathbf{A}^{-1}$ and $\mathbf{A}^{-1}\mathbf{A}$ do, in fact, equal the 3×3 identity matrix $\mathbf{I}$.

Exercise AI.5

Find the inverse of the following matrices:

$$\begin{pmatrix} 3 & 2 & -4 \\ 2 & -3 & 2 \\ 4 & -2 & -3 \end{pmatrix}, \quad \begin{pmatrix} 1 & 2 & 0 \\ 2 & 0 & -3 \\ 0 & -1 & 2 \end{pmatrix}$$

Verify that in each case $\mathbf{A}\mathbf{A}^{-1} = \mathbf{I}$.

Exercise AI.6

Show that the inverse of the matrix $\mathbf{A} = \begin{pmatrix} a & b \\ c & d \end{pmatrix}$ is

$$\mathbf{A}^{-1} = \frac{1}{ad - cb} \begin{pmatrix} d & -b \\ -c & a \end{pmatrix}$$

Solution of linear equation systems

Recall that, at the beginning of Section AI.4 we suggested that $n \times n$ equation systems of the type $\mathbf{A}\mathbf{x} = \mathbf{b}$ could be solved along the lines of (AI.13) provided that an inverse matrix $\mathbf{A}^{-1}$ could be found. As we are now able to derive an inverse matrix, we next illustrate how this method of equation solving proceeds.

Consider the equation system

$$\begin{aligned}
-4x_1 \qquad\quad + 2x_3 &= 6 \\
x_1 - 3x_2 + x_3 &= 3 \\
-2x_1 + x_2 \qquad\quad &= -2
\end{aligned} \tag{AI.29}$$

We can express (AI.29) in matrix notation as

$$\begin{pmatrix} -4 & 0 & 2 \\ 1 & -3 & 1 \\ -2 & 1 & 0 \end{pmatrix} \begin{pmatrix} x_1 \\ x_2 \\ x_3 \end{pmatrix} = \begin{pmatrix} 6 \\ 3 \\ -2 \end{pmatrix}$$

so that, following (AI.13), we have

$$\begin{pmatrix} x_1 \\ x_2 \\ x_3 \end{pmatrix} = \begin{pmatrix} -4 & 0 & 2 \\ 1 & -3 & 1 \\ -2 & 1 & 0 \end{pmatrix}^{-1} \begin{pmatrix} 6 \\ 3 \\ -2 \end{pmatrix} \tag{AI.30}$$

The matrix that has to be inverted in (AI.30) is, in fact, (AI.17). Its inverse is given by (AI.28). Thus we have

$$\begin{pmatrix} x_1 \\ x_2 \\ x_3 \end{pmatrix} = \begin{pmatrix} \frac{1}{6} & -\frac{1}{3} & -1 \\ \frac{1}{3} & -\frac{2}{3} & -1 \\ \frac{5}{6} & -\frac{2}{3} & -2 \end{pmatrix} \begin{pmatrix} 6 \\ 3 \\ -2 \end{pmatrix} = \begin{pmatrix} 2 \\ 2 \\ 7 \end{pmatrix}$$

Thus the solution to the equation system (AI.29) is $x_1 = 2$, $x_2 = 2$ and $x_3 = 7$.

Note that if the matrix $\mathbf{A}$ in the system $\mathbf{Ax} = \mathbf{b}$ is singular (i.e. its determinant equals zero) then $\mathbf{A}^{-1}$ will not exist, and the above procedure will break down. In such a situation a unique solution to the equation system cannot be obtained.

Exercise AI.7

Using the matrix inverses found in Exercise AI.5, solve the equation systems in Exercise AI.3.

AI.7 Linear dependence and rank

A set of m vectors $\mathbf{a}_1$, $\mathbf{a}_2$, $\mathbf{a}_3$, ..., $\mathbf{a}_m$, all of order $n \times 1$ are said to be **linearly dependent** if there exists a set of scalars λ_i, not all zero, such that

$$\lambda_1 \mathbf{a}_1 + \lambda_2 \mathbf{a}_2 + \lambda_3 \mathbf{a}_3 + \cdots + \lambda_n \mathbf{a}_n = \mathbf{o} \tag{AI.31)]}$$

where $\mathbf{o}$ is the null vector. For example, consider the column vectors

$$\mathbf{a}_1 = \begin{pmatrix} 4 \\ -2 \\ 3 \end{pmatrix}, \quad \mathbf{a}_2 = \begin{pmatrix} 0 \\ 3 \\ 1 \end{pmatrix}, \quad \mathbf{a}_3 = \begin{pmatrix} 6 \\ 0 \\ \frac{11}{2} \end{pmatrix}$$

Since $3\mathbf{a}_1 + 2\mathbf{a}_2 - 2\mathbf{a}_3 = \mathbf{o}$, these vectors are linearly dependent. Similarly, the vectors

$$\mathbf{a}_1 = \begin{pmatrix} 2 \\ 3 \\ 4 \end{pmatrix}, \quad \mathbf{a}_2 = \begin{pmatrix} 0 \\ 0 \\ 0 \end{pmatrix}, \quad \mathbf{a}_3 = \begin{pmatrix} -3 \\ 12 \\ 2 \end{pmatrix}$$

are also linearly dependent since $0\mathbf{a}_1 + \lambda_2\mathbf{a}_2 + 0\mathbf{a}_3 = \mathbf{o}$ for any $\lambda_2 \neq 0$. However, the vectors

$$\mathbf{a}_1 = \begin{pmatrix} 5 \\ 2 \\ 4 \end{pmatrix} \quad \text{and} \quad \mathbf{a}_2 = \begin{pmatrix} 15 \\ 10 \\ -3 \end{pmatrix}$$

are **linearly independent**, since, as should be clear, it is impossible to find scalars λ_1 and λ_2 such that $\lambda_1\mathbf{a}_1 + \lambda_2\mathbf{a}_2 = \mathbf{o}$.

In the above we have applied the notions of linear dependence and independence to column vectors. They can of course be equally well applied to row vectors.

Rank of a matrix

An $m \times n$ matrix $\mathbf{A}$ can be regarded as a set of n $(m \times 1)$ column vectors laid side by side. That is,

$$\mathbf{A} = (\mathbf{a}_1 \quad \mathbf{a}_2 \quad \mathbf{a}_3 \quad \ldots \quad \mathbf{a}_n) \tag{AI.31}$$

The **rank** of the matrix $\mathbf{A}$, which we write as $r(\mathbf{A})$, is defined as *the maximum number of linearly independent columns in the matrix*. For example, the matrices

$$\mathbf{A} = \begin{pmatrix} 6 & 1 \\ 12 & 2 \\ 3 & \frac{1}{2} \end{pmatrix} \quad \text{and} \quad \mathbf{B} = \begin{pmatrix} 3 & -3 \\ 6 & -6 \\ 4 & -4 \end{pmatrix}$$

have a rank of 1 only, since in each case their two columns are linearly dependent. However, the matrices

$$\mathbf{A} = \begin{pmatrix} 3 & 0 \\ -2 & 5 \\ 4 & -1 \end{pmatrix} \quad \text{and} \quad \mathbf{B} = \begin{pmatrix} 2 & 6 \\ 3 & 9 \\ 5 & -1 \end{pmatrix}$$

are both of rank 2, since in both cases the two columns are linearly independent.

An $m \times n$ matrix $\mathbf{A}$ can also be written as m $(1 \times n)$ row vectors, $\mathbf{a}'_1, \mathbf{a}'_2, \mathbf{a}'_3, \ldots, \mathbf{a}'_n$ stacked on top of one another. It can be shown that the rank of a matrix can also be defined as *the maximum number of linearly independent rows in the matrix*. It is always the case that the maximum number of linearly independent rows equals the maximum number of linearly independent columns.

It is possible to show that for the rank of an $m \times n$ matrix to be k, it is necessary

(a) that every minor of order $k+1$ should equal zero, and

(b) that at least one minor of order k should be non-zero.

For example, consider the matrix

$$\mathbf{A} = \begin{pmatrix} 4 & -2 & 3 \\ 8 & -4 & 6 \\ 2 & -1 & -3 \end{pmatrix}$$

This matrix has rank 2, because its first two rows are linearly dependent. We can only obtain a 'minor' of order 3 by taking the determinant of the whole matrix $\mathbf{A}$. It can easily be seen that $|\mathbf{A}| = 0$. However, we can find a minor of order 2 that is non-zero by striking out the first row and column of $\mathbf{A}$. This confirms that $r(\mathbf{A}) = 2$. Thus one way of determining the rank of a matrix is to search for the largest non-zero determinant that can be formed from its rows and columns.

If rank is defined in terms of the largest non-zero determinant, then we see that for an $n \times n$ square matrix to be non-singular, it must have a rank of n. It follows that an $n \times n$ equation system $\mathbf{Ax} = \mathbf{b}$ will have a unique solution only if $r(\mathbf{A}) = \mathbf{n}$.

Finally in this section, we quote an important result concerning the rank of matrix products. It can be shown that *the rank of a matrix product* $\mathbf{AB}$ *cannot exceed the smaller of the ranks of* $\mathbf{A}$ *and* $\mathbf{B}$.

This result is of relevance in Section 9.1, when we consider the $k \times k$ matrix product $\mathbf{X'X}$, $\mathbf{X}$ being an $n \times k$ matrix of observations on k variables. Since $n > k$, the maximum rank that $\mathbf{X}$ and $\mathbf{X'}$ can have is therefore k. Suppose, however, that perfect multicollinearity exists between the k variables. This implies that the columns of $\mathbf{X}$ are linearly dependent, so that the ranks of $\mathbf{X}$ and $\mathbf{X'}$ must both be less than k. Hence, by the above result, the rank of $\mathbf{X'X}$ must be less than k. It follows that the matrix $\mathbf{X'X}$ is singular, so its inverse does not exist.

AI.8 Matrix differentiation

Consider

$$\mathbf{a'x} = (a_1 \quad a_2 \quad a_3 \quad \ldots \quad a_n) \begin{pmatrix} x_1 \\ x_2 \\ x_3 \\ \vdots \\ x_n \end{pmatrix} = a_1 x_1 + a_2 x_2 + a_3 x_3 + \cdots + a_n x_n$$

Partially differentiating $\mathbf{a'x}$ with respect to each x_i in turn simply yields the scalars in the vector $\mathbf{a}$. That is, $\partial(\mathbf{a'x})/\partial x_i = a_i$ for all i. If we arrange the n partial derivatives as a column vector then we can write

$$\frac{\partial(\mathbf{a'x})}{\partial \mathbf{x}} = \mathbf{a} \tag{AI.33}$$

where we use the notation on the left-hand side of (AI.33) to denote the process of differentiating $\mathbf{a'x}$ with respect to the x_i in the vector $\mathbf{x}$.

Note that since the scalar $\mathbf{a'x}$ can also be written as $\mathbf{x'a}$, we can also write

$$\frac{\partial(\mathbf{x'a})}{\partial \mathbf{x}} = \mathbf{a} \tag{AI.34}$$

Next consider

$$\mathbf{x'Ax} = (x_1 \quad x_2 \quad x_3 \quad \cdots \quad x_n) \begin{pmatrix} a_{11} & a_{12} & a_{13} & \cdots & a_{1n} \\ a_{12} & a_{22} & a_{23} & \cdots & a_{2n} \\ a_{13} & a_{23} & a_{33} & \cdots & a_{3n} \\ \vdots & \vdots & \vdots & \vdots & \vdots \\ a_{1n} & a_{2n} & a_{3n} & \cdots & a_{nn} \end{pmatrix} \begin{pmatrix} x_1 \\ x_2 \\ x_3 \\ \vdots \\ x_n \end{pmatrix}$$

(AI.35)

Notice that the matrix **A** is symmetric. Expanding $\mathbf{x'Ax}$ results, after collecting terms, in

$$\begin{aligned}
\mathbf{x'Ax} = a_{11}x_1^2 \quad &+ 2a_{12}x_1x_2 \quad + 2a_{13}x_1x_3 \quad + \quad \cdots \quad + 2a_{1n}x_1x_n \\
&+ a_{22}x_2^2 \qquad + 2a_{23}x_2x_3 \quad + \quad \cdots \quad + 2a_{2n}x_2x_n \\
&\qquad\quad + a_{33}x_3^2 \qquad + \quad \cdots \quad + 2a_{3n}x_3x_n \\
&\qquad\qquad\qquad\qquad\qquad\qquad\qquad\quad \vdots \\
&\qquad\qquad\qquad\qquad\qquad\qquad\qquad + a_{nn}x_n^2
\end{aligned}$$

(AI.36)

$\mathbf{x'Ax}$ is an example of what is known as a **quadratic form**. Partially differentiating (AI.36) with respect to each of the x_i gives

$$\frac{\partial}{\partial x_1}(\mathbf{x'Ax}) = 2(a_{11}x_1 + a_{12}x_2 + a_{13}x_3 + \cdots + a_{1n}x_n)$$

$$\frac{\partial}{\partial x_2}(\mathbf{x'Ax}) = 2(a_{12}x_1 + a_{22}x_2 + a_{23}x_3 + \cdots + a_{2n}x_n)$$

$$\vdots$$

(AI.37)

$$\frac{\partial}{\partial x_n}(\mathbf{x'Ax}) = 2(a_{1n}x_1 + a_{2n}x_2 + a_{3n}x_3 + \cdots + a_{nn}x_n)$$

The quantities in parentheses on the right-hand side of Equations (A1.37) can be seen to be the scalars in the matrix product $\mathbf{Ax}$ (recall that **A** is symmetric, so that $a_{ij} = a_{ji}$). If we place these scalars in the form of a column vector, we can write

$$\frac{\partial}{\partial \mathbf{x}}(\mathbf{x'Ax}) = 2\mathbf{Ax}$$

(AI.38)

where the left-hand side of (A1.38) represents the process of differentiating with respect to the x_i in the vector **x**.

The above rules for differentiating matrices with respect to all the scalars in a vector are used in Chapter 7 to move from Equation (7.11) to (7.12). In this case we are differentiating with respect to the vector of regression estimators $\hat{\boldsymbol{\beta}}$.

The first term in (7.11), $\mathbf{Y'Y}$, is, in fact, a scalar, which can be treated as constant when differentiating with respect to $\hat{\boldsymbol{\beta}}$. Differentiating this constant with respect to each element in $\hat{\boldsymbol{\beta}}$ simply yields a column vector of zeros.

The second term in (7.11) is $-2\hat{\boldsymbol{\beta}}'\mathbf{X'Y}$. Since $\mathbf{X'Y}$ is a column vector, we can differentiate this second term with respect to $\hat{\boldsymbol{\beta}}$ by using the result (A1.34). This gives $-2\mathbf{X'Y}$, the first term in (7.12).

The third term in (7.11) is $\hat{\boldsymbol{\beta}}'\mathbf{X}'\mathbf{X}\hat{\boldsymbol{\beta}}$. Since $\mathbf{X}'\mathbf{X}$ is a symmetric matrix, this is a quadratic form of the type (AI.35). We may therefore differentiate with respect to $\hat{\boldsymbol{\beta}}$ using the result (AI.38). This yields $2\mathbf{X}'\mathbf{X}\hat{\boldsymbol{\beta}}$, the second term in (7.12).

Notes to Appendix I

1. While mathematicians usually denote the scalar in the ith row and jth column as a_{ij}, econometricians sometimes like to do things in reverse! For example, the scalar in the ith row and jth column of the matrix $\mathbf{X}$ in Chapter 7 is written as X_{ji}.

2. We have seen that if we multiply a row or column of a square matrix into the cofactors corresponding to that row or column, we obtain the determinant of the matrix. If, however, we multiply a row or column into the cofactors corresponding to some other row or column of the matrix then it can be shown that the resultant sum always equals zero. This operation is sometimes termed 'expanding in terms of alien cofactors'. It is this operation that yields the zeros in the matrix $|\mathbf{A}|\mathbf{I}$ in (AI.25).

appendix

appendix

II Answers to numerical exercises

Chapter 2

2.1 Probability distribution is

X	0	1	2	3	4
$p(X)$	1/16	1/4	3/8	1/4	1/16

2.2 Probability distribution is

X	0	1	2
$p(X)$	2/7	4/7	1/7

2.3 $E(X)=2$, Var $(X)=1$, $E(X^3)=14$, $E[1/(1+X)]=0.3875$

2.4 (a) 0.1 (b) 0.5 (c) 0.5

2.5 $E(Y)=11$, Var $(Y)=175$

2.6 Probability distribution is

X	0	1	2	3	4	5
$p(X)$	0.3277	0.4096	0.2048	0.0512	0.0064	0.0003

2.7 (a) 0.0916 (b) 0.999 665

2.8 (a) 0.0367 (b) 0.6904 (c) 0

2.9 69

2.10 (a) Sample space

X	Y		X	Y		X	Y		X	Y	
(1,1)	1	1	(2,1)	2	1	(3,1)	3	1	(4,1)	4	1
(1,2)	2	1	(2,2)	2	2	(3,2)	3	2	(4,2)	4	2
(1,3)	3	1	(2,3)	3	2	(3,3)	3	3	(4,3)	4	3
(1,4)	4	1	(2,4)	4	2	(3,4)	4	3	(4,4)	4	4

(b) Joint and marginal distributions

Y \ X	1	2	3	4	$g(Y)$
1	1/16	2/16	2/16	2/16	7/16
2	0	1/16	2/16	2/16	5/16
3	0	0	1/16	2/16	3/16
4	0	0	0	1/16	1/16
$f(X)$	1/16	3/16	5/16	7/16	

(c) $E(X) = 3.125$, Var $(X) = 0.859$

2.11 (a)

Y	1	2	3	4
$g(Y \mid X=4)$	2/7	2/7	2/7	1/7

(b)

X	1	2	3	4
$f(X \mid Y=2)$	0	1/5	2/5	2/5

(c) $E(Y \mid X=4) = 2.29$, Var $(Y \mid X=4) = 1.06$

2.12 (a) $E(XY) = 6.25$, $E(X) = 3.125$, $E(Y) = 1.875$, Cov $(X,Y) = 0.391$
(b) Var $(X) = 0.859$, Var $(Y) = 0.859$, Correlation $\rho = 0.455$

2.13

Outcome	RRR	WRR	RWR	RRW	WWR	WRW	RWW
X	0	1	1	1	2	2	2
Y	3	2	2	2	1	1	1
Prob.	5/12	1/6	1/6	1/6	1/36	1/36	1/36

Joint and marginal distributions

X \ Y	1	2	3	$f(X)$
0	0	0	5/12	5/12
1	0	1/2	0	1/2
2	1/12	0	0	1/12
$g(Y)$	1/12	1/2	5/12	

Cov $(X,Y)=-0.389$, Var $(X)=0.389$, Var $(Y)=0.389$, $\rho=-1$
Correlation is -1 because there is an exact linear relationship between X and Y. That is, $Y=9-X$.

2.14 $E(U)=-5$, Var $(U)=162$, $E(V)=-1$, Var $(V)=36$,
$E(W)=24$, Var $(W)=72$

2.15 $E(A)=12$, Var $(A)=80$, $E(B)=1$, Var $(B)=70$
$E(X^2)=$ Var $(X)+(EX)^2=35$
$E(Y^2)=$ Var $(Y)+(EY)^2=24$
$E(XY)=$ Cov $(X,Y)+E(X)E(Y)=15$
Hence $E(AB)=-23$ and Cov $(A,B)=-35$

2.16 $E(X)=1.5$, $E(Y)=2$, $E(XY)=3$, Cov $(X,Y)=0$
Thus X and Y are uncorrelated but are not independent, since joint probabilities are not the product of marginal probabilities.

2.17   Joint distribution is

X / Y	1	2	3	4	5	$g(Y)$
3	0.03	0.06	0.09	0.06	0.06	0.3
6	0.04	0.08	0.12	0.08	0.08	0.4
9	0.03	0.06	0.09	0.06	0.06	0.3
$f(X)$	0.1	0.2	0.3	0.2	0.2	

$E(X)=6$, $E(Y)=3.2$, $E(XY)=19.2$

Chapter 3

3.1 $\bar{X}$ is N(480,220.4) (a) 0.8898 (b) 0.0885

3.2 $\bar{X}$ is N(20,0.625) Pr $(\bar{X} < 18.5)=0.0228$, Pr $(\bar{X} < 18)=0.0057$

3.3   Safety limit is exceeded if mean parcel weight is greater than 328. Assuming weights are normally distributed,
$\bar{X}$ is N(300,100), Pr $(\bar{X} > 328)=0.0026$

3.4   (a) $\bar{X} = 36.5$ (b) $s^2=0.823$

3.5 25 ± 1.147

3.6 135 ± 9.21, $n=803$

3.7   TS $= \dfrac{1460 - 1500}{110/\sqrt{80}} = -3.25$. Reject H_0 at 0.05 and 0.01 levels of significance.

3.8   One-tail test because claim is that breaking strength can be increased.
H_0: $\mu=905$, H_A: $\mu > 905$
TS $= \dfrac{930 - 905}{50/\sqrt{40}} = 3.16$. Reject H_0 at 0.05 level of significance. Sufficient evidence to justify claim.

3.9   Pr (type I error) $=0.0179$
Pr (type II error) $=0$, 0.0475, 0.3372

3.10 Two-tail test

$$TS = \frac{8 - 6.5}{2.4/\sqrt{200}} = 8.83.$$ Reject H_0 at 0.05 and 0.01 levels of significance.

Sufficient evidence to reject claim.

3.11 Two-tail test

$$TS = \frac{92.8 - 95}{10.3/\sqrt{100}} = 2.14.$$ Reject H_0 at 0.05 level but not at 0.01 level of significance.

3.12 Upper-tail test

$$TS = \frac{340(24)}{300} = 27.2, \chi^2_{0.05} = 36.415.$$ Do not reject H_0.

Insufficient evidence to say bulb fails to meet specification.

3.13 Upper-tail test. $\bar{X} = 42, s^2 = 8$

$$TS = \frac{42 - 40}{2.83/\sqrt{10}} = 2.24, t_{0.05} = 1.833.$$ Reject H_0.

Sufficient evidence to say claim is incorrect.

3.14 Testing H_0: $\mu = 0.5$ against H_A: $\mu \neq 0.5$

$$TS = \frac{0.49 - 0.5}{0.0134/\sqrt{11}} = 2.475, t_{0.025} = 2.228.$$ Reject H_0.

Testing H_0: $\sigma^2 = 0.0001$ against H_A: $\sigma^2 > 0.0001$

$$TS = \frac{0.00018(10)}{0.0001} = 18, \chi^2_{0.05} = 18.307.$$ Do not reject H_0.

Machine appears to be working properly.

3.15 42 ± 2.907

3.16 Testing H_0: $\sigma_1^2 = \sigma_2^2$ against H_A: $\sigma_1^2 > \sigma_2^2$

$TS = 2500/400 = 6.25$, $F_{0.05} = 3.03$. Reject H_0.

Testing H_0: $\sigma^2 = 625$ against H_A: $\sigma^2 < 625$

$$TS = \frac{400(9)}{625} = 5.76, \sigma^2_{0.95} = 3.325.$$ Reject H_0.

Chapter 4

4.1 (b) $\sum y^2 = 2246.1$, $\sum x^2 = 27.6$, $\sum xy = -143.6$

(c) $\hat{\beta} = -5.20$, $\hat{\alpha} = 203.14$

(e) Elasticity $= 1.63$

4.2 (a) $\hat{\beta} = -7.00$, $\hat{\alpha} = 81.1$ (b) \$24.4 billion

4.3 $\hat{A} = 542.1 - 9.01Q$

4.4 $R^2 = 0.332$, $R = -0.577$

4.5 $R^2 = 0.70$

4.6 $\hat{\beta} = 0.235$, $\hat{\alpha} = 1.84$, $R^2 = 0.995$

4.7 (a) $\hat{P} = 18.18 - 0.01365Q$, $\hat{P} = 2.44Q^{-0.51}$

(c) Elasticity $= 1.96$

4.8   (a) $\hat{\beta} = 4853.9$, $\hat{\alpha} = 51.24$, $R^2 = 0.70$
      (c) $R^2 = 0.70$ and $R^2 = 0.99$

4.9   (a) $\hat{W} = 8.99 - 2.84U$, $R^2 = 0.673$
      (b) $\hat{W} = 6.60 - 4.84 \ln(U)$, $R^2 = 0.738$
      (c) $\hat{W} = 2.36$. Suggests upward shift in relationship for 1967.

Chapter 5

5.1   (a) The biases are 3, $80/n$ and $-\mu/(n+1)$. For the given values, μ has the largest bias.
      (b) Variances are σ^2/n, σ^2/n and $n\sigma^2/(n+1)^2$.

5.3   MSEs equal sums of variances and squared biases found in 5.1. For the given values, $\tilde{\mu}$ has the smallest MSE

Chapter 6

6.1   (a) $\hat{S} = 6.99 + 4.57P$
      (b) $s_{\hat{\alpha}} = 1.79$, $s_{\hat{\beta}} = 0.336$
      (c) $\text{TS} = \hat{\beta}/s_{\hat{\beta}} = 13.6$, $t_{0.05} = 1.943$. Price does influence supply.
      (d) 6.99 ± 4.38

6.2 $s_{\hat{\alpha}} = 12.03$, $s_{\hat{\beta}} = 2.61$
      (a) $\text{TS} = \hat{\beta}/s_{\hat{\beta}} = -1.99$, $t_{0.05} = 1.860$. Price does influence demand.
      (b) 203.14 ± 27.74

6.3 $s_{\hat{\alpha}} = 6.38$, $s_{\hat{\beta}} = 1.033$
      H_0: $\beta = -10$, H_A: $\beta \neq -10$
      $\text{TS} = (\hat{\beta} + 10)/s_{\hat{\beta}} = 2.90$, $t_{0.025} = 2.447$. Reject claim.

6.4 H_0: $\beta = 0.2$, H_A: $\beta > 0.2$
      $\text{TS} = (\hat{\beta} - 0.2)/s_{\hat{\beta}} = 6.48$, $t_{0.05} = 1.833$. Reject H_0.

6.5 52.7 ± 7.9
      Since $S = 56$ lies within this interval, there is no evidence of a change in the relationship.

6.6 $s_{\hat{\alpha}} = 13.4$, $s_{\hat{\beta}} = 237.45$
      H_0: $\beta = 4000$, H_A: $\beta > 4000$
      $(\text{TS} = \hat{\beta} - 4000)/s_{\hat{\beta}} = 3.60$, $t_{0.05} = 2.132$
      Reject H_0. Evidence suggests fixed costs exceed 4000.

6.7   (a) $\sum X = 10.49$, $\sum Y = 25.70$, $\hat{S} = 9.59P^{0.726}$
      (b) 0.726 ± 0.095

6.8 H_0: $\beta = -1$, H_A: $\beta > -1$
      $\text{TS} = (\hat{\beta} + 1)/s_{\hat{\beta}} = 30.1$, $t_{0.05} = 2.132$
      Reject H_0. Evidence suggests elasticity is greater than unity.

6.9   Residuals are $+1.6$, -0.4, -2.8, -2.2, $+0.4$, $+3.5$
      Durbin–Watson statistic $= 0.94$

Chapter 7

7.1   (a) $\sum x_2 x_3 = 540$
     (b) $\hat{Y} = 109.4 + 2.836 X_2 + 5.126 X_3$
     (c) 0.910
     (d) 0.885

7.2   (a) $\hat{\alpha} = 0.638$, $\hat{\beta} = 0.627$
     (b) $\widehat{\ln(A)} = -1.220$, $\hat{A} = 0.295$

7.3 $\hat{\beta}_2 = 0.6$, $\hat{\beta}_3 = 0.1$, $\hat{\beta}_4 = 1.4$. $R^2 = 0.826$

7.4   (a) $s_{\hat{\beta}_2} = 2.83$, $s_{\hat{\beta}_3} = 5.24$
     (b) 2.836 ± 6.69
     (c) H_0: $\beta_3 = 0$. TS $= \hat{\beta}_3 / s_{\hat{\beta}_3} = 0.978$, $t_{0.05} = 1.895$. Do not reject H_0.

7.5   (a) $s_{\hat{\alpha}} = 0.0603$, $s_{\hat{\beta}} = 0.0645$
     (b) H_0: $\alpha = 1$. TS $= (\hat{\alpha} - 1)/s_{\hat{\alpha}} = -6.00$, $t_{0.05} = 1.67$. Reject H_0.
        H_0: $\beta = 1$. TS $= (\hat{\beta} - 1)/s_{\hat{\beta}} = -5.78$, $t_{0.05} = 1.67$. Reject H_0.

7.6   (a) $s_{\hat{\beta}_2} = 0.738$, $s_{\hat{\beta}_3} = 0.639$, $s_{\hat{\beta}_4} = 0.976$
     (b) t-ratios are 0.81, 0.16 and 1.43. $t_{0.25} = 2.086$
        None of the X variables appear to influence Y.
     (c) H_0: $\beta_3 = 5$. TS $= (\hat{\beta}_3 - 5)/s_{\hat{\beta}_3} = 7.67$, $t_{0.05} = 1.725$ Reject H_0.

7.7   (a) $\hat{\beta}_2 = 2.4$, $\hat{\beta}_3 = -1.4$, $\hat{\beta}_4 = -0.9$
       $s_{\hat{\beta}_2} = 0.444$, $s_{\hat{\beta}_3} = 0.628$, $s_{\hat{\beta}_4} = 0.719$

Chapter 9

9.3 $h = 3$, TS $= 2.31$, $F_{0.05} = 2.79$. Restrictions are data-acceptable.

9.4   SSR$_U = 116.76$, SSR$_R = 158.34$
     $h = 2$, TS $= 7.12$, $F_{0.05} = 3.23$. At least one restriction is invalid.

9.5   Testing (II) against (I): TS $= 20.69$, $F_{0.05} = 4.06$. Reject restriction.
     The restriction imposed on (III) is $\beta_3 = 0$.
     Testing (III) against (II): TS $= 1.86$, $F_{0.05} = 4.07$. Restriction is data-acceptable.
     Estimate $Y_t = \beta_1 + \beta_2 X_t + \beta_4 Y_{t-1} + \epsilon_t$

9.6   (a) $\hat{\beta}_2 = 1.2$, $\hat{\beta}_3 = 0.2$, $\hat{\beta}_4 = 1.2$
       $s_{\hat{\beta}_2} = 0.696$, $s_{\hat{\beta}_3} = 0.762$, $s_{\hat{\beta}_4} = 1.10$
     (b) H_0: $\beta_2 = \beta_3 = \beta_4 = 0$, TS $= 26.8$, $F_{0.05} = 2.99$. Reject H_0.
     The X-variables are clearly multicollinear.

9.7 H_0: $\beta_3 = \beta_4 = 0$, TS $= 3.0$, $F_{0.05} = 3.32$. Do not reject H_0.

9.8   (a) H_0: $\beta_3 = 0$, t-ratio $= 0.71$, $t_{0.025} = 2.03$. Do not reject H_0.
       H_0: $\beta_4 = 0$, t-ratio $= 0.89$, $t_{0.025} = 2.03$. Do not reject H_0.
     (b) SSE for Y on X_2 alone is $11.2(25) = 280$.
       H_0: $\beta_3 = \beta_4 = 0$, TS $= 11.91$, $F_{0.05} = 3.27$. Reject H_0.
     X_3 and X_4 are collinear.

9.9 For regression of Y on X_4 alone, $\hat{\beta}_4 = -0.931$, $SSE_1 = 202.03$
$H_0: \beta_2 = \beta_3 = 0$, $TS = 43.74$, $F_{0.05} = 3.19$. Reject H_0.

9.11 $H_0: \beta_2 = \beta_3$, $TS = (\hat{\beta}_2 - \hat{\beta}_3)/u$, where $u^2 = s^2(x^{22} + x^{33} - 2x^{23})$
$s^2 = 2$, $u^2 = 0.08$, $TS = 1.06$, $t_{0.025} = 2.11$. Do not reject H_0.

9.12 (a) $TS = 17.8$, $\chi^2_{0.05} = 3.841$. Reject restriction.
(b) $TS = 2.4$, $\chi^2_{0.05} = 3.841$. Do not reject restriction.
(c) $TS = 20.2$, $\chi^2_{0.05} = 5.991$. At least one restriction is invalid.

9.13 Restrictions are $\beta_2 = \beta_3$ and $\beta_4 + \beta_5 = 1$, i.e. $h = 2$.
(a) $TS = 3.89$, $F_{0.05} = 3.25$
(b) $TS = 7.44$, $\chi^2_{0.05} = 5.991$
(c) $TS = nR^2 = 7.31$, $\chi^2_{0.05} = 5.991$.
All tests suggest at least one restriction is invalid.

9.14 $SSR_1 = 0.028\,18$ ($n_1 = 21$), $SSR_2 = 0.042\,20$ ($n_2 = 18$), $SSR_P = 0.079\,99$
$TS = 1.06$, $F_{0.05} = 2.68$. Parameters appear stable.

9.15 $SSR_1 = 7250.4$, $SSR_P = 9118.2$
$TS = 1.84$, $F_{0.05} = 2.11$. Predictive failure test is passed.

9.16 $SSR_1 = 144.2$, $SSR_2 = 65.9$, $SSR_P = 286.8$
Chow Test I: $TS = 6.08$, $F_{0.01} = 4.22$. Test failed.
Chow Test II: $TS = 2.29$, $F_{0.01} = 2.42$. Test passed.
More information is used in the first test. It is therefore more powerful.

Chapter 13

13.1 (a) $\Delta y_t = \lambda \beta_0 + b_1 \Delta x_t + c_1 \Delta z_t - \lambda y_{t-1} + \lambda \beta_1 x_{t-1} + \lambda \beta_2 z_{t-1} + \epsilon_t$

(b) (i) $\beta_1 = \beta_2$, so coefficients of x_{t-1} and z_{t-1} are equal.
(ii) $b_1 = c_1$, so coefficients of Δx_t and Δz_t are equal.
(iii) $\beta_1 + \beta_2 = 1$, so coefficients of x_{t-1}, z_{t-1} and y_{t-1} sum to zero.
(iv) $b_2 = c_2 = 0$ implies $b_1 = \lambda \beta_1$ and $c_1 = \lambda \beta_2$, so coefficients of Δx_t and x_{t-1} are equal and coefficients of Δz_t and z_{t-1} are equal.

(c) (i) $\Delta y_t = \lambda \beta_0 + b_1 \Delta x_t + c_1 \Delta z_t - \lambda y_{t-1} + \lambda \beta_1 (x_{t-1} + z_{t-1}) + \epsilon_t$
(ii) $\Delta y_t = \lambda \beta_0 + b_1 (\Delta x_t + \Delta z_t) - \lambda y_{t-1} + \lambda \beta_1 x_{t-1} + \lambda \beta_2 z_{t-1} + \epsilon_t$
(iii) $\Delta y_t = \lambda \beta_0 + b_1 \Delta x_t + c_1 \Delta z_t - \lambda (y_{t-1} - z_{t-1})$
$\quad + \lambda \beta_1 (x_{t-1} - z_{t-1}) + \epsilon_t$
(iv) $\Delta y_t = \lambda \beta_0 + b_1 x_t + c_1 z_t - \lambda y_{t-1} + \epsilon_t$

(d) Equation (I) is the full error correction model.
Testing (II) against (I):
$H_0: \beta_1 + \beta_2 = 1$, $F = 9.68$, $F_{0.05} = 4.10$. Reject H_0.
Testing (III) against (I):
$H_0: \beta_1 = \beta_2$, $F = 0.66$, $F_{0.05} = 4.10$. Do not reject H_0.
Testing (IV) against (III):
$H_0: b_1 = c_1$, $F = 5.34$, $F_{0.05} = 4.09$. Reject H_0.
Testing (V) against (I):
$H_0: \beta_1 = \beta_2$, $b_2 = c_2 = 0$, $F = 6.45$, $F_{0.05} = 2.86$. Reject H_0.

Testing (V) against (III):

H_0: $b_2 = c_2 = 0$, $F = 9.43$, $F_{0.05} = 3.24$. Reject H_0.

Equation (III) is the preferred equation. However, Δx_t in this equation has a t-ratio of only 0.83, and should therefore be dropped.

In error correction form, Equation (III) is

$$\Delta y_t = 0.218\,\Delta x_t + 0.834\,\Delta z_t$$
$$- 0.721(y_{t-1} - 2.25 - 0.849x_{t-1} - 0.849z_{t-1})$$

Long-run elasticities with respect to X and Z are both 0.849, while short-run elasticities are 0.218 and 0.834 respectively. 72% of any disequilibrium in any period is made up in the following period.

When X and Z grow at a proportionate rate g, Y grows at a rate of $1.698g$. The long-run relationship is therefore

$$Y = K(XY)^{0.849}, \qquad \text{where} \quad K = e^{2.25 - 0.90g}$$

13.2 (a) (i) $\hat{\beta}_0 = 1.227$, $\hat{\beta}_1 = 0.943$, $\hat{\lambda} = 0.418$

(ii) $b_1 = 0.344$, $b_2 = -0.152$, $b_3 = 0.202$, $\hat{\mu}_1 = 0.776$, $\hat{\mu}_2 = -0.194$

(b) (II) $b_3 = \mu_2 = 0$, (III) $b_2 = b_3 = \mu_2 = 0$

(IV) $\beta_1 = 1$, (V) $\beta_1 = 1$, $b_3 = \mu_2 = 0$

(c) Testing (II) against (I): $F = 2.45$, $F_{0.05} = 3.19$. Do not reject H_0. Restrictions are data-acceptable.

Testing (III) against (II): $F = 10.60$, $F_{0.05} = 4.05$. Reject H_0. Restriction is invalid.

Testing (IV) against (I): $F = 0.87$, $F_{0.05} = 4.04$. Do not reject H_0. Restriction is data-acceptable.

Testing (V) against (IV): $F = 2.40$, $F_{0.05} = 3.19$. Do not reject H_0. Restriction is data-acceptable.

Testing (V) against (II): $F = 0.72$, $F_{0.05} = 4.05$. Do not reject H_0. Restriction is data-acceptable.

Testing (V) against (I): $F = 1.88$, $F_{0.05} = 2.80$. Do not reject H_0. Restrictions are data-acceptable.

Equation (V) is the preferred equation. The short-run elasticity of Y with respect to X is 0.345, whereas the long-run elasticity is unity. 43% of the disequilibrium in any period is made up in the following period. The long-run relationship between X and Y is

$$Y = KX, \qquad \text{where} \quad K = e^{1.1406 - 1.520g}$$

Appendix I

AI.1 (a) $\mathbf{AC} = \begin{pmatrix} 0 & -18 & 24 & -20 \\ 1 & -6 & 5 & -9 \\ -15 & -7 & 24 & 7 \end{pmatrix}$, $\quad \mathbf{AB} = \begin{pmatrix} 76 & 40 & 46 \\ 22 & 14 & 18 \\ 50 & 25 & 2 \end{pmatrix}$,

$$\mathbf{BA} = \begin{pmatrix} 71 & 62 & 33 \\ 41 & 6 & -1 \\ 44 & 27 & 15 \end{pmatrix}, \qquad \mathbf{Ax} = \begin{pmatrix} 6 \\ 0 \\ 23 \end{pmatrix},$$

$$\mathbf{DA} = \begin{pmatrix} -16 & -5 & -3 \\ 8 & -6 & -6 \end{pmatrix}, \qquad \mathbf{DB} = \begin{pmatrix} -4 & -1 & -26 \\ 4 & 24 & -14 \end{pmatrix}$$

DE, **yC** and **BD** are not defined.

AI.3 (a) $\mathbf{A} = \begin{pmatrix} 3 & 2 & -4 \\ 2 & -3 & 2 \\ 4 & -2 & -3 \end{pmatrix}, \qquad \mathbf{x} = \begin{pmatrix} x_1 \\ x_2 \\ x_3 \end{pmatrix}, \qquad \mathbf{b} = \begin{pmatrix} 15 \\ -8 \\ 6 \end{pmatrix}$

(b) $\mathbf{A} = \begin{pmatrix} 1 & 2 & 0 \\ 2 & 0 & -3 \\ 0 & -1 & 2 \end{pmatrix}, \qquad \mathbf{x} = \begin{pmatrix} a \\ b \\ c \end{pmatrix}, \qquad \mathbf{b} = \begin{pmatrix} 11 \\ 3 \\ -2 \end{pmatrix}$

AI.4 (a) 54 (b) 7, -16, 36, 0

AI.5 $\begin{pmatrix} \frac{13}{35} & \frac{14}{35} & -\frac{8}{35} \\ \frac{14}{35} & \frac{7}{35} & -\frac{14}{35} \\ \frac{8}{35} & \frac{14}{35} & -\frac{13}{35} \end{pmatrix}, \begin{pmatrix} \frac{3}{11} & \frac{4}{11} & \frac{6}{11} \\ \frac{4}{11} & -\frac{2}{11} & -\frac{3}{11} \\ \frac{2}{11} & -\frac{1}{11} & \frac{4}{11} \end{pmatrix}$

AI.7 $x_1 = 1$, $x_2 = 2$, $x_3 = -2$
   $a = 3$, $b = 4$, $c = 1$

appendix

The data sets and the floppy disk

The floppy disk contains 12 data files in all, giving the data sets for the computer exercises in the main part of this book. Six of these files are for use with the computer package MICROFIT, and have names of the form DATASET*.FIT. The remaining six files are ASCII raw data files with names of the form DATASET*.DAT. On these files the data is entered variable by variable and is in free format. These files are for use with other packages.

AIII.1 Data sets 1, 2 and 3

These refer to the demand for food in the USA, the UK and Japan respectively. These data sets are stored on MICROFIT files named DATASET1.FIT, DATASET2.FIT and DATASET3.FIT respectively and on ASCII raw data files named DATASET1.DAT, DATASET2.DAT and DATASET3.DAT respectively. Each file contains annual data on 4 variables for the years 1963–1992. *On the data disk*, the variables are named as follows for the MICROFIT files:

$$NF = \text{expenditure on food in current prices}$$
$$RF = \text{expenditure on food in constant prices}$$
$$NTE = \text{total expenditure in current prices}$$
$$RTE = \text{total expenditure in constant prices}$$

On the ASCII files the variables are entered in the above order. The US data is in $ billions the UK data in £ billions and the Japan data in billions of Yen.

RF corresponds to the variable Q (demand for food) in the main text and NTE corresponds to the variable X (total expenditure). The variable P (price of food) in the main text can be created as NF/RF, and the variable G (general price index) as NTE/RTE. These data sets are reproduced in Tables AIII.1, AIII.2 and AIII.3.

AIII.2 Data set 4

This data set contains quarterly data on UK consumption and disposable income for the period 1974Q1–1984Q4. It is stored on a MICROFIT file named DATASET4.FIT and on an ASCII file named DATASET4.DAT. On the MICROFIT file the variables are named as in the main text. That is,

C = consumers' expenditure in constant prices
Y = disposable income in constant prices

On the ASCII file they are entered in that order. This data set is reproduced in Table AIII.4. The figures are in £ billions

AIII.3 Data set 5

This data set contains simulated data on a cross-section of 50 households. It is stored on the MICROFIT file DATASET5.FIT and on the ASCII file DATASET5.DAT. On the MICROFIT file the three quantitative variables are named as in the main text. That is,

E = average hourly earnings of household (£)
A = age of household
S = schooling of household

The variable DUM corresponds to the dummy variable D_i defined in Section 16.4. On the ASCII file the variables are entered in the above order. This data set is reproduced in Table AIII.5.

AIII.4 Data set 6

This data set contains quarterly time series data relating to the German economy for 1972Q1–1989Q4. It is stored in the MICROFIT file DATASET6.FIT and in the ASCII file DATASET6.DAT. On the MICROFIT file the variables are named as follows:

$M0$ = narrow money supply in current prices
GNP = gross national product in current prices
P = consumer price index
I = central bank discount rate

On the ASCII file the variables are entered in the above order. The variables in Appendix 15A in the main text can be created as $M = M0/P$, $Y = GNP/P$ and $R = 1 + I/100$. This data set is reproduced in Table AIII.6.

Table AIII.1 Data set 1

Year	NF	RF	NTE	RTE
1963	57 381.4	155 385.0	379 212.1	975 441
1964	60 626.4	161 358.0	405 934.2	1 029 447
1965	65 126.8	169 269.0	436 171.6	1 087 325
1966	70 744.0	174 606.0	471 369.0	1 142 935
1967	72 403.0	179 328.0	496 863.1	1 176 228
1968	77 396.6	185 036.0	545 714.7	1 241 160
1969	82 529.0	187 976.0	591 206.8	1 286 474
1970	89 011.6	192 614.0	632 131.3	1 316 125
1971	90 970.9	193 006.0	685 725.1	1 367 139
1972	96 692.4	194 204.0	752 398.9	1 446 381
1973	107 674.4	186 513.0	832 352.3	1 448 779
1974	122 492.6	183 111.0	910 673.2	1 434 678
1975	134 398.5	188 207.0	1 005 438	1 466 942
1976	144 213.7	199 261.0	1 123 621	1 548 702
1977	154 860.0	205 585.0	1 250 754	1 617 373
1978	168 781.5	202 052.0	1 393 873	1 683 404
1979	188 198.2	204 581.0	1 549 308	1 714 752
1980	204 542.0	204 542.0	1 711 662	1 711 662
1981	217 892.0	201 449.0	1 895 379	1 736 843
1982	224 738.6	201 133.0	2 024 198	1 750 610
1983	232 016.8	204 832.0	2 207 199	1 825 259
1984	245 859.1	208 603.0	2 407 035	1 914 548
1985	256 367.7	213 900.0	2 603 585	1 996 650
1986	265 875.3	216 483.0	2 774 282	2 076 802
1987	276 767.7	215 630.0	2 969 222	2 136 452
1988	293 333.5	218 899.0	3 211 440	2 220 540
1989	313 861.7	219 327.0	3 442 326	2 271 500
1990	337 636.0	222 720.0	3 673 863	2 308 922
1991	346 499.2	222 198.0	3 814 636	2 306 381
1992	351 817.1	222 720.0	4 035 737	2 371 061

Source: *OECD National Accounts*

Table AIII.2 Data set 2

Year	NF	RF	NTE	RTE
1963	4 980.0	16 638.0	14 320.0	46 978.0
1964	5 564.0	18 001.0	16 681.0	52 437.0
1965	6 279.0	18 837.0	18 822.0	55 389.0
1966	7 033.0	20 271.0	21 445.0	60 001.0
1967	7 923.0	22 068.0	24 538.0	66 120.0
1968	8 946.0	23 120.0	28 357.0	72 445.0
1969	10 099.0	24 727.0	32 637.0	79 440.0
1970	11 503.0	25 925.0	37 807.0	85 913.0
1971	12 468.0	26 682.0	42 595.0	90 940.0
1972	13 888.0	28 839.0	49 124.0	99 565.0
1973	16 375.0	30 372.0	59 366.0	108 744.0
1974	20 340.0	29 860.0	71 782.0	108 544.0
1975	23 763.0	31 304.0	83 591.0	113 511.0
1976	26 557.0	31 740.0	94 444.0	117 467.0
1977	28 942.0	32 628.0	105 398.0	122 182.0
1978	30 331.0	33 202.0	115 960.0	128 223.0
1979	31 623.0	34 099.0	127 601.0	136 401.0
1980	34 045.0	34 045.0	138 585.0	138 585.0
1981	36 043.0	34 388.0	147 103.0	140 267.0
1982	37 479.0	35 454.0	157 994.0	146 832.0
1983	39 037.0	35 807.0	166 632.0	151 849.0
1984	40 193.0	35 414.0	175 383.0	155 979.0
1985	41 537.0	36 137.0	185 335.0	161 241.0
1986	42 043.0	36 421.0	192 327.0	166 206.0
1987	42 825.0	37 430.0	200 704.0	172 830.0
1988	43 888.0	38 229.0	210 185.0	180 571.0
1989	46 090.0	39 509.9	222 719.0	188 082.0
1990	48 877.0	40 518.0	237 375.0	195 707.0
1991	51 213.0	40 641.0	248 746.0	200 216.0
1992	52 003.0	40 917.0	258 154.0	203 356.0

Source: *Economic Trends Annual Supplement*

Table AIII.3 Data set 3

Year	NF	RF	NTE	RTE
1963	4 689.0	34 274.0	20 279.0	170 874.0
1964	4 889.0	34 695.0	21 643.0	176 044.0
1965	5 059.0	34 673.0	23 044.0	178 493.0
1966	5 297.0	35 054.0	24 373.0	181 550.0
1967	5 485.0	35 631.0	25 618.0	185 985.0
1968	5 696.0	35 817.0	27 591.0	191 209.0
1969	6 035.0	35 919.0	29 292.0	192 366.0
1970	6 429.0	36 280.0	31 907.0	197 873.0
1971	7 105.0	36 312.0	35 763.0	204 139.0
1972	7 614.0	36 248.0	40 439.0	216 752.0
1973	8 751.0	37 120.0	46 213.0	228 615.0
1974	10 028.0	36 470.0	53 256.0	225 317.0
1975	12 313.0	36 480.0	65 590.0	224 580.0
1976	14 459.0	36 866.0	76 225.0	225 666.0
1977	16 596.0	36 547.0	87 165.0	224 892.0
1978	18 373.0	37 217.0	100 524.0	236 909.0
1979	20 988.0	38 046.0	119 212.0	247 212.0
1980	23 655.0	38 095.0	138 564.0	247 185.0
1981	24 946.0	37 849.0	154 274.0	247 402.0
1982	26 490.0	37 942.0	169 372.0	249 852.0
1983	28 061.0	38 582.0	185 611.0	261 200.0
1984	29 274.0	37 925.0	198 820.0	266 486.0
1985	30 657.0	38 402.0	217 485.0	276 742.0
1986	32 574.0	39 610.0	241 554.0	295 622.0
1987	34 402.0	40 621.0	265 290.0	311 234.0
1988	36 491.0	41 542.0	299 449.0	334 591.0
1989	39 143.0	42 249.0	327 363.0	345 406.0
1990	41 816.0	41 816.0	347 527.0	347 527.0
1991	44 061.0	41 880.0	364 972.0	339 915.0
1992	45 476.0	42 581.0	382 240.0	339 946.0

Source: *OECD National Accounts*

Table AIII.4 Data set 4

Obs	C	Y	Obs	C	Y
74Q1	42 065.0	48 856.0	79Q3	48 664.0	55 014.0
74Q2	43 636.0	48 921.0	79Q4	51 326.0	58 841.0
74Q3	44 994.0	50 727.0	80Q1	48 272.0	55 814.0
74Q4	47 521.0	50 929.0	80Q2	47 527.0	56 151.0
75Q1	42 667.0	51 138.0	80Q3	49 480.0	56 968.0
75Q2	43 979.0	49 695.0	80Q4	50 546.0	56 949.0
75Q3	44 492.0	50 061.0	81Q1	47 483.0	56 763.0
75Q4	46 362.0	49 525.0	81Q2	47 892.0	55 902.0
76Q1	42 364.0	49 371.0	81Q3	49 457.0	55 520.0
76Q2	43 657.0	49 445.0	81Q4	51 179.0	55 962.0
76Q3	44 940.0	51 344.0	82Q1	47 360.0	55 325.0
76Q4	47 318.0	49 539.0	82Q2	47 842.0	55 568.0
77Q1	42 264.0	47 278.0	82Q3	50 190.0	55 919.0
77Q2	42 981.0	47 895.0	82Q4	52 588.0	56 232.0
77Q3	44 484.0	48 996.0	83Q1	49 438.0	55 950.0
77Q4	47 754.0	51 164.0	83Q2	50 081.0	57 203.0
78Q1	44 845.0	50 232.0	83Q3	52 852.0	57 563.0
78Q2	45 560.0	52 379.0	83Q4	54 561.0	58 234.0
78Q3	47 574.0	53 388.0	84Q1	50 653.0	57 961.0
78Q4	49 531.0	54 314.0	84Q2	51 526.0	58 954.0
79Q1	46 356.0	53 412.0	84Q3	52 830.0	58 975.0
79Q2	49 318.0	55 033.0	84Q4	55 950.0	61 041.0

Source: *Economic Trends Annual Supplement*

Table AIII.5 Data set 5

House-hold	A	S	E	DUM	House-hold	A	S	E	DUM
1	0	6.0	4.71	0	26	25.0	2.0	12.80	0
2	1.0	3.0	3.60	0	27	25.0	0	5.20	0
3	2.0	0	4.37	0	28	27.0	4.0	8.12	1.0
4	2.0	4.0	4.64	0	29	28.0	7.0	17.54	1.0
5	3.0	1.0	3.27	0	30	28.0	4.0	22.52	1.0
6	5.0	0	4.26	0	31	30.0	3.0	5.47	0
7	6.0	7.0	6.14	1.0	32	31.0	1.0	13.67	0
8	7.0	5.0	6.74	0	33	32.0	0	4.84	0
9	8.0	0	6.11	0	34	34.0	5.0	38.52	1.0
10	8.0	2.0	5.53	1.0	35	34.0	2.0	9.98	1.0
11	8.0	6.0	5.53	0	36	37.0	6.0	27.73	1.0
12	10.0	1.0	5.36	0	37	37.0	0	5.06	0
13	11.0	7.0	8.73	1.0	38	37.0	1.0	4.36	0
14	13.0	0	5.85	0	39	38.0	7.0	23.96	1.0
15	15.0	0	6.88	0	40	38.0	4.0	30.77	1.0
16	15.0	2.0	7.17	1.0	41	39.0	0	20.68	1.0
17	15.0	7.0	10.80	1.0	42	40.0	2.0	50.90	1.0
18	18.0	0	5.06	0	43	42.0	3.0	3.96	0
19	19.0	6.0	13.69	1.0	44	42.0	0	7.58	0
20	21.0	0	8.01	0	45	43.0	4.0	6.18	1.0
21	21.0	2.0	17.13	1.0	46	44.0	3.0	43.25	0
22	23.0	1.0	7.75	1.0	47	44.0	1.0	32.04	0
23	24.0	0	6.20	0	48	45.0	0	3.35	0
24	24.0	5.0	17.72	1.0	49	45.0	2.0	18.35	0
25	24.0	3.0	8.80	1.0	50	46.0	0	4.95	0

Table AIII.6 Data set 6

Obs	M0	GNP	P	I
72Q1	117.1	799.6	54.9	3.0
72Q2	121.8	813.6	55.5	3.0
72Q3	125.7	829.2	56.2	3.0
72Q4	128.4	858.0	57.2	4.5
73Q1	131.8	899.6	58.4	5.0
73Q2	127.3	904.8	59.6	7.0
73Q3	126.1	922.0	60.1	7.0
73Q4	130.6	949.2	61.3	7.5
74Q1	131.5	959.6	62.7	7.5
74Q2	134.7	975.2	63.8	7.5
74Q3	138.5	999.2	64.3	7.0
74Q4	144.5	1008.8	65.2	6.0
75Q1	148.3	995.2	66.5	5.0
75Q2	154.3	1020.4	67.7	4.5
75Q3	161.5	1037.2	68.3	3.5
75Q4	165.0	1064.8	68.8	3.5
76Q1	166.2	1092.0	69.9	3.5
76Q2	172.5	1125.2	70.7	3.5
76Q3	173.5	1132.8	70.9	3.5
76Q4	170.6	1154.8	71.4	3.5
77Q1	177.7	1176.8	72.6	3.5
77Q2	182.2	1193.6	73.4	3.5
77Q3	188.6	1189.2	73.6	3.5
77Q4	191.4	1237.6	73.9	3.0
78Q1	202.5	1256.0	74.8	3.0
78Q2	207.7	1284.8	75.5	3.0
78Q3	213.8	1298.4	75.4	3.0
78Q4	219.2	1327.2	75.6	3.0
79Q1	223.6	1350.4	77.0	4.0
79Q2	224.0	1384.0	78.0	4.0
79Q3	225.4	1411.6	79.0	5.0
79Q4	225.9	1440.0	79.7	6.0
80Q1	226.8	1476.8	81.2	7.0
80Q2	227.8	1478.4	82.6	7.5
80Q3	232.9	1490.4	83.1	7.5
80Q4	234.9	1495.2	83.8	7.5

continued

Table AIII.6 continued

Obs	M0	GNP	P	I
81Q1	230.0	1516.0	85.8	7.5
81Q2	232.0	1530.8	87.4	7.5
81Q3	230.2	1547.2	88.6	7.5
81Q4	231.3	1568.0	89.8	7.5
82Q1	234.0	1580.4	90.9	7.5
82Q2	239.0	1584.4	92.0	7.5
82Q3	242.5	1590.8	93.1	7.0
82Q4	247.8	1602.4	94.0	5.0
83Q1	258.7	1645.6	94.6	4.0
83Q2	265.3	1660.4	95.1	4.0
83Q3	266.9	1675.2	96.0	4.0
83Q4	268.0	1717.2	96.5	4.0
84Q1	269.0	1748.4	97.3	4.0
84Q2	270.4	1722.8	97.8	4.5
84Q3	274.2	1774.0	97.8	4.5
84Q4	284.0	1801.6	98.5	4.5
85Q1	278.7	1791.2	99.7	4.5
85Q2	280.0	1820.8	100.2	4.5
85Q3	288.6	1860.0	99.9	4.0
85Q4	303.0	1878.0	100.2	4.0
86Q1	306.2	1890.0	100.4	3.5
86Q2	311.5	1926.0	100.1	3.5
86Q3	320.9	1960.4	99.6	3.5
86Q4	327.5	1979.2	99.3	3.5
87Q1	332.0	1955.2	99.9	3.0
87Q2	342.6	2005.6	100.2	3.0
87Q3	350.1	2012.0	100.2	3.0
87Q4	351.6	2044.0	100.2	3.5
88Q1	365.7	2061.6	100.8	3.5
88Q2	377.2	2092.4	101.4	3.5
88Q3	383.0	2117.6	101.5	3.5
88Q4	392.6	2154.8	101.9	3.5
89Q1	400.5	2218.4	103.3	4.0
89Q2	396.5	2220.4	104.3	5.0
89Q3	401.4	2248.8	104.3	5.0
89Q4	415.4	2289.6	104.9	6.0

Source: *International Financial Statistics*

appendix

appendix

IV Statistical tables

Areas under the standard normal curve

z'	0.00	0.01	0.02	0.03	0.04	0.05	0.06	0.07	0.08	0.09
0.0	0.0000	0.0040	0.0080	0.0120	0.0160	0.0199	0.0239	0.0279	0.0319	0.0359
0.1	0.0398	0.0438	0.0478	0.0517	0.0557	0.0596	0.0636	0.0675	0.0714	0.0753
0.2	0.0793	0.0832	0.0871	0.0910	0.0948	0.0987	0.1026	0.1064	0.1103	0.1141
0.3	0.1179	0.1217	0.1255	0.1293	0.1331	0.1368	0.1406	0.1443	0.1480	0.1517
0.4	0.1554	0.1591	0.1628	0.1664	0.1700	0.1736	0.1772	0.1808	0.1844	0.1879
0.5	0.1915	0.1950	0.1985	0.2019	0.2054	0.2088	0.2123	0.2157	0.2190	0.2224
0.6	0.2257	0.2291	0.2324	0.2357	0.2389	0.2422	0.2454	0.2486	0.2517	0.2549
0.7	0.2580	0.2611	0.2642	0.2673	0.2704	0.2734	0.2764	0.2794	0.2823	0.2852
0.8	0.2881	0.2910	0.2939	0.2967	0.2995	0.3023	0.3051	0.3078	0.3106	0.3133
0.9	0.3159	0.3186	0.3212	0.3238	0.3264	0.3289	0.3315	0.3340	0.3365	0.3389
1.0	0.3413	0.3438	0.3461	0.3485	0.3508	0.3531	0.3554	0.3577	0.3599	0.3621
1.1	0.3643	0.3665	0.3686	0.3708	0.3729	0.3749	0.3770	0.3790	0.3810	0.3830
1.2	0.3849	0.3869	0.3888	0.3907	0.3925	0.3944	0.3962	0.3980	0.3997	0.4015
1.3	0.4032	0.4049	0.4066	0.4082	0.4099	0.4115	0.4131	0.4147	0.4162	0.4177
1.4	0.4192	0.4207	0.4222	0.4236	0.4251	0.4265	0.4279	0.4292	0.4306	0.4319
1.5	0.4332	0.4345	0.4357	0.4370	0.4382	0.4394	0.4406	0.4418	0.4429	0.4441
1.6	0.4452	0.4463	0.4474	0.4484	0.4495	0.4505	0.4515	0.4525	0.4535	0.4545
1.7	0.4554	0.4564	0.4573	0.4582	0.4591	0.4599	0.4608	0.4616	0.4625	0.4633
1.8	0.4641	0.4649	0.4656	0.4664	0.4671	0.4678	0.4686	0.4693	0.4699	0.4706
1.9	0.4713	0.4719	0.4726	0.4732	0.4738	0.4744	0.4750	0.4756	0.4761	0.4767
2.0	0.4772	0.4778	0.4783	0.4788	0.4793	0.4798	0.4803	0.4808	0.4812	0.4817
2.1	0.4821	0.4826	0.4830	0.4834	0.4838	0.4842	0.4846	0.4850	0.4854	0.4857
2.2	0.4861	0.4864	0.4868	0.4871	0.4875	0.4878	0.4881	0.4884	0.4887	0.4890
2.3	0.4893	0.4896	0.4898	0.4901	0.4904	0.4906	0.4909	0.4911	0.4913	0.4916
2.4	0.4918	0.4920	0.4922	0.4925	0.4927	0.4929	0.4931	0.4932	0.4934	0.4936
2.5	0.4938	0.4940	0.4941	0.4943	0.4945	0.4946	0.4948	0.4949	0.4951	0.4952
2.6	0.4953	0.4955	0.4956	0.4957	0.4959	0.4960	0.4961	0.4962	0.4963	0.4964
2.7	0.4965	0.4966	0.4967	0.4968	0.4969	0.4970	0.4971	0.4972	0.4973	0.4974
2.8	0.4974	0.4975	0.4976	0.4977	0.4977	0.4978	0.4979	0.4979	0.4980	0.4981
2.9	0.4981	0.4982	0.4982	0.4983	0.4984	0.4984	0.4985	0.4985	0.4986	0.4986
3.0	0.4987	0.4987	0.4987	0.4988	0.4988	0.4989	0.4989	0.4989	0.4990	0.4990

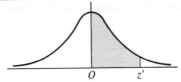

The above table shows the area beneath the standard normal curve between zero (the mean of the N(0, 1) distribution) and z', a point on the horizontal axis. It therefore gives areas such as that shaded in the figure. For example, if $z' = 1.47$ then the shaded area is 0.4292. Thus if z is N(0, 1) then $\Pr(0 < z < z') = 0.4292$.

Since (a) the standard normal curve is symmetrical about the vertical axis and (b) the total area under it is unity, the area beneath the curve between any two points on the z-axis can be found using the table.

Percentage points of the Student's *t* distribution

Area α under right-hand tail

v	0.4	0.25	0.1	0.05	0.025	0.01	0.005	0.0025	0.001	0.0005
1	0.325	1.000	3.078	6.314	12.706	31.821	63.657	127.320	318.310	636.620
2	0.289	0.816	1.886	2.920	4.303	6.965	9.925	14.089	22.327	31.598
3	0.277	0.765	1.638	2.353	3.182	4.541	5.841	7.453	10.214	12.924
4	0.271	0.741	0.533	2.132	2.776	3.747	4.604	5.598	7.173	8.610
5	0.267	0.727	1.476	2.015	2.571	3.365	4.032	4.773	5.893	6.869
6	0.265	0.718	1.440	1.943	2.447	3.143	3.707	4.317	5.208	5.959
7	0.263	0.711	1.415	1.895	2.365	2.998	3.499	4.029	4.785	5.408
8	0.262	0.706	1.397	1.860	2.306	2.896	3.355	3.833	4.501	5.041
9	0.261	0.703	1.383	1.833	2.262	2.821	3.250	3.690	4.297	4.781
10	0.260	0.700	1.372	1.812	2.228	2.764	3.169	3.581	4.144	4.587
11	0.260	0.697	1.363	1.796	2.201	2.718	3.106	3.497	4.025	4.437
12	0.259	0.695	1.356	1.782	2.179	2.681	3.055	3.428	3.930	4.318
13	0.259	0.694	1.350	1.771	2.160	2.650	3.012	3.372	3.852	4.221
14	0.258	0.692	1.345	1.761	2.145	2.624	2.977	3.326	3.787	4.140
15	0.258	0.691	1.341	1.753	2.131	2.602	2.947	3.286	3.733	4.073
16	0.258	0.690	1.337	1.746	2.120	2.583	2.921	3.252	3.686	4.015
17	0.257	0.689	1.333	1.740	2.110	2.567	2.898	3.222	3.646	3.965
18	0.257	0.688	1.330	1.734	2.101	2.552	2.878	3.197	3.610	3.922
19	0.257	0.688	1.328	1.729	2.093	2.539	2.861	3.174	3.579	3.883
20	0.257	0.687	1.325	1.725	2.086	2.528	2.845	3.153	3.552	3.850
21	0.257	0.686	1.323	1.721	2.080	2.518	2.831	3.135	3.527	3.819
22	0.256	0.686	1.321	1.717	2.074	2.508	2.819	3.119	3.505	3.792
23	0.256	0.685	1.319	1.714	2.069	2.500	2.807	3.104	3.485	3.767
24	0.256	0.685	1.318	1.711	2.064	2.492	2.797	3.091	3.467	3.745
25	0.256	0.684	1.316	1.708	2.060	2.485	2.787	3.078	3.450	3.725
26	0.256	0.684	1.315	1.706	2.056	2.479	2.779	3.067	3.435	3.707
27	0.256	0.684	1.314	1.703	2.052	2.473	2.771	3.057	3.421	3.690
28	0.256	0.683	1.313	1.701	2.048	2.467	2.763	3.047	3.408	3.674
29	0.256	0.683	1.311	1.699	2.045	2.462	2.756	3.038	3.396	3.659
30	0.256	0.683	1.310	1.697	2.042	2.457	2.750	3.030	3.385	3.646
40	0.255	0.681	1.303	1.684	2.021	2.423	2.704	2.971	3.307	3.551
60	0.254	0.679	1.296	1.671	2.000	2.390	2.660	2.915	3.232	3.460
120	0.254	0.677	1.289	1.658	1.980	2.358	2.617	2.860	3.160	3.373
∞	0.253	0.674	1.282	1.645	1.960	2.326	2.576	2.807	3.090	3.291

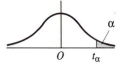

The table gives critical values for t, written t_α, cutting off an area α under the right-hand tail as indicated by the shaded area in the figure. $v =$ number of degrees of freedom. For example, if $v = 24$ and $\alpha = 0.05$ then $t_{0.05} = 1.711$; if $v = 12$ and $\alpha = 0.025$ then $t_{0.025} = 2.179$.

Percentage points of the χ^2 distribution

Area α under distribution

v	0.995	0.99	0.975	0.95	0.05	0.025	0.01	0.005
1	0.0000393	0.000157	0.000982	0.00393	3.841	5.024	6.635	7.879
2	0.0100	0.0201	0.0506	0.103	5.991	7.378	9.210	10.597
3	0.0717	0.115	0.216	0.352	7.815	9.348	11.345	12.838
4	0.207	0.297	0.484	0.711	9.488	11.143	13.277	14.860
5	0.412	0.554	0.831	1.145	11.070	12.832	15.086	16.750
6	0.676	0.872	1.237	1.635	12.592	14.449	16.812	18.548
7	0.989	1.239	1.690	2.167	14.067	16.013	18.475	20.278
8	1.344	1.646	2.180	2.733	15.507	17.535	20.090	21.955
9	1.735	2.088	2.700	3.325	16.919	19.023	21.666	23.589
10	2.156	2.558	3.247	3.940	18.307	20.483	23.209	25.188
11	2.603	3.053	3.816	4.575	19.675	21.920	24.725	26.757
12	3.074	3.571	4.404	5.226	21.026	23.337	26.217	28.300
13	3.565	4.107	5.009	5.892	22.362	24.736	27.688	29.819
14	4.075	4.660	5.629	6.571	23.685	26.119	29.141	31.319
15	4.601	5.229	6.262	7.261	24.996	27.488	30.578	32.801
16	5.142	5.812	6.908	7.962	26.296	28.845	32.000	34.267
17	5.697	6.408	7.564	8.672	27.587	30.191	33.409	35.718
18	6.265	7.015	8.231	9.390	28.869	31.526	34.805	37.156
19	6.844	7.633	8.907	10.117	30.144	32.852	36.191	38.582
20	7.434	8.260	9.591	10.851	31.410	34.170	37.566	39.997
21	8.034	8.897	10.283	11.591	32.671	35.479	38.932	41.401
22	8.643	9.542	10.982	12.338	33.924	36.781	40.289	42.796
23	9.260	10.196	11.689	13.091	35.172	38.076	41.638	44.181
24	9.886	10.856	12.401	13.848	36.415	39.364	42.980	45.558
25	10.520	11.524	13.120	14.611	37.652	40.646	44.314	46.928
26	11.160	12.198	13.844	15.379	38.885	41.923	45.642	48.290
27	11.808	12.879	14.573	16.151	40.113	43.194	46.963	49.645
28	12.461	13.565	15.308	16.928	41.337	44.461	48.278	50.993
29	13.121	14.256	16.047	17.708	42.557	45.722	49.588	52.336
30	13.787	14.953	16.791	18.493	43.773	46.979	50.892	53.672

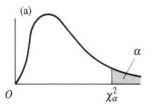

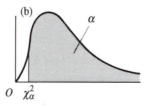

The table gives critical values for χ^2, written χ^2_α, cutting off the area α, to the *right* of χ^2_α, under the distribution as indicated by the shaded areas in the figures. Note that α can be a small area, as in (a) or a large area as in (b). $v =$ number of degrees of freedom. For example, if $v = 24$ and $\alpha = 0.05$ then $\chi^2_{0.05} = 36.415$; if $v = 12$ and $\alpha = 0.95$ then $\chi^2_{0.95} = 5.226$.

0.05 and 0.01 points of the F distribution

$F_{0.05}$ points

Degrees of freedom for numerator

	1	2	3	4	5	6	7	8	9	10	12	15	20	24	30	40	60	120	∞
1	161	200	216	225	230	234	237	239	241	242	244	246	248	249	250	251	252	253	254
2	18.5	19.0	19.2	19.2	19.3	19.3	19.4	19.4	19.4	19.4	19.4	19.4	19.4	19.5	19.5	19.5	19.5	19.5	19.5
3	10.1	9.55	9.28	9.12	9.01	8.94	8.89	8.85	8.81	8.79	8.74	8.70	8.66	8.64	8.62	8.59	8.57	8.55	8.53
4	7.71	6.94	6.59	6.39	6.26	6.16	6.09	6.04	6.00	5.96	5.91	5.86	5.80	5.77	5.75	5.72	5.69	5.66	5.63
5	6.61	5.79	5.41	5.19	5.05	4.95	4.88	4.82	4.77	4.74	4.68	4.62	4.56	4.53	4.50	4.46	4.43	4.40	4.37
6	5.99	5.14	4.76	4.53	4.39	4.28	4.21	4.15	4.10	4.06	4.00	3.94	3.87	3.84	3.81	3.77	3.74	3.70	3.67
7	5.59	4.74	4.35	4.12	3.97	3.87	3.79	3.73	3.68	3.64	3.57	3.51	3.44	3.41	3.38	3.34	3.30	3.27	3.23
8	5.32	4.46	4.07	3.84	3.69	3.58	3.50	3.44	3.39	3.35	3.28	3.22	3.15	3.12	3.08	3.04	3.01	2.97	2.93
9	5.12	4.26	3.86	3.63	3.48	3.37	3.29	3.23	3.18	3.14	3.07	3.01	2.94	2.90	2.86	2.83	2.79	2.75	2.71
10	4.96	4.10	3.71	3.48	3.33	3.22	3.14	3.07	3.02	2.98	2.91	2.85	2.77	2.74	2.70	2.66	2.62	2.58	2.54
11	4.84	3.98	3.59	3.36	3.20	3.09	3.01	2.95	2.90	2.85	2.79	2.72	2.65	2.61	2.57	2.53	2.49	2.45	2.40
12	4.75	3.89	3.49	3.26	3.11	3.00	2.91	2.85	2.80	2.75	2.69	2.62	2.54	2.51	2.47	2.43	2.38	2.34	2.30
13	4.67	3.81	3.41	3.18	3.03	2.92	2.83	2.77	2.71	2.67	2.60	2.53	2.46	2.42	2.38	2.34	2.30	2.25	2.21
14	4.60	3.74	3.34	3.11	2.96	2.85	2.76	2.70	2.65	2.60	2.53	2.46	2.39	2.35	2.31	2.27	2.22	2.18	2.13
15	4.54	3.68	3.29	3.06	2.90	2.79	2.71	2.64	2.59	2.54	2.48	2.40	2.33	2.29	2.25	2.20	2.16	2.11	2.07
16	4.49	3.63	3.24	3.01	2.85	2.74	2.66	2.59	2.54	2.49	2.42	2.35	2.28	2.24	2.19	2.15	2.11	2.06	2.01
17	4.45	3.59	3.20	2.96	2.81	2.70	2.61	2.55	2.49	2.45	2.38	2.31	2.23	2.19	2.15	2.10	2.06	2.01	1.96
18	4.41	3.55	3.16	2.93	2.77	2.66	2.58	2.51	2.46	2.41	2.34	2.27	2.19	2.15	2.11	2.06	2.02	1.97	1.92
19	4.38	3.52	3.13	2.90	2.74	2.63	2.54	2.48	2.42	2.38	2.31	2.23	2.16	2.11	2.07	2.03	1.98	1.93	1.88
20	4.35	3.49	3.10	2.87	2.71	2.60	2.51	2.45	2.39	2.35	2.28	2.20	2.12	2.08	2.04	1.99	1.95	1.90	1.84
21	4.32	3.47	3.07	2.84	2.68	2.57	2.49	2.42	2.37	2.32	2.25	2.18	2.10	2.05	2.01	1.96	1.92	1.87	1.81
22	4.30	3.44	3.05	2.82	2.66	2.55	2.46	2.40	2.34	2.30	2.23	2.15	2.07	2.03	1.98	1.94	1.89	1.84	1.78
23	4.28	3.42	3.03	2.80	2.64	2.53	2.44	2.37	2.32	2.27	2.20	2.13	2.05	2.01	1.96	1.91	1.86	1.81	1.76
24	4.26	3.40	3.01	2.78	2.62	2.51	2.42	2.36	2.30	2.25	2.18	2.11	2.03	1.98	1.94	1.89	1.84	1.79	1.73
25	4.24	3.39	2.99	2.76	2.60	2.49	2.40	2.34	2.28	2.24	2.16	2.09	2.01	1.96	1.92	1.87	1.82	1.77	1.71
30	4.17	3.32	2.92	2.69	2.53	2.42	2.33	2.27	2.21	2.16	2.09	2.01	1.93	1.89	1.84	1.79	1.74	1.68	1.62
40	4.08	3.23	2.84	2.61	2.45	2.34	2.25	2.18	2.12	2.08	2.00	1.92	1.84	1.79	1.74	1.69	1.64	1.58	1.51
60	4.00	3.15	2.76	2.53	2.37	2.25	2.17	2.10	2.04	1.99	1.92	1.84	1.75	1.70	1.65	1.59	1.53	1.47	1.39
120	3.92	3.07	2.68	2.45	2.29	2.18	2.09	2.02	1.96	1.91	1.83	1.75	1.66	1.61	1.55	1.50	1.43	1.35	1.25
∞	3.84	3.00	2.60	2.37	2.21	2.10	2.01	1.94	1.88	1.83	1.75	1.67	1.57	1.52	1.46	1.39	1.32	1.22	1.00

Degrees of freedom for denominator

$F_{0.01}$ points

Degrees of freedom for numerator

	1	2	3	4	5	6	7	8	9	10	12	15	20	24	30	40	60	120	∞
1	4052	5000	5403	5625	5764	5859	5928	5982	6023	6056	6106	6157	6209	6235	6261	6287	6313	6339	6366
2	98.5	99.0	99.2	99.2	99.3	99.3	99.4	99.4	99.4	99.4	99.4	99.4	99.4	99.5	99.5	99.5	99.5	99.5	99.5
3	34.1	30.8	29.5	28.7	28.2	27.9	27.7	27.5	27.3	27.2	27.1	26.9	26.7	26.6	26.5	26.4	26.3	26.2	26.1
4	21.2	18.0	16.7	16.0	15.5	15.2	15.0	14.8	14.7	14.5	14.4	14.2	14.0	13.9	13.8	13.7	13.7	13.6	13.5
5	16.3	13.3	12.1	11.4	11.0	10.7	10.5	10.3	10.2	10.1	9.89	9.72	9.55	9.47	9.38	9.29	9.20	9.11	9.02
6	13.7	10.9	9.78	9.15	8.75	8.47	8.26	8.10	7.98	7.87	7.72	7.56	7.40	7.31	7.23	7.14	7.06	6.97	6.88
7	12.2	9.55	8.45	7.85	7.46	7.19	6.99	6.84	6.72	6.62	6.47	6.31	6.16	6.07	5.99	5.91	5.82	5.74	5.65
8	11.3	8.65	7.59	7.01	6.63	6.37	6.18	6.03	5.91	5.81	5.67	5.52	5.36	5.28	5.20	5.12	5.03	4.95	4.86
9	10.6	8.02	6.99	6.42	6.06	5.80	5.61	5.47	5.35	5.26	5.11	4.96	4.81	4.73	4.65	4.57	4.48	4.40	4.31
10	10.0	7.56	6.55	5.99	5.64	5.39	5.20	5.06	4.94	4.85	4.71	4.56	4.41	4.33	4.25	4.17	4.08	4.00	3.91
11	9.65	7.21	6.22	5.67	5.32	5.07	4.89	4.74	4.63	4.54	4.40	4.25	4.10	4.02	3.94	3.86	3.78	3.69	3.60
12	9.33	6.93	5.95	5.41	5.06	4.82	4.64	4.50	4.39	4.30	4.16	4.01	3.86	3.78	3.70	3.62	3.54	3.45	3.36
13	9.07	6.70	5.74	5.21	4.86	4.62	4.44	4.30	4.19	4.10	3.96	3.82	3.66	3.59	3.51	3.43	3.34	3.25	3.17
14	8.86	6.51	5.56	5.04	4.70	4.46	4.28	4.14	4.03	3.94	3.80	3.66	3.51	3.43	3.35	3.27	3.18	3.09	3.00
15	8.68	6.36	5.42	4.89	4.56	4.32	4.14	4.00	3.89	3.80	3.67	3.52	3.37	3.29	3.21	3.13	3.05	2.96	2.87
16	8.53	6.23	5.29	4.77	4.44	4.20	4.03	3.89	3.78	3.69	3.55	3.41	3.26	3.18	3.10	3.02	2.93	2.84	2.75
17	8.40	6.11	5.19	4.67	4.34	4.10	3.93	3.79	3.68	3.59	3.46	3.31	3.16	3.08	3.00	2.92	2.83	2.75	2.65
18	8.29	6.01	5.09	4.58	4.25	4.01	3.84	3.71	3.60	3.51	3.37	3.23	3.08	3.00	2.92	2.84	2.75	2.66	2.57
19	8.19	5.93	5.01	4.50	4.17	3.94	3.77	3.63	3.52	3.43	3.30	3.15	3.00	2.92	2.84	2.76	2.67	2.58	2.49
20	8.10	5.85	4.94	4.43	4.10	3.87	3.70	3.56	3.46	3.37	3.23	3.09	2.94	2.86	2.78	2.69	2.61	2.52	2.42
21	8.02	5.78	4.87	4.37	4.04	3.81	3.64	3.51	3.40	3.31	3.17	3.03	2.88	2.80	2.72	2.64	2.55	2.46	2.36
22	7.95	5.72	4.82	4.31	3.99	3.76	3.59	3.45	3.35	3.26	3.12	2.98	2.83	2.75	2.67	2.58	2.50	2.40	2.31
23	7.88	5.66	4.76	4.26	3.94	3.71	3.54	3.41	3.30	3.21	3.07	2.93	2.78	2.70	2.62	2.54	2.45	2.35	2.26
24	7.82	5.61	4.72	4.22	3.90	3.67	3.50	3.36	3.26	3.17	3.03	2.89	2.74	2.66	2.58	2.49	2.40	2.31	2.21
25	7.77	5.57	4.68	4.18	3.86	3.63	3.46	3.32	3.22	3.13	2.99	2.85	2.70	2.62	2.53	2.45	2.36	2.27	2.17
30	7.56	5.39	4.51	4.02	3.70	3.47	3.30	3.17	3.07	2.98	2.84	2.70	2.55	2.47	2.39	2.30	2.21	2.11	2.01
40	7.31	5.18	4.31	3.83	3.51	3.29	3.12	2.99	2.89	2.80	2.66	2.52	2.37	2.29	2.20	2.11	2.02	1.92	1.80
60	7.08	4.98	4.13	3.65	3.34	3.12	2.95	2.82	2.72	2.63	2.50	2.35	2.20	2.12	2.03	1.94	1.84	1.73	1.60
120	6.85	4.79	3.95	3.48	3.17	2.96	2.79	2.66	2.56	2.47	2.34	2.19	2.03	1.95	1.86	1.76	1.66	1.53	1.38
∞	6.63	4.61	3.78	3.32	3.02	2.80	2.64	2.51	2.41	2.32	2.18	2.04	1.88	1.79	1.70	1.59	1.47	1.32	1.00

Degrees of freedom for denominator

Tables give F_α as indicated in the figure for $\alpha = 0.05$ and 0.01. For example, if d.f. in numerator = 8 and d.f. in denominator = 12 then $F_{0.05} = 2.85$.

d_L and d_U points for the Durbin–Watson statistic

0.05 significance points

n	$k'=1$ d_L	$k'=1$ d_U	$k'=2$ d_L	$k'=2$ d_U	$k'=3$ d_L	$k'=3$ d_U	$k'=4$ d_L	$k'=4$ d_U	$k'=5$ d_L	$k'=5$ d_U
15	1.08	1.36	0.95	1.54	0.82	1.75	0.69	1.97	0.56	2.21
16	1.10	1.37	0.98	1.54	0.86	1.73	0.74	1.93	0.62	2.15
17	1.13	1.38	1.02	1.54	0.90	1.71	0.78	1.90	0.67	2.10
18	1.16	1.39	1.05	1.53	0.93	1.69	0.82	1.87	0.71	2.06
19	1.18	1.40	1.08	1.53	0.97	1.68	0.86	1.85	0.75	2.02
20	1.20	1.41	1.10	1.54	1.00	1.68	0.90	1.83	0.79	1.99
21	1.22	1.42	1.13	1.54	1.03	1.67	0.93	1.81	0.83	1.96
22	1.24	1.43	1.15	1.54	1.05	1.66	0.96	1.80	0.86	1.94
23	1.26	1.44	1.17	1.54	1.08	1.66	0.99	1.79	0.90	1.92
24	1.27	1.45	1.19	1.55	1.10	1.66	1.01	1.78	0.93	1.90
25	1.29	1.45	1.21	1.55	1.12	1.66	1.04	1.77	0.95	1.89
26	1.30	1.46	1.22	1.55	1.14	1.65	1.06	1.76	0.98	1.88
27	1.32	1.47	1.24	1.56	1.16	1.65	1.08	1.76	1.01	1.86
28	1.33	1.48	1.26	1.56	1.18	1.65	1.10	1.75	1.03	1.85
29	1.34	1.48	1.27	1.56	1.20	1.65	1.12	1.74	1.05	1.84
30	1.35	1.49	1.28	1.57	1.21	1.65	1.14	1.74	1.07	1.83
31	1.36	1.50	1.30	1.57	1.23	1.65	1.16	1.74	1.09	1.83
32	1.37	1.50	1.31	1.57	1.24	1.65	1.18	1.73	1.11	1.82
33	1.38	1.51	1.32	1.58	1.26	1.65	1.19	1.73	1.13	1.81
34	1.39	1.51	1.33	1.58	1.27	1.65	1.21	1.73	1.15	1.81
35	1.40	1.52	1.34	1.58	1.28	1.65	1.22	1.73	1.16	1.80
36	1.41	1.52	1.35	1.59	1.29	1.65	1.24	1.73	1.18	1.80
37	1.42	1.53	1.36	1.59	1.31	1.66	1.25	1.72	1.19	1.80
38	1.43	1.54	1.37	1.59	1.32	1.66	1.26	1.72	1.21	1.79
39	1.43	1.54	1.38	1.60	1.33	1.66	1.27	1.72	1.22	1.79
40	1.44	1.54	1.39	1.60	1.34	1.66	1.29	1.72	1.23	1.79
45	1.48	1.57	1.43	1.62	1.38	1.67	1.34	1.72	1.29	1.78
50	1.50	1.59	1.46	1.63	1.42	1.67	1.38	1.72	1.34	1.77
55	1.53	1.60	1.49	1.64	1.45	1.68	1.41	1.72	1.38	1.77
60	1.55	1.62	1.51	1.65	1.48	1.69	1.44	1.73	1.41	1.77
65	1.57	1.63	1.54	1.66	1.50	1.70	1.47	1.73	1.44	1.77
70	1.58	1.64	1.55	1.67	1.52	1.70	1.49	1.74	1.46	1.77
75	1.60	1.65	1.57	1.68	1.54	1.71	1.51	1.74	1.49	1.77
80	1.61	1.66	1.59	1.69	1.56	1.72	1.53	1.74	1.51	1.77
85	1.62	1.67	1.60	1.70	1.57	1.72	1.55	1.75	1.52	1.77
90	1.63	1.68	1.61	1.70	1.59	1.73	1.57	1.75	1.54	1.78
95	1.64	1.69	1.62	1.71	1.60	1.73	1.58	1.75	1.56	1.78
100	1.65	1.69	1.63	1.72	1.61	1.74	1.59	1.76	1.57	1.78

0.01 significance points

n	$k'=1$ d_L	$k'=1$ d_U	$k'=2$ d_L	$k'=2$ d_U	$k'=3$ d_L	$k'=3$ d_U	$k'=4$ d_L	$k'=4$ d_U	$k'=5$ d_L	$k'=5$ d_U
15	0.81	1.07	0.70	1.25	0.59	1.46	0.49	1.70	0.39	1.96
16	0.84	1.09	0.74	1.25	0.63	1.44	0.53	1.66	0.44	1.90
17	0.87	1.10	0.77	1.25	0.67	1.43	0.57	1.63	0.48	1.85
18	0.90	1.12	0.80	1.26	0.71	1.42	0.61	1.60	0.52	1.80
19	0.93	1.13	0.83	1.26	0.74	1.41	0.65	1.58	0.56	1.77
20	0.95	1.15	0.86	1.27	0.77	1.41	0.68	1.57	0.60	1.74
21	0.97	1.16	0.89	1.27	0.80	1.41	0.72	1.55	0.63	1.71
22	1.00	1.17	0.91	1.28	0.83	1.40	0.75	1.54	0.66	1.69
23	1.02	1.19	0.94	1.29	0.86	1.40	0.77	1.53	0.70	1.67
24	1.04	1.20	0.96	1.30	0.88	1.41	0.80	1.53	0.72	1.66
25	1.05	1.21	0.98	1.30	0.90	1.41	0.83	1.52	0.75	1.65
26	1.07	1.22	1.00	1.31	0.93	1.41	0.85	1.52	0.78	1.64
27	1.09	1.23	1.02	1.32	0.95	1.41	0.88	1.51	0.81	1.63
28	1.10	1.24	1.04	1.32	0.97	1.41	0.90	1.51	0.83	1.62
29	1.12	1.25	1.05	1.33	0.99	1.42	0.92	1.51	0.85	1.61
30	1.13	1.26	1.07	1.34	1.01	1.42	0.94	1.51	0.88	1.61
31	1.15	1.27	1.08	1.34	1.02	1.42	0.96	1.51	0.90	1.60
32	1.16	1.28	1.10	1.35	1.04	1.43	0.98	1.51	0.92	1.60
33	1.17	1.29	1.11	1.36	1.05	1.43	1.00	1.51	0.94	1.59
34	1.18	1.30	1.13	1.36	1.07	1.43	1.01	1.51	0.95	1.59
35	1.19	1.31	1.14	1.37	1.08	1.44	1.03	1.51	0.97	1.59
36	1.21	1.32	1.15	1.38	1.10	1.44	1.04	1.51	0.99	1.59
37	1.22	1.32	1.16	1.38	1.11	1.45	1.06	1.51	1.00	1.59
38	1.23	1.33	1.18	1.39	1.12	1.45	1.07	1.52	1.02	1.58
39	1.24	1.34	1.19	1.39	1.14	1.45	1.09	1.52	1.03	1.58
40	1.25	1.34	1.20	1.40	1.15	1.46	1.10	1.52	1.05	1.58
45	1.29	1.38	1.24	1.42	1.20	1.48	1.16	1.53	1.11	1.58
50	1.32	1.40	1.28	1.45	1.24	1.49	1.20	1.54	1.16	1.59
55	1.36	1.43	1.32	1.47	1.28	1.51	1.25	1.55	1.21	1.59
60	1.38	1.45	1.35	1.48	1.32	1.52	1.28	1.56	1.25	1.60
65	1.41	1.47	1.38	1.50	1.35	1.53	1.31	1.57	1.28	1.61
70	1.43	1.49	1.40	1.52	1.37	1.55	1.34	1.58	1.31	1.61
75	1.45	1.50	1.42	1.53	1.39	1.56	1.37	1.59	1.34	1.62
80	1.47	1.52	1.44	1.54	1.42	1.57	1.39	1.60	1.36	1.62
85	1.48	1.53	1.46	1.55	1.43	1.58	1.41	1.60	1.39	1.63
90	1.50	1.54	1.47	1.56	1.45	1.59	1.43	1.61	1.41	1.63
95	1.51	1.55	1.49	1.57	1.47	1.60	1.45	1.62	1.42	1.64
100	1.52	1.56	1.50	1.58	1.48	1.60	1.46	1.63	1.44	1.65

n = number of observations, k' = number of explanatory variables (excluding intercept).

bibliography

bibliography

Almon S. (1965). The distributed lag between capital appropriations and expenditures. *Econometrica*, **33**, 178–96

Amemiya T. (1980). Selection of regressors. *International Economic Review*, **21**, 331–54

Anderson T.W. (1966). The choice of degree of a polynomial regressor as a decision problem. *Annals of Mathematical Statistics*, **33**(1), 255–65

Banerjee A., Dolado J.J., Hendry D.F. and Smith G.W. (1986). Exploring equilibrium relationships in econometrics through static models: some Monte Carlo evidence. *Oxford Bulletin of Economics and Statistics*, **48**, 253–77

Banerjee A., Dolado J., Galbraith J.W. and Hendry D.F. (1993). *Co-integration, Error Correction, and the Econometric Analysis of Non-Stationary Data*. Oxford: Oxford University Press

Box G.E.P. and Cox D.R. (1964). An analysis of transformations. *Journal of the Royal Statistical Society*, **B26**, 211–52

Breusch T. (1978). Testing for autocorrelation in dynamic linear models. *Australian Economic Papers*, **17**, 334–55

Breusch T. and Pagan A. (1979) A simple test for heteroskedasticity and random coefficient variation. *Econometrica*, **47**, 1287–94

Charemza W.W. and Deadman D.F. (1992). *New Directions in Econometric Practice*. Aldershot: Edward Elgar

Chiang A.C. (1984). *Fundamental Methods of Economics* 3rd edn. International Student Edition. New York: McGraw-Hill

Cochrane E. and Orcutt G.H. (1949). Application of least squares regressions to relationships containing autocorrelated error terms. *Journal of the American Statistical Association*, **44**, 32–61

Cochrane L.J.W. (1988). How big is the random walk in GNP? *Journal of Political Economy*, **96**, 893–920.

Cooley T.F. and LeRoy S.F. (1985). Atheoretical macroeconomics. *Journal of Monetary Economics*, **16**, 283–308

Cuthbertson K. and Taylor M.P. (1986). Monetary anticipation and the demand for money in the UK: testing rationality in the shock absorber hypothesis. *Journal of Applied Economics*, **1**, 355–65.

Cuthbertson K. and Taylor M.P. (1988). Monetary anticipations and the demand for money in the US: further results. *Southern Economic Journal*, **55**, 326–35.

Cuthbertson K., Hall S.G. and Taylor M.P. (1992). *Applied Econometric Techniques*. Hemel Hempstead: Harvester Wheatsheaf

Davidson J.E.H., Hendry D.F., Srba F. and Yeo S. (1978). Econometric modelling of the aggregate time series relationship between consumers' expenditure and income in the UK. *Economic Journal*, **88**, 661–92

Davidson R. and MacKinnon J.G. (1981). Several tests for model specification in the presence of alternative hypotheses. *Econometrica*, **49**, 781–93

Dickey D.A. and Fuller W.A. (1979). Distributions of the estimators for autoregressive time series with a unit root. *Journal of the American Statistical Association*, **74**, 427–31

Dickey D.A. and Fuller W.A. (1981). The likelihood ratio statistics for autoregressive time series with a unit root. *Econometrica*, **49**, 1057–72

Durbin J. (1970). Testing for serial correlation in least squares regression when some of the regressors are lagged dependent variables. *Econometrica*, **38**, 410–21

Durbin J. and Watson G.S. (1971). Testing for serial autocorrelation in least squares regression III. *Biometrica*, **37**, 1–19

Engle R.F. and Granger C. (1987). Co-integration and error correction: interpretation, estimation and testing. *Econometrica*, **66**, 251–76

Engle R.F., Hendry D.F. and Richard J.-F. (1983). Exogeneity. *Econometrica*, **51**, 277–304

Farrar D.E. and Glauber R.R. (1967). Multicollinearity in regression analysis: the problem revisited. *Review of Economics and Statistics*, **49**, 92–107

Friedman M. (1953). The methodology of positive economics. In *Essays in Positive Economics*. Chicago: Chicago University Press

Friedman M. (1957). *A Theory of the Consumption Function*. Princeton: Princeton University Press

Fuller W.A. (1976). *Introduction to Statistical Time Series*. New York: Wiley

Gilbert C.L. (1986). Professor Hendry's econometric methodology. *Oxford Bulletin of Economics and Statistics*, **48**, 283–307

Glejser H. (1969). A new test for homoscedasticity. *Journal of the American Statistical Association*, **64**, 316–23

Godfrey L.G. (1978). Testing for higher order serial correlation in regression equations when the regressors contain lagged dependent variables. *Econometrica*, **46**, 1303–10

Granger C.W.J. (1969). Investigating causal relations by econometric models and cross-spectral methods. *Econometrica*, **37**, 24–36

Granger C.W.J. and Newbold P. (1974). Spurious regressions in economics. *Journal of Econometrics*, **35**, 143–59.

Greene W.H. (1993). *Econometric Analysis* 2nd edn. New York: Macmillan

Griffiths W.E., Judge G.G. and Hill R.C. (1993). *Learning and Practising Econometrics*. New York: Wiley

Hall R.E. (1978). Stochastic implications of the stochastic life cycle–permanent income hypothesis: theory and evidence. *Journal of Political Economy*, **86**, 971–87

Hausman J. (1978). Specification tests in econometrics. *Econometrica*, **46**, 1251–71.

Hendry D.F. (1980). Econometrics – alchemy or science? *Economica*, **47**, 387–406.

Hendry D.F. (1983). Econometric modelling: the consumption function in retrospect. *Scottish Journal of Political Economy*, **30**, 193–220

Hendry D.F. (1987). Econometric methodology: a personal perspective. In *Advances in Econometrics: 5th World Congress*, Vol. 2 (Bewley T.F., ed.), pp. 236–61. Cambridge: Cambridge University Press

Hendry D.F. and Ericsson N.R. (1991). An econometric analysis of UK money demand. In *Monetary Trends in the United States and the United Kingdom* (Friedman M. and Schwartz A.J. eds.) *American Economic Review*, **81**, 8–38.

Hendry D.F. and Richard J-F. (1983). the econometric analysis of economic time series. *International Statistical Review*, **51**, 111–63.

Hildreth C. and Lu J.Y. (1960). *Demand Relations with Autocorrelated Disturbances*. Michigan: Michigan State University

Holden K. and Thompson J. (1992). Co-integration: an introductory survey. *British Review of Economic Issues*, **14**, 1–55

Jarque C.M. and Bera A.K. (1980). Efficient tests for normality, homoskedasticity and serial independence of regression residuals. *Economic Letters*, **6**, 255–9

Johansen S. (1988). Statistical analysis of cointegration vectors. *Journal of Economic Dynamics and Control*, **12**, 231–54.

Johnston J. (1984). *Econometric Methods* 3rd edn. Singapore: McGraw-Hill

Jorgenson D.W. (1963). Capital theory and investment behavior. *American Economic Review, Papers and Proceedings*, **53**, 247–53.

Judge G.G., Hill R.C., Griffiths W.E. Lutkepohl H. and Lee T.-C. (1988). *Introduction to the Theory and Practice of Econometrics* 2nd edn. New York: Wiley

Klein L.R. (1958). The estimation of distributed lags. *Econometrica*, **26**, 559–65

Kendall M.G. and Stewart A. (1973). *The Advanced Theory of Statistics*. London: Griffin

Kmenta J. (1986). *Elements of Econometrics*. New York: Macmillan

Liu T.C. (1960) Underidentification, structural estimation and forecasting. *Econometrica*, **28**, 855–65

Lovell M.C. (1983). Data mining. *Review of Economics and Statistics*, **65**, 1–12

Lucas R.E. (1976) Economic policy evaluation: a critique. In *The Phillips Curve and Labour Markets* (Brunner K. and Meltzer D., eds.). Amsterdam: North-Holland.

McAleer M. and Peseran M.H. (1986). Statistical inference in non-nested economic models. *Applied Mathematics and Computation*, **20**, 271–311

McCallum R.T. (1976). Rational expectations and the estimation of econometric models: an alternative procedure. *International Economic Review*, **17**, 484–90

McFadden D. (1974). The measurement of urban travel demand. *Journal of Public Economics*, **25**, 303–28

MacKinnon J.G. (1991). Critical values for co-integration tests. In *Long Run Equilibrium Relationships* (Engle R.F. and Granger C.W.J., eds.) pp. 267–76 Oxford: Oxford University Press

Maddala G.S. (1988). *Introduction to Econometrics*. New York: Macmillan

Meullbauer J. (1983). Surprises in the consumption function. *Economic Journal*, **93**, Conference Papers 34–49

Mizon G.E. and Richard J.-F. (1986). The encompassing principle and its application to testing non-nested hypotheses. *Econometrica*, **54**, 657–78

Nelson C.R. and Plosser C.I. (1982). Trends and random walks in macroeconomic time series. *Journal of Monetary Economics*, **10**, 139–62

Park R. (1966) Estimation with heteroskedastic error terms. *Econometrica*, **34**, 888

Permon R. (1991). Cointegration: an introduction to the literature. *Journal of Economic Studies*, **18**, 3–30

Perron P. (1989). The great crash, the oil shock and the unit root hypothesis. *Econometrica*, **57**, 1361–402

Phillips P.C.B. (1986) Understanding spurious regressions in econometrics. *Journal of Econometrics*, **33**, 311–40

Phillips P.C.B. and Perron P. (1988). Testing for a unit root in time series regressions. *Biometrica*, **75**, 335–46

Pindyck R.S. and Rubinfeld D.L. (1991). *Econometric Models and Economic Forecasts* 3rd edn. New York: McGraw-Hill

Prais S.J. and Winsten C. (1954). Trend estimators and serial correlation. *Cowles Commission Discussion Paper*, No. 383. Chicago: University of Chicago

Ramsey J.B. (1969) Tests for specification error in classical least squares regression analysis. *Journal of the Royal Statistical Society*, **B31**, 250–71

Rao B.B. (1994). *Cointegration for the Applied Economist*. Basingstoke: Macmillan

Samuelson P.A., Koopmans T.C and Stone J.R.N. (1954). Report of the evaluative committee for *Econometrica*. *Econometrica*, **22**, 141–6

Sargan J.D. (1964). Wages and prices in the United Kingdom. In *Econometric Analysis for Economic Planning* (Mort P.E., Mills G. and Whitaker J.K., eds.) London: Butterfield pp. 25–54.

Sargan J.D. and Bhargava A. (1983). Testing residuals from least squares regression for being generated by the Gaussian random walk. *Econometrica*, **51**, 153–74

Sims C.A. (1980). Macroeconomics and reality. *Econometrica*, **48**, 1–48

Silvey S.D. (1975). *Statistical Inference*. London: Chapman and Hall

Stewart J. (1991). *Econometrics*. London: Philip Allen

Stock J.H. (1987). Asymptotic properties of least squares estimators of cointegrating vectors. *Econometrica*, **55**, 1035–56

Thomas R.L. (1993). *Introductory Econometrics: Theory and Applications* 2nd edn. Harlow: Longman

White H. (1980). A heteroskedasticity-consistent covariance matrix estimator and a direct test of heteroskedasticity. *Econometrica*, **48**, 817–38

Yule G.U. (1926). Why do we sometimes get nonsense correlations between time series? A study in sampling and the nature of time series. *Journal of the Royal Statistical Society*, **89**, 1–64

Zarembka P. (1968) Functional form in the demand for money. *Journal of the American Statistical Association*, **63**, 502–11

index